Advanced Composite Materials in Bridges and Structures

Matériaux composites d'avant-garde pour ponts et charpentes

1st   International Conference

1re Conférence internationale

Sherbrooke, Québec, Canada

1992

Edited by:

K.W. Neale
P. Labossière

Éditeurs

DOCUMENTATION

The papers herein are published in the form submitted by the authors. Minor changes have been made where obvious errors and discrepancies were detected, and to standardize visual presentation.

The opinions expressed in the papers are solely those of the authors. Neither the Canadian Society for Civil Engineering nor the Organizing Committee accept responsibility for the accuracy of the statements made therein.

Les articles apparaissant dans ce volume sont publiés dans la forme sous laquelle ils ont été soumis. Des corrections mineures ont été faites là où des erreurs évidentes ou des incompatibilités ont été détectées, de même que pour uniformiser la mise en page.

Les opinions exprimées dans ces articles sont la seule responsabilité de leurs auteurs. Ni la Société canadienne de génie civil, ni le Comité d'organisation de la conférence n'acceptent la responsabilité des propos exprimés par les auteurs.

Published by / *Publié par*:

The Canadian Society for Civil Engineering
La Société canadienne de génie civil
2050 Mansfield, Bureau 700
Montréal (Québec) H3A 1Z2 CANADA

ISBN: 0-921303-41-6

FOREWORD

Preparations for ACMBS-I began more than two years ago, immediately following the Canadian Society for Civil Engineering's approval of a proposition it had received from its Technical Committee on Advanced Composite Materials in Bridges and Structures. Announcements for this conference have attracted wide interest from around the world, a strong indication that the time is ripe for a meeting to discuss recent developments and prospects for the future in this fascinating new field.

I am deeply indebted to all who have contributed to the success of the conference. The efforts of the members of the Technical Committee and Organizing Committee are greatly appreciated. The papers offered by the three Keynote Lecturers are valuable original contributions, for which I am very grateful. Many thanks of course to all the authors, representing 13 different nations, for their participation. I also wish to acknowledge the financial support of our sponsor, the Canadian Society for Civil Engineering, as well as the administrative and financial assistance provided by the Université de Sherbrooke and its Département de génie civil.

Finally, I wish to express my sincere appreciation to three dedicated, assiduous colleagues whose help has been indispensable, and with whom it is always a genuine pleasure to collaborate: Dominique Lefebvre for his extremely efficient cooperation as Chair of the Organizing Committee, Pierre Labossière for his exceptionally meticulous work as Co-Editor of the conference proceedings, and Lise Dutrisac for her extraordinary patience and unfailing professionalism in carrying out the demanding duties of Conference Secretary.

Kenneth W. Neale / Chair — ACMBS-I

AVANT-PROPOS

Suite à l'approbation accordée par la Société canadienne de génie civil à une proposition soumise par son Comité technique sur les matériaux composites d'avant-garde pour ponts et charpentes, nous avons entrepris il y a deux ans l'organisation de MCAPC-I. Les annonces de cette conférence ont suscité un intêret marqué de la communauté internationale, ce qui démontre que nous sommes à un moment opportun pour discuter des développements récents et des perspectives d'avenir de ce nouveau domaine fascinant.

Je suis très reconnaissant à tous ceux qui ont contribué au succès de la conférence. Les efforts des membres du Comité technique et du Comité d'organisation sont grandement appréciés. Les communications des trois conférenciers invités représentent des contributions originales très importantes et je les en remercie vivement. Merci bien sûr à tous les auteurs, représentant treize pays différents, pour leur participation. Je tiens aussi à remercier la Société canadienne de génie civil pour son soutien financier, ainsi que l'Université de Sherbrooke et son Département de génie civil pour leur assistance administrative et financière.

Finalement, je voudrais exprimer ma plus grande gratitude à trois collègues dévoués et assidus dont l'aide a été indispensable, et avec qui j'ai toujours un véritable plaisir à collaborer: Dominique Lefebvre pour sa coopération très efficace en sa qualité de Président du Comité d'organisation, Pierre Labossière pour son travail extrêmement méticuleux dans la préparation et la rédaction des comptes rendus de la conférence, et Lise Dutrisac pour son professionalisme de tous les instants et sa patience extraordinaire dans la réalisation des tâches très exigeantes de Secrétaire de la conférence.

Kenneth W. Neale / Président — MCAPC-I

ORGANIZING COMMITTEE
COMITÉ D'ORGANISATION

Chair / *Président*:   D. Lefebvre
Secretary / *Secrétaire*:   L. Dutrisac
Treasurer / *Trésorier*:   A.E. Lahoud
Members / *Membres*:   C. Carbonneau
    D. Green
    P. Labossière
    K.W. Neale
    A. Makinde
    P. Paultre

TECHNICAL COMMITTEE / *COMITÉ TECHNIQUE*

B. Bakht, *Canada*
C.J. Burgoyne, *U.K.*
F. Ellyin, *Canada*
M.-A. Erki, *Canada*
M. Faoro, *Germany*
H. GangaRao, *U.S.A.*
A. Gerritse, *Holland*
P. Hamelin, *France*
S.L. Iyer, *U.S.A.*

P. Labossière, *Canada*
C. Lim, *Canada*
U. Meier, *Switzerland*
A.A. Mufti, *Canada*
K.W. Neale, *Canada*
H. Okamura, *Japan*
S. Rizkalla, *Canada*
R.N. Swamy, *U.K.*

This Conference is sponsored by the
Canadian Society for Civil Engineering

Cette conférence est parrainée par la
Société canadienne de génie civil

PREFACE

Wood, steel and concrete are the materials traditionally used to build our bridges and other structures. Such structures are built to last, with the result that structural engineering is generally perceived as a rather conservative discipline. Since civil engineering structures must invariably be designed to conform to strict regulations and codes, ways of introducing innovative materials are not usually obvious. In fact, the unimaginative observer will rarely conceive of a structure built from non-conventional materials. However, even if innovations may be slow to catch the public eye, material technologies are continually changing modern bridge and building construction. Although very few of our contemporaries question the use of steel — a construction material barely over a century old — or hesitate to build with reinforced concrete, which is an even younger technology, the application of plastics or advanced fibre-reinforced materials in structural applications has so far not been given much thought.

The rapid technological evolutions in today's society is constantly triggering the development of numerous innovations, among which is the use of advanced composite materials (ACM) in civil engineering construction. We are now submerged in a sea of novelties in the areas of computer and information technologies, as well as in various sectors of transportation and telecommunications. New, engineered materials are being developed for all kinds of purposes. In aeronautical and space applications, for example, progress in the area of advanced composites has been phenomenal over the last two decades. The need for lighter, faster and safer aircraft required innovation, and the development of advanced materials was a major part of the answer.

Structural engineering now faces comparable challenges. While most of the world tries to catch up with the so-called advanced nations, it is ironic that the infrastructure of the world's more developed countries is rapidly becoming inadequate. The deterioration of structures built forty or fifty years ago, an increase in the loads carried by bridges designed for conditions not as demanding as today's, an ever-increasing concern about the environment, and an improved awareness of the importance of aesthetics are but a few of the more obvious sources of pressure for technological innovation in structural engineering. An added impetus for innovation is the increasing need to do more within the limits of shrinking budgets. It is almost certain that new materials, notably advanced composites, will be prominent in the quest to meet these challenges.

The themes of the contributions from the four continents represented at this 1st *International Conference on Advanced Composite Materials in Bridges and Structures* (ACMBS-I) fall into strategic areas previously identified by the Canadian Society for Civil Engineering technical committee on this subject. In their book *Advanced Composite Materials With Application to Bridges,* published by CSCE in 1991, the most promising potential applications of advanced composites mentioned were *(i)* the reinforcement of concrete with ACM, in particular using prestressing tendons; and *(ii)* the rehabilitation and strengthening of existing structures using ACM. The papers contained in these proceedings are related somehow to one or the other of these topics.

In order to put the development of advanced composite materials in bridges and other structures into a proper perspective, the texts of three *Invited Lectures* by leading international authorities in this field appear at the beginning of these proceedings. First, C.A. Ballinger presents an historic retrospective and his vision for future prospects in his paper *Development of Fibre-Reinforced Plastic Products for the Construction Market — How Has and Can It Be Done?* To direct our attention to more specific bridge applications, P.R. Head contributes the paper *Design Methods and Bridge Forms for the Cost Effective Use of Advanced Composites in Bridges.* In the paper *Smart Structures — A Revolution in Civil Engineering,* R.M. Measures demonstrates that advanced composite materials can, in addition to their structural applications, offer fascinating possibilities for monitoring the performance of bridges and structures.

It seemed appropriate to begin the contributed papers with those reviewing the *Properties of Rods, Cables, and Laminates.* The papers included in this section contain experimental results for a variety of glass, carbon or graphite fibre-reinforced plastics. Measurements of short and long-term properties are presented, and the list of topics includes the evaluation of the tensile strength of cables and rods, and the effects of impact on strength. The variation of rod and laminate properties after being exposed to harsh environmental conditions, and the effects of fatigue and relaxation are also presented.

One reason to use advanced composite materials in bridges and other structures is to avoid corrosion problems in situations where these can be quite critical. Thus, the first type of application treated in these proceedings is that of *Concrete Beams With FRP Rebars.* Comparisons between experimental results and analytical predictions are considered. The calculation of the strengths of sections is discussed, together with topics related to the bond between rebars and concrete, cracking, and deflection behaviour.

When long concrete spans are needed, prestressing is generally required. The third series of contributed papers is grouped in a section on *Concrete Beams With Prestressed Composite Tendons.* The papers include discussions on the behaviour of prestressed sections, both pre-tensioned and post-tensioned. Experimental results on sections reinforced with glass-epoxy, carbon-epoxy or aramid prestressing tendons are presented. The development of bond strength between the tendons and concrete is also discussed.

The rehabilitation of existing structures is one of the most severe problems faced by structural engineers. *The Strengthening and Rehabilitation of Concrete Structures* with advanced composites may provide part of the solution to this urgent need, as is demonstrated by the papers grouped in this section. These include experimental and theoretical results on concrete beams reinforced externally by fibre-reinforced composite plates. Actual case studies are also presented. The external retrofitting of columns using ACM is also discussed.

Producers of composite materials rival in creating new products, for which users seek innovative applications. In the following section we find papers which report experimental studies of manufactured products such as *Pultruded Sections and Grids.* These are tested either in their original form, or used in innovative ways. For example, pultruded sections loaded in compression or used as handrail or barrier structures, and the reinforcement of panels and slabs with advanced composite grids are considered here.

Some advanced composite materials are notorious for their fragile behaviour in areas where holes and other discontinuities are present. Some of the papers presented in the section on *Anchorages and Connections* attempt to deal with this serious problem. Connections designed for special applications, and the development of ground anchors are also presented here.

The *Bridge Applications* section should be of interest to all structural engineers as it complements the previous topics with full-scale examples of application. The contributions here provide a state-of-the-art perspective on the use of composite materials in bridges on three continents. The bridges discussed here vary in size from entirely composite, small span pedestrian footbridges, to a wood-composite bridge structure, to large-scale traffic bridges with prestressed composite tendons. The variety of bridge projects is followed by another section on other *Innovative Applications of Composite Materials*. This section demonstrates the wide range of applications which have been thought of recently for advanced composites — among these the reader will no doubt discover many appealing and perhaps surprising ideas. The contributions submitted under these two headings actually comprise the largest section of this book.

A conference on the use of composite materials in bridges and other structures would definitely be incomplete without contributions dealing with *Analytical and Design Methods.* Finite element analyses are used by many of the authors of this group to predict the behaviour of bridge and structural components made from composite materials. Others examine special topics of interest in the fields of optimization, buckling analysis, and the development of design codes.

Altogether, the reader will find more than sixty papers, contributed by 136 authors from 13 countries. We hope that these proceedings will provide engineers from industrial, research and academic institutions with a clear and global picture of the current state-of-the-art in the rapidly changing world of advanced composite materials in civil engineering structures, and that this will stimulate added interest and promote further progress in this exciting new field.

K.W. Neale and P. Labossière
Université de Sherbrooke

PRÉFACE

La plupart de nos ponts et structures sont construits de bois, d'acier ou de béton. Comme la plupart de ces constructions survivent pendant longtemps, le génie civil et en particulier le génie des structures sont souvent perçus comme des disciplines conservatrices. En fait, puisque les charpentes doivent être dimensionnées de façon à assurer la sécurité du public, se conformer à des réglementations et des normes strictes, les innovations ne sont pas toujours apparentes. Un observateur non averti peut difficilement s'imaginer une structure construite autrement qu'avec ces matériaux traditionnels, et les innovations sont lentes à frapper l'attention du public. Cependant, l'innovation a sa place même en génie des structures... Très peu de nos contemporains réalisent que l'acier est un matériau de construction âgé d'à peine un siècle, et que le béton armé est une technologie encore plus récente. Dans ce contexte, l'utilisation des plastiques et des matériaux renforcés de fibres est encore loin de faire l'unanimité.

Il est prévisible que l'évolution de la société mènera éventuellement au développement complet de son potentiel technologique, y compris l'utilisation de nouveaux matériaux composites dans l'industrie de la construction. Par exemple, nous sommes maintenant submergés par un océan de nouveautés dans les domaines de l'informatique et des technologies de l'information, des transports et des télécommunications. De nouveaux matériaux sont créés pour toutes sortes d'usages. Les progrès des matériaux composites d'avant-garde pour des applications en aéronautique et en aérospatiale ont été phénoménaux durant les vingt dernières années. La nécessité étant la mère de l'invention, le développement des composites d'avant-garde répondait partiellement au besoin d'avoir des avions plus légers, plus économiques et plus sécuritaires.

L'ingénierie des structures sera maintenant confrontée à des défis comparables. Alors que la plupart des pays du monde tentent de rattraper les pays appelés avancés, il est évident que l'infrastructure de ces derniers se détériore rapidement. A titre d'exemple, l'augmentation des charges sur des ponts dimensionnés pour des conditions moins exigeantes que celles d'aujourd'hui, un souci de plus en plus grand des effets de l'environnement, et même l'importance accrue de l'esthétique, ne sont que quelques-unes des sources de pression. Sans parler de la nécessité de faire toujours plus à l'intérieur de budgets réduits. Il est bien possible que les nouveaux matériaux, et notamment les composites d'avant-garde, nous aideront à trouver des solutions aux problèmes techniques de notre époque.

Les projets présentés dans ces comptes rendus, qui nous proviennent de quatre continents, sont pour la plupart dans des domaines identifiés par un Comité technique de la Société canadienne de génie civil sur l'utilisation des composites d'avant-garde. Dans le livre *Advanced Composite Materials with Application to Bridges*, que ce comité a publié en 1991, les deux plus importantes applications potentielles des matériaux composites d'avant-garde étaient présentées comme: a) le renforcement de sections de béton, et en particulier par des tendons de précontrainte, et b) la réhabilitation et le renforcement de charpentes existantes. Les articles inclus dans ces comptes rendus sont pour la plupart reliés à l'un ou l'autre de ces sujets.

Afin de mettre le développement des matériaux composites d'avant-garde pour ponts et charpentes dans une juste perspective, trois **Conférences générales** de spécialistes dans le domaine apparaissent au début de ces comptes rendus. D'abord, C.A. Ballinger nous présente une rétrospective historique accompagnée de sa vision de l'avenir dans un article sur *Development of Fiber Reinforced Plastic Products for the Construction Market - How Has and Can It Be Done ?* Afin de concentrer notre attention plus spécifiquement sur des applications reliées aux ponts, un article sur *Design Methods and Bridge Forms for the Cost Effective Use of Advanced Composites in Bridges* nous est offert par P.R. Head. Enfin, R.M. Measures nous indique que les matériaux composites d'avant-garde pourraient, en complément à leurs avantages structuraux, servir au contrôle permanent des ponts et charpentes, dans un article sur les *Smart Structures - A Revolution in Civil Engineering*.

Il semble approprié de présenter un premier groupe de communications techniques par celles dans le domaine des **Propriétés des tiges, câbles et stratifiés**. Les articles inclus dans cette section présentent les résultats d'essais expérimentaux variés sur des plastiques renforcés de fibres de verre, de carbone ou de graphite. On y présente des mesures des propriétés à court et à long terme, et la liste des sujets comprend des évaluations de la résistance en tension des câbles et tiges, et les effets des impacts sur la résistance. La variation des propriétés des tiges et stratifiés exposés à des conditions environnementales sévères, les effets de la fatigue et de la relaxation sont aussi traités dans cette section.

Une bonne raison d'utiliser des composites d'avant-garde dans les ponts et charpentes est pour éviter les problèmes de corrosion, qui peuvent être très critiques dans les ponts et garages de stationnement. Aussi, la première application des composites traitée dans ces comptes rendus est le cas des **Poutres de béton avec armature de FRP** (Le terme FRP est utilisé dans ces comptes rendus pour désigner les plastiques renforcés de fibres.) Des résultats expérimentaux et le traitement analytique du sujet sont comparés dans plusieurs articles. Le calcul de la résistance des sections est discuté, de même que des sujets reliés a l'adhérence entre les armatures et le béton, la fissuration, et les déflexions.

Lorsque de longues portées en béton sont nécessaires, on applique de la précontrainte. La troisième série de communications techniques regroupe sous le titre **Poutres de béton précontraint avec tendons composites** des articles discutant de la précontrainte en pré- ou en posttension. Des résultats expérimentaux sur des sections précontraintes par des tendons de verre-époxy, de carbone-époxy, ou d'aramide, sont présentés. Le transfert des contraintes entre les tendons et le béton y est également discuté.

La réhabilitation des structures existantes est un des problèmes les plus urgents auxquels doivent faire face les ingénieurs. Le **Renforcement et la réhabilitation de structures en béton** avec des matériaux composites d'avant-garde sont des solutions possibles à ce problème pressant, comme le démontrent les articles regroupés sous ce titre. Ceux-ci comprennent des résultats expérimentaux et théoriques pour des poutres de béton renforcées extérieurement par des plaques de composites; on présente même des cas d'application sur des structures en service. La réhabilitation des colonnes est également discutée.

Les fabricants de produits en matériaux composites rivalisent dans la création de nouveaux produits pour lesquels les utilisateurs inventent constamment de nouvelles applications. Dans la section suivante sont regroupés les articles dans lesquels on rapporte les résultats d'essais expérimentaux, soit sur les sections fabriquées, soit sur certaines de leurs utilisations novatrices. Des sections pultrudées en compression, ou utilisées comme rampes ou barrières, sont présentées sour le titre **Sections pultrudées et maillages**, de même que le renforcement de panneaux et dalles avec des grilles en matériaux composites d'avant-garde.

Il est notoire que les matériaux composites d'avant-garde ont un comportement fragile dans les zones de discontinuités. Quelques-uns des articles présentés dans la section portant sur les **Ancrages et assemblages** discutent de ce problème sérieux. Des assemblages pour des applications spéciales de même que le développement d'ancrages de fondation sont également présentés dans cette section.

Les **Applications aux ponts** complètent les études précédentes avec des applications réelles, et devraient ainsi intéresser un large public. Les contributions soumises des trois continents projettent un éclairage nouveau sur le sujet. Les ponts dont il est question dans cette section varient en format des passerelles piétonnières entièrement en composites, aux structures de ponts bois-composites, aux ponts routiers en béton précontraint avec tendons composites. La variété des projets de ponts est complétée par une autre section portant sur toutes les autres **Applications novatrices des matériaux composites.** On y trouve un vaste éventail d'applications, parmi lesquelles le lecteur choisira ses préférées et y fera, nous l'espérons, quelques découvertes surprenantes. Les contributions regroupées dans ces deux sections constituent la grande partie de ce volume.

En tout, ces comptes rendus regroupent plus de soixante articles, auxquels ont contribué 136 auteurs de 13 pays. Nous espérons que ces comptes rendus de MCAPC-I fourniront aux chercheurs, qu'ils soient dans un milieu industriel ou universitaire, un portrait global et un éclairage nouveau sur un domaine en évolution constante, celui des matériaux composites d'avant-garde pour ponts et charpentes.

Une conférence portant sur l'utilisation des matériaux composites d'avant-garde dans les ponts et charpentes ne saurait être complète sans un volet consacré aux **Méthodes analytiques et de design.** Des analyses par éléments finis y sont présentées par plusieurs auteurs, qui les ont utilisées pour prédire le comportement des ponts et éléments structuraux en matériaux composites. D'autres auteurs démontrent un intérêt particulier pour les problèmes d'optimisation ou ont concentré leurs efforts sur la prédiction du flambement de sections en composites, et sur les normes de design.

K.W. Neale et P. Labossière
Université de Sherbrooke

TABLE OF CONTENTS / *TABLE DES MATIÈRES*

Keynote Lectures

Conférences générales

ADVANCED COMPOSITE MATERIALS IN BRIDGES AND STRUCTURES
K.W. Neale and P. Labossière, Editors; Canadian Society for Civil Engineering, 1992

Matériaux composites d'avant-garde pour ponts et charpentes
K.W. Neale et P. Labossière, éditeurs; Société canadienne de génie civil, 1992

DEVELOPMENT OF FIBRE-REINFORCED PLASTIC PRODUCTS FOR THE CONSTRUCTION MARKET – HOW HAS AND CAN IT BE DONE?

C.A. Ballinger
Craig Ballinger and Associates
Vienna, Virginia, USA

ABSTRACT

This paper presents a brief introduction and overview of the development and current uses of fibre-reinforced plastics for civil engineering structures and structural members in the United States and abroad; including cables, highway lighting poles, reinforcing bars for concrete and for building construction. The paper also covers ongoing structural FRP research that is being conducted at several universities, on concrete reinforcement, pultruded structural shapes, and on a modular, totally fibreglass, bridge deck. The paper also presents some suggestions for developments and future applications of fibre-reinforced plastic composites. The paper strongly recommends that such developments may be expedited by a team or consortium approach, in which the prospective users, engineers, composites industry representatives and standards organizations would work together in focused Research and development programs. With regard to economics, the most important factor is not the cost per pound of the materials, but rather what is the cost effectiveness of the finished product, INSTALLED, and the life expectancy – and what are the costs of the alternatives.

RÉSUMÉ

Cet article présente une brève introduction et une vue d'ensemble du développement et des utilisations actuelles des plastiques renforcés de fibres (FRP) dans les structures de génie civil, et dans les éléments structuraux, tant aux États-Unis qu'ailleurs dans le monde. Ceci inclut les câbles, les lampadaires d'autoroutes, les barres d'armature pour le béton. Cet article couvre également la recherche sur le FRP dans plusieurs universités, les armatures pour le béton, les sections structurales pultrudées, et un tablier de pont modulaire et entièrement en fibres de verre. L'article propose également des suggestions sur le développement et les applications futures des composites de FRP. On y recommande que de tels développements soient entrepris par une équipe ou un consortium, qui serait formé des utilisateurs potentiels, ingénieurs, représentants des industries concernées et organismes de normalisation, lesquels travailleraient en collaboration dans des programmes conjoints de R & D. D'un point de vue économique, le facteur le plus important n'est pas le rapport coût/poids des matériaux, mais l'efficacité économique du produit fini, installé, en tenant compte de sa durée de vie et du prix des alternatives.

INTRODUCTION

This conference has been established to start a continuing effort to promote the development and use of composite materials for bridges and structures. I think that this objective is not only technically feasible it is economically justifiable. However, if it is to be accomplished within a reasonable period of time, it will require a sustained effort by several groups of individuals and companies working together as a team, not individually and sequentially. It will also require forging new types of industry- university-government alliances that have rarely been used for the development of more conventional civil engineering materials, products and technology. Even so, such research and development work may be expensive and time consuming to complete, but much less than if the work was not done synergistically.

As taxpayers we cannot justify the expenditure of huge amounts of public funds to develop products for private companies. On the other hand it is not reasonable to expect private industry to develop (by themselves) a broad range of construction products that would use an entirely new class of materials that have different physical properties in all three directions; for which extremely little structural testing has been done; and for which there are no applicable specifications or test methods that government or private sector designers and owners of buildings and other types of structures may use for purchasing such products. Moreover, the two technologies that are so different and new that those with expertise do not even know the 'language' of the other group; that is, the composite industry (including the materials suppliers, the aerospace and defense contractors, and government officials involved with civilian construction). Thus, much work will have to be done, and a teamwork approach is the only viable alternative. Each of the three (or more) groups, with a vested interest in the outcome, have different knowledge, expertise and requirements. By working together they complement each other. By not working together they strongly inhibit such developments.

BACKGROUND

Traditional Materials

Almost since the beginning of recorded time 'modern man' has used composite materials for civil engineering-type construction; including timber (a natural composite), straw reinforced clay, steel reinforced concrete and plywood. Note that the materials are made integrally and not just connected together, as is a reinforced concrete bridge deck on the supporting girders. Thus, the concept of using composite materials for civil engineering structures should not be considered overly revolutionary, but merely a logical evolution of this technology as new materials are developed and research and development work is conducted to characterize the physical and structural properties of the constituent materials and combinations of them, and to develop analytical criteria and procedures for engineers to design and build structures with them.

Fiber Reinforced Plastic Composites for Military and Defense

Development of fiber reinforced plastic (FRP) composites essentially began in the early 1940's, for military and aerospace applications; such as rockets and satellites, wing skins for aircraft and even main rotor blades for helicopters. The main attributes of composites are high strength, light weight, resistance to chemicals, and good fatigue strength and non-magnetic properties. Over the years, billions of dollars have been spent on development of fibers, resins and techniques for designing, manufacturing and testing composites. For many of these applications the value of weight reduction was as high as several hundred thousand dollars per pound, thus research and the expenditure of considerable money was justified.

With regard to advanced composites, it is possible to build very sophisticated products, with the fibers oriented in the directions to carry principal stresses. A wide range of service conditions can be accommodated and long term durability under extreme temperatures may be achieved. However, precise stress analyses and structural designs are still very difficult to do, even for the simplest of the products. Almost all of the (single, and very special purpose) products are still developed through an iterative process of design, build, test, redesign and retest until the product meets agreed upon criteria. It is then that very specialized ASTM-type tests and specifications are developed; basically for quality control and quality assurance, so that exactly the same product is produced and accepted for the specified application.

It should be noted, however; that most of these applications of FRP composites are really non-structural; that is they are not load bearing or do not carry significant loads over long periods of time; as do primary building and bridge members. This is evident from the fact that many of the composite products are rather thin sheets of materials (laminates) that are used for such applications as wing skins ('control' surfaces) for aircraft and to enclose various types of structures; where reduced weight, high stiffness and certain serviceability criteria are required.

The cost of the constituent materials was frequently over 100 dollars a pound and the cost of the work to develop the materials and the final products was extremely high. Nonetheless, it is this research and development work that permitted space travel to the moon and the development of stealth bombers; that could not be done with conventional construction materials. Continued research and development work has also led to a substantial reduction in material costs for lower performance fibers and resins.

It is also important to recognize that such products are developed through a teamwork approach in which the end users, the materials scientists, engineers, and manufacturing experts all work together – through the entire process of research and development. This, in itself, is extremely important.

MATERIALS, MANUFACTURING AND DESIGN

Materials

Fibers

A variety of types of fibers are now available; including several types of glass, aramid (kevlar), graphite, boron, silicon carbide and alumina. They offer a wide range of structural properties, including strengths that range between 100,000 psi and 600,000 psi and elastic moduli that range between 10 million and over 100 million psi. However, it should also be noted that the fibers have different properties in all three directions (tension, compression and radially). In addition aramid and graphite fibers (by themselves) have a negative thermal coefficient of expansion.

Resins

Many types of resins may be used; including epoxies and polyesters. Some resins are classed as thermoplastics and others as thermosets – depending on whether they may be melted, and even remelted; e.g. the thermoplastics. Obviously the physical and strength properties of the latter resins will change with changes in temperature. Moreover, as we know from the use of epoxies for construction and repair of portland cement concrete, the properties of resin formulations may be changed with the additions of even small amounts of catalysts, retarders and fillers.

Manufacturing Methods

One of the biggest attributes of composites is the ability to use a variety of manufacturing processes and materials. In addition, as the automotive manufacturers eventually recognized, it is possible to make one composite part that replaces, as many as, ten individual parts. Although the cost of the basic materials may be high, developments in the materials and technology are occurring and the costs are steadily becoming less. Perhaps the most important factor to remember is not the cost per poud of the materials, but rather what is the cost effectiveness of the finished product, installed, and the life expectancy – and what are the costs of the alternatives.

Layup

This process involves hand or machine buildup of sheets of fibers, that are bound together with a plastic (resin). This may be the simple concept that is used for patching major rust holes in cars or the very complex approach used for manufacturing wing skins of military aircrafts, using computer controlled laser cutters and highly automated and precise equipment. However, it is not too different than cutting out parts for a ladies dress, orienting the pattern for the individual pieces on the cloth so that they are 'on the bias' and they will not warp.

Pultrusion

This is a continuous process of pulling fibers through a resin bath and then through a heated die to produce constant cross-section and structural shapes. Although many of the fibers are uniaxial, it is possible to pull off-axis fibers and continuous strand mat.

Filament Winding

This is an automated process in which resin-wetted fibers are wound around a mandrel to produce circular shapes, as well as very complex solid shapes when special techniques are used. This process permits wide variations in the angle of winding the various layers and the thickness of the completed circular part.

Design Principles and Concepts

The general philosophy of composite design is perhaps best depicted by the layup process, in which the strong fibers are oriented and built up in the directions to carry the expected structural loads. It may be noted that the early design concepts were an outgrowth of 'plywood' design. However, fibers may now be oriented at almost any angle, rather than being limited to plus or minus 90 degrees. In addition, like the plywood design, layers of fibers for sheet products (laminates) are frequently balanced and symmetrical on both sides of the center layer – to prevent warping during curing.

Another factor that must be recognized is that resin systems are subject to long-term deformation under static or cyclic loads, and the magnitude of such deformation (with time) is primarily a function of (1) the type of resin used, (2) the relative percentage and orientation of the fibers, (3) the magnitude of the load, (4) the temperature. For civil engineers, the phenomenon is somewhat like the time dependent behavior of prestressed concrete; with the added factor that the strength elements (the fibers) may be oriented in all three planes.

From the above, it is obvious that doing a classical (or even a simple) design with fiber reinforced plastics could be a very complex and difficult task; especially for almost every civil or structural engineer in America. Moreover, there are very few universities in the U.S.A. that teach courses in structural composite design but some are being developed and taught. Very very few civil engineers, architects, government officials and building owners know anything at all about structural composites.

As noted above, it should be recognized that many of the military and aerospace applications have been of relatively thin sheet-type layers of composites (for such things as wing skins on aircraft) whereas most civil engineering structures are required to carry significant loads over long periods of time – in changing environments, often without the benefit of periodic inspection and maintenance. Moreover there is very limited available information on design criteria, standards or test and evaluation criteria that is directly applicable to thick-section composites, that will be needed for civil engineering style structures or structural members made with fiber reinforced plastics.

CURRENT CIVILIAN APPLICATIONS OF COMPOSITES

Although this conference is primarily focused on advancing the development and use of advanced composites for civil engineering-type applications it is important to recognize the current state-of-the-art and actual use of FRP composites for civilian construction work. This is important for two reasons:

1. The need to recognize the sort of products that are being made, for what type of applications; and what are their limitation – that might be minimized with advanced composite materials, and
2. The level of acceptance of FRP composites by civilian government and code-writing organizations highlights how our developments should proceed.

There is no question that most of the current FRP products used in the civil sector construction are made with glass fiber materials and there are only a few that are made with aramid and carbon fibers. Nonetheless, these developments and use have served us well, to set the stage for uses of more advanced composite materials or improved designs for currently made products. That is, to begin making civil engineers, architects and government officials aware of the fact that FRP composites can carry structural loads, be reliable and be cost effective, at least for very specific types of applications.

The principal applications have been where corrosion resistance and non-magnetic properties are required. In some cases they are subjected to significant (and not well defined) loads over long periods of time, in the very aggressive outdoor environment – without periodic inspections and maintenance. There are also many composite construction products that are not subjected to primary loads but which must sustain minor loads and maintain a serviceability function in an aggressive environment. The following is a brief summary of the more important types of products, that provides some insight into the products that are being used at this time.

8

Filament Wound Products

Several types of filament wound products are being made and sold.

Storage Tanks

One of the largest, and most well known, markets for structural fiberglass is for double wall tanks for storage of gasoline, chemicals, and food products. The stiffening ribs for some of these tanks are made with graphite materials.

Pipe Products

Several companies manufacture, up to 12 feet diameter, filament wound high- and low-pressure pipe systems that are used for the construction of both new pipelines and for structurally relining deteriorated existing lines, without necessitating digging up the existing line, that may cross under expressways, railroads or buildings.

What is most important is that these manufacturers have worked together to establish the SPI's 'Fiberglass Pipe Institute' and to establish industry standards for filament wound pipe that are based on criteria from the American Water Works Association (AWWA) and other organizations. In addition, appropriate ASTM test methods and specifications have been developed for testing and acceptance of these products by governmental agencies and building owners, through the competitive bidding process.

Poles for Highway Lighting

Several U.S. companies make poles for roadway lighting. The most noteworthy are the poles recently developed by the Shakespeare Company, that are designed to break away at the base when hit by a car. This Research and Development effort was based on criteria of the Federal Highway Administration and the American Association of State Highway and Transportation Officials (ASSHTO), but was conducted with private industry funds, with technical support and some testing by the FHWA.

Pultruded Products

A few U.S. companies have been making constant cross-section pultruded fiberglass structural-type shapes, for many years, These are primarily used for the construction of:

– walkways for chemical plants and platforms for offshore structures
– non-magnetic buildings
– non conductive ladders and booms for man-lift bucket trucks
– custom made throughs, racks and enclosures.

It should be noted that there are several major drawbacks to some of these 'general purpose' products, that has limited their acceptance and use.

1. Because of the low elastic modulus of the products (in the range of 6 million psi, or one fifth of that of steel) structural designs are based on deflection criteria rather than on strength criteria,
2. The results of recent structural research (funded by the National Science Foundation) tests have indicated that the currently made pultruded shapes have severe problems under overload or failure load levels and improved concepts are needed for connecting pultruded structural shapes.

With the exception of the ladder industry, there has been extremely little interaction between the pultrusion companies, structural engineers, governmental agencies, or the end users. Although the SPI has a 'Pultrusion Industry Council', it is the opinion of the SPI that standards (and improved designs for pultruded shapes) should be developed by the ASTM; which is not consistent with the normal activities of ASTM.

9

Cable, Rod and Grid Systems

Several types of FRP cable, rod and grid products have been developed for the construction market.

Guy Cables

One of the most spectacular applications is for the 1300 feet tall Sutro Tower in the San Francisco area, that supports television and communications antennas. The 300 feet tall antennas at the top are guyed with flexible kevlar ropes which are anchored in resin-filled end sockets. Limited studies indicated that although graphite materials may be non-magnetic they are not electrically invisible, and they cause distortion of electronic signals.

Aramid and graphite cable systems have been developed and used to anchor off-shore platforms and other types of structures. Aramid cables are widely used to support communications and electrical power lines.

Research work funded by the FHWA is also leading to the development of a fiber-dominated eye-bar (or link) type of cable that will be installed in a tied-arch highway bridge in California. Although the cable is primarily glass, the eye ends are reinforced with kevlar and graphite.

Prestressing Systems for Concrete

Several companies throughout the world have been developing cable systems for prestressing concrete.

Germany : The companies of Bayer and Strabag have developed a fiberglass system for bridge construction. Although it was developed in the mid-1980's it has not been widely used.

Netherlands : The HBG construction company and AKZO have developed the "Arapree" aramid type of pretensioning system, that has been used to some extent in Germany and in Japan, but not in the U.S.

Japan : Several Japanese companies are developing aramid and carbon systems for prestressing concrete; including Mitsubishi Kasei, Mitsui Construction, Teijin, and Tokyo Rope.

It is very important to note that although these products have only been used to a limited extent many of them are being developed under the Japanese Government's 5-year "Comprehensive Technological Development Project" being coordinated by the Building Research Institute of the Ministry of Construction.

Cable Stayed Bridges

Research is underway at the Swiss Federal Institute for Research and Testing (EMPA) to develop a carbon fiber type stay cable system, that may look somewhat like the Bayer-Strabag prestressing system, but have much superior structural properties.

Grid Systems

The Japanese company Shimizu has developed a grid system for reinforcing concrete and to retain earth and rock embankments. This unique FRP product may be made entirely with glass, with aramid or with carbon fibers – or combination of these fibers. A Canadian company has recently been licensed to manufacture this product line for the North American market. A limited amount of research is being conducted in the U.S. on concrete reinforced with this product.

Structural Strengthening Systems

One of the most interesting, and perhaps the most economically viable, application of currently available advanced composite materials is for strengthening damaged or structurally inadequate buildings and bridges.

Switzerland

A Swiss company has developed a concept for strengthening structures with adhesively bonded graphite-epoxy laminated plates; that advances the concept of strengthrening such structures with adhesively bonded steel plates has been used in Europe for well over 10 years. The plates, that are 28 times lighter than the weight of steel plates that would be needed to provide the same strength, are easier and less expensive to install.

Japan

Several companies have been strengthening tall chimneys by wrapping them with carbon fiber tape materials.

U.S.

The California highway department has recently strengthened several bridge columns in the Los Angeles area by wrapping them with fiberglass-polyester materials, to provide increased structural strength and safety against earthquake damage. The technology and State specifications for this concept were developed with private money and some State support, through structural tests at the University of California in San Diego, as an alternate to their more common practice of jacketing the columns with structural steel plates.

Bridge Decking

A very interesting concept that is being developed by the U.S. Department of Transportations's Federal Highway Administration is a modular, totally fiberglass, bridge deck. Although such a deck would certainly be expensive, the economic advantage envisioned is that such a deck could be used to replace a deteriorating reinforced concrete deck on a low load classification bridge with a composite deck that might weigh only 30 percent of the existing deck, and thereby allow an increase in the load classification of the bridge. Research on this concept is underway at the FHWA's structures laboratory in McLean, Virginia. The concept also has potential application for the construction of new wider or longer lift span bridges, where weight reduction would also be important.

DEVELOPMENT OF COMPOSITE PRODUCTS FOR THE CONSTRUCTION MARKET

It is possible to develop advanced composite products for the construction market, but it will take a considerable amount of concentrated effort. Also, as noted previously, it should be done by the teamwork approach; with the prospective users, engineers, composites industry representatives and strandards organizations working together in an iterative fashion to:
- identify serviceability and strength criteria
- develop and evaluate prototype models through design and test programs
- develop methods for testing and accepting the products

Although this has rarely been done in the civil engineering arena it has been done for military and aerospace applications for at least 40 years.

This approach is also compatible with professors doing research and the need of private companies to have secrets from their competition. However, there is one significant difference in that the 'researchers' must also become involved in the 'D' of 'R and D', the development phase. Heretofore, too many university professors have restricted their activities to only the research phase, with the result that their good work may not result in advancing technology, at least within a reasonable period of time. We really cannot afford that luxury.

It is possible to develop a wide variety of both individual products and standardized ones, through a focused effort that will encourage the investment of private, commercial and government money, and technical support, to develop new advanced composite products for civilian construction. Although it is relatively new, the concept of cost sharing and teamwork is essential for the development and use of new concepts. There are several broad areas of applications that can be considered; that includes advancement of the concepts and products that are now being developed outside of North America.

Individual Structural Members

General purpose shapes that could be used by designers to create a variety of types of structures. This could include I- and box-beams, channels, etc. This may also include improved concepts for connecting them together. The shapes could also be used in combination with other materials so as to improve their structural efficiency and economy. Examples might include:

– hybrid beams which could include a fiberglass I-beam core with graphite-epoxy plates bonded to the flanges, to place premium materials where they are needed to carry the highest tension and compression stresses; which would permit longer spans with less material, at a lower unit cost.

– graphite-epoxy beams that are combined with a fiberglass grid deck to act together in the same manner as a reinforced concrete bridge deck is connected to and structurally works together with its supporting steel of concrete girders.

– lightweight filament wound graphite-epoxy couplers to connect oceanic pipelines, that are now connected with very heavy steel connections, by divers working at great depths, under very hazardous conditions.

– chopped carbon fiber reinforced concrete panels, hatches, floor units, manhole covers, etc., that would be strong but lightweight. The electrical conductivity of the panels would be particularly applicable for floors in hospitals, computer rooms, etc., where static electricity must be dissipated to prevent sparks, explosions or interference with electronics.

Structural Systems, or Assemblies

These would be assemblies of individual components, that provide an integrated product that may be used for special applications. There could be two broad areas of structural systems that could be developed: (1) building systems that would be installed by contractors and (2) construction equipment assemblies that would simplify or expedite the construction work – because of their light weight, stiffness, etc.

The first group of systems could be those that are designed to serve a special function, such as the group of new and unusual shapes that have been designed to work together for ceramic cooling towers.

The latter types of applications may actually be the most promising, and saleable – to contractors, construction companies, etc. because those companies are more sensitive to the cost of doing business; the cost of men and equipment – and the time required to actually build something. This could include lightweight, strong and durable platforms, formwork or other construction 'hardware' that could more easily be moved and used by contractors.

Non-Structural Systems

There may also be a variety of types of advanced composite specialty products that would not generally be load bearing, but marketable because of their light weight, corrosion resistance and time necessary for construction, and other attributes. This could include building facia panels, such as the chopped carbon fiber reinforced concrete ones developed and used in Japan.

Prestressing (cable) Systems

The research work in Europe and Japan has shown that there is some potential for advanced composite systems for very specialized products or applications; primarily for prestressing concrete and for ground anchors and tie-backs for retaining walls. In addition, such products are also being evaluated for certain portions of airport runways, where metallic reinforcement causes interference with control-tower to aircraft communications.

One of the largest possible applications of advanced composite prestressing systems may be for construction of guideway systems for Mag-Lev trains; which will probably require non-magnetic reinforced concrete.

One of the few applications of fiberglass reinforcing bars in the U.S. is for the construction of MRI facilities in hospitals. It is possible to develop specialized prestressed concrete girders and floor members that would be even more economical.

In addition to the above there will also be a need to develop equipment and techniques for inspecting and accepting advanced composite construction products and also for maintaining and repairing them.

CONCLUSION

In summary, there are many potential opportunities for using advanced composite materials for the construction market.

The public and private owners of structures are always looking for new materials and structural concepts which are less expensive, more durable and longer lasting than those currently used. Unfortunately, they are not familiar with advanced composite materials, so it will be more difficult and time consuming to prove that they are reliable and economically viable.

It is also necessary to be aware of applicable codes and specifications that control the design and construction of buildings and bridges, even though they may not directly recognize FRP composites, their philosophy and general criteria will control structural behavior as well as safety issues, such as fire, smoke and toxicity behavior. Nonetheless, it will also be possible to develop products that are accepted on the basis of their particular characteristics; providing that necessary test and performance data has been provided.

It is also possible to use the consortium approach that is not only feasible, it is perhaps the best way to make significant advancements into this entirely new area of civilian technology – within a reasonable amount of time. Such an approach should encourage funding and technical support from the suppliers of advanced composite materials, manufacturers, and government agencies for programs that would be properly managed, and conducted at a variety of locations – under close supervision of all organizations that have a vested interest in the developments. The guiding committee would also play a vital role in establishing the necessary design and performance criteria, specifications and ultimate introduction of such products in engineering practice.

Again, the most important factor to remember is not the cost per pound of the materials, but rather what is the cost effectiveness of the finished product, installed, and the life expectancy – and what are the costs of the alternatives.

ADVANCED COMPOSITE MATERIALS IN BRIDGES AND STRUCTURES
K.W. Neale and P. Labossière, Editors; Canadian Society for Civil Engineering, 1992

Matériaux composites d'avant-garde pour ponts et charpentes
K.W. Neale et P. Labossière, éditeurs; Société canadienne de génie civil, 1992

DESIGN METHODS AND BRIDGE FORMS FOR THE COST EFFECTIVE USE OF ADVANCED COMPOSITES IN BRIDGES

P.R. Head
Maunsell Structural Plastics
Beckenham, Kent, England

ABSTRACT

An analysis of the factors influencing the cost effectiveness of advanced composites in bridges is followed by a review of design methods and specifications being used for the design and construction of advanced composite structures, including bridges. Presentations of different bridge forms showing how advanced composites can be used, sometimes in conjunction with other materials, to the clients and bridge users' benefit, are given.

RÉSUMÉ

Une analyse des facteurs portant sur l'économie relative à l'emploi de matériaux composites d'avant-garde dans la construction des ponts est suivie d'une revue des méthodes de calcul et des descriptifs couramment employés pour la conception et la mise en oeuvre de structures comportant de tels matériaux, y compris les ponts. Nous présentons les différents types de ponts montrant l'emploi de matériaux composites d'avant-garde, parfois conjointement avec d'autres matériaux, au bénéfice du maître d'oeuvre et des usagers.

INTRODUCTION

Advanced composite materials are now being used successfully in a wide range of structural applications in the construction industry around the world (Fig. 1). Generally, these applications are in prototype structures which are demonstrating the capability of the materials to achieve the designer's objectives either when used on their own or when used in conjunction with other materials. The construction and evaluation of prototypes is an essential part of the development of any new material, to address matters such as long term structural performance, how materials stand up to construction in a civil engineering site environment and how they weather and change appearance if exposed. However a key question rarely answered by prototype projects is whether the materials have a future in the construction market, in other words, whether the applications will be "cost effective". Many fine words have been written about the promise of these materials but the lack of progress into widespread use illustrates just how difficult it is to achieve cost effectiveness.

Ten years ago we realised that a quantum leap in design, manufacture and fabrication technology would be needed if advanced composites were to make the transition from low volume, high performance and high cost markets such as Aerospace and Defence to the high volume, high performance and low cost market of construction. A research and development programme was initiated in 1984 to address these fundamental problems and this paper provides an up to date summary of the progress that has been made in the bridge sector of the construction market, concentrating particularly on the design and specification linked to the developments in manufacture.

Fig. 1: Variable Message Sign Gantry

ADVANCED COMPOSITE MATERIALS

It is essential to understand the meaning the author attaches to Advanced Composite Materials, since the interpretation varies from country to country. The following definition has been adopted by the British Plastics Federation and is used by the author:

"Composite materials consist normally of two discrete phases, a continuous matrix which is often a resin, surrounding a fibrous reinforcing structure. The reinforcement has high strength and stiffness while the matrix binds the fibres together, allowing stress to be transferred from one fibre to another and producing a consolidated structure.

In advanced or high performance composites, high strength and high modulus fibres are used in relatively high volume fractions while the orientation of the fibres is controlled to enable high mechanical stresses to be carried safely. In the anisotropic nature of these materials lies their major advantage. The reinforcement can be tailored and oriented to follow the stress patterns in the component leading to much greater design economy than can be achieved with traditional isotropic materials".

Different fibre types and resin matrices have been continually developed over the last thirty years and together with many different highly automated manufacturing techniques they offer considerable scope to the designer. There are three main types of fibre which are currently available for advanced composites, glass fibres, aramid fibres and carbon fibres. Suitable resins for construction are polyester, vinylester or epoxy.

COST EFFECTIVENESS

General

Cost effectiveness is proven if a client chooses to purchase a product and it performs to the client's satisfaction. In bridge engineering these choices are complex and the criteria adopted by clients in decision making vary widely and are unpredictable.

Client choice will be examined in more detail. Also the factors driving the costs of applications of advanced composites in bridges will be examined to set the background to the technical part of the paper.

Client Evaluation

Capital Design and Construction Cost

First cost is the major and often the only parameter used by clients in decision making. A particular problem to be overcome by the advanced composites industry is to provide the essential element of competition that will be sought by clients. If a design is fully specified around a particular system clients will need to be assured that an element of competition is present in the manufacturing procurement. However often the developments are linked to particular manufacturing processes only available from limited sources. Advanced composite solutions for bridges are very unlikely to use the internationally standardised products that are seen in the steel industry because there are so many ways in which different fibres and resins can be combined. On the other hand design costs are so high that some standardisation of product components is necessary to ensure competitiveness, as will be shown later. There are many more questions than answers here but it is clear that designs that can be sourced from several suppliers in competition are essential.

Whole Life Costing

Clients for bridges in the United Kingdom such as the Department of Transport, British Rail and National Rivers Authority usually now require whole life costing to be carried out which takes account of the predicted inspection and maintenance costs over the lifetime of the bridge, usually taken as 100 to 120 years. Costs are evaluated by calculating the net present value of the expenditure stream using a cash discount rate of between 2 and 8%. Advanced composite materials benefit considerably compared with steel in such comparisons, but the benefits vary with the cash discount rate chosen. The Department of Transport currently uses 6% at which level costs more than 40 years in the future become negligible. Advanced composite materials having a life to maintenance of over 40 years clearly benefit as long as inspection cost are minimised. Hence "smart structures" technology allowing remote inspection and condition monitoring, perhaps by using optical fibres embedded in the composite, will be important in the future.

Bridge User Benefits

The infrastructure in Europe has been overwhelmed by traffic growth over the last twenty years and inspection and maintenance of bridges causes great disruption of traffic. The Department of Transport is one of the first government authorities in the world to introduce a method of evaluation of alternative bridge designs which takes account of the traffic disruption and accident costs caused by inspection and maintenance over the lifetime of the bridge (Ref. 1). Disruption and accident costs are assessed against delay times and accident statistics using a standardised computer program that allows for alternative traffic routes. The net present value of these costs is added to the whole life cost to provide a comparative cost for deciding on the bridge form. Traffic disruption costs for busy motorways can be a very high proportion of the capital cost and therefore this approach is greatly encouraging an interest in low maintenance bridge designs in the United Kingdom.

Construction Speed

High interest rates for borrowing money is forcing some clients to look for greater construction speed and where construction is over busy roads or railways this speed also leads to the direct benefits described above in terms of user delay reductions. Since lightweight advanced composite structures can offer lower lead times and shorter construction times on site, this is an important aspect in client choice.

Environmental Aspects

Global environmental considerations are now beginning to influence client decision making in Europe as far as materials selection is concerned (Ref. 2). Matters such as energy consumption during manufacture, the depletion of valuable resources and recycling of materials are beginning to have an impact and this trend is expected to accelerate as legislation and taxation are introduced. Advanced composite materials have much to offer an environmentally conscious client particularly in replacing the use of hardwoods from tropical rain forests, and in reducing energy consumption.

Advanced Composite Costs

Materials

The material costs of fibre and resin constituents are a greater proportion of total cost than the constituents of concrete and steel. Hence it is of the utmost importance to minimise the quantity of fibre and resin in construction applications where first cost is still an overriding consideration. This means design methods have to be very sophisticated to avoid conservatism and material wastage. Associated manufacturing methods have to have low scrap rates combined with the highest possible quality to reduce variability. Current design work shows that glass fibres are much more cost effective for spanning bridge members such as decks. This is shown graphically in Figure 2 in which the cost effectiveness is compared with conventional steel construction. Also typical weight savings are shown. However in very long spans, in prestressing applications and some strengthening applications aramid and carbon fibres may be appropriate. This was reported more fully in Ref. 3. This paper will concentrate on the larger volume glass fibre applications.

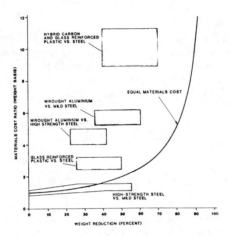

Fig. 2: Cost of Substituting Lightweight Materials for Steel in Short Span Structures

Design

Design costs of advanced composite applications are very high because of the great complexity of the design process and the need to optimise material content. Design costs of steel and concrete structures may typically be 2 to 4% of construction cost whereas with advanced composites design may cost at least 10 to 20%. This premium may render a design too expensive and therefore reduction of costs through the use of standard modular system designs is attractive to the designer.

Manufacture

Since material costs are so high it is paramount in the high volume, high quality, low cost construction environment that manufacturing costs are minimised without sacrifice in quality. Hence automated processes with low labour input such as pultrusion supplemented by filament winding and resin injection moulding are ideally suited to meeting these demands. Labour intensive manufacturing methods used in aerospace will never be cost effective for construction.

Fabrication and Erection

Advanced composite structures need to avoid the labour intensive fabrication shop and site practices still prevalent in steel and concrete bridges if they are to be successful commercially. Modular systems that can be rapidly assembled without drilling and bolting are most likely to achieve these objectives. The lightness of structures, which can be as low as 10% of the weight of conventional bridges, means that structures can be built with much lower craneage and transport costs, and the use of modular systems provides shorter lead and construction times. Conversion from constituent materials to a finished high quality structure can be achieved in days rather than months.

Other Aspects of Bridge Cost

The use of lightweight materials means that foundation costs are reduced and where earthquake design is important these can be reduced even further. Since foundation costs are typically 50% of bridge costs, these savings can be very significant.

Conclusion

It is clear from the forgoing that a modular advanced composite system, manufactured by an automated process such as pultrusion, which can be rapidly assembled into a large range of different structural forms for bridges is likely to have a good chance of success. The design method and specifications that follow have been developed specifically to enable such a system, using pultruded glass reinforced components to be developed.

DESIGN METHODS

Limit State Design

The design method developed for advanced composite materials in construction applications is based on Limit State Design principles whose development in Europe began in the 1960's. The Joint Committee on Structural Safety (JCSS) agreed in 1974 that these principles should form part of an international system of unified standard codes of practice for structures. The first volume of this work entitled "Common Unified Rules for Different Types of Construction and Materials" was published in 1978 (Refs. 4 and 5) and deals with a common basis for setting up codes to ensure adequate treatment of safety and reliability.

Limit State Design provides a logical design procedure which identifies the limit state at which a structure ceases to fulfill its design functions. The aim of Limit State Design is to achieve acceptable probabilities that the relevant limit states will not be reached during the intended life of the structure. The assessment of these probabilities sets up a framework within which the uncertainities in test data, loading, stress analysis, etc. can be quantified and understood.

The method is particularly suited to design of composite structures (Ref. 6) and for bridge applications the following limit states are appropriate: –

(a) Serviceability

The serviceability limit states that need to be considered include deflection/deformation, first damage, and local buckling, including effects of creep and environmental damage as appropriate.

(b) Ultimate State

The ultimate limit states to be considered include rupture under elastic stress distributions and fatigue loading including the effects of creep and environmental damage as appropriate.

Variables are dealt with by the use of partial coefficients. Two types of partial coefficient are used, one type for the loads or load effects and the other for strength of materials or elements. The partial coefficients vary depending on the load type, the material, the component, and the consequences of the limit state being exceeded.

Partial coefficients are applied to a characteristic value and the resulting value is termed a design value. The design value for a particular variable changes for different limit states (whereas the characteristic value is constant). Thus, for a particular limit state the design value of the different types of variables is given by:

$$F_d = \gamma_f F_k$$
$$f_d = f_k / \gamma_m$$

Where F_d is the design value of a load
F_k is the characteristic value of the load
γ_f is the partial coefficient for the load
f_d is the design material property (e.g. strength)
f_k is the characteristic property
γ_m is the partial material coefficient for the property

Laminate characteristics including partial material coefficients are derived using a combination of laminate test specimen data, properties of the constituent materials from test data and laminate properties derived from theory. A special computer program LAMINA has been written for the purpose of calculating laminate properties. The design method has been independently assessed by the National Physical Laboratory in the United Kingdom.

Loading

The design loading, for bridge applications in the United Kingdom is taken from BS 5400 (Ref. 7) which is also written in limit state format.

Design Criteria

The design criteria at the Serviceability Limit State are as follows:

Deflection:
Deflection limits for bridges are associated with dynamic response under various loadings. The criteria given in BS 5400 have been adopted. These criteria are important for the design of footbridge applications but are not as onerous as might be expected because of favourable mass to stiffness ratios combined with the good damping properties of advanced composite materials.

First Damage:
The maximum strain in any direction in any lamina is limited to 0.25%.

Buckling:
Calculated stresses do not exceed the buckling limit calculated as:

$$\text{Buckling Limit} = \frac{\text{Minimum critical buckling stress}}{\text{Buckling factor}}$$

The minimum critical buckling stress is calculated using standard theoretical solutions for orthotropic plates with appropriate edge restraints and applied stress distributions using plate stiffnesses factored by the appropriate material factors. The buckling factor is chosen from test results for particular applications.

21

The design criteria at the Ultimate Limit State are as follows:

Rupture:
The design of the structure under the design loads appropriate to the ultimate limit state ensures that prior collapse does not occur as a result of rupture of one or more critical sections. Ultimate factored stresses calculated using linear elastic methods are checked to ensure that they do not exceed design strengths. Also sections in compression are checked to ensure that ultimate factored stresses do not exceed post-buckling rupture strengths. These strengths are assessed from test results. Finally laminates are checked for the combined effects of biaxial stress membrane stress and shear using a failure criterion such as a generalisation of the well known von Mises criterion.

Fatigue:
An overall assessment of the loads likely to cause cumulative fatigue damage of the bridge enclosure and footbridge structures designed so far shows that in these cases significant loads do not have sufficient frequency of occurrence to make fatigue a critical limit state design parameter. Bridge decks subject to wheel loads would be a different matter however.

Fire Resistance:
A programme of fire tests has been carried out in order to establish the design criteria for fire resistance. The specification of resin type, structural performance and Class 2 performance in accordance with surface spread of flame test BS 476 Part 7 has been established in these tests as satisfactory to ensure that bridge materials will not support combustion for significant distances away from a fire source and will not contribute significantly to the heat generated by the burning source material. A high glass content is found to be a significant factor in the satisfactory performance of the materials in these tests.

Methods of Analysis

Global analysis of the structure is undertaken for each of the most severe loading conditions appropriate to each part. Linear elastic methods of analysis, typically using finite elements, are used for both serviceability and ultimate limit states with appropriate allowances for loss of stiffness due to creep. Particular care is taken to model the structure so that stresses due to all the following aspects of structural behaviour are calculated:
(a) Stresses due to axial forces and global bending moments, both longitudinal and transverse including the influence of shear lag;
(b) shear stresses including those due to torsion;
(c) warping stresses due to torsion and distortion of box members;
(d) transverse stresses due to distortion of the members;
(e) stresses due to creep;
(f) stresses occurring in the vicinity of major stress concentrations, around local loads or near supports.

Partial Factors for Strength and Stiffness

The partial material factors for laminate strength and stiffness used for design are calculated by multiplying together component factors for the effects of variations in laminate thickness and reinforcement position, creep, weathering and constituent glass weight. In each case the range of each variable is carefully assessed by discussions with experts in manufacture and testing and by detailed analysis of available test data. Specification limits and test methods are decided upon for each variable and then the limits are used to calculate the appropriate partial material factors. It is found necessary to make separate calculations for membrane, in plane and shear effects, flexural and torsional effects. Also different values for long and short term loading are required because of the effects of creep and weathering. A matrix of 28 different partial material factors have been developed for each laminate configuration. Those familiar with limit state design in concrete and steel will appreciate the great complexity this introduces.

MANUFACTURING SPECIFICATION

General

The vital importance of developing a detailed specification for manufacture, testing, assembly and erection of advanced composite bridge structures was recognised at an early stage in the development of the design method. For example the evaluation of partial material factors for strength and stiffness is dependent on a knowledge of the maximum variation in laminate thickness and glass content or position. These tolerances need to be realistic in relation to the manufacture of complete advanced composite sections and therefore extensive consultations were carried out within the industry on an international basis as the specifications and design methods have been developed.

The design–specification–manufacture interfaces have been carefully studied at all stages of the design development and a performance specification has been evolved based on defined material types and structural geometry. A full programme of type approval, batch and panel assembly tests, is specified including tests for fire resistance and effects of weathering. The main elements of the specification are summarised below.

Laminates and Profile

The designer gives typical fibre layouts for each laminate. The manufacturer is required to select the final laminate material and proportions of materials within the defined geometry to satisfy the short and long term strength, stiffness, durability and fire resistance requirements of the specification as established by type approval.

Materials – Resin, Glass, Additives and Surface Veil

A detailed resin specification is given covering physical properties, keeping properties, packaging, labelling, quality control and batch acceptance. It is anticipated that filled resin will be supplied to the manufacturer and therefore tolerances are specified on filled resin properties for quality assurance purposes covering viscosity, volatile matter, gel time and density. Glass fibre grades and relevant British Standards are specified together with a particular specification for specialist mats. Pigments and ultra violet absorbers are specified and other additives such as fillers, flame retardant substances and low profile additives are permitted as long as performance requirements are achieved. A surface veil is generally specified on exposed profile surfaces.

Type Approval

A type approval process is required to be carried out before resin and glass are supplied for manufacture of the finished profiles. This consists of obtaining certificates of conformity for constituent materials and carrying out a series of tests on pultruded laminate samples to demonstrate satisfactory performance. These tests include the following:
- short term flexural strength and stiffness
- long term flexural stiffness
- long term flexural strength
- weathering test
- fire resistance test

The mechanical test methods specified are those given in Royal Aircraft Establishment Technical Report 84102, CRAG test methods for the measurement of the Engineering Properties of Fibre Reinforced Plastics. Ultrasonic C-scan of test samples is specified for long term test samples to check for fibre debonding during each test.

Pultrusion Process

A detailed specification for the manufacturing process such as pultrusion is prepared covering handling and storage of materials, splicing of glass reinforcement, cutting of sections, gripper design, quality control, packaging and labelling. The manufacturer is required to have the certificate of registration under the British Standard Institution System for the Registration of Firms of Assessed Capability to BS 5750: Part 2. Records are required to enable full Lot Traceability to be carried out for each pultruded section and batch sizes are defined.

Physical Properties

Requirements for physical properties of the finished pultruded profiles are specified in terms of appearance, selection of test pieces for destructive tests, mechanical properties, tolerances, quality control, batch acceptance and proof testing. Minimum requirements are given for strength, stiffness, glass content and barcol hardness, all to be established generally by destructive tests on each batch of material. Figure 3 shows the locations from which test pieces are required to be taken for the typical components. The tests on these test pieces included the following for short term strength and stiffness:
- tensile properties
- flexural properties
- compression properties
- interlaminar shear strength

As for type approval, the current CRAG test methods are specified, with strength being defined as failure of the first lamina.

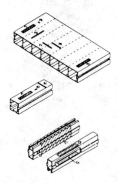

Fig. 3: Destructive Test Coupon

BRIDGE FORMS

General

A wide ranging review of the potential for the use of advanced composite materials in bridges is given in Ref. 2. Since that paper was written considerable progress has been made in the United Kingdom in developing a range of specific applications and it is these that are presented. It is already clear that these materials will be important for bridge construction, but they should not be viewed as providing only complete replacements for steel, concrete and timber. It is likely in most bridges that a combination of different materials, each being used to its maximum effectiveness, will provide the optimal solutions. Indeed the introduction of advanced composite materials may open up the possibilities of new structural forms in steel and concrete.

It is the durability of composite materials and the attendant reduction in maintenance cost which is so attractive to clients, and the forms of bridge now being developed take full advantage of this property.

Bridge Enclosure and Aerodynamic Fairings

The concept of 'Bridge Enclosure' was a prize winner in the 1981 Civil Engineering Competition organised in the United Kingdom. The proposal was to suspend a floor beneath the girders of steel composite bridges to provide inspection and maintenance access and then to seal the floor onto the underside of the edge girders to enclose the steelwork and protect it from further corrosion (Fig. 4). Trial enclosures of this type, undertaken by the United Kingdom Transport and Road Research Laboratory, have shown that the corrosion rate of steel within such enclosures drops to negligible level (Ref. 8).

Glass reinforced composites have been found to be ideal materials for such enclosure floors because they add little weight to the bridge and are highly durable particularly as they are protected from ultraviolet light under the bridge (Ref. 9). An advanced composite construction system concept, was used in the design of the world's first major bridge

Fig. 4: A19 Tees Viaduct Bridge Enclosure

enclosure completed in 1989 in the United Kingdom. This cellular glass reinforced plastic floor, consisting of interlocking pultruded planks (Fig. 5) was manufactured and installed as a permanent enclosure to the A19 Tees Viaduct. The floor area is $16\,000\,m^2$ and contains 250 tonnes of advanced composite materials. Other bridge enclosure projects have followed (Fig. 6) in which steel is completely enclosed with an advanced composite skin.

Fig. 5: Advanced Composite Construction System

The concept of bridge enclosure may have even more important implications for the future design of long span bridges. Currently steel box girders are often used for the deck girders of such bridges in order to provide an aerodynamic shape, to minimise exposed steel areas and to give good torsional stiffness. However the development of cable-stayed bridges and the reduction in fabricated cost of steel plate girders compared with the labour intensive steel boxes has resulted in a recent increase in the use of plate girders for long span bridges. The addition of fibre reinforced plastic enclosures around such structures not only enables maintenance costs to be greatly reduced, but also enables the shape of the cross section to be optimised by extending the enclosure into a fairing to give minimum drag consistent with aerodynamic stability (Fig. 7).

Fig. 6: Nevilles Cross Bridge Enclosure

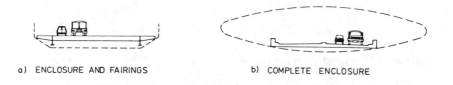

a) ENCLOSURE AND FAIRINGS   b) COMPLETE ENCLOSURE

Fig. 7: Enclosures Around Long Span Bridge Decks

The concept could be further extended to complete enclosure of the deck and traffic for extremely long span bridges in which the design for lateral wind is likely to dominate the structural form (Ref. 3).

Alternative forms of steel deck, such as space frame trusses, can be considered for use inside enclosures (Fig. 8). These forms were previously ruled out because of high maintenace cost. Research work is proceeding on designs in which advantage can be taken of robotic welding of steel components. The reinforced plastics skin will act completely with the steel and contribute to the overall bridge stiffness.

Also forms of enclosure in which the edge panels act as permanent formwork for casting deck concrete cantilevers are now being designed for a series of small bridges on the approaches to the Second Severn Crossing in the United Kingdom (Fig. 9). These bridges are also highly suited to new construction over live motorways and railways since the enclosure can be used as a complete working platform for constructing the deck slab.

27

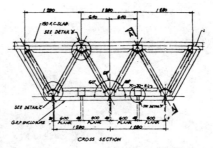

CROSS SECTION

Fig. 8: Alternative Form of Enclosed Steel Deck

Fig. 9: Bridge Enclosures for Motorway Bridges

Advanced Composite Bridge Decks

The glass reinforced polyester Advanced Composite Construction System (ACCS) has been used to build two 18 metre long and 2 metre wide bridge beams which are entirely bonded and have no mechanical fasteners (Fig. 10). The System consists of three pultruded interlocking sections. These beams are part of a major test programme, partly funded by the Department of Transport, to prove the design and long term performance of advanced composite bridge decks (Fig. 11). The beams have performed outstandingly well so far having been test loaded under full design live load for five months. Designs for many footbridge applications are now complete and show competitiveness with steel and concrete across a wide range of span lengths. This success is partly the result of a European industrial collaboration in which material scientists, production engineers, structural engineers, construction engineers and end users have worked as a team. The companies involved with Maunsell were DSM Resins, Vetrotex (UK) Ltd., Ciba Geigy Plastics and CU Bridges.

This technology has enabled the design to be completed for the world's longest span advanced composite bridge to be built over the River Tay in Scotland (Fig. 12). This 65 metre main span cable stayed footbridge will have deck and towers manufactured by bonding ACCS components and will use aramid fibre cable stays. Construction will be reported further at the conference.

Work is now proceeding on the development of designs for trafficked roadway decks which will also use ACCS.

Fig. 10: ACCS LINK Beams During Manufacture

Fig. 11: ACCS LINK Beams Under Load

29

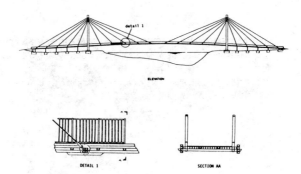

Fig. 12: Aberfeldy Footbridge – Linksleader Project

CONCLUSION

Limit State Design techniques, combined with sophisticated manufacturing specifications for automated manufacture, have enabled optimised bridge forms to be developed which use advanced composite materials. The modular Advanced Composite Construction System concept has demonstrated that the design and construction of these bridges can be cost effective in the current market place and there are several factors which are likely to increase their competitiveness in the future. Many new forms of bridge are emerging as a result of this technological breakthrough. It is now clear that the great expectations are beginning to be fulfilled and advanced composite materials will take their place alongside steel and concrete as bridge construction materials of the 21st Century.

REFERENCES

1. BD36/88 *Evaluation of Maintenance Costs in Comparing Alternative Designs for Highway Structures*, Department of Transport, November 1988.

2. Head, P.R., *The Future of FRP in Structures From an Engineer/Designer's Viewpoint*, British Plastics Federation Congress, November 1990.

3. Head, P.R. and Richmond, B. *Alternative Materials in Long Span Bridge Structures*, Kerenskey Memorial Conference, June 1988.

4. *Common Unified Rules for Different Construction Materials*, Vol. 1, International System of Unified Standard Codes of Practice for Structures, CEB–FIP, 3rd Edition, 1978.

5. *General Principles on Reliability for Structural Design*, Joint Committee on Structural Safety (JCSS), IABSE, Report 35 Part II, 1981.

6. Head, P.R. and Templemen, R.B., *The Application of Limit State Design Principles to Fibre Reinforced Plastics*, British Plastics Federation RP Group Congress, 1986.

7. BS 5400 *Code of Practice for the Design of Steel, Concrete and Composite Bridges*, London, British Standards Institute, 1978 onwards.

8. Bishop, R.R., Transport and Road Research Laboratory, *Report 83*.

9. Head, P.R. and Churchman, A.E., *Design, Specification and Manufacture of a Pultruded Composite Flooring System*, "Mass Production of Composites" Symposium, Imperial College of Science and Technology, 19th and 20th September, 1989.

ADVANCED COMPOSITE MATERIALS IN BRIDGES AND STRUCTURES
K.W. Neale and P. Labossière, Editors; Canadian Society for Civil Engineering, 1992

Matériaux composites d'avant-garde pour ponts et charpentes
K.W. Neale et P. Labossière, éditeurs; Société canadienne de génie civil, 1992

SMART STRUCTURES – A REVOLUTION IN CIVIL ENGINEERING

R.M. Measures
University of Toronto
Downsview, Ontario, Canada

ABSTRACT

Smart Structure technology could usher in a "new age of civil engineering". In this era many major new structures would be constructed with built-in optical sensing systems and this could lead to a civil infrastructure: bridges, highways, railways, dams, pipelines, port facilities, airports and buildings, that is self-monitoring and even self- scheduling of its maintenance and repair. This revitalization would come from the marriage of: fibre optics, sensors, lasers, microelectronics, integrated optics and artificial intelligence with the more traditional areas of material and structural engineering. Improvements in safety, reductions in cost, and enhancement of the environment are some of the benefits expected.

RÉSUMÉ

La technologie des "structures intelligentes" pourrait marquer le début d'un "nouvel âge du génie civil". Des structures majeures seraient construites en intégrant des systèmes de senseurs optiques. Ces infrastructures, incluant les ponts, routes, chemins de fer, barrages, pipelines, ports et aéroports, en plus des édifices, pourraient s'auto-diagnostiquer et même prévoir leurs besoins propres en entretien et réparations. Cette revitalisation serait issue d'une combinaison de fibres optiques, senseurs, lasers, de la micro-électronique et de l'intelligence artificielle, avec les domaines plus traditionnels de l'ingénierie des structures et des matériaux. Il est à prévoir que les bénéfices incluraient des améliorations de la sécurité et de l'environnement, de même qu'une réduction des coûts.

INTRODUCTION AND BACKGROUND

Need for Smart Structures in Civil Engineering
Buildings, bridges, dams, tunnels, seaports, highways, railways, pipelines and airports represent an enormous financial investment. There is a growing need for a built-in sensing system for monitoring these structures due to increasing: traffic, air pollution, corrosive precipitation (acid rain) and the rising costs of labour intensive inspection, maintenance and repairs. If resident optical fiber sensors can improve concrete evaluation, the ramifications could have enormous value to the multi-billion dollar annual construction business as aging and deterioration of many highway bridges is recognized as one of the major problems facing structural engineers in the US, EC and Japan. In cold-climate countries this deterioration has been greatly accelerated by the use of de-icing salts. In Europe, a large scale research effort has been directed at using advanced composite materials (ACM) in bridges. This research has addressed issues of corrosion, rehabilitation and monitoring and has led to new concepts and designs in bridge repair and construction. One of the most signicant advances is the replacement of steel prestressed tendons with ones made of ACM. These fiber reinforced polymers are practically immune to corrosion and also lend themselves to internal monitoring by means of embedded fiber optic sensors.

A structurally integrated sensing system could monitor the state of a structure throughout its working life. It could determine the: strain, deformation or deflection, load distribution, temperature or environmental degadation, experienced by this valuable asset and warn if any excursions deviate from accepted values. Such an integrated sensing system could also monitor the various structural components during construction, possibly leading to improved quality control. In certain instances this resident sensing system could also provide valuable information on the usage of the structure. For example, in the case of a bridge the sensing system could be used to generate information on the traffic itself. It is quite conceivable that a suitably instrumented bridge could monitor not only the number of vehicles per minute, but their weight (even the distribution of this weight) size, direction of travel and the speed of each vehicle. In terms of degradation, especially chemical, it may be possible to have sufficient warning of its onset and location that a low cost repair is possible. The impact on civil engineering of structurally integrated sensing could be profound, leading to a revitalization of the field. For optimum progress civil engineers should work closely with those developing fiber optic sensors in order to ensure that full use is made of the wealth of knowledge and experience currently available.

Smart Structure Definitions
The simplest definition of a *Smart Structure* is one that possesses a structurally integrated sensor system for determining its state [**Measures, 1989**]. Most important of all a Smart Structure should maintain a constant vigilance over its structural integrity and indicate if damage is inflicted or fatigue problems developing. In more advanced Smart Structures the information provided by the sensor system could be used for controlling some aspect of the structure such as its: stiffness, shape, position, or orientation, such systems might be called "Adaptive (or Reactive) Smart Structures" [**Ahmad, et al.,1990**] to distinguish them from the simpler "Passive Smart Structures" which only sense their state. Eventually, Smart Structures will be developed that will be capable of adaptive learning and these might be more correctly termed "Intelligent Structures". Indeed, if we consider the confluence of the four fields: Materials and Structures; Sensor Systems; Actuator Control Systems and Neural Network Systems, we can appreciate that there is the potential for a broad class of structures, **figure 1**. According to this designation *Sensing Structure* would be more appropriate than the Passive Smart Structure term used above.

Overview of Potential for Smart Structures
The successful development of Smart Structures Technology could lead to: bridges and tunnels that are remotely self monitoring and also track the flow of traffic; dams and buildings that check their internal integrity and their response to loads to which they are subjected; aircraft that are safer, lighter, more efficient, easier to maintain and to service; pipelines, pressure vessels and storage tanks that constantly monitor their structural integrity and immediately issue an alert if any problem is detected; space platforms that check for pressure leaks, unwanted vibration, excess thermal buildup, and deviation from some preassigned shape. In many situations this optical sensing

network would be part of a active actuation control system that could take some appropriate action such as modifying the stiffness, shape or motion.

The considerable potential of "Smart Structure Technology " to a broad range of civil and industrial sectors: from Bridges and Dams to Aircraft and Submarines, is gaining recognition and as a consequence is being taken seriously within the: US, EC and Japan. Several substantial research programs have been initiated within the past few years and the Japanese have identified " Intelligent Materials " as one of their National Goals for the 21st Century. Indeed, Smart Structures may eventually be recognized as a revolution in many branches of engineering, and especially in civil engineering.

SMART STRUCTURE FIBER OPTIC SENSING SYSTEMS

Merits of Fiber Optic Sensors

Fiber optic sensors are: extremely small and light weight, resistant to corrosion and fatigue, immune to electrical interference, safe and practically incapable of initiating fires or explosions. They are also particularly attractive as they: serve the dual role of sensor and pathway for the signal, are dielectric in nature and are therefore compatible with ACM, and avoid the creation of electrical pathways within the structure. They also have a high sensitivity and very large bandwith and are consequently well suited as sensors for embedding within ACM and concrete. The fact that no protection is required against lightning and various forms of electromagnetic interference also figure prominently in their choice for a sensing system in large civil structures. Even in the absence of a direct lightning strike, magnetic field coupling can generate voltages that can burnout various components and fragile circuits used in many electronic systems, especially if distributed over a large structure. It is expected that the increased use of fiber optics for communications will help reduce the cost of this technology and if it is also used substantially in the construction business this, in itself, could bring down the costs due to the potential scale of this market.

Structurally Integrated Fiber Optic Sensor Measurements

Optical fibers can either be bonded to the surface of most structures or embedded within: advanced composite materials (ACM), concrete or low temperature melting metals. These sensors are capable of measuring: strain, vibration frequencies, structural deformation and temperature. They could possibly detect and locate internal damage generated by: impacts, manufacturing flaws, excessive loading or fatigue, and assess the growth in the extent of these damage zones. Structurally imbedded optical fibers sensors might also monitor the cure state of thermoset composites or concrete. This could lead to improvements in the quality control of structures made from these materials. In terms of ACM the combination of improved quality control and a resident sensing system could greatly enhance confidence in their use and expand their role as a primary building material. This might avoid structural overdesign and provide the opportunity of evaluating the true fatigue life based on the actual load history of each component. Monitoring the dynamic response of structural components during operation might also provide insight into the structural integrity of the system.

Types of Fiber Optic Sensor

Structurally Integrated Fiber Optic Remote Sensor (SIFORS) technology [**Measures, 1989**] is in its infancy, nevertheless, the optical fiber sensors are fairly well developed. In general we can characterize optical fibers sensors as either "distributed" or "localized." Distributed sensors are, in principle, very attractive for they would permit the use of fewer sensors and represent a more effective use of the optical fibers, in that *each element of the optical fiber is used for both measurement and data transmission purposes*. In essence by making a time of flight measurment along the optical fiber the value of the measurand is determined along the entire length of the optical fiber. In practice the spatial resolution attainable is somewhat limited. This is particularly true if the measurements have to be made in real time. Furthermore, the need for high resolution, flexible sensing architecture and graceful degradation is not satisfied with distributed sensors. Often a single break in the optical fiber effectively takes out of commission a large proportion of the sensing capacity.

Localized fiber optic sensors *determine the measurand over a specific segment of the optical fiber* and are similar in that sense to conventional strain or temperature gauges. If a scalar field, like pressure or temperature, is to be mapped a grid of such localized line integrated sensors can be used in conjunction with an inverse Radon transform. Indeed, direct measurements of angular orientation can be directly made with such line integrated sensors [**Turner et al., 1989**] and have specific value in certain forms of structural control situations. However, a grid of line integrated optical fiber sensors, in general, cannot be used to map a vector or tensor field, such as strain. Exceptions can arise where the field is constrained in such a way that it is not truly two dimensional in nature. Where the field is two dimensional, three independent measurements are required at each point to uniquely specify the field. This can be accomplished, in certain situations, by using an optical strain rosette sensor, comprising three small identical fiber optic sensors set at different orientations, **figure 2**, [**Valis et al., 1990**]. Under these conditions high spatial resolution is important as each sensor must have a gauge length that is small compared to the scale length for the field gradient.

Information about the state of the structure is impressed upon the transmitted (or in many instances the reflected) light by a number of mechanisms. These include interactions that change the: intensity, phase, frequency, polarization, wavelength or modal distribution of the radiation propagating along the optical fiber. Fiber optic sensors can be classified into two major categories: Intensiometric and Interferometric.

Intensiometric Sensors - depend upon a variation of the radiant power transmitted through a multimode optical fiber. The simplest form of this sensor involves the presence or absence of light. For example, fracture of an optical fiber can serve as the basis of a damage sensing systems. A full scale leading edge of an aircaft wing instrumented with a grid of damage sensing optical fibers demonstrated in ground impact tests the potential of such a system [**LeBlanc and Measures, 1992**]. It has long been recognized that small bends in an optical fiber leads to a loss of its light as the curvature permits core radiation to leak into the cladding from which it escapes the fiber. The smaller the radius of curvature the greater the loss. Microbend fiber optic sensors rely on this principle, using either some device or the intrinsic corrugations of the composite material to convert an applied force into a microbend in the optical fiber and thereby reduce its transmission of light, **figure 3**. Unfortunately, such sensors have very limited sensitivity, measurement range and accuracy. Furthermore, many phenomena that are unrelated to strain can also cause attenuation and using a transduction mechanism that restricts the optical signal is not sound. Optical time domain reflectometry (OTDR) uses a time of flight measurement to not only detect but also locate breaks in an optical fiber by means of Fresnel reflection from the fracture. If an optical fiber has several intrinsic mirrors along it length then OTDR can be used to evaluate large strain excursions with a spatial resolution of meters and a strain resolution of probably 1000 μstrain {1 mm in 1 m - gauge length}, **figure 4**, [**Zimmermann et al., 1989**]. Other types of intensiometric fiber optic sensors that can measure temperature are based on fluorescence decay, differential absorption and blackbody emission [**Measures, 1989**]. Raman backscattering has been used to make a "distributed" fiber optic temperature sensor, [**Dakin, 1989**] with a few degrees resolution within about 1 m spatial resolution. In principle, it could also provide distributed strain measurements.

Interferometric Sensors - represent a large class of extremely sensitive optical fiber sensors. These primarily function by sensing the measurand induced phase change in light propagating along a single mode optical fiber. There are two basic types of interferometric (or phase modulated) fiber optic sensor that are well suited for use with Smart Structures: the Fabry-Perot and the intracore Bragg grating. In the Fabry-Perot fiber optic sensor a cavity comprising two mirrors that are parallel to each other and perpendicular to the axis of the optical fiber forms the localized sensing region. A change in the optical path length between the mirrors leads to a shift in the frequencies of the cavity modes. In this way the reference and sensing optical fiber are one and the same, up to the first mirror that constitutes the start of the sensing region. The Fabry-Perot sensor is normally configured to be single ended, and if built with low reflectivity mirrors will provide a sinusoidal phase strain relationship. Fabry-Perot sensors can be configured as either "intrinsic", **figure 5(a)** [**Hogg et al., 1991**] or "extrinsic", **figure 5(b)** [**Kruschwitz et al., 1992**]. The former has the advantage of being the least perturbative, capable of being used in the form of a strain rosette,

34

and possibly the more robust. As a consequence of the separation between gauge length and cavity length in the latter, it can be built with long gauge lengths yet work with lasers of modest coherence length. The extrinsic sensor has less transverse coupling and can therefore evaluate more directly the axial component of strain in a host material **[Sirkis   and Haslach, 1991]**.

The intracore Bragg grating fiber optic sensor **[Morey et al., 1989]** relies on the narrow band reflection from a region of periodic variation in the core index of refraction of a single mode optical fiber. In this sensor the centre (Bragg) wavelength of the reflected signal is linearly dependent upon the product of the scale length of the periodic variation (the periodicity) and the mean core index of refraction. Changes in strain or temperature, to which the optical fiber is subjected, will consequently shift this Bragg wavelength leading to a wavelength encoded optical measurement that can be determined by a simple wavelength dependent ratiometric technique, **figure 6,** **[Melle et al., 1992 and Measures et al., 1992]**.

The high sensitivity of both the Bragg grating and the Fabry-Perot sensor make it possible to use them with short gauge lengths. However, in civil structures it is possible that large gauge lengths (of the order of a meter) might be adequate, if not desirable. Under these circumstances a modalmetric or a polarimetric fiber optic sensor might be satisfactory. To some extent the modalmetric sensor is simpler to use and has slightly higher sensitivity than the polarimetric sensor. The most well developed form of modalmetric sensor is called a two mode sensor and involve changes in the transverse spatial distribution of light within the optical fiber, **figure 7** **[Blake et al.,1988, Lu and Blaha, 1991]**. In these sensors modal interferometry is exploited in circular or elliptic core single mode optical fibers excited with light below the cut off wavelength (the wavelength above which light propagates in only a single spatial mode) in the sensing region of the optical fiber.

Unfortunately, the nonlinear (cosine) relationship between the signal and the measurand (strain and or temperature) in the host structure is common to all of the interferometric sensors with the exception of the Bragg grating. This relationship gives rise to serious problems of signal fading and ambiguity in regard to the direction of phase change. There are, however, a number of quadrature detection schemes for overcoming this difficulty, **[Liu and Measures, 1992]**. However, a fairly sophisticated commercial demodulation system is now available, **figure 8**. For sensitive fiber optic interferometric sensors, the circular symmetry of the optical fiber may not be adequate to stabilize the two orthogonal linear polarization eigenmodes and this can lead to *polarization-fading* and the possibility of cross coupling between the modes.   These effects represent a source of noise in interferometric sensors.   One of the most common methods of avoiding this problem is to use polarization maintaining single mode optical fibers. The high birefringence designed into this kind of optical fiber stabilizes the polarization because the two eigenmodes are forced to have an appreciable difference in their respective propagation constants and this limits the exchange of energy between the two modes. This high birefringence is created either through asymmetry, such as an elliptic core, or by thermal stress loading the core. Several optical fiber designs have been introduced to this end, **[Measures 1989]**.

Smart Structure Criteria and Choice of Sensor
In order to develop fiber optic sensors that are well suited for Smart Structures we have built and tested several different kinds, including: Michelson, Polarimetric, Two mode and Fabry-Perot sensors. We have also explored the use of the Bragg grating sensor. This has allowed us to compare their relative strengths and weaknesses, **[Turner et al.,1989]** A set of criteria that can serve as a guide for judging any fiber optic sensor's suitability for use with Smart Structures would require an ideal sensor to be:
1.   *Intrinsic* in nature for minimum perturbation and stability
2.   *Localized,* so it can operate *remotely* with *insensitive leads*
3.   Able to *discern* the direction of measurand field change
4.   *Well-behaved* with *reproducible* response
5.   Able to determine *measurand field directly* or with additional measurement
6.   *All-fiber* for operational stability
7.   Able to provide a *linear response* - most interferometric sensors require *quadrature* detection

35

8. A *single optical fiber* for minimum perturbation and *common mode rejection*
9. *Single-ended* for ease of installation and connection
10. Sufficiently *sensitive* (for detection of acoustic emission) with adequate *dynamic range*
11. *Insensitive* to phase interruption at the structural interface
12. *Nonperturbative* to the structure and *robust* for installation
13. Interrupt immune and capable of *absolute measurement*
14. Amenable to *multiplexing* to form sensing networks within structures
15. *Easily* manufactured and adaptable to *mass production*

If a single sensor could be developed for all of the measurements required by Smart Structures the cost would be minimized. Such a sensor might have to be sufficiently sensitive to detect acoustic emission, while exhibiting a measurement range adequate for monitoring the general loading of the structure. This requires an interferometric fiber optic sensor and the choice seems to lie between the Fabry-Perot and the intracore Bragg grating sensor. However, for large civil type structures the Two Mode sensor may be adequate for some applications. A careful comparison will have to be undertaken to determine which has the greatest advantage in practice. The Fabry-Perot may have the edge when it comes to sensitivity but the Bragg grating offers more direct absolute measurement capability and a very simple (low cost) demodulation system.

Critical Issues for Smart Structure Sensing
Implementation of Smart Structure technology will require a number of critical issues [**Measures et al., 1992**] to be addressed. These can be divided into micromechanic issues and system architecture issues. The former includes:

• *Influence of Embedded Optical Fibers on the Material Properties*
If optical fibers are to be embedded within practical ACM or concrete structures they must not: compromise the tensile or compressive strength, increase the damage vulnerability or reduce the fatigue life of these materials. Although preliminary evidence suggests that degradation of the material properties is minimal [**Czarnek et al 1988, Blagojevic et al., 1989, Loken 1990, Roberts and Davidson, 1992**] providing that the diameter of the optical fiber is less than about 125 μm, fractographic studies reveal that in the case of ACM optical fibers embedded at an angle to the adjacent ply directions of the composite material create resin cavities (termed "resin-eyes" because of their shape). The formation of resin-eyes leads to high stress concentrations at the host/optical fiber interface which may over a period of time and under occassional high loading conditions lead to debonding of the optical fiber from the host. Clearly, more definitive research will be needed before optical fibers can be imbedded with confidence within structures intended to have a 20 (plus) year working life.

• *Sensor/Host Interface, Coatings and Sensor Performance Life*
It is possible that this high stress concentration around the optical fiber may be diminished with coatings of appropriate size and stiffness, [**Sirkis and Dasgupta, 1990**]. Debonding between the optical fiber and the host represents a potentially serious concern in terms of sensor performance. Careful consideration will have to be given to the diameter of optical fibers and their type of coating if they are to be embedded within composite structures and function correctly with no performance degradation for the useful life of the structure. When the optical fibers are embedded collinear with the ply direction there is no appearance of a resin eye and minimal stress concentration is expected. However for this configuration a resin void is formed on the end of the optical fiber and this could lead to initiation of debonding from the host material. This suggests that it may not be prudent to locate the sensing region at the end of an embedded optical fiber intended for extensive use. More research is needed to ascertain the seriousness of this problem.

• *Sensing System Damage Vulnerability and Degradation*
A sensing system within a practical Smart Structure will have to be fairly robust and degrade gracefully when the structure suffers modest damage. Special coatings, a judicious choice of location and orientation may help to reduce premature fracture of the optical fiber and use of a cellular sensing architecture minimize the loss of any particular set of optical fibers.

The latter includes:
• *Sensing System Architecture*
The type of measurement to be undertaken will dictate whether the fiber optic sensors should be localized or distributed, while the nature of the structure will determine if they are multilayered or limited to form a single layer. Optical fiber orientation and placement, especially in an ACM layup, spatial resolution and constraints imposed by the finite bend radius are all important factors to be considered. It will also be important to identify any special structural features or regions of high stress concentration. The power budget and signal to noise factors will certainly play a key role in defining the sensing system architecture. Sensing system damage vulnerability and ease of fabrication represent other considerations to be taken into account.

• *Multiplexing Strategies*
Multiplexing is the merging of data from several channels into one channel, while demultiplexing is the inverse. The primary parameters used in optical multiplexing schemes are: wavelength, time, frequency, phase and space. Consequently, there are five multiplexing techniques. In the case of large civil structures, Time Division Multiplexing, can be practical and is also the least expensive. However, as discussed above there are other reasons for not placing all of the sensors on a single optical fiber and winding it throughout the structure. It may make good sense to have a few sensors on each optical fiber and use a cellular sensing architecture as indicated in the generic illustration, **figure 9**.

• *Structural Interconnect/Interface*
The nature of the structural interconnect problem hinges on whether the output from the structure is optical or electrical. Current thinking is predicated on optical signals flowing into and out of the structure via the structural interface. In general this interface must have minimal structural perturbation, be easy to fabricate and introduced during fabrication of the structure. If multiplexing is not used each sensor would have its own input/output and a ribbon or bundle of optical fibers would have to egress from the structure. Nevertheless, the structural interconnect problem might be simplified if each major sensing cell were connected through a single electrical cable to the central computer facility charged with interpreting the data. The development of a multisensor signal processing optoelectronic chip would certainly simplify the interconnect issue and provide a number of advantages, **figure 10**, [**Measures et al., 1992**]. One of the most important, however, is the great reduction of unit cost when so much of the system is reduced to the form of an optoelectronic chip. This includes: multiplexing, multisensor signal processing and possible conversion to single electrical output.

SMART STRUCTURE APPLICATIONS TO CIVIL ENGINEERING

Advances in Bridge Technology
The Institution of Structural Engineers (1989) reported that severe corrosion of bridge prestressing strands in structures built only tweny years ago had been discovered and related failures had occurred. This has prompted research into the use of alternative noncorrosive materials, especially ACM, for bridges. In order to permit the continued use of some bridges that have suffered serious deterioration, ACM plates have been bonded to the structure. Although, these materials cost more than steel, their lighter weight, better corrosion resistance (especially to sodium chloride) and lower cost of fabrication and installation have encouraged their use.

In the last few years bridge designers have looked to the use of ACM (carbon fiber/epoxy and fiberglass/epoxy) in the construction of new bridges due to their corrosion resistance, especially in high saline environments. In particular, the use of ACM tendons for prestressing of concrete girders and decks represents one of the most promising applications of this new material for bridges. Although, there has been no long term studies on ACM use in bridge construction, the prospect of instrumenting each ACM tendon with a built-in fiber optic sensing system makes their use worthy of serious consideration. Indeed, several bridges have already been built in Europe using ACM as a major constituent:

-- The Ulenbergtrasse Bridge in Dusseldorf, is the first highway bridge to be constructed using glass reinforced prestressing strands (Polystar Tendons).
-- The Marienfelde Bridge in Berlin, is the first civil engineering structure to be built with external prestressing polystar tendons.
-- The Schiessbergstrasse Bridge in Leverkusen, uses 27 polystar prestressing tendons, several of which have fiber optic sensors in their core.
-- Finally, the A19 Tees-Viaduct in Northeast England, is a composite steel-concrete bridge with the world's first major ACM bridge enclosure. [**Mufti et al., 1991**]

More recently researchers at South Dakota School of Mines and Technology, Rapid City, have built a 9 meter long and 5 meter wide bridge for demonstrating the potential of using carbon fiber composite cables for prestressing concrete bridge decks [**Advanced Materials and Processes, 15, June 1992**]

ACM prestressing tendons are made of parallel filaments of glass, carbon, or aramid embedded within a resin matrix. The general advantages of ACM tendons as compared to steel are:
(a) High strength to mass ratio, which ranges between 10 to15 times that for steel.
(b) Excellent fatigue characteristics, three times that of steel for carbon and aramid fiber tendons.
(c) Superior corrosion resistance, especially for high saline environments.
(d) Low thermal expansion coefficient, especially for carbon fiber tendons.

It should be noted that the glass fiber reinforced material tendons may have a fatigue strength which is significantly lower than that of prestressing steel. Unfortunately, the high ratio of the axial to lateral strength of ACM tendons, means that conventional systems used for steel tendons cannot ensure a reliable anchorage for ACM systems, and can result in premature anchorage zone failure.

Types of Measurement and Sensing Strategy

Types of Measurement Relevant to Civil Engineering
A selection of some of the more important measurements that should be undertaken with the implementation of Smart Structure Sensing to large civil structures:
-- Vibration frequencies of: support columns, floors, windows, bridge decks and cables....
-- Spatial vibration modes of: walls, floors, bridge decks and cables....
-- Thermal strain and deformations caused by sunlight to one side of the structure.
-- Construction loads (excessive loading, pressures, impacts....).
-- Wind monitoring and wind pressure on: bridges, buildings.....
-- Long-term health monitoring including load history and excessive loads.
-- Shear forces on bridge bearings.
-- Internal strain distribution and hydropressure for dams.
-- Onset of internal crack formation in concrete structures.
-- Impact detection and localization.
-- Damage assessment (delamination in ACM).
-- Debonding of reinforcing bars and prestressing tendons in concrete structures.
-- Corrosion degradation.
-- Chemical sensor for: acid rain, smog, bird droppings, deicing salt solution.......
-- Real time truck/aircaft weight and load distribution.
-- Traffic flow patterns (number of vehicles, weight and velocity).
-- Ground creep or seismic movement.
-- Temperature distribution and anomalous hot spot detection.

Some of the characteristic problems of facing the designer of a structurally integrated sensing system for monitoring concrete civil structures are:
-- Small strains so need for high strain sensitivity.
-- Rough handling and a hard casting process.
-- Harsh environment (high levels of moisture, large temperature excursions).
-- Large dimensions and exposure to electrical interference.

Types of Sensor and Sensing Strategy
Since it will be necessary to make the unit cost of this sensing technology as low as possible for its implementation to be economic, one sensor should be capable of undertaking as many different measurements as possible for then it could be used in a diverse range of applications. Some of the most important measurements for civil engineering include: strain distribution, acceleration, vibration frequency, spatial vibration mode, pressure, temperature, elongation, cure for ACM or concrete, corrosion degradation, damage assessment. It may also be necessary, in certain situations, to be capable of undertaking chemical sensing.

It has been established that a Fabry-Perot (and possibly a Bragg grating) fiber optic sensor has sufficient sensitivity to undertake: strain distribution, acceleration, vibration frequency, spatial mode, pressure, temperature and elongation measurements, either directly or by suitable mounting, **figure 11**. First the Fabry-Perot fiber optic sensor represents an extremely sensitive strain gauge if bonding to, or embedded within, a structure. If such a Fabry-Perot optical strain gauge is mounted on the diaphragm of a suitably constructed cell it can be used as an effective pressure gauge or it can serve as an accelerometer if mounted so that it measures the force exerted by a small mass that is free to accelerate. For many practical situations, the temperature has to be measured to account for thermally induced apparent strain. This can be quite considerable (of the order of 1000 µstrain) for structures like bridges which may be subject to 60 °C temperature excursions. A Fabry-Perot fiber optic sensor can measure the temperature directly by preventing it from experiencing any strain coupling from the structure, [**Hogg et al., 1992**]. Cure monitoring of ACM with Fabry-Perot optical strain gauges could be feasible through the use of optoacoustic probing, [**Ohn et al., 1992**]. It is also possible that some form of optoacoustics may also enable cure monitoring of concrete to be undertaken with an embedded fiber optic sensing system, [**Fuhr et al., 1992**]. It may even be possible for a Fabry-Perot fiber optic sensor to undertake some degree of chemical sensing.

The optimum sensing strategy for any given situation is very dependent on the measurements to be undertaken. For example, if it desirable to measure the wind loading on a tall building the best sensing configuration might be to use a distributed fiber optic sensor (or many time division multiplexed sensors along an optical fiber) that is bonded to an ouside wall of the building. On the other hand, a highly flexible sensing cell architecture may be more desirable in the case of a bridge where: various loads are to be recorded; structural vibrations monitored; the traffic flow is tracked; and corrosive degradation is assessed.

Current Integrated Sensing for Bridges and Other Civil Structures

Most bridges comprise three basic structural components: one or more deck spans; piers (or supports); and bearings, **figure 12**. The bearings serve to: transmit load from the deck to the supports; provide a degree of freedom from physical constraints and damp dynamic effects. The Bearings are constructed of alternating layers of elastomer sheet and steel plates and are subject to vertical compression, horizontal shear and rotation. Special hard cladding, multimode microbend optical fiber sensors were integrated into the elastomer sheets and the sensors were used both in transmission and back reflecting modes, [**Caussignac et al., 1992**]. Although the attenuation of light in these optical fibers varied both with normal and shear forces applied to the Bearing, its nonlinear and inconsistent dependence limits its usefulness, **figure 13**. Nevertheless, this initial work clearly indicates the value of pursuing this research with reliable, calibrated optical strain gauges having a linear response.

The Schiessbergstrasse triple span road bridge (53m long, 10m across) in Leverkusen is one of the first of a new generation of civil structures which will use ACM tendons and built-in fiber optic sensors, **figure 14**. A combination of microbend sensors and elongation sensors are designed to evaluate the load on the tendons and monitor strain within the concrete. There are, in addition, built in chemical sensors and the bridge deck is protected by an epoxy coating and foil sealing achieved with polyurethane. [**Wolf and Miesseler, 1992**]. The bridge is designed with limited prestressing using 27 glass fibers prestressing tendons, three of which are instrumented with fiber optic microbend strain sensors to monitor excessive loading and deformation. These sensors check the integrity of the tendons or locate the damage. The tensile zone above the piers and the spans are monitored permanently with integrated optical fiber sensors with an accuracy of ± 0.15mm. There are also nine fiber optic sensors integrated into the concrete to track the chemical changes taking place. These corrosion cells monitor the progression of carbonation and eventual penetration of chlorides. Information extracted by an on site computer is transmitted to client along a phone line. This constant survelliance permits early detection of problems and reduced cost of maintenance and repair.

Detailed knowledge of the reinforcement strains in reinforced concrete structures is a prerequisite to a thorough understanding of how such structures actually behave. Strain distributions are profoundly affected by the formation of cracks and can change during the life of a structure due to effects such as creep, shrinkage and load history. To avoid affecting the steel/concrete interface and thereby weakening the structure, a set of electrical strain gauges were mounted within the rebars by milling two solid bars and bonding them together with the gauges and wiring included, [**Scott and Gill, 1992**]. The technique has been refined to the point where 3mm long strain gauges can be mounted about 12 mm apart (100 gauges to bar). These were able to pick up cracks in the concrete before they reached the surface. It is expected that strain gauge instrumented concrete structures could warn if any component was approaching its overload stress and in general monitor the state of internal strain. This might provide insight into weakness developing due to corrosion. Although this useful research has been undertaken to date using conventional foil strain gauges it demonstrates the kind of information that could be attained with much less work using fiber optic strain gauges.

Excessive displacements or deformations in large civil structures can lead to critical states of stability that can endanger public safety. The use of electrical based measurement systems in hydraulic plants is undesirable as they are susceptible to: corrosion of the metallic guides (due to the high atmosphic humidity), and electromagnetic interference (from lightening strikes, overvoltage). These problems are magnified by the vast distances involved (km) in major civil structures, like Dams. Two types of optical fiber system for monitoring span joints and structural stability in Dams is currently under consideration, [**Holst et al., 1992**].

Extinsic Fabry -Perot optical fiber sensors have been developed and used with short gauges lengths to measure strain and temperature within concrete specimens [**Kruschwitz et al., 1992**]. Although these sensors can be spatially multiplexed along a linear sensor data bus they are likely to be limited to short gauge lengths and represent somewhat of a perturbation if embeddedwithin composite materials. Nevertheless, strain direction ambiquity can be overcome in these sensors using two slightly different wavelengths or two adjacent sensors with different cavity lengths. Physically decoupling one end of the sensor head from the structure also permits the temperature to be determined. Two such sensors were embedded in 15cm x 20cm x 122cm reinforced cement concrete specimen during fabrication. Cylindrical metal washers ensured effective longitudinal strain coupling for sensors embedded directly in concrete, while the other sensors were attached to metal reinforcing rods prior to embedding. A 5% difference in the strain was observed between the rod mounted sensors and those directly embedded-suggesting some slip between the sensor, the rod, and the matrix, or nonparallel alignment of the sensor axes. Four of these sensors were attached, using two part epoxy adhesive, to the under surface of a simple span bridge made of reinforced concrete with a wooden bottom. A maximum reading of 12 μstrain was recorded when a 12,000 lb truck was driven slowly over the bridge and an asymmetry between the front and rear wheel loading was evident , **figure 15**, [**Kruschwitz et al., 1992**].

The University of Vermont is in the process of constructing a five-story, 65,000 square foot concrete (Stafford) Building, that has been equipped with fiber optic and conventional sensors embedded into the concrete superstructure [**Fuhr et al., 1991**]. Specifically, these sensors were embedded into the concrete itself - in the floor, the load bearing support columns, the walls and ceilings. This network of sensors will provide information about the buildings structural integrity, its response to both microvibrations (traffic) and macrovibrations (earthquakes), the strain levels of the reinforcement bars within the concrete, local wind pressures being applied to the outer surface of the building, and any thermal deformations of the building caused by sun induced heating of only a part of the building. Both conventional sensors (e.g. strain gauges and accelerometers) and fiber optic and optical sensors are being used. Although, not all of these sensors require components to be embedded into the concrete structural elements, a key aspect of developing a Smart Structure arises from the presence of the sensing components within the structure itself. This fact is particularly evident when attempting to monitor the curing of the concrete and stresses incurred during the construction phase, or determine if a section has developed internal cracks which aren't visible on the outside [**Fuhr et al., 1992**].

CONCLUDING REMARKS AND FUTURE PROSPECTS

An enormous financial investment is associated with the established civil infrastructure: bridges, highways, railways, dams, pipelines, port facilities, airports and buildings. Aging of these structures represents a financial problem of immense proportions. Instrumentation of these structures with fiber optic sensors that could accurately assess their useful remaining life and schedule repair or replacement when required, could lead to substantial cost savings. Furthermore, we are witnessing a major change in the design and fabrication of large civil structures, like bridges, based on the replacement of steel with composite materials. It just happens that these new materials are quite conductive to the incorporation of resident fiber optic sensing systems which will allow the future custodians of these engineering investments to monitor the structure in a comprehensive way. This built-in inspectability will enhance confidence in using these new materials so that the two advances (use of composites and sensing) will reinforce each other and greatly accelerate the implementation of Smart Structure technology. In the last few years considerable progress has been made in the development of fiber optic sensors and their associated signal processing systems. Rapid and successful implementation of sensing systems into major new civil structures will best be achieved if there is the correct marriage of sensor developers with the civil engineers charged with the responsibly for these structures. There is a danger that progress could be impeded if there is not strong communication and cooperation across the disciplines.

In the 21st Century Smart Structure technology could lead to a civil infrastructure that is self monitoring and even self scheduling of its maintenance and repair. This level of self monitoring might make modular design more attractive, wherein a section is replaced as soon as it degrades beyond a certain point. This revolution in technology could usher in a "new age of civil engineering". This era would see the marriage of fiber optic technology and artificial intelligence with material science and structural engineering. Major structures constructed in this period would be constructed with built-in optical neurosystems and active actuation control that would make them more like living entities than the inanimate edifices we are familiar with today. To carry this biological paradigm one step further, it may even be possible to contemplate future structures that have the capacity for limited self repair. Indeed, if we think of the new frontiers for civil engineering as being in space or underwater, self diagnosis, self control and self healing may not be so much esoteric as vital.

Like all technology this will have its bright and dark side. The future highway that senses and alerts a truck driver that one of his tires is dangerously underinflated, or that his load is incorrectly balanced, will not only prevent many of the accidents that haunt us today........it will most certainly also take away our freedom to speed!

ACKNOWLEDGEMENTS

This work was supported by the Ontario Laser and Lightwave Research Centre, the Natural Science and Engineering Research Council of Canada and the Ontario Centre for Materials Research. Some of the work reported in this paper was undertaken by: T. Alavie, D. Hogg, M. LeBlanc, K.Liu, S. Melle, M. Ohn and T. Valis.

REFERENCES

Ahmad, A., Crowson, A., Rogers,C. A., and Aizawa, M., (1990), US-Japan Workshop on Smart/Intelligent Materials and Systems, Technomic Publishing.

Blagojevic, B., Tsaw,W., McEwen, K., and Measures, R.M., (1989), " The Influence of Embedded Optical Fibers on the Interlamina Fracture Toughness of Composite Materials", Review of Progress in Quantitative NDE, Brunswick, Maine, July 23-28.

Blake, J.N., Huang, S.Y. and Kim, B.Y., (1988), "Ellipitical: Core Two-Mode Fiber Strain Gauge", SPIE, 838-862.

Caussignac , J.M., Chabert, A., Morel, G., Rogez, P., and Seantier, J., (1992) "Bearing of a Bridge Fitted with Load Measuring Devices Based on Optical Fiber Technology", 207-210, 1st Europ. Conf. Smart Structures & Materials, Glasgow.

Czarnek, R., Guo, Y.F., Bennett, K.D., and Claus, R.O., (1988), "Interferemetric Measurements of Strain Concentrations Induced by an Optical Fiber Embedded in a Fiber Reinforced Composite", SPIE, Vol 986, Fiber Optic Smart Structures & Skins I, Boston, 43-54.

Dakin, J. P., "Distributed Optical Fiber Sensor Systems," Chap. 15, (1989), 575-598, Optical Fiber Sensors, Ed. B. Culshaw and J. Dakin, Artech House.

Fuhr, P.L., Huston, D.R., Kajenski, P.J., Ambrose, T.P., (1991) "Performance and Health Monitoring of the Stafford Medical Building Using Embedded Sensors", Private Communication.

Fuhr, P.L., Huston, D.R., Kajenski, P.J., Ambrose, T.P.,W.B. Spillman, (1992), " Installation and Preliminary Results from Fiber Optic Sensors Embedded in a Concrete Building", 409-412, 1st Europ. Conf. Smart Structures & Materials, Glasgow.

Hogg, D.,Valis, T., Mason, B. and Measures, R.M., (1992) "Temperature Compensated Strain Measurements Using Fiber Fabry-Perot Strain Gauges", Optical Fiber Sensor-Based Smart Materials and Structures Conference, Blacksburg, Virginia.

Holst, A., W. Habel and Lessing, R., (1992) "Fiber Optic Intensity Modulated Sensors for Continous Observations of Concrete and Rock-Fill Dams", 223-226, 1st Europ. Conf. Smart Structures Materials, Glasgow.

Housner, G.W., Masri, S.F., and Soong, T.T., (1992) "An Overview of Active Structural Control", 201-206, 1st Europ. Conf. Smart Structures & Materials, Glasgow.

Kruschwitz, B., Claus, R.O., Murphy, A., May, R.G., and Gunther, M.F., (1992) "Optical Fiber Sensors for the Quantitative Measurement of Strain Concrete Structures", 241-244, 1st Europ. Conf. Smart Structures & Materials, Glasgow.

LeBlanc, M., and Measures, R.M., (1992), "Impact Damage Assessment in Composite Materials with Embedded Fiber Optic Sensors," J. Composite Engineering, Vol 2, 573-596.

Liu, K., and Measures, R.M.,"Signal Processing Techniques for Localized Interferometric Fiber-Optic Strain Sensors", (1992), Accepted for the Journal of Intelligent Material Systems and Structures.

Loken, D., (1990), "Effect of Fiber Straightness on Fatigue of Aligned Continuous CFRP Composites ", University of Toronto (Chemical Eng.) M.A.Sc Thesis.

Lu, Z.J., and Blaha, F.A., (1989), "A Fiber Optic Stgrain and Impact Sensor System for Composite Materials", SPIE, vol. 1170, 239-242.

42

Lu, Z.J., and Blaha, F.A., (1991), "Application Issues of Fiber Optics in Aircraft Structures", SPIE. vol. 1588, 276-281.

Mathews, C.T., and Sirkis, J.S., (1990), " The Interaction of Interferometric Optical Fiber Sensors Embedded in a Monolithic Structure, "SPIE, Vol. 1370, Fiber Optic Smart Structures and Skins III, San Jose, 142-153.

Measures, R.M.," Smart Structures with Nerves of Glass", (1989), Progress in Aerospace Sciences, Vol 26, 289-351.

Measures, R.M., (1992), "Smart Composite Structures with Embedded Sensors", Jr. Composites Eng. vol. 2. 597-618.

Measures, R.M., Melle, S.M., and Liu, K., (September 5-6.1992), "Wavelength Demodulated Bragg Grating Fiber Optic Sensing Systems for Addressing Smart Structure Critical Issues", Jr. Smart Mater. Struct. vol.1., 36-44.

Melle, S.M., Liu, K., and Measures, R.M., (1991), "Strain Sensing Using a Fiber Optic Bragg Grating," SPIE, Vol. 1588, OE/Fibers' 91 - Conference: Fiber Optic Smart Structures and Skins IV, Boston.

Melle, S. M., Liu, K., and Measures, R. M., (1992), "A Passive Wavelength Demodulation System for Guided-Wave Bragg Grating Sensors", IEEE Phot.Tech. Lett. vol.4, 516-518.

Morey, W.W., Meltz ,G., and Glenn, W.H., (1989), "Fiber Optic Bragg Grating Sensors", SPIE Vol. 1169, Fiber Optic & Laser Sensors VII, 98-107.

Mufti, A.A., Erki, M-A, Jaeger, L.G., Editors, Advanced Composite Materials with Application to Bridges, (1991), "Anchorages for Prestressing Tendons and Cables", 238-239, Pub. Can .Soc. Civil Eng.

Murphy, K. A., Gunther, M. F., Vengarkar, A. M., and Claus R. O. , Optics Letters 16, 273.

Murphy, K.A., Miller, M.S, Vengsarkar, A.M., Claus, R.O., and Lewis, N.E., (1989), "Embedded Modal Domain Sensors Using Elliptical Core Optical Fibers", SPIE. vol. 1170, 566-573.

Ohn, M., Davis , A., Liu, K. , and Measures, R. M., (1992), "Embedded Fiber Optic Detection of Ultrasound and its Application to Cure Monitoring", Optical Fiber Sensor-Based Smart Materials and Structures Conference, Blacksburg, Virginia, April.

Roberts, S.S.J., and Davidson, R., (1992) "Short Term Fatigue Behaviour of Composite Materials Containing Embedded Fiber Optic Sensors and Actuators", 255-262, 1st Europ. Conf. Smart Structures & Materials, Glasgow.

Scott, R.H. and Gill, P.A.T., (1992) " Possibilites for the Use of Strain Gauged Reinforcement in Smart Structures", 211-214, 1st Europ. Conf. Smart Structures & Materials, Glasgow.

Sirkis, J.S., and Dasgupta, A., (1990), "Optimal Coatings for Intelligent Stucture Fiber Optic Sensors", SPIE Vol. 1370, Fiber Optic Smart Structures & Skins III, San José, 129-140.

Sirkis, J.S., and Haslach Jr., H.W., (1990), "Full Phase-Strain Relation for Structurally Embedded Interferometric Optical Fiber Sensors", SPIE, Vol. 1370, Fiber Optic Smart Structures and Skins III, San Jose, 248-259..

Turner, R.D., Valis, T., Hogg, W. D., and Measures, R. M., (1989), " Fiber Optic Strain Sensors for 'Smart ' Structures," J. of Intelligent Material Systems and Structures, Vol. 1, 26-49.

Valis, T., Hogg, D., and Measures, R. M, (1990), "Composite Material Embedded Fiber Optic Fabry-Perot Strain Rosette," SPIE, Vol. 1370, Fiber Optic Smart Structures and Skins III, San Jose, 154-161.

Wolf, R. & Miesseler, H.J., (1992) "Monitoring of Prestressed Concrete Structures with Optical Fiber Sensors", P.23-29, 1st Europ. Conf. Smart Structures & Materials, Glasgow.

Zimmermann, B. Claus, R., Kapp, D., and Murphy, K., "Optical Time Domain Reflectometry for Local Strain Measurements, SPIE, vol. 1170, 534-541, 1989.

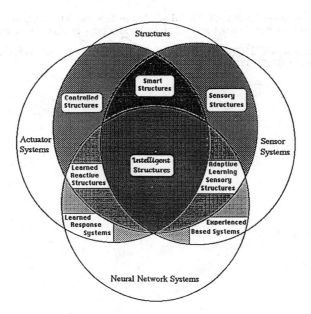

Figure 1. Structures possible by the confluence of four disciplines: structures, sensors, actuator control systems, and neural networks.

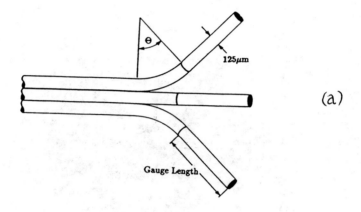

125μm

Θ

Gauge Length

Detail of the FFP fiber-optic strain rosette.

(a)

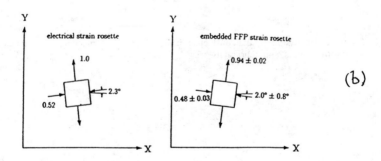

Y

electrical strain rosette

1.0

2.3°

0.52

Y

embedded FFP strain rosette

0.94 ± 0.02

2.0° ± 0.8°

0.48 ± 0.03

X

X

(b)

Figure 2.   (a) Fiber optic strain rosette based on three Fabry-Perot fiber optic sensors: (b) A comparison of the laminar strain tensor measured by the fiber optic strain rosette embedded within a composite cantilever beam with the results obtained from a surface adhered conventional foil electrical strain rosette.

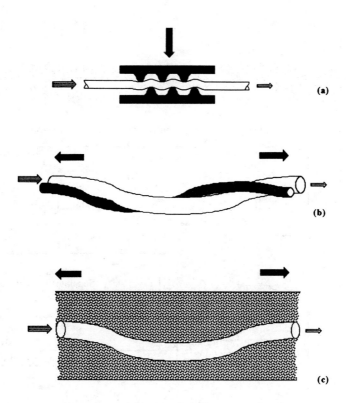

Figure 3.   Three microbend sensor arrangements: (a) Optical fiber is squeezed by small microbend jaws. (b) Optical fiber is wound around a wire or another optical fiber. (c) Microbend in the optical fiber is produced by physical inhomogeneitious in the composite material.

OTDR Quasi-Distributed Fiber Optic Strain Sensor

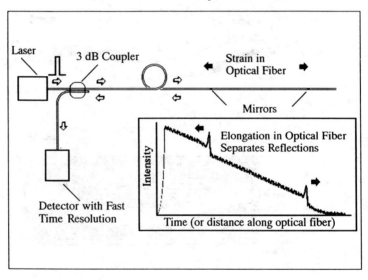

Figure 4.   Quasi-distributed strain sensing based on mirror separation measurement along the fiber.

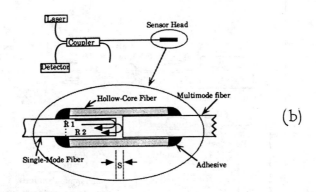

(b)

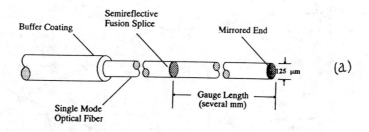

(a)

Figure 5.   Fabry-Perot fiber optic sensor configurations: (a) Intrinsic [Hogg eta l., 1992], and (b) Extrinsic [Kruschwitz et al., 1992].

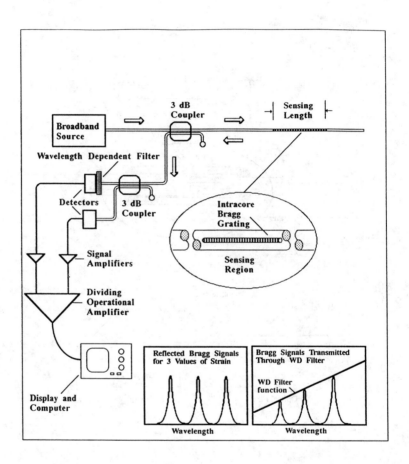

Figure 6. Intracore Bragg grating fiber optic sensor. Small inset on bottom left indicates Bragg reflected signals for three values of strain. Small inset on bottom right reveals how these three signals are affected by transmission through a wavelength dependent linear filter. Wavelength demodulation of the Bragg sensor is achieved from the ratio of the signals from the two sensors indicated, one receiving its light after passage through the wavelength dependent filter, the other receiving its light directly and serves as a reference.

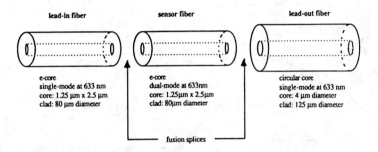

lead-in fiber

sensor fiber

lead-out fiber

e-core
single-mode at 633 nm
core: 1.25 μm x 2.5 μm
clad: 80 μm diameter

e-core
dual-mode at 633nm
core: 1.25μm x 2.5μm
clad: 80μm diameter

circular core
single-mode at 633 nm
core: 4 μm diameter
clad: 125 μm diameter

fusion splices

Figure 7.   Two mode e-core fiber optic sensor configuration [Murphy et al., 1989].

Demodulated Fabry-Perot Fiber Optic Sensor

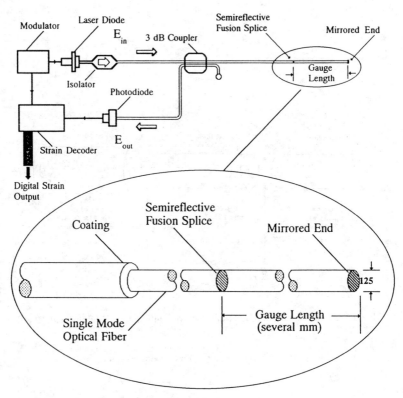

Close up of Fabry-Perot Fiber Optic Sensor

Figure 8.   Demodulation system for the Fabry-Perot fiber optic sensor.

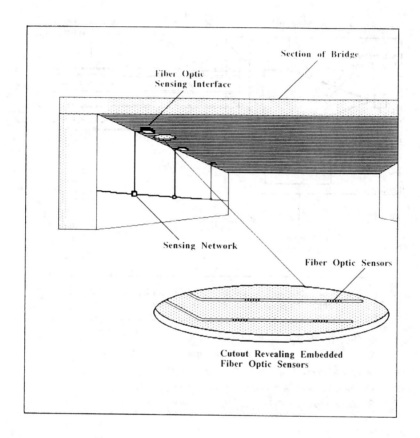

Figure 9. Schematic of a future bridge instrumented with a fiber optic cellular sensing architecture.

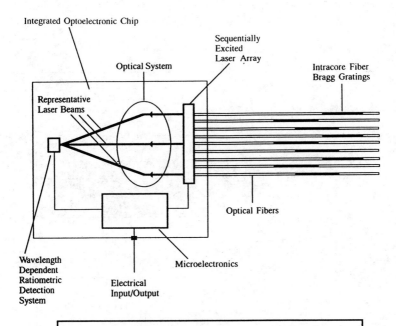

Integrated Optoelectronic Chip

Sequentially
Excited
Laser Array

Optical System

Intracore Fiber
Bragg Gratings

Representative
Laser Beams

Optical Fibers

Wavelength
Dependent
Ratiometric
Detection
System

Electrical
Input/Output

Microelectronics

Merits of Multiplexed Multiple Bragg Laser Sensor Array
with Single Wavelength Demodulated Detection System

● *Multiplexing Within Structural Interface*
● *Many Sensors Processed on Single Optoelectronic Chip*
● *Optoelectronic Chip within Structural Interface*
● *Optoelectronic Chip Performs Optical/Electrical Conversion*
● *Single Electrical Cable with User Friendly Interconnection*

Figure 10. Schematic of an optoelectronic chip for signal processing of many Bragg laser sensors.

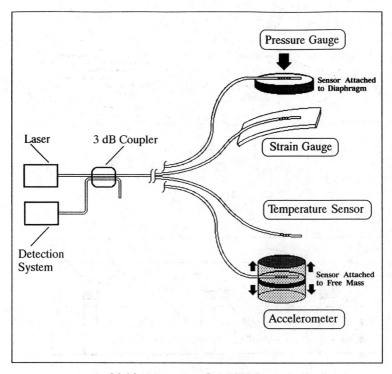

Multimeasurement Capability
of Fiber Optic Sensors

Figure 11. Schematic illustration of how a fiber optic sensor can be used as a: pressure gauge, strain sensor, temperature sensor, and an accelerometer.

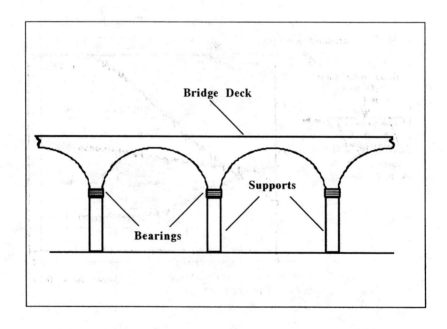

Figure 12. Generic elements of a bridge.

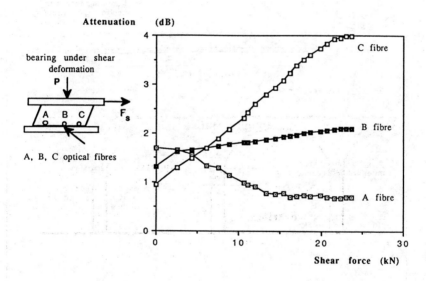

Figure 13. Attenuation observed in three fiber optic sensors embedded within a shear loaded bridge bearing. Small inset indicates location of sensors and loads applied to the bearing, [Caussignac et al. 1992].

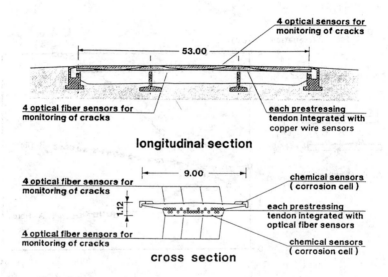

Figure14. Arrangement of optical fiber sensors and chemical sensors in the triple span Schiessbergstrasse road bridge, [Wolf and Miessler, 1992].

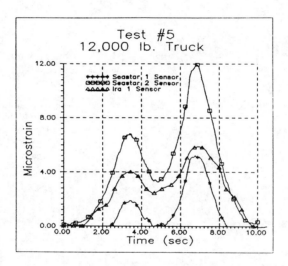

Figure 15. Microstrain signals versus time recorded by a pair of extrinsic Fabry-Perot fiber optic sensors adhered to a concrete bridge deck subjected to a 12,000 lb truck with an asymmetric load. This strain variation is compared with a conventional strain gauge, [Kruschwitz et al., 1992].

Properties of Rods, Cables, and Laminates

Propriétés des tiges, câbles et stratifiés

ADVANCED COMPOSITE MATERIALS IN BRIDGES AND STRUCTURES
K.W. Neale and P. Labossière, Editors; Canadian Society for Civil Engineering, 1992

Matériaux composites d'avant-garde pour ponts et charpentes
K.W. Neale et P. Labossière, éditeurs; Société canadienne de génie civil, 1992

EVALUATION OF TENSILE STRENGTH OF FRP RODS WITH ALIGNED CONTINUOUS FIBRES

T. Uomoto and **H. Hodhod**
University of Tokyo
Tokyo, Japan

ABSTRACT

A procedure for evaluating tensile strength of FRP rods is introduced. Three fibre/matrix systems are used for testing the procedure. First, system constituents are characterized experimentally. The procedure is then explained for a proposed failure path. The procedure simulates the propagation of failure within the rods and employs random numbers for assigning tensile strength to the fibres. The procedure is applied for the three characterized fibre/matrix systems and strength distributions are obtained. Experimental verification of the results is made and, based on this, the behaviour of the three composites is explained.

RÉSUMÉ

Une procédure pour évaluer la résistance en tension de barres de FRP est présentée. Trois systèmes fibres/matrice sont utilisés pour tester la procédure. Premièrement, les constituants des systèmes sont caractérisés expérimentalement. La procédure est alors expliquée pour un cheminement de rupture précis. La procédure simule la propagation de la rupture à l'intérieur des barres et établit arbitrairement la résistance des fibres. La procédure est appliquée pour les trois systèmes fibres/matrice et les distributions de contraintes sont obtenues. Une vérification expérimentale des résultats sert à expliquer le comportement des trois composites.

INTRODUCTION

The evaluation of composite strength under the ideal conditions, without grips effect or manufacturing defects, has a special importance. It gives the tensile capacity of the composite and helps the assessment of adverse factors effects on the strength. Besides, the assumed mechanism for strength evaluation and its comparison with the actual behavior gives idea about the effect of different mechanisms on composite strength. This is of great importance for the design of the composite, choice of fiber/matrix combination.

For strength evaluation, there exist the law of mixtures and the bundle theory. The former is an oversimplification that ignores the effect of the size on the strength of fibers. It even does not define the length at which the strength of fibers is to be determined. The latter considers the binding effect of the matrix, and the size effect on fibers strength. However, it consider the matrix as a rigid medium capable of distributing the load of broken fibers equally to all the fibers in the damaged section, which is contradictory to reality.

There is a need for a comparative study on the effect of different mechanisms on the strength of different systems, and development of new methodology for calculating the strength of composites. This method should be capable of adopting different modifications in the studied system and, hence, should consider the damage evolution from the most elementary member of the composite, that is single fiber.

CONSTITUENTS CHARACTERIZATION

Fibers Strength Distributions

Monofilament experiments were conducted on the three materials considered in this research, aramid, carbon and glass. About 150 standard testpieces were prepared for each material, according to the Japanese Industrial Specifications JIS-R7601. Standard Test-piece is shown in Fig. 1-a. Single fiber is attached to the central portion of card paper frame. The frame is 20 x 40mm rectangle with a central opening, 25 mm long, across which the fiber is pasted. The testpiece is mounted in the testing machine using bolts. Then, the frame is cut on both sides of the fiber, as shown in Fig. 1-b.

All the experiments were conducted in an average temperature of 20°C and fixed stroke rate of 0.4mm/min. The Load-displacement relationships were monitored, in real time, using a plotter connected to the testing machine. These relationships were transformed, later, into stress-strain relationships. The load axis was transformed into stress axis by measuring fibers diameters and division by the area. The displacement axis was transformed into strain axis given fiber length, stroke rate and chart speed. The stress-strain relationships were reproducible and typical ones are shown in Fig.2.

Strength values, for each material, were characterized statistically, as well as the failure strain and Young's modulus. The results are shown in Table 1. The strength distributions were fitted to Weibull Distribution in the following form:

$$f(\sigma) = \frac{m}{\alpha^m} \sigma^{m-1} \exp[-(\frac{\sigma}{\alpha})^m]$$ (1)

where $f(\sigma)$: strength probability density function
σ : filament tensile strength
m : Weibull modulus (material constant)
α : constant dependent on the material and specimen size

The distributions are shown in Fig. 3, and the values of the parameters m and α are given in Table 1. The variance of strength values increases with the brittleness of the material. This agrees with the known brittleness of the tested materials: maximum for glass and minimum for aramid.

Matrix Stress-Strain Relationship

FRP producer has selected two types of resins to bind the fibers. The resins are members of vinylester resin family with brand names Ripoxy-R802 and Ripoxy-H600. The former is used for aramid and glass fibers and the later is used for carbon fibers. Three standard specimens were prepared for each type. The standard specimen is shown in Fig. 4, JIS-K7113.

For each specimen, two resistance strain gages were attached to the central portion of each face: one in the axial direction and the other in the transverse direction. The strain gages, and testing machine load terminal, were connected to a data logger to monitor load and strain development. The experiments were conducted in 20°C and the stroke rate was 2mm/min, according to the above specifications.

Typical stress-strain relationships are shown in Fig.5. The mean strength, failure strain, initial tangent Young's moduli and Poisson's ratios are given in Table 2.

STRENGTH EVALUATION

Simulation Strategy

The fibers inside rod section are assumed to be uniformly distributed. Therefore, the hexagonal array is chosen for fibers arrangement. The matrix is considered as fibers binders and its strength, in tension, is neglected. This is justified by comparing the figures of filament and matrix strengths given above. A perfect bond is assumed between the fibers and matrix in all load levels. Hence, rod failure will propagate in one section, with thickness equal to fibers critical length. The weakest section, in the rod, is studied. The fibers in the section are assigned, randomly, strengths and moduli according to the experimentally obtained distributions. Random numbers were used for this purpose. A strain increment is, then, applied to the composite and the resulting stresses are calculated. These stresses are compared with the assigned strengths and a fiber is coded as broken one when its strength is exceeded. The loads of the broken fibers are distributed to the surrounding sound fibers, in the section. The overstressed fibers are only the six fibers surrounding the broken one, according to Riley (Riley, 1968). When more than one adjacent fibers fail, their loads are distributed to the first layer of fibers surrounding them. The previous two rules are explained in Fig. 6. Then, the overstressed fibers are checked again to determine whether their strengths are exceeded. The process of stress calculation and strength check is repeated until the stable equilibrium is reached: no more fibers fail upon loads redistribution. Then, a subsequent strain increment is applied.

If the stable equilibrium is not reached for many iterations, the ratio of broken fibers, to total number of fibers, is compared with an arbitrary value, set in this study to 0.9. If this value is exceeded, rod failure is declared. The strength, of the rod, is calculated as the sum of fibers loads divided by total rod cross-sectional area. This process is explained in the flow chart shown in Fig. 7.

The above process is repeated many times, using different sets of randomly selected fibers strengths and moduli. Then, the distribution of rods strengths is obtained.

Calculation of Section Depth (Fibers Critical Length)

When Fiber breaks in the composite, its load is transferred to the surrounding medium through interfacial shear stresses at its ends. The equilibrium, between the normal and shear forces, at fiber end, yields the following equation for transfer length (Jayatilaka, 1979)

$$\frac{\sigma_f}{2\tau_y} = \frac{l_t}{r_f} \tag{2}$$

where σ_f :   fiber tensile strength
    τ_y :   matrix shear yield stress
    l_t :   fiber transfer length
    r_f :   fiber radius

This equation assumes rigid plastic matrix behavior. The value of matrix shear yield stress is considered as half of tensile yield stress (Jayatilaka, 1979). In case of the brittle matrix Ripoxy-H600, the matrix might fail in shear. However, the asperity of failure surface allows the transfer of shear stresses by bearing. The assumption made herein is that the equivalent value of τ_y is half of matrix tensile strength.

This length calculated from the above equation is needed for load transfer at one end. The critical length is that needed for load transfer at both ends, which is double the transfer length.

Fibers Strength at Critical Length

The transfer lengths as calculated for aramid, carbon and glass fibers are 0.57, 0.31 and 0.38 mm respectively. The strength distributions at theses lengths are to be extrapolated from the available results at the standard length, 25 mm. The rule chosen is that based in the weakest link concept introduced in Weibull distribution (Weibull, 1951). Simply, the number of links is proportional to the length of the fiber. Hence, following (Van der Zwaag, 1989) and (Jayatilaka, 1979), the parameter α in Weibull distribution will be related to the length through

$$\alpha = \frac{K}{l^{1/m}} \tag{3}$$

where K is a constant. If the parameter α is determined at a certain length, the constant K can be obtained and then α, for any other length, can be calculated. Weibull modulus m is defined as a material constant that does not vary with length. Hence, the parameters of the distribution can be determined at the critical length, given their values at the standard length. These distributions, at critical lengths, are used in the simulation process described above, as failure propagates within this length.

Simulated Strength Distributions

The simulation process is applied 100 times for each type of composite. The resulting values were fitted to Gaussian distributions, shown in Fig. 8. The distributions have small variances compared to those of their fibers strengths. The mean values of rods strengths are not proportional to those of the fibers. This contradicts rules like the law of mixtures that assumes composite strength to be proportional to that of the fibers.

EXPERIMENTAL VERIFICATION

In order to investigate the validity of the proposed failure mechanism, special specimens were prepared for tensile testing. The specimens are, as shown in Fig.9, 6 mm diameter FRP rods with aligned continuous fibers. As the current anchorage system results in rods failure at the grips, ultimate loads and failure shapes are not corresponding to uniaxial tension. Therefore, the rods were machined at the middle of their length, 40cm, to a diameter of 2 mm. This process aimed at forcing the failure away from the field of stresses at end grips. The length of this reduced section was 2 mm.

10 rods of each type were prepared at volume fractions of 0.55 and 0.45. They were tested in 20°C and stroke rate 5 mm/min for AFRP and GFRP and 2 mm/min for CFRP rods. The mean strength values are shown in Table 3. The Failure shape is shown in Fig. 10.

DISCUSSION

The strength mean values, for the special FRP specimens, agree well with the simulated values for the case of CFRP and GFRP. The case of AFRP, however, seems to be underestimated by the proposed technique. A separate study showed that aramid fibers does not show the expected strength increase for short lengths, and the strength can be considered to be constant at any length. This implies that the size effect rule applied herein should have given an overestimate to the strength. A study of the failure pattern might give some explanation. In the simulation process, an inherent assumption is that the failure surface will be plane-like with maximum height difference (δz = critical length). The fulfillment of this assumption in case of CFRP means that the assumption made for evaluating the transfer length was acceptable, as shown in Fig.10. Obviously, this is not the case for AFRP rods, that has a failure surface with $\delta z = 10$cm. This can be understood if stress-strain relationship and strength distribution for aramid fibers, and stress-strain relationship for matrix Ripoxy-R802 are put together as shown in Fig. 11. The strength distribution for aramid fibers shows that no fiber failure occurs before strain of about 3.2%. At this value, the matrix has already entered the yield stage. Hence, the assumption that it can exert shear stress to transfer the load of broken fiber at its end is invalid, as the additional strain results in almost no stress at this level. The equivalent value for τ_y in Eq.(2) becomes, then, zero resulting in an infinite transfer length. The infinite length means that the fibers will behave as if they were bundle of unbound fibers. In this case, the load of broken fiber is distributed to all the fibers in the rod regardless of their positions relative to the broken ones. The strength of a bundle of fibers can be calculated from the following equation (Coleman, 1959)

$$\sigma_b = \alpha(em)^{\frac{-1}{m}} \qquad (4)$$

where e is natural logarithm base, and α and m are Weibull distribution parameters. This yields a value of 3390 MPa which is close to the experimental values. Besides, the failure pattern of AFRP rods , as shown in Fig. 10, agrees well with that of fiber bundle.

It remains to consider the case of GFRP. Glass fibers starts failure at very low stresses, as shown in their distribution. GFRP strain at failure is about 3%. This value is within the range of matrix yield. Then, it is expected that GFRP will behave like a bundle of fibers at the final failure stages. The strength of glass fibers at bigger lengths is smaller than the value at critical length. This implies that the simulation process should have yielded higher strengths than they have. This can be understood referring to the results of measuring Poisson's ratio for FRP rods, in a different work. The value for GFRP was

0.25. If this figure is compared with the figure given for the matrix alone in Table 2, an inevitable conclusion will be made on the lower value of fibers Poisson's ratio. This means that during rods loading, there exist transverse compressive stresses at the interface between fiber and matrix. The modeling of (Kelly et. al., 1976) and (Pinchin, 1976) is used for explaining the current results. The fibers are considered as cylinders contained in a cylindrical shell of matrix. The inner radius of the hollow cylindrical shell is the same as that of the fibers, prior to loading. During loading, the difference in Poisson's ratio for the two cylinders restrains the full contraction of matrix shell. The matrix is, consequently, subjected to internal pressure due to the constraint made by the included fiber. This results in hoop tensile stresses in the walls of the matrix shell. This effect increases the axial stresses needed for the same strain, under uniaxial tension. Hence, the matrix response will be more stiff than that obtained for the standard specimens. Similar effect was reported also by (Kelly and Lilholt, 1969). It means that the value of τ_y used for calculating the transfer length should be higher than the employed one. This implies that the critical length would be shorter and the strength distribution would move to the higher range. Hence, higher strength values should have been obtained from the simulation technique, and the aforementioned effect of matrix yield would adjust it to the measured value. Closer view of the failure surface of GFRP specimen, as shown in Fig. 12, shows that the failure did not propagate on a plane but rather on a surface, and the final stages occurred in bundle-like failure.

CONCLUSIONS

A simulation procedure is introduced for evaluating the strength distribution of FRP rods with aligned continuous fibers. The procedure depends on the random numbers for distributing the strength of the fibers in rod section, and assumes failure propagation in almost plane perpendicular to rod axis. It was applied for three kinds of FRP rods; namely aramid, carbon and glass FRP rods. The results showed good agreement for the case of CFRP. The case of AFRP was underestimated by the assumed mechanism, and the behavior of AFRP in the considered system was better described as a bundle of fibers without any binding material. This gives higher strengths than the case of good binding matrix, mainly due to the low variance strength distribution of aramid fibers that magnifies the effect of stress concentration, when fibers are well bound by the matrix.

The case of GFRP showed early behavior as assumed by the proposed mechanism, but later failure stages were similar to the case of AFRP. This is due to the large failure strain of glass fibers that correspond to the yield of the binding matrix.

REFERENCES

Coleman, B.D. (1959). On the Strength of Classical fibers and Fibers Bundles. J. Mech. Phys. Solids, **7**, 60-70.
Jayatilaka, A.(1979).Fracture of Engineering Brittle Materials. Applied Science Publishers Ltd. London, 242 ,241,122-123 p.
Kelly, A. and Lilholt, H.(1969). Stress-Strain Curve of a Fiber Composite. Philos. Mag., 311-328.
Kelly, A. and Zweben, C. (1976). Poisson Contraction in Aligned Fiber Composites Showing Pull-out. J. Mat. Sc. Let., **11**, 582-587.
Pinchin, D.J. (1976). Poisson Contraction Effects in Aligned Fiber composites. J. Mat. Sc. Let., **11**, 1578-1581.

Riley, V.R. (1968). Fiber/Fiber Interaction. J. Comp. Mat., **2**, 4, 436-446.
Van der Zwaag, S.(1989).The concept of Filament Strength and Weibull Modulus. Journal of Testing and Evaluation JTEVA, **17**, 5, 292-298.
Weibull, W. (1951). A Statistical Distribution of Wide Applicability. J. Appl. Mech., , 293-297.

Table 1 Fibers Diameters and Tensile Parameters Characterization

Parameter		Aramid[*]	Carbon[†]	Glass[‡]
Diameter	Mean (μm)	12.2	6.7	12.7
Number of Experiments		150	150	150
	Mean (MPa)	3830	3240	2460
	Standard Deviation (MPa)	345	520	590
Strength	Variation Coefficient	0.09	0.16	0.24
	m	13.2	7	5
	α (MPa)	4210	3350	2560
Failure Strain	Mean (%)	4.6	1.4	2.9
Young's Modulus	Mean (GPa)	84	227	86

* Technora aramid
† Pan based carbon fibers
‡ S-Glass

Table 2 Mean Values of Matrices Tensile Parameters

Matrix	Strength (MPa)	Failure Strain (%)	Young's Modulus (GPa)	Poisson's Ratio
Ripoxy-R802	82	5.30	3.05	0.34
Ripoxy-H600	70	1.95	3.92	0.34

Table 3 Simulated and Experimental Tensile Strength for Different FRP rods

Material	Mean Tensile Strength (MPa)/V_f		
	$V_f = 0.45$	$V_f = 0.55$	Simulated
AFRP	3310	3100	3000
CFRP	3150	3200	3250
GFRP	3000	2950	3060

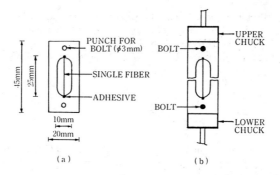

Fig. 1   Standard Fiber Testpiece and Configuration Before Testing

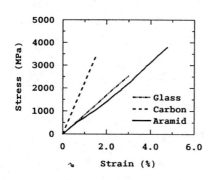

Fig. 2   Stress-Strain Relationships
for Different Fibers

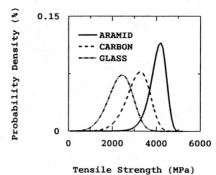

Fig. 3   Strength Distributions for
Different Fibers

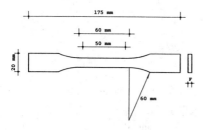

Fig. 4   Standard Matrix Specimen
F= 1-10 mm (3 mm for the current work)

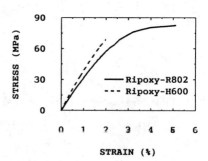

Fig. 5   Stress-Strain Relationships
for Different Matrices

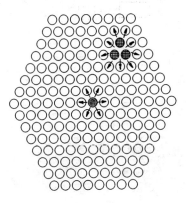

Fig. 6   Distribution of Broken Fibers
         Loads

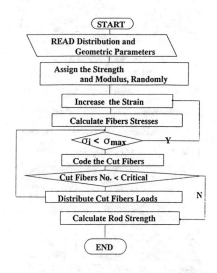

START

READ Distribution and
Geometric Parameters

Assign the Strength
and Modulus, Randomly

Increase the Strain

Calculate Fibers Stresses

$\sigma_i < \sigma_{max}$ Y

Code the Cut Fibers

Cut Fibers No. < Critical

Distribute Cut Fibers Loads   N

Calculate Rod Strength

END

Fig. 7   Flow Chart of Simulation Program

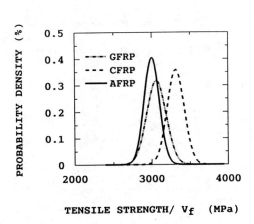

Fig. 8   Simulated Strength Distributions
         for FRP Rods

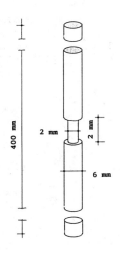

Fig. 9   Rod Specimen with
         Reduced Section

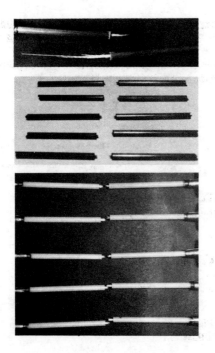

Fig. 12　Failure shape of GFRP Rods

Fig. 10　Failure Shape of FRP Rods
　　　　　(Downwards: AFRP,CFRP, GFRP)

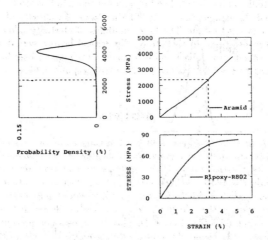

Fig. 11　Matrix Strain at First Failure of Aramid Fibers

ADVANCED COMPOSITE MATERIALS IN BRIDGES AND STRUCTURES
K.W. Neale and P. Labossière, Editors; Canadian Society for Civil Engineering, 1992

Matériaux composites d'avant-garde pour ponts et charpentes
K.W. Neale et P. Labossière, éditeurs; Société canadienne de génie civil, 1992

EVALUATION OF GRAPHITE COMPOSITE CABLES FOR PRESTRESSING CONCRETE

S.L. Iyer and **A. Khubchandani**
School of Mines and Technology
Rapid City, South Dakota, USA

ABSTRACT

Corrosion is a severe problem for prestressed concrete structures. It influences the service life of the structures significantly. Various solutions to the problem of corrosion have been suggested but none of them has so far been proved to be viable. Therefore efforts had to be redirected towards the search of new materials which have high tensile and bond strengths, low modulus and noncorrosive properties. Carbon fibres (AS-4 and AS-2) supplied by Hercules and pultruded by Polygon were used in this study. The pretensioning system was used throughout this study. The modulus of elasticity of graphite cables is lower than that of steel cables. The lower modulus of elasticity adds to the advantage of lesser losses in prestress. In this study, slip critical beams were designed and tested for static and cyclic flexure which had inadequate development length. The transfer and development lengths were determined for steel and graphite cables.

RÉSUMÉ

La corrosion est un grave problème pour les structures en béton précontraint et influence leur serviceabilité. Des solutions variées au problème de la corrosion ont été suggérées mais aucune d'elles n'est satisfaisante. C'est pourquoi on recherche de nouveaux matériaux ayant une grande résistance, un bas module, et qui sont résistants à la corrosion. Des fibres de carbone (AS-4 et AS-2), fournies par Hercules et pultrudées par Polygon, ont servi ici à l'étude d'un système de prétension. Le module d'élasticité des câbles de graphite est plus bas que celui de câbles d'acier. De plus, leurs pertes de précontrainte sont moins importantes. Dans cette étude, des poutres dimensionnées et testées en flexion statique et cyclique ont permis de déterminer les longueurs d'ancrage des câbles d'acier et de graphite.

INTRODUCTION

Steel has been used for prestressing ever since the prestressed concrete came into practice without facing any challenge because of its economy and the ductility. The problem of corrosion of steel reinforcements in bridges and the structures exposed to marine environment has not been fully solved despite the exhausting financial and man-power efforts. Corrosion poses a severe problem for prestressed concrete structures because of the lesser area of reinforcement involved. Even the minor loss in the area of reinforcement leads to unmanageable stress levels. Therefore the search for the new non corrosive reinforcements for prestressed concrete with good bond and stability in concrete environment began.

S-2 Glass fiber was first tried but its use was constrained by the preliminary findings of a lower safe stress level of 983 MPa (142.5 ksi) in the alkaline concrete environment. Carbon fiber composites are inert in nature and have good corrosion resistance to acidic as well as alkaline environment. AS-4 carbon fiber composite (with Vinylester 8084 resin system) has a high ultimate tensile strength of 2243 MPa (325 ksi) and the modulus of elasticity of 158.8 GPa (23 million psi) which is lower than that of steel. Both the facts add on to the advantage of prestressing with this graphite composite besides offering the advantage of being a non-corrosive reinforcement. AS-2 carbon fiber was also studied which has an ultimate tensile strength of 2070 MPa (300 ksi) and the modulus of 151.8 GPa (22 million psi).

General Review

The Corps of Engineers (1,2) tried to use the fiberglass cables for prestressing but was not able to develop a satisfactory anchorage system. In 1987, Dr. Iyer developed a satisfactory commercially viable anchorage system for prestressing with the composite cables at South Dakota School of Mines and Technology.

Carbon Fiber Composite Cables

Carbon fiber composite cables (CFCC) were used for two small bridges in Japan. Due to the low density of carbon fibers (1.5 gm/cc), they exhibit specific mechanical properties which exceed those of high strength metals considerably(3). Carbon fiber composites are superior in strength and stiffness in comparison to glass and aramid fiber composites. The other extremely useful characteristics are:

Good corrosion resistance to acidic as well as alkaline environment, Good damping behavior, High fatigue resistance, Very little relaxation under stress.

Relaxation experiments were performed on CFCC and steel cables under equivalent conditions over a period of 100 hours by Zoch, Kimura, and others (3). CFCC relaxed two percent against eight percent for steel cables. Relaxation experiments to simulate the temperature profile of steam curing of concrete at 80 percent of the proof load showed two and a half percent relaxation for CFCC against five and three quarters percent for steel cables.

Carbon fibers are well known to be unaffected by the acidic and alkaline environments (3). Due to the resin system being used in the composite cables, CFCC was tested in alkaline conditions. CFCC was exposed to aqueous solution of sodium and calcium hydroxide (pH = 13) heated to 60 degree Celsius. Specimens were stressed to 70 percent of proof load for 2500 hours (3). There was a very little loss of prestress and the ultimate tensile strength.

Vinylester 8084 resin system was tested for alkaline concrete environment in the stressed condition at Owens Corning Laboratory by coating the strand with 25.4 mm x 25.4 mm (1 in. x 1 in.) cement mortar. No damage to the resin system was reported for a safe stress level of 983 MPa (142.5 ksi).

All this review directed to the selection of graphite composite cables for this particular study for the search of a new non-corrosive material for prestressing.

TESTING OF CABLES AND BEAMS

Static Tension Test On Graphite Cables

Graphite (AS-4) rods of 3.2 mm (0.125 inch) diameter were tested for their ultimate tensile strength. The aluminum alloy tabs which contoured to the shape of the rod were used as grips as per ASTM D3916 (5). The ultimate tensile strength was found to be 2195 MPa (318 ksi).

Graphite Cables were made by using seven graphite rods 1066 mm (42 inches) long and 3.2 mm (0.125 inch) diameter. The seven strands were twisted at the rate of 1 twist per 304.8 mm (1 foot). The nominal cross sectional area is equivalent to that of #3 steel bar. The anchorage system developed by Dr. Iyer (6) was provided at both ends of the cable to leave a gage length of 535 mm (21 inches) to be tested. Quick release chucks of 15 mm (0.6 inch) diameter were used as the grips. Two strain gages were mounted on graphite rods. The results of the static tension tests for AS-4 and AS-2 graphite cables are shown in Fig. 1.

Short Term Sustained Tension Test on Graphite Cables

In order to simulate the field condition of pretensioning system (where cables are stressed for 24 hours for concrete to gain transfer strength with steam curing), cables were stressed to 60 percent of their ultimate strength. Stress level used was 1366 MPa (197.9 ksi). Figure 2 shows the variation in strain with respect to time. It is evident from the figure that no significant prestress loss was noticed during this time period.

Long Term Sustained Tension Test on Graphite Cables

A long term sustained tension test similar to the short term was carried out for six months to study the creep in graphite cables. The cables were subjected to different stress levels; Cable #1 943 MPa, Cable #2 989 MPa, and Cable #3 1066 MPa. Figure 3 shows the variation in strains with respect to time. There was a little drop in the strain values over this time period.

Bond Strength of Graphite Cables

The first few beams prestressed with graphite cables failed in bond irrespective of the flexural bond lengths. A maximum of 458 mm (18 inches) beyond the transfer length was tested. The slip of cables was usually associated very close to the first crack. The bond strength of the graphite cables was improved by coating the cables with a resin system and then sprinkling fine sand over the resin. Resin was allowed to cure for 24 hours and the excess sand was brushed off. Concrete of 34.5 MPa (5000 psi) strength was used to cast 76.20 mm x 76.20 mm x 304.8 mm (3" x 3" x 12") specimens for comparing the bond strengths of unsanded and sanded graphite cables. Average bond strength of 3.83 MPa (556 psi) and 7.11 MPa (1030 psi) was observed for unsanded and sanded graphite cables respectively.

Transfer Length

Transfer length was measured for steel and unsanded graphite cables. Strains at regular intervals were measured from the free end to the center of the beam. The curve plotted between the distance from free end and the strain in concrete was averaged as shown in Fig. 4. Transfer lengths of 558 mm (22 inches) for a stress level of 911 MPa (132 ksi) in steel and 813 mm (32 inches) for a stress level of 994 MPa (144 ksi) in graphite cables were determined. Both values are higher than the ACI recommended values of one third of the effective prestress (in ksi) times the nominal diameter of the cable (in inches).

Static Flexure Tests

Preliminary dimensions of the beams were selected to initiate beam failure and cable slip (8). Cable slip condition was designed on the basis of the insufficient flexural bond length. The beam failure condition was designed by increasing either the length or depth of beams. The slip was measured by dial gages fixed on exposed ends of the cables so that the spindles of the dial gages rested against the beam face. Beams prestressed with sanded graphite cables and steel cables which were 2040 mm (8 feet) long showed no slip and the observed moment of resistance was close to the theoretical values. The beam prestressed with unsanded graphite cables and 2440 mm (8 feet) long failed in bond. The rest of the beams tested were 1525 mm long and failed in bond. The bond failure was usually associated very close to the first crack. The comparison of the theoretical and experimental values of first crack and ultimate moments are shown in Table-1.

Deflections and strains for beams prestressed with steel and graphite cables were nearly equal even after cracking.

Cyclic Flexure Tests

Beams prestressed with unsanded and sanded graphite cables were tested for non-reversible cyclic flexure. The beams were loaded to their first crack values. An amplitude of 9.9 KN (2000 lbs.) to their first crack value was used for loading sinusoidally at a frequency of 7 Hz. Both beams were 1525 mm (5

76

feet) long. the beam with sanded graphite cables showed slipping of cables near 500,000 cycles whereas the beam with unsanded graphite cables showed slip near 400,000 cycles. Minimum and maximum strains in concrete started rising with the slip initiation because of micro-cracking. The strains in cables tried to increase every time but kept dropping with the continuous slip.

Losses in Prestressing

The main loss in this study was the jack transfer loss because of the shorter length 7.17 m (23.5 feet) of prestressing bed. The unsanded graphite cables showed a loss due to elastic shortening (7.8% for beam ID # 2UG8)) greater than the theoretical value of 3.14% which indicates that the cables slipped during the prestress transfer. For unsanded graphite cables, shrinkage and creep losses were also more than expected.
The elastic shortening loss for the sanded cables is 3.0% against a theoretical value of 3.14% indicating no cable slip. The sanded graphite cables showed the loss due to elastic shortening in proportion to their modulus. The losses were in the proportion of 1:0.75 for steel and sanded graphite cables. Relaxation loss for graphite cables could not be determined but it should be definitely less than steel cables as reported in the literature (3).

Development Length of Sanded Graphite Cables

The beam which was 2440 mm (8 feet) long and prestressed with sanded graphite cables was tested in center point load static flexure. The total development length available was 1182 mm (3.875 feet). The strains in cables at the location of crack started rising after the first crack. The failure occurred by the tension failure of the cables because no slip was noticed on dial gages mounted on the exposed cable ends. Concrete had a maximum strain of 2310 when the cables had reached nearly the ultimate strain. The measured moment of resistance was nearly equal to the theoretical moment of resistance proving that this was the total development length for sanded graphite cables.
The development length of all the beams were compared with the ACI 318-89 equation by considering f_{ps} as the stress at slip initiation. The experimental values agree with the ACI equation for beams prestressed with steel cables where as they differ for the beam prestressed with graphite cables.

Total Development Length = $(f_{ps}-2/3*f_{se})*d_b$ . . . .(1)
f_{ps} = stress in steel at nominal strength (in ksi)
f_{se} = effective prestress in steel cable (in ksi)
d_b = nominal diameter of bar (in inches)

CONCLUSIONS

The above described investigation brings out the following conclusions:
Transfer lengths of steel and unsanded graphite cables were

61 and 85 diameters respectively. Both values are higher than the ACI 318-89 recommended values.

Surface preparation (as described) doubled the bond strength of graphite cables.

The losses for sanded graphite cables to that of steel cables were in the proportion of 1:0.75.

Unsanded graphite cables slipped during transfer of prestress showing poor bond strength with concrete.

Measured values of development length for steel cables agree to the ACI 318-89 recommended values. Sanded graphite cables showed lesser values than the ACI recommended values and the unsanded graphite cables showed higher values than the ACI recommended values.

The slip failure mode was similar for steel, sanded graphite and unsanded graphite cables.

Non-reversible cyclic flexure initiated slip at a lesser load than the static flexure. Cyclic loading for two million cycles did not significantly affect the ultimate strength of the beam prestressed with sanded graphite cables.

The long term (6 months) sustained tension test on graphite cables did not show any significant creep.

ACKNOWLEDGEMENTS

The authors would like to thank Hercules and Shell Oil Company for supplying materials. Part of this project was sponsored by South Dakota Department of Transportation. The authors would like to thank South Dakota School of Mines and Technology for providing facilities at the Structural Engineering Laboratory.

REFERENCES

1. Wines, J. C., and Hoff, G. C. (1966). Laboratory Investigation of Plastic Glass Fiber Reinforcement for Reinforced and Prestressed Concrete. Report 1, February 1966, U.S. Army Engineering waterways Experiment Station, Corps of Engineers, Vicksburg, Mississippi.

2. Wines, J. C., Dietz, R. J., and Hawley, J.L. (1966). Laboratory Investigation of Plastic Glass Fiber Reinforcement for Reinforced and Prestressed Concrete. Report 2, July 1966, U.S. Army Engineering Waterways Experiment Station, Corps of Engineers, Vicksburg, Mississippi.

3. Zoch, P., Kimura, H., Iwasaki, T., and Heym, M. Carbon Fiber Composite cables.

4. Khubchandani, A. (1991). Evaluation of Graphite Composite Cables for Prestressing Concrete. M.S. Thesis 1991, South Dakota School of Mines and Technology.

5. ASTM D 3916

6. Iyer S. L., and Kumaraswamy C. (1988). Performance Evaluation of Glass and Fiber Composite Cables for Prestressed Concrete Units. 33rd International SAMPE Symposium, March 7-10, 1988, Anaheim, California

7. Anigol, M. U.(1991). Testing Mechanical Properties of Fiber Glass and Graphite Composite Cables. M.S. Thesis 1991, South Dakota School of Mines and technology.

8. Iyer S. L., Khubchandani A., and Feng, J. (1991). Fiberglass and Graphite Composite Cables for Bridge Decks. Proceedings of Specialty Conference on Advanced Composite Materials in Civil Engineering, January 31- February 1, 1991.

TABLE-1

COMPARISON OF THE THEORETICAL AND EXPERIMENTAL VALUES OF THE FIRST CRACK AND ULTIMATE MOMENTS

BEAM IDENTI-FICATION	FIRST CRACK MOMENT		ULTIMATE MOMENT		MODE OF FAILURE
	THE.	EXP.	THE.	EXP.	
4ST8	21.57	20.62	30.22	26.40	Compression
3ST5	7.94	11.46	16.30	12.72	Slip
4ST5	9.15	16.12	30.21	20.96	Slip
4UG8	12.19	18.40	35.29	20.11	Slip
4UG5	13.60	11.28	35.29	20.11	Slip
3UG5	11.35	6.45	19.30	8.47	Slip
2SG8	17.73	18.40	33.96	29.02	Cable Tension
2SG5C	15.20	16.12	33.96	29.02	Slip & Shear
2SG5	14.86	19.34	33.96	21.69	Slip
2UG8	12.48	15.78	33.96	21.69	Slip
2UG5	5.97	12.08	33.96	13.69	Slip
2UG5C	12.05	9.68	33.96	9.68	Slip

ST: Steel, UG: Unsanded Graphite, SG: Sanded Graphite
THE.-THEORETICAL, EXP.-EXPERIMENTAL
All moments in KN.m
Cross section of all beams is 152 mm x 216 mm (6.0 inches x 8.5 inches).
Beam Identification 4ST8 indicates 4 cables of steel used in 2440 mm (8 feet) long beam.

Theoretical First Crack Moments are based on ACI 318-89 recommended value of modulus of rupture of $7.5(f_c')^{1/2}$ where f_c' is in psi.
Theoretical Ultimate Moments are based on the assumption of sufficient development length.
All the beams were tested in static flexure except 2UG5C and 2SG5C which were tested after 2 million cycles of non-reversible cyclic flexure.

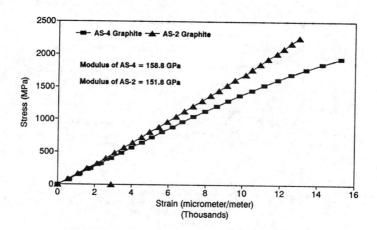

Fig. 1 Stress Strain Diagrams for Graphite Cables

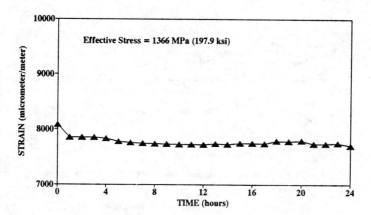

Fig. 2 Short Term Sustained Tension Test on Graphite Cable

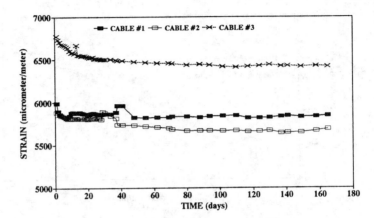

Fig. 3 Long Term Sustained Tension Test on Graphite Cables

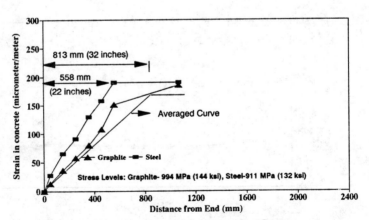

Fig. 4 Transfer Lengths for Unsanded Graphite and Steel Cables

ADVANCED COMPOSITE MATERIALS IN BRIDGES AND STRUCTURES
K.W. Neale and P. Labossière, Editors; Canadian Society for Civil Engineering, 1992

Matériaux composites d'avant-garde pour ponts et charpentes
K.W. Neale et P. Labossière, éditeurs; Société canadienne de génie civil, 1992

IMPACT TENSILE STRENGTH OF CARBON FIBRE COMPOSITE CABLE

Y. Kobayashi and **Y. Tanaka**
Ministry of Transport
Tokyo, Japan

ABSTRACT

This paper reports on the results of impact tensile tests of carbon fibre composite cable for prestressed concrete. The test results include the strain-rate dependence of strength, elongation, elastic modulus, and absorbed energy. In the stress-strain relationship, the proportional limit corresponds to the breaking point in static tension, but it arises before the failure of the cable in impact tension and it results in damage. The damage point implies that an impact produces various kinds of failure; i.e., interfacial cracks, failure of fibre, and deformation of the strand shape.

RÉSUMÉ

Cet article présente les résultats de tests d'impact pour un câble de précontrainte en composite renforcé de fibres de carbone et en tension. Les résultats du test permettent d'étudier l'effet du taux de déformation sur la résistance, l'élongation, le module élastique, et l'absorption d'énergie. Dans la relation contrainte-déformation, la limite de proportionnalité correspond à la rupture en tension statique, mais elle se produit avant la rupture du câble soumis à un impact sous tension, et correspond au dommage. L'endommagement suite à l'impact génère différentes sortes de rupture telles que : fissures interfaciales, rupture des fibres, et déformation de la forme du filin.

INTRODUCTION

The durability of marine concrete structures is dominated by corrosion resistance of reinforcing steels, therefore fiber reinforced plastic rods and cables have been developed as the substitutive materials for reinforcing steels. Carbon or aramid fiber reinforced plastic strands are useful for the prestressing cables of prestressed concrete structures in corrosion environment. These new materials have the properties of light weight, high strength, and excellent corrosion resistance, but they are lacking in plastic deformation and ductility compared with reinforcing steels. In the collisions between thin prestressed concrete and a truck on shore or a ship on sea, impact tension will arise in prestressing cables. However the impact characteristics have not been published, therefore the impact data for new materials are necessary for the design of structural members. Carbon Fiber Composite Cable (CFCC, Tokyo Rope MFG, 1991) is a kind of carbon fiber reinforced plastic which is made of PAN base carbon fiber and an epoxy resin. The cables are on sail for 1.3 to 40mm in diameter (18.7 to 1,072kN in breaking load).

This paper reports the results of impact tensile test of CFCC 1x7 strand. The stress–strain relationships are obtained from the strain and load responses and the results are studied on the strain–rate dependence of breaking strength, elongation, elastic modulus, and absorbed energy. The evaluation is expressed by the relative value; i.e. the ratio of the impact value to the static value.

EXPERIMENTAL PROCEDURE

Materials and Specimen

The test cable is 1x7 construction and 5mm in outer diameter. It consists of one central element material and six side ones surrounding the central element material. The element material is a kind of carbon fiber reinforced plastic which is impregnated two prepregs with the denatured epoxy resin. One prepreg consists of 12,000 pieces of carbon fiber. The carbon fiber is PAN base system and 7 microns in diameter. The effective cross section area of the cable is $10.1mm^2$ and the volume fraction of reinforcement is 64%. These mechanical properties are shown in Table 1.

The specimen was 750mm long and the cable length between anchor chucks was 250mm as shown in Fig.1. Both ends of the cable were anchored by resin filling a steel pipe. Impact tensile load was applied through the screw of the pipe end.

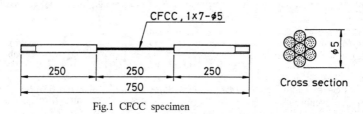

Fig.1 CFCC specimen

Table 1 Mechanical properties of materials and specimen

	Breaking load P_{us} kN	Tensile strength σ_{us} MPa	Elastic modulus E_s GPa	Elonga- tion ε_{us} %	Absorbed energy E_{uo} J/cm^3
Carbon fiber[*]	—	3630	235	1.5	—
Denatured epoxy resin[*]	—	88.2	3.53	4.2	—
CFCC (1x7 ⌀5)	21.7	2150	145	1.52	15.3

[*] CFCC technical data

84

Testing Procedure

Impact tension was tested by a rotating disk type machine with a capacity of 100kN for 100m/s. The schematic diagram of test and measuring system are shown in Fig.2. When the speed of hammer reached the demand value, the specimen was tensed by the tensile block with the hammer. Load was detected by a load cell of strain gage system and elongation by the strain gages of 70mm and 30mm in length. The above measuring analog data were transformed into the digital data with a sampling rate of 4 micro second by using an A/D translator of 12 bit resolving power. Finally the data were stored on a floppy disk in a personal computer. In the measurement of strain, the 70mm gage was located at the middle of the cable and 30mm gages at both ends. The strain gages and adhesive were enough to bear elongation of 5%. Rubber sheets were pasted on both faces of the tensile block to absorb the pulses by strike.

The strain-rate, $\dot\varepsilon$, is given by $\dot\varepsilon = \Delta l/(l\Delta t)$, where $\Delta l/\Delta t$ corresponds to the hammer speed, V_h, l is the length of specimen cable. The relationships between V_h and $\dot\varepsilon$ are shown in Fig.3. When the cable is fixed rigidly at both

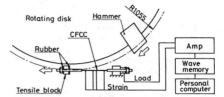

Fig.2 Schematic diagram of test and measuring system

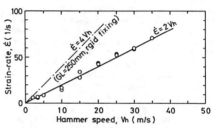

Fig.3 Relationships between strain-rate and hammer speed

ends of the cable, the strain rate becomes $\dot\varepsilon = 4V_h$. But the experimental measured strain-rate decreased to a half of the above value. This is caused by the elongation of both anchor chucks and the jig in loading system, because the capacity of inertia moment of the rotating disk is enough to break the cable.

RESULTS AND DISCUSSIONS

Characteristics in Static Tension

The average values of three static tensile results are shown in Table 1. The stress was proportional to the strain in stress-strain diagram. Each breaking stress was almost same. The elongation at breaking point, $i.e.$ the strain, ε_{us}, agreed approximately with the fiber's value. According to the estimated values obtained from the law of mixture to loading direction, the experimental breaking stress, σ_{us}, and elastic modulus, E_s, were 91% and 95% of the estimated value respectively. The two measuring systems were adopted for the measurement of elongation in static tension; one was measured by the above strain gage at the middle of specimen and the other by a laser extensometer in the gage length of 150mm. Same behaviors were shown in the stress-strain or stress-elongation diagrams, and each proportional limit corresponded to the breaking point. The good response of strain gage is based on the reason that the elongation of the resin in the cable is more than that of the carbon fiber. From this experimental fact, the strain gage method is very useful for the measurement of elongation in impact tension.

Characteristics in Impact Tension

Breaking Position of Cable

The breaking position could be decided from the strain response in addition to observations after test. Many specimens broke firstly at the anchor end of the striking side as shown in Fig.4 and secondly at the anchor end of the load cell side. Static test specimens did not always break at the anchor ends, but impact specimen became to break at anchor ends in high strain-rate. Cable breaks generally at an anchor end on account of stress concentration. However, when the cable broke at the anchor end, the compressive failure arose at the other end. This is caused by the recoverable energy in tension. In relation to the breaking position of CFCC, the estimate for propagation velocity of stress wave was approximately 8,800m/s from the strain response at both ends.

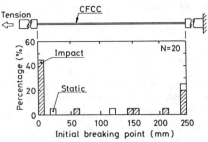

Fig.4 Breaking point of cable in tension

Strain and Load responses, Stress–strain Diagram

Each example of strain and load variation with time is shown in Fig.5. The time lag was observed between both variations because of the different measuring positions. The strain variation had a part of a constant strain–rate, but it had the unstable range before the break of strain gage. The load variation had also a linear portion for some time. The rising responses were not linear by the effect of the rubber sheets. Therefore these rising times are obtained from the extrapolation of constant strain–rate or load for convenience.

Stress–strain diagram was drawn by the following procedure. The maximum load was regarded as the breaking load. As the test was constant tensile speed, the strain variation with time ought to be linear up to the break of the strain gage. Therefore the unstable variation does not show the correct tensile strain of the cable. From this reason, the top (open circle) of the constant strain–rate was regarded as the correspondent point to the maximum load. Of course each rising time must be same. From the above-mentioned reasons, the stress–strain diagram can be made by moving the time at the maximum load to the time at the top of the constant strain–rate and by corresponding to both rising times. According to the analysis of strain and load variation with time in $\dot{\varepsilon} > 10(1/s)$, the time lag between both rising times was approximately equal to that between the time at the top of the constant strain–rate and the time at the maximum load.

The stress–strain diagram of Fig.6 was obtained from Fig.5, and the marks show the correspondent points in both figures with the exception of the triangle. A proportional limit appeared in the stress–strain relationship. The

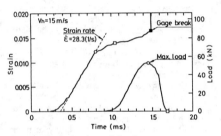

Fig.5 Strain and load responses

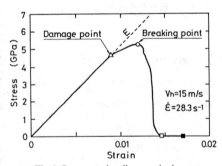

Fig.6 Stress–strain diagram in impact

authors call the proportional limit the damage point (triangle) in impact. Since impact is apt to produce damages at the location of ununiform volume fraction of reinforcement because of the shear–lag between fiber and matrix, it is considered that the damage point is caused by various kinds of damage; *i.e.* interfacial cracks, break of fiber, cracks of matrix, and loosening between a center element material and side ones.

Effect of Strain–rate on Strength and Elongation

σ_d and σ_u represent the damage stress and the breaking stress respectively. The relationships between the relative stresses, σ_d/σ_{us} and σ_u/σ_{us}, and the strain–rate are shown in Fig.7. The strain–rate was $2.5 \times 10^{-5}(1/s)$ in static tension and then the static value was plotted at $\dot\varepsilon=0$ for convenience. There was no effect of strain-rate on σ_d/σ_{us} and σ_u/σ_{us} in $\dot\varepsilon\leq10(1/s)$, but there were significant effects of strain-rate in $\dot\varepsilon>10(1/s)$. The relative values increased in $10<\dot\varepsilon\leq32(1/s)$ and decreased in $\dot\varepsilon>32(1/s)$. It is assumed that the maximum values were $\sigma_d/\sigma_{us}\approx2.2$ and $\sigma_u/\sigma_{us}\approx2.5$ for $\dot\varepsilon=32(1/s)$ and they were gradually approaching the fixed values in high strain-rate; i.e. $\sigma_d/\sigma_{us}\approx0.2$ and $\sigma_u/\sigma_{us}\approx0.5$.

In these behaviors, it can be considered that the increase of strength was caused by the strain-rate dependence of the resin and the decrease of strength is caused by the break of fiber with the brittleness of the resin in high speed tension. In other words, stress distributes uniformly to the cross section in low strain-rate, but it is concentrated at the location of less volume fraction in high strain-rate and cracks tend to initiate by shear-lag. According to the simulations of dynamic failure process of CFRP single plate (Kimpara and Ozaki, 1987), it is shown that the stress, deformation and strain energy are concentrated at a loading point in high strain-rate and the failure becomes to concentrate the limited area.

ε_d and ε_u represent the damage strain and the breaking strain in impact tension respectively. Fig.8 shows the strain-rate dependence on the relative values, $\varepsilon_d/\varepsilon_{us}$ and $\varepsilon_u/\varepsilon_{us}$. The relative damage strain decreased linearly. The breaking strain decreased remarkably in $\dot\varepsilon\leq32(1/s)$, but it was approximately constant, $\varepsilon_u/\varepsilon_{us}=0.73$, for $\dot\varepsilon>32(1/s)$. Elongation decreases generally with the increase of strength. As for the high breaking strain in high strain-rate, it is considered to be the phenomenon with the strain-rate dependence of the epoxy resin in high speed tension. On the other hand the decrease of damage strain means that impact produces interfacial cracks and break of fiber in the cable. Furthermore the extrapolated value became $\varepsilon_d/\varepsilon_{us}=0.73$ for $\dot\varepsilon=0$ on the equation by the least squares method of the damage strain. Therefore this suggests that the cable has some damages in 73% of the elongation of static tension.

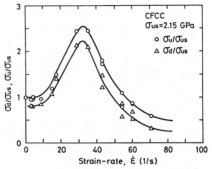

Fig.7 Effect of strain-rate on strength

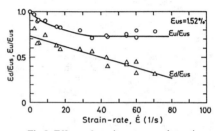

Fig.8 Effect of strain-rate on elongation

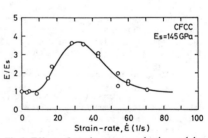

Fig.9 Effect of strain-rate on elastic modulus

Effect of Strain-rate on Elastic Modulus

Elastic modulus, E, can be obtained from a stress-strain diagram or the ratio of stress-rate $\Delta\sigma/\Delta t$ to $\dot\varepsilon$. The relationship between the relative elastic modulus, E/E_s, and the strain-rate is shown in Fig.9. The maximum was $E/E_s\approx3.7$ for $\dot\varepsilon=32(1/s)$, and it approached gradually the static elastic modulus ($E/E_s\approx1.0$) in high strain-rate. Although the strain-rate dependence of elastic modulus is caused by the interaction between the increase of stress and the decrease of damage strain, $E/E_s>1$ is brought primarily by the increase of stress. If the strain is measured at the localized failure point, a large strain-rate is given and small elastic modulus will be obtained. E/E_s right after impact gave large value in $\dot\varepsilon<10(1/s)$, but it was not considered in this paper since the range influenced was comparatively small in the stress-strain relation.

Effect of strain-rate on Absorbed Energy

E_d and E_u represent the absorbed energy per unit volume in the damage point and the breaking point respectively. E_d/E_{us} and E_u/E_{us} represent the relative values, where E_{us} is the absorbed energy in static tension. The relative values depended on the strain-rate as shown in Fig.10, and the trend was similar to the strain-rate dependence on strength. The maximum relative absorbed energies gave $E_d/E_{us} \approx 1.4$ and $E_u/E_{us} \approx 2.4$ for $\dot{\varepsilon}=32(1/s)$, but these were gradually approaching the fixed values in high strain-rate; *i.e.* $E_d/E_{us} \approx 0.1$ and $E_u/E_{us} \approx 0.5$.

Damage Ratio

The damage ratios, σ_d/σ_u, $\varepsilon_d/\varepsilon_u$, and E_d/E_u, are defined as the ratio of the value at the damage point to the value at the breaking point respectively. These relationships are shown in Fig.11. Each damage ratio was approximately constant; *i.e.* $\sigma_d/\sigma_u \approx 0.9$, $\varepsilon_d/\varepsilon_u \approx 0.75$ and $E_d/E_u \approx 0.6$ for $\dot{\varepsilon} \leq 32(1/s)$, and decreases linearly with the increase of strain-rate in $\dot{\varepsilon}>32(1/s)$. It is clear that the damage occurs at the approximate fixed level to the break and that the absorbed energy decreases markedly by the additive effects of decrease in stress and strain.

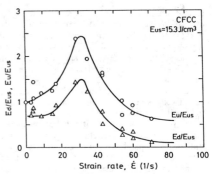

Fig.11 Effect of strain rate on damage ratio

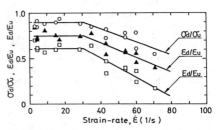

Fig.10 Effect of strain-rate on absorbed energy

CONCLUDING REMARKS

Carbon Fiber Composite Cable (CFCC) for prestressed concrete was tested under impact tension. Examining the effect of strain-rate on mechanical properties, the results are as follows.
1. In the stress-strain relationship, the proportional limit corresponded to the breaking point in static tension, but it was observed before the break of the cable in impact tension and it means the damage of the cable. From the strain-rate dependence on the strength and elongation, the damage is caused by initiation of interfacial cracks, failure of fiber and deformation of strand shape etc.
2. Similar trend was observed in the strain-rate dependence of strength, elastic modulus and absorbed energy. Each strain-rate dependence showed different characteristics in $\dot{\varepsilon} \leq 10(1/s)$, $10<\dot{\varepsilon} \leq 32(1/s)$, and $\dot{\varepsilon}>32(1/s)$. In the case of the breaking stress, there was no effect of strain-rate in $\dot{\varepsilon} \leq 10(1/s)$. The strength increased in $10<\dot{\varepsilon} \leq 32(1/s)$ as the strain-rate increased, but it decreased in $\dot{\varepsilon}>32(1/s)$. It can be considered that the increase of strength is caused by the strain-rate dependence of the resin, and that the decrease of strength by the growth of the above damage with the brittleness of the resin in high speed tension.
3. From the damage point is observed in impact, low cycle impact test will be useful for the evaluation of cable and anchor strength. Furthermore impact strength will improve through a good selection of resin and uniformity of volume fraction in process of production.

REFERENCES

Kimpara,I. and Ozaki,T.(1987). Study on Reliability Assessment System of composite Material(3rd report),-Establishment of Dynamic Failure Model and Examination on Dynamic Failure Process-. J. Society of Naval Architects of Japan, Vol.161, 382-389.

Tokyo Rope MFG. Co., Ltd. CFCC Technical Data, Jan. 1991.

ADVANCED COMPOSITE MATERIALS IN BRIDGES AND STRUCTURES
K.W. Neale and P. Labossière, Editors; Canadian Society for Civil Engineering, 1992

Matériaux composites d'avant-garde pour ponts et charpentes
K.W. Neale et P. Labossière, éditeurs; Société canadienne de génie civil, 1992

CÂBLES COMPOSITES POUR LA PRÉCONTRAINTE : ÉTUDE DE LA RELAXATION

S. Kaci
Université de Tizi-Ouzou
Tizi-Ouzou, Algérie

RÉSUMÉ

Un des problèmes posés par les câbles composites à base de kevlar dans leur utilisation comme armature de précontrainte est leur comportement en relaxation à long terme. Comme il est inconcevable d'étudier ce problème en temps réel (plusieurs années), nous nous sommes orientés vers une caractérisation accélérée en mettant au point une machine de relaxation originale et en appliquant le principe d'équivalence temps-température. À partir des essais de relaxation de courte durée (1 min à 120 h) mais à différentes températures (25–70 C), nous avons établi la courbe maîtresse à la température ambiante du module de relaxation sur une période proche de cinq ans. Le module de relaxation a tendance à se stabiliser à environ 85 pour cent de sa valeur initiale. De plus, contrairement aux aciers de précontrainte, il est montré que la relaxation est indépendante de la contrainte initiale appliquée.

ABSTRACT

One of the main problems of the Kevlar composite cables when used as prestressing reinforcement is their long time relaxation behaviour. As it is inconceivable to study this problem in real time (many years), our research has focused on accelerated caracterisation by setting up an original relaxation machine and applying the principle of time-temperature equivalence. From short time relaxation tests (1 min to 120 h), but at different temperatures (25–70 C), we have established the base curve at room temperature of the relaxation modulus for a period of about five years. A long-time relaxation modulus has a tendency to stabilize at a value around 85 percent of its initial value. It has also been shown that the relaxation is independent of the applied initial stress.

INTRODUCTION

Les matériaux composites bien connus dans de nombreuses industries (aéronautique, aérospatiale, etc.) s'introduisent actuellement sous forme de câbles, dans le domaine du génie civil. Ils sont déjà utilisés dans de nombreux emplois techniques et plus récemment encore dans le haubanage des pylônes. Leurs performances exceptionnelles (résistance élevée à la traction, excellente tenue à la corrosion) incitent de nombreux industriels à vouloir les substituer aux aciers de précontrainte qui, par suite surtout de leur corrosion, sont très souvent à l'origine de nombreux désordres dont certains très graves, sur les ouvrages en béton-précontraint. Un des problèmes posés par ces câbles composites lors des premières applications (Gerritse et Schurhoff, 1986) et que l'on se propose d'étudier dans cet article est le comportement en relaxation à long terme. On se propose d'abord de déterminer les caractéristiques mécaniques en traction du matériau étudié puis de présenter les différents résultats d'essais obtenus à l'aide d'une machine de relaxation originale dont la description et le principe de fonctionnement seront exposés. L'application du principe d'équivalence temps-température aux résultats d'essais effectués à différentes températures nous permet d'obtenir une courbe maîtresse du module longitudinal de traction, s'étalant sur une longue période. Nous terminons par une étude comparée de ces câbles avec les aciers de précontrainte en guise de conclusion.

MATÉRIAU ÉTUDIÉ : CORDON DE KEVLAR.0.95.TW.A2

Le matériau que nous étudions est un cordon tressé de Kevlar haut module, imprégné d'une résine thermodurcissable de polyester-uréthane; il se présente sous forme cylindrique de faible diamètre (0.95 mm). La tresse est obtenue à partir de deux groupes constitués chacun de quatre brins (le premier groupe tressé dans le sens S, l'autre dans le sens Z). Chacun de ces brins, formé par un assemblage de 768 filaments de Kevlar 49 tous parallèles entre-eux, a une masse linéaire de 1270 dtex (Photo 1). Un tel assemblage par tressage à pas long, permet de conserver le plus possible les caratéristiques mécaniques des fibres de Kevlar; quant au produit d'imprégnation (polyester-uréthane) en plus du rôle de lubrifiant qu'il joue entre les fibres constituant la tresse, il permet de conserver la cylindricité de cette dernière. Au contact de la tresse, ce polyester-uréthane présente une liason élastique adhérente qui procure au cordon réalisé une grande souplesse. La fraction massique en fibre est de l'ordre de 80%.

CARATÉRISTIQUES MÉCANIQUES DE TRACTION

Les caratéristiques mécaniques de traction ont été obtenues à l'aide d'une machine ADAMEL l'HOMARGY (modèle DY 25) et d'un extensomètre optique de haute résolution. Quant au diamètre, il est déterminé à l'aide d'un projecteur de profil (3A3EM.P.500). Les résultats obtenus sont indiqués ci-dessous : résistance à la traction (MPa), 2201 ± 22; allongement à la rupture (%), 2.13 ± 0.05; module d'élasticité longitudinal (GPa), 103.2 ± 3.4; diamètre de cordon (mm), 0.95 ± 0.05. Le diagramme de traction obtenu est semblable à celui de la fibre élémentaire de Kevlar; il est représenté par une courbe linéaire jusqu'à la rupture (Fig. 1).

ÉTUDE DE COMPORTEMENT EN RELAXATION

Nous nous proposons de mettre en évidence un phénomène de relaxation par un essai technologique simple, qui permettra de déterminer le comportement rhéologique du matériau testé (cordon de Kevlar 0.95 TW.A2) et de mettre en place une chaîne de mesure qui permettra de déterminer les grandeurs caractéristiques du matériau (notamment le module de relaxation).

Essai retenu pour définir l'état de relaxation du matériau

Ce choix est imposé par la nature du matériau à tester; en effet, compte tenu de sa grande flexibilité (souplesse) et surtout sa fragilité à toute sollicitation transversale, nous avons volontairement écarté aussi bien les essais de relaxation en flexion, qu'en torsion; nous avons par contre opté pour un essai de relaxation en traction en raison de son éventuel futur emploi et aussi pour la répartition uniforme des contraintes auxquelles il conduit.

Principe de fonctionnement de la machine de relaxation (Photo 2)

Un système de mise en tension (1) approprié permet de tendre l'éprouvette (2), placé entre un ancrage passif (3) et un ancrage actif (4); tous deux situés à l'intérieur d'un bâti, métallique (5). Le dispositif de mise en tension (1) a la particularité de bloquer l'armature juste après la fin de sa mise en charge. Un capteur de force (6) positionné juste sous l'ancrage actif permet de connaître à tout instant la valeur de la tension résiduelle existante dans l'armature. Cette machine permet donc de mettre le cordon (2) en traction et de maintenir l'allongement ainsi créé constant pendant toute la durée de l'essai.

Programme expérimental d'essais

Afin d'atteindre les objectifs que nous nous sommes fixés, trois séries d'essais ont été exécutées sur ces cordons de Kevlar de type 0.95 TW.A2: Une première série d'essai de relaxation pure portant sur de longues durées. Une deuxième série d'essai de relaxation pure dont le paramètre variable est le niveau de contrainte initiale. Et enfin une troisième série d'essai de relaxation pure dont le paramètre variable est la température.

Résultats

Les essais de la première série ont été effectués à une température constante $(25^{\circ}C)$ et pour un niveau de contrainte égal à 50% de la contrainte de rupture. Les résultats sont représentés sur la Fig. 2. On peut écrire:

$$D\sigma(t) = A\log t + B \qquad \text{ou bien} \qquad \rho(t) = A'\log t + B' \qquad (1)$$

Avec t =temps; $\sigma(t)$ = contrainte à l'instant t; σi = contrainte initiale; $D\sigma(t) = \sigma i - \sigma(t)$ = pertes de contraintes à l'instant t; $\rho(t) = \dfrac{D\sigma(t)}{\sigma i} \times 100$ = pourcentage de relaxation; et enfin A, B, A', B' sont des constantes.

$$\frac{dD\sigma(t)}{dt} = \frac{A}{t} \qquad \text{ou} \qquad \dot{\rho}(t) = \frac{d\rho(t)}{dt} = \frac{A'}{t} \tag{2}$$

La relaxation du cordon de Kevlar suit une loi expérimentale de type logarithmique; sa vitesse suit une loi hyperbolique. Au bout de huit heures, on remarque que les pertes de contraintes ont déjà atteint les trois quarts de pertes totales; les valeurs de la relaxation à des temps caractéristiques de 120 heures et 1000 heures sont respectivement d'environ 12.1% et 13.5%. Par simple extrapolation, sa valeur au bout de 10^6 heures est de 18.9%.

Les essais de la deuxième série ont été effectués à température constante (25^oC) et à différents niveaux de contraintes initiales (30%, 50%, 60%, et 70% Tr; avec Tr = contrainte de rupture du matériaux). Les résultats des essais sont representés sur la Fig. 3. Pour des niveaux de contraintes initiales supérieurs ou égaux à 30% de la contrainte de rupture, le pourcentage de relaxation est constant (Fig. 4).

Application du principe d'équivalence temps-température

Une augmentation de la température a, sur les propriétés mécaniques d'un corps viscoélastique, la même influence qu'une augmentation du temps de mesure. Le principe d'équivalence temps-température dans lequel on fait intervenir l'équation du facteur temps (Tobolsky, 1967)

$$\tau(T1) = \tau(T0) \times a(T1/T0) \tag{3}$$

nous permet de déterminer le comportement à une température ($T0$) connaissant celui de la température ($T1$); $a(T1/T0)$ étant le facteur de translation, $\tau(T1)$ le temps à la température $T1$ et $\tau(T0)$ le temps à la température (To). L'application de ce principe nous permet d'obtenir une courbe maitresse à la température (To) (Fig. 6). Au bout de 1702 jours ($\approx$ 5 ans) le module de relaxation a atteint une valeur égale à 84% du module initial et a tendance à se stabiliser; ce résultat est en bon accord avec celui obtenu pour un même temps avec l'Eq. (1).

CONCLUSION

Contrairement à l'acier de précontrainte, pour lequel les pertes de tension, par suite du phénomène de relaxation sont décrites par une loi de puissance (Fig. 7),

$$\rho(t) = bt^n \tag{4}$$

celles du cordon de Kevlar suivent une loi logarithmique. Sa vitesse de relaxation de type hyperbolique diminue au cours du temps d'une façon plus rapide que celle de l'acier précontraint. Après 120 heures d'essai, le pourcentage de relaxation de contrainte du Kevlar s'évalue à quatre fois celui de l'acier de précontrainte traditionnelle dit de relaxation normale (R.N.), qui lui pour une même durée et pour un niveau de contrainte égal à 70% de la contrainte de rupture, présente un pourcentage de l'ordre de 3%. Mais au bout de 1000 heures, ce rapport de quatre diminue et n'est que de 1,5. Et à long terme, ce rapport aura tendance à s'inverser (Fig. 7).

L'influence du niveau de contrainte initiale a conduit à un résultat particulièrement avantageux: le pourcentage de perte de tension est indépendant du niveau de contrainte initiale, alors que pour l'acier de précontrainte, il évolue d'une manière exponentielle (Fig. 8).

L'application du principe d'équivalence temps-température à des résultats de courbes obtenues à différentes températures nous a permis de déduire une courbe maîtresse du module de relaxation longitudinal, qui semble se stabiliser à une période proche de cinq ans pour une température de $25^{o}C$.

Au vu de ces résultats de relaxation, ces nouveaux matériaux à base de fibres synthétique (Kevlar) durables sous n'importe quelle attaque environnante, incluant même les sels et les solutions alcalines, et combinant à la fois des qualités de très grandes résistances et de manutention, peuvent être utilisés très avantageusement comme outil de précontrainte, surtout dans les milieux aggressifs et ce sans obliger un entretien.

Cependant compte tenu du diagramme de traction ne présentant aucune phase de plasticité, il est conseillé d'imposer un coefficient de sécurité élevé; il est également utile de réduire au plus possible l'important pourcentage de relaxation se produisant lors des premières heures, et ce en le soumettant à des méthodes de traitement thermique par exemple.

Comme perspectives, il serait intéressant d'établir une théorie qui puisse permettre d'établir des formules pratiques de calcul des pertes de tensions. Et enfin de créer de nouvel appareillage d'essai rhéologique afin d'analyser le problème réel, tel qu'il se pose dans un ouvrage en béton précontraint. Il est recommandé d'envisager une étude en vraie grandeur, donc de résoudre le problème des pertes différées non pas des composites seuls, mais d'un système de renfort en composites tendus et d'un béton comprimé. Cette interdépendance permet de résoudre le problème de relaxation des composites combiné au fluage et retrait du béton.

RÉFÉRENCES

Burgoyne, C.L. (1988). Proceedings of Symposium on Parafil Ropes. Imperial College of Science and Technology, London.

De Charentenay, F.X.(1970). Propriétés Viscoélastiques Morphologie. École Nationale Supérieure des Techniques Avancées.

Ferry, J.D. (1970). Viscoelastic Properties of Polymers. Wiley.

Fujisaki, T., Matsuzaki, Y., Sekijma, K., and Okamura, H. (1987). New Materials for Reinforced Concrete in Place of Reinforcing Steel Bars. Technical Contribution to IABSE Symposium, Paris.

Gerritse, A. and Werner, J. (1988). Arapree: The Prestressing Element Composed of Resin Bonded Twaron Fibres. Rapport interne AKZO.

Gerritse, A., Schurhoff, H.J., and Maatjes, E. (1987). Prestressed Concrete Structure with Arapree; Relaxation. Technical Contribution to IABSE Symposium, Paris.

Gerritse, A. and Schurhoff, H.J. (1987). Heavy Duty Composite Material for Prestressing of Concrete Structures. Technical Contribution to IABSE Symposium, Paris.

Gerritse, A. and Schurhoff, H.J. (1986). Aramid Reinforced Concrete (ARC). Technical Contribution to RILEM 3rd Symposium, Sheffield.

Gerritse, A. and Schurhoff, H.J. (1986). Prestressing with Aramid Tendons. Technical Contribution to FIP sath congress, New Delhi.

Kaci, S. (1989). Câbles Composites pour la précontrainte : Étude de la relaxation. Thèse Université de Bordeaux I.

Tobolsky, A.V. (1967). <u>Properties and Structure of Polymers</u>. Wiley.

Morlier, P. (1972). Influence de la température sur le comportement des matériaux: L'environnement mécanique, sa mesure et ses effets. Comportement des matériaux. Rapport ADERA – ASTE, Bordeaux.

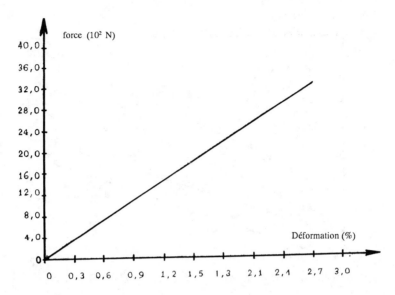

Figure 1 : Diagramme de traction du cordon de Kevlar (type 0,95 TWA2)

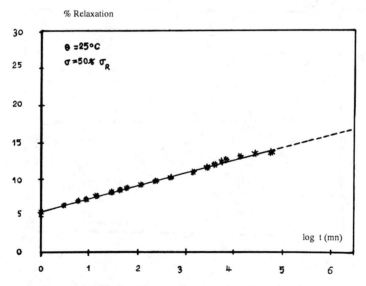

Figure 2 : Relaxation du cordon de Kevlar à température constante (25°)

95

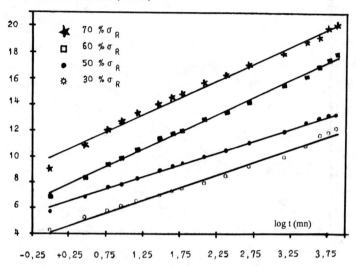

Pertes de contraintes (10 MPa)

Figure3 : Influence du niveau de contrainte initiale

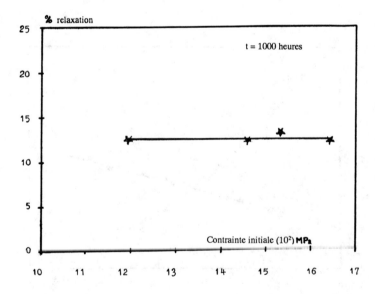

Figure4 : Evolution du pourcentage de relaxation en fonction du niveau de contrainte initiale

Pertes de contraintes (10 MPa)

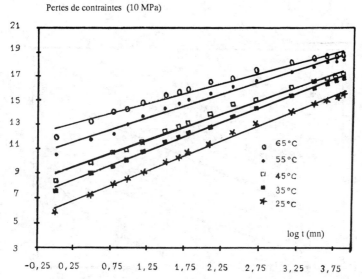

Figure5 : Influence de la température

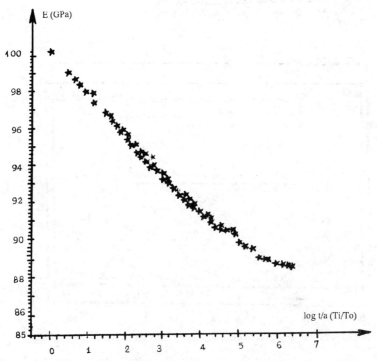

Figure 6 : Courbe maîtresse du module de relaxation du cordon de Kevlar

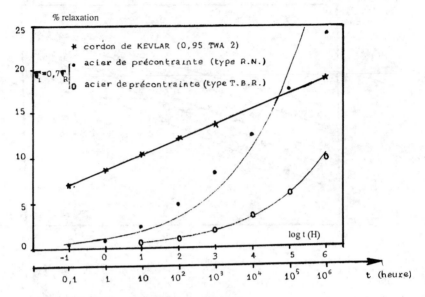

Figure 7 : Comparaison du comportement en relaxation

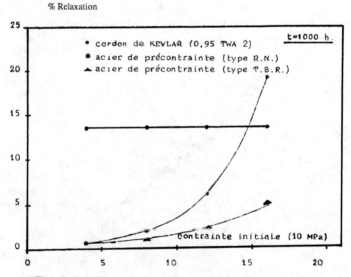

Figure 8 : Comparaison du comportement en relaxation à differentes contraintes initiales

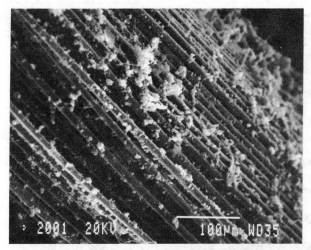

photo 1 : Vue microscopique de quelques filaments élémentaires du Kevlar 49, d'un même brin, imprégnés de resine de polyester-urethane.(diametre d'un filament = 13um).

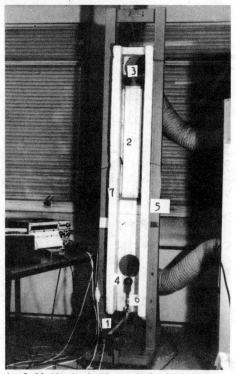

Legende :

1 : Systeme de mise en tension
2 : Cordon de Kevlar
3 : Ancrage passif
4 : Ancrage actif
5 : Bati metallique rigide
6 : peson à jauge de contrainte
7 : Enceinte thermique

photo2 : Machine de relaxation munie d'une chaine de mesure

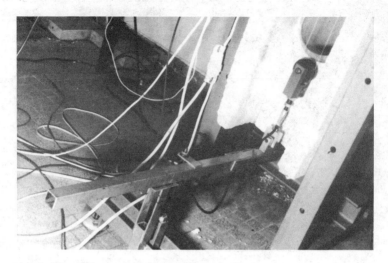

photo 3 : Dispositif de mise en tension

photo 4 : chaine d'acquisition de mesure

ADVANCED COMPOSITE MATERIALS IN BRIDGES AND STRUCTURES
K.W. Neale and P. Labossière, Editors; Canadian Society for Civil Engineering, 1992

Matériaux composites d'avant-garde pour ponts et charpentes
K.W. Neale et P. Labossière, éditeurs; Société canadienne de génie civil, 1992

DURABILITY OF BRAIDED EPOXY-IMPREGNATED ARAMID FRP RODS

A. Nanni
Pennsylvania State University
University Park, Pennsylvania, USA

S. Matsubara and **K. Hasuo**
Mitsui Construction
Tokyo, Japan

ABSTRACT

Fibre-reinforced plastic (FRP) rods are suitable for reinforcing and/or prestressing concrete members, provided that their durability and long-term performance can be assured. Among the questions that need to be addressed are chemical reactivity (with particular emphasis on alkali), moisture sensitivity, stress-rupture, and loss of ultimate elongation. Understanding of FRP material properties is complicated by the lack of standardized accelerated testing procedures. This paper presents some preliminary experimental data on the environmental behaviour of braided, epoxy-impregnated, aramid FRP rods under alkali exposure (solution form and concrete embedment) with and without rod pretension. Results are encouraging and indicate good potential.

RÉSUMÉ

Les barres en FRP sont appropriées pour le renforcement et/ou la précontrainte de pièces en béton, à condition que leur durabilité et leur performance à long terme puissent être assurées. Notons parmi les questions qui doivent être résolues, la réactivité chimique (en particulier avec les alcalis), la sensibilité à l'humidité, la contrainte à la rupture, et l'élongation ultime. La compréhension de ces propriétés est compliquée par l'absence de méthodes accélérées d'essais pour les FRP. Cet article présente quelques résultats expérimentaux sur le comportement de barres en FRP d'aramide, imprégnées d'époxy et tressées, sous une exposition d'alcalis (en solution ou dans le béton), avec ou sans prétension des barres. Les résultats d'essais sont encourageants.

INTRODUCTION

Worldwide concrete structures are undergoing accelerated deterioration as the result of corrosion of the embedded reinforcing steel. The use of fiber-reinforced-plastic (FRP) reinforcement may be an alternative solution to the several active and passive protection methods that have been considered and used to extend the service life of concrete structures. It is therefore of fundamental importance to address the long-term durability of FRP reinforcement before its use in the field.

Chemical Resistance of FRP. In FRP composites, chemical resistance has been traditionally attributed to the resin matrix. Based on manufacturers data, the appropriate resin can be selected for a given application environment (i.e., temperature, concentration of corrosive substances, moisture, and time of exposure). However, since the volume of resin in FRP rods is minimized, the degree of corrosion resistance offered by the resin may be questioned. Furthermore, any matrix cracking or crazing, resin-fiber debonding, and porosity will weaken the resin barrier effect. It is also known that absorbed water from the surrounding environment plasticizes the resin (epoxy) and causes softening, swelling, and reduction of the glass transition temperature. Finally, absorbed water may be the vehicle for corrosion agents to enter in contact with the fibers. It is therefore important that FRP rods be made of fibers with a good chemical resistance of their own. For the case of aramid (which is the material of interest in this paper), fibers show a good resistance to chemical attack except by strong acids and bases at high concentration and elevated temperature (Dobb 1985). A schematic representation of the chemical degradation of aramid and aramid-epoxy FRP is compared to that of steel in Fig. 1 (Gerritse May 1990).

In order to determine the long-term durability of FRP reinforcement in concrete, FRP rods should be tested under several aggressive conditions which include combinations of environments with high pH ($Ca(OH)_2$, NaOH, and KOH from portland cement), chlorides ($CaCl_2$ from accelerating agents and NaCl from seawater and deicers), and sulfates (SO_3 from cement, soil, or contaminants). Different solution concentrations and temperatures should be considered. Even though these specific test conditions are unique to the needs of the construction industry, there is a number of experimental and analytical works that have been performed on composites to assess their long-term durability (O'Brien March 1982; Springer 1981, 1984 and 1987). These works can offer valuable guidance and can complement others with more direct implications on construction industry needs (Glaser et al. 1984; Holloway, L. 1990).

Braided Epoxy-Impregnated Aramid FRP Reinforcement. Braided, epoxy-impregnated, aramid FRP rods are manufactured in different sizes (nominal diameters varying between 3 and 20 mm). A rod is made with 8 fiber strands and each strand may be composed of 1 to 32 yarns. Each yarn consists of 4,000 Kevlar-49 filaments (6,000 denier industrial grade). The gross cross-section of a rod is approximately 65 percent aramid and 35 percent epoxy by volume. The data presented in Table 1 summarize some of the mechanical properties of both the aramid fiber and the epoxy resin used to manufacture the FRP rods described in this paper.

The stress-strain behavior of the composite after epoxy hardening is practically linear-elastic up to failure. Both the composite ultimate strength and elastic modulus are about 80 percent of the corresponding volume of aramid, with efficiency slightly decreasing as the rod diameter increases (Hasuo et al. Sept. 1991). By controlling the bond between fiber strands, rigid or flexible rods can be manufactured. The latter type is preferable for prestressing tendons for ease of shipment and workmanship. Before epoxy hardening, silica sand can be adhered to the rod surface to further improve mechanical bond with concrete. Table 2 summarizes some of the mechanical properties of the two rod types used in this project. Among the listed properties, it should be noted that Column 5 shows the value of the rated capacity P_r, whereas Column 6 shows the average ultimate capacity P_u. The value of P_r is recommended by the manufacturer for design computations and it is derived as P_u minus 2.5 times the standard deviation (i.e., 99.4% of the sample population has an ultimate capacity equal to or better than P_r).

RESISTANCE TO ALKALI ATTACK

Alkali Solution without Pretensioning. A total of 72 aramid FRP rods 4 mm in diameter (K16 type) and 1400 mm long were placed in a solution containing $Ca(OH)_2$, NaOH, and KOH in concentrations of 0.027, 0.25 and 0.25 mol/l (0.2, 1.0 and 1.4% by weight), respectively, and NaCl in a concentration of 3% by weight. The pH of the resulting solution was 13. This selection was an attempt to reproduce an environment typical of portland cement concrete saturated with seawater. As a term of reference, alkalies in portland cement are in the range of 0.2 to 1.5% equivalent Na_2O, with a pH of the pore fluid in concrete between 12.5 and 13.5 (Mehta 1986). Most seawaters contain about 3.5% of soluble salts by weight with NaCl accounting for the highest concentration (Mehta 1986).

Four constant temperature levels were maintained in four separate tanks, varying from 20 to 80°C. Eighteen rods were fully immersed in each tank for a period of time varying between 3 and 90 days. After selected times of immersion, three rods from each tank were tested under uniaxial tension with the average tensile strength results shown in Table 3. The coefficient of variation in each of these 3-specimen groups varied between values of 2.0 and 6.6%. The tensile strength ratio with respect to a virgin, unexposed sample (P_u=17.36 kN) is plotted in Fig. 2 as a function of the time of immersion in the log scale. Based on available data, the expected strength retention ratio at 500,000 hours (57 years) is 98.2% at the lowest tank temperature (20°C), and 94.8% at the highest tank temperature (80°C).

Alkali Solution with Pretensioning. Twelve samples of FRP rods 8 mm in diameter (K64 type) were pretensioned at values of 0.6, 0.7, and 0.8 of the rated capacity of the rod (P_r=62.78 kN). The central segment of the rod (1000 mm) was immersed in the solution described in the previous paragraph (maintained at a constant temperature of 60°C). The sketch in Fig. 3 shows the test apparatus. The results of this test are summarized in Table 4. Columns 1 and 2 show the initial pretensioning force (P_i) and its ratio with the rated capacity (P_r). Column 3 shows the time of failure of each specimen resulting from a combination of stress-rupture and chemical corrosion. Column 4 shows the recorded level of pretension at the time of rod failure (since each test frame was provided with a load-cell). The loss of initial prestress which resulted from tendon relaxation and anchorage slip/creep, is consistent with tendon relaxation data obtained in separate tests. For the case of a rod of the same diameter (K64 type), in air, at constant temperature of 60°C, and with an initial prestress ratio of 0.7, relaxation varied between 8.2% at 100 hours and 10.7% at 1000 hours (linear relationship when time is in the log scale). Specimens which did not fail after 11 months of exposure (Column 6) were removed from the tank and tested under uniaxial tension a month later. The results of these tensile test are given in Columns 7 and 8, the latter being the ratio with respect to the rated strength.

Fig. 4 shows a plot of the initial prestress ratio versus time of exposure in a log scale. Because of the limited number of data points, it is not possible to accurately predict the safe value of initial prestress for a life of 500,000 hours (57 years) under the described testing conditions.

Embedment in Concrete with Pretension. A third series of durability tests consisted of embedding a pretensioned rod with diameter of 8 mm (K64 type), along the centroidal axis of a concrete prism, 360 mm long and 100 by 100 mm in cross-section. Thirty specimens were fabricated. The concrete was maintained wet and at constant temperatures of 20 and 60°C. Three values of initial prestress were used, namely: 0.5, 0.6, and 0.8 of the rated capacity (P_r= 62.78 kN). After 1, 3 and 12 months from construction, the tendons were pulled to failure with the results shown in Table 5. The concrete used for all specimens had the following proportions in kg/m^3: portland cement 360; free water 155 (W/C ratio=0.50); sand 663; and gravel 1185 (maximum aggregate size=10 mm). A water reducing agent was used to produce a slump of 18 cm. Material tests conducted on 10 by 20 cm cylinders at 28-day showed a compressive strength of 35 MPa.

In Fig. 5, the strength retention ratio with respect to the rated capacity is plotted as a function of the exposure time in a log scale. The diagram is limited to specimens maintained at the higher temperature (60°C). For the rods at 0.6 pretensioning, the expected retention ratio at 500,000 hours (57 years) is 110%.

DISCUSSION

The expected strength retention for rods without pretensioning and exposed to an alkali solution similar to that of seawater-saturated concrete is satisfactory (see Fig. 2). When the tank temperature is $80^{\circ}C$, the expected average strength at 500,000 hours remains 4.8% higher than the rated strength. Even if useful for background information, these results cannot be used to predict the life of FRP reinforcement because of the lack of stress in the rods. From the data collected in the case of rods subjected to pretension and exposed to alkali solution, it appears that the combined effects of stress-rupture and chemical corrosion impose a threshold of at least 0.6 on the value of the initial prestress ratio (P_j/P_r) (see Fig. 4). More work is needed to confirm the value of this threshold. A study on durability of aramid-epoxy rods of different composition and manufacturing (Schurhoff and Gerritse 1986), has indicated that, for exposure to a similar alkali solution at a temperature of $60^{\circ}C$, a more conservative threshold of 0.4 is appropriate.

The data obtained from pretensioned rods embedded in wet concrete show encouraging results (see Fig. 5). For a P_j/P_r ratio of 0.6 and temperature of 60°, the predicted residual strength (50% confidence level) at 500,000 remains well above the rated capacity. Concrete embedment was less detrimental to strength than the alkali solution.

CONCLUSIONS

The experimental work presented in this paper, even though limited and incomplete, shows that braided, epoxy-impregnated, aramid FRP rods have a promising behavior with respect to the corrosive environment of portland cement concrete. Investigations on the long-term performance of FRP rods need to continue before the widespread use of advanced composites as reinforcement to concrete structures. In addition to experimental results, there is the need for standardized testing procedures to be used for acceptance (chemical resistance) of any potential FRP reinforcing rod type.

ACKNOWLEDGMENTS

The first author gratefully acknowledges the support of the National Science Foundation under Grant No. MSS-8918592 for his long-term research visit to Mitsui Construction Co., Tokyo, Japan.

REFERENCES

Dobb, M.G., (1985). "The Production, Properties and Structure of High-Performance Poly (p-Phenylene Terephthalamide) Fibers," Handbook of Composites, Vol. 1, W. Watt and B.V. Perov, Editors, Elsevier, London, U.K., pp. 673-704.

Gerritse, A. (May 1990). "Applications and Design Criteria for Aramid Fibrous Tensile Elements," Proc., Composite Materials in Building: State-of-the-Art, Research, and Prospects, Consiglio Nazionale Ricerche, Milan, Italy, pp. 317-333.

Glaser, R.E., Moore, R.L., and Chiao, T.T. (1984). "Life Estimation of Aramid/Epoxy Composites Under Sustained Tension," Composites Technology Review, Vol. 6, No. 1, pp. 26-35.

Hasuo, K., et al. (Sept. 1991). "Study on Braided Aramid Fiber Rods (Part 14. Tensile Properties and Their Distribution)," Proc., Arch. Inst. of Japan, Tokyo, Japan, 2 pp., (in Japanese).

Holloway, L. (1990). "Polymer, Fiber and Composite Material Properties and Manufacturing Techniques," in Polymers and Polymer Composites in Construction, L. Holloway, Editor, Thomas Telford Ltd., London, pp. 5-31.

Mehta, P.K. (1986). Concrete - Structure, Properties, and Materials. Prentice-Hall, Englewood Cliffs, NJ, 450 pp.

O'Brien, T.K., Editor (March 1982). "Long-Term Behavior of Composites," ASTM STP 813, Am. Soc. Test. Mat., Philadelphia, PA.

Schurhoff, H.J and Gerritse, A. (1986). "Aramid Reinforced Concrete," Proc. of III Rilem Symposium, Developments in Fibre Cement and Concrete, Univ. of Sheffield, Sheffield, U.K., 10 pp.

Springer, G.S., Editor (1981, 1984, and 1987). "Environmental Effects on Composite Materials," Vol. 1, 2, and 3, Technomic Publishing Co., Westport, CT.

Table 1: Properties of aramid and epoxy

Material	Ultimate Strength (MPa)	Elastic Modulus (GPa)	Ultimate Elongation (%)
(1)	(2)	(3)	(4)
aramid	2845	108.9	2.4
epoxy (at 23°C)	74	2.9	3.1

Table 2: Properties of braided aramid FRP rods

Rod Code	Nominal Dia. (mm)	Total Area (mm^2)	Fiber Area (mm^2)	Rated Strength P_r (kN)	Ult. Strength P_u (kN)	Elastic Mod. E (GPa)	Ult. Elong. ε_u (%)
(1)	(2)	(3)	(4)	(5)	(6)	(7)	(8)
K16	4	10.5	7.4	15.70	17.36	63.76	2.2
K64	8	42.0	29.6	62.78	68.87	63.76	2.2

Table 3: Ultimate tensile load (average) for rods in alkali solution without pretensioning

Time (hr)	Tensile Strength (kN) at 20°C	40°C	60°C	80°C
(1)	(2)	(3)	(4)	(5)
72	17.27	17.24	17.59	17.48
168	17.62	17.45	17.07	16.84
336	16.97	16.80	17.50	16.93
720	16.97	17.45	-	17.02
1440	17.43	16.98	17.07	16.84
2160	17.17	17.10	16.58	16.80

Table 4: Summary of results for rods in alkali solution with initial pretension (60°C)

Initial Preten. P_i (kN)	P_i/P_r	Time of Failure (hr)	Preten. at Failure (kN)	P_e/P_r	Time of Removal (hr)	Residual Strength (kN)	P_u/P_r
(1)	(2)	(3)	(4)	(5)	(6)	(8)	(9)
50.2	0.8	444	43.6	0.69	-	-	-
50.2	0.8	775	39.8	0.63	-	-	-
50.2	0.8	456	42.7	0.68	-	-	-
50.2	0.8	353	43.9	0.70	-	-	-
43.9	0.7	1794	39.0	0.62	-	-	-
43.9	0.7	-	-	-	7814	70.39	1.12
43.9	0.7	1111	37.3	0.59	-	-	-
43.9	0.7	1543	35.8	0.57	-	-	-
37.7	0.6	-	-	-	7814	70.95	1.13
37.7	0.6	-	-	-	7814	68.99	1.10
37.7	0.6	-	-	-	7814	70.71	1.13
37.7	0.6	-	-	-	7814	72.84	1.16

Table 5: Tensile strength of rods embedded in concrete with pretension

Concrete Temp. ($^\circ$C)	Initial Preten. (kN)	P_i/P_r	Residual Tensile Strength (kN) at		
			1 mos.	3 mos.	12 mos.
(1)	(2)	(3)	(4)	(5)	(6)
20	50.2	0.8	-	78.65	-
				82.08	
				76.19	
20	37.7	0.6	-	-	79.96
					79.92
					81.10
20	31.4	0.5	-	-	80.12
					86.49
					82.24
60	50.2	0.8	73.25	77.33	-
			73.25	80.61	
			77.17	N/A	
60	37.7	0.6	71.94	78.48	72.92
			72.10	79.14	73.08
			77.82	73.74	70.31
60	31.4	0.5	-	63.60	73.57
				77.33	69.82
				71.12	78.48

106

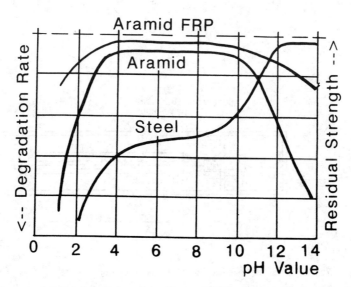

Fig. 1: Schematic chemical degradation of aramid, aramid FRP, and steel (Gerritse May 1990)

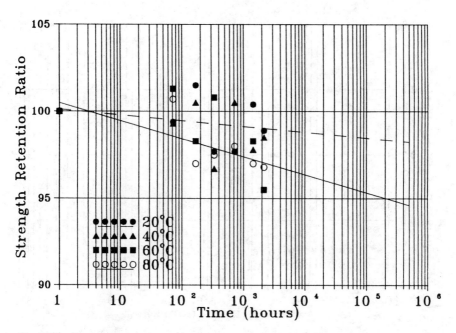

Fig. 2: Tensile strength retention vs. time (alkali solution without pretension)

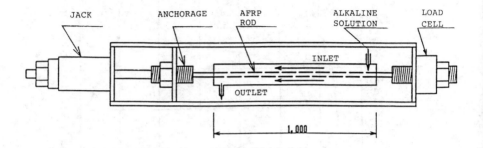

Fig. 3: Test apparatus for pretensioned rods in alkali solution

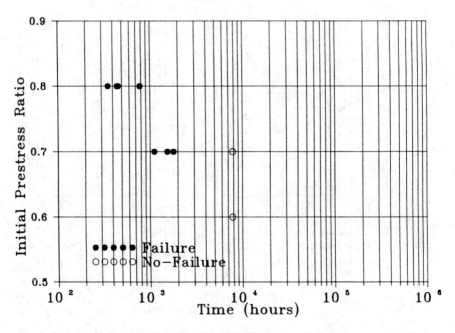

Fig. 4: Initial pretension rate vs. time for rods in alkali solution

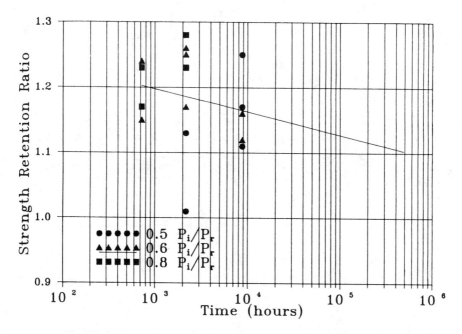

Fig. 5: Residual tensile strength for pretensioned rods embedded in concrete

ADVANCED COMPOSITE MATERIALS IN BRIDGES AND STRUCTURES
K.W. Neale and P. Labossière, Editors; Canadian Society for Civil Engineering, 1992

Matériaux composites d'avant-garde pour ponts et charpentes
K.W. Neale et P. Labossière, éditeurs; Société canadienne de génie civil, 1992

FATIGUE TESTING AND LIFE PREDICTION OF FIBREGLASS-REINFORCED COMPOSITES

F. Ellyin and **D. Kujawski**
University of Alberta
Edmonton, Alberta, Canada

ABSTRACT

Designers of structural/mechanical components generally have a long experience and a good appreciation of the behaviour of metals. In contrast, the experience with structural components fabricated with composite materials is limited. A short review highlighting differences in fatigue behaviour of fibre-reinforced composites and metals is given first. Following this, fatigue test results of a fibreglass-epoxy laminate under unidirectional loading are presented. The results indicate a significant influence of loading frequency on the cyclic stress-strain behaviour. In particular, the effect of frequency on cyclic creep and fatigue life is discussed. Cyclic creep resulting from the mean-stress and the material sensitivity to the rate of loading are found to have a major influence on the fatigue life.

RÉSUMÉ

Les concepteurs d'éléments structuraux ou mécaniques connaissent généralement bien le comportement des métaux. Par contre, leur expérience des matériaux composites est plus limitée. On présente d'abord dans cet article une courte revue des différences de comportement entre les composites et les métaux. Ensuite, des essais en fatigue sur un stratifié sont présentés. Les résultats indiquent une influence significative de la fréquence du chargement sur le comportement contrainte-déformation. On note, en particulier, l'effet de la fréquence sur le fluage cyclique et sur la durée de vie. On montre que cette dernière est influencée par le fluage cyclique résultant de la contrainte moyenne et par la sensibilité du matériau au taux de chargement.

INTRODUCTION

Fibre-reinforced composites (FRC's) are currently used in almost all engineering fields, including transport, civil engineering and chemical industry. Usually, they are composed of thin layers or laminae reinforced unidirectionally or multidirectionally with high strength fibres embedded in a relatively weak and ductile matrix.

The matrix constitutes an indepensible component of the composite aggregate and its role is multifunctional, e.g. it transfers applied load to the fibres, protects the reinforced filaments from mechanical damage and environmental attack, and also holds the fibres aligned in the important stressed directions (Harris, 1982). The matrix strength and modulus are often neglected in calculating composite properties, however, the quality of the adhesion between fibre and matrix affects the overall performance of the composite.

At present, some of the important engineering properties of the FRC's, e.g. stiffness and elastic behaviour, are successfully predicted on the basis of simple mathematical models, but toughness, fatigue performance and time-dependent behaviour are not be accurately predicted. Therefore, a designer must consult available experimental evidence, and design with caution to accommodate this state of uncertainty of the FRC's (Gerharz, 1982).

Designers of structural/mechanical components generally have a long experience and a good appreciation of the behaviour of metals. In contrast, the experience with the FRC products is limited. Therefore, it would be helpful to compare the behaviour of these two groups of materials. It is hoped that this will assist designers when assessing the use of advanced composite materials in load bearing structural components.

It is the objective of this paper to point out differences in fatigue behaviour of the FRC's and metals. The results of an investigation on the tensile fatigue performance of $[\pm45°]_{5S}$ fibreglass-epoxy laminate under unidirectional tension-tension cyclic loading are presented, and some conclusions are drawn.

DIFFERENCES IN FATIGUE PERFORMANCE OF FIBRE-REINFORCED COMPOSITES AND METALS

Fibre-reinforced composites are inherently heterogeneous, and this results in a rather complex behaviour under cyclic loading. For example, the state of stress and strain are multiaxial in a laminated composite even under a simple tensile load. This is due to interlaminar shear and normal stresses between the layers. Moreover, fibre/matrix composite systems are often rate sensitive.

Typical damage mechanisms observed in FRC's are: matrix cracking, fibre-matrix debonding, delamination, void growth and fibre breakage which usually do not occur separately but are interconnected (Hahn, 1979; Stinchcomb and Reifsnider, 1979). The combination of particular mechanisms depends to a certain extent on composite constituent materials (fibres and resin), the laminate stacking sequence, environment, cyclic frequency and loading conditions (uniaxial or multiaxial with different amounts of tension, compression or shear stresses). The combined modes of damage described above result in different fatigue behaviour of FRC's in comparison with metals in many respects.

The most striking differences observed between metals and FRC's are with respect to the following aspects:

- damage mechanisms,
- material degradation,
- non-self-similar crack growth,
- mean stress effect, and
- notch sensitivity.

Simultaneous generation of different damage mechanisms results in a successive material degradation which is manifested in reduced stiffness and residual strength of an FRC component. An observed change in stiffness or compliance is seen as a simple combined measure of material degradation rate (Lemaitre and Dufailly, 1987; Talreja, 1986). Fatigue degradation of the fibre/matrix composite materials is one of the most significant differences between metals and FRC's.

Various modes of damage mechanisms generally do not combine to form a single dominant crack growing in a self-similar manner as in the case of metals (Ellyin and El Kadi, 1990). In a laminate, a rather complex damage state is observed under cyclic loading. For example, in multidirectional laminates cracks in 90° piles usually occur first and increase in density, leading subsequently to delamination or transverse cracking in closely oriented plies. Final fracture occurs when 0° plies fail. In the case of compression load, 0° plies might fail first due to the buckling of the brittle fibres.

In contrast to metals, the fatigue strength of FRC materials decreases with increasing compressive mean stress. Therefore, the fatigue strength of composites in tension-compression fatigue cannot be predicted in a manner analogous to that used in metals.

Another significant difference observed between metals and FRC's is in the way they respond to a notch. Contrary to metals, FRC materials show a large detrimental influence of a notch on static strength and low cycle fatigue, and only a small influence in the case of high cyclic fatigue regime.

Most of the presently used methods for life prediction of FRC's are of the empirical nature. In order to better understand rate (frequency) - dependent fatigue behaviour of FRC materials, more experimental data is needed.

In the following section an experimental study of tensile fatigue behaviour of fibreglass (non-woven) reinforced plastic under unidirectional cyclic loading, is described. In particular, the effects of test frequency are discussed.

UNIAXIAL FATIGUE BEHAVIOUR OF
FIBREGLASS-EPOXY COMPOSITE LAMINATES

Material, Specimen and Experimental Method

The material employed in this investigation was supplied in procured form of unidirectional roll (0.305 m × 66 m in size) by the 3-M company designated as Scotchply Reinforced Plastic Type 1003. The fibreglass used is a continuous filament "E" type glass within the epoxy resin (resin content 36 ± 3% by weight).

Specimens with the geometry shown in Fig. 1 were fabricated from the prepreg by laminating five layers of two plies (with fibre orientation +45° and -45°) symmetric with respect to the mid-plane of the sample, i.e. $[\pm45°]_{5S}$ (20 ply laminate). Once the samples were laminated (three at a time) in a specially designed mold, they were cured at 150°C (300°F) for 12 hours. After curing, the ends of the sample were reinforced by gluing aluminum tabs for the gripping purpose (see Fig. 1).

The loading system employed in the fatigue tests was an electro-hydraulic servo-controlled MTS unit. The specimens were mounted in tapered wedge grips located in series with the reaction frame, load cell, and actuator. The tests were conducted at room temperature by initially applying a mean load to the specimen and then superimposing an alternating load with a load ratio $R = \sigma_{min}/\sigma_{max} \approx 0.05$.

4.75

15°

Grip tabs made of aluminum

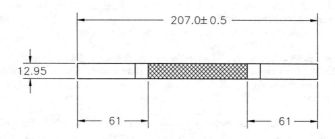

207.0± 0.5

12.95

61

61

Fig. 1   Specimen dimensions

Two frequencies of sinusoidal load cycle wave form were used: a low frequency, 0.417 Hz (25 cpm), and a high frequency, 3.6 Hz (217 cpm). The signals from the load cell and from a 25.4 mm (one inch) gauge length extensometer were recorded using an X-Y plotter and an IBM-PC computer at low and high frequencies, respectively. In the case of high frequency the IBM-PC computer was also used to provide a sinusoidal command signal.

Results and Discussion

Fatigue test results obtained at two frequencies, i.e. 0.417 Hz (25 cpm) and 3.6 Hz (217 cpm), are summarized in Table 1.

114

Table 1   Fatigue Test Results of Fibreglass Laminate $[\pm45°]_{5S}$

Specimen Number	Frequency Hz	Peak Stress σ_{max} (MPa)	Stress Range $\Delta\sigma$ (MPa)	Cycles to Failure N_f
C1	0.417	101.4	93.4	2 552
B2	0.417	85.5	81.1	17 730
C2	0.417	74.0	69.5	62 500
D1	0.417	65.3	61.0	168 100
E2	3.6	97.4	89.0	2 813
D3	3.6	86.6	82.4	8 578
F1	3.6	71.7	68.7	136 508
E3	3.6	65.0	60.4	702 984

Young's modulus E = 10 070 MPa

Typical cyclic stress-strain diagrams obtained at the highest applied stress levels for both slow and fast tests, are shown in Figs. 2a and 2b, respectively. It is seen that permanent strain accumulates after each cycle up to the final fracture. At the unloading point the stress-strain curve does not follow an elastic path, but bends forward, thereby indicating the existence of a viscous strain. For these relatively high stress ranges ($\Delta\sigma \approx 90$ MPa) the material exhibits a moderate hysteresis loop and significant cyclic creep. The cyclic creep, i.e. accumulated strain at minimum load (stress), results from the mean stress and the material sensitivity to the rate (frequency) of loading.

The area of the hysteresis loop represents energy loss for each load cycle. Most of this energy is converted to heat and is dissipated during the test. For relatively high stresses and frequencies the rise of temperature may reduce fatigue life (Dally and Broutman, 1967). In the tests reported here no significant heating of the specimen was observed.

The variation of the accumulated strain at minimum load with number of cycles for both frequencies is shown in Figs. 3a and 3b for high (~ 90 MPa) and low (~ 60 MPa) stress ranges, respectively. The curves in Fig. 3 resemble typical creep curves observed for metals under constant load.

It is seen that the value of accumulated strain, for a particular number of cycles, depends on both applied stress range and frequency. In the case of ~ 60 MPa stress range, Fig. 3b, the accumulated strain at a given number of cycles is larger for the lower frequency than for the higher one. On the other hand, the opposite trend is observed at the higher stress ranges (see Fig. 3a). The detrimental influence of the cyclic creep resulting from the material sensitivity to the rate (frequency) of loading on fatigue life is evident from examining Figs. 3a and 3b.

The fatigue test results, for both frequencies, are plotted in Fig. 4 in terms of applied stress amplitude, $\Delta\sigma/2$, against number of reversals to failure, $2N_f$. The least square regression lines (best fit) of the type

$$\frac{\Delta\sigma}{2} = \sigma_f'\,(2N_f)^b \qquad (1)$$

are also shown in the figure.

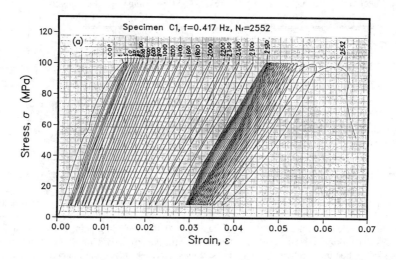

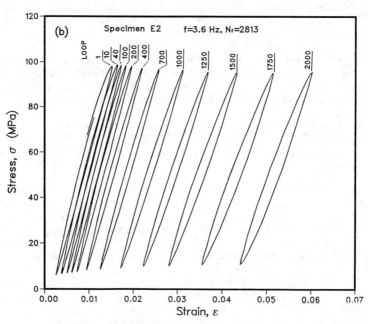

Fig. 2 Stress-strain response of fibreglass laminate under uniaxial tension-tension loading
(a) Slow test, (b) Fast test

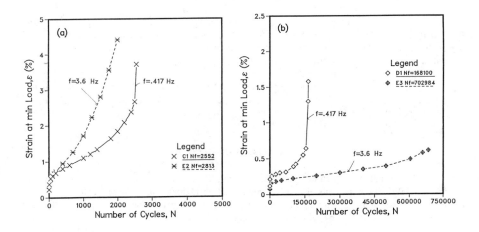

Fig. 3   Accumulated strain at minimum load versus number of cycles
(a) $\Delta\sigma \approx 90$ MPa, (b) $\Delta\sigma \approx 60$ MPa

It is noted that the "best fit" lines cross-over at a point corresponding to ~ 39 MPa of stress amplitude and 3.4×10^4 reversals to failure. The slope of the regression line for the low frequency tests is steeper than that of the high frequency.

The results presented in Fig. 4 demonstrate that the lower frequency is more damaging in high-cycle fatigue whereas the reverse is true in the low-cycle region. This behaviour is governed by pertinent cyclic creep development (compare Figs. 3 and 4) and its detrimental influence on the fatigue life of the material.

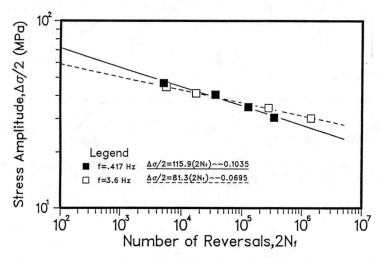

Fig. 4   Applied stress amplitude versus number of reversals to failure

CONCLUSIONS

The results presented herein demonstrate that the effect of test loading frequency on tensile fatigue performance of fibreglass $[\pm45]_{5S}$ laminate is associated with the development of cyclic creep. At lower stress amplitudes the cyclic creep increases and the fatigue life decreases with reduced cyclic frequency.

In contrast, at higher stress amplitudes ($\Delta\sigma/2 > 39$ MPa) the effect of loading frequency on both cyclic creep and fatigue life is opposite to that at lower stresses. That is, fatigue life decreases with higher frequency.

ACKNOWLEDGEMENTS

The results presented here are part of a general investigation on the long term durability and relaibility of components made of advanced composite materials. The research is supported, in part, by the Natural Science and Engineering Council of Canada, Operating Grant A-3808, and NSERC CRD grant 120764 with Esso Resources of Canada Limited.

REFERENCES

Dally, J.W. and Broutman, L.J. (1967). Frequency Effects on the Fatigue of Glass Reinforced Plastics, J. Composite Materials, **1**, 424-442.

Ellyin, F. and El Kadi (1990). Predicting Crack Growth Direction in Unidirectional Composite Laminae, Engng. Fract. Mech., **36**, 27-37.

Gerharz, J.J. (1982). Mechanisms of Fatigue Damage and Fatigue Testing, in: Practical Considerations of Design, Fabrication and Tests for Composite Materials, AGARD Lecture Series No. 124, 7.1-7.20.

Hahn, H.T. (1979). Fatigue Behaviour and Life Prediction of Composite Laminates, ASTM STP 674, 383-417.

Harris, B. (1982). The Nature of Fibre Composite Materials, in: Practical Considerations of Design, Fabrication and Tests for Composite Materials, AGARD Lecture Series No. 124, 1.1-1.5.

Lemaitre, J. and Dufailly, J. (1987). Damage Measurements, Engng. Fract. Mech., **28**, 648-661.

Stinchcomb, W.W. and Reifsnider, K.L. (1979). Fatigue Damage Mechanisms in Composite Materials, ASTM STP 675, 762-787.

Talreja, R. (1986). Stiffness Properties of Composite Laminates with Matrix Cracking and Interior Delamination, Engng. Fract. Mech., **25**, 751-762.

ADVANCED COMPOSITE MATERIALS IN BRIDGES AND STRUCTURES
K.W. Neale and P. Labossière, Editors; Canadian Society for Civil Engineering, 1992

Matériaux composites d'avant-garde pour ponts et charpentes
K.W. Neale et P. Labossière, éditeurs; Société canadienne de génie civil, 1992

EVALUATION OF THE DURABILITY OF ADVANCED COMPOSITES FOR APPLICATIONS TO PRESTRESSED CONCRETE BRIDGES

K. Katawaki, I. Nishizaki and **I. Sasaki**
Ministry of Construction
Ibaraki, Japan

ABSTRACT

One application of advanced composite materials in civil engineering is prestressing of concrete structures. In order to standardize design codes for these materials, we have performed tests under actual environmental conditions. We selected the splash zone (marine atmospheric location) as the typical corrosive condition. The materials include carbon fibre composites, aramid fibre composites, and glass and vinylon fibre composites. Their deterioration was measured as a function of exposure duration. It was found that deterioration was almost non existent or only negligible. Thus good resistance of these materials to sea water and chloride particles will make fibre composites advantageous over steel for bridge structures in/over the sea water. The data related to the durability of fibrous reinforced plastic composites evaluated under actual marine conditions are summarized in this article.

RÉSUMÉ

La précontrainte de structures en béton est une application potentielle des matériaux composites en génie civil. Afin de standardiser les normes de design pour ces matériaux, nous avons effectué des essais sous des conditions environnementales réelles. Une portion de structure exposée à l'effet des vagues a été sélectionnée comme milieu de corrosion typique. Les matériaux incluent des composites à fibres de carbone, d'aramide, et de verre et vinylon. Leur détérioration a été mesurée en fonction de la durée d'exposition. On a trouvé que la détérioration était inexistante ou négligeable. La résistance à la corrosion de ces matériaux les rend donc utiles en cas d'utilisation dans des ponts ou structures exposés à l'eau de mer. Les résultats obtenus lors de nos essais sont compilés dans cet article.

INTRODUCTION

When designing a new marine structure or sea bridge of superior quality anticorrosive and highly durable members are required. This has led to a strong demand to expedite the development of durable, anticorrosive composite materials.

The purpose of this study is to evaluate and confirm the durability of composite materials for use in prestressed concrete members. We have evaluated the durability of fibrous composite materials by exposing specimens at an actual sea site for two periods.

DETAILS OF STUDY

The splashed zone of a marine structure is a harsher environment than any other zone. In the splashed zone, the environment is corrosive because chloride ions adhere directly to the surface of members.

The composite materials that can be expected to be used include FRP (resin matrix composite materials) which are reinforced fiber materials, such as carbon fiber, aramid fiber, glass fiber and vinylon fiber. These composite materials are characterized by their light weight, namely a high strength per unit weight (specific strength) and a high specific elasticity.

This study comprises the following two parts:

Stage 1 Test: In this test, we tested specimens of two types of carbon fiber and aramid fiber to exposure using 5–ton common loads under the condition of tension strength.

Stage 2 Test: In this test, we tested the anticorrosiveness of carbon fiber, aramid fiber, and other fibers. When fabricating the models of prestressed concrete members, we set the load to the optimum for the materials.

CONCRETE SPECIMENS

Specimens for Stage 1 Test

We tested two AFRP materials with different molecular structures and matrix resins, and two carbon fiber CFRP materials with different fiber raw materials and wire shapes. The material characteristics and mechanical properties are shown in Table 1. The reinforcing fibers used in the tests were an improved type of reinforcing fiber with an improved elastic modulus, current on the market. The shapes of these members are shown in Fig. 1.

Specimens for Stage 2 Test

Eight types of tendon beams were used for the rectangular concrete members ($L =$ 1.0 m). The conditions were varied by a combination of prestressing forces, location to exposure and other factors, and they were prestressed by the open cable formula.

The materials applied were fiber-reinforced plastic wires of carbon, aramid, glass and vinylon fibers. From the carbon and aramid fibers, we fabricated stranded and braided materials, and also fabricated prestressing bars and prestressing strands for comparison.

120

When designing a prestressed concrete beam, the maximum prestressing level for the ultimate strength (P_u) of tendons is important. However, factors such as the elasticity of the material and its delayed failure behavior may make it impossible to decide the target level of prestressing load. We thus selected the tension to be introduced by measuring the tensile strength of the material, then inferred the characteristic value of its rupture strength. Table 2 lists the composition and fabricating methods of the materials used and shows the results of the tensile strength test.

The prestressing load was set at about $0.8P_u$, the ordinary tension level by prestressing steel, and $0.6P_u$ at which rather satisfactory results had been obtained in our relaxation test or in materials previously exposed.

For the vinylon composite with little past data and for glass with possible problem of delayed failure, we set low prestressing levels and fabricated members using the prestressing loads.

TEST METHODS

Sea Exposure Test

We conducted the Stage 1 test at the Marine Test Station at Suruga Bay in Shizuoka and conducted the Stage 2 test at both the Marine Test Station and on the self elevating platform (SEP) in Okinotorishima Island in tropical maritime environments. The sea exposure test was conducted not only for these members but also for prestressing steel for comparison. Photos 1 and 2 show the installation of specimens at the Marine Test Station.

SURVEY METHODS

Deterioration of Stage 1 Test Specimens

The deterioration of materials was surveyed for carbon fiber-reinforced plastic (CFRP) and aramid fiber-reinforced plastic (AFRP) after exposure for 1.5 years.

Deterioration of Stage 2 Test Concrete Members

We visually examined the members periodically. After severe deterioration, we will conduct a tensile test and examine such details as EPMA.

SURVEY RESULTS

Results of Stage 1 Test

We measured the deterioration of the fibrous composite materials after exposure under tension for 1.5 years at a constant strain. Table 3 shows the results of the material characteristics and mechanical properties for the two types of AFRP and the two types of CFRP. The change in ultimate tensile strength and elastic modulus are reported in the table.

The reduction of tension during exposure represents a relaxation while exposed outdoors. Indoor exposure (exposure in the premises of the Public Works Research Institute) produced a relaxation of more than 10% for the aramid fiber composite and $10 \sim 20\%$ for the carbon fiber composite.

When exposed to the sea (Suruga Bay Marine Test Station), cracks developed in AFRP(1) indicating a great reduction in residual tension. For materials other than AFRP(1), the results were much the same as for indoor exposure. Aramid will become weak when exposed to ultaviolet rays because it is an organic polymer, and AFRP(1) which is made of a vinylester resin that is more resistant to ultraviolet rays than epoxy, still showed a little deterioration.

Except for CFRP(2), the ultimate tensile strength declined regardless of the extent of relaxation. Since the initial value is the proof strength of the material, the actual initial strength is probably somewhat larger than this and the extent to which the strength declines is also somewhat greater. All the materials showed little change in their elastic coefficient and, so far, there has been no change of rigidity due to exposure.

Fiber-reinforced plastics are made into composites by orienting reinforcing lints in matrices such as epoxy resin. So the physical deterioration of the fibers and the resins in addition to the reduction in the interlocking bond betwen fibers and resins presumably cause the reduction in mechanical properties in these materials .

Results of Stage 2 Test

In our follow-up survey conducted five months after the installation of specimens, the following phenomena were observed:
(a) The prestressing steel became very rusty (Photo 3).
(b) Cracks developed in the glass composite material regardless of the prestressing load (Photo 4). This is due to the level of the applied tension which is relatively high. So, it will be necessary to retest at a level of tensile load more appropriate for this material.
(c) The surface of the vinylon fiber composite material was somewhat frosted. This is for want of an effective surface protective layer. When using FRP, a surface layer is deemed to be positively necessary.
It seems that in the short term, the glass fiber composite has a durability problem under a prestressing load. However, the other fibrous composite materials showed no problems in the sea test.

CONCLUSION

We conducted an actual exposure tests using various fiber reinforced plastic materials. As a result we conclude that carbon fiber composite material and aramid fiber composite material have strength characteristics comparable to steel, exhibit excellent anti-corrosion properties required for maritime structures, and can be used effectively in a concrete composite. However, some types exhibit inferior durability, hence it is important to draw up specifications, taking into account quality and durability effects.

Exposure caused cracks in the glass fiber composite material. So far, surface deterioration started in the vinylon fiber composite due to exposure. Therefore quality improvement and surface protection of materials will be reevaluated for improving durability.

For composite materials with large tensile elongation or high Poisson's ratio, the anchoring method must be improved because slips in anchorage occur in these materials when under tension or exposed.

Future applications of fibrous composite materials (fiber-reinforced plastics) include concrete reinforcing bars, prestressing tendons, anticorrosive formwork, suspenders and mooring equipment, and there is every likelihood that these will be used in marine environments. New materials for maritime structures have previously not been objectively evaluated under practical conditions for a long period, therefore, hardly any quantitative data on durability sufficient for structural design is available. We will continue to accumulate practical data on the durability of these materials.

REFERENCES

1. K. Katawaki and I. Nishizaki, "The Test Report of Prestressed Tendon Applied with Composite Materials," *Journal of Prestressed Concrete* (1988).

2. K. Katawaki and I. Sasaki, "The Report of Development for Utilization and Maintenance Technology of Maritime Structure," Public Works Research Institute (1991).

3. K. Katawaki and I. Sasaki, "The Study Report of the Durability Evaluation Related to the Composite Materials in Marine Atmosphere," Public Works Research Institute (1989).

Table 1 Materials for Exposure Test

Name		AFRP (1)	AFRP (2)	CFRP (1)	CFRP (2)
Type		Bar	Bar	Bar	Strand
Nominal diameter	(mmø)	8	8	8	12.4
Real diameter	(mmø)	8.04	7.8	7.9	12.2
Sectional area	(mm^2)	50.8	47.8	49.0	93.9
Fiber		Aramid (*1)	Aramid (PPTA *2)	Carbon (pitch)	Carbon (PAN)
Fiber content	%	65	65	65	65
Fiber diameter	(μm)	12	12	7	7
Matrix resin		Vinylester	Epoxy	Epoxy	Epoxy
Specific gravity	(g/cm^3)	1.28	1.35	1.57	1.53

(*1) Copolyphenylen · 3,4' oxydiphenylen · terephthalamid
(*2) Poly · p-phenylen terephyhalamid

Table 2 Introduced Tensile Load (Stage 2 Test)

Name	Fiber	Resin	Tensile (Pu ton f)	Target tension ratio × f Pu	Target tensile load (ton f)	Measured tensile load (ton f)	Measured elastic modulus kgf/mm^2
CFRP (a)	Carbon (PAN)	Epoxy	13.40	0.8	10.72	9.54 9.28 9.33	11,020 12,520 13,440
				0.6	8.04	7.67 7.69 8.03	13,510 14,020 13,780
CFRP (b)	Carbon (pitch)	Epoxy	6.58	0.8	5.26	5.07 4.89 4.79	13,260 13,970 14,090
				0.6	3.95	3.94 4.02 3.87	13,630 14,280 14,160
AFRP (a)	Aramid (*)	Vinylester	5.42	0.8	4.33	4.15 4.37 4.43	5,890 5,410 5,017
				0.6	3.25	3.06 3.03 3.12	3,220 4,130 4,620
AFRP (b)	Aramid (PPTA)	Epoxy	5.72	0.8	4.58	4.31 4.48	4,930 4,530
				0.6	3.44	2.90 3.54	5,330 4,670
GRFP	E-grass	Vinylester	4.13	0.55	2.27	2.30 2.25	5,220 6,280
				0.4	1.65	1.72 1.67 1.69	4,650 5,380 5,230
				0.25	1.03	1.05 1.09	5,270 5,330
VFRP	Vinylon	Epoxy	2.06	0.6	1.24	1.35 1.25 1.34	2,780 2,590 2,800
				0.4	0.82	0.91 0.94 0.89	2,990 2,760 3,120
Steel	Steel bar for prestressed concrete JIS G 3109		12.61	0.8	10.09	9.74 9.70	17,350 17,200
	Steel strand for prestressed concrete JIS G 3538		16.30	0.8	12.51	11.46 11.65	15,950 19,440

* Copolyphenylen · 3,4' · oxydiphenylen · terephthalamid

Table 3 Strength Reduction After 1.5 Years of Exposure (Stage 1 Test)

Name of material	No.	Initial tension	Residual tension	Difference (*1)	Guaranteed tensile strength	Tensile strength after exposure	Difference (*2)	Elastic modulus before exposure	Elastic modulus after exposure
		(ton f)		(ton f)	(ton f)		(ton f)	($\times 10^6$ kgf/cm^2)	
AFRP (1) ø8mm (*3)	A	5.03	0.70	4.33		Cannot be measured	–	0.57	–
	B	5.32	1.40	3.92	7.40	Cannot be measured	–	0.53	–
	C	5.18	4.10	1.08		6.80	0.60	0.51	0.50
AFRP (2) ø8mm	A	5.16	4.80	0.36		Slip out	–	0.84	–
	B	5.02	3.70	1.32	7.60	7.36	0.24	0.85	0.84
	C	5.06	4.00	1.06		7.62	−0.02	0.88	0.84
CFRP (1) ø8mm	A	5.24	5.10	0.14		7.56	1.54	1.48	1.48
	B	5.21	4.90	0.31	9.10	7.72	1.38	1.50	1.49
	C	5.30	4.90	0.40		8.82	0.28	1.54	1.49
CFRP (2) ø12.5mm	A	5.16	4.30	0.86		14.60	−0.10	1.41	1.42
	B	5.36	4.50	0.86	14.50	14.55	−0.05	1.33	1.40
	C	5.21	4.60	0.61		14.55	−0.05	1.43	1.48

(*1) Corresponding to stress relation
(*2) Corresponding to strength difference
(*3) At Stage 2, the quality of materials had been improved and their weatherability imporved.

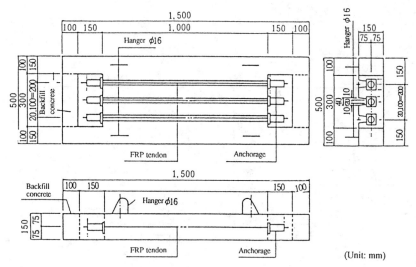

FRP tendon   Anchorage   (Unit: mm)

Fig. 1 Exposure Specimen

Photo 1 The Marine Test Station

Photo 2 The Installation of Specimens at the Marine Test Station

Photo 3 Corrosion of the Prestressing Steel

Photo 4 Appearance of Glass Composite Material (Occuring Exposure)

ADVANCED COMPOSITE MATERIALS IN BRIDGES AND STRUCTURES
K.W. Neale and P. Labossière, Editors; Canadian Society for Civil Engineering, 1992

Matériaux composites d'avant-garde pour ponts et charpentes
K.W. Neale et P. Labossière, éditeurs; Société canadienne de génie civil, 1992

DURABILITY CRITERIA FOR NON-METALLIC TENDONS
IN AN ALKALINE ENVIRONMENT

A. Gerritse
Hollandsche Beton Groep
Rijswijk, The Netherlands

ABSTRACT

The use of advanced composite materials, like non-metallic tendons based on high strength fibres in a polymeric matrix, introduces materials of which the characteristics and their long term behaviour is not well known up to now. Most high strength fibres are perfectly resistant in environments where steel will corrode, but in the alkaline environment of the concrete matrix – where steel behaves perfectly – they face problems. This inherently means the long term interaction with concrete may become a critical criterion. To assess the reliability of applications on the longer term, the extrapolation of the residual strength based on the Arrhenius approach is discussed.

RÉSUMÉ

Les caractéristiques et le comportement à long terme des matériaux composites d'avant-garde, composés de fibres très résistantes dans une matrice à base de polymères, sont mal connus. Même si la plupart des fibres sont parfaitement résistantes dans des milieux corrosifs pour l'acier, elles sont sujettes à des problèmes dans les environnements alcalins tels le béton. Ceci indique qu'un critère critique de design pourrait être l'interaction entre les fibres et le béton sur une longue durée. On discute dans cet article de l'extrapolation de la résistance résiduelle à long terme, basée sur l'approche d'Arrhenius.

INTRODUCTION

General Remarks

Concrete elements or concrete structures are commonly reinforced with steel reinforcement and/or prestressed with prestressing steel to accomodate for tensile forces. In recent years however interesting developments have emerged in the field of non-metallic tensile elements (Reinhardt, Gerritse and Werner 1990). These alternatives are mainly based on the availability of high strength, high modulus artificial fibres, which are embedded in a polymeric matrix.
They can appropriately be applied in case of:
- very thin concrete elements
- aggressive or corrosive environments (e.g. seawater, de-icing salts)
- need for non-electrical or non-magnetic conductive materials.

In these and comparable cases, use of such high strength fibrous (non-metallic) tensile elements can be advantageous. However they still have to comply with the essential performance criteria as usual expected from concrete structures.

Satisfactory application of these tensile elements can only be achieved if basic requirements are fulfilled, such as:
- adequate physical and mechanical properties
- durability in environments occurring in actual practice
- ability to transfer force

Concrete elements and concrete structures are expected to last many years (a "lifetime") and perform adequately during such a period; say 50 to 100 years. This means continuous fulfillment of the function for which the elements or structures are designed ("Fitness for use").

Developments

A range of developments in bars and tendons, consisting of continuous high strength, high modulus fibres -usually- embedded in a polymeric matrix, is aiming at structural applications in concrete (Clark 1992). The fibres concerned are (fig. 1):
- glass fibres
- aramid fibres
- carbon fibres

Their strength capacities are in the range of prestressing steel. However several other material characteristics differ considerably from those of the well known steels. This is especially important for those -less familiar- phenomena or characteristics of which nobody would expect them to become critical or decisive.

The assumed common practice in use of these material in the near future by structural engineers necessitates the need for reliable data for these elements, specificly with respect to their long term behaviour. So we have to investigate and evaluate the behaviour as well as the mechanical, physicial and chemical properties in relation to long term use. Adapted design criteria will have to be developed with emphasis on:
- behaviour under sustained stress and in aggressive (alkaline) environment
- warning behaviour of the structure

An additional argument to define methods to extrapolate on long term behaviour may be found in the less positive behaviour recently experienced with epoxy-coated steel bars (Sagues, Powers and Zayed 1992). Practical use of new material has to be based on reliable extrapolation.

CRITERIA TO BE CONSIDERED FOR TENSILE ELEMENTS IN PRESTRESSED CONCRETE

From the practical points of view of application as well as from the structural point of view of designing with adequate safety for an adequate life span at least the following items are to be considered:

Physcial properties
- Density
- Coëfficient of thermal expansion (axial and radial)
- Electrical conductivity
- Water uptake

Mechanical properties
- Stess-strain diagram; shape
  * strength
  * strain at failure (fracture mode)
  * stiffness (elastic modulus)
- Long-term behaviour under sustained load
  * Stress-rupture (static fatigue) /Residual strength
  * Creep (Stress-decay)
  * Relaxation
- Fatigue behaviour

Durability: Behaviour in different environments
- Cementitious matrix
  * alkaline environment   (pH > 12)
  * carbonated concrete   (ph < 10)
- Presence of chlorides ($CaCl_2$, seawater, de-icing salts)
- Other aggressive environments (like SO_3, Pure H_2O etc)
- Temperature effects (very high; very low)
- Stress Corrosion
- UV resistance

Force transfer
- By bond (direct contact with cementitious matrix)
  * fatigue on bond
- By anchorage (full force to anchorge device)
  * temporary (mainly pretensioning)
  * remaining during service life (mainly post-tensioning)
- Secondary reinforcement

General
- Cost effectiviness
- Workability

CRITERIA TO GIVE SPECIAL ATTENTION

General remarks

Data for most of the items mentioned in the former chapter must be available to make design and application possible and the design philosophy is not different from which is commonly used in structural engineering (Gerritse 1990). Still it seems useful to give some of the items additional attention becuase behaviour or effect can differ considerably from what is expected (Gerritse and Schürhoff 1986).

Coëfficient of thermal expansion

The value for the axial coëfficient of thermal expansion is slightly negative for aramid and carbon fibres. In combination with the resin the result for the tendon will be circa zero; still a difference with the surrounding concrete to take into account. However of more importance is the large positive value for the coëfficient of thermal expansion in the radial direction which has to be worked out in combination with the resin. Values up to 50×10^{-6} /°C are possible and to be evaluated -in the case of pretensioning- also with a relative high value of the poisson ratio.

Warning behaviour

Concrete structures are assumed to possess an adequate "warning behaviour" before failure. This means limited, but significant, deformations (e.g., deflections, cracks) should occur before an eventual failure. Therefore, structural design is based on the assumption that failure of the tensile elements has to occur before concrete fails in compression (before brittle failure). This in turn requires a minimum strain capacity of the tensile elements. (de Sitter and Gerritse 1992).

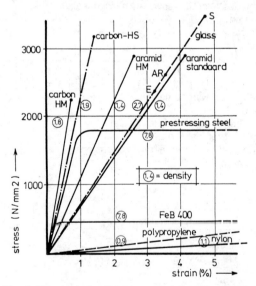

Fig. 1. Stress-strain diagrams of reinforcing materials

Stress rupture

With most materials, which are subjected to sustained relatively high stress (which is common in prestressed concrete), the failure strength will decrease with time. This is commonly not critical for prestressing steel, but he rate of this decrease and the available residual strength just before failure is urgent for polymeric (organic) materials. This phenomenon is called stres rupture if in air (fig.2). Stress corrosion is the same phenomenon, but in a particular chemical environment (e.g. alkaline environment).

Relaxation

The plastic behaviour of a material under constant load is called creep. Of more importance is the loss of stress in a material held under constant deformation, which is called relaxation. Both are however expressions of the same phenomenon. There exists a large degree of hesitation in the field of structural engineering to this kind of phenomena, using polymeric materials (Gerritse, Maatjes and Schürhoff 1987). So sufficient data to overcome this hesitation must be available.

Durability: Long term behaviour in different environments

It is essential for tensile elements to be used in prestressed/pretensioned concrete to retain sufficient strength capacity, during the normal lifetime of the concrete structure, in any of the environments which might be encountered in practice. In case of direct contact the embedment in a cementitious matrix which will cause, in the first instance, alkaline exposure (pH > 12) as well as later on, possible in carbonated concrete (pH < 10). The major argument to use non-steel, tensile elements is that steel corrodes in carbonated concrete, which will be seriously enhanced if chlorides are present (coastal area, de-icing salts, etc.).

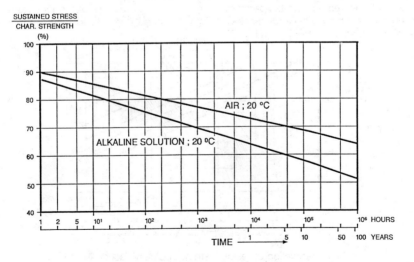

Fig. 2. Stress-rupture behaviour of Arapree

Alternative materials, based on glass-, polymeric- or carbon fibres behave generally satisfactory in carbonated concrete, however, some, with the emphasis on glass, will deteriorate in an alkaline environment. So durability (or residual strength) of any fibre in alkaline environments will define its practical applicability in concrete elements, if in direct contact with the cementitious matrix. To put it a bit bluntly, all efforts to improve the bond of this kind of bars to the cementitious - concrete- matrix (direct contact) is of no use if the tensile elements do not retain sufficient strength over a sufficiently long period.

ESTIMATING RESIDUAL STRENGTH IN ALKALINE ENVIRONMENT

General Remarks

From the above it is obvious that the survival of these alternative reinforcements in alkaline environment is an imperative requirement to practical application in direct contact with concrete. The degradation of some fibres in alkaline environment is in principle governed by the attack by OH^- ions emerging from the hydration process and reaching the fibres. It is a relative slow process of which the effects will only be observed after a considerable time-lap. To avoid disappointing evidence after years it is urgent to develop or define accelerated methods to extrapolate the behaviour to be expected after years.

Not all fibre types are equally sensitive, glass is relatively prone to alkaline attack, aramid much, much less (fig. 4) and carbon is more or less insensitive to it. The recent evidence given by the research of Sen and Issa (1992) is an additional reason to evalute or define testmethods with a reliable background.

The phenomenon is not new. The experience with the original applications of GRC (glass-reinforced cement) must be a warning. The investigation and evaluation of "accelerated aging" (Litherland et al 1981) has shown that the Arrhenius approach to this process is very sensible. The Arrhenius approach accelerates the process by increasing the temperature (increasing the movement of the ions) and when no disturbing other processes occur (in the range from 0°C to 100°C) it is a valid investigation.

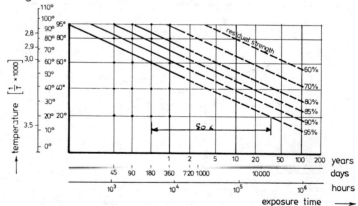

Fig. 3. Extrapolation of residual strength plotting according to Arrhenius, Aramid-epoxy tendon in saturated $CaOH_2$

134

Proposed testmethod

The Arrhenius approach can be worked out mathematically by estimating the activation energy, which indicates -in this case- the temperature dependance of the proces of diffusion and attack on the fibres by OH⁻ions. It can however also be carried out in a relative simple grafical way, by inserting measured values in a graph like fig..At each temperature the proces develops at a certain velocity.
By measuring the residual strength values of samples at regular intervals, the rate of decrease in strength can be determined at each temperature. It will prove that, if a range of measurements is carried out at several temperatures (minimum 3) contourlines can be drawn connecting the same residual strength levels (fig.3). In this approach the temperature indications -on the vertical axis are to be plotted on a linear scale with the factor $1/T$, were T is the temperature in degrees Kelvin.

The contour-lines found ought to be straight to signify that no different -chemical- processes have interfered. The sloping contour-lines found do indicate which residual strength can be expected at each chosen temperature level. Thus if a significant part of these contour-lines -which are principally parallel- can be established an extrapolation of the rate of degradation to be expected, e.g. at roomtemperature in the given environment, can be established from measurements at higher temperatures. If measurements over a sufficient long period at higher temperatures are available the acceleration factor can be defined.

Representative measurements

The next step is to decide how the above approach can be applied in praxis to evaluate the durability of high strength fibrous tensile elements in a concrete matrix.

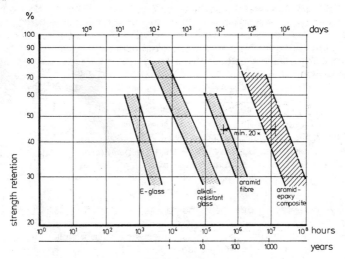

Fig. 4. Extrapolation of residual strength of some fibres
in alkaline environment (pH > 12,5 20°C)

The alkaline resistance of the tensile elements (pure fibres, impregnated fibres or bar shaped elements) can all be evaluated by immersing samples in bathes with a certain -but maintained- alkalinity (e.g. pH value > 13) at different temperatures. The contour-lines given in fig.3 are determined on Arapree, a tendon based on aramid fibres in epoxy resin immersed in a saturated $CaOH_2$ solution.

Several kinds of alkaline solutions can be assumed to be representative from cement slurry to sodium hydroxyde. The latter being largely overdone, but if a relation to reality can be investigated it can give a very quick result. Basically some relation to the alkalinity of the pore-water in concrete has to be established. After some previous experiments (like fig.3) the rather severe alkaline solution used by the author and his team, to establish the reliable service life of Arapree, was chosen as saturated $CaOH_2$+0.4N KOH.

The contour-lines will shift to the left if less resitant fibres (e.g. glass) or less protected (e.g. pure fibres) are chosen. The slopes can differ slightly dependant on the particular resin chosen. But roughly it can be concluded from fig..that an acceleration factor of more than 50 can be applied by increasing the temperature from room temperature up to 60°C and even a factor of more than 200 by increasing it up to 80°C.

Discussion

Residual strength investigations comparable to the one given in fig... can be made for different tensile elements and for different circumstances. Besides estimating the capacity of the elements in a solution it might be more appropriate to insert them in concrete products and prestress those before immersion in heated water. This will assumably give the most correct information. From evidence by the author Arapree tendons in prestressed concrete elements show no sign of any strength decrease after 3 years exposure at 60°C. It will be understandable that the movement of ions in solution is much more active than in the concrete matrix. Results with glass tendons reported by Sen and Issa (1992) are much less positive.

From fig.3 its obvious that the tested aramid based tendons do retain more than 80% of their original capacity after 100 years at room temperatures. Since the slope of the contour-lines will prove to be comparable in different cases it could be argued from the above that investigating 1 single point (e.g. 180 days in alkaline solution at 80°C) can already indicate an extrapolated residual strength of over 80% after 100 years real time. Evalutions -partly based on other results like (Litherland et al 1981)- lead to an indicative estimate as given in fig. 4.

The author has no evidence on comparable investigations with carbon based tensile elements, but from the known insensitivity of carbon fibres to most chemicals an even better residual strength can be expected.

SUMMARY

The durability of advanced composite materials used in concrete can become critical due to unsufficient knowledge and experience. The experience gathered on steel reinforced concrete is sometimes not applicable to these types of material. Some of the items which deserve special attention are given with emphasis on estimating a reasonable, more or less reliable, approach to define the durability of these materials if embedded in -alkaline- concrete.

From the authors investigations it might be clear that aramid based tendons will survive "a lifetime" which is essential for concrete structures. For other materials and/or other phenomena only indications are given.

REFERENCES

Reinhardt, H.W., Gerritse, A. and Werner, J. (1990) ARAPREE - A new prestressing material going into practice *FIP-congres* Hamburg.

Clarke, J.L. (1992). Tests on slabs with on-ferrous reinforcements *FIP-notes* 92/1 and 92/2.

Sagues, A., Powers, R. and Zayed, A. (1990). Marine environment corrosion of epoxy-coated reinforcing steel. *Corrosion of Reinforcement in concrete* (p. 539-549).

Gerritse, A. (1990). ARAPREE a non-metallic prestressing tendon. *Conference on "Durable reinforcements for aggressive environments"* B.C.A. Luton 1990.

Gerritse, A. and Schürhoff, J.H. (1986). ARAPREE the prestressing element. *FIP-congres* Delhi.

De Sitter, W.R. and Gerritse, A. (1992). Elastoplastic design of composite structural members with brittle base materials. Technologie und Anwendung der Baustoffe (Ernst & Sohn). *Publication on the celebration of the 60th anniversary of prof. Rostàsy.*

Gerritse, A., Maatjes, E. and Schürhoff, H.J. (1987). Prestressed concrete structures with Arapree: Relaxation *IABSE-congress Paris*

Sen, R. and Issa, M. (1992). Feasability of Fiberglass pretensioned piles in an marine environment. *College of Engineering University of South Florida*

Litherland, K.L. et all (1981). The use of accelerated aging to predict long term strength of GRC. *Cement and Concrete Research Vol. 11.*

Concrete Beams With FRP Rebars

Poutres de béton avec armature de FRP

ADVANCED COMPOSITE MATERIALS IN BRIDGES AND STRUCTURES
K.W. Neale and P. Labossière, Editors; Canadian Society for Civil Engineering, 1992

Matériaux composites d'avant-garde pour ponts et charpentes
K.W. Neale et P. Labossière, éditeurs; Société canadienne de génie civil, 1992

FUNDAMENTAL CONSIDERATIONS IN THE DESIGN OF FLEXURAL CONCRETE MEMBERS WITH NON-PRESTRESSED FRP REINFORCEMENT

M.B. Stetson and **C.H. Goodspeed**
University of New Hampshire
Durham, New Hampshire, USA

ABSTRACT

This paper presents the results of "typical" calculations of two FRP-reinforced and two steel-reinforced sections representative of common designs for bridge decks, retaining walls and heavy floor slabs. The relationships between their expected service-level moments and deflections and their ultimate moments and deflections are discussed. Finally, the impact of these results (which are consistent with on-going laboratory testing) upon the development of design procedures is discussed.

RÉSUMÉ

Cet article présente les résultats de calculs "typiques" pour deux sections renforcées de FRP et deux sections renforcées d'acier pour le design des tabliers de pont, murs de soutènement, et dalles lourdes de plancher. Les relations entre les moments en niveau de service et les déflexions, et entre les moments ultimes et les déflexions, sont discutées. Finalement, l'impact de ces résultats (qui sont consistants avec les essais expérimentaux en laboratoire) sur le développement de procédures de design est discuté.

INTRODUCTION

Several structural design problems may be solved by using concrete reinforced with fiber-reinforced plastic (FRP) bars rather than steel bars. Among these problems are bridge decks which are subject to attack by road salts and structures housing experimental, medical, or communications equipment for which non-magnetic reinforcing is desirable.

FRPs are not, however, non-corroding, non-magnetic steels. Bars made of FRP have a variety of physical and mechanical properties depending upon the fibers and resins used, the volume fraction of the fibers, and the fabrication processes. Two properties are of particular interest in the design of reinforced concrete flexural members -- the modulus of elasticity, E, and the ultimate stress, f_{ult}. (None of the FRP products available exhibit a yield stress, fy, as do structural steels). A variety of combinations of fibers, resins, and manufacturing processes can produce bars with E $\cong$ 69,000 MPa (10,000 ksi) and f_{ult} $\cong$ 690 MPa (100 ksi). Bars with high volume fractions of aramid fibers (greater than about 60%) may exhibit higher values of E and f_{ult}, but this study will focus upon the values cited above which can be achieved readily. No available bar exhibits E approaching 200,000 MPA (29,000 ksi).

CALCULATIONS FOR PURE FLEXURE

Consider the behavior of a 304.8 mm x 304.8 mm (12 in. x 12. in.) section reinforced with a 645 mm² (1.0 in²) FRP bar centered 50.8 mm (2.0 in.) from the bottom fiber, with concrete strength f_c' = 34.5 MPA (5.0 ksi). (A relatively high value of f_c' is selected to achieve a higher modulus of elasticity of concrete, in addition to increasing strength). The section and the stress-strain models for the materials are shown in Figure 1.

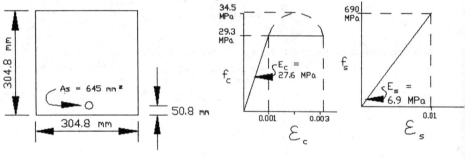

Concrete stress-strain curve

FRP stress-strain curve

Figure 1   Data for Flexural Calculations.

"Typical" calculations imposing equilibrium and compatibility reveal the following bending moment, reinforcing stress and curvature, respectively, at the elastic limit, which corresponds to the onset of concrete yielding:

$$M_e = 49.9 \ kN\text{-}m \ (441.3 \ in\text{-}k)$$

$$f_s = 324.4 \ MPa \ (47.0 \ ksi)$$

$$\frac{1}{R} = 0.0227, \ \frac{1}{m}$$

For the purpose of these calculations, allowable stresses are based on interpretations of "working stress" provisions (ACI 318-89, Appendix A), recognizing that FRP lacks a "yield stress".

$$f_c = 0.45 f_c' = 15.5 \ MPa \ (2.25 \ ksi)$$

$$f_s = 0.40 \ f_{ult} = 276.1 \ MPa \ (40 \ ksi)$$

the FRP-reinforced section has service-level or allowable moment, reinforcing stress, and curvature:

$$M_a = 26.4 \ kN\text{-}m \ (233.6 \ in\text{-}k)$$

$$f_s = 172.1 \ MPa \ (24.9 \ ksi)$$

$$\frac{1}{R} = 0.0121, \ \frac{1}{m}$$

At ultimate (without any "capacity reduction"), initiated by concrete crushing

$$M_u = 100.4 \ kN\text{-}m \ (888.3 \ in\text{-}k)$$

$$f_s = 677.9 \ MPa \ (98.2 \ ksi)$$

$$\frac{1}{R} = 0.0504, \ \frac{1}{m}$$

Assuming an initially cracked section, the moment-curvature relation can be described as in Figure 2. Because there is no yielding in the reinforcing, the moment-curvature function of the section is only slightly non-linear, unlike that of a steel-reinforced flexural section designed according to either allowable stress or ultimate strength methods. To help in interpreting curvature, the mid-span deflection of a 4.6 m (15 ft.) span simple beam loaded by equal and opposite moments at the ends is shown in Figure 3. (These midspan deflections are about twice those which would be created by lateral loads producing the maximum moment).

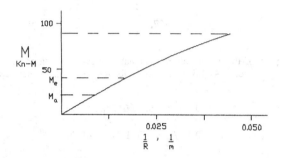

Figure 2   Moment-Curvature Function of the FRP-Reinforced Section

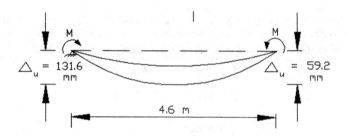

Figure 3   Midspan Deflections at the Elastic Limit and at
Ultimate for the FRP-Reinforced Section

A variety of steel-reinforced sections might be considered to be "equivalent" to this FRP reinforced section. Only two will be considered here:

- the section with the same ultimate moment
- the section with the same service-level moment, as defined by
  working stress limits.

The steel-reinforced section with the same ultimate moment as the FRP reinforced section, M_u = 100.4 kN-m (888.3 in-k), has 1058.0 mm² (1.64 in²) of Gr. 60 steel reinforcement. Typical calculations produce the moment curvature function shown in Figure 4.

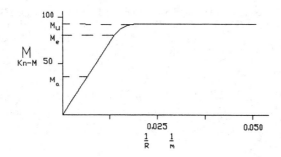

Figure 4   Moment-Curvature Function for the Steel Reinforced
Section Having the Same M_u as the FRP Reinforced Section

Comparison of the moment-curvature functions for these FRP-reinforced and steel-reinforced sections, Figure 2 and Figure 4, respectively, reveals a significant difference in the ductility of the sections.   Again, to aid in visualizing the effect of curvature, deflections of the steel-reinforced section used in a 4.6 m (15 ft.) span loaded by equal and opposite end moments is shown in Figure 5.

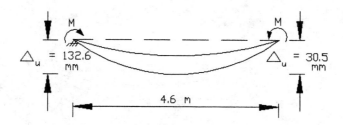

Figure 5   Midspan Deflections at the Elastic Limit and at Ultimate
for the Steel-Reinforced Section Having the Same M_u

Using Gr 60 (minimum yield stress 414.2 MPa) steel bars, a steel-reinforced section has allowable stresses.

$$f_c = 15.5 \ MPa \ (2.25 \ ksi)$$

$$f_s = 165.7 \ MPa \ (24 \ ksi)$$

The steel-reinforced section having the same service-level moment as the FRP-reinforced section, $M_a = 26.4$ kN-m (233.6 in-k), has 709.7 mm² (1.1 in²) of Gr. 60 steel reinforcement. The moment-curvature function for that section is shown in Figure 6, and the deflections of a 4.6 m span simple beam are shown in Figure 7.

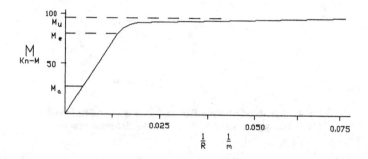

Figure 6 Moment-Curvature Function for the Steel Reinforced Section Having the Same M_a as the FRP Reinforced Section

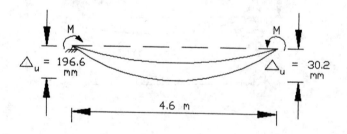

Figure 7 Midspan Deflections at the Elastic Limit and at Ultimate for the Steel-Reinforced Section Having the Same Allowable Moment

146

Figures 3,5 and 7 show that the deflection in the elastic range for the FRP-reinforced section is about twice that of the steel-reinforced section - not very surprising given the smaller modulus of FRP. The deflections at ultimate load are about the same, however, a consequence of yielding in steel bars which does not occur in FRP bars. This comparison suggests that another basic FRP section should be considered: an FRP-reinforced section which would have about the same elastic deflections for a given load level as the steel-reinforced sections. That section has about 3.5 times the FRP reinforcing area as the original section. At its elastic limit

$$M_e = 86.8 \ kN\text{-}m \ (768 \ in\text{-}k)$$

$$f_s = 142.2 \ MPa \ (20.6 \ ksi)$$

$$\frac{1}{R} = 0.0123, \ \frac{1}{m}$$

At ultimate capacity

$$M_u = 155.3 \ kN\text{-}m \ (1374 \ in\text{-}k)$$

$$f_s = 323.8 \ MPa \ (46.9 \ ksi)$$

$$\frac{1}{R} = 0.0303, \ \frac{1}{m}$$

The moment curvature function is shown in Figure 8 and the deflections under equal and opposite end moments in Figure 9.

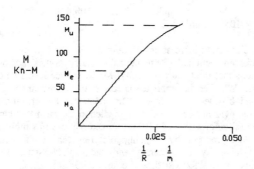

Figure 8   Moment-Curvature Function for 2,258 mm² of FRP Reinforcement

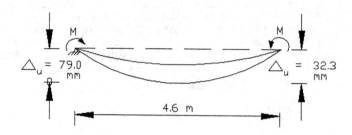

Figure 9 Midspan Deflections at the Elastic Limit
and Ultimate for the 2,258 mm² of FRP Reinforcement

Table 1. Summary of Key Moment Data

Section	M_a kN-m	M_c	M_u	M_u/M_a
FRP A_s = 645 mm²	26.4	49.9	100.4	3.80
FRP A_s = 2258 mm²	46.0	86.8	155.3	3.38
Steel A_s = 709.7 mm²	26.4	66.0	69.7	2.64
Steel A_s = 1058.0 mm²	39.2	90.6	100.4	2.56

Table 1 reveals a significant increase in the ratio M_u/M_a for FRP-reinforced sections as compared to steel reinforced sections. (Remember that it is hypothesized for the purpose of making these comparisons that the flexural capacity, M_a, at service levels be determined from working stress methods. Whether that approach is correct or not remains to be determined by further investigation and broader discussion). This relatively higher ratio M_u/M_a might be considered to balance the evident lack of ductility prediction for the FRP reinforced sections. This model for the flexural deformation of FRP-reinforced sections in simply-supported beams agrees well with test data produced by on-going joint research by the University of New Hampshire, Catholic University of America and the United States Federal Highway Administration (Schmeckpeper, 1992; Goodspeed et al., 1990).

Designers may expect essentially elastic-brittle flexural behavior, and that because of increased crack-widths and reduce compressive stress block size, shear strengths of beams may be significantly lower than predictions which presume steel reinforcement. Preliminary results of the testing of cantilever beams at the University of New Hampshire also suggest small compressive stress blocks and lower than expected thresholds for shear failure.

CONCLUSIONS

These basic comparisons suggest the following conclusions:

- the lack of section ductility suggests that if a design methodology for FRP reinforced concrete is based on ultimate strength criteria, higher load factors or lower capacity reduction factors, or both may be required. While neither of these factors were intended to address the issue of section ductility, their adjustment for FRP-reinforced section design is a pragmatic choice available.
- Working stress design is a rational alternative. A reduction in allowable stresses to compensate for lower section ductilities may be appropriate.
- The lack of section ductility should restrict the use of FRP-reinforced sections in critical members of structures in areas of high seismic risk.
- Manufacturers of FRP reinforcement should focus upon development of higher elastic moduli and some degree of classical for ductility rather than upon high ultimate strength. These may result from improving resins rather than fibers.

This discussion covers only the pure flexural behavior of beams with discrete non-prestressed FRP reinforcing. The sections studied here represent only a limited portion of the domain of flexural reinforced concrete design -- similar studies of sections different concrete strengths, section depths and reinforcing properties will produce very different analysis results. (The conclusions drawn from those results may not differ greatly from those here, however). The section discussed here was selected not because of the breadth of parameters it offered, but because of its breadth of usage -- building floor slabs, bridge decks, cantilever retaining walls and other such thin flexural sections.

REFERENCES

American Concrete Institute (1989). Building Code Requirements for Reinforced Concrete, ACI 318-89, Detroit, Michigan.

Goodspeed, C., Gross, T., Henry, R., Schmeckpeper, R., Yost, J., Zhang, M., "Fiber Reinforced Plastic Grids for the Structural Reinforcement of Concrete", Proceedings of the First materials Engineering Congress. American Society of Civil Engineers, New York, 1990.

Schmeckpeper, R.S. (1992). "Performance of Concrete Beams and Slabs Reinforced With FRP Grids", Doctoral Dissertation submitted to the University of New Hampshire.

ADVANCED COMPOSITE MATERIALS IN BRIDGES AND STRUCTURES

ADVANCED COMPOSITE MATERIALS IN BRIDGES AND STRUCTURES
K.W. Neale and P. Labossière, Editors; Canadian Society for Civil Engineering, 1992

Matériaux composites d'avant-garde pour ponts et charpentes
K.W. Neale et P. Labossière, éditeurs; Société canadienne de génie civil, 1992

PRE- AND POST-CRACKING DEFLECTION BEHAVIOUR OF CONCRETE BEAMS REINFORCED WITH FIBRE-REINFORCED PLASTIC REBARS

S.S. Faza and **H.V.S. GangaRao**
West Virginia University
Morgantown, West Virginia, USA

ABSTRACT

The load-deflection behaviour of concrete beams reinforced with fibre-reinforced plastic (FRP) rebars is investigated extending the current methods used for steel reinforced beams. In addition, certain recommendations to compute post-cracking deflections in beams reinforced with FRP rebars are presented.

RÉSUMÉ

Le comportement charge-déflexion de poutres de béton armé avec des barres de plastique renforcé de fibres (FRP) est étudié en utilisant les méthodes conventionnelles pour les poutres renforcées d'armature en acier. De plus, certaines recommandations pour le calcul des déflexions après la fissuration des poutres renforcées de barres de FRP sont présentées.

INTRODUCTION

Concrete reinforced with mild steel rebars is commonly used in the construction of bridge decks, parking garages, and numerous other constructed facilities. The extensive use of deicing chemicals is reducing the service life of these facilities. In addition, concrete structures exposed to highly corrosive environments, such as coastal and marine structures, chemical plants, water and wastewater treatment facilities, have been experiencing drastically reduced service life and causing user inconveniences.

The gradual intrusion of chloride ions into concrete eventually leads to corrosion of steel reinforced concrete structures and concrete cracking; which may be due to shrinkage, creep, thermal variations, or some unexpected design inadequacies due to external loads (Nawy, 1990). A corrosion protection system that would extend the performance of our constructed facilities would have a payoff in billions of dollars, since their replacement runs twice the original construction cost (America's Highways, 1984).

Several recommendations have been adopted in the design of concrete structures to prevent the corrosion of steel reinforcement such as use of waterproofing admixtures in concrete, impermeable membrane, epoxy-coated steel rebars, and others without a complete success. Therefore, use of noncorrosive fiber reinforced plastic (FRP) rebars in place of mild steel rebars has been researched as an alternative to improve the longevity of structures.

RESEARCH SIGNIFICANCE

The performance of FRP rebars embedded in concrete is not fully understood, even though FRP rebars have been used in structural applications for over ten years (Nawy, 1977). The current mathematical models and design equations of concrete beams reinforced with mild steel cannot be applied directly to beams reinforced with FRP rebars without fully understanding the following issues:

1) Lower modulus of elasticity of FRP than steel.
2) Bond behavior.
3) Long term degradation.
4) Post-cracking behavior of the concrete beams with FRP rebars.

The primary focus of the research conducted at the Constructed Facilities Center, West Virginia University is to study the behavior of reinforcing concrete beams and bridge decks with FRP rebars. The main objectives of this paper include two aspects of the behavior of FRP rebars used as reinforcement in concrete: (1) Investigation of the pre- and post-cracking deflection behavior under bending of concrete beams reinforced with FRP rebars; (2) Development of post-cracking deflection design equations for FRP reinforced concrete, which are practical and simple to use for structural design applications.

TEST PROGRAM

Fiber Reinforced Plastic Rebar Characteristics

Since the 1950s, glass has been considered a good substitute to steel for reinforcing or prestressing concrete structures. For example, a typical continuous E-glass fiber reinforced plastic rebar has 55 percent glass volume fraction embedded in a matrix of vinylester and an appropriate coating to prevent alkaline reaction (Rubinski 1954).

In order to develop good bond strength between FRP rebars and concrete, different surface conditions for rebars were developed. Among them, 45 degree angular wrapping or helical ribs produce a deformed surface on the rebar. Coating FRP rebars with epoxy and rolling them in a bed of sand creates a roughened surface and is one of the alternatives that would improve bond strength.

Experimental results indicate that the average tensile stiffness depends on the fiber type and volume fraction and is virtually independent of manufacturer, bar size, bar type (with or without ribs), test procedure, and type of resin. A mean tensile stiffness of 48.26 GPa for 55% fiber volume fraction was reported by Wu (1991). However, ultimate tensile strength is sensitive to bar diameter, quality control in manufacturing, matrix system, fiber type, and gripping mechanism. The ultimate tensile strength of continuous glass fiber reinforced rebars with vinylester resin decreases rapidly with increase in bar diameter (Table 1). Considering the fact that FRP rebars do not exhibit a yield plateau as steel, it is necessary to assume a 20% reduction for an effective yield strength of the rebar for reasons of safety; hence minimum of six rebars have to be tested to obtain an average ultimate rebar strength, f_{ult}.

The reduction factor was arrived at after extensive testing of samples from a variety of manufacturers (Wu, 1991, Faza, 1992). If testing of rebar samples is not possible, the following results outlined in Table 1 can be used as the effective yield strength, f_{yf}, of FRP rebars.

Table 1 Effective Yield Strength of FRP Rebars (MPa)

REBAR SIZE	#3	#4	#5	#6	#7	#8
f_{ult}*	897.4	738.6	655.8	621.3	586.8	552.2
f_{yf}	717.9	590.9	524.6	497.0	469.4	441.8

* Based on test data on Kodiak Rebars

Concrete Properties

In order to take advantage of the high tensile strength of the FRP rebars, concrete strength of 34.5 - 69.0 MPa was used in the testing program. Class K concrete from a local mixing plant was used in all the specimens. For each batch of concrete delivered, eight 101.6 x 203 mm (4 x 8 in.) cylinders were cast, cured and tested with the specimens.

153

Beam Specimens

Twenty five rectangular beams, 152.4 x 304.8 mm by 3048 mm (6 x 12 in. by 10 ft), were tested under pure bending (as simply supported under four point bending), using different configuration of FRP reinforcement and concrete strength. The variables are:
   a) Rebar size (#3, #4, #7, #8).
   b) Type of rebar (smooth, ribbed, sand coated).
   c) Type of stirrups (steel, smooth FRP, ribbed FRP).
   d) Reinforcement distribution (3#4 versus 5#3).
   e) Concrete compressive strength, 29 - 69 MPa, ($f_c{}' = 4.2, 5.0, 6.5, 7.5,$ and 10 ksi).

EXPERIMENTAL RESULTS

The major emphasis of our test program was to investigate the FRP reinforced concrete beam behavior and compare with the steel reinforced beam, in terms of:
   - Pre- and Post-Cracking Behavior
   - Load-Deflection and Stress-Strain Variations
   - Elastic and Ultimate Load Carrying Capacities
   - Crack Patterns (spacing, width, propagations)
   - Modes of Failure.

The simply supported rectangular beams were tested under pure bending using different configurations of FRP reinforcements. In order to take advantage of the high tensile strengths of FRP rebars, beams with higher strength concrete ($f_c{}' = 34.5 - 69$ MPa) were tested for the purpose of maximizing the bending resistance of the beams. In this paper, the pre- and post-cracking deflection behavior are emphasized.

Pre- and Post-Cracking Behavior

The precracking segments of load-deflection curves in all specimens are essentially straight lines indicating the full elastic behavior. The maximum tensile stress in concrete beams in this region is less than the tensile strength of concrete. The flexural stiffness EI of the beams can be estimated using Young's modulus E_c of concrete and the moment of inertia of the uncracked reinforced concrete cross section. The load-deflection behavior before cracking is dependent on the stress-strain relationship of concrete.

When flexural cracking develops, contribution of concrete in the tension zone is neglected. Thus the slope of a load-deflection (or stiffness) curve is less steep than in the precracking stage. The stiffness continues to decrease with increasing load, reaching a lower limit that corresponds to the moment of inertia of the cracked section, I_{cr}.

The post-cracking experimental deflection of FRP reinforced beams (Beam #9 & #H1) were about four times larger than the beam reinforced with steel rebars (Beam #11) as shown in Fig. 1. The larger post-cracking deflections were expected due to the low modulus of elasticity of FRP rebars, which is about 4.83 GPa. The deflection behavior was vastly improved when sand coated rebars were used as shown in Fig 2. This behavior is attributed to the reduction in crack widths, and the improvements in the distribution and propagation of the cracks when sand coated FRP rebars are used (Faza, 1992).

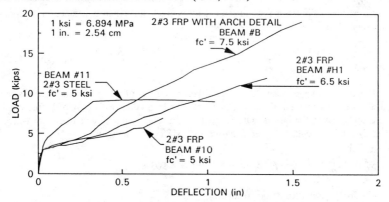

Figure 2 Experimental Load vs Deflection

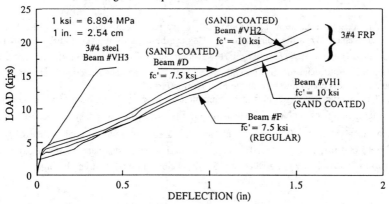

Figure 3 Load vs Deflection (using sand coated FRP bars)

THEORETICAL CORRELATION OF EXPERIMENTAL DEFLECTIONS

The theoretical correlation of the experimental deflections utilizes, as a first step, the current mathematical models and design equations for concrete reinforced with mild steel rods. The results from these equations are checked with the experimental deflections and modified as necessary to accommodate FRP reinforcement.

Various methods have been considered by researchers in an attempt to calculate post cracking deflections of concrete beams reinforced with steel (Nawy 1990). The differences among the various methods consist mainly of the ways to compute the modulus of elasticity, E, and the moment of inertia, I. Both quantities are difficult to define in a steel reinforced concrete member. Considering that cracking behavior of concrete beams reinforced with FRP bars is different from that of steel reinforced concrete beams, the effective cracked moment of inertia, I_{eff}, would be different from that of conventional steel reinforced beams. Such difference can be attributed mainly to the extent of cracking, which is a function of the bond between concrete and rebar.

Precracking Stage

The precracking segments of load-deflection curves in all specimens were essentially straight lines indicating the full elastic behavior. The load-deflection behavior before cracking is dependent on EI of the beams and the stress-strain relationship of concrete from which the value of E_c can be calculated either using the ACI 318 code expression

$$E_c = 57,000 \sqrt{f_c'} \text{ , where } E_c \& f_c' \text{ (psi, 1 psi = 6.903 KPa)} \tag{1}$$

or the ACI 363R committee recommendation

$$E_c = 40,000 \sqrt{f_c'} + 1 \times 10^6 \qquad \text{, where } E_c \& f_c' \text{ (psi, 1 psi = 6.903 KPa)} \tag{2}$$

An accurate estimation of the moment of inertia I necessitates the consideration of FRP reinforcement A_f in the computations. This can be done by replacing FRP bar area by an equivalent concrete area $(E_f/E_c)A_f$. However, the use of gross moment of inertia resulted in acceptable results in the precracking stage with the uncracked section and neglecting additional stiffness contribution from the FRP reinforcement.

The precracking stage stops at the initiation of the first flexural crack when concrete reaches its modulus of rupture, f_r, which is typically $7.5 \sqrt{f_c'}$, (f_c' , psi) The ACI 363R recommends a value of $11.7 \sqrt{f_c'}$ for normal weight concretes with strength in the range of 3000 to 12,000 psi, (1 psi = 6.903 KPa). For curing conditions such as seven day moist curing followed by air drying, a value of $7.5 \sqrt{f_c'}$ is closer to the full strength range.

Postcracking Stage

When flexural cracking develops, tensile strength of concrete is neglected. The slope of a load-deflection (or stiffness) curve is less steep than in the precracking stage as shown in load-deflection curves in Figs 3 and 4. The stiffness continues to decrease with increasing load, reaching a lower limit that corresponds to the moment of inertia of the cracked section, I_{cr}. The moment of inertia of a cracked section can be obtained by computing the moment of inertia of the cracked section about the neutral axis resulting in the following relationship after neglecting the concrete section below the neutral axis:

$$I_{cr} = \frac{bc^3}{3} + n A_f (d - c)^2 \tag{3}$$

where,

n = Modular ratio, (E_f / E_c)
c = Distance from top fiber to the neutral axis

156

In actual cases, only a portion of a beam along its length is cracked. The uncracked segments below the neutral axis possess some degree of stiffness which contributes to the overall beam rigidity. The actual stiffness of the beam lies between $E_c I_g$ and $E_c I_{cr}$. As the load approaches the ultimate value, beam stiffness approaches $E_c I_{cr}$. The major factors that influence the beam stiffness are:

        1) Extent of cracking.

        2) Contribution of concrete below the neutral axis.

The ACI 318 code specifies that deflection shall be computed with an effective moment of inertia, I_e as follows, but not greater than I_g.

$$I_e = (M_{cr}/M_a)^3 \ \ I_g \ + (1-(M_{cr}/M_a)^3) \ \ I_{cr} \tag{4}$$

where, $M_{cr} = \dfrac{f_r I_g}{Y_t}$, $M_a = Applied\ Moment$, and $\quad Y_t = h/2$

The effective moment of inertia adopted by the ACI 318-89 is considered sufficiently accurate for use in control of deflection of beams reinforced with steel. I_e was developed to provide transitional moments of inertia between I_g and I_{cr} and it is a function of $(M_{cr}/M_a)^3$

By investigating the experimental versus theoretical load-deflection curves using I_e as prescribed by eq. (4), a large discrepancy is found in deflections after the first crack as shown in Figs. 3 and 4.

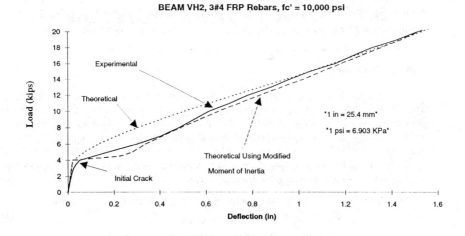

Figure 3 Load vs Deflection (Theoretical vs Experimental)

157

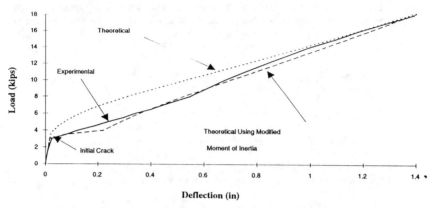

Figure 4   Load vs Deflection (Theoretical vs Experimental)

The equation for deflection of a simply supported beam of span L, loaded with two concentrated loads P (Fig. 5), in kips, at a distance a from each end is written as:

$$\Delta_{max} = \frac{P\,a}{24\,E_c\,I_e}\,(3L^2 - 4a^2),\quad(in,\ 1\ in = 25.4\ mm)\qquad(5)$$

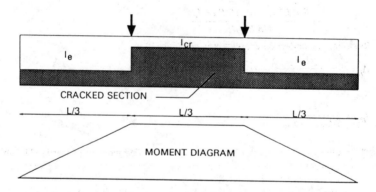

Figure 5   Load, Moment and Cracking Section of Loaded Beam

for $a = L/3$, $\Delta_{max} = \dfrac{23\,P\,L^3}{648\,E_c\,I_e}$ \qquad(6)

in which , E_c = Concrete modulus of elasticity (experimental values, psi)

I_e — Effective moment of inertia (in^4)

L = 108 in. the deflection expression can be rewritten as

$$\Delta_{max} = \frac{44712\,P}{E_c\,I_e}\,(in,\ 1\ in. = 25.4\ mm)\qquad(7)$$

For evaluating I_e, the experimental cracking moment M_{cr}, observed from the tests was used.

It is seen from the load-deflection curves, Figs. 3 and 4, that the deflection by Eq. (6) overestimates the moment of inertia of the beam after the first crack. Thus, the calculated deflection values from Eq. (8) are lower than the observed values. A better estimate of the moment of inertia is needed. In the following subsection, a new expression for the effective moment of inertia has been proposed by the authors.

Modified Moment of Inertia

Due to the nature of crack pattern and propagation and the height of the neutral axis which is very small for FRP reinforced concrete beams, a new method in calculating the effective modulus of elasticity is introduced for FRP reinforced concrete beams. The new expression is based on the assumption that concrete section between the point loads is assumed to be fully cracked, while the end section are assumed to be partially cracked (Fig. 5). Therefore, expression for I_{cr} is used in the middle third section, and I_e is used in the end sections.

Using the moment area approach or other methods to calculate the maximum deflection at the center of the beam, as shown in Fig. 5, would result in an expression for maximum deflection that incorporates both I_e and I_{cr} as shown in equation (8).

$$\Delta_{max} = \frac{8\,P\,L^3\,EI_{cr} + 15\,P\,L^3\,EI_e}{648\,EI_{cr}\,EI_e}, \; in, \; (1\; in. = 25.4\; mm) \tag{8}$$

$$= \frac{8\,P\,L^3\,I_{cr} + 15\,P\,L^3\,I_e}{648\,EI_{cr}I_e} \tag{9}$$

Rewriting the deflection expression in equation (9)

$$\Delta_{max} = \frac{23\,P\,L^3}{648\,E_c\,I_m} \; (in) \tag{10}$$

in which,

$$I_m = \frac{23\,I_{cr}\,I_e}{8\,I_{cr} + 15\,I_e} \tag{11}$$

The resulting deflection equation (10) and the modified moment of inertia (11) which is valid for two concentrated point loads that are applied at the third points on the beams are plotted as shown in Fig. 3 and 4.

Using the same approach as in the case of two concentrated point loads, expressions for maximum deflection and modified moment of inertia are derived for a concentrated point load and for a uniform distributed load. However, no experimental information is available to check their validity.

For a concentrated point load applied at the center of the beam, the maximum deflection expression can be written as:

$$\Delta_{max} = \frac{P\,L^3}{48\,E_c\,I_m} \; (in) \quad where, I_m = \frac{54\,I_{cr}\,I_e}{23\,I_{cr} + 45\,I_e} \tag{12}$$

For a uniform distributed load applied on the beam, the maximum deflection expression can be written as:

$$\Delta_{max} = \frac{5\,W\,L^4}{384\,E_c\,I_m} \; (in) \quad where, \; I_m = \frac{240\,I_{cr}\,I_e}{45\,I_{cr} + 202\,I_e} \tag{13}$$

159

SUMMARY AND CONCLUSIONS

Based on the mechanical properties of FRP rebars obtained by Wu (1991), twenty five concrete beams were designed and tested under bending. Test variables included concrete strengths (29 - 69 GPa), type of FRP rebar (smooth, ribbed, sand coated), and rebar size. The response of concrete beams reinforced with FRP rebars were investigated in terms of pre- and post-cracking load-deflection behavior. The use of sand coated FRP rebars in addition to high strength concretes improved the overall behavior of concrete beams in terms of the ultimate moment capacity, crack width and propagation, thus improving the load-deflection behavior.

Theoretical correlations with our experimental deflections were conducted using current provisions. The current design methodology for steel reinforced concrete beams cannot be applied directly to FRP reinforced concrete beams. New design equations for deflections similar to the ACI 318-89 building code provisions were established based on the experimental results outlined. Theoretical equations were established to compute modified moment of inertia.

Due to the nature of crack formation and propagation in FRP reinforced concrete beams and the low modulus of elasticity of FRP rebars, a modified effective moment of inertia equation is proposed herein to estimate deflection. The modified effective moment of inertia incorporates both the cracked moment of inertia as well as the current ACI code equation, and is valid for sand coated FRP rebars which exhibit a bond strength of at least 1500 psi (eq. 11).

REFERENCES

ACI Building Code Requirements for Reinforced Concrete (ACI 318-89), American Concrete Institute, Detroit, MI, 1989.

America's Highway, Accelerating the Search for Innovation, Transportation Research Board, Special Report #202, 1984.

Faza, S.S., Ph.D. Dissertation, West Virginia University, Morgantown, West Virginia, 1991, *"Bending and Bond Behavior and Design of Concrete Beams Reinforced with Fiber Reinforced Plastic Rebars"*.

Faza, S.S, and GangaRao, H.V.S., Advanced Composites Materials, ASCE, Edited by Iyer S.L., 1991, pp. 262, *"Bending Response of Beams Reinforced with FRP Rebars for Varying Concrete Strengths"*.

Nawy, E.G., and G.E. Neuwerth, ASCE Journal of the Structures Division, Vol. 103, No. ST2, Feb. 1977.

Nawy, E.G., Reinforced Concrete, A Fundamental Approach, 2nd edition, Prentice Hall International, 1990.

Rubinski I., and Rubinski, A., Magazine of Concrete Research, (6), 71-78, 1954.

Wu, W. P., "Thermomechanical Properties of Fiber Reinforced Plastic Bars," Ph.D. Dissertation, West Virginia University, 1991.

ADVANCED COMPOSITE MATERIALS IN BRIDGES AND STRUCTURES
K.W. Neale and P. Labossière, Editors; Canadian Society for Civil Engineering, 1992

Matériaux composites d'avant-garde pour ponts et charpentes
K.W. Neale et P. Labossière, éditeurs; Société canadienne de génie civil, 1992

RENFORCEMENT DU BÉTON PAR ARMATURES EN COMPOSITE FIBRES DE VERRE-MATRICE VINYLESTER À RELIEF AJOUTÉ PAR TRAME TEXTILE

F. Buyle-Bodin
Institut Universitaire de Technologie de Béthune
Béthune, France

M. Convain
Société Cousin Frères
Wervicq, France

RÉSUMÉ

La Société Cousin a développé une armature en composite fibres de verre-matrice vinyl-lester à relief ajouté par trame textile. L'adhérence de ces barres dans le béton a été quantifiée par une série de tests et le comportement de la liaison armature-béton analysé par essais de poutres soumises à des cycles charge-décharge. Des essais sur minipoutres soumises à des cycles thermiques en enceinte permettent d'apprécier l'importance de la différence des modules de dilatation des deux produits. L'étude présentée ici devrait contribuer à une meilleure connaissance de la contribution mécanique réciproque du béton et de l'armature en composite et proposer de premiers outils de calcul de structures en béton ainsi renforcé.

ABSTRACT

The Cousin Company has developed a novel rod for reinforcing concrete using composite materials (glass fibres/vinylester matrix with textile woof added surface). The bond strength of the bars has been quantified through a series of beam tests and the behaviour of the reinforcement/concrete adherence analysed through a series of tests on beams submitted to loading and unloading phases. Tests on mini-beams submitted to thermal cycles enable us to appreciate the importance of the difference of the dilatation moduli of both products. This study should lead to a methodology for designing reinforced concrete structures reinforced in this way.

INTRODUCTION

Le département composites de la société COUSIN, par son savoir-faire dans le textile linéaire, a développé une armature en composite fibres de verre - matrice vinylester dont l'originalité réside dans un relief ajouté par trame textile. Cette armature devrait connaître un débouché dans la réalisation de structures en ambiance corrosive ou sous conditions amagnétiques, ainsi qu'en réhabilitation de structures bétons.

L'adhérence des barres en composite comme armatures dans le béton est le premier phénomène à étudier car le fonctionnement mécanique du béton armé est essentiellement dû au transfert de charges du béton aux armatures.

L'étude présentée ici apporte une meilleure connaissance de la contribution mécanique réciproque du béton et de l'armature en composite en vue de proposer à terme des outils de calcul de structures en béton ainsi renforcées.

L'ARMATURE JITEC

La Société COUSIN produit une armature pour béton en composite fibre de verre vinylester dont l'originalité réside dans l'ajout d'un relief par un procédé textile.

Cette armature dénommée JITEC comprend 80 % en poids et 65 % en volume de fibres de verre type E. La forte proportion de fibres par rapport à la matrice est obtenue par un procédé de tressage et d'essorage décrit figures 1 et 2. Le savoir-faire de COUSIN dans le textile linéaire a permis de développer un procédé original de création de relief en surface de jonc, ce qui permet d'obtenir une adhérence élevée avec le béton. Les principales caractéristiques du composite sont présentées tableau 1 en en regard de celles de l'acier inoxydable.

Le comportement, en terme de contraintes en fonction de l'allongement par essai de traction est exposé figure 3 pour l'acier, le polyester et JITEC.

Il est à noter que le module d'Young du verre, donc celui du JITEC en traction, est 3 à 4 fois plus faible que celui de l'acier, ce qui n'est pas sans conséquences sur la rigidité des structures en béton renforcé de composite.

Le comportement est par contre parfaitement élastique jusqu'à rupture, ce qui présente de nombreux intérêts pour des structures soumises à des sollicitations variables.

Enfin, le composite est insensible à la corrosion que peut connaître l'armature classique en acier. Cela permet de diminuer les épaisseurs d'enrobage, et donc d'alléger les structures, ou pour le moins d'augmenter les moments résistants.

L'armature en composite JITEC devient un substitut de l'armature classique en acier dès que se présentent des conditions particulières de corrosion, de poids, d'amagnétisme ou de conductivité électrique.

ESSAIS D'ADHERENCE

Le fonctionnement mécanique du béton armé tient essentiellement au bon transfert des efforts de traction du béton vers les armatures.

C'est le phénomène d'adhérence béton-armature, qui combine des effets géométriques d'imbrication, mécaniques d'épaulement et de serrage, chimiques de collage.

L'essai simple et classique d'arrachement d'une barre ancrée dans un cylindre de béton plus ou moins fretté néglige les effets mécaniques.

L'essai dit "Beam Test" prend en compte l'ensemble des effets en se rapprochant du mode de fonctionnement réel des armatures tendues des pièces fléchies. Cet essai décrit figure 4, est l'objet d'une recommandation RILEM [RILEM, 1982], et nous l'avons retenu, après d'autres [Schaller, De Larrard, Fuchs, 1990] pour caractériser l'adhérence de JITEC.

Une série d'essais, sur HA 10 et HA 16 (armatures acier conventionnelles type TOR), et sur JITEC Ø 10 avec des bétons de structure classiques (type FAURY) ou plus riches en sable (type BOLOMEY) ont été menés pour caractériser l'adhérence et distinguer l'influence de différents paramètres sur les effets énoncés ci-dessus [Dreux, 1981].

Des résultats présentés par ailleurs [Buyle-Bodin, Adry Ramos, 1992] nous ne retiendrons que les valeurs de contrainte d'adhérence définies conventionnellement pour un glissement de 100 mm, reportées tableau 2 et qui sont du même ordre pour l'acier et pour le JITEC. La figure 5 présente un exemple de courbe glissement-charge.

COMPORTEMENT DU BETON RENFORCE AVEC DES ARMATURES EN COMPOSITE JITEC

L'adhérence est donc du même ordre pour l'acier haute adhérence et pour le JITEC dans le cas de sollicitations régulièrement croissantes.

Les comportements différents du composite et de l'acier amènent à s'interroger sur le comportement réel d'une structure soumise à sollicitations variables.

Nous avons pour cela réalisé 10 poutres de section 15 X 24 et longueur 3,30 m. Ces poutres sont d'une dimension classique en France dans l'étude de la rupture du BA [Dreux 1981]. Elles sont chargées en flexion trois points comme indiqué figure 6. Trois types de ferraillage sont réalisés : MA sous-armées avec 2 barres de 10, NA normalement armées avec 4 barres de 10, PA sur-armées avec 6 barres de 10.

Différents types d'essai ont été entrepris: essai charge-décharge par palier jusqu'à rupture ou essai de fatigue par palier. Le premier type pour une poutre MA, NA et PA avec les deux types d'armature. Le deuxième type pour une poutre NA avec les deux types d'armature.

De l'état actuel d'avancement des essais et de leur dépouillement, il apparaît les résultats suivants :   - un module de rigidité environ deux fois plus faible pour les poutres renforcées en composite.

- avant rupture, un comportement en réversibilité très semblable

- après rupture, un retour presque complet pour les poutres renforcées en composite, et un non retour complet pour les poutres renforcées en HA.

L'ensemble des résultats est en cours de dépouillement et une courbe d'essai est présentée en figure 5

ETUDE DE L'INFLUENCE DES COEFFICIENTS DE DILATATION DU COMPOSITE ET DU BETON

Le béton se voit classiquement attribué un coefficient de dilatation voisin de celui de l'acier. On considère en valeur moyenne pour le béton 8 à 12.10^{-6} et 11.10^{-6} pour l'acier [Guerrin, Lavaur, 1973]. Or le composite vinylester-fibre de verre présente un coefficient de 6.10^{-6} (coefficient du verre).

Cette différence peut faire craindre une dégradation de la liaison armature-béton au cours de la vie d'un ouvrage à la suite des fluctuations naturelles ou artificielles de la température.

Par ailleurs, l'insensibilité du composite aux agressions atmosphériques permet de réduire l'épaisseur d'enrobage de béton. Or celui-ci ne sert pas uniquement à protéger l'armature, mais contribue à l'adhérence et au transfert des charges du béton à l'armature.

L'étude entreprise pour éclaircir ces deux points utilise des éprouvettes prismatiques de taille réduite 10 X 10 X 40, affinées en partie centrale au niveau tendu figure 5. Trois types avec enrobage de 1,2 ou 3 cm sont actuellement en cours d'étude figure ....

Le chargement est constant et obtenu par des masses. L'essai est donc du type essai de fluage. La température de l'enceinte dans laquelle est placé le dispositif de chargement varie deux fois par jour d'un palier - 5° C à un palier + 25° C figure 6.

L'exploitation des résultats de l'influence de l'épaisseur d'enrobage est présentée dans un autre papier à paraître [Buyle-Bodin, Convain, 1992]. Une application immédiate de la faible épaisseur d'enrobage nécessaire pour les armatures en composite peut en effet se trouver dans la réhabilitation des structures béton armé endommagées.

CONCLUSION

La présente communication est l'exposé d'un travail de collaboration entre un industriel du textile développant un produit utilisable en Génie Civil, et un laboratoire universitaire de recherche et développement du matériau béton et des structures en béton renforcé de diverses façons.

Les premiers résultats d'une recherche systématique sur la collaboration entre le béton et l'armature en composite viennent d'être présentés. Il s'agit essentiellement des valeurs de l'adhérence.

Les essais en cours sur poutres et sur prismes sous cycles thermiques devraient permettre d'optimiser l'épaisseur d'enrobage minimale, de lever tout doute sur le comportement à long terme sous variations de température, et d'amorcer un travail de réflexion sur le développement d'outils de calcul de structures ainsi renforcées.

La réflexion de base portera sur la définition de l'état limite de service à admettre.

Les structures renforcées en composite sont plus souples que les structures en béton armé. Elles se déforment donc plus et fissurent d'avantage. Mais cette fissuration n'est en principe pas préjudiciable aux armatures, insensibles aux agressions atmosphériques.

De plus, le matériau composite est parfaitement élastique. La rupture n'est donc pas annoncée par des déformations irréversibles, et la structure devrait être plus résistante aux solliciations alternées, variables, voire dynamiques.

Tout ceci reste à préciser et devra nécessiter de nombreux essais dans un avenir proche.

REFERENCES

Buyle-Bodin F. et Adry Ramos M. (1992). Bond in Concrete of Glass Fiber-Epoxy Composite with Relief Adding Framework as Reinforcement. Second Int. Symp. Textile Composites in Building Construction. 23-25 Juin 1992. Lyon (France).

Buyle-Bodin F. et Convain M. (1992). Réhabilitation des Structures B.A. par emploi d'armatures en composite fibre de verre- matrice en polymères organiques à relief ajouté par trame textile. Colloque européen "Construction Réhabilitation: apport des polymères organiques". 8-10 septembre 1992. Lyon (France).

Dreux G. (1981). Nouveau Guide du Béton. Eyrolles. Paris. 312 p.

Dreux G. (1981). Calcul Pratique de Béton Armé. Eyrolles. Paris. 244p.

Guerrin A. et Lavaur R.C. (1973). Traité de Béton Armé. Tome 1. Dunod. Paris. 324p.

RILEM. (1982). Recommendations on reinforcement steel for reinforced concrete RC5.

Schaller I., De Larrard F. et Fuchs J. (1990). Adhérence des Armatures Passives dans le Béton à Très Hautes Performances. *Bulletin de Liaison du Laboratoire Central des Ponts et Chaussées. 167. Mai-Juin 1990.*

Tableau 1: caractéristiques comparées du JITEC et de l'acier

Caractéristiques	Unités	JITEC/verre	INOX 18NCD6
Densité		1,95	7,85
Contrainte de rupture en traction	daN/mm2	170	113
Module d'élasticité	daN/mm2	4400	21000
conductibilité élec.	Ohms.cm	non conducteu	1,3
conductibilité therm.	W/mK	1	30
Module/densité	daN/mm2	2256	2675

Tableau 2: résultats du Beam Test

	méthode	Faury	méthode	Bolomey
glissement (microns)		100		100
steel HA 10		7,55		
steel HA 16		10,6		
JITEC		11,88		
JITEC				10,42

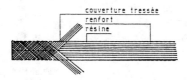

Figure 1: Fabrication des barres en composite COUSIN

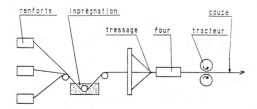

Figure 2: Fabrication des barres en composite COUSIN

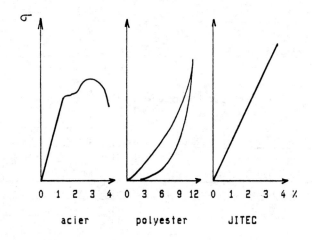

Figure 3 : Comportement mécanique en traction de différents matériaux

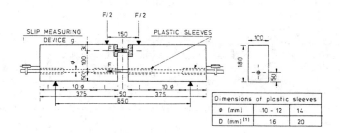

Figure 4: Essai Beam Test (d'après RILEM)

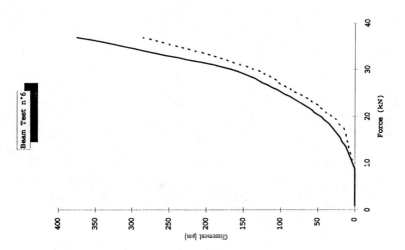

Figure 5: exemple de courbe de Beam Test

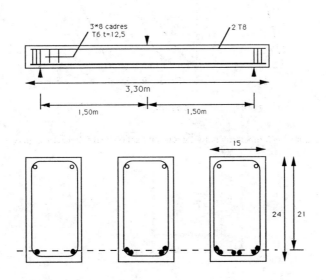

Figure 6: Essai de poutres

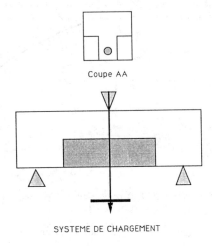

Coupe AA

SYSTEME DE CHARGEMENT

Figure 7: Essai de mini poutres en cycles thermiques

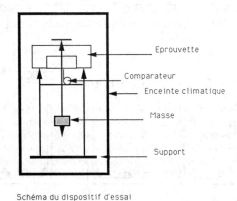

Eprouvette

Comparateur

Enceinte climatique

Masse

Support

Schéma du dispositif d'essai

Figure 8: Dispositif d'essai des mini-poutres

ADVANCED COMPOSITE MATERIALS IN BRIDGES AND STRUCTURES
K.W. Neale and P. Labossière, Editors; Canadian Society for Civil Engineering, 1992

Matériaux composites d'avant-garde pour ponts et charpentes
K.W. Neale et P. Labossière, éditeurs; Société canadienne de génie civil, 1992

AN INNOVATIVE GLASS-FIBRE COMPOSITE REBAR FOR CONCRETE STRUCTURES

O. Chaallal, B. Benmokrane and **R. Masmoudi**
Université de Sherbrooke
Sherbrooke, Québec, Canada

ABSTRACT

The paper reports on results of a laboratory investigation of a glass-fibre composite rod to be used as a rebar for concrete structures. The investigation includes two parts: (a) characterization of the rod, that is its physical and mechanical properties, and (b) behaviour of concrete beams reinforced with glass-fibre composite rods. In light of the results, prospective uses of glass-fibre rods as structural reinforcement in concrete structures are discussed and a design method proposed.

RÉSUMÉ

Cet article présente les résultats d'une investigation en laboratoire d'une nouvelle tige d'armature à base de fibres de verre. L'investigation comprend deux parties : (a) la caractérisation de la tige, dont notamment les propriétés physiques et mécaniques, et (b) le comportement de poutres en béton renforcées avec la tige en fibres de verre. Par ailleurs, sur la base de ces résultats, les perspectives d'utilisation de cette tige d'armature à base de fibres de verre pour le renforcement de structures en béton sont discutées.

INTRODUCTION

Severe deteriorations were reported during the last decade in reinforced concrete structures built in corrosive environment particularly those in contact with de-icing salt such as bridges and multi-storey parking garages. It is admitted that these deteriorations are mainly due to corrosion of steel rebars embedded in concrete (Saadatmanesh and Ehsani, 1991).

One of the alternatives to using steel reinforcement is to use glass-fibre composite (GFC) rod. The latter presents many advantages but also drawbacks (for the time being) that limit its use to specific applications (Laverne, 1990).

Although there is a growing body of knowledge on how best to manufacture GFC rods, little is known about their mechanical behaviour as concrete reinforcement. This Study is part of a large-scale experimental and theoretical programme aimed to gain insight into the characteristics and behaviour of GFC rod. This paper reports on some of GFC rod properties. The performance of such a rod when used as a rebar in concrete beams is also being investigated; however the results are not readily available by the time the paper is submitted but will be reported during the conference.

DESCRIPTION OF GFC ROD

The glass-fiber plastic rods used in this study were made of continuous longitudinal glass-fiber strands bound together with a thermosetting polyester resin using a pultrusion process (Chaallal and Benmokrane, 1992a). The resulting rod has a smooth surface around which glass-fiber strands are wrapped and bonded with polyester resin. Sand particles of a specific grain-size distribution coat the surface to further enhance bonding potential. The final product (Fig. 1) is ideal as concrete reinforcement or as an anchoring system.

The percentage of type E glass-fiber ranges from 73 to 78%, depending on rod diameter. Different diameters can be produced by changing the diameter of the die (see Fig. 1a). The most common diameters are 9.5 (3/8"), 12.7 (1/2"), 15.9 (5/8"), 19.1 (3/4"), and 25.4 mm (1").

OVERALL EXPERIMENTAL PROGRAMME

The large-scale experimental programme, which has been carried out at the Université de Sherbrooke, was designed to investigate

(a) physical properties such as specific gravity and coefficients of thermal expansion;

(b) mechanical and elastic properties such as tensile, compressive, shear and flexural strength, modulus of elasticity, Poisson's ratio, stress-strain relation, maximum elongation, bond, loss of strength with elevated temperatures, loss of stress due to relaxation, fatigue endurance, etc.; and

(c) performance of GFC rod as a rebar of concrete structural elements and as anchoring systems

PROPERTIES OF GFC ROD

General Properties

The average mechanical and elastic properties of GFC rod obtained experimentally are summarized in Table 1 along with those of conventional steel rebar for comparison. Typical stress-strain curves of GFC rod and steel rebar are displayed in Fig. 2.

170

It can be seen that GFC rod is substantially lighter than steel. It behaves elastically and linearly up to failure. It possesses a high tensile strength compared to steel. However its ultimate elongation and modulus of elasticity are substantially lower than those of steel. The longitudinal coefficient of thermal expansion (α_L) of GFC rod is similar to that of steel and hardened concrete while that in the transverse direction α_r is five times α_L.

Loss of Tensile Strength at Elevated Temperatures

Loss of tensile strength of bare GFC rod at elevated temparatures as preliminary to considering the performance of concrete structure reinforced with GFC rod in fire was investigated. Tension tests at temperatures up to 400°C were carried out. Residual tensile strength of GFC rod and steel rebar versus temperature curve is presented in Fig. 3 along with that of concrete in compression [Draft of ASCS, 1985, cited by Chew, 1988]. Results showed that strength loss of GFC rod at 100°, 200°, 300° and 400°C was respectively 31, 45, 60 and 71% of reference tensile strength. Losses are seen to be higher in terms of percentage than those experienced by conventional steeel ($\sim$ 14% at 400°C). However due to GFC rod's high intial strength, a strength loss of 50%, for instance, results in a residual elastic strength as high as 345 MPa.

Fatigue and Relaxation

Fatigue tests were carried out under a sinusoïdal type of loading having a frequency of 10 Hz. Preliminary results are compared to deformed steel rebars in Fig.4. It is seen from these limited data that GFC rod withstood fewer cycles than steel rebar. The endurance limit (more than one million cycles) is seen to correspond to a stress range Sr = 120 MPa approximately.

In this investigation a relaxation testing system was developed, and the apparatus is displayed in Fig. 5. The GFC specimen is placed inside a meter-long steel instrumented tube. A washer and a freyssinet-type-cone anchor are placed at one end. At the other end, where the loading is to be applied, a washer, a specially designed lifting device and a cone-type anchor are mounted in that order. By skrewing the lifting device, the anchor is lifted and thereby the rod is tensioned and the steel tube is compressed. By equilibrium, the tension in the rod equals the compression in the steel tube. Therefore, changes of the tensile force in the rod can be monitored by measuring the changes in the steel tube compressive force.

Successfull short-term (2000 hours) relaxation tests were performed with this apparatus, and typical results are shown in Fig. 6. It is observed on this figure, which represents results of 15.9 mm-d rod, that for an initial stress of 70% of ultimate strength the stress loss due to relaxation, is around 5% after 2000 hours.

Bond Strength and Development Length

Pullout tests were undertaken to evaluate bond strength as well as development length of GFC rod when embedded in normal strength concrete (NSC), high-strength concrete (HSC), and grout (Chaallal and Benmokrane, 1992b). Three different diameter were used and the anchored length varied from five times the rod diameter (d) to ten times d. The average bond strengths are seen in Table 2. It is observed that bond strength is around 12 MPa for both NSC and HSC and around 5 MPa for grout.

Development length is defined as the minimum embedded length required to develop the ultimate tensile force, F_u, of the rod. Table 3 gathers the average development lengths for 12.7, 15.9 and 19.1 min-diameter rods. It is seen that development length can be taken around 20d for both NSC and HSC.

APPLICATION TO CONCRETE BEAMS

To demonstrate the applicability of test results, it was thought useful to develop design approaches for basic structural elements as part of a large-scale programme. These approaches will be supplemented by full-scale tests on the laboratory. This paper reports on the most commonly used structural element: concrete beam.

171

Design Approach

When designing a concrete beam reinforced with GFC rods, engineers can use the conventional non linear concrete stress-strain distribution method. The only difference is that GFC rod does not possess a yield stress and that $f_f = E_f \, \varepsilon_f$. Note that $f_{f\,max} = f_y = f_u = 690$ MPa and $\varepsilon_{f\,max} = 1.8\%$ (Table 1). Fig. 7 a shows a beam of rectangular section reinforced with GFRPR and subjected to a moment M. Strain and stress distributions are illustrated in Fig. 7 b and c, and the assumed stress block in Fig. 7 d.

With reference to Fig. 7 d, the resulting compressive and tensile forces are:

$$C = 0.85 \, \phi_c \, f'_c \, ab; \qquad T = \phi_f \, A_f \, f_y \qquad (1)$$

where $\phi_c = 0.6$ and ϕ_f has been assumed equal to $\phi_s = 0.9$, although ϕ_f has not been established yet for GFC rod. Writing C = T and taking into account that $\rho = A_f/bd$, it follows that:

$$a = \frac{\phi_f \, f_y \, d \, \rho}{0.85 \, \phi_c \, f'_c} \qquad (2)$$

The resisting moment can be derived from:

$$M = jd \times C = jd \times T = \phi_f \, A_f f_y \left(d - \frac{a}{2}\right) \qquad (3)$$

Equation (3) can also be used to determine A_f if M is known.

Experimental Behaviour of Concrete Beams Reinforced with GFC Rod

Flexutal tests on concrete beams reinforced with GFC rod are on going in our laboratory. The beams, which are made of NSC, are 3m-long and have a section of 200 x 300 mm. The beams are instrumented with strain gages, tiltmeters, and LVDTs to measure deformations as well as displacements and rotations due to applied loadings. The reinforcing bars are also instrumented with strain gages before casting of concrete to measure bond properties of GFC rod.

Results of this experimental investigation are not readily available but will be reported during the conference by the authors. In particular the load versus vertical displacement at midspan and versus rotation at beam ends will be reported. The crack patterns, as well as the cracking sequence will be discussed and compared to conventionally reinforced beams. Experimental results will finally be compared to theoretical results derived from design approach.

CONCLUSION

Glass-fibre composite rod has potentials as a rebar for concrete structures. The experimental results substantiate the possible use of GFC rod in the building industry. In specific applications such as concrete structures built in corrosive environment, the cost of GFC rod reinforced concrete can be lower than conventionally reinforced concrete, if one takes into account the added cost of repairing and maintenance during the life span of the structure.

ACKNOWLEDGEMENTS

This study was made possible by financial support from the National Research Council of Canada, and from Pultrall Inc., Thetford Mines, Quebec. The experimental work was conducted with the collaboration of Mr. Claude Dugal, technician at the Department of Civil Engineering, Université de Sherbrooke.

REFERENCES

Chaallal, O., Benmokrane, B. (1992a) "Physical and Mechanical Performance of an Innovative Glass-Fiber Reinforced Plastic Rod for Concrete and Grouted Ancorages". To be published in Canadian Journal of Civil Engineering.

Chaalal, O., Benmokrane, B. (1992b) "Pullout and Bond of Glass-Fiber Rods Embedded in Concrete and cement Grout". To be published in RILEM Materials and Structures Journal.

Chew, N.Y.L. (1988). "Assessing heating Concrete and Masonry with Thermoluminescence", ACI Materials Journal, V85, N°6, November/December, pp. 537-543.

Collins, M.P., Mitchell, D. (1987) "Prestressed Concrete Basics", CPCI, 614 p.

Laverne, L. (1990) "Rebuilding the Infrastructure with Advanced Composites", Advanced Composites, May/June, pp. 43-47.

MacGregor, J.G. (1988) Reinforced Concrete - Mechanics and Design, Prentice Hall, 799 p.

Saadatmanesh, H., Ehsani, M.R. (1991) "Fiber Composite Bar for Reinforced Concrete Construction" Journal of Composite Materials, Vol 25. February, pp. 188-203.

LIST OF SYMBOLS

a	depth of concrete compressive block
A_f	tensile GFC rod section
b	beam section width
C	internal resulting compressive force
d	effective depth of beam section
d	rod diameter
E_f	modulus of elasticity of GFC rod in tension
f'_c	concrete compressive strength
f_y	yield strength of GFC rod
F_u	ultimate force Supported by GFC rod = A_f x F_u
f_u	ultimate Strength of GFC rod
f_f	tensile GFC rod stress
jd	distance between internal resulting compressive force (C) and tensile force (T)
M	applied bending moment
T	internal resulting tensile force = Af x f_f
E_f	GFC rod strain
ϕ_c	Resistance factor for concrete
ϕ_f	Resistance factor for GFC rod
ρ	tensile reinforcement ratio

Table 1 - Mechanical and elastic properties of GFC rod and steel rebar

		GFC	Steel
Tensile strength (f_y)	(MPa)	690	450
Compressssive strength	(MPa)	540	450
Modulus of elasticity in tension	(GPa)	45	200
Modulus of elasticity in compression	(MPa)	40	200
Strain at rupture	(%)	1.8	15
Poisson's ratio		0.28	0.3
Coefficient of longitudinal expansion	(/°C)	9×10^{-6}	11.7×10^{-6}
Coefficient of transverse thermal expansion	(/°C)	53×10^{-6}	11.7×10^{-6}
Density	(kg/m^3)	2000	7800

Table 2 - Average bond strength (MPa)

NSC	HSC	Grout
12.9	12.1	4.7

Table 3 - Development length

Diameter mm	NSC	HSC	Grout
12.7	21d	14d	26d
15.9	16d	21d	26d
19.1	21d	21d	30d

d = rod diameter
Values based on 4 tests per diameter

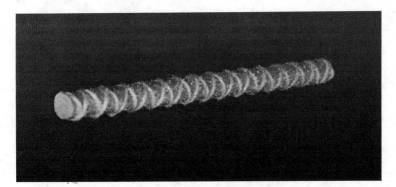

Fig. 1 GFC rod - final product

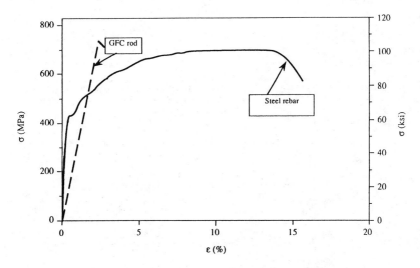

Fig. 2 Tensile stress-strain relations of GFC rod and steel

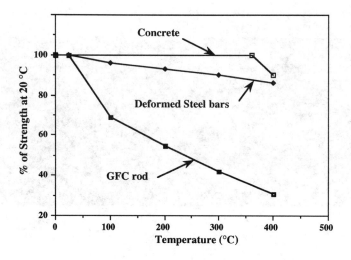

Fig. 3 Effect of elevated temperature on GFC rod,
concrete [1] and steel [2]

(1) (Draft ASCS, 1985, cited by Chew, 1988)
(2) (CPCI, 1982, cited by, Collins and Mitchell, 1987)

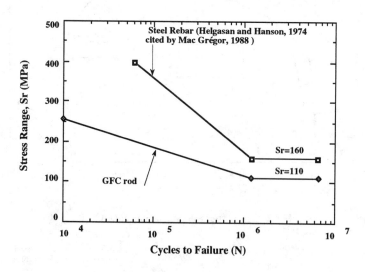

Fig. 4 Fatigue life of GFC rod and steel

176

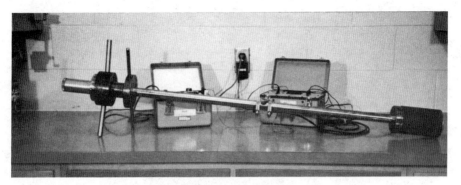

Fig. 5 Relaxation test apparatus

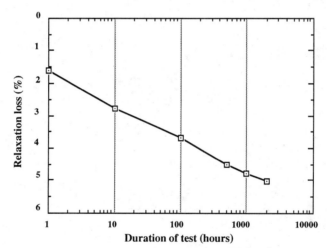

Fig. 6 Short-term relaxation test result:
loss due to relaxation of stress versus time

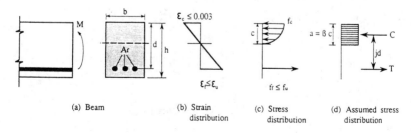

(a) Beam   (b) Strain distribution   (c) Stress distribution   (d) Assumed stress distribution

Fig. 7 Rectangular stress-block concept

ADVANCED COMPOSITE MATERIALS IN BRIDGES AND STRUCTURES
K.W. Neale and P. Labossière, Editors; Canadian Society for Civil Engineering, 1992

Matériaux composites d'avant-garde pour ponts et charpentes
K.W. Neale et P. Labossière, éditeurs; Société canadienne de génie civil, 1992

DEVELOPMENT LENGTH FOR FIBRE-REINFORCED PLASTIC BARS

S. Daniali
Lamar University
Beaumont, Texas, USA

ABSTRACT

Bond strength of fibre-reinforced plastic rebars was experimentally investigated in this study. A total of 30 concrete beams were tested. The beam specimens were reinforced with #4, #6, or #8 FRP bars and #3 FRP shear reinforcements. The FRP bars were made of glass fibres and vinylester binder. The specimens reinforced with #4 rebars developed adequate bond and all of them failed in tension. The specimens containing #6 bars with 610 mm (24 in.) embedment length developed the full tensile strength of the #6 bars. The other specimens reinforced with #6 bars failed due to inadequate bond or splitting of their covering concrete in the constant moment region. All the specimens with #8 rebars failed due to inadequate bond or splitting of their covering concrete.

RÉSUMÉ

Dans cette étude, 30 poutres en béton armé de barres #4, #6 ou #8 en FRP, et d'étriers #3 en FRP, ont été testées expérimentalement afin de déterminer la résistance d'ancrage. Les barres de FRP consistent en fibres de verre dans une résine de vinylester. Les poutres renforcées de barres #4 ont développé un bon ancrage et ont rupturé en tension. Les spécimens contenant des barres #6 ont développé leur pleine résistance avec une longueur d'ancrage plus grande ou égale à 610 mm. Tous les spécimens renforcés de barres #8 ont rupturé à cause d'un ancrage insuffisant, ou par éclatement du béton d'enrobage.

INTRODUCTION

Corrosion of steel reinforcement in concrete by chloride ions has been determined to be the major cause of premature deterioration of concrete structures (ACI Committee 208, 1958). Sources of chloride ions include de-icing salts used on highways, bridge decks, and parking garages slabs, and seawater spray in coastal regions. During the pass 20 years several methods were being developed and used to prevent corrosion of steel reinforcement. These methods could be divided in to two categories: I. Use of treatments which seal the surface of the concrete structures or the entire concrete matrix. II. Use of reinforcing steel with protective coating such as galvanized and epoxy-coated steel. The use of epoxy-coated steel rebars has been used extensively in bridges and parking buildings. However, the recent discovery of extensive premature corrosion of epoxy-coated bars in new bridges indicates that the corrosion of steel reinforcement in concrete has not yet been solved and more efficient techniques or new non-corrosive reinforcing materials are needed. In contrast to conventional materials in construction, fiber reinforced plastics offer significant advantages such as high corrosion resistance, high electro-magnetic transparency, and high strength-to- weight ratios which make these materials ideally suitable to replace steel reinforcement in concrete. Recently reinforcement made of FRP were used in chemical plants, seawalls, hospitals , and airports.

RESEARCH SIGNIFICANCE

Design and analysis of reinforced concrete elements are based on the development of adequate bond between reinforcing bars and the surrounding concrete. The bonding of the bars to the concrete is due to several factors, including the chemical adhesion between concrete and the surface of the bars, the friction due to surface roughness of the bars, the mechanical anchorage of the bars surface deformation (ribs) against the hardened concrete, and shrinkage pressure of the hardened concrete against the bars. Because of the complex relationship between bond, shear, and moment, the bond between steel reinforcement and concrete was subject of numerous comprehensive theoretical and experimental studies (ACI, Committee 318, 1989, Johnson, 1982 and Jirsa, 1981). The current ACI design procedure for development of reinforcement is based on the results of these studies. However, these results cannot be used for FRP bars due to the several major differences between steel and FRPs. FRP materials have very soft matrices, they process very low tensile modulus and they are viscoelastic. The main objective of the present study was to investigate the bond strength of FRP bars and their modes of failure.

MATERIALS

Reinforcement: The FRP bars were made of vinyl ester resin and type E glass fibers with a glass content of 60% to 70% by weight. The bars had deformed surfaces. The surface deformations were made by wrapping the bars with a fiberglass strand in a 45° helical pattern previous to entering in the heated die where the polymerization of the resin occurred.
   Concrete: Four batches of typical 5-sack mix concrete were procured from a ready-mix company to cast the beam specimens. The concrete mixes were made of portland cement type I and round coarse aggregate (gravel). Maximum size of the concrete aggregate was 19 mm (3/4 in.). Nine standard 152.5 x 305 mm (6 x 12 in.) cylinders were casted from each concrete batch. Average compressive strengths of 27.6±2.07 MPa (4000±300 psi) were obtained at 28 days of age.

SPECIMENS

The specimens were 3,048 mm (10 ft) long and had a rectangular cross-section of 203 x 457 mm (8 x 18 in.). The beams were essentially of the type described in the report of the ACI Committee 208 [1]. In the first phase of this study 27 specimens grouped in nine sets of three identical specimens were tested. The specimens were reinforced with one #4, #6 or #8 FRP bar. The specimens were also reinforced with #3 stirrups along the shear spans. In second phase, three additional specimens were tested. These specimens were reinforced with one #6 bar and the stirrups were located along the entire length of the specimens. A covering concrete of 38 mm (1.5 in.) was used for #4 and #6 bars, and 44.5 mm (1.75 in.) for #8 bars. In order to eliminate the effect of reaction forces on the end of the bars over the supports, the ends of the main bars were separated from the concrete by means of two 102 mm (4 in.) long oversized steel pipes. The reinforcement layout for different sets of specimens is shown in Fig. 1.

INSTRUMENTATION

In order to measure the strain in the main reinforcement, two strain gages were installed on each bar, at the end of the constant moment region inside the recess notches. Also, the slippage of the free ends (unloaded ends) of the main bars was monitored by means of two dial gages located at the ends of each specimens. Steel yokes were used to hold dial gages. Deflection at the mid-span was measured by two dial gages. Location of these instruments are shown in Fig. 2.

TESTING PROGRAM

The beam specimens were tested as simply supported beams over a span of 2845 mm (112 in.). The specimens were loaded by two equal concentrated loads applied to the beams at two ends of the constant moment region. The specimens were loaded in increments of 17.8 kN (4000 lb). Strain in the main reinforcement, slip at both free ends, and deflection at mid-span were recorded after each load increment was completed or after a new crack was developed. Location of each crack and the width of major cracks were also measured during the test.

In order to determine the tensile force developed in the main reinforcement, twelve tensile specimens were prepared from different bars, including the shear reinforcement (#3 bar). The specimens were tested in a universal testing machine. To prevent premature failure of the specimens inside the grips, both ends of the specimens were reinforced. A strain gage similar to those used for the beam specimens was installed on each tensile specimen.

TEST RESULTS

Tensile tests: The results of these tests are summarized in Table 1. The FRP material behaved linearly for the entire range of loading. The specimens made of #4 bar developed higher tensile and tensile modulus than the specimens made of #6 and #8 bars. Low tensile strength of the #3 bars prepared from the shear reinforcement could be due to low glass content and/or production method (chemical polymerization rather than thermal polymerization).

Beam Tests: A total of 30 beam specimens were tested. The following modes of failure were observed during these tests: 1. Tension failure of the main reinforcement. 2. Pull out failure: In contrast to steel reinforcement which shears concrete located between bar surface deformation, concrete shears the ribs on the surface of the FRP bars, causing large slippage and bond failure. The two types of pullout failure are shown in Fig. 3. 3. Splitting failure: This mode of failure occurred when the specimens experienced large deflections. The cover splitting could be prevented by providing shear reinforcements in the constant moment regions as it is shown in phase two of the beam tests. 4. Failure due to creep deformation: FRP materials are viscoelastic; consequently, their ultimate load-carrying capacity and their long-term performance depends upon different factors such as level of loading and duration of loading. Specimen T8-2 was loaded until 70% of its ultimate tensile strain was developed in the bar. Then the load was kept constant. The specimen failed after 20 minutes. The results of the beam tests are summarized in Table 2. The crack distribution of the specimens tested in the first phase are shown in Figs. 5 to 7.

During the first phase of the beam tests, several specimens failed due to the splitting of their covering concrete in the constant moment region. This type of failure occurred when the specimen experienced large deflections. In order to eliminate this type of failure, three additional beam specimens similar to the specimens T6-4 were prepared and tested. Shear reinforcement was provided in both shear regions as well as the constant moment region. These specimens failed in tension. The results of these tests are presented in the lower portion of Table 2. Also, the reinforcement layout and the cracks patterns of these specimens are shown in Fig. 4.

CONCLUSIONS

The following conclusions may be drawn from the test results presented in this paper:
1. The tensile modulus of pultruded FRP bars ranges from 35,000 to 48,000 MPa (5,000 to 7000 ksi) which is approximately 20% to 25% of the tensile modulus of steel bars. Low tensile modulus limits the serviceability of the concrete member reinforced with FRP bars.
2. Crack pattern were the same in identical specimens. The cracks were generally very wide prior to failure.
3. A development length of 203 mm (12 in.) was adequate for developing ultimate tensile strength of #4 bar. Full strength of #6 bar could be developed over 440 mm (18 in.) embedment length if shear reinforcement was provided along the entire length of the specimens.
4. All specimens reinforced with #8 bars failed in bond. However, these specimens had developed 70% to 90% of their ultimate tensile strains at failure.
6. Under sustained load, premature bond failure might occur. Additional study is needed to address this problem.

Table 1- RESULTS OF TENSILE TESTS

Bar Size	Tensile Strength (MPa)	Tensile Modulus (MPa)	Ultimate Strain (mm/mm x 10^{-6})
#3	276-297	20,700	>10,000
#4	725-760	47,600-49,700	>14,000
#6	518-538	38,000-42,100	>12,000
#8	470-483	34,500-41,400	>12,000

Table 2- RESULTS OF BEAM SPECIMENS

Tests	Bar Size	l_{emb} mm	l_{emb}/d_{bar}	$\epsilon_{max}/\epsilon_{ult}$ %	Free End Slip mm	Mode of Failure
T4-1	#4	203	16	100	.74	Tension
T4-2	#4	203	16	100	.46	Tension
T4-3	#4	203	16	100	.51	Tension
T4-4	#4	610	24	100	.12	Tension
T4-5	#4	610	24	100	.05	Tension
T4-6	#4	610	24	100	.05	Tension
T4-7	#4	406	32	100	.05	Tension
T4-8	#4	406	32	100	.03	Tension
T4-9	#4	406	32	100	.05	Tension
T6-1	#6	305	16	>90	1.01	Bond
T6-2	#6	305	16	>90	1.01	Bond
T6-3	#6	305	16	>90	.94	Bond
T6-4	#6	457	24	>90	.10	Cover Splitting
T6-6	#6	457	24	>90	.10	Cover Splitting
T6-7	#6	457	24	100	.05	Tension
T6-8	#6	610	32	100	.20	Tension
T6-9	#6	610	32	100	.01	Tension
T8-1	#8	508	20	>85	2.52	Bond
T8-2	#8	508	20	>70	2.03	Bond (Creep)
T8-3	#8	508	20	>85	3.30	Bond
T8-4	#8	635	25	>90	.78	Bond
T8-5	#8	635	25	>90	.58	Bond
T8-6	#8	635	25	>80	1.37	Bond
T8-7	#8	762	30	>70	.25	Bond
T8-8	#8	762	30	>80	.22	Cover Splitting
T8-9	#8	762	30	>80	.15	Cover Splitting
T6-4*	#6	457	24	100	1.20	Bond
T6-5*	#6	457	24	100	.72	Bond
T6-6*	#6	457	24	100	.75	Bond

* Additional beam specimens tested in the second phase

REFERENCES

ACI Committee 208 (1958). Test Procedure to Determine Relative Bond Value of Reinforcing Bars. ACI J., 5, 1-16.

ACI Committee 318 (1989). Building Code Requirements for Reinforced Concrete. ACI 318-89, ACI, Detroit.

ACI Committee 222 (1985). Corrosion of Metals in Concrete. ACI J., 3-32.

Jirsa, J. O., and Bearn, J. E. (1981). Influence of Casting Position and Shear on Development and Splice Length -Design Recommendations, Research Report 242-3F, Center for Transportation Research, The University of Texas at Austin, Texas.

Johnson, D. W., and Zia, P. (1982). Bond Characteristics of Epoxy Coated Reinforcing Bars, Report No. FHWA/NC/82-002, Department of Civil Engineering, North Carolina State University, North Carolina.

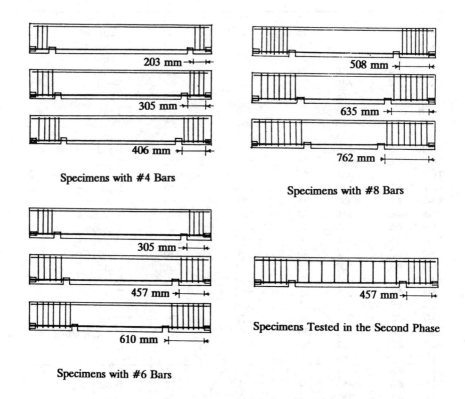

Specimens with #4 Bars

Specimens with #8 Bars

Specimens with #6 Bars

Specimens Tested in the Second Phase

Fig. 1- Reinforcement Layout

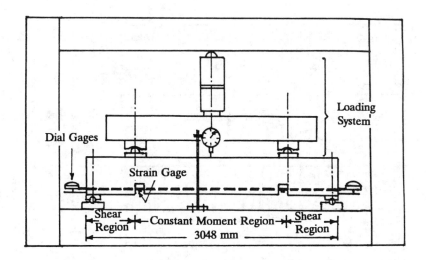

Fig. 2- Test Set-up

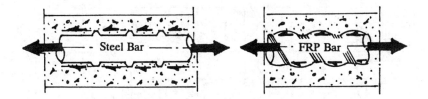

Fig. 3- Pullout Failure

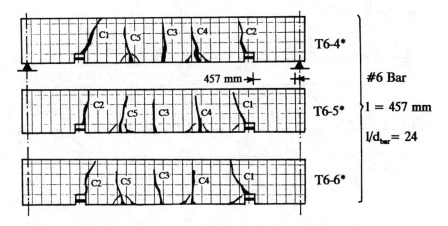

Fig. 4- Specimens Tested in the Second Phase at Failure

185

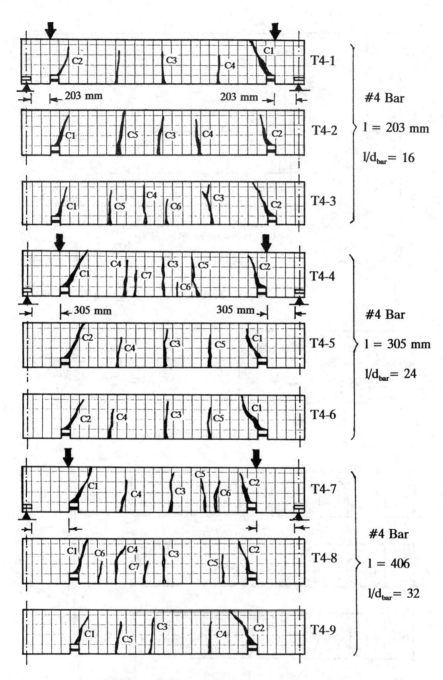

Fig. 5- Specimens Reinforced with #4 Bars at Failure

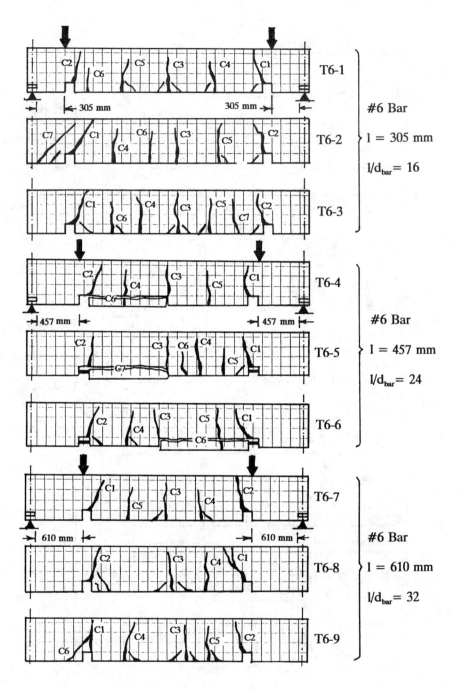

Fig. 6- Specimens Reinforced with #6 Bars at Failure

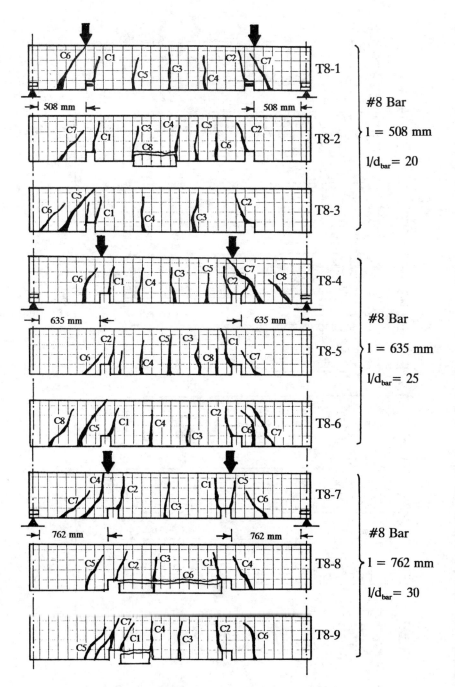

Fig. 7- Specimens Reinforced with #8 Bars at Failure

Concrete Beams With Prestressed Composite Tendons

Poutres de béton précontraint avec tendons composites

ADVANCED COMPOSITE MATERIALS IN BRIDGES AND STRUCTURES
K.W. Neale and P. Labossière, Editors; Canadian Society for Civil Engineering, 1992

Matériaux composites d'avant-garde pour ponts et charpentes
K.W. Neale et P. Labossière, éditeurs; Société canadienne de génie civil, 1992

FRP TENDONS FOR POST-TENSIONED CONCRETE STRUCTURES
ACCEPTANCE TESTING, REQUIREMENTS AND
MECHANICAL BEHAVIOUR

C. Hankers and **F.S. Rostásy**
Technical University of Braunschweig
Braunschweig, Germany

ABSTRACT

In post-tensioning tendons, which consist of FRP tensile elements and of efficient ancho-rages, the advantages of a high tensile strength with an excellent corrosion resistance can be combined. In comparison with prestressing steel no consented basis for the testing of FRP elements and tendons yet exists. On the basis of the mechanical behaviour of FRP elements and dependent on the requirements for FRP tendons in practice this report submits proposals for the necessary test work and for the requirements to be met for acceptance and quality control.

RÉSUMÉ

Les torons de précontrainte, qui se composent d'éléments de tension en synthétique renforcé de fibres (FRP) et d'ancrages efficaces, allient les avantages d'une haute ré-sistance à la traction à ceux d'une excellente résistance à la corrosion. En comparaison avec l'acier de précontrainte, aucune base convenue n'existe encore pour tester les élé-ments et les torons FRP. Sur la base du comportement mécanique d'éléments FRP et en fonction des exigences dans la pratique envers les torons FRP, ce rapport soumet des propositions concernant le travail nécessaire pour les tests et pour les exigences à établir pour l'acceptation et le contrôle de qualité.

INTRODUCTION

For the post-tensioning of concrete structures, the tendons currently consist primarily of a plurality of high-strength prestressing units (wire, strand), placed within the ducts and anchored at the tendon-assembly, by wedges, etc.. Especially for corrosion protection, the tendons and the anchorages are usually placed within the concrete of structure, with the ducts being cement-grouted upon stressing operation.

In recent years this method has come, however, into dispute, as corrosion damages emerged. Deficiencies of the grouting work and subsequent steel corrosion often required costly repair. These problems led to counter-measures. Single strand tendons with anti-corrosion fat filling of ducts were developed. Extensive development and application of exterior tendons (placed outside of the concrete section) with non-grout corrosion protection are under way, following the new demands: inspectability of corrosion protection, maintainability and eventual replaceability of tendons. With the development of fiber reinforced plastic tensile elements (FRP) another alternative has emerged due to the excellent corrosion resistance in combination with high tensile strength of FRP.

For tendons with prestressing steel vast experimental experience has been gathered. International rules for acceptance testing and requirements have been established by FIP /1/. In comparison with this status, no common, consented basis for the testing of FRP-tensile elements and tendons exists yet. The report submits, on basis of the mechanical behaviour of FRP elements and dependent on the requirements for FRP tendons in practice, proposals for the necessary test work and for the requirements to be met for the acceptance and quality control. The mechanical behaviour of FRP tendon-anchorage assemblies (TA) in such tests will be discussed. The relevance of the proposed requirements will be related to those of the structural design. The major differences in the mechanical behaviour between FRP tendons and prestressing steel tendons will be elucidated.

A post-tensioning system must meet several requirements with respect to reliability, safety, serviceability and practicality. The tendon-anchorage assembly (TA) should retain the characteristic strength of the tendon and should be secure under all conditions /1/.

FRP-ELEMENTS FOR THE POST-TENSIONING

There are many types of FRP, with more to expect in the future. FRP consist of thin and strong fibers of different chemical origin embedded in a polymeric matrix. For high-strength tensile elements for the post-tensioning only the unidirectional (ud) arrangement of endless fibers is of interest. Table 1 presents examples of commercially available FRP-elements.

Several types of fibers and matrix materials are used. For linear tensile elements only glass fibers, carbon fibers and aramid fibers have been used successfully up to now. Also the matrix

Table 1: Some high-strength FRP tensile elements

Tensile Element	Type of FRP	Fiber Volume Vol.-%	Tensile Strength GPa	Young's Modulus GPa	Producer
ARAPREE	AFRP	44	1.23	54	AKZO (NL)
Polystal	GFRP	68	1.56	51	BAYER STRABAG (D)
CFCC	CFRP	60	1.90	140	TOKYO ROPES (Jap)

192

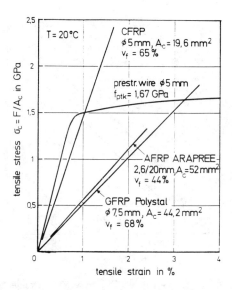

Fig. 1: Stress-strain lines of various FRP-elements in comparison with prestressing steel

materials show a great variety but only three are commonly used today for FRP-elements: polyester, epoxy and vinylester resin. For a tendon with FRP-elements the axial composite strength of the FRP is of special interest. Because the fiber is much stronger than the matrix, the contribution of the latter to the axial strength of the FRP is generally negligible. Fig. 1 depicts composite stress-strain lines of several FRP-elements in comparison with the σ_p-ε_p line of a high-strength, cold-drawn, stress-relieved prestressing steel wire. The behaviour of the FRP-elements is ideal-elastic and brittle.

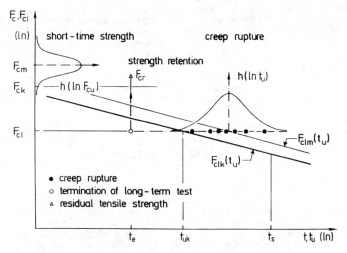

Fig. 2: Creep Rupture and Strength Retention of FRP

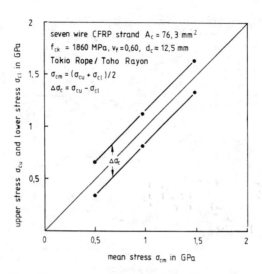

Fig. 3: Smith diagram of fatigue strength of CFRP seven wire strands for 10^6 load cycles (Tokyo Rope)

The FRP elements of a tendon are primarily subjected to long-term static stresses, in combination with the relevant environment of the structure within the structural member. Experiments show that long-term static stresses may reduce the tensile strength of FRP. The admissible permanent tensile stress of FRP must take into consideration the phenomena of creep rupture strength and of strength retention. The phenomenon of creep rupture is irrelevant for prestressing steel if the permissible stress does not exceed $\sigma_{pmo} \leq 0,75\, f_{ptk}$, provided reliable protection against corrosion has been ensured. Fig. 2 shows schematically the time-dependence of the tensile rupture force.

Up to now only a few tests are available /2/, /3/. For Polystal-bars the characteristic long-term strength at 10^6 hours could be assessed to $F_{clk} = 0,7 \cdot F_{ck}$ (air, 20 °C). In alkaline solution the endurance is rather low. AFRP are less sensitive to alkaline solutions than GFRP. CFRP are the least sensitive FRP material to any kind of environmental influence.

When using FRP for post-tensioned concrete bridges their fatigue behaviour must be known. The fatigue strength of FRP elements differs widely, with the following ranking: CFRP, AFRP, GFRP.

In Fig. 3 fatigue test results for CFRP seven wire strands are depicted. For an upper stress of $\sigma_{cu} \approx 1150$ MPa a stress range of $\Delta\sigma_c = 310$ MPa was endured for $2 \cdot 10^6$ load cycles. Under such condition prestressing steel strand St 1570/1770 exhibits a fatigue stress range of about $\Delta\sigma_p \approx 200$ MPa.

POST-TENSIONING TENDONS

General Remarks

The economic and efficient use of FRP elements for tendons necessitates the development of suitable tendon-anchorage assemblies (TA). FRP are sensitive to transverse pressure when subjected to high axial stress. High transverse pressure and surface notching reduce the effective tensile strength of FRP. Consequently, many of the usual methods developed for the anchorage of high-strength prestressing steel like teethed steel wedges, threads, etc. cannot be adopted.

194

Due to these facts new ways had to be sought for FRP. The TA have to be designed in such a way that the tensile strength of the FRP is not significantly reduced by anchorage effects when subjected to static and dynamic actions. Three kinds of anchorage principles are possible: Resin bond anchorage, wedge anchorage and clamp anchorage. The literature sources /4/ to /8/ present an overview on anchorage development. The mechanical behaviour of the TA depends on that of the FRP-elements and the intermediary materials, on the design and on the mechanism of force transfer of the TA. Because the bond anchorage is the one which is at present already being used in practice, it will be dealt with in sequel. Nevertheless, the general statements are essentially valid for other types of force transfer.

Acceptance Testing, Requirements and Mechanical Behaviour

<u>Short-Term Rupture Strength</u>

The static strength of the FRP-tendon is determined with a tendon consisting of n FRP-elements and with TA on both ends of tendon. The force is incrementally increased to the force max $P_{m,o}$ for overstressing and kept constant for 1 hour. Then the force is increased until failure of the first FRP-element at the TA, with measurement of the strain ε_c, slip of FRP-elements and deformations of the TA. The rupture force is denoted F_{Tu}. It has to be compared with the theoretical rupture force F_{cu} of the tendon without TA

$$F_{cu} = n\, A_c\, f_{cm}, \tag{1}$$

with f_{cm} the mean tensile strength of the FRP-elements of the tendon. Both, F_{cu} and F_{Tu}, are scattering properties.

In Fig. 4 the relation between the strength of the FRP-tendon and of the TA is schematically depicted. On the F_c-ε_c-line of the FRP-material the forces F_{cu} and F_{Tu} can be plotted. The extent of utilization of the tensile strength of the FRP is expressed by the anchorage efficiency factor η_A:

$$\eta_A = \frac{F_{Tu}}{F_{cm}} \leq 1 \tag{2}$$

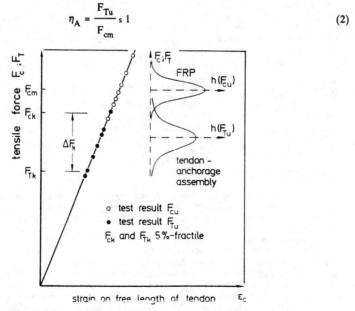

Fig. 4: Force-strain line of FRP-elements and of the TA

195

Fig. 5: Test-setup for the static rupture test for HLV-tendons

The FIP recommendations /1/ for prestressing steel tendons require that the mean anchorage efficiency factor shall not fall below 0,95. In combination with a total steel strain measured on the free length of the tendon of at least 2,3 % at the rupture force F_{Tu} sufficient ductility at failure is ensured. FRP are ideally elastic materials. Nevertheless the requirement of a sufficient total strain ε_{cu} at failure of the tendon is essential to ensure adequate ductility of the prestressed concrete element. At present no international requirements for tendons with FRP elements exist yet. A reasonable set of requirements is expressed in terms of the mean values:

$$\text{meas } \eta_{Am} \geq \text{nec } \eta_{Am} = 0,95 \tag{3}$$

$$\text{meas } \varepsilon_{Tum} \geq \text{nec } \varepsilon_{Tum} = 2 \% \tag{4}$$

Comprehensive tests have been performed with HLV-tendons of STRABAG. They consist of Polystal GFRP bars, d = 7,5 mm. Optimization of anchorage led to a high and consistent anchorage efficiency of $\eta_{Am} \approx 0,96$. Moreover, the coefficients of variation v_c and v_T were very similar and about 2 %. Fig. 5 shows schematically test set-up of the static rupture test.

Static Long-Term Strength

For the tendon-anchorage assembly, also the strength under long-term static force (e.g. prestress) must be known. The question arises whether the long-term static strength of the FRP-elements is adversely affected by the multiaxial stresses within the anchorage. Only a few experimental results are available. It was found that the long-term static strength of the Polystal HLV-tendons extrapolated for about 10^6 hours (= 114 years) does not significantly fall below the long-term static strength of the FRP-elements ($F_{clk} = F_{Tlk} = 0,70 \cdot F_{ck}$ at 10^6 hours). Fig. 6 shows the test results of HLV-tendons with 8 bars, Fig. 7 the test set-up.
The static long-term behaviour must be investigated on at least three distinctly different force levels F_{Tli}, e.g.: 0,8; 0,7; and 0,6 · F_{ck}. The force F_{Tli} is maintained constant until break of first element occurs, the fracture times t_{ui} are recorded. The range of endurance times t_u should cover up to 10^4 hours. Experience shows that at least 10 results t_{ui} per force level are neccessary to establish the characteristic endurance line $F_{clk}(t)$.

196

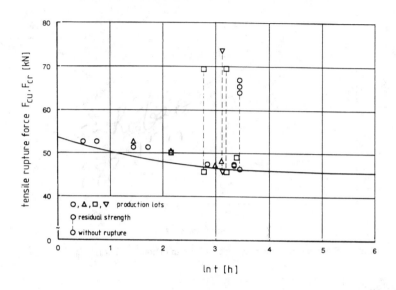

Fig. 6: Static long-term behaviour of HLV-tendons, 8 bars

Fig. 7: Test set-up for static long-term testing

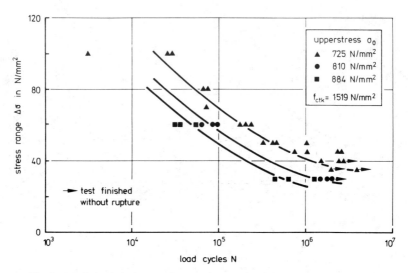

Fig. 8: S-N-lines of single polystal bars 7,5 mm in bond anchorage (l_b = 300 mm)

Dynamic Strength

For prestressing steel tendons a constant stress amplitude test to determine the dynamic behaviour of the TA is demanded. In this test the constant upper force corresponds to a steel stress of 0,65 f_{ptk}. Fatigue strength of tendon is defined as the stress range $\Delta\sigma_p$ for two million load cycles which can be endured without a loss of more than 5 % of the initial cross-section due to fatigue. Fatigue strength $\Delta\sigma_p$ (2 · 10^6) is in range of 90 to 150 MPa and thus only 1/4 to 1/2 of the steel itself.

The fatigue strength of FRP-tendons is influenced by the properties of the chosen anchorage. It was shown for GFRP-tendons with a polymer mortar bond anchorage that the differential slip of the bar at its entry into the bond anchor may cause superficial wear. This may be eliminated by protective sheating of the element but even so, the fatigue strength of GFRP is markedly below the one of wedge-anchored prestressing wire. In Fig. 8 the S-N-curves for single GFRP bars ø 7,5 mm anchored by polymer bond in steel tubes are shown. For many p/c-applications the fatigue strength is sufficient. Nevertheless, further development is needed.

Permissible Prestressing Force for Post-Tensioning

The permissible prestress of the FRP-element must be determined on basis of test results and of a suitable design format by which the variability of the actions and resistances can be taken into account. Such design format is given in the Eurocode EC 2, pt. 1 /9/. For FRP-elements under permanent high tensile stress the long-term strength $F_{clk}(t)$ is the relevant resistance of the material. Hence, the designer has to decide the nominal service life t_s of the concrete element (Fig. 9).

At first the permissible initial prestressing force is derived the bonded tendon with the existance of the TA not being taken into account. Both the prestressing force and the long-term strength of FRP-elements decrease in course of time. The permissible initial prestressing force $P_{m,o}$ (at t = 0) can be derived with the action and resistance at the design level

$$S_d(t_s) \le R_d(t_s) \tag{5}$$

at the end t_s of service life. The loss of prestress will be written as usual

198

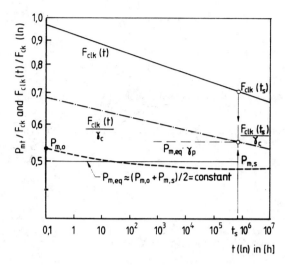

Fig. 9: Derivation of permissible prestressing force

$$\omega_s = \frac{P_{m,eq}}{P_{m,o}}, \tag{6}$$

The reduction of the characteristic short-term tensile strength of the FRP-element due to long-term load and environmental effects can be expressed by

$$\alpha_s = \frac{F_{clk}(t_s)}{F_{ck}}. \tag{7}$$

Now the design format Eq. (5) can be formulated:

$$P_{m,o} \cdot \omega_s \cdot \gamma_p \leq \frac{\alpha_s F_{ck}}{\gamma_{cl}} \tag{8}$$

For the partial safety of prestress γ_p a value of 1,2 can be chosen /9/. The partial safety factor of the long-term strength γ_{cl} depends on the coefficient of variation of F_{clk}. Tests show that a value of 1,15 ÷ 1,25 is acceptable. Hence, we arrive at the permissible initial prestress of the bonded tendon:

$$P_{m,o} \leq \frac{\alpha_s \ F_{ck}}{\omega_s \ \gamma_p \gamma_{cl}} \tag{9}$$

Evaluation of test data shows that for GFRP and AFRP-exposed to normal air - the initial prestress is in the range of

$$P_{m,o} \approx 0,5 ÷ 0,6 \ F_{ck} \tag{10}$$

For unbonded tendons the influence of the TA must be considered. Hence, the relevant factors α_{Ts} and γ_{Tl} of the TA have to derived from tests. In this case we obtain:

199

$$Pm,o \leq \frac{\alpha_{Ts} \; F_{ck}}{\omega_s \; \gamma_p \, \gamma_{Tl}} \tag{11}$$

Tests with HLV-tendons showed that because of $\alpha_s \approx \alpha_{Ts}$ and $\gamma_{cl} \approx \gamma_{Tl}$ the TA does not reduce the permissible prestress of the GFRP elements (at normal air).

REFERENCES

/1/ FIP Recommendations for Acceptance and Application of Post-tensioning Systems. Cement and Concrete Association, Wexham Springs, March 1981

/2/ Rehm, G.; Franke, L.: Kunstharzgebundene Glasfaserstäbe als Bewehrung im Betonbau. Deutscher Ausschuß für Stahlbeton, Heft 304, 1979

/3/ Gerritse, A.; Maatjes, E.; Schürhoff, H.J.: Prestressed Concrete Structures with High-Strength Fibres. IABSE Report Vol. 55, Zürich, 1987, pp.425/432

/4/ Rostásy, F.S.: New Materials for Prestressing. Proc. FIP Symposium -Israel '88, Jerusalem, September 1988

/5/ Rostásy, F.S.; Budelmann, H.: FRP-Tendons for the Post-Tensioning of Concrete Structures. ASCE Spec. Conf.: Advanced Composite Materials in Civil Engineering Structures, Las Vegas, 1991, pp. 155/156

/6/ Waaser, E.; Wolff, R.: Ein neuer Werkstoff für Spannbeton. HLV-Hochleistungs-Verbundstab aus Glasfasern. beton, No. 7, pp. 245/250, 1987

/7/ Kepp, B.: Zum Tragverhalten von Verankerungen für hochfeste Stäbe aus Glasfaserverbundwerkstoff als Bewehrung im Spannbetonbau. Diss. TU Braunschweig, 1984

/8/ Gerritse, A.: Application and Design Criteria for Aramid Fibreous Tensile Elements. Symp. Design of Composite Structures. Milano, May 1990

/9/ Eurocode No.2: Design of Concrete Structures. Part 1: General Rules and Rules for Buildings, March 1991

200

ADVANCED COMPOSITE MATERIALS IN BRIDGES AND STRUCTURES
K.W. Neale and P. Labossière, Editors; Canadian Society for Civil Engineering, 1992

Matériaux composites d'avant-garde pour ponts et charpentes
K.W. Neale et P. Labossière, éditeurs; Société canadienne de génie civil, 1992

POUTRES DE BÉTON DE POLYMÈRE PRÉCONTRAINTES PAR CÂBLES COMPOSITES VERRE-ÉPOXY

P. Hamelin
Université Claude-Bernard - Lyon 1
Villeurbanne, France

RÉSUMÉ

Nous présentons des résultats expérimentaux concernant le comportement mécanique de poutres précontraintes par câbles composites et mettant en oeuvre des bétons de résine. Le procédé technologique de mise en tension des câbles est présenté ainsi que l'analyse du comportement en flexion des poutres.

ABSTRACT

We present experimental results concerning the mechanical behaviour of beams prestressed by means of composite cables. The concrete used here is polymer concrete. We describe the process developed for the application of the tensile load on the cable as well as the analysis of the flexural behaviour of the beams.

INTRODUCTION

L'utilisation des cables composites pour appliquer des efforts de précontrainte présente un intérêt technologique certain dans la mesure où les pertes de précontrainte par fluage et relaxation sont minimisées. En effet, les modules d'élasticité des cables composites sont plus faibles que les cables métalliques. D'autre part, la stabilité physico-chimique des matrices polymères confère à ces nouveaux matériaux une bonne résistance à la corrosion. Les caractéristiques mécaniques des fibres, les notions de résistance spécifique et de rigidité spécifiques sont rapportés dans les tableaux 1 et 2 ci-dessous selon WEISS (1983).

Filament	Diam. (μ)	Densité	Traction (MPa)	Module (MPa)	Allon (%)	Fusion (°C)
Verre E	3-30	2,54	3 400	73 000	4,5	850
Verre D	3-30	2,14	2 500	55 000	4,5	
Verre R	3-30	2,48	4 400	86 000	5,2	990
Carbone HT	8	1,78	2 800	200 000	1	2500
Carbone HM	8	1,8	2 200	400 000	0,5	2500
Carbone thornel P	12	2,02	2 200	380 000		2500
Carbone GY70	8	1,95	1 800	530 000	0,38	2500
Aramide HR	12	1,45	3 100	70 000	4,0	480
Aramide HM	12	1,45	3 100	130 000	2,0	480

Tableau 1 - Caractéristiques mécaniques des fibres

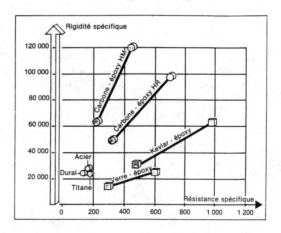

Tableau 2 - Résistances et rigidités spécifiques des composites

202

Dans le cas des ouvrages d'art, ces caractéristiques sont particulièrement intéressantes dans la mesure où elles permettent de minimiser le poids propre et par suite d'augmenter considérablement les performances de l'ouvrage.

Dans le cadre du présent article, nous présentons des résultats de recherche portant sur la caractérisation du comportement mécanique de poutres expérimentales de faible portée mettant en oeuvre des bétons de polymère précontraint par adhérence à l'aide de cables composites.

CARACTERISATION DES CABLES COMPOSITES DE PRECONTRAINTE

Nous utilisons des cables composites fabriqués par pultrusion mettant en oeuvre une matrice polymère époxyde DER 332 combinée à un durcisseur D 260 et un catalyseur DY 070. Les renforts filamentaires utilisés sont les suivants :

```
52    R0     5122   2400 tex      verre  E
4     P9            1600 tex      verre  R
2     P9            2450 tex      verre  R
4     carbone HTA 7w    3000
```

Principales caractéristiques mécaniques des cables :

Volume de fibres.. 65%
Densité... 2.1
Module d'élasticité longitudinal............................. 53500 Mpa
Diamètre... 10,5 mm
Allongement maximum.. 2.1%

Le principe de pultrusion est décrit par la figure 1 ci-dessous et les principaux paramètres influençant le procédé de transformation sont abordés par GEIER M. (1985). Dans notre cas, la température moyenne de la tête de pultrusion est de 160° C et la vitesse d'étirement de 750 mm/mn.

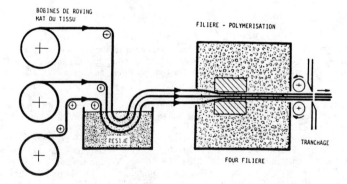

Figure 3 - Schématisation du procédé de pultrusion

La loi de comportement de ces câbles est quasi linéaire jusqu'à rupture et le mode d'endommagement ainsi que le comportement à la fatigue et au fluage a été étudié par ZERMENO (1988) et BOUFERA A. & HAMELIN P. (1992).

Nous retenons que les contraintes à rupture sont comprises entre 1100 et 1300 MPa, et vis-à-vis de critères de durabilité, le coefficient de pondération est de 0,6 pour des tenues à la fatigue supérieures à 10^8 cycles.

Pour améliorer l'adhérence avec le béton, chaque cable est recouvert par des mèches de fibres de verre imprégnées de résine et disposées avec un pas hélicoïdal le long du cable.

FORMULATION DU BETON DE POLYMERE

Des études et recherches antérieures conduites au laboratoire par D. PRIN (1974) et D. PRIN & P. HAMELIN (1972) ont permis de formuler des bétons de polymère à forte compacité mettant en oeuvre des matrices polyester, epoxydes et vinylester.

Pour la présente application, nous avons choisi une résine vinylester DERAKANE 411-45 pour ses propriétés intrinsèques et notamment ses intéressantes facultés de mouillage des charges minérales et ses facilités de transformation (thermodurcissement par polymérisation classique : catalyseur + accélérateur).

Nous utilisons des granulats de silice définis par le tableau ci-dessous :

Fillers S2   :   d ≤ 100 µm
F3   :   0,1 < d < 0,8 mm
G2   :   0,5 < d < 1,5 mm
G5   :   1,5 < d < 4 mm
G6   :   2,5 < d < 6 mm
G7   :   5   < d < 10 mm

A partir d'une étude granulométrique, visant à augmenter la compacité du matériau et à minimiser le pourcentage de liant (pour des raisons économiques) nous retenons la formulation suivante : (pourcentage en poids).

S2   :   16,90%
F3   :   12,02%
G2   :   6,14%
G5   :   7,04%
G6   :   10,32%
G7   :   36,60%
Résine :   12,00%

La polymérisation de la matrice est obtenue par l'ajout de catalyseur, 2% du poids de résine, 0,5% pour l'accélérateur et 0,5% pour l'ajout anti-retrait. Dans ces conditions, la durée de polymérisation à température ambiante (20°C) est de 30 mm.

L'évaluation des caractéristiques mécaniques du béton de polymère est réalisée sur des éprouvettes cylindriques 16 x 32 cm instrumentées de capteurs ohmiques de déformation.

Les modules d'élasticité sont compris entre 23000 et 25000 MPa, les coefficients de Poisson entre 0,21 et 0,23. Les résistances à la compression instantanées varient entre 72 et 80 MPa. La loi de comportement est quasi linéaire jusqu'à 80% de la charge de rupture. L'allongement à la limite de linéarité est compris entre 3000 et 4000 µm/m en compression et 700 et 1000 µm/m en traction.

POUTRES EXPERIMENTALES

Après une étude préalable conduite par J.C. BAUD & P. FRALON (1988), dans le cas de poutrelles préfabriquées de 4 m de long, précontraintes par des cables rectilignes sur toute la longueur de la poutre, soumises à des charges d'exploitaion de 300 kg/m2, nous retenons le prédimensionnement suivant :

Largeur	:	a = 0,15 m
Hauteur	:	b = 0,20 m
Effort de précontrainte	:	P = 0,09 MN
Nombre de cables	:	n = 2
Excentricité des cables	:	e = 0,05 m.

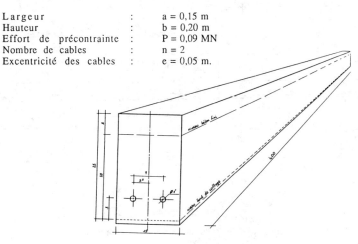

Figure 2 - Plan de coffrage de la poutre.

Vis-à-vis de l'effort tranchant, nous retenons le plan de ferraillage ci-dessous calculé suivant les règles de BAEL 80 (Figure 3).

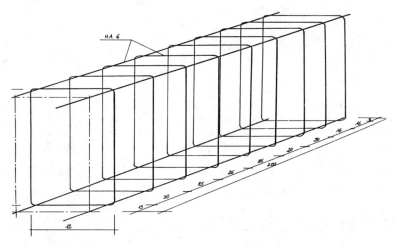

Figure 3 - Armatures d'effort tranchant.

205

Pour appliquer les efforts de tension sur les cables et de compression sur la section, nous réalisons un banc de précontraitne décrit par la figure 4 ci-dessous.

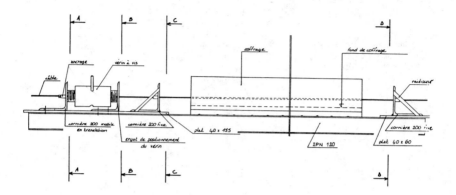

Figure 4 - Banc de mise en précontrainte

Le suivi de la mise en tension sur les cables est assuré par la mesure des déformations (capteurs ohmiques). Les enregistrements portent sur l'évaluation des pertes instantanées après polymérisation du béton et sciage des cables et des pertes secondaires durant 9 jours après la mise en précontrainte (Figures 5 et 6).

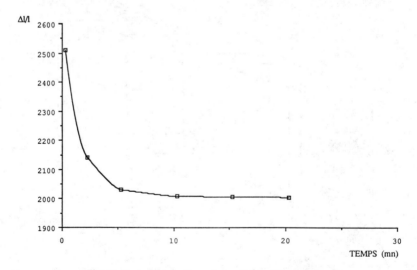

Figure 5 - Pertes de précontraintes instantanées.

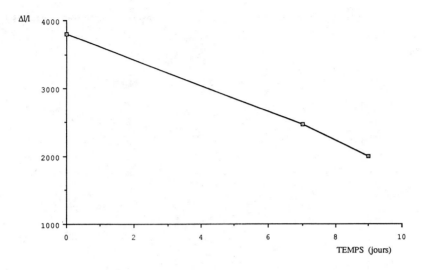

Figure 6 - Pertes de précontraintes différées.

Nous remarquons que les pertes les plus importantes sont obtenues lors du sciage des cables : la charge de précontrainte est égale à 80% de la tension appliquée aux cables. La prise en compte des pertes est impérative pour appliquer un effort de précontrainte majoré initialement de 20%.

COMPORTEMENT MECANIQUE DES POUTRES DE BETON POLYMERE PRECONTRAINTE PAR CABLE COMPOSITE

Les poutres sont sollicitées en flexion circulaire suivant le croquis ci-dessous (Figure 7).

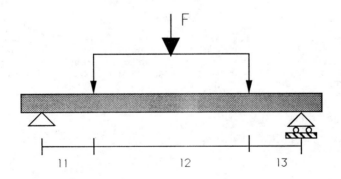

Figure 7 - Principe de chargement de la poutre.

207

L'évolution de la déformée en fonction de la charge est représenté par les courbes de la figure 8.

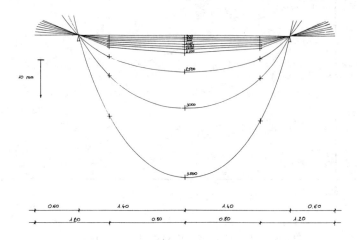

Figure 8 - Evolution des flèches en fonction de la charge

Il est intéressant de remarquer qu'au delà de la charge de 2100 daN, la fissuration intervient brutalement en zone tendue. Ceci ce traduit par une perte importante de rigidité. La contrainte en traction du béton de résine est de 11 MPa et la contrainte maximum supporté par le béton en zone comprimée est de 55 MPa.
La force de rupture pour un cable est de 8500 daN. Ces constats confirment la bon dimensionnement de la poutre. Le seul point qui n'est pas satisfaisant est le ferraillage d'effort tranchant qui semble créer des points de fragilité dans le béton.

CONCLUSION

Le principe d'une poutre composite combinant béton de résine et précontrainte par cable verre-résine adhérent est particulièrement intéressant pour des applications exceptionnelles (rapidité de réparation, tenue à la corrosion). L'analyse expérimentale a montré que ces structures présentaient une grande réserve de déformation vis-à-vis de la charge ultime. En conséquence, l'énergie correspondante est importante. La limite de charge de service est, dans le cas actuel toujours dépendante des résistances à rupture en traction et cisaillement du béton et des travaux de recherches sont engagés à ce jour pour améliorer le comportement en traction par l'ajout de fibres et pour optimiser la section géométrique de la poutre.

REFERENCES BIBLIOGRAPHIQUES

WEISS J., BORD C. (1983) - Les matériaux composites. Editions de l'Usine Nouvelle. Paris 1983, Vol. I - 640 p.

GEIER M., DUEDAL D. (1985) - Guide pratique des matériaux composites. Paris. Technique et documentation. Lavoisier. 349 p.

ZERMENO DE LEON (1988) - Contribution à l'étude du comportement mécanique de cables compsoites. Application à la mise en précontrainte d'ouvrage du Génie Civil. Thèse de Doctorat. Institut National des Sciences Appliquées de Lyon. Mai 1998.

A. BOUFERA, P. HAMELIN (1992) - Comportement à la fatigue de composites unidirectionels. Actes du colloque : "Textiles composites in building construction" 23-25 Juin 1992. Editions Pluralis, St. Etienne.

D. PRIN (1974) - Béton de résine polyester. Application au domine du Génie Civil. Thèse de Docteur Ingénieur. Institut National des Sciences Appliquées de Lyon. 1974.

J.C. BAUD, FRALON P. (1988) - Précontrainte par cables composites. Projet de fin d'études. Institut National des Sciences Appliquées de Lyon. 1988.

ADVANCED COMPOSITE MATERIALS IN BRIDGES AND STRUCTURES
K.W. Neale and P. Labossière, Editors; Canadian Society for Civil Engineering, 1992

Matériaux composites d'avant-garde pour ponts et charpentes
K.W. Neale et P. Labossière, éditeurs; Société canadienne de génie civil, 1992

STRUCTURAL BEHAVIOUR OF CONCRETE BEAMS PRESTRESSED WITH GLASS FIBRE TENDONS

L. Taerwe
University of Ghent
Ghent, Belgium

H.-J. Miesseler
SICOM GmbH
Cologne, Germany

ABSTRACT

After a brief review of the general characteristics of glass fibre prestressing bars and optical fibre sensors, the results of loading tests on concrete beams prestressed with glass fibre tendons are discussed. It follows that the structural behaviour of these members can well be predicted by making use of the usual assumptions that apply for steel tendons, and that sufficient flexural ductility at ultimate can be provided.

RÉSUMÉ

Après un bref aperçu des caractéristiques générales des barres de précontrainte en fibres de verre, l'article présente les résultats d'essais de mise en charge effectués sur des poutres en béton, précontraintes à l'aide de câbles de ce type. Les auteurs démontrent que les méthodes courantes, établies pour les câbles en acier, évaluent bien le comportement des poutres étudiées. Une ductilité suffisante en flexion peut être assurée en phase ultime.

INTRODUCTION

A few years ago, composite prestressing bars containing glass fibres have become available for practical use. These bars are not sensitive to the usual types of corrosion that affect the durability of prestressing steel. In this paper attention is paid to the prestressing system developed in Germany (Wolff, 1987 ; Wolff and Miesseler, 1989 ; Franke and Wolff, 1988) that already found application in a few road bridges and other structures (Taerwe, Lambotte, Miesseler, 1992). An important feature of the glass fibre bars is that they allow integration of optical sensors. In this way it is possible to realize permanent monitoring of the integrity of prestressed concrete structures.

When applying new materials for the reinforcement of concrete, questions arise about the influence on the structural behaviour of concrete members as compared to conventional steel reinforcement. Hence the necessity for large scale tests on concrete members prestressed with glass fibre tendons. In the sequel, this aspect is addressed by making use of loading tests, performed in the Magnel Laboratory of Ghent University in the framework of the BRITE-program "Monitoring of prestressing force by integrated sensors". "BRITE" stands for "Basic Research in Industrial Technologies for Europe" and is sponsored by the Commission of the European Communities. Different German research institutes were also involved in the tests, more particularly for the application of different non-destructive measuring techniques. The main aim of the research program was to assess the reliability of these techniques and to compare the results with conventional deformation measurements. At the same time, these tests provide useful information about the structural behaviour of the concrete members. In the first part of the program, 3 beams with a span of 2 m were loaded up to failure. These beams will be termed "short beams". In this case the sensor-techniques could be tested for short concrete members. In the second stage, a "long beam" with a span of 20 m was tested. The dimensions approach those of a real prestressed girder and thus scale effects are eliminated to a large extent.

In the next two sections, a survey of the material characteristics and the main features of the optical sensors is given. Subsequently, the test program and the structural behaviour will be discussed.

GLASS FIBRE BARS

The so-called "Polystal" bars consist of 68 % glass fibres (by volume) and 32 % resin. The glass fibre content by weight is about 80 %. A cross section of the composite bars, having a diameter of 7.5 mm consists of some 60,000 glass fibres embedded in a modified unsaturated polyester resin matrix. A polyamide coating protects the bar against mechanical and chemical attack. The bars or tendons are placed in the usual steel sheet ducts which are grouted with a resin having appropriate properties for this purpose.

The stress-strain curve of a Polystal bar is perfectly linear until the ultimate stress is reached whereby sudden brittle failure takes place. The tensile strength (about 1500-1600 MPa) is comparable to that of usual prestressing steel. The ultimate strain is only 3.3 % which is significantly lower than for steel. However, the loading tests discussed later in the paper, show that sufficient strain capacity is available in order to provide the required flexural ductility. Long-term sustained loading results in a strength loss of 30 % i.e. the long-term strength is 70 % of the short-term strength.

OPTICAL SENSORS

Optical fibres have already been in use for almost a decade in the telecommunication sector as signal transmitters. The light transmitted by an optical fibre is subject to losses due to absorption and scattering caused by impurities present in the glass. For the optical fibres, light attenuation has been reduced to the lowest possible value. However, when the optical fibres have to be applied as strain sensor, light attenuation will just be used as test signal and a certain dependency between this attenuation and mechanical changes in the sensor should exist. Hence the problem is to select the most appropriate optical fibre type for this purpose. This appeared to be a so-called gradient-index fibre which has a gradually decreasing index of refraction from the centre towards the outer surface. In order to obtain a higher attenuation, and hence a more sensitive signal, the optical sensor is provided with a fine spiral wire. When the sensor is submitted to tension, the spiral wire exerts radial compression on the sensor, which causes microbending and results in increased attenuation.

The attenuation of the light signal is defined as

$$A = -10 \log (P_i/P_o)$$

where A stands for the attenuation and P_i and P_0 respectively denote the input and output power. Attenuation is measured in decibels (dB) per unit length, typically dB/km. An almost linear relationship is found between the attenuation (in dB) and the applied strain which allows strain evaluation on the basis of attenuation measurements.

Further details and practical applications of this technique are discussed in (König, Oetes, Giegerich and Miesseler, 1987 ; Nanni, Yang, Pan, Wan and Michael, 1991).

TESTS ON SHORT BEAMS

General characteristics of beams and test set-up

The dimensions of the beams, the arrangement of the reinforcement and the test set-up are indicated in fig. 1. The two-point loads were applied by means of hydraulic actuators. Two hinging supports were provided, one of which was fixed while the other one was free to roll. Prior to prestressing, the beams were placed on their final supports in the test set-up. Prestressing was realized by means of two separate glass fibre bars. The total prestressing force equals 66 kN which corresponds to an initial stress σ_{po} in the composite bar equal to 750 MPa. Prestressing was applied stepwise and at the same time the point loads were gradually increased up to F = 20 kN. This load was held constant until the start of the loading test. Ages of prestressing and testing are mentioned in table 1. Grouting of beams 1 and 3 took place immediately after prestressing. Beam 2 was not grouted.

TABLE 1 - Characteristics of short beams

Beam no.	Age at prestressing (days)	Age at loading test (days)	Cracking load F_r, kN	Ultimate load F_u, kN
1	21	28	105	307
2	28	28	110	327
3	83	111	130	324

The concrete used to cast the beams had a W/C-ratio of 0.50 and the fresh concrete had a slump of 40 mm and a value of 1.54 in the flow test. Compressive strength of concrete cylinders (diameter 150 mm, height 300 mm) was 42 MPa on the mean at the age of the loading test. Flexural tensile strength of concrete prisms with dimensions 150 x 150 x 600 mm was 5.1 MPa. More details on material properties may be found in (Taerwe, Lambotte and Miesseler, 1992). At 7 days age the grouting resin used for beam 1 showed a flexural tensile strength of 12.8 MPa on prisms 40 x 40 x 160 mm and a compressive strength of 38.2 N/mm^2 (test on two halves resulting from bending test). The limit of elasticity of the reinforcing bars equals 561 MPa.

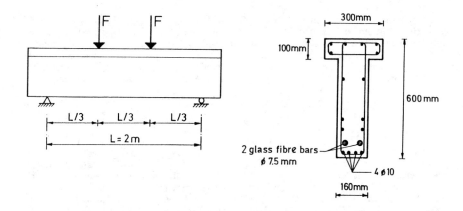

Fig. 1 - Test set-up and cross-section of short beams

Measurements

Deflections were measured by means of dial gauges and LVDT's. Prior to casting of the beam, strain gauges were applied to the reinforcing bars and the two glass fibre bars. Measurements were taken by means of an automatic data acquisition system. Deformations at the concrete surface were measured by means of mechanical deformeters. During the tests, cracks in the concrete were indicated at the side faces of the beams and crack widths were measured by means of a small microscope. Longitudinal optical sensors were provided in the prestressing bars, at different locations in the beams and at the beams' surface.

Test results

The cracking loads F_r, given in table 1, correspond to the appearance of the first crack observable by the naked eye. During the loading test, the load was increased stepwise and time was taken for making the different measurements and indicating the cracks. For beam 3 however, the time spent at each level was only a few minutes because only the automatic measurements were executed. Hence, only an approximate value of F_r is indicated in table 1.

Failure was caused by rupture of the glass fibre bars. The ultimate loads F_u given in table 1 are fairly comparable, also for beam 2 with the unbonded tendons. It has to be noted that the beams act like tied arches and that about 60 % of the beam capacity is derived from the reinforcing steel (see "Discussion"). For beam 1 the three main flexural cracks occur under the two point loads and in between these sections. For beam 2, the two main flexural cracks occur under the point loads. Failure of beam 1 took place in between the point loads, where the tensile strain capacity of the tendons was reached. For beam 2, the tendons were stressed more uniformly over their entire length and failure occured under one of the point loads. As regards beam 3, it has to be noted that the loading test took place at an age of 111 days, instead of 28 days for the two other short beams (see table 1).

The load-deflection curve of beam 1 is shown in Fig. 2. The first descending branch is due to intentional unloading of the beam. The second descending part corresponds to rupture of one of the glass fibre bars. Strain measurements for beam 1 are shown in Fig. 3. The transition from the uncracked to the cracked state is clearly visible in the diagrams. Once the ordinary reinforcement starts yielding, it can be seen that the strain increase in the glass fibre tendons occurs at a faster rate than before, which is also reflected in the load-deflection curve (Fig. 2).

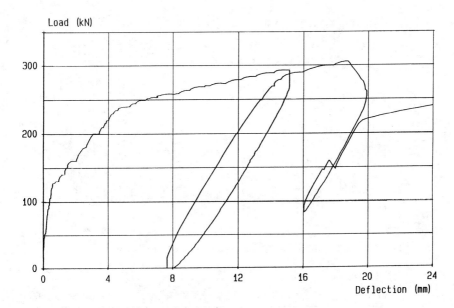

Fig. 2 - Load-deflection curve of beam 1

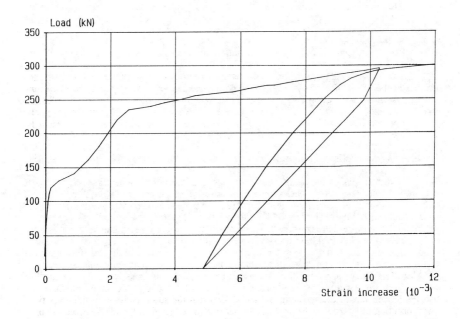

Fig. 3 - Mean strain increase in a glass fibre reinforcing bar (beam 1)

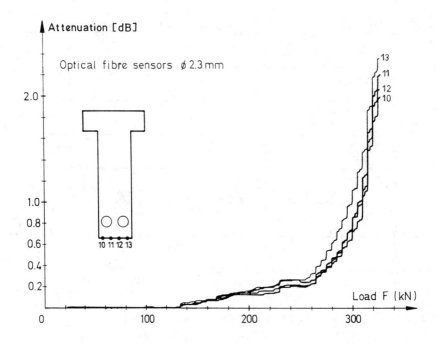

Fig. 4 - Attenuation of signals transmitted through optical sensors (beam no. 3)

Figure 4 shows the results of measurements performed with optical sensors located in notches at the lower face of beam 3. The experimental curves are completely similar to those obtained with the conventional deformation measurement techniques.

TEST ON LONG BEAM

General characteristics of the beam and test set-up

The dimensions of the beam, the arrangement of the reinforcement and the tendon lay-out are indicated in Fig. 5. The beam was prestressed at an age of 14 days by means of a tendon consisting of 19 glass fibre bars (7.5 mm in diameter) with parabolic profile. Immediately after the application of the full prestressing force, the tendon was grouted. The magnitude of the prestressing force P_0 equals 660 kN, which corresponds to an initial stress $\sigma_{po} = 787$ MPa. This value is obtained by multiplying the tensile strength first by a factor 0.7 to take into account the long-term strength reduction and secondly by the usual safety factor of 0.7. At mid span, the initial compressive stresses in the concrete due to prestressing and dead weight were limited to 2.42 MPa at the upper fibre and 2.03 MPa at the lower fibre. These stresses are fairly low because in this case the design was made in such a way that the tendon should certainly fail.

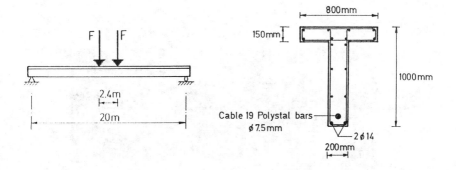

Fig. 5 - Test set-up and dimensions of long beam

After prestressing, the beam was placed on its final supports with a span of 20 m. The beam was loaded at two points located 1.2 m from the centre (Fig. 5). The load was applied by means of hydraulic actuators and due to their limited stroke, special arrangements were necessary with respect to the large deflections at ultimate.

The concrete used to cast the beam had a W/C-ratio of 0.50 and the fresh concrete showed a slump of 190 mm and a value of 2.40 in the flow test. Mechanical properties of the hardened concrete were comparable to those given for the short beams. The limit of elasticity of the reinforcing bars was 556 MPa.

Testing schedule

The same type of deformation and deflection measurements were executed as outlined previously. The testing schedule was as follows :
- Gradual increase of the load up to F = 35 kN which is slightly higher than the cracking load of 33 kN.
- Application of 28000 load cycles between F_{max} = 35 kN and F_{min} = 25 kN at a mean frequency of 0.45 Hz.
- Unloading and stepwise increase of the loads. At F = 55 kN, yielding of reinforcing steel occured and at F = 70 kN the tendon reached its long-term strength equal to $0.7 \, f_{pt}$.
- Failure of the beam at F = 137 kN.

Test results

Fig. 6 shows the beam after failure. Figure 7 gives the evolution of the mean strain increase in the glass-fibre bars during the final loading stage up to failure. The ultimate deflection amounted to 730 mm which is about 3.5 % of the span length.

Although the glass fibre bars as such show a brittle behaviour, the tests indicated that failure of concrete members prestressed with these bars is accompanied by extensive deformations, similarly as for members prestressed with steel wires or strands.

217

Fig. 6 - Long beam after failure

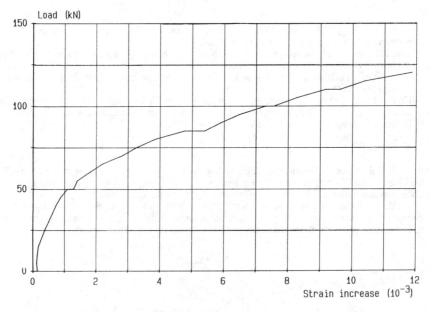

Fig. 7 - Mean strain increase in the glass fibre prestressing bars (long beam)

DISCUSSION

Contribution of reinforcing steel

Judgement of the structural behaviour must also take into account the presence of ordinary reinforcing steel. In table 2, some quantities characterizing the structural behaviour of the tested beams are given :
- the cross-section area of the ordinary reinforcing steel (A_s) and the prestressing bars (A_p).
- the products AE which are a measure of the relative contribution of both reinforcing types to the tensile resultant as long as the steel is not yielding.
- the products $A_s f_y$ en $A_p f_{pt}$ which are a measure for the contribution of both reinforcement types to the tensile resultant at ultimate.

It follows that the reinforcing steel contributes significantly to the resisting moment but that the relative contribution of the glass fibre bars increases considerably towards the failure stage.

Design procedure

As concerns the design method, the usual approach can be applied on condition that the appropriate initial stress for the tendons is introduced. This was confirmed by the good agreement between calculated and observed structural characteristics and deformations.

TABLE 2 - Some mechanical characteristics of the beams

	Short beams ($\ell = 2$ m)	Long beam ($\ell = 20$ m)
Reinforcement section A_s , mm^2 A_p , mm^2	314 88	308 839
Product AE $A_s E_s$, kN $A_p E_p$, kN	62800 4500	61600 42800
Tensile forces at ultimate $A_s f_y$, kN $A_p f_{pt}$, kN	176 134	171 1347

Cracking load

As mentioned previously for the long beam, the initial compressive stress in the concrete at the lower fibre of the section at mid-span equals 2.03 MPa. Assuming a loss of prestress of 1% at the age of 28 days, this concrete stress is slightly reduced to 1.93 MPa. Assuming a modulus of rupture of 4.28 MPa the cracking load can be calculated as 31.3 kN. This value is in good agreement with the observed cracking load of 33 kN.

Ultimate load

The ultimate moment capacity of the long beam is calculated assuming a parabolic stress-strain curve for the concrete with top at $e_c = 2‰$ and peak stress equal to $f'_c = 43.3$ MPa. The ultimate stress in the glass fibre bars is $f_{ps} = f_{pt} = 1606$ MPa. From strain compatibility with $e_{cu} = 1.65 ‰$ and $\Delta e_p = 16.21 ‰$ it follows that the depth of the compression zone at ultimate equals 84.2 mm. The equilibrium conditions further yield $M_u = 1094$ kNm. As the moment due to dead weight equals $M_g = 361.6$ kNm, it follows that

$F_{u, calc} = 124$ kN. This value has to be compared with $F_{u, exp} = 137$ kN. The difference between calculated and experimental values must partly be attributed to the fact that the tensile strength of the bars in the tendon is higher than the value found in a tensile test on a single bar. The first reason for this increase is the fact that the bars are embedded in the resin grout and thus better protected against interlaminar shear. The second influencing factor is that in a tensile test on a single bar, there still can be a detrimental influence of the anchorages, while for the tendon in the central zone of the beam this influence does not exist.

CONCLUSIONS

- Two short concrete beams with a span of 2 m and one long beam with a span of 20 m were tested up to failure in the Magnel Laboratory of the University of Ghent (Belgium) in the framework of a BRITE research program. The structural behaviour of these elements with realistic dimensions proved to be completely satisfactory and in very good agreement with predicted behaviour.
- Glass fibre bars may offer an interesting alternative to the classical prestressing steel tendons. The optical sensor techniques could turn out to be extremely useful to monitor long-term behaviour both of new and older structures.
- It has to be realized that the whole system is still in an experimental stage and that different aspects of it need to be the subject of more detailed investigations. Actually research is going on to increase the knowledge on material characteristics, interaction of non-metallic reinforcement and surrounding concrete and structural behavior of concrete members. Also flexural ductility and long-term behaviour require further attention.

REFERENCES

FRANKE L., WOLFF R. (1988). Glass fibre tendons for prestressed concrete bridges. 13th IABSE Congress, Helsinki, Congress Report, 51-56.

KOENIG G., OETES A., GIEGERICH G., MIESSELER H.J. (1987). Monitoring of the structural behaviour of bridge Uhlenbergstrasse in Düsseldorf. IABSE 1987 Bergamo Colloquium, "Monitoring of large structures and assessment of their safety", IABSE Reports Vol. 56, 325-337.

NANNI A., YANG C., PAN K., WANG J.-S., MICHAEL R. (1991). Fibre-optic sensors for concrete stress/strain measurement. ACI Materials Journal, May-June issue, 257-264.

TAERWE L., LAMBOTTE H., MIESSELER H.-J. (1992). Loading tests on concrete beams prestressed with glass fibre tendons. Journal of the Prestressed Concrete Institute, Vol. 36, No. 4.

WOLFF R. (1987). Heavy duty composite material for prestressing of concrete structures. IABSE Paris-Versailles Symposium, IABSE Reports Vol. 55, 419-424.

WOLFF R., MIESSELER H.J. (1989). New Materials for prestressing and monitoring heavy structures. Concrete International, Vol. 11, No. 9, 86-89.

ADVANCED COMPOSITE MATERIALS IN BRIDGES AND STRUCTURES
K.W. Neale and P. Labossière, Editors; Canadian Society for Civil Engineering, 1992

Matériaux composites d'avant-garde pour ponts et charpentes
K.W. Neale et P. Labossière, éditeurs; Société canadienne de génie civil, 1992

ARAMID TENDONS IN PRETENSIONED
CONCRETE APPLICATIONS

K.S. McKay and **M.-A. Erki**
Royal Military College of Canada
Kingston, Ontario, Canada

ABSTRACT

The durability of reinforced concrete structures has become an increasing concern as our infrastructure ages. Of particular concern is the deterioration of steel reinforcements when used in concrete structures exposed to severe corrosive environments. This paper investigates the feasibility of using non corroding aramid fibre-reinforced plastic (AFRP) tendons as a substitute for steel strand in pretensioned concrete applications. Three AFRP pretensioned beams, 150 mm x 300 mm x 2100 mm, were tested under both static and cyclic loading. Test results indicate that load capacities of the beams were not affected by the cyclic loading. Ultimate strengths were generally greater than predicted, primarily as a result of the ability of the AFRP rods to develop greater tensile stresses than expected.

RÉSUMÉ

La durabilité des structures de béton armé pose de plus en plus de problèmes avec le vieillissement des infrastructures. La détérioration des armatures en acier dans des structures exposées à des milieux corrosifs est particulièrement inquiétante. Cet article étudie la possibilité d'utiliser des tendons non corrosifs en plastiques renforcés de fibres d'aramide (AFRP) comme substitut aux barres d'acier dans le béton. Trois poutres en béton précontraint ont été testées sous des chargement statiques et cycliques. Les résultats des tests indiquent que la résistance des poutres n'a pas été affectée par le chargement cyclique. Les résistances ultimes ont été généralement plus grandes que prévu, principalement à cause de la résistance supérieure des barres de AFRP.

INTRODUCTION

In recent years, there has been increasing concern with the durability of prestressed concrete structures, because of corrosion of the prestressing steel tendons, especially in corrosive environments such as parking garages and bridge decks. In these chloride rich environments, the loss of steel to corrosion or corrosion embrittlement is accelerated. The last decade has seen increasing interest in the use of advanced composite materials (ACM) as a replacement for steel reinforcements. ACM consist of strong fibres embedded in a resin matrix. ACM have several key properties that make them particularly suitable for prestressed concrete applications. These are high strengths, which are comparable or greater than that of steel, low tensile modulus of elasticity, which result in lower concrete prestress losses due to shrinkage and relaxation, and resistance to corrosion.

This paper reports the results of a research program which investigated the potential of aramid fibre reinforced plastic (AFRP) tendons for pretensioned concrete structures. The relaxation properties, anchorage bond, and static and fatigue strengths of the beams under partially prestressed conditions were investigated.

General

The ACM used in this study is manufactured by TEIJIN Limited of Japan. The ACM consists of continuous aramid fibre, trade name TECHNORA, and a vinylester resin matrix. The materials are combined in a 2 to 1 ratio by volume. The rods used in this research were 6 mm diameter and had been modified by the manufacturer by winding a smaller bundle of fibres around the rod in a helical fashion and fixing this bundle in place with resin (Fig. 1). The published mechanical properties are shown in Table 1.

Previous fatigue testing of the AFRP rods (Kakihara et al, 1990) indicated fatigue strengths comparable to steel strand at average service loads. A detailed comparison is difficult due to the limited number of tests with the AFRP rods; however, the rods do appear to be more sensitive to the minimum cycling stress with the fatigue life dropping off sharply at minimum stresses of 1400 MPa.

When conventional strand is initially stressed at less than 55% of yield, the steel shows no relaxation. The testing done to date on the AFRP rods does not show this proportional limit (Kobayashi et al, 1988). The AFRP rods have been reported to show a relatively linear relaxation with time at initial stresses ranging from 330 MPa to 1380 MPa. Relaxation losses at seven days were about 12% to 7% respectively. Comparable losses for low relaxation steel strand would be 0% to 0.5%. In a modified tensioning method, the rods are initially stressed to 1380 MPa and then fixed at a lower stress. It was found that if the rod was fixed at less than 870 MPa, significant reductions in relaxation were realized. Although no design formulas are presented, Kobayashi estimated a 20% relaxation loss at 30 years, with an initial stress of about 1100 MPa.

EXPERIMENTAL PROGRAM

Three pretensioned beams were fabricated and tested to confirm the performance of the AFRP rods subjected to static and cyclic loading. Beam dimensions are shown in Fig. 2. The beam fabrication details are outlined in Table 2. During fabrication, a load cell was used to provide an independent load monitor during jacking. The data from this load cell was also used to monitor the relaxation in the system prior to release.

The jacking force was limited to 80% of the guaranteed tensile strength of the AFRP rods, as for normal steel strand. Stresses were transferred to the concrete through a sudden release of tension in the rods. Electrical strain gauges were attached to the surface of the beam using an epoxy base. Following release, several readings were taken from each gauge. The strain readings were used to determine the transfer of the prestress into the concrete and to estimate the transfer lengths.

All beams were loaded in four point bending using a MTS Servo Hydraulic Control Test System with a 250 kN load cell. Data was collected using a Digital PDP11 computer. The midspan deflection was monitored for each test using two linear variable displacement transformers (LVDT's) attached to the beam. The load and ram stroke were monitored automatically by the MTS system. Although not intended for this purpose, the strain gauges which were attached during fabrication were left in place, and the concrete strains at several locations were monitored during testing. LVDT's were also attached to the free ends of the AFRP rods of specimen B1 to check for rod slip during loading.

Specimen B1 was loaded in two stages. Stage 1 loaded the beam past cracking to near ultimate before the load was released. Stage 2 loaded the beam to failure. The loading was applied at a constant displacement rate of approximately 0.1 mm/sec.

Specimen B2 was initially subjected to two static load cycles, from 0 to 60 kN, to ensure the beam was cracked. The load deflection curves were recorded, and the sinusoidal loading was begun at a speed of 4 Hz. The maximum and minimum loads were set at 53 kN and 43 kN respectively. These values were chosen in order to simulate partially prestressed conditions in the beam. The lower load is just below the theoretical cracking load, and the upper load induces a theoretical stress change in the rod of 200 MPa, with a maximum stress of about 80% of the guaranteed strength. These would be considered severe conditions for steel prestressing strand. The loading was stopped at 103500, 604000 and 1600500 cycles to obtain the new load deflection curve. It should be noted that the loading system was experiencing some problems at this time, and the system came to a standstill for up to 18 hours, which allowed some elastic recovery to take place. The beam was loaded to failure after 1.96 million cycles.

Specimen B3 was subjected to the same loading conditions as B2; however, the cycling was not intentionally stopped before 2.1 million cycles in order to minimize any elastic recovery behaviour. Load deflection curves were obtained for the initial static cycles and for the final loading to failure. All cyclic testing was conducted using load control to ensure that any creep in the moduli of the materials was not translated into a reduction in stress. The maximum and minimum strokes of the hydraulic ram were recorded at short regular intervals during the cyclic loading.

RESULTS AND DISCUSSION

Figure 3 show the strain gauge readings taken on the surface of beam B3 following release of the prestress force. The transfer length appears to be in the order of 150 mm to 300 mm. Previous measurements (Noritake et al, 1990) indicated that the transfer length for the 6 mm rod were about 250 to 300 mm. Using transfer length equations for steel strand provided in the Canadian Standards Association CAN3 A23.3 (1984) and Ontario Highway Bridge Design Code (OHBDC 1983), the predicted lengths could vary from 165 mm to 330 mm.

Figure 4 shows the measured stress losses for the three beams as a percentage of the original fixing stress. The data follows a linear stress-time relationship, similar to steel strand. The test results from Kobayashi (1988) are also plotted. A comparison of the relaxation curves show reasonable agreement, although the values from this program are slightly lower. This can be attributed to the fabrication procedure which involved fastening both AFRP rods to a steel plate which was tied to a short length of steel strand. Since the steel strand relaxes at a slower rate, the overall system relaxation is slightly reduced.

A linear regression analysis of the data was performed which ignored the small differences in fixing stresses. The analysis resulted in Equation 1.

223

$$\frac{f_p}{f_{p\,i}} = 1.009 - \frac{logt}{65.19}$$

$$where:\ t = time\ (mins)$$

$$f_{p\,i} = fixing\ stress$$

(1)

The correlation was approximately 0.92. For the initial stresses used here, the expected relaxation of the rods in 50 years would be about 10%. The more elaborate testing conducted by Kobayashi would predict relaxation values closer to 12%, over this time period. The expected stress loss for low relaxation steel strand under similar conditions would be less than 4%.

The last few load cell readings taken for B1 were not included in the analysis. The readings seemed excessively low compared to the rest of the data, and it was suspected that the stressing bed had been jarred prior to the data being recorded, which possibly shifted the rods. The strains in the concrete at release show reasonable agreement with the theoretical strains so the low readings do not appear to result from an instrumentation problem.

The failure mode for all beams was a tensile failure in the AFRP rods at a midspan crack. The internal forces at failure were calculated using rectangular stress block factors for the concrete. These calculated stresses are summarized in Table 3. The ultimate factored moment for the beams, calculated from clause 9-11.1.1 of the OHBDC (1983), was 20.4 kN·m. It is apparent that there is considerable reserve capacity in the rods, beyond the manufacturers guaranteed strength of 1767 MPa.

At ultimate load, the increase in tensile stress in the rod at a crack location is about 1100 MPa to 1500 MPa. A previous study (McKay, 1992) indicated that the ultimate strength of the rods is based on a shear failure condition in the grouted anchorages during tensioning. It appears that the ability of the rod to sustain these larger tensile stresses is likely due to the reduction in bond shear at the crack location, as compared to the stress conditions which exist in the anchors.

The theoretical cracking moment for the three beams was calculated to be 17.5 kN·m. Experimental cracking moments were estimated as 17.2, 17.2 and 18.1 kN·m for B1, B2 and B3 (Fig. 5), respectively. The close agreement with the theoretical value indicates that the analysis procedures used for conventionally pretensioned concrete may be equally applicable to the AFRP pretensioned members.

In order to provide a basic comparison between steel strand development length requirements and the AFRP rod performance in the beams tested herein, the end sections of the beams were analyzed at ultimate. Figure 6 shows the theoretical forces in the beams over the uncracked length at the supports. If a transfer length of 150 mm is assumed for the AFRP rods, the bond stresses generated are in line with those allowed for steel strand.

Specimens B2 and B3 showed no reduction in strength following two million cycles of sinusoidal loading. Material fatigue properties are generally highly variable. Therefore, making any firm conclusions based on two tests would be unreasonable; however, the results do tend to indicate that the fatigue strength of the rods in service is at least as good as steel strand.

As was noted earlier, technical problems with the loading system caused a number of halts in the testing which allowed some elastic recovery in beams B2 and B3. Despite the equipment problems, the cumulative damage effect on the rods should be about the same as an uninterrupted test. There may have been some elastic recovery in the rods which may have reduced the contribution of any creep rupture effects to the overall damage in the rods; however, given the short time frame of the loading, the extra damage contribution is considered to be minimal.

The increase in deflection for both beams during the cycling was in the order of 10% to 20% of the original deflection, with most of this increase occurring within the first 100,000 to 200,000 cycles. In a normally pretensioned beam subjected to fatigue loading, the increase in deflection is due primarily to creep in the concrete and a reduction in tension stiffening. Balaguru (1981) has proposed equations to predict the effect of these two factors on the deflection behaviour. Using these equations, the predicted loss in stiffness for the beams would be about 37%. If the contribution of the time dependent creep in the concrete is neglected, the stiffness loss would still be about 18%. These calculations disregard any creep in the reinforcing and any reduction in tension stiffening. Based on these estimates, there appears to be little, if any, contribution to the beam deflection as a result of any potential loss of stiffness of the AFRP rods resulting from the cyclic loading. It should be noted that following the initial static loading for these beams, B2 was fully cracked while the exterior flexural shear cracks in B3 were not yet formed. This appears to have had a significant effect on the cycling behaviour of the two beams with B2 showing a larger increase in deflection.

Following beam failure, the exposed rod sections were examined for damage. The rods showed an almost horizontal failure surface at the crack location. For specimens B2 and B3, the winding fibres showed progressively worse damage closer to the failure crack location. This type of damage was not as pronounced in specimen B1 suggesting that the damage was caused by the continuous relative movement between the rod and the concrete during cycling. The load deflection curve for B3 in Fig. 7 shows the load increasing in a step-like fashion after the maximum cycling load was passed. Since this behaviour was not seen in B1, it is possible that these load drops were caused as the damaged rod was able to slip more easily within the concrete. This slip would result in a sudden increase in the size of the concrete cracks and a consequent loss in stiffness.

CONCLUSIONS AND RECOMMENDATIONS

The major conclusions and recommendations of the work herein can be summarized as follows:

1. The relaxation losses in AFRP rods are higher than for normal steel strand. Values of 10 to 12% for a 50 year design life appear to be reasonable design values for the initial stresses used in this investigation.

2. The AFRP rods are capable of achieving tensile strengths, in service, 20% to 50% higher than the guaranteed tensile strength. This appears to be due to the more gradual distribution of bond stresses on either side of a beam crack than is present in the prestressing anchorage.

3. The use of present design theory for steel pretensioned beams provides an adequate prediction of AFRP pretensioned beam behaviour, including cracking behaviour, development length, transfer length and ultimate moment. Post-cracking deflection calculations may be overly conservative due to the wide crack spacing which results in significant tension stiffening.

4. The fatigue strength of AFRP rods in service is at least as good as that for steel strand under the stress conditions used in this investigation.

5. The ability of the rods to sustain high tensile stresses under service conditions should be investigated further. There was a large range in the theoretical stresses attained in these tests. Before this reserve capacity can be used, the variables controlling the strength must be determined.

6. A reasonable approximation of the relaxation losses for AFRP at initial stresses in the 1200 MPa range can be found from Equation 1.

7. Pending further research, AFRP prestressed members should only be designed as fully prestressed. This recommendation could be safely ignored for low risk or non critical structural members.

REFERENCES

Balaguru, P.N. (1981). Analysis of Prestressed Concrete Beams for Fatigue Loading. *PCI Journal*, May-June 1981, 70-94.

Kakihara, R., Kamiyoshi, M., Kumagi, S. and Noritake, K. (1990). A New Aramid Rod for the Reinforcement of Prestressed Concrete Structures. *Advanced Composite Materials In Civil Engineering Structures*. Proceedings of the Specialty Conference Las Vegas Nevada. January 30-February 1 1990, ASCE New York, 132-142.

Kobayashi, K., Cho, R., Nishimura, T. and Nakai, H. (1988). Relaxation Characteristics of Aramid Fibre Reinforced Plastic Rod Tendons. *Seisan Kenkyu, Kenkyu Sokuho*, Volume 40 No 8, August 1988.

McKay, K.S. (1992). Aramid Fibre Reinforced Plastic Tendons In Pretensioned Concrete Applications. Master of Engineering Thesis, Royal Military College of Canada, Kingston, Ontario.

Noritake, K., Kumagi, S., Mizutani, J. and Mashiko, H. (1990) Aramid FRP Pretensioned Road Bridge. *International Symposium on Innovation in the Applications of Precasting and Prestressing*, Singapore, 27-29 November 1990, 65-70.

ACKNOWLEDGEMENTS

The authors gratefully acknowledge the generosity of SUMITOMO Construction Company of Japan, for supplying the aramid rods with grouted anchorages for the beams tested herein. The authors would also like to thank Mr. Floyd Clapp of PRECON Limited, Belleville, Ontario, for his assistance in fabricating the beams. The technical advice received from both SUMITOMO and PRECON was greatly appreciated.

Table 1: Published Rod Properties

Volume of fibre (%)	65
Guaranteed Tensile Strength (MPa)	1767
Theoretical Strength	2500
Longitudinal Modulus (MPa)	53000
Poisson Ratio	0.35
Ultimate Strain (%)	3.7
Relaxation (%)	7-14

Table 2: Beam Fabrication Details

Beam	Fixing stress (MPa)	Stress at release (MPa)	f_{ci} (MPa)	f_c at test (MPa)	E_c at test (MPa) (avg)	A_{ps} (mm²)	A'_s (mm²)
B1	1290	1135	31.2	40.5	25360	57.6	200
B2	1205	1154	32.3	39.5			
B3	1208	1143	36.5	40.3			

Table 3: Ultimate Loads For Beams

Beam	Failure Load (kN)	Failure Moment kN·m	AFRP Stress (MPa)	Ultimate: Allowable (stress)	Ultimate: Theoretical (stress)
B1	87	34.8	2200	1.25	.88
B2	83	33.2	2100	1.19	.84
B3	100	40.0	2600	1.47	1.03

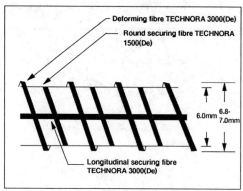

Figure 1 Deformed AFRP Rod

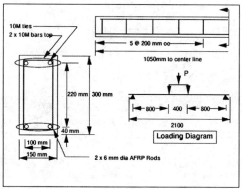

Figure 2 Beam Dimensions

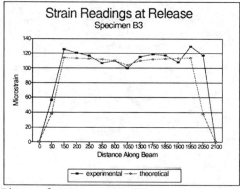

Figure 3 Strain Readings at Release (B3)

228

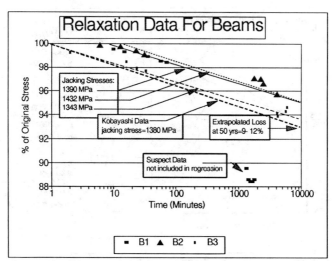

Figure 4 Short Term Relaxation Behaviour

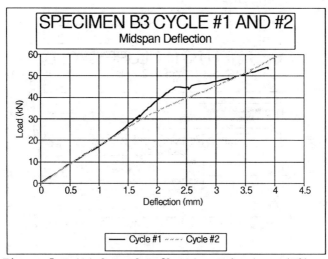

Figure 5 Initial Load Deflection Behaviour (B3)

229

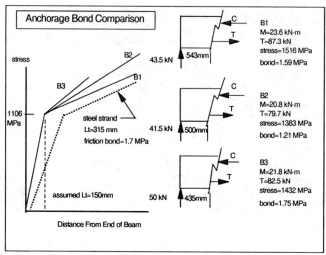

Figure 6 Estimated Anchorage Bond At Ultimate

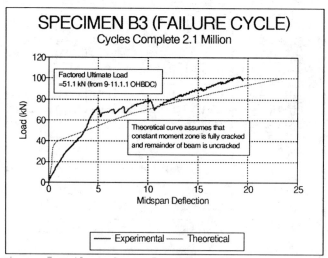

Figure 7 Failure Curve Specimen B3

230

ADVANCED COMPOSITE MATERIALS IN BRIDGES AND STRUCTURES
K.W. Neale and P. Labossière, Editors; Canadian Society for Civil Engineering, 1992

Matériaux composites d'avant-garde pour ponts et charpentes
K.W. Neale et P. Labossière, éditeurs; Société canadienne de génie civil, 1992

TESTS ON BEAMS PRESTRESSED WITH POLYARAMID TENDONS

C.J. Burgoyne
University of Cambridge
Cambridge, UK

ABSTRACT

The paper describes tests on two concrete beams, prestressed with aramid ropes which consist of parallel yarns of aramid fibres without any resin. The anchoring and stressing system for the ropes are described. One beam was stressed with a single, straight, unbonded tendon in a duct on the centreline; the other had two external deflected tendons. The beams were loaded in bending until they failed in flexure. In both cases, the ultimate load was reached when compressive failure of the concrete occurred, with the tendons remaining intact. Although both aramid and concrete are brittle materials, the beams demonstrated a considerable ability to absorb energy at failure. In one beam, the variation of force in the tendons was recorded for 65 days after first stressing. Losses were seen to be comparable with those in steel tendons. After the tests, the tendons were removed and were tested in simple tension, and were found not to have lost any strength. Implications for the design of beams using aramid ropes are also presented.

RÉSUMÉ

Cet article décrit des tests sur deux poutres en béton précontraint avec des câbles d'aramide, lesquels consistent en brins parallèles d'aramide sans aucune résine. Les systèmes d'ancrage et de tensionnement sont décrits. Une poutre a été tendue avec un seul tendon linéaire et sans liant, dans une gaine centrale; l'autre comprenait deux tendons extérieurs fléchis. Les poutres ont été chargées en flexion jusqu'à la rupture. Dans les deux cas, la charge ultime correspondait à la rupture en compression, et les tendons étaient intacts. Dans une poutre, la variation de la force dans les tendons a été mesurée pendant 65 jours après la mise sous contrainte. Les pertes étaient comparables à celles observées dans des tendons en acier. Après ces tests, les tendons, retirés et testés en tension simple, n'avaient perdu aucune résistance. Les implications pour le dimensionnement de poutres utilisant des câbles d'aramide sont présentées.

INTRODUCTION

Tests have been carried out on two beams prestressed with parallel-lay aramid ropes (Parafil), to demonstrate the feasibility of producing structural elements in this way. This paper summarises the tests that have been carried out, and the results that were obtained. Full details of the tests are given elsewhere (Burgoyne, Guimaraes and Chambers, 1991; Chambers, 1986; Guimaraes, 1989). The tests were carried out by the author and his co-workers at Imperial College in London. The work was sponsored by Linear Composites Ltd.

PARAFIL ROPES

Parafil ropes contain a core of *parallel filaments* of yarn within a thermoplastic sheath. A variety of core yarns can be used; in the case of the Type G Parafil, the yarn used is a stiff polyaramid yarn. The combination of high yarn strength (2760 N/mm²) and stiffness (126 kN/mm²) makes this version of the rope suitable for structural applications, particularly prestressing tendons for concrete.

Figure 1 shows the short term stress-strain curve for a 60 Tonne nominal breaking load (NBL) tendon, as used in these tests. The response is essentially linear, with a slight stiffening once the load exceeds about 50% of the NBL. This stiffening is also observed in the response of the fibres themselves and is not due to the rope construction.

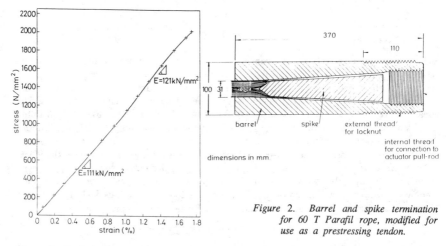

Figure 2. Barrel and spike termination for 60 T Parafil rope, modified for use as a prestressing tendon.

Figure 1. Typical stress-strain response for a Type G Parafil rope.

Terminal details

In tension members, the design of the terminations is clearly critical, since the rope is of no use unless the force can be transmitted to the rope. The terminals used for the Parafil ropes have been designed by the manufacturer and are used on all tests of the rope. The basic geometry consists of an internal spike which grips the fibres against an external conical barrel. In this system, every fibre is subjected to an evenly distributed gripping force, which allows friction to develop the full strength of each yarn; this contrasts with external wedge

232

systems which tend to develop hoop compression in the outer layers of circular ropes and do not fully anchor the inner fibres. To modify the terminals for prestressing operations, two threads are placed on the end of the terminals, as shown in Figure 2. The inner thread is used to connect to a pull-rod which is used to apply the prestressing force, while the external thread is used for a back-nut which transmits the force to the concrete itself.

DESIGN OF TEST BEAMS

The ropes cannot be bonded to concrete, and indeed, with materials which do not show plastic yielding, this would be undesirable; thus, from the outset it was expected that these ropes would be used as external or unbonded tendons. Two designs were produced; the first (Beam A) had a single, straight tendon, contained within a duct on the centreline of a simple I-beam, while the second (Beam B) had two external deflected tendons, one on each side of a T-shaped cross-section (Figure 3).

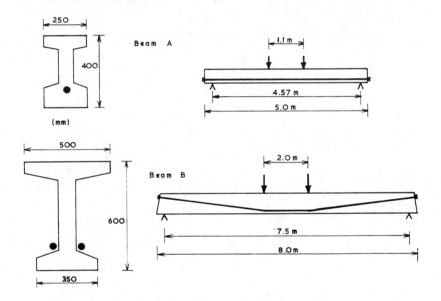

Figure 3. General Arrangement of Test beams.

Beam A was stressed with a 60 tonne Type G Parafil tendon stressed initially to 70% NBL. To enable the end anchorages to be accommodated and to limit the anchorage bearing stresses the main I-section of the beam was splayed-out to a full rectangular section at the beam ends.

Beam B was prestressed with two external 60 tonne Type G Parafil tendons, deflected by an angle of 4.57 degrees. Other tests (Chambers, 1986) had shown that there is no reduction in the breaking load of the ropes when deflected in this way. To avoid direct contact between the ropes and the rough surface of the concrete at the deflection points, which could damage the sheath of the ropes during the prestressing operation, a steel shoe was fitted to the concrete. This was formed from a piece of steel tube, of slightly larger diameter than the rope, cut in half along its longitudinal axis and bent to a smooth curve.

For an internal tendon, as in Beam A, the terminals have to be fitted before the rope is placed in position in the beam; since the terminals are too large to pass through the duct, this is built up around the tendons. This was done in a straightforward way by making the duct in several pieces, which could then be easily joined together. In the second beam, the tendons were to be placed outside the concrete, so there was no need to assemble the rope in a duct prior to casting. Holes were formed in the thickened end blocks to receive the rope terminations, by casting-in plastic pipes.

PRESTRESSING OPERATIONS

The principles of the stressing procedure are shown in Figure 4. The tendon is placed in the structure, and a pull-rod fitted to the internal thread of the termination. The pull-rod is then passed through the centre hole of a hydraulic jack, and secured by means of a nut. The jack is held away from the beam by means of a trestle, which allows access to the terminal to secure the back-nut. Force is applied by the jack, which brings the terminal just outside the face of the concrete; the back-nut can then be fitted to lock the tendon in position in its stressed state. The jack, trestle and pull-rod can be removed, and a security cap fitted to prevent dirt and debris getting into the termination, and also to contain the anchorage in the unlikely event of a rope failure.

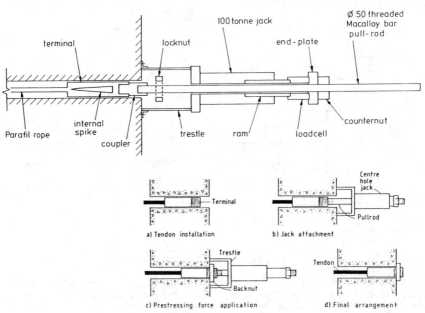

Figure 4. Prestressing system and sequence used in laboratory tests.

The prestress was applied to Beam A forty days after casting and 20 hours before testing, while the beam remained on the soffit shutter. The rope was first pretensioned to 60% of the nominal breaking load (in the usual manner specified by the manufacturers). One hour later, a prestress of 42 tonnes (70% NBL) was applied to the beam. The strain distribution gave good agreement with predictions, indicating a negligible loss of prestress due to friction between the rope and the prestressing duct, as would be expected.

The prestressing apparatus for Beam B was similar to that used in the earlier test; two identical jacks were used, one for each tendon, both connected to the same hydraulic cabinet. The prestress force measurements were taken by load cells fitted to one of the jacks at the live load end, and to both anchorages at the dead end. The beam had been designed with sufficient reinforcement to take its own weight without cracking, but for extra security during lifting, a partial prestressing force was applied, with the beam resting on the soffit formwork, ten days after casting. The beam was then lifted to allow the removal of the bottom shutter and placed on its bearing plates.

At the age of 33 days, the force in the tendons was removed and the initial readings of displacements and strains were taken with the beam subjected to the action of its own weight. The total initial prestressing force applied to the beam was 626 kN. The force at the dead-end of the tendons was measured while the prestressing was underway. This indicated that 5% of the prestressing force was being lost to friction; taking the standard relationship for friction in deflected tendons ($P_x = P_o e^{-\mu\theta}$), with $\theta = 0.16$ radians, this gives $\mu = 0.32$. This value is slightly higher than would be expected with steel tendons, but could be brought down by a better selection of sheath and deflector material. Measurement of the force in the tendon, after the force had been transferred from the jack to the permanent back-nut, indicated that no loss of prestress occurred at this stage.

ELASTIC TESTS

Both beams were tested in four point bending rigs with loads being applied by hydraulic jacks. The beams were taken through several elastic loading cycles; the second beam was kept under sustained load for 42 days to monitor the effects of creep and relaxation.

Tests were carried out on the beams at working (uncracked) load levels, before the tests to determine the load carrying capacity. In the case of Beam A, these tests were merely to get the short term elastic response, but for Beam B, the working load was applied for a period of 42 days, in order to monitor the combined effects of creep and shrinkage of the concrete together with relaxation effects in the tendons.

The elastic test on Beam A was designed to apply a load that would induce the allowable flexural tensile stress in the bottom fibre of the beam. The load-deflection curve was essentially linear, and 94% of the maximum mid-span deflection being recovered 5 minutes after the load was removed.

Beam B was subjected to two loading cycles at the service load. In the first cycle, the load was applied in increments until a small tensile strain was observed in the bottom flange. No visible cracks were present under this load. The beam was maintained under this load for 42 days, after which the load was removed. The second load cycle started immediately afterwards and consisted of the application of the same load as cycle 1, using the same load increments, followed by its immediate removal.

Time dependent variations

The relationship between the applied load and the deflection at the centre of the beam is shown in Figure 5; this is similar in form to the response of the concrete strain at the top fibres. On the application of the load, the response is almost linear, with the portions of the curves corresponding to loading and unloading being parallel. The instantaneous camber produced by the prestressing is indicated by the horizontal part of the curve at zero load. The increase of deflection due to the effects of shrinkage and creep of concrete after 42 days was 59% of the instantaneous deflection caused by the applied load. This figure is not affected by relaxation of the tendon, being due to loss of stiffness of the concrete.

In prestressed concrete only minor changes in stress are induced in the tendons when the dead and live loads are applied to the member; this is particularly true when the tendons are unbonded. The resistance to external bending moment is almost exclusively due to an increase of the lever arm between the internal compression and tension forces whose magnitudes remain

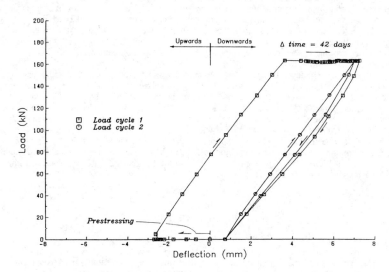

Figure 5. Load-deflection results for first two working load cycles for Beam B.

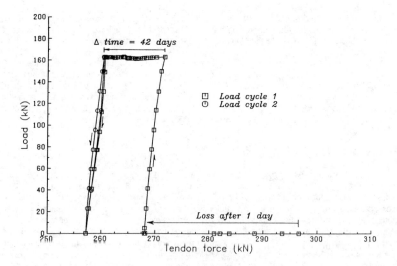

Figure 6. Load versus tendon force for tendons in Beam B.

relatively unchanged. This is shown in Figure 6 where the slope of the curves indicate a very small variation of the forces in the tendons due to the application of the load; the figure shows the expected linear variation of tendon force with applied load - small since the tendons are unbonded - together with time dependent variations due to creep and relaxation.

The total loss of prestress in both tendons, due to shrinkage and creep of concrete and due to stress relaxation in the tendons, is shown in Figure 7. The tendons were tensioned initially to approximately 22% of their tensile strength, when the age of concrete was 10 days. Losses of 13% and 14% (of the initial force) in tendons 1 and 2 respectively were observed after 23 days when the full prestressing force was applied. Over this period of time the beam was subjected only to the action of its own weight. 43 days after the application of the full prestressing, the losses of prestress under service load were 12% in tendon 1 and 11% in tendon 2. It can be seen in the figure that most of the losses occurred 1 day after prestressing. From then on the curves show a very low rate of loss.

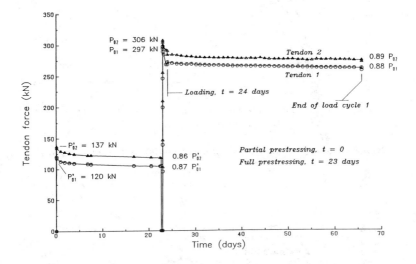

Figure 7. Variation of prestressing force with time for tendons in Beam B.

ULTIMATE LOAD TESTS

Ultimate load tests were carried out on both beams, which responded as expected. After passing the cracking load, the stiffness reduced considerably; when unloaded from the cracked (but still elastic) state, the stiffness remained lower until the cracks had closed up but the full elastic stiffness was recovered and there was virtually no permanent set when unloaded.

When loaded until failure, both beams showed considerable curvature at virtually constant load, with large cracks forming in the bottom of the beam. Failure occured in both beams by crushing of the top flange. Figure 8 shows the load deflection curves for Beam A; the results for Beam B are similar.

There were slight differences in the final failure mode of the two beams. In both cases, the top flange failed by crushing, but in the first beam, as the tendon was constrained in the bottom flange, the beam did not completely collapse. The compression zone passed down through the web, and into the top of the bottom flange, with a consequent reduction in load. However, the bottom flange did not fail, remaining axially prestressed. After the test, the tendon was found still to be carrying a force of 330 kN.

237

In the second beam, the tendon was outside the bottom flange, which could thus deflect while leaving the tendon in its original position relative to the ends of the beam. The beam thus failed suddenly and completely, with a total loss of prestress.

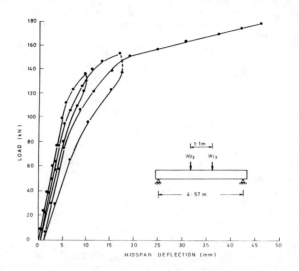

Figure 8. Load-deflection curve for ultimate load tests on Beam A.

TENSILE PROPERTIES OF THE TENDONS AFTER BEAM FAILURE

It was not practical to remove the tendon from Beam A without damaging it, so it was impossible to test whether the loading to which it had been subjected caused any reduction in tendon strength. However, in Beam B the tendons were external, so they were removed and subsequently tested 63 days later. The breaking loads were 668 kN for tendon 1 and 686 kN for tendon 2, and the elastic modulus for both tendons was 120 kN/mm². The breaking loads of both tendons were greater than the mean value (597 kN), and even greater than the maximum value (626.6 kN), observed in the tensile tests conducted on similar ropes (Chambers, 1986) tested in the same way.

This effect is probably due to increased creep in the more heavily loaded filaments, which will even out variations in the slack in the yarns. In subsequent loading, the rope acts as a bundle of yarns with less variabilty, and hence increased strength. Work is now underway at Cambridge University to study the implications of bundle theory when influenced by visco-elastic effects; it is hoped that this will shed more light on this phenomenon.

238

PRACTICAL LESSONS FOR THE DESIGN OF CONCRETE PRESTRESSED WITH PARAFIL

The results of the tests show that basic design principles for prestressed concrete do not need radically altering; the following are additional points which a designer should take into account when designing a beam with Parafil tendons.

1. The tendon should be pretensioned, with the terminals in place, to a load level in excess of that expected during both the initial stressing operation, or the service life of the structure. This will have the effect of ensuring that the terminal spike is properly bedded, and will also give a check on the tendon length before being placed in the structure.

    It is normal practice, according to the manufacturer's instructions, to pretension ropes to 60% of the nominal breaking load prior to use, whenever possible. These ropes, when used in conventional rigging arrangements, are normally stressed to much lower load levels than those in use in prestressing tendons; in these cases, 60% is perfectly adequate as a pretensioning load. However, in prestressing tendons, where high force levels are normal, a higher pretensioning level may be needed to ensure adequate bedding of the termination.

2. Any deflector points should be properly flared to ensure no damage to the sheath during stressing operations; this should not be difficult to arrange if taken into account at the design stage.

3. The coefficient of friction between the tendon and the duct (or the deflector) should be reduced wherever possible. This may mean undertaking some studies of friction coefficients between various possible sheathing materials and alternative duct materials. Alternatively, coating materials, such as PTFE or Nylon tapes, might be considered.

4. The working load design of prestressed concrete beams should be based on allowable stress limits taking account of the design prestressing force, after allowing for losses, and the ultimate strength of the section should be based on the assumption that only minimal increases of force take place due to geometry changes as the beam deflects.

5. The compression zone of the concrete should be provided with confining reinforcement to increase the ductility of the concrete in that area.

6. If the tendons are external to the concrete, they should pass through loose rings so that, in the event of failure, the tendons are forced to deflect with the beam. This will ensure that failure occurs in the more controlled manner of Beam A, rather than in the more sudden manner of Beam B.

Recommendations 4, 5 and 6 apply also to beams prestressed with steel tendons.

REFERENCES

Burgoyne C.J., Guimaraes G.B and Chambers J.J. (1991). Tests on beams prestressed with unbonded polyaramid tendons, Cambridge University Engineering Dept. Tech Rep. CUED/D - Struct/TR 132.

Chambers J.J. (1986). Parallel-lay aramid ropes for use as tendons in prestressed concrete, PhD Thesis, University of London.

Guimaraes G.B. (1989). Parallel-lay aramid ropes for use in structural engineering, Ph.D. Thesis, University of London.

Strengthening and Rehabilitation of Concrete Structures

Renforcement et réhabilitation de structures en béton

242

ADVANCED COMPOSITE MATERIALS IN BRIDGES AND STRUCTURES
K.W. Neale and P. Labossière, Editors; Canadian Society for Civil Engineering, 1992

Matériaux composites d'avant-garde pour ponts et charpentes
K.W. Neale et P. Labossière, éditeurs; Société canadienne de génie civil, 1992

STRENGTHENING OF STRUCTURES WITH CFRP LAMINATES : RESEARCH AND APPLICATIONS IN SWITZERLAND

U. Meier, M. Deuring, H. Meier and G. Schwegler
Swiss Federal Laboratories for Materials Testing and Research (EMPA)
Dübendorf, Switzerland

ABSTRACT

The results of a comprehensive research programme at EMPA show that the calculation of flexure in reinforced concrete elements post-strengthened with untensioned or with tensioned CFRP plates can be performed analogous to conventional reinforced or prestressed concrete. Longtime fatigue tests on 7 m girders displayed an outstanding fatigue performance of this strengthening technique. A new approach also allows an increase of shear strength of the post-strenghthened systems. In 1991, for the first time real structures were strengthened with CFRP in Switzerland, e.g., the multispan box beam Ibach Bridge near Lucerne with a total length of 228 meters. The City Hall of Gossau St. Gall followed in 1992. In addition, the historic wooden bridge near Sins was strengthened for heavy trucks.

RÉSUMÉ

Les résultats d'un vaste programme de recherche entrepris à l'EMPA montrent que la méthode de dimensionnement classique peut être appliquée par analogie au dimensionnement des poutres sollicitées en flexion renforcées ultérieurement au moyen d'une armature collée, précontrainte ou non, en plaques de FRP. Des essais de fatigue de longue durée ont démontré les excellentes caractéristiques de comportement à la fatigue de cette technique de renforcement. Une méthode nouvellement développée permet aussi d'augmenter la résistance au cisaillement d'un système porteur. En 1991, on a procédé pour la première fois en Suisse au renforcement ultérieur d'ouvrages d'art au moyen de FRP. On a ainsi, par exemple, renforcé le pont de l'Ibach, long de 228 m, situé près de Lucerne et l'Hôtel de Ville de Gossau dans le canton de St-Gall, suivis en 1992 par le renforcement du pont de bois historique de Sins qui a dû être à nouveau ouvert au trafic lourd.

INTRODUCTION

Preserving the existing values is becoming increasingly important. This also includes the field of civil engineering. Wherever larger structures have to be strengthened and supplemented to meet future needs the technique of post-strengthening through the bonding of steel plates has gained in significance. Nowadays in western Europe this technique is largely state of the art for the strengthening of existing reinforced and prestressed concrete structures.

In previous papers (Meier 1987, Kaiser 1989, Meier and Kaiser 1991, Meier 1992) the advantages and disadvantages of post-strengthening by means of steel plates have been discussed at length as well as the reasons for replacing steel plates with carbon-fiber reinforced plastics (CFRP), above all in bridge construction. The most important reason is clear from the following observations: Within the framework of long-term creep tests on beams strengthed with steel plates at the EMPA, the residual strength was determined after 15 years of exposure to weathering. In several cases, traces of corrosion were discovered at the joint steel/adhesive.

RESEARCH AT THE SWISS FEDERAL LABORATORIES
FOR MATERIALS TESTING AND RESEARCH (EMPA) IN DUEBENDORF

Strengthening with Non-Pretensioned CFRP Sheets

In the years 1984 to 1989, carbon-fiber reinforced epoxy-resin was successfully employed for the first time at the EMPA for post-strengthening purposes. Loading tests were performed on 26 flexure beams having a span of 2 m and 1 beam having a span of 7 m (Kaiser 1989). The research work shows the validity of the strain-compatibility method in the analysis of cross-sections. This implies that the calculation of flexure in reinforced concrete elements post-strengthened with cabon-fiber reinforced epoxy-resin sheets can be performed analogous to conventional reinforced concrete elements. The work also shows that possible occurrence of shear cracks may lead to a peeling-off of the strengthening sheet. Thus, the shear crack development represents a dimensional criterion. Flexural cracks are spanned by the CFRP sheet and do not influence the loading capacity. In comparison to the unstrengthened beams, the strengthening sheets lead to a much finer cracking distribution (Meier and Kaiser 1991). A calculation model (Kaiser 1989), developed for the CFRP sheet anchoring agrees well with experimental results.

Differences in the temperature expansion coefficients of concrete and the carbon-fiber reinforced epoxy resin result in stresses at the joints with changes of temperature. After one hundred frost cycles ranging from +20 °C to -25 °C, no negative influence of the loading capacity of the post-strengthened 3 beams was found (Kaiser 1989).

The following failure modes were observed in the load tests (see also Fig. 1):
– Tensile failure of the CFRP sheet (1). The sheets failed more or less suddenly, with a sharp explosive snap. The impending failure was always announced far in advance by cracking sounds.
– Classical concrete failure in the compressive zone (2) of the beam.
– Continuous peeling-off of the CFRP sheets due to an uneven concrete surface (3). For thin sheets (less than 1 mm) applied with a vacuum bag, an extremely even bonding surface is required. If the surface is too uneven, the sheet will slowly peel off during loading.
– Shearing of the concrete in the tensile zone (3) (also observed as secondary failure).
– Interlaminar shear (4) within the CFRP sheet (observed as secondary failure).
– Failure of the reinforcing steel in the tensile zone (5). This failure mode was only observed during fatigue tests.

244

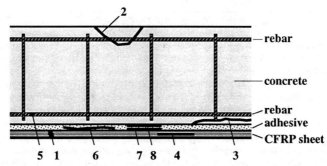

Figure 1: Failure modes.

The following failure modes were not yet observed but are theoretically possible:
– Cohesive failure within the adhesive (6)
– Adhesive failure at the interface CFRP sheet/adhesive (7)
– Adhesive failure at the interface CFRP concrete/adhesive (8).

For post-strengthening with CFRP sheets we recommend the design rule that the CFRP sheets should fail during yielding of the steel reinforcing bars before failure of the concrete in the compressive zone. Yielding of the steel bars should not occur before reaching the permitted loads.

Kaiser (1989) investigated a beam with a 2.0 m span under fatigue loading. The cross-section was 300 mm wide and 250 mm deep. The existing steel reinforcement consisted of 2 rebars of 8 mm diameter in the tension as well as in the compression zones. This beam was post-strengthened with a hybrid sheet with the dimensions 0.3 x 200 mm (see Table 1, sheet type Nr. 1). The fatigue loading was sinusoidal at a frequency of 4 Hz. The test set-up corresponded to a four-point flexure test with loading at the one-third points. The calculated stresses in the hybrid sheet and the steel reinforcement are listed in Table 2. After 480,000 cycles the first fatigue failure occurred in one of the two rods in the tension zone. After 560,000 cycles the second rod broke at another cross-section. After 610,000 cycles a further break was observed in the first rod and after 720,000 cycles, in the second rod. The first damage appeared after 750,000 cycles. It was in the form of fractures of individual rovings of the sheet. The beam exhibited gaping cracks, which however were bridged by the hybrid sheet. The relatively sharp concrete edges rubbed against the hybrid sheet at every cycle. After 805,000 cycles, the sheet finally failed. This test was executed with unrealistically high steel stresses. The goal of the test however was to gain insight into the failure mechanism after a complete breaking of the steel reinforcement. This goal was achieved. It was remarkable to observe how much the hybrid sheet could withstand after failure of the steel reinforcement.

Property	Sheet type Nr.				
	1	2	3	4	5
Fiber type	2/3 T 300 1/3 E-glass	T 300	–	T 700	M 46 J
Fiber volume fraction [%]	–	70	51	50	–
Longitudinal strength [MPa]	960	2,000	1,900	2,100	2,600
Longitudinal Young's modulus [GPa]	80	147.5	129	130	305
Strain at failure [%]	1.15	1.36	1.47	1.62	0.85
Density [g/cm³]	–	1.58	1.46	1.45	–

Table 1: Properties of Hybrid and CFRP sheets

Loads [kN]	Stresses [MPa]	
	rebars	hybrid sheet
minimum 1	21	11
maximum 19	407	205

Table 2: Fatigue loading and stresses of the 2 m beam

Loads [kN]	Stresses [MPa]	
	rebars	CFRP sheet
minimum 125.8	131	102
maximum 283.4	262	210

Table 3: Fatigue loading and stresses of the 6 m beam

In 1991/92 (Deuring 1993) the EMPA performed a further fatigue test on a beam with a span of 6.0 m under more realistic conditions. The dimensions and reinforcement of the beam can be seen in Fig. 2. The total carrying capacity F of this beam amounted to 610 kN without the CFRP. Through the bonding of a CFRP sheet having the dimensions 200 x 1 mm (sheet type Nr. 2, Table 1), the carrying capacity was increased by 32% to 815 kN. In Fig. 3, typical force/ deflection diagrams are presented for this type of beam. The calculated stresses in the CFRP sheet and the steel reinforcement are given in Table 3. The beam was subjected to this loading for 10.7 million cycles. The crack development was observed after every 2 million cycles (Deuring 1993). After 10.7 million cycles the tests were continued in a climatic room. The temperature was raised from room temperature to 40ºC and the relative humidity to at least 95%. The goal of this test phase was to verify that the bonded CFRP sheet can withstand very high humidity with simultaneous fatigue loading. Already at the beginning of this test phase the CFRP sheet was nearly completely saturated with water. After a total of 12.0 million cycles the first reinforcement steel failed due to fretting fatigue. The joint CFRP sheet/ concrete did not present even the slightest of problems. In the continuation of the test, the external loads were held constant (Table 3) whereas the stresses in the reinforcement steel and the CFRP sheet correspondingly increased. After 14.09 million cycles the second reinforcement steel failed, likewise due to fretting fatigue. The cracks bridged by the CFRP sheet rapidly grew. After failure of the third reinforcement rod due to yielding of the remaining overloaded steel the CFRP sheet was sheared off.

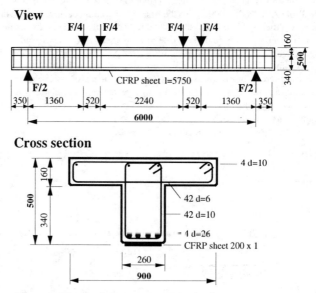

Figure 2: View and cross section of the 6 m beam.

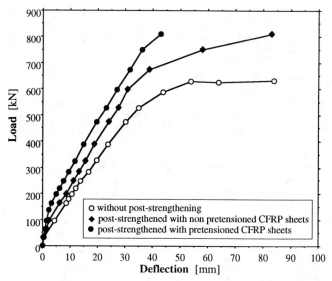

Figure 3: Typical load/deflection curves for beams shown in Figure 2.

STRENGTHENING WITH PRETENSIONED CFRP SHEETS
AND SHEAR STRENGTHENING

At the present time a fatigue test is being carried out at the EMPA, analogous to that described in the previous section. The only difference is that the CFRP sheet was prestressed (50% of strength of sheet type Nr. 2). Up to now, 30 million cycles were performed without any evidence of damage whatever.

In the last months a new method was developed and tried out in several tests. This allows an effective strengthening of the shearing force areas without the use of steel. One possible implementation is illustrated in the beam cross-section of Fig. 4. The inner stirrup reinforcement is supplemented by a stressed or limply applied external strengthening, made of advanced composite materials. These are braided or unidirectional in form. Depending on the application, carbon fiber may be employed as well as aromatic polyamid and glass fibers. The pretensioning material is wrapped around the cross-section on one side and anchored on the opposite side in the compression zone. The modulus of elasticity and geometry should be chosen so as to minimize the loss of tensioning force due to creep of the element to be strengthened and relaxation of the prestressing material.

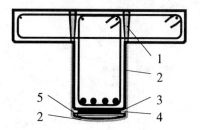

(1) anchorage zone
(2) shear strengthening element of advanced composites
(3) adhesive
(4) CFRP sheet for flexural strengthening
(5) CFRP plate for load distribution

Figure 4: Cross section of beam with shear strengthening arrangement

Many bridges in need of rehabilitation are deficient not only with respect to flexural resistance. Often it is necessary to strengthen mainly the shear resistance. In order to contribute at once to the strengthening and to relieve the inner stirrup reinforcement, the reinforcement located externally to the element should be additionally prestressed. In this way, crack formation in the shear force region can be precluded or the cracks more finely distributed, in case shear cracks develop.

In some cases it can be advantageous to provide additional prestressing to the flexure-strengthening sheets. In this way, the serviceability of the structure can be improved and the shearing off of the sheets due to shear failure of the concrete in the tension zone can be avoided. An initial publication of this EMPA research effort appeared recently (Triatafillon, Deskovic, Deuring 1992). Detailed results will soon follow (Deuring 1993). The procedure for applying a prestressed sheet is shown schematically in Fig. 5. When the pretensioning force is too high, failure of the beam due to pretension release will occur at the two ends, because of the development of high shear stresses in the concrete layer just above the CFRP sheet. Therefore the design and construction of the end regions requires careful attention. Tests and calculations have shown that without special end anchoring, CFRP sheets shear off from the end zones immediately with a prestress of over 5% of their failure strength. In order to achieve a technically and economically rational prestress considerably higher degrees of prestressing in the range of 50% are necessary.

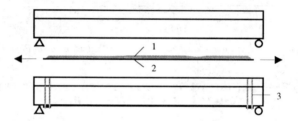

Figure 5: Procedure for applying a prestressed sheet
(1) adhesive
(2) prestressed CFRP sheet
(3) shear strengthening arrangement according to Figure 4.

At the EMPA end anchorings for flexure beams in accordance with Figures 4 and 5 were developed and successfully tested. In contrast to pure shear strengthening, the advanced composites which wrap around the sheet must most definitely be prestressed. This will built up a multi-axial stress condition in the concrete as much as possible and also interlock cracks. This way failure at the two ends of the CFRP sheets can be avoided.

THE IBACH BRIDGE

The bridge to be repaired (Fig. 6), located in the County of Lucerne, was completed in 1969. It is designed as a continuous, multispan box beam with a total length of 228 meters. The damaged span of the bridge has a length of 39 meters. The box section is 16 meters wide, with a central, longitudinal web.

Core borings were performed to mount new traffic signals. In the process, a prestressing tendon in the outer web was accidentally damaged, with several of its wires completely severed by means of an oxygen lance. As a result, the granting of authorizations for special, heavy convoys across the bridge was suspended until after completion of the repair work. Since the damaged span crosses Highway N2, the traffic lanes in direction Lucerne on this highway had to be closed during the repair work, which could therefore only be conducted at night.

Figure 6: Ibach bridge

Carbon fiber-reinforced plastics (CFRPs) are fifty times more expensive, per kilogram, than the steel used to this date (Fe 360) for the reinforcement of existing structures. Do the unquestionably superior properties of CFRPs justify their high price? When one considers that, for the repair of the Ibach bridge, 175 kg of steel could be replaced by a mere 6.2 kg of CFRP, the high prices suddenly no longer seem so outrageous. Furthermore, all the work could be carried out from a mobile platform, thus eliminating the need for expensive scaffolding.

The bridge was repaired with 3 CFRP sheets of the dimensions 150 x 5000 x 1.75 mm (2 sheets) and 150 x 5000 x 2.00 mm (1 sheet) according to sheet type Nr. 3 in Table 1. A loading test with 840 kN vehicle demonstrated that rehabilitation work with the CFRP sheets was very satisfactory. The experts participating in the repair of the Ibach bridge were pleasantly surprised about the simplicity of applying the 2 mm thick and 150 mm wide CFRP sheets.

HISTORIC WOODEN BRIDGE IN SINS

The covered wooden bridge in Sins/Switzerland was built in 1807 in accordance with the design of Josef Ritter of Luzern. On the Sins side the original supporting structure is almost completely preserved, even today. The Chams side was blown up for strategic purposes on November 10, 1847 during the Civil war. In 1852, the destroyed half of the bridge was rebuilt with a modified supporting structure. These differing systems can clearly be seen in the Fig. 7. On the Sins side, the supporting structure consists of arches. These are strengthened with suspended and trussed members. On the Chams side, the supporting structure is made up of a combination of suspended and trussed members with interlocking tensioning transoms. Originally the bridge was dimensioned for horse-drawn vehicles. Today, vehicles with a load of 200 kN are permitted.

Sins   **Cham**

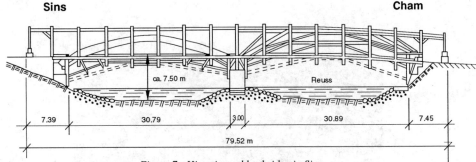

ca. 7.50 m   Reuss

| 7.39 | 30.79 | 3.00 | 30.89 | 7.45 |

79.52 m

Figure 7: Historic wodden bridge in Sins

In the 185 year history of the bridge a great variety of rehabilitation efforts were undertaken. Loading tests performed by the EMPA and the ETH Zürich indicated that the pavement and several crossbeams no longer met the requirements of heavy traffic. A project involving the construction of a pretensioned concrete bridge several hundred meters upstream was opposed by the residents. Thus, in 1992 the wooden bridge urgently had to be rehabilitated. It was decided to replace the old wooden pavement with 20 cm thick bonded wooden planks, transversely pretensioned. This technique described in the Ontario Bridge Design Code in 1983 was further developed at the ETH Zürich. Two of the most highly loaded cross-beams were strengthened by the EMPA using carbon fibre reinforced epoxy resin sheets. Each of these cross-beams were constructed of two solid oak beams placed one upon the other. A cross section of the bridge with the strengthening is shown in Fig. 8. In order to increase the thickness, wooden blocks were inserted between the beams. The lower beams were 37 cm high and 30 cm wide, the upper beams 30 cm thick and 30 cm wide.

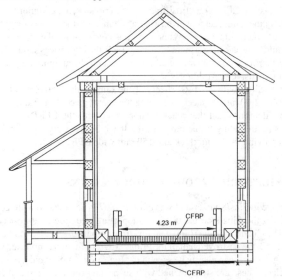

CFRP

4.23 m

CFRP

Figure 8: Cross section of historic wooden bridge in Sins.
Selected cross beams were strengthened with CFRP sheets

Cross-beam Nr. 14 was strengthened with 1.0 mm thick CFRP sheets made of high-modulus Toray M46J fibres; on the upper side the width amounted to 250 mm and and on the lower side 200 mm. Cross-beam Nr. 15 was strengthened on the upper side with a 1.0 mm thick CFRP sheet made of high-strength Toray T700 fibres having a width of 300 mm.

Before bonding the sheets, the bonding surface was planed with a portable system. The bonding and installation were accomplished with the same material and the analogous clamping system as for the Ibach bridge (Meier, Deuring 1991).

The strengthened cross-beams of the Sins bridge, subjected to extremely high loading and reinforced with CFRP sheets, help to gain practical experience and confidence in this method for preservation of historic bridges. Thus, in the future, similar structures may be rehabilitated in this manner.

The historic wooden bridge in Sins is a valuable structure, both from esthetic and technical viewpoints. It is also of value historically and under protection as a national monument. For the post-strengthening of such structures the technique with CRP plates is especially suited since the thin but extremely stiff and strong plates are hardy noticed and therefore do not detract from the original design of the structure.

REFERENCES

Deuring, M. (1993). Post-strengthening of Concrete Structures with Pretensioned Advanced Composites. Will be published in German in summer 1993 by the EMPA as Research Report No. 224, EMPA Duebendorf, CH-8600 Duebendorf/Switzerland.

Kaiser, H.P. (1989). Strengthening of Reinforced Concrete with Epoxy-Bonded Carbon-Fiber Plastics. Doctoral Thesis, Diss. ETH Nr. 8918, ETH Zürich, CH-8092 Zürich/Switzerland (in German).

Meier, U. (1987). Bridge Repair with High Performance Composite Materials. Material und Technik, 15, 125–128 (in German and in French).

Meier, U. and Kaiser H.P. (1991). Strengthening of Structures with CFRP Laminates. Proceedings Advanced Composite Materials in Civil Engineering Structures. MT Div / ASCE / Las Vegas, Jan 31, 1991.

Meier, U. and Deuring, M. (1991). The application of fiber composites in bridge repair. Strasse und Verkehr, 77, page 775.

Meier, U. (1992). Carbon Fiber-Reinforced Polymers: Modern Materials in Bridge Engineering. Structural Engineering International, 2, 7–12.

Triantafillou, T.C., Deskovic, N. and Deuring, M. (1992). Strengthening of Concrete Structures with Prestressed Fiber reinforced Plastic Sheets. ACI Structural Journal, 89, 235–244.

ADVANCED COMPOSITE MATERIALS IN BRIDGES AND STRUCTURES
K.W. Neale and P. Labossière, Editors; Canadian Society for Civil Engineering, 1992

Matériaux composites d'avant-garde pour ponts et charpentes
K.W. Neale et P. Labossière, éditeurs; Société canadienne de génie civil, 1992

STRENGTHENING OF R/C- AND P/C-STRUCTURES
WITH BONDED FRP PLATES

F.S. Rostásy, C. Hankers and **E.-H. Ranisch**
Technical University of Braunschweig
Braunschweig, Germany

ABSTRACT

In Europe the external strengthening of reinforced and prestressed concrete members by epoxy bonded steel plates has become a well-proven technology. To cope with the danger of corrosion FRP plates are a promising alternative to steel. Extensive shear and bending tests with R/C-members were performed to assess the suitability of commercial UP- and EP-laminates with glass fibres. A multispan hollow box P/C-bridge was strengthened with GFRP plates in order to increase the reinforcement in the cracked coupling joints and to reduce the dynamic prestressing steel stresses in the couplers of the tendons. Load testing of the bridge proved the envisaged efficiency of the strengthening with GFRP plates.

RÉSUMÉ

Le renforcement externe d'éléments en béton armé et précontraint à l'aide de plaques en acier collées avec une colle à base de résine époxyde est devenu, en Europe, une technologie confirmée. Pour éliminer les risques de corrosion, les plaques synthétiques renforcées de fibres (FRP) représentent une alternative prometteuse à l'acier. Dans le but d'estimer l'applicabilité de stratifiés commerciaux en polyesters insaturés et en époxyde avec fibres de verre, des essais au cisaillement et à la flexion ont été exécutés sur des éléments en béton armé. Un pont (à poutres-caissons) à travées multiples en béton précontraint a été renforcé par des plaques composites en fibres de verre pour augmenter le renforcement et pour diminuer les contraintes dynamiques de l'acier précontraint dans les coupleurs de torons. Des tests de chargement ont prouvé l'efficacité envisagée du renforcement par plaques FRP.

INTRODUCTION

The strengthening of concrete structures with epoxy-bonded steel plates has become a proven technology. Long-term tests in artificial, humid laboratory climate and observations in practice have shown that the durability of the adhesive bond between concrete and the steel plate's inner surface may be reduced by the diffusion of water vapour to the joint and by the on-set of corrosion /1/, /2/, /3/. Effective countermeasures against corrosion are appropriate shop primers on or the zinc-coating of the steel plates. Also chromium-nickel alloyed steel has been used. Corrosion can be entirely eliminated if fiber reinforced plastic (FRP) plates are used because ionic reactions cannot occur on their surfaces. The FRP materials for the external strengthening will essentially consist of unidirectional glass, aramid or carbon fibers embedded in epoxy or polyester resin. Their fiber volume should be high to obtain an adequate axial stiffness. FRP plates can be produced by several processes. The use of FRP for strengthening raises new questions which have to be studied by experiment and analysis. First applications proved the suitability of the strengthening of concrete structures with FRP plates /4/, /5/.

OVERVIEW ON RESEARCH AT THE IBMB

In the past years extensive experimental and theoretical work on the strengthening with steel and FRP plates has been performed at the Institute for Structural Materials, Concrete Construction and Fire Protection (IBMB). The materials exclusively used for tests and applications were glass fiber reinforced plastics (GFRP). Table 1 shows some of the GFRP tested. In basic tests the properties of GFRP and the bond strength of GFRP plates epoxy-glued to concrete were studied. Bond strength was investigated on concrete tension specimen with double lap joints. Long-term bond strength was studied on beams subjected to load and moist environment /6/. Extensive tests were performed on one-way r/c-slabs strengthened with FRP plates and also alternatively with steel plates /7/. For the strengthening of prestressed concrete bridges with FRP plates the suitability of FRP plates to reduce the crack width and to increase the stiffness of cracked members had to be studied. These tests will be dealt with. On basis of their results the Kattenbusch roadway bridge could be strengthened in 1987.

EXPERIMENTAL WORK

Aim and Program of Tests

For the strengthening of the prestressed concrete roadway bridge with externally bonded FRP plates as described in the next section tests became necessary. The bottom slab of the hollow box cross-section of the continious multispan bridge exhibited severe transverse cracks. They were caused by thermal restraint. As the reinforcement of the bottom slab proved to

Table 1: Properties of GFRP elements

property	unit	Bayer (Polystal)	Grilla	Röchling-Haren
fiber arrangement	-	ud	ud	95 % ud
matrix resin	-	unsat. polyester	unsat. polyester	epoxy
fiber content	Vol.-%	68	42	51
Young's mod F_u	GPa	55	29	39
ax. tensile str. f_c	MPa	1800	520	700
shape	mm	round, ø 7,5	10 x 100	10x100,5x200 etc

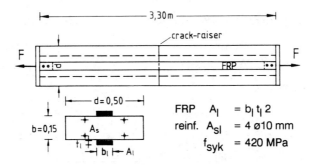

Fig. 1: Specimen for axial tension test

be to low to control the crack widths and the dynamic stress amplitude in the tendon couplers, additional reinforcement became necessary. In previous bridges steel plates were bonded to the bottom slab's inner surface /8/. Now FRP plates were chosen.

If the hollow box section is subjected to a high positive bending moment and to a normal force due to prestress the bottom slab can be regarded as an axially stressed concrete tension member. Hence, the test specimens had to simulate a cut-out of the slab. They were subjected to axial force incrementally increased to failure. Measurement of crack widths, local strains and of strains on a long basis was performed.

Test specimen and test procedure

The test specimen was a concrete member of a length of 3,30 m, of a breadth of 0,50 m and of a thickness of 0,15 m (as in the structure). Its concrete strength at test at the age of 28 days was 30 MPa. The inner reinforcement consisted of 4 deformed BSt 420/500 RK bars with d_s = 10 mm (act $f_{sy} \approx f_{syk}$; $E_s \approx 200$ GPa). The external FRP reinforcement of GFRP plates of 10 mm thickness was glued on the broad sides of the concrete member. The GFRP plates were fabricated by Röchling-Haren (last column of Table 1). Two specimens with external FRP plates were tested: BT1 with plates 10 x 100 mm and BT2 with plates 10 x 200 mm. For bonding the epoxy glue XB3074 of CIBA-GEIGY AG was used which is commonly applied for the bonding of steel plates. The surface treatment of concrete is the same as for steel plates. The surface of FRP has to be slightly roughened with sand paper and then be cleaned with an organic solvent. Additional details are given in /6/.

The specimen was tested in axial tension in a vertical test machine. Introduction of force was performed via steel end plates to which the inner reinforcement and additional deformed bars were welded. Also the FRP plates were fastened by bolts to the end plates. In the middle of the specimen's length a thin steel plate was arranged as crack raiser. The test specimen was loaded incrementally. The total strain ε_m of specimen across cracks was measured with LVDT on a length of 2,5 m. At the section of the crack-raiser the steel strains of the FRP plates an of the bars were measured. At each load stage the cracks were mapped, their widths measured. At service force level 10^5 load cycles were performed.

Theoretical relations

Purpose and assumptions

For the interpretations of the test results and for the valuation of the suitability of the external strengthening with FRP plates theoretical relations are necessary. These relations pertain to the distribution of forces, to the stiffness and strengthening efficiency. The concrete member, symmetrically reinforced and strengthened, under axial tension is regarded. Fig. 2 shows the stress-strain lines of the components. It is assumed that the bond stiffness and the bond transmission length of the deformed bar, embedded in concrete, and of the FRP plate, glued to the concrete, do

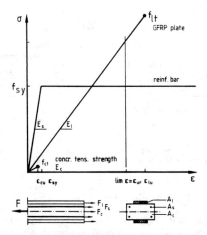

Fig. 2: Stress-strain lines, total areas and total forces of the components

not differ significantly. The areas A_c, A_s, A_l are the total cross-section, the forces F_c, F_s and F_l are the forces pertaining to the areas.

<u>Stiffness factors</u>

The mechanical behaviour of a member consisting of different materials will be influenced by the extensional stiffnesses of the components. The stiffness in the uncracked stage is

$$K_{id} = E_c A_c + E_s A_s + E_l A_l \quad , \tag{1}$$

and in the cracked section (ε_r crack strain):

$$K_{cr} = \frac{F_r}{\varepsilon_r} \tag{2}$$

The mean stiffness of the member in the cracked stage is:

$$K_{crm} = \frac{F}{\varepsilon_m} \tag{3}$$

with ε_m the mean strain across cracks, hence with tension stiffening. In the sequel relative stiffness values are used:

$$k_c = \frac{E_c A_c}{E_l A_l} \qquad k_s = \frac{E_s A_s}{E_l A_l} \qquad k_l = \frac{E_l A_l}{E_l A_l} = 1 \tag{4a) to (4c}$$

<u>Forces and strains in the uncracked stage</u>

The strains of all components are identical:

$$\varepsilon_c = \varepsilon_s = \varepsilon_l = \varepsilon \quad \text{and} \quad \varepsilon_c \leq \varepsilon_{cu} = \frac{f_{ct}}{E_c}$$

256

Hence we obtain (Fig. 2):

$$F = F_c + F_s + F_l \tag{5}$$

$$F = \varepsilon\, E_1\, A_1(k_c + k_s + 1) \tag{6}$$

The cracking force is attained at $\varepsilon = \varepsilon_{cu}$

$$F_{cr} = \varepsilon_{cu}\, E_1\, A_1(k_c + k_s + 1) \tag{7}$$

Forces and strains in the cracked section

a. Elastic reinforcement $(\varepsilon_r < \varepsilon_{sy})$

With the common strain ε_r in the crack

$$\varepsilon_r \le \varepsilon_{sy} = \frac{f_{sy}}{E_s} \qquad \text{and with } \varepsilon_s = \varepsilon_l = \varepsilon_r$$

we obtain the forces in the crack:

$$F_r = F_{sr} + F_{lr} \qquad F_{sr} = \frac{k_s}{1 + k_s} F_r \qquad F_{lr} = \frac{1}{1 + k_s} F_r \tag{8a) to (8c}$$

In terms of the strain in the crack the forces can be expressed by:

$$F_r = \varepsilon_r\, E_1\, A_1(1 + k_s)\,, \quad F_{sr} = \varepsilon_r\, E_1\, A_1\, k_s \quad \text{and } F_{lr} = \varepsilon_r\, E_1\, A_1 \tag{9a) to (9c}$$

Yielding of the reinforcement occurs under the total force

$$F_{yr} = \varepsilon_{sy}\, E_1\, A_1(1 + k_s) \tag{10}$$

b. Yielding reinforcement $(\varepsilon_r > \varepsilon_{sy})$

Because of

$$F_{syr} = f_{sy}\, A_s \tag{11}$$

and of

$$F_l = \varepsilon_r\, E_1\, A_1 \tag{12}$$

the total force is

$$F_r = \varepsilon_r\, E_1\, A_1(1 + k_s \frac{\varepsilon_{sy}}{\varepsilon_r}) \tag{13}$$

Fig. 3 shows the relations (6) and (9).

257

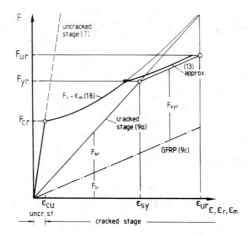

Fig. 3: Dependence of force on strain in different stages (schematically; numbers in brackets refer to Eq.)

c. Ultimate force

The ultimate force based on the failure of either steel or FRP in tension can only be expressed as a nominal value. It is assumed that an eventual bond failure does not prematurely occur. By introduction of a limit strain $\varepsilon_{ur} < \varepsilon_{lu}$ we obtain with Eq. (13) and Fig. 3:

$$F_{ur} = f_{sy} A_s + \varepsilon_{ur} E_l A_l \tag{14}$$

or

$$F_{ur} = \varepsilon_{mr} E_l A_l \left(1 + k_s \frac{\varepsilon_{sy}}{\varepsilon_{ur}}\right) \tag{15}$$

For the strain ε_{ur} a value of e.g. 5 ^{o}/oo can be chosen, which is less than ε_{su} and ε_{lu}.

Tension stiffening

It can be shown with /9/ that the mean axial strain ε_m of the tension member across cracks follows the relation

$$\varepsilon_m \approx \varepsilon_r \left[1 - \left(\frac{F_{cr}}{F_r}\right)^2 \rho\right] \tag{16}$$

with F_{cr} acc. to Eq. (7) and F_r acc. to Eq. (9) and with

$$\rho = \frac{k_c}{1 + k_s + k_c}. \tag{17}$$

With Eq. (7) and (9) the relation between the force F_r and the mean strain is obtained:

$$F_r = \frac{\varepsilon_m E_l A_l (1 + k_s)}{2} \left[1 + \sqrt{1 + \left(\frac{\varepsilon_{cu} (1 + k_c + k_s)}{\varepsilon_m (1 + k_s)}\right)^2 4\rho}\right] \tag{18}$$

258

Its dependence on the strain ε_m is shown in Fig. 3. Eq. (18) is valid as long as the reinforcement does not yield.

Strengthening and stiffening factor

The gain of strength by externally bonded FRP plates can be expressed by the strengthening factor

$$\eta = \frac{F_{sy} + \varepsilon_{ur} E_l A_l}{F_{sy}} \geq 1 \tag{19}$$

Exterior strengthening is often applied to reduce the static and/or dynamic steel stresses of the reinforcement or the crack width under the service load F_r. It is assumed that the section is cracked, the reinforcement stress yet elastic. The reduction of the steel stress in the crack can be expressed by

$$\frac{\sigma_{sr}}{\sigma_{sro}} = \frac{k_s}{1 + k_s} < 1; k_s = \frac{E_s A_s}{E_l A_l} \tag{20}$$

with σ_{sro} the steel stress of the unstrengthened member and σ_{sr} of the strenghtened member. External reinforcement increases the stiffness. With the stiffness of cracked section of the unstrenghtened member K_o and with the stiffness K_{st} after strengthening, we obtain the stiffening factor:

$$\omega = \frac{K_{st}}{K_o} = \frac{E_s A_s + E_l A_l}{E_s A_s} = \frac{1 + k_s}{k_s} > 1 \tag{21}$$

Table 2 contains important theoretical values of the test specimens BT1 and BT2. For comparison the values of the specimen HV-1 from /10/ are included. This specimen is identical with BT1 and BT2, however it was strengthened with two steel plates 3 x 100 mm (f_{ly} = 220 MPa; $E_l \approx 200$ GPa).

Table 2: Main data and values of the test specimens

specimen	plate material	E	A_l	A_s (4 ∅ 10mm)	F_{ur}	η	ω
		GPA	mm^2	mm^2	kN	strength. factor	stiffening factor
BT1	GFRP	30	2000 (2x10x100)	314	432	3.3	2.0
BT2	GFRP	30	4000 (2x10x200)	314	732	5.5	2.9
HV1	steel	200	600 (2x3x100)	314	264	2.0	2.9

Main results

Force-strain relations

Fig. 4 shows the measured relation between the total force F and the mean strain ε_m over a measuring basis of 2,50 m. Because of the crack-raiser at half-length the cracking force F_{cr} cannot be registered, it is estimated to be 150 kN with f_{ct} = 2 MPa. The force-strain loops between 15 and 132 kN for 10^5 cycles are not depicted. They lead to a decrease of the tension stiffening. The test

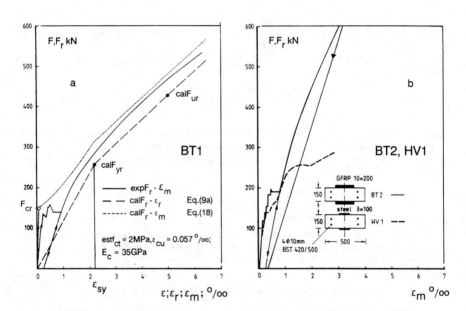

Fig. 4: Measured and calculated force-strain relation of specimens BT1, BT2 and HV1

was terminated at 580 kN without failure of bond or of the components. This corresponds to a strain of 7 °/oo, recovery was elastic. The dashed line in Fig. 4a is the theoretical force-crack strain relation F_r - ε_r of Eq. (9a) and (13). The dotted line is the F_r - ε_m-relation with tension stiffening acc. to Eq. (18). The observed behaviour is well described by the theory.

The specimens BT2 and HV1 were strengthened in such a way to have the same stiffness in the service load range (elastic steel stresses), s. Table 2 and Fig. 4b. The test BT2 was terminated at about 620 kN without failure. The test HV1 was terminated once excessive yielding of reinforcement and steel plates occured. The 10^5 load-cycles of BT2 between 60 and 170 kN and the $2 \cdot 10^5$ cycles of HV1 between 64 and 170 kN are not depicted. Stiffness of both specimens is equivalent.

Stiffening

In Fig. 5 the measured values of the mean extentional stiffness K_{IIII} are plotted vs. the mean strain. It can be seen that in the range of the service load steel stresses - corresponding to $\varepsilon_m < 0.5$ °/oo; $\varepsilon_{sr} \approx 2 \varepsilon_m$ - the stiffness of all specimens is very similar.

Crack width

The specimen HV1 with the steel plate strengthening shows slightly lower crack widths than the GFRP specimens. However, for all specimens the crack width in the service load range of 150 to 200 kN is small: 0.15 - 0.20mm.

260

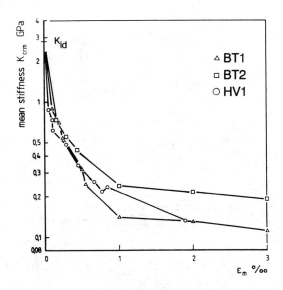

Fig. 5: Measured mean extensional stiffness vs. mean strain

STRENGTHENING OF THE KATTENBUSCH BRIDGE

Construction of bridge and cracks

The Kattenbusch bridge is a continious post-tensioned concrete roadway bridge with 11 spans (l = 36,5 m) consisting of two seperate hollow box girders (Fig. 6). It was built spanwise, with the working joints at the points of contraflexure. At these points all tendons were coupled. After several years many of these bridges exhibited wide cracks at the working joints. These cracks cut through the bottom slab and reached also into the webs of the girders. The main cause of the cracks is a temperature restraint in summer times which was not considered in the design. Because the bottom slab is only slightly reinforced wide cracks formed. However more important is the transformation of the working joints into a cracked section. An abrupt increase of the dynamic steel stresses in the tendon couplers - excess of the permissible value of $adm2\sigma_{pa}$ = 56 MPa for the PZ A 100 tendon - was the consequence. Their fatigue strength was in danger. Hence, additional reinforcement to control the crack width and to reduce the dynamic steel stresses became necessary.

Exterior plate strengthening

All working joints of both box girders were strengthened: 8 joints with steel plates (St 37, $f_{sy} \approx 240$ MPa; plates 10 x 100 x 3,0 m) and 2 joints with GFRP plates (s. Table 1, last column; 30 x 150 x 3,2 m) per box girder. Procedure of strengthening is described in /5/. The principal aim of the strengthening was the increase of stiffness of the bottom slab by additional reinforcement. The design for the steel plate strengthening led to a total cross-section of steel:

A_{ls} = 17 · 10 · 100 = 17.000 mm^2

261

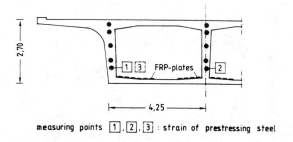

measuring points $\boxed{1}$, $\boxed{2}$, $\boxed{3}$: strain of prestressing steel

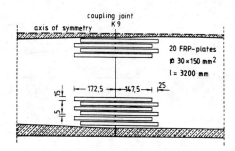

Fig. 6: Kattenbusch roadway bridge

With the total cross-section of GFRP plates of

$$A_{lGFRP} = 20 \cdot 15 \cdot 150 = 90.000 \text{ mm}^2$$

nearly the same stiffening factor $\omega \approx 4$, Eq. (21) related to the inner reinforcement of 8 ø 10/m is attained with GFRP plates. Fig. 6 shows the arrangement of GFRP plates in the ground plan of the half box.

Load test

In addition to the laboratory tests a load test of the bridge - before and after strengthening - was performed to study the suitability of GFRP plates in comparison with steel plates to reduce crack widths and dynamic steel stresses. The test load consisted of gravel-loaded trucks with a total load of 22 tons per truck. The trucks travelled side by side over the bridge. In several working joints the strain amplitudes of the couplers of the tendons closest to bottom edge of box girder were measured with LVDT (Fig. 6; couplers 1, 2 and 3). For this, the web and the duct had to be opened. The coupler consisted of threaded bars with d = 56 mm and a coupling sleeve with an inner thread. The strain amplitude $\Delta\sigma_p$ was measured on the coupler and then transformed into the stress amplitude of the prestressing steel.

In Fig. 7 the dependence of the measured stress change $\Delta\sigma_p$ on the position of the test load in two adjacent spans is shown. The maximum stress change in the unstrengthened stage was between 20 and 30 MPa. It was drastically reduced by strengthening with steel or FRP plates. The strengthening effect of both materials is identical. The work was performed in 1987. It is in perfect function.

262

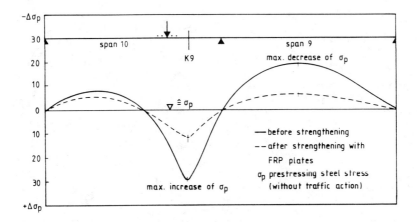

Fig. 7: Measured reduction of stress change $\Delta\sigma_p$ in the lowest tendon by external strengthening

REFERENCES

/1/ Ladner, M.; Weder, Ch.: Langzeitversuche an Stahlbetonbalken mit geklebter Bewehrung. In: Festschrift 100 Jahre EMPA, Dübendorf 1980, pp.44/51.

/2/ Lloyd, G.O.; Calder, A.J.J.: The microstructure of epoxy bonded steel-to-concrete joints. TRRL Chrowthorne Berkshire: TRRL 1982, Sup. Rep. 705.

/3/ Rostásy, F.S.; Ranisch, E.-H.: Einfluß von Temperaturen bis 60 °C und hoher Luftfeuchtigkeit auf das Dauerverhalten von tragenden Verklebungen von Beton und Stahl. Forschungsbericht Land Niedersachsen, 1988.

/4/ Meier, U.; Deuring, M.: The Application of Fiber Composites in Bridge Repair. Straße und Verkehr, 9/1991

/5/ Amtliche Materialprüfanstalt für das Bauwesen (MPA) Braunschweig, Untersuchungsbericht Nr. 3126/1429, Ankleben von Stahl- und GFK-Laschen im Bereich der Koppelfugen, Talbrücke Kattenbusch, Braunschweig, 1987.

/6/ Rostásy, F.S.; Ranisch, E.-H.: Sanierung von Betontragwerken durch Ankleben von Faserverbundwerkstoffen. Forschungsbericht Land Niedersachsen, 1984.

/7/ Rostásy, F.S.; Ranisch, E.-H.: Verstärkung von Stahlbetonplatten durch angeklebte Laschen aus glasfaserverstärktem Kunststoff. Forschungsbericht Land Niedersachsen, 1986.

/8/ Rostásy, F.S.; Ranisch, E.-H.: Strengthening of Bridges with epoxy bonded steel plate. IABSE Symposium: Maintenance, Repair and Rehabilitation of Bridges, Washington DC, 1982.

/9/ Rostásy, F.S.; Alda, W.: Rißbreitenbeschränkung bei zentrischem Zwang von Stäben aus Stahlbeton und Stahlleichtbeton. In: Beton- und Stahlbetonbau, 6/1977, pp. 149/156.

/10/ Rostásy, F.S.; Ranisch, E.-H.: Nachträgliche Verstärkung von Spannbetonbrücken im Koppelfugenbereich durch geklebte Stahllaschen. In: Forschung Straßenbau und Straßenverkehrstechnik, Heft 326, 1981, pp. 95/142.

ADVANCED COMPOSITE MATERIALS IN BRIDGES AND STRUCTURES
K.W. Neale and P. Labossière, Editors; Canadian Society for Civil Engineering, 1992

Matériaux composites d'avant-garde pour ponts et charpentes
K.W. Neale et P. Labossière, éditeurs; Société canadienne de génie civil, 1992

RENFORCEMENT DE POUTRES EN BÉTON ARMÉ À L'AIDE DE MATÉRIAUX COMPOSITES : ÉTUDES THÉORIQUE ET EXPÉRIMENTALE

M. Deblois, A. Picard et **D. Beaulieu**
Université Laval
Ste-Foy, Québec, Canada

RÉSUMÉ

Cet article traite du renforcement en flexion de poutres en béton armé, à l'aide de plaques minces en matériau composite. Un modèle théorique, basé sur la théorie fondamentale du béton armé, a d'abord permis d'étudier l'effet des paramètres les plus significatifs sur le comportement en flexion de poutres renforcées. Les prédictions du modèle théorique ont été vérifiées en réalisant deux séries d'essais, l'une sur des poutrelles (1000 x 125 x 125 mm) et l'autre sur des poutres (4100 x 300 x 200 mm). Ces essais ont démontré qu'il est possible d'obtenir une augmentation appréciable de la résistance en flexion. Dans cet article, on présente une partie des résultats théoriques et expérimentaux.

ABSTRACT

This paper deals with the flexural strengthening of reinforced concrete beams by means of thin composite plates. A theoretical model was first developed to study the effects of the most significant parameters on the flexural behaviour of strengthened beams. To verify the theoretical results, two series of tests were carried out, one on small beams (1000 x 125 x 125 mm) and the other on larger beams (4100 x 300 x 200 mm). These tests have shown a significant increase in flexural strength. Some theoretical and experimental results are presented in this paper.

INTRODUCTION

La recherche dont il est question dans cet article s'inscrit dans la problématique du renforcement des ponts, en particulier ceux en béton armé. Le sous-dimensionnement de nombreux ponts est un problème bien connu. Il résulte principalement de l'augmentation des surcharges routières (environ 40% en quarante ans), qui, combinée à des conditions environne-mentales particulièrement difficiles, a conduit à une dégradation des ouvrages.

Le renforcement de poutres en béton armé à l'aide de plaques d'acier, collées ou ancrées mécaniquement, est une technique assez répandue à cause de sa relative simplicité et à cause du fait qu'elle convient bien aux ouvrages à courtes et moyennes portées (10 à 30 m), les plus nombreux. L'utilisation de plaques en matériaux composites est une alternative intéressante parce que leur masse volumique est environ quatre fois moindre que celle de l'acier, ce qui facilite la manipulation et l'installation. De plus, le problème de la corrosion ne se pose pas. Les plaques dont il est question dans cet article, sont constituées de fibres de verre noyées dans une matrice faite d'une résine synthétique.

Pour l'analyse du comportement en flexion de poutres renforcées, nous avons utilisé un modèle théorique basé sur la théorie fondamentale du béton armé. On s'est d'abord limité au renforcement en flexion; le renforcement à l'effort tranchant fera l'objet d'études ultérieures. Ce modèle théorique a permis d'étudier l'effet des paramètres les plus significatifs sur le comportement en flexion de poutres renforcées. Ces paramètres sont le pourcentage d'armature passive, l'épaisseur de la plaque de renforcement et les propriétés du composite, en particulier, le module d'élasticité.

Une des hypothèses fondamentales du modèle théorique, c'est l'adhérence parfaite du composite au béton. Dans le but de vérifier cette hypothèse et aussi les prédictions du modèle théorique, deux séries d'essais furent planifiées. La première série fut réalisée sur des poutrelles en béton armé (1000x125x125mm), la deuxième sur des poutres en béton armé de section rectangulaire (300x200mm), ayant 4100 mm de longueur. Les plaques en matériaux composites furent soit collées, soit collées et ancrées mécaniquement.

Au moment d'écrire cet article, l'analyse de tous les résultats n'étant pas complétée, on ne présente donc qu'une partie des résultats théoriques et expérimentaux.

ÉTUDE THÉORIQUE

Le modèle théorique qui est utilisé pour l'analyse du comportement en flexion de poutres renforcées par une plaque placée sur la surface des fibres extrêmes en traction, permet de calculer la courbe charge-flèche jusqu'à la charge ultime. Seules les équations permettant de calculer la résistance ultime en flexion sont présentées ici. En plus des hypothèses conventionnelles du béton armé, on admet les deux hypothèses suivantes: l'adhérence de la plaque de renforcement au béton est parfaite, ce qui signifie aucun glissement relatif de la plaque par rapport au béton; le comportement du matériau composite reste linéaire, c'est-à-dire que la contrainte (σ) est toujours proportionnelle à la déformation unitaire ($\sigma = E_{com}\,\varepsilon$; E_{com} = module d'élasticité du composite).

Cette dernière hypothèse est vérifiée parce que les essais de traction montrent que la courbe $\sigma-\varepsilon$ des composites est linéaire jusqu'à la rupture.

La figure 1 montre les trois forces internes agissant sur une section rectangulaire à l'état limite ultime. La force de compression dans le béton est égale à:

$$C_u = (0,85f'_c)\,(\beta_1 c)\,b \qquad (1)$$

Dans cette équation, f'_c représente la résistance ultime du béton en compression et c représente la profondeur de l'axe neutre à l'état limite ultime.

La force de traction dans les armatures passives (T_u) dépend de la déformation unitaire au niveau de ces armatures (ε_s), à l'état limite ultime, donnée par:

$$\varepsilon_s = \varepsilon_u\left(\frac{d-c}{c}\right) \qquad (2)$$

On admet, comme en béton armé, que l'armature passive a un comportement élasto-plastique parfait. Par conséquent, si $\varepsilon_s < \varepsilon_y$, on a $\sigma_s = \varepsilon_s E_s$, où $E_s = 200\ 000$ MPa. Si $\varepsilon_s \geq \varepsilon_y$, on a $\sigma_s = f_y$. Les paramètres f_y et ε_y représentent respectivement la limite élastique et la déformation unitaire correspondant à la limite élastique ($\varepsilon_y = f_y/E_s$). Si A_s désigne l'aire de la section des armatures passives, on a donc:

$$T_u = \varepsilon_s\, E_s A_s \quad (\text{si } \varepsilon_s < \varepsilon_y) \tag{3}$$

$$T_u = f_y\, A_s \quad (\text{si } \varepsilon_s \geq \varepsilon_y) \tag{4}$$

La déformation unitaire au niveau du composite, à l'état limite ultime, est donnée par

$$\varepsilon_{com} = \varepsilon_u \left(\frac{h + 0,5t - c}{c} \right) \leq \varepsilon_{uc} = \frac{f_{uc}}{E_{com}} \tag{5}$$

L'équation (5) indique que la déformation unitaire du composite, à l'état limite ultime, ne doit pas dépasser la déformation unitaire ultime du composite (ε_{uc}) égale à la contrainte ultime du composite (f_{uc}) divisée par le module d'élasticité (loi de Hooke valide jusqu'à la rupture du composite).

La force de traction dans le composite est égale à:

$$T_{com} = (\varepsilon_{com}\, E_{com})(wt) \tag{6}$$

Les paramètres géométriques des équations (5) et (6) sont définis sur la figure 1. L'équilibre des forces donne:

$$C_u = T_u + T_{com} \tag{7}$$

Si l'acier d'armature ne se plastifie pas à l'état limite ultime de résistance à la flexion ($\varepsilon_s < \varepsilon_y$), les équations (1) (2) (3) (5) (6) et (7) donnent l'équation quadratique suivante pour le calcul de la position de l'axe neutre (c):

$$(0,85\beta_1\, f_c' b)c^2 + \varepsilon_u (E_s A_s + E_{com} wt)c - \varepsilon_u [E_s A_s d + E_{com}\, wt\, (h+0,5t)] = 0 \tag{8}$$

Si l'acier d'armature se plastifie ($\varepsilon_s \geq \varepsilon_y$), les équations (1) (4) (5) (6) et (7) donnent l'équation quadratique suivante pour le calcul de la position de l'axe neutre:

$$(0,85\beta_1\, f_c' b)c^2 + (\varepsilon_u\, E_{com} wt - A_s f_y)c - \varepsilon_u\, E_{com}\, wt\, (h+0,5t) = 0 \tag{9}$$

En résolvant l'une des deux équations quadratiques précédentes, on obtient la position de l'axe neutre à l'état limite ultime, ce qui permet de calculer le moment fléchissant ultime que peut supporter la section.

$$M_u = T_u (d - 0,5\beta_1 c) + T_{com} (h+0,5t - 0,5\beta_1 c) \tag{10}$$

À l'aide de cette théorie, on peut étudier l'influence de certains paramètres sur la capacité ultime en flexion. Sur la figure 2, on montre l'influence de l'épaisseur de la plaque de renforcement (t), l'influence du module d'élasticité du composite (E_{com}) et celle de la résistance en compression du béton (f_c'). La section utilisée pour les calculs est celle des poutres du programme expérimental ($h = 300$ mm, $d = 250$ mm, $b = 200$ mm, $w = 150$ mm, $A_s = 400$ mm^2, $f_y = 400$ Mpa). Les valeurs de f_c' indiquées sur la fig. 2 peuvent sembler faibles mais, dans le cas de renforcement de vieux ponts, ces valeurs sont réalistes.

On note sur la fig. 2 que, pour une épaisseur donnée, la résistance ultime en flexion augmente lorsque le module d'élasticité du composite augmente. Toutefois, il s'agit d'une augmentation à taux décroissant. On observe également une augmentation à taux décroissant de la résistance en fonction de l'épaisseur, pour une valeur fixe quelconque du module d'élasticité du composite. La résistance ultime en flexion augmente aussi lorsque la résistance du béton en compression augmente, mais contrairement aux cas précédents il s'agit d'une augmentation à taux croissant. En effet, l'augmentation est plus significative lorsque le module d'élasticité du composite est élevé.

ÉTUDE EXPÉRIMENTALE

Propriétés des composites

Deux types de composites ont été utilisés lors des essais: un composite bidirectionnel dont les fibres sont orientées selon les directions longitudinale et transversale de la plaque de renforcement; un composite unidirectionnel dont les fibres sont orientées uniquement dans la direction longitudinale. Les deux types sont constitués de fibres de verre de catégorie E noyées dans une résine polyester. Quelques propriétés de ces composites sont présentées dans le tableau 1.

Si on compare deux composites ayant un même pourcentage volumique de fibres, l'un unidirectionnel l'autre bidirectionnel, ce dernier a évidemment moins de fibres dans le sens longitudinal, c'est-à-dire dans le sens d'application de l'effort de traction, d'où une résistance en traction moins élevée. Toutefois, si on utilise des ancrages mécaniques pour relier la plaque de renforcement au béton (ancrages placés dans des trous forés dans la plaque et le béton), il est essentiel d'utiliser un composite bidirectionnel. En effet, la butée des ancrages contre un composite unidirectionnel produit le défilage du composite, d'où une résistance faible à la butée et l'inefficacité des ancrages. Dans un composite bidirectionnel, les fibres transversales augmentent la résistance à la butée parce qu'elles permettent de mieux distribuer les contraintes autour des trous.

Description des spécimens

Une première série d'essais fut réalisée sur des poutrelles en béton armé de section carrée (125x125mm), ayant une longueur totale de 1000 mm. Cette première série d'essais avait d'abord pour but de vérifier l'efficacité de la colle commerciale choisie à la suite d'essais préliminaires sur différents types de colle.

Le béton des poutrelles avait une résistance moyenne en compression de 22,5 MPa. L'armature des poutrelles comprenait deux barres no 10 (A_s = 200 mm^2) et 26 étriers no 2 carrés (85x85mm) espacés de 40 mm (A_v = 2x32 = 64 mm^2). Les sections des six poutrelles testées sont montrées sur la fig. 3. Le spécimen de référence, non renforcé, est dénoté 125-01. Le spécimen 125-1/4-C est renforcé à l'aide d'une plaque collée ayant une épaisseur de 1/4 de pouce (6,35 mm; composite bidirectionnel). Le spécimen 125-1/4-CA est identique au précédent sauf que la plaque est collée et ancrée mécaniquement. Le spécimen 125-3/16-C est renforcé à l'aide de deux plaques collées ayant une épaisseur de 3/16 de pouce (4,75 mm; composite unidirectionnel). Le spécimen 125-3/16-CRC est identique au précédent sauf que les faces verticales ont été renforcées à l'aide de plaques collées (t = 6,35 mm; composite bidirectionnel). Le dernier spécimen, dénoté 125-S1/4-CARC, est un spécimen spécial. Il est renforcé sur sa face inférieure par une plaque ayant une épaisseur de 6,35 mm, collée et ancrée, et par deux plaques ayant une épaisseur de 4,75 mm, collées sur la plaque de 6,35 mm d'épaisseur. De plus, les faces verticales de ce spécimen sont renforcées comme celles du spécimen précédent.

La deuxième série d'essais a été réalisée sur des poutres de section rectangulaire (300x200mm), ayant une longueur totale de 4100 mm. Le béton de ces poutres avait une résistance moyenne en compression de 28,6 MPa. L'armature comprenait deux barres no 15 (A_s = 400 mm^2) et 32 étriers no 10 rectangulaires (230x140 mm) espacés de 120 mm (A_v = 2x100 = 200 mm^2). Seuls les résultats des essais sur les deux premières poutres sont présentés plus loin. La poutre de référence, non renforcée, est dénotée G-01. L'autre poutre est dénotée G-1/4-CA6. Elle est renforcée sur sa face inférieure par une plaque d'épaisseur 1/4 de pouce (6,35 mm; composite bidirectionnel), ayant 150 mm de largeur, collée et ancrée à l'aide de six ancrages mécaniques, trois à chaque extrémité de la plaque.

Le mode de chargement des poutres et des poutrelles ainsi que les dimensions longitudinales des plaques de renforcement sont montrés sur la fig. 4. Lors des essais sur les poutrelles, en plus de la charge appliquée, on a mesuré les flèches au centre à l'aide de deux déflectomètres mécaniques. Lors des essais sur les poutres, l'instrumentation a été beaucoup plus importante. Des jauges électriques ont permis de mesurer les déformations unitaires du béton et du composite. Les flèches et le glissement relatif de la plaque de renforcement ont été mesurés à l'aide de LVDT. Toutes les lectures ont été prises automatiquement à l'aide d'un système d'acquisition de données.

Collage et ancrage

Pour le collage des plaques de renforcement, on a utilisé une colle commerciale composée d'un époxy et d'un durcisseur (colle vendue sous le nom de MAGNOBOND 56). Les surfaces de collage ont été soigneusement préparées. La surface de béton a été nettoyée à l'acide muriatique. Quant à la surface du composite, elle a été sablée à l'aide d'un papier abrasif à gros grains pour enlever le fini lustré et augmenter l'adhérence de la colle, sans toutefois abimer les fibres. Ensuite, elle été nettoyée au propanol pour enlever les particules fines laissées par le sablage.

Pour certains spécimens, en plus d'être collées, les plaques de renforcement ont été ancrées mécaniquement à l'aide d'ancrages de type "Kwik-bolt" fabriqués par la compagnie Hilti. Les propriétés de ces ancrages sont données dans le tableau 2. Dans le cas des poutrelles, on a négligé la contribution de la colle à la résistance au cisaillement sur l'interface dans le calcul du nombre d'ancrages. Par contre, pour les poutres, on a admis que la colle reprenait la moitié du cisaillement et les ancrages l'autre moitié. La disposition transversale et longitudinale des ancrages est montrée sur les figures 3 et 5. On rappelle qu'avec des ancrages mécaniques, il est recommandé d'utiliser un composite bidirectionnel.

Résultats expérimentaux

Les courbes montrant les flèches mesurées au centre des poutrelles et des poutres, en fonction de la charge appliquée, sont présentées sur les figures 6 et 7. Dans le tableau 3, on compare la charge ultime obtenue expérimentalement à la charge ultime théorique, calculée avec les propriétés mécaniques mesurées des matériaux.

On note dans le tableau 3 que la charge ultime mesurée est toujours inférieure à celle calculée, sauf pour la poutrelle 125-3/16-CRC. On note également plusieurs ruptures en cisaillement dans les poutrelles. Sur la figure 6, on remarque que ce type de rupture cause une cassure dans la courbe charge-flèche. Dans le but d'éliminer ce type de rupture, les deux dernières poutrelles ont été renforcées en cisaillement en collant des plaques sur les faces verticales (fig. 3). Si on compare les charges ultimes expérimentales des spécimens 125-3/16-C et 125-3/16-CRC, on note que le renforcement des faces latérales a produit une augmentation de la résistance mais le type de rupture n'a pas changé. Il convient de souligner que les charges ultimes théoriques des deux dernières poutrelles ont été calculées sans tenir compte du renforcement des faces verticales.

Pour la poutre renforcée G-1/4-CA6, la rupture s'est produite à la suite du décollement de la plaque de renforcement à une des extrémités. Après ce décollement, la plaque a buté très fortement contre les ancrages et les trous se sont ovalisés d'au moins 15 mm.

On note, sur les figures 6 et 7 et dans le tableau 3, une augmentation significative de la résistance relativement aux spécimens non renforcés. Dans le cas des poutres, cette augmentation, qui est d'environ 65%, s'accompagne d'une réduction de la ductilité (fig. 7). La flèche mesurée avant la rupture de la poutre renforcée est quand même importante (L/60).

Comparaison avec une plaque d'acier

Pour compléter cette étude, on a calculé l'épaisseur de la plaque d'acier qu'il faudrait utiliser à la place du composite pour obtenir la même résistance ultime que celle de la poutre G-1/4-CA6. La plaque est en acier G40.21M-300W (F_y = 300 MPa) et elle a la même largeur que la plaque composite (w = 150 mm). On a obtenu une plaque d'acier de 3,2 mm d'épaisseur, ce qui donne un poids d'environ 3,8 kg/m pour la plaque d'acier, comparé à 1,6 kg/m pour la plaque composite. Le coût de la plaque d'acier a été évalué à $6,70/m alors que celui de la plaque composite est de $20,30/m. Toutefois, selon Meier et Kaiser (1991), le coût des matériaux lors du renforcement d'un pont ne représente que 20% du coût total, alors que le coût de la main d'oeuvre représente 80%. Ce dernier coût pourrait être réduit de façon significative par l'utilisation de plaques composites à cause de leur poids plus faible, ce qui facilite la manipulation et la pose.

CONCLUSION

Selon les résultats préliminaires présentés dans cet article, on peut envisager l'utilisation de matériaux composites pour renforcer des poutres en béton armé et possiblement en béton précontraint. Il faut cependant reconnaître que plusieurs questions n'ont pas encore été abordées, entre autres la préparation des surfaces de béton en chantier, les effets thermiques, le contrôle de la qualité des composites, leur disponibilité, ... Il est vraisemblable que, pour le renforcement de structures existantes, l'utilisation d'ancrages mécaniques sans collage soit une solution plus réaliste, à cause de la difficulté de contrôler la qualité d'exécution du collage.

RÉFÉRENCE

MEIER, U., KAISER, H. (1991). Strengthening of Structures with CFRP Laminates. Proceedings of the ASCE Specialty Conference: Advanced Composite Materials in Civil Engineering Structures, p. 224-232.

REMERCIEMENTS

Les auteurs désirent remercier M. Michel Deblois de la firme PKD Consult Inc. (Beauport, Québec) pour ses nombreux conseils et son expertise sur l'utilisation de matériaux composites.

Tableau 1 - Principales propriétés des composites utilisés

Propriétés	Composite bidirectionnel	Composite unidirectionnel
Pourcentage volumique de fibres	40-45%	65-70%
Résistance à la traction longitudinale (MPa)	210	690
Module d'élasticité longitudinal, E_{com} (MPa)	17 240	41 380
Déformation unitaire à la rupture, ε_{uc}	1,22%	1,67%
Coefficient de dilatation thermique longitudinal (mm/mm/°C)	$5,2 \times 10^{-6}$	$3,0 \times 10^{-6}$

Tableau 2 - Propriétés des ancrages mécaniques

Propriétés	Poutrelles	Poutres
Type d'ancrage	KB38-312	KB12-512
Diamètre de l'ancrage (mm)	9,5	12,7
Profondeur d'enfoncement recommandée (mm)	60	85
Résistance au cisaillement * (kN)	24	37
Résistance à la traction* (kN)	18	32
Torque appliquée (N•m)	35	90

*Propriétés mécaniques pour f_c = 25 MPa

Tableau 3 - Comparaison des charges ultimes

Spécimen	Charge ultime mesurée (kN)	Charge ultime théorique (kN)*	Type de rupture
125-01	35,7	36,6	compression
125-1/4-C	47,1	48,6	compression
125-1/4-CA	48,0	48,6	cisaillement
125-3/16-C	42,1	55,0	cisaillement
125-3/16-CRC	56,5	55,0	cisaillement
125-S1/4-CARC	62,8	63,1	cisaillement
G-01	57,4	58,2	compression
G-1/4-CA6	95,4	102,4	décollement

*Calculée avec les propriétés mécaniques mesurées (f_c, f_y)

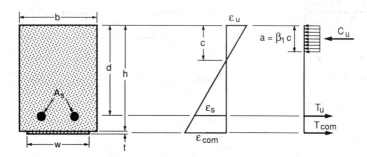

Notes: $f'_c \leq 30$ MPa , $\beta_1 = 0{,}85$

$f'_c \geq 30$ MPa , $\beta_1 = 1{,}09 - 0{,}008 \, f'_c \geq 0{,}65$

ε_u (théorique) = 0,003

Fig. 1 - Forces internes à l'état limite ultime.

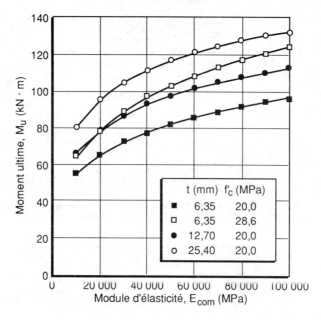

Fig. 2 - Quelques résultats théoriques.

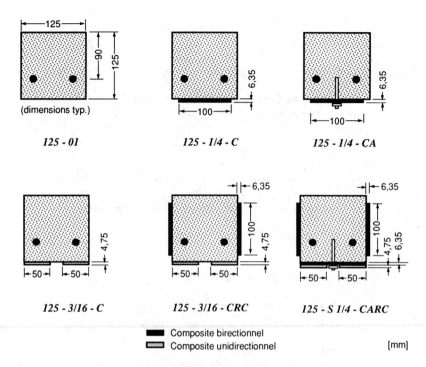

125 - 01   125 - 1/4 - C   125 - 1/4 - CA

125 - 3/16 - C   125 - 3/16 - CRC   125 - S 1/4 - CARC

■ Composite birectionnel
▨ Composite unidirectionnel   [mm]

Fig. 3 - Section transversale des poutrelles.

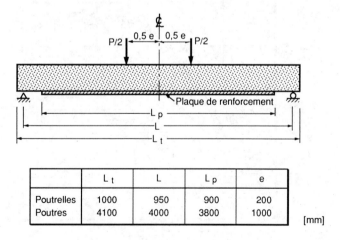

	L_t	L	L_p	e
Poutrelles	1000	950	900	200
Poutres	4100	4000	3800	1000

[mm]

Fig. 4 - Mode de chargement.

273

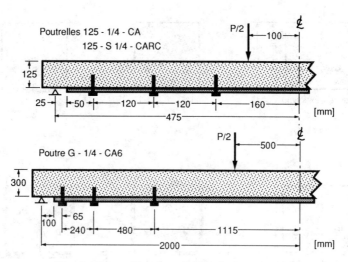

Fig. 5 - Disposition longitudinale des ancrages.

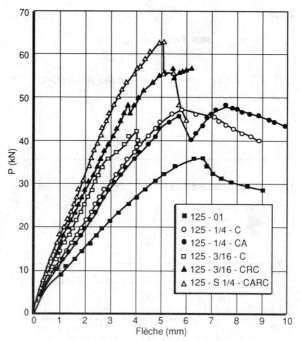

Fig. 6 - Courbes charge-flèche des poutrelles.

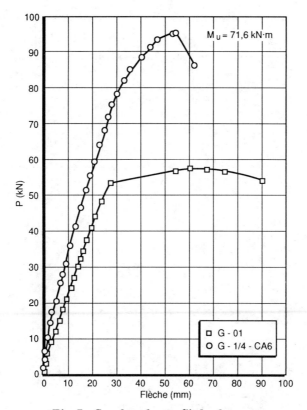

Fig. 7 - Courbes charge-flèche des poutres.

ADVANCED COMPOSITE MATERIALS IN BRIDGES AND STRUCTURES
K.W. Neale and P. Labossière, Editors; Canadian Society for Civil Engineering, 1992

Matériaux composites d'avant-garde pour ponts et charpentes
K.W. Neale et P. Labossière, éditeurs; Société canadienne de génie civil, 1992

OPTIMAL DESIGN FOR PRESTRESSING WITH FRP SHEETS IN STRUCTURAL MEMBERS

G.N. Karam
Massachusetts Institute of Technology
Cambridge, Massachusetts, USA

ABSTRACT

The short term mechanical behaviour of prestressing structural members with externally bonded FRP sheets is reviewed from a design point of view. The efficiency of this method is controlled by the maximum achievable prestress level so that the FRP-prestressed system does not fail near the anchorage zones due to the shear stress concentration that arises from the discontinuity at the end of the member when the prestressing agent is released. At failure, only a small portion of the structural member reaches a critical load when FRP sheets of uniform width and thickness are used. It is proposed to increase the efficiency of the technique by specially designing the anchorage zones. The condition of uniform shear stress and strain in the adhesive layer is proposed as a design constraint. The feasibility of theoretical solutions and practical schemes to implement them are investigated.

RÉSUMÉ

Le comportement à court terme des charpentes précontraintes par collage de plaques en FRP est présenté du point de vue de la conception. L'efficacité de cette méthode dépend du niveau maximum de précontrainte avant la rupture des zones d'ancrage. Cette rupture est due à la concentration des contraintes de cisaillement causées par la discontinuité aux extrémités de l'élément lorsque le mécanisme de précontrainte est relâché. Dans le cas de plaques d'épaisseurs et de largeurs uniformes, seule une petite partie de la charpente atteint des charges critiques à la rupture. L'efficacité du renforcement peut être accrue par une conception spéciale des zones d'ancrage. La faisabilité des solutions théoriques et les moyens pratiques de les appliquer sont étudiés.

INTRODUCTION

After years of being confined to aerospace and high technology applications Fibre Reinforced Plastic (FRP) composites are finding their way into civil engineering helped by lower prices and the need to repair, rehabilitate and replace the ageing infrastructure of the industrialised world namely North America, Japan and Europe. These composites are becoming increasingly important in the construction industry and their future role and applications have been investigated in a state of the art report (Mufti et al. 1991). The use of externally bonded FRP sheets as reinforcement in structural members has been recently investigated theoretically and experimentally showing good promise of higher ratios of strength to weight and stiffness to weight in the structural systems considered (Triantafillou and Plevris, 1990, 1992, Saadatmanesh and Ehsani 1991a, 1991b). The efficiency of the FRP sheet-reinforced structural member can be increased by prestressing the FRP sheet prior to bonding it, hence introducing an initial prestress in the member that can be used to balance applied dead and live loads as in conventional prestressed structures. A simplified theoretical approach to the problem was presented by Peterson (1965) in an investigation of glulam beams reinforced by prestressed steel sheets bonded on the tensile fibre side. Triantafillou and Deskovic (1991) have recently presented an analytical model for the short term mechanical behavior of rectangular structural members prestressed with externally bonded FRP sheets of uniform width and thickness and the theoretical predictions were in good agreement with experimental results (Triantafillou and Deskovic, 1992, Triantafillou et al., 1992). In this paper a theoretical analysis of prestressing with externally bonded FRP sheets is performed from the same basic principles as Triantafillou and Deskovic, (1991) but in a more generalised form that is also amenable to a design procedure. The mechanics of prestressing and failure are further investigated and the design of anchorage zones is studied theoretically and practically.

MECHANICS OF PRESTRESSING WITH EXTERNALLY BONDED FRP SHEET

General Derivation Of The Governing Equations

In this prestressing technique the composite sheet is first pretensionned by an initial force P^o then bonded to the tensile face of the beam. Upon curing of the adhesive the prestressing agent is released and the tension in the sheet is then balanced by compressive stresses that develop in the tensile fibre of the beam (Fig. 1). The loads between the composite sheet and the beam are transmitted by shear stresses in the adhesive layer. The mechanics of this structural system can be investigated by using the principles of displacement or strain compatibility, static equilibrium of the reinforced beam section, static equilibrium of the FRP sheet and the boundary conditions.

Consider a beam of length l, with a generic section of width b, height h, cross section area A, and moment of inertia I. It is reinforced with a FRP sheet of uniform area a, and uniform width b_f with $b_f{\le}b$, bonded with an adhesive layer of thickness d (Fig. 1). The material properties are as follows E_f=modulus of elasticity of the FRP, E_b=modulus of elasticity of the beam, G_a=shear modulus of the adhesive. The composite sheet is pretensionned by a load P^o that drops after the release of the pretensioning agent to P(x) with a compressive stress $\sigma_p(x)$ developping in the bottom fibre of the beam and a shear stress $\tau(x)$ developping in the adhesive. After the pretension is released the system shortens axially with the displacements at a section x of the three components shown in Fig. 2. Let $u_b(x)$=the shortening of the beam , $u_f^o(x)$=the initial extension of the FRP and $u_f(x)$=the extension of the FRP after the pretension is released. Assuming that all the materials are linear elastic and that the adhesive deforms mainly by shear, then from the displacement compatibility the shear strain, γ, in the adhesive layer at a section x can be written as:

$$\gamma = \frac{u_f^o - u_f + u_b}{d} \tag{1}$$

and the interface shear:

$$\tau = \frac{G_a}{d}(u_f^o - u_f + u_b) \tag{2}$$

differentiation of Eq. 2 with respect to x gives:

$$\frac{d\tau}{dx} = \frac{G_a}{d}(\varepsilon_f^o - \varepsilon_f + \varepsilon_b) \tag{3}$$

where ε_f^o, ε_f and ε_b are respectively: the initial strain in the FRP, the strain in the FRP after pretension release and the compressive strain in the bottom fibre of the beam.

The prestress σ_p, in the bottom fibre of the beam can be expressed as:

$$\sigma_p = -\left(\frac{1}{A} + \frac{h'^2}{I}\right)P = -\beta P \tag{4}$$

where h' is the distance from the bottom compressive fibre to the centroid of the reinforced section and β is a section property . Note that in most cases the effect of the FRP sheet on the moment of inertia can be neglected and h' will be very close to h/2.

From the equilibrium of a FRP strip of length dx, the following equation for the shear in the adhesive layer and at its interface is obtained:

$$\tau = \frac{-1}{b_f}\frac{dP}{dx} \tag{5}$$

Furthermore Eq. 3 can be rewritten in terms of P by using Eq. 4 and the constitutive law of the elastic materials :

$$\frac{d\tau}{dx} = \frac{G_a}{d}\left(\frac{1}{E_f a}(P^o - P) - \frac{1}{E_b}\beta P\right) \tag{6}$$

let n=E_f/E_b , differentiating Eq. 6 with respect to x and replacing dP/dx by its value from Eq. 5 a differential equation in τ is obtained:

$$\frac{d^2\tau}{dx^2} = w^2\tau \tag{7a}$$

$$w = \sqrt{\frac{G_a b_f(1 + n\beta a)}{E_f a d}} \tag{7b}$$

The solution to this differential equation is of the form:

$$\tau = Ae^{-wx} + Be^{wx} = C\cosh(wx) + D\sinh(wx) \tag{8}$$

A, B, C and D are constants determined from the boundary conditions. In fact due to the symmetry of the problem we always have $\tau(x=0)=0$, hence a priori C=0 and only one constant, D, is to be determined.

In the following sections these governing equations are used to find the minimum required FRP area and the pretensionning force needed to achieve a given prestress level at the middle section of the beam, $\sigma_p(x=0)$, without failure of the system upon pretension release.

Analysis In The Elastic Range

In this section all components are required to stay in the elastic range and the system is considered to have failed when a limit yield or fracture shear stress τ^* is reached. This maximum shear stress can correspond to either the yield stress of the adhesive or that of the beam (plastic yielding stress for steel and wood or cracking stress for concrete). From Eq. 8 it is seen that the shear stress will increase monotonically from the centre of the beam towards the edges where it will be maximum at x=l/2. Hence putting $\tau(x=l/2)=\tau^*$, Eq. 8 gives:

$$\tau = \tau^* \frac{\sinh(wx)}{\sinh(\frac{wl}{2})} \qquad (9)$$

Combining Eq. 6, 7b and 9 an equation for P is obtained:

$$P = \frac{1}{(1+n\beta a)}\left[P^0 - \sqrt{\left(\frac{E_f}{G_a}adb_f(1+n\beta a)\right)}\tau^*\frac{\cosh(wx)}{\sinh(\frac{wl}{2})}\right] \qquad (10)$$

Using the boundary condition P(x=l/2)=0, the initial pretension P^0 level can be found:

$$P^0 = \sqrt{\left(\frac{E_f}{G_a}adb_f(1+n\beta a)\right)}\coth\left(\frac{wl}{2}\right)\tau^* \qquad (11)$$

note that for most practical FRP sheet-prestressed systems wl/2>5, resulting in useful simplifications such as coth(wl/2)=1 in Eq. 11.

In the design problem it is required to achieve a prestress σ_p^* at the middle section of the beam, hence from Eq. 4 and 10 and assuming wl/2>5 :

$$\sigma_p^* = \beta P(x=0) = \frac{\beta}{(1+n\beta a)}P^0 \qquad (12)$$

and replacing P^0 by its value from Eq. 11:

$$\sigma_p^* = \beta\sqrt{\left(\frac{E_f adb_f}{G_a(1+n\beta a)}\right)}\tau^* \qquad (13)$$

With this last equation the design problem can be solved given the materials properties and the dimensions of the beam. The area of the sheet and its width have to satisfy two requirements: first achieve the required prestress σ_p^* found from Eq. 13 and second be strong enough to support the pretensionning load P^0:

$$\frac{P^0}{a} \leq \varepsilon_f^* E_f \qquad (14)$$

where ε_f^* is the tensile strain at failure, or the maximum allowable strain in the FRP composite. Assuming a value for $b_f \leq b$, Eq. 12, 13 and 14 can be solved iteratively for the required FRP area in the case of a feasible solution. For a given beam reinforced by a uniform FRP sheet there exists a maximum achievable prestress which cannot be exceeded without either exceeding τ^* or loading the FRP sheet beyond ε_f^*.

Analysis With Plastic Yielding In The Anchorage Zones

Triantafillou and Deskovic (1991) have derived the maximum initial prestress which upon release will just cause the failure of the system. The derivation is based on the elastic analysis with the addition of the contribution of the yielding or cracking in the anchorage zones. They have treated two cases:

1-Failure by cracking in the case of a concrete member: a very small crack evolves near the concrete-adhesive interface at the ends of the structural member. In this cracked anchorage zone the shear is reduced and the prestress transmitted can be calculated by solving a nonlinear system of equations (Triantafillou and Deskovic, 1991, Triantafillou et al., 1992). As it is unsafe to allow cracking in highly stressed concrete structures it is recommended to design for uncracked systems following the elastic analysis or to strengthen the anchorage regions to reduce cracking. This can be done by either specially designing the FRP sheet as presented in a subsequent section or by reinforcing the beam itself against shear stresses.

2-Failure by yielding of either the adhesive or the beam near the interface in an idealised elastic-perfectly plastic manner: the shear stress reaches its maximum value τ^* at some distance before the end of the beam and stays constant till the end while the strains increase in the yielding zone until an ultimate rupture value is reached (Triantafillou and Deskovic, 1991, 1992). This case is treated in the rest of the section.

When the pretension is released the shear stresses in the adhesive layer build up from the middle of the beam until a distance $x=l'/2 \leq l/2$ where $\tau(x=l'/2)=\tau^*$ and the shear strain $\gamma(x=l'/2)=\gamma^{el}$, γ^{el} being the elastic limit strain (Fig. 3). From $l'/2$ to the end of the beam at $l/2$ the shear stress remains constant while the shear strains increase until γ^*, the rupture strain, is reached causing failure. The shear strain in the elastic zone is described similarily to the shear stress by taking $\tau=\gamma G_a$ in Eq. 9, furthermore it is assumed that the equation so obtained for γ holds also in the plastic region (Triantafillou and Deskovic, 1991, 1992) :

$$\gamma = \gamma^{el}\frac{\sinh(w\,x)}{\sinh(\frac{w\,l}{2})}; 0 \leq x \leq \frac{l}{2} \qquad (15)$$

The length of the yielding zone $(l-l')/2$ is obtained by solving $\gamma(x=l/2)=\gamma^*$ in Eq. 15; noting that for $wl'/2 \geq 2$, $\sinh(wl'/2)=0.5e^{wl'/2}$ and $\sinh(wl/2)=0.5e^{wl/2}$ the solution is:

$$\frac{(l-l')}{2} = \sqrt{\left(\frac{E_f a d}{G_a b_f(1+n\beta a)}\right)}\ln\left(\frac{\gamma^*}{\gamma^{el}}\right) \qquad (16)$$

Assuming that the load in the FRP sheet decreases to zero linearly from $l'/2$ to $l/2$, P^o can be found as:

$$P^o = \left[\sqrt{\left(\frac{E_f}{G_a}adb_f(1+n\beta a)\right)}\coth(\frac{w\,l'}{2}) + b_f(1+n\beta a)\frac{(l-l')}{2}\right]\tau^* \qquad (17)$$

for all practical systems $wl'/2 \geq 2$ and $\coth(wl'/2)$ is equal or very close to unity. Eq. 17 replaces Eq. 11 in the elastic analysis and can be used with Eq. 12, 14 and 16 to design the prestressing of a structural element where yielding is allowed in the adhesive layer or in the beam. By contrast with Eq. 11, Eq. 17 shows two contributions to the pretensioning force: a first elastic term from the central part of the beam and a second plastic term from the anchorage zones. The second term is often the dominant one as seen in the FRP-prestressed systems that were investigated so far (Triantafillou and Deskovic, 1992). The efficiency of the technique, measured by the prestress introduced in the beam, is greatly improved by the presence of these plastic yield zones that transmit the prestress at the maximum possible shear stress level. It is however unsafe to allow extensive yielding and large plastic strains to take place in an engineering structural system in order to reach high prestresses. In the design of structures such as bridges and long spanning members it is expected that safety and reliability will confine the prestressing to the elastic range allowing very little or no yielding. Because of their controlling effect on the achievable prestress level, the anchorage or end zones in the system need to be specially designed to transmit the prestress safely and efficiently as will be shown in the next section.

Special Design Of The Anchorage Zones

It is proposed to create in the anchorage zones a region of highly efficient prestress transmission from the sheet to the beam at a constant maximum shear stress τ^* without however allowing the shear strains to increase causing yielding or cracking. Similarily to the previous section for a given prestress let $\tau(x=l'/2)=\tau^*$ with $l'/2 \leq l/2$. To keep the end zone $(l-l')/2$ in the elastic range, the shear stress and strain must stay constant at the limit of elasticity : $d\tau/dx=d\gamma/dx=0$; hence the area of the FRP sheet must increase. Assuming b_f to be constant while a varies, Eq. 5 shows P to decrease linearly to zero from $l'/2$ to $l/2$:

$$P(x) = \tau^* b_f \left(\frac{l}{2} - x \right); \frac{l'}{2} \leq x \leq \frac{l}{2} \tag{18}$$

and putting $d\tau/dx=0$ in Eq. 6 and solving for $a(x)$:

$$a = \frac{1}{n\beta} \left(\frac{P^o}{P} - 1 \right) = \frac{1}{n\beta} \left(\frac{P^o}{\tau^* b_f \left(\frac{l}{2} - x \right)} - 1 \right); \frac{l'}{2} \leq x \leq \frac{l}{2} \tag{19}$$

Thus it is possible to develop a highly efficient anchorage zone $(l-l')/2$, where the materials are not stressed beyond their elastic limit, by letting the FRP area increase hyperbolically. Note that mathematically $a(x=l/2)$ will tend to infinity, but practically it will have to be limited to the maximum practical area a_{max}. The value of P^o is given by Eq. 17 where a is the value of the FRP area over the uniform part l'.

FROM THEORY TO PRACTISE

Optimal Design Of Prestressing Sheet

The optimal design is defined as the one that minimizes the volume of FRP needed to achieve a required prestress level σ_p^* at the middle of a given beam with minimal or no cracking or yielding taking place in the component materials of the system; if cracking and plastic strains are reached, they should remain below rupture values. The following procedure is recommended:
1-Combining Eq. 12 and 14 the minimum FRP area, a_{min}, to support the pretension P^o is found as:

$$a_{min} = \frac{\sigma_p^*}{\beta \left(\varepsilon_f^* E_f - n\sigma_p^* \right)} \tag{20}$$

2-Assuming a value for b_f, $(l-l')/2$ is found from Eq. 17 with $a=a_{min}$. The increase in the area of FRP can then be calculated from Eq. 19 and the location $l*/2$ at which the maximum feasible FRP area is reached can also be found. In the region $(l-l*)/2$ at the end of the member the FRP area will be constant at a_{max}.

3-If $(l-l*)/2$ is not much smaller than the critical cracking length for concrete (Triantafillou and Deskovic, 1991) or $(l-l')/2$ obtained from Eq. 16 with $a=a_{max}$, the area a_{min} has to be increased and steps 2 and 3 repeated until a satisfactory solution is obtained.

The hyperbolic profile of the required FRP area in the anchorage zone can be approximated by either successive sheet laminations to increase the thickness or by flaring the ends of the sheet increasing its width. The lamination solution is the most practical and the area profile can be approximated by a series of equal steps corresponding to the thickness of sheet used. b_f was assumed constant throughout the analysis; if however it is possible to increase the area of the sheet by increasing its width, and be able to bond this added width to the bottom of the beam or even to its sides, this will result in a drop in the transmission shear stress hence increasing the capacity and safety of the assembly. These solutions are shown in Fig. 4.

Numerical Example

It is proposed to optimise the FRP prestressing sheet for a system analysed and tested by Triantafillou and Deskovic (1992). A small rectangular wood beam, l=800 mm, b=45 mm, h=60 mm was reinforced with an epoxy bonded (d=1 mm) CFRP sheet of uniform dimensions: b_f=44 mm and a=33 mm^2. The material properties are as follows: E_f=115 GPa, ε_f*=0.0122, G_a=2.8 GPa, E_w=13.5 GPa, $\tau*$=40 MPa, γ^{el}=0.012, $\gamma*$=0.039. At maximum achievable pretension the system fails by yielding of the wood near the adhesive interface. Noting that n=8.52 and β=1481.5 m^{-2} following the plastic yield analysis, Eq. 17, 16, and 12 give: P^o=25.3 kN, σ_p*=26.5 MPa and $(l-l')/2$=5.5 mm in agreement with the theoretical and experimental results of Triantafillou e and Deskovic (1992); and the volume of FRP used for this beam is 0.264 cm^3.

The FRP sheet design is now optimised while providing the same prestress σ_p*=26.5 MPa. Assuming b_f=44 mm, Eq. 20 yields a_{min}=15.2 mm^2, Eq. 12 gives P^o=21.3 kN and Eq. 17 gives $(l-l')/2$=6.7 mm. Eq. 19 gives $a(x=l'/2)$=63.9 mm^2, this sudden increase in the area corresponds to the discontinuity in $d\tau/dx$ at $l'/2$ (Fig. 3 and 4). Assuming that the FRP area can only be increased to a maximum of 128 mm^2 over the last 7mm then $(l-l*)/2$=4.6 mm and using $a=a_{max}$=128 mm^2 in Eq. 16 it is found that $(l-l')/2$=8.0 mm which almost twice $(l-l*)/2$. The FRP volume used in the optimised design is a little less than 0.137 cm^3 about half that needed for the non optimised system.

CONCLUSION

A theory for the optimal design of externally bonded FRP sheets for prestressing structural members was presented and practical ways of implementing it discussed. By minimising the volume of FRP needed it promises to keep the cost of using FRP composites at a minimum. Experimental investigation of the different anchorage designs is urgently needed to validate the approach and develop practical procedures for its application in the strengthening and repair of old structures and the construction of new ones.

REFERENCES

Mufti, A.A., Erki, M-A. and Jaeger L.G. editors (1991). Advanced Composite Materials with Application to Bridges. Published by the Canadian Society of Civil Engineers, Montréal, Canada, 297p.

Peterson, J. (1965). Wood Beams Prestressed with Bonded Tension Elements. *J. Struct. Div.,* ASCE, **91**(1), 103-119

Saadatmanesh, H. and Ehsani, M.R. (1991a). RC Beams Strengthened with GFRP Plates I: Experimental Study. *J. Struct. Engrg.,* ASCE, **117**(11), 3417-3433

Saadatmanesh, H. and Ehsani, M.R. (1991b). RC Beams Strengthened with GFRP Plates II: Analysis and Parametric Study. *J. Struct. Engrg.,* ASCE, **117**(11), 3434-3455

Triantafillou, T.C. and Deskovic, N. (1991). Innovative Prestressing with FRP Sheets: Mechanics of Short-Term Behavior. *J. Engrg. Mech.,* ASCE, **117**(7), 1652-1672

Triantafillou, T.C.and Deskovic, N. (1992). Prestressed FRP Sheets as External Reinforcement of Wood Members. *J. Struct. Engrg.,* ASCE, **118**(5), 1270-1284

Triantafillou, T.C., Deskovic, N. and Deuring, M. (1992). Strengthening of Concrete Structures with Prestressed Fiber Reinforced Plastic Sheets. *ACI Struct. J.,* **89**(3), 235-244

Triantafillou, T.C. and Plevris, N. (1990). Flexural Behavior of Structures Strengthened with Epoxy-Bonded Fiber-Reinforced Plastics. *International Seminar on Structural Repairs/Strengthening by the Plate Bonding Technique,* University of Sheffield, England, Sept. 1990

Triantafillou, T.C. and Plevris, N. (1992). Strengthening of RC Beams with Epoxy-Bonded Fiber-Composite Materials. to appear in *Materials and Structures,* RILEM, 1992

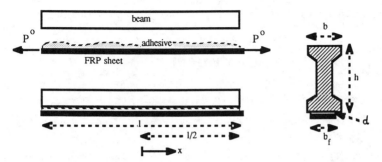

Fig. 1 Pretensionning a beam with a FRP sheet

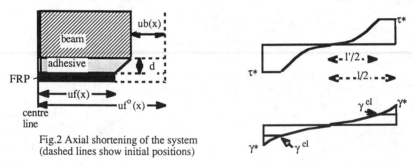

Fig.2 Axial shortening of the system
(dashed lines show initial positions)

Fig. 3 Shear stress and strain
distribution at yielding

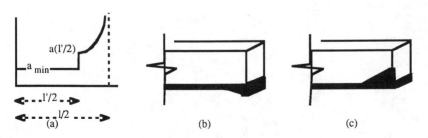

(a)   (b)   (c)

Fig. 4 (a) Optimal area profile (b) Area increase by lamination (c) Area increase by end flaring

285

ADVANCED COMPOSITE MATERIALS IN BRIDGES AND STRUCTURES
K.W. Neale and P. Labossière, Editors; Canadian Society for Civil Engineering, 1992

Matériaux composites d'avant-garde pour ponts et charpentes
K.W. Neale et P. Labossière, éditeurs; Société canadienne de génie civil, 1992

COLUMN SEISMIC RETROFIT USING
FIBREGLASS/EPOXY JACKETS

M.J.N. Priestley and **F. Seible**
University of California at San Diego
La Jolla, California, USA

E. Fyfe
Fyfe Associates, Inc.
Del Mar, California, USA

ABSTRACT

The concept of retrofitting bridge columns to enhance flexural and shear performance using fibreglass/epoxy composite jackets in critical regions is discussed. Results of tests of three large-scale flexural columns with longitudinal reinforcement lapped in the flexural plastic hinge region, and of four shear columns tested under double bending are reported. The experimental results indicate that properly designed composite jackets can inhibit lap-splice failures in hinge regions, and provide sufficient shear strength to columns with shear strength deficiency to ensure ductile flexural response.

RÉSUMÉ

Le renforcement de piliers de ponts par des gaines de fibre de verre/époxy, afin d'en améliorer la performance en flexion et en cisaillement, est discuté. Des résultats expérimentaux sont présentés pour trois colonnes en flexion avec le renfort installé dans la région de la rotule plastique, et de quatre colonnes en cisaillement testées en double flexion. Ces résultats indiquent que des gaines composites dimensionnées correctement peuvent prévenir la rupture dans la région de la rotule, et fournir suffisamment de résistance au cisaillement pour garantir une réponse ductile en flexion.

INTRODUCTION

As a consequence of failures of bridge columns in recent earthquakes [Fung et al. 1971, Priestley 1988, Buckle et al. 1990] a substantial research effort has been mounted to develop techniques for retrofitting circular and rectangular reinforced concrete columns to enhance flexural ductility and shear strength. One successful and widely implemented technique involves the use of cylindrical steel jackets of circular or elliptical shape [Chai et al. 1991, Priestley and Seible 1991].

When placed over the flexural plastic hinge regions with grout or concrete filling the void between the jacket and the column, ductile flexural response can be assured, even when longitudinal reinforcement is lap-spliced in the hinge region. Properly designed steel jackets on squat columns subjected to double bending can convert brittle shear failures to ductile flexural modes of inelastic deformation with remarkable ductility capacity.

This paper discusses an alternative method of retrofitting, using a combination of active and passive confinement provided by a jacket of fiberglass/epoxy composite material. For flexural plastic hinge regions, a layer of the material is first placed over the full extent of the potential hinge, and pressure grouted with either epoxy or cement grout. The process of pressure grouted induces reasonably large hoop strains in the jacket, ensuring that the grouted pressure is maintained, with little loss, after the grout has hardened. A second, passive layer of the composite material is placed over the end portion of the plastic hinge to provide additional passive confinement in the region where high longitudinal compression strain in the column indicates a need for extra confinement, or where the presence of lap-spliced longitudinal bars indicates the need for additional restraint. It should be noted that active confinement was expected to improve the seismic performance compared with passive confinement, since the dilation of the concrete core which is necessary to activate confinement in a passive system, and which implies the presence of significant longitudinal microcracking, is not essential in an actively confined system.

Regions between potential plastic hinges in a column subjected to high shear force may also be strengthened with the same active/passive combination. However, simple passive confinement provided by unstressed fiberglass/epoxy jackets may often provide adequate shear strength at less cost than an active, or active/passive combination.

THEORETICAL CONSIDERATIONS

Flexural Integrity of Column-Base Lap Splices for Circular Columns

Bridge columns designed in the 1950's and 1960's commonly included lap splices of longitudinal reinforcement at the base. This is a location where inelastic flexural actions must develop to provide the ductile response necessary to enable the bridge to survive intense seismic attack. Invariably lap-splices break down under the cyclic inelastic action, with a consequent reduction in flexural strength and energy absorption. Figure 1 shows typical lateral force-displacement hysteresis curves for a circular column with lap-spliced longitudinal reinforcement illustrating this behavior.

Failure of lap-splices can be inhibited, provided adequate confining pressure is developed across the potential splitting cracks, before excessive dilation of the crack surfaces develops. Experiments on lap-spliced columns indicate that the critical radial dilation strain is about 0.001. From consideration of the probable disposition of fracture surfaces within the lap-splice region, it can be shown [Priestley 1991] that the critical confining stress f_ℓ needed to ensure that the ultimate strength of the bars in a lap splice can be developed is

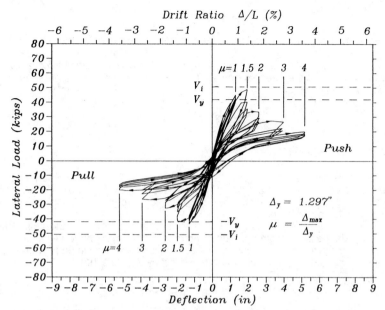

FIG.1 Lateral Force-Deflection Hysteresis Loops of an 'As-Built' Circular Bridge Column with Lap-Spliced Starter Bars

$$f_\ell \geq \frac{A_b f_y \qquad s}{[0.5\pi D/n + 2(d_b + c)]} \qquad (1)$$

where A_b is the area of one of the n spliced bars, of yield strength f_y, D is the diameter of the longitudinal reinforcement pitch circle, d_b is the bar diameter, c is the cover, and ℓ_s is the splice length.

With a fiberglass/epoxy wrap consisting of an active wrap of thickness t_a and modulus of elasticity E_a, stressed to produce an active confining stress of f_a in the column, and an additional passive wrap of thickness t_p and modulus of elasticity E_p, the equilibrium of forces when the jacket expand to $\varepsilon_d = 0.001$ requires that

$$t_a E_a + t_p E_p \geq 500 (f_\ell - f_a) \qquad (2)$$

Equation (2) can be used to design thicknesses t_a and t_b and active pressure f_a, given the required confining stress f_ℓ and the marked properties.

Flexural Confinement of Column Plastic Hinges

Where column bars are not spliced in the plastic hinge region, confinement will still be needed to impart adequate ductility. The required jacket thickness can be assessed from energy considerations related to required ductility capacity [Priestley and Seible 1991]. The critical parameter of the analysis is the ultimate compression strain of the concrete imparted by the confinement, and given for a fiberglass/epoxy composite as

$$E_{cu} = 0.004 + \frac{0.5 \, \rho_s \, f_u \, \varepsilon_u}{f'_{cc}} \qquad (3)$$

where f_u is the ultimate tensile strength of the jacket material, ε_u is the ultimate strain, f'_{cc} is the confined concrete strength and e_s, the effective volumetric ratio of confinement provided by the jacket is

$$\rho_s = \frac{4(t_a + t_p)}{D} \qquad (4)$$

Shear Strength

Shear failures of bridge columns under seismic actions are common for shorter bents subjected to double-bending. The force-deformation behavior is characterized by rapid degradation of lateral strength, stiffness and energy absorption, as illustrated by the example shown in Fig. 2.

The retrofit design requirement is to enhance the shear strength sufficiently so that it exceeds the flexural strength, enabling ductile flexural action to develop.

For a circular jacket, the enhancement in column shear strength provided by a fiberglass/epoxy jacket can be shown to be [Priestley & Seible 1991]

$$V_{sj} = \frac{\pi}{2} \left[(t_a E_a + t_p E_p) \, \varepsilon_p + T_a \right] D \cot\theta \qquad (5)$$

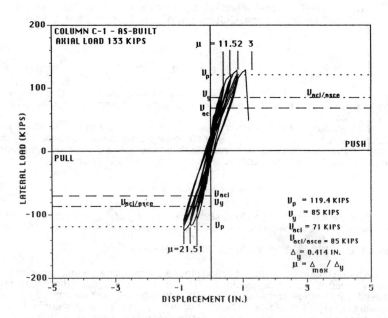

FIG. 2   Lateral Force-Deflection Hysteresis Loops of an 'As-Built' Circular Bridge Column Failing in Shear

where $T_a = f_a \, D/2$ (6)

is the jacket active tension force per unit height due to active pressure f_a, and ε_p is the design limit to tensile strain in the jacket, which may be taken conservatively as 0.004. The angle θ between the column axis and the principal diagonal compression strut may be taken as 30°, provided longitudinal reinforcement is not terminated in the region under consideration.

For rectangular columns retrofitted with a passive wrap of thickness t_p, the enhancement of shear strength will be

$$V_{sj} = t_p \, E_p \, \varepsilon_p \, h\cot\theta \qquad (7)$$

where h is the column section dimension in the direction being considered.

EXPERIMENTAL PROGRAM

In order to validate the theoretical considerations summarized above, an experimental program involving large-scale testing of circular and rectangular bridge columns is currently under way. To date, seven tests have been carried out; three tests on circular columns with lap-spliced column reinforcement expected to be dominated by flexural action, and two tests each of shorter rectangular and circular columns subjected to double bending where shear failure of the unretrofitted companions had occurred. Figs. 3 and 4 show the flexural and shear test set-ups, and general dimensions.

Flexural Tests

In each case the basic column was identical in size, reinforcement content and material strengths to the 'as-built' reference column whose behavior is given in Fig. 1. Column diameter was 610 mm, with a clear height to the point of load application of 3.66 m. Reinforcement was provided by 26 #6 [19 mm] bars lap-spliced for a length of 20 bar diameters at the column base. Transverse reinforcement was #2 [6.35 mm] hoops, lap spliced in the cover concrete at 125 mm centers. Material strengths were $f_y = 315$ MPa, and $f'_c = 34.5$ MPa (nominal). The columns were considered to represent typical 1950-70 details, at a scale of 0.4 : 1.

Three different retrofit designs were tested, based on active/passive combinations of fiberglass/epoxy confinement layers.

Column 1: The retrofit consisted of an active E-glass fiberglass/epoxy layer of nominal thickness $t_a = 2.44$ mm. This was epoxy pressure-grouted to achieve an active confinement stress of 1.72 MPa. All fibers of the E-glass layers were oriented in the circumferential direction to maximize confinement efficiency. The height of the active confinement jacket was 1.22 m or 33% of the column height. In addition, a passive wrap of high modulus fiberglass/epoxy extending over the bottom 305 mm of column height, and with a thickness of $t_p = 3.25$ mm was added to increase the potential confining pressure in the critical region at the column base.

Column 2: The active composite wrap for Column 2 was reduced from eight layers of circumferentially oriented E-glass to four layers, giving a nominal thickness $t_a = 1.22$ mm. The active wrap extended over the lower 1.22 m of column height, and was pressure-grouted to 0.69 MPa active pressure using an epoxy injection grouting procedure. The passive wrap of high modulus fiberglass/epoxy composite material was the same as for Column 1, at nominal thickness $t_p = 3.25$ mm and height 305 mm.

291

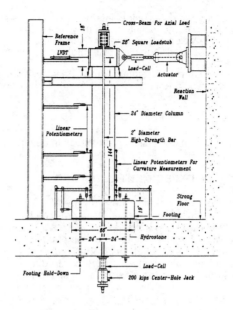

FIG. 3　Flexural Test Set Up

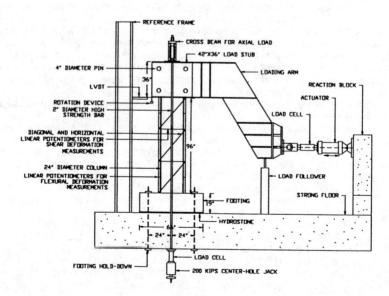

FIG. 4　Shear Test Set Up

292

Column 3: The most important change from Columns 1 and 2 involved the use of cement grout to pressurize the active wrap rather than epoxy grout. Test problems were experienced in cement grouting, resulting in circumferential fracture of the active wrap at about 1.4 MPa grouting pressure. It was not felt that this was a function of the use of cement grout rather than epoxy, but was perhaps related to dynamic fluctuations of pumping pressure at the much higher pumping speeds achieved for the cement grout. Coupled with the low vertical strength of the active wrap resulting from the unidirectional (hoop) fibre orientation, and Poisson's ratio vertical tensile stresses as the jacket was pressurized, fracture occurred. To avoid this happening in the test column, this column was wrapped with six layers of E-glass in the circumferential direction, giving an effective active layer thickness of $t_a = 1.83$ mm, and finished with two layers with the fibre oriented vertically. These would not contribute in any significant fashion to the strength or stiffness of the active wrap in the hoop tension direction. Because of the lower active wrap thickness, the active pressure was set at $f_a = 1.38$ MPa.

Since the earlier tests had not indicated any problems at the upper levels of the jacket, it was decided to reduce the height of the active wrap for Column 3 from 1.22 m to 0.91 m. The passive wrap was the same as that for Column 1 and 2.

Force-Deflection Hysteretic Behavior

Experimental lateral force-lateral displacement hysteresis curves are show in Figs. 5, 6 and 7 for Columns 1,2 and 3 respectively. Each plot includes the theoretical load-deflection envelope based on a nominal concrete compression strength of $f'_c = 34.55$ MPa (shown as a dashed curve). The ideal lateral strength based on $f'_c = 34.5$ MPa, $f_y = 315$ MPa, and ultimate compression strain of 0.006, and a model for confined concrete [Mander et al. 1987] is also indicated as V_i.

The response of Column 1, with the highest level of effective confinement, is excellent, with stable hysteresis loops up to the third cycle to displacement ductility levels of $\mu_\Delta = +8, -6$. It will be seen that there is no sign of the structural degradation associated with bond-failure of the starter bars, apparent for 'as-built' columns (compare with Fig. 1). Behavior is very close to that of a steel jacket retrofit column reported by Chai et al. (1991). Strength and stiffness differences between Column 1 and steel jacket retrofit columns appear to be primarily due to differences in concrete compression strength. However, structural degradation with the fiberglass/epoxy retrofit did not occur until significantly higher displacements than with equivalent steel jacket columns. This apparent improvement in performance may have been a result of more effective confinement at the base of the column, combined with a spread of plasticity up into the column, resulting from the lower stiffness of the retrofit scheme.

The behavior of Column 2, shown in Fig. 6, is very similar to that of Column 1 until a displacement of approximately 150 mm ($\mu = \pm 6$) when peak loads at each cycle degrade as a consequence of bond failure. It should be noted, however, that the degradation is very gradual and appears to be stabilizing at $\mu = \pm 7$. It is felt that this is a consequence of the clamping pressure provided across the failing lap-splice. Although this pressure was insufficient to eliminate eventual bond failure, it resulted in a dependable friction force across the failing lap-splice which resisted movement in both directions of loading. It will be noted that the width of the hysteresis loop, measured in the direction of the load axis, at zero displacement decreases after initiation of the bond failure and results in a reduction to the total energy absorbed per cycle.

Despite the higher effective confining stress of Column 3, the force-deflection hysteresis behavior, as shown in Fig. 7, is very similar to that exhibited by Column 2 except that degradation of Column 3 after bond slip commenced seems to be more

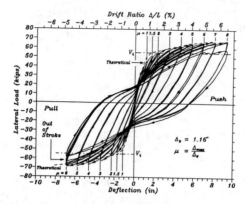

FIG. 5   Force-Deflection Behavior for Column 1

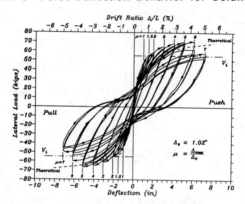

FIG. 6   Force-Deflection Behavior for Column 2

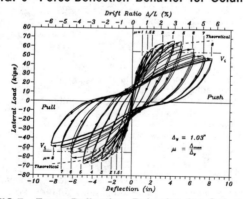

FIG.7   Force-Deflection Behavior for Column 3

gradual than with Column 2, and appears to be stabilizing at a higher force level for Column 3. It should be noted that Column 3 was taken to higher displacements than Column 2.

Shear Tests

Basic column section dimensions, longitudinal and transverse reinforcement and material properties for circular columns were the same as for the flexural tests. Rectangular column sections had section dimensions of 610 mm x 406 mm, similar longitudinal reinforcement ratios (ρ_ℓ = 0.0025) and transverse details [peripheral #2 hoops at 125 mm centers] as the circular columns. All columns were subjected to double bending in the test rig shown in Fig. 4, with total height to depth ratios of 4. For these columns longitudinal reinforcement had a strength of 469 MPa in order to maximize the shear force corresponding to flexural strength of the column. 'As-built' circular and rectangular columns without retrofit measures [Priestley et al. 1991] suffered brittle shear failures at low displacements.

Column 4: The fibre/epoxy jacket consisted on three separate regions: (1) over the end 610 mm top and bottom a "class C" active wrap consisting of two 1.14 mm layers was expanded using 0.69 MPa grouting pressure, and cement grout; (2) over the end 305 mm top and bottom, an additional passive wrap of eight layers of 0.406 mm high-modulus E-glass was added (t_p = 3.25 mm); and (3) over the center 1.2 m of the column, a passive wrap of three 1.14 mm layers (= 3.43 mm) was bonded directly to the column without grouting. The design was based on a maximum usable strain of 4000×10^{-6} in. the shear region.

Column 5: Column 5 differed from Column 4 only in that over the center 1.2 m of the column, the passive wrap was reduced to two 1.14 mm layers (= 2.28 mm effective thickness). This meant that higher strains were expected in resisting the shear force associated with development of flexural strength. The design usable strain was increased to 6000×10^{-6} in the shear region.

Column 6: A rectangular column was wrapped with a fiberglass/epoxy bonded directly to the column surfaces. Thus no membrane action from the curved shape of an elliptical jacket existed, though the corners of the column were rounded to spread the corner confining forces. It was expected that a confinement failure in the plastic hinge region would eventually occur. Within the central 1.2 m of the column, three 1.14 mm. (= 3.43 mm) layers of fiberglass/epoxy was used. In the end region an additional three layers, giving a total thickness of 6.86 mm were placed. Note that the system was entirely passive. No grouting was used to develop active pressure.

Column 7: The three earlier shear column tests utilized a comparatively low axial compression force of 503 kN, since higher axial force was expected to enhance shear strength more than flexural strength, and thus represent less critical conditions. However, the failure mode of Column 6 was expected to result from inadequate confinement of the compression zones of the plastic hinge regions, which is more critical for columns with high axial compression. Consequently Column 7 duplicated the details of rectangular Column 6, but with a higher axial compression force of 1780 kN.

Results of Shear Tests

All four shear-retrofitted columns performed exceptionally well. For the circular columns, stable hysteresis loops were obtained for drift ratios of more than 5%, corresponding to the deflection limits of the test rig. Figure 8 shows hysteresis loops for Column 5, which because of the thinner jacket within the central region, represented the critical case for the circular columns. It will be seen that exceptionally stable loops, with little strength or stiffness degradation were measured, up to the maximum displacement ductility of $\mu = 8$.

Strains were recorded at different heights of the jacket during testing. An example of the strain-deflection hysteresis loops obtained for a gauge close to midheight of Column 5 is included in Fig. 9. Note that the strain is increasing as the

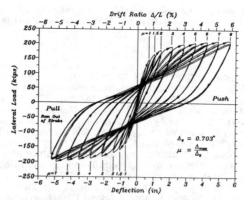

FIG. 8   Measured Horizontal Load-Deflection Hysteresis
Loops for Column No. 5 (Circular)

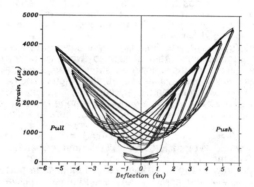

FIG. 9   Average Strain 39 Inches Above Base for Column No. 5

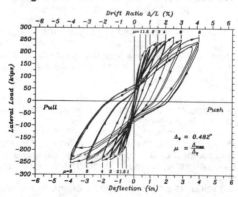

FIG. 10   Measured Horizontal Load-Deflection Hysteresis
Loops for Column No.7 (Rectangular)

296

displacement is increased despite the shear force being essentially constant at displacements from 50 mm (2 in.) onwards. It is clear that the strength of concrete shear resisting mechanism was degrading with increased ductility, even for regions outside the plastic hinge region. It should be noted that peak shear force sustained by these columns was approximately 20% above nominal ultimate flexural strength based on measured material properties. Peak strains, at about 4500 $\mu\epsilon$ were somewhat lower than the design value of 6000 $\mu\epsilon$.

The rectangular columns also performed extremely well, with stable hysteresis loops being achieved to displacement ductility factors of $\mu_\Delta = \pm6$. At high ductilities, as expected, confinement failures occurred within the plastic hinge regions, by fracture of the jacket, followed by longitudinal bar buckling and collapse of the concrete compression zone. The ductilities achieved, however, were significantly higher than expected. It is felt that the enhanced performance resulted, at least in part, from the ability of the fiberglass/epoxy jacket to deform from its original flat surface to a curved surface as the compression zone of the concrete dilated. The high elastic strain limit of the jacket material enabled significant membrane action to thus develop, resisting collapse of the compression zone until very large ductilities were obtained. Figure 10 shows the hysteresis loops recorded for the more heavily loaded Column 7. The stable loops up to $\mu_\Delta = 6$, followed by rather rapid strength degradation at higher ductilities, should be noted.

CONCLUSIONS

Tests on large scale columns retrofitted with fiberglass/epoxy composite jackets have shown that the procedure can inhibit lap-splice failure, enhance flexural ductility, and increase shear strength of squat columns to the extent that brittle shear failure modes are converted to ductile inelastic flexural deformation modes. Stress levels on the jacket have been conservatively predicted by analytical models, and lend confidence to the use of the rather simple design models developed for flexural ductility and shear strength enhancement.

ACKNOWLEDGMENTS

The research reported in this paper has been partially funded by the California Department of Transportation (Caltrans). Any conclusions or recommendations in the paper are those of the authors alone, and should not be construed to be endorsed by Caltrans.

REFERENCES

Buckle, I.G. et al. (1990). "Loma Prieta Earthquake Reconnaissance Report," (Supplement to Volume 6) *Earthquake Spectra*. Earthquake Engineering Research Institute, May 1990, 448 pp.

Chai, Y.H., M.J.N. Priestley and F. Seible.(1991). "Seismic Retrofit of Circular Bridge Columns for Enhanced Flexural Performance." *ACI Structural Journal*, 88 (5):572-584, Sept./Oct. 1991.

Fung, G.C., et al. (1971). "Field Investigation of Bridge Damage in the San Fernando Earthquake." *Technical Report, Bridge Department, Division of Highways, California Department of Transportation*, Sacramento, CA, 209 pp.

Mander, J.B., M.J.N. Priestley and R. Park (1988). "Theoretical Stress-Strain Model for Confined Concrete." *ASCE Journal*, 114(8), 1804-1826, August 1988.

Priestley, M.J.N. (1988). "Damage of the I-5/I-605 Separator in the Whittier Earthquake of October 1987." *Earthquake Spectra*, 4(2): 389-405.

Priestley, M.J.N.(1991). "Seismic Assessment of Existing Concrete Bridges," in *Seismic Assessment and Retrofit of Bridges*, University of California, San Diego, Structural Systems Research Project Report No. SSRP 91/03, July 1991, 84-149.

Priestley, M.J.N and F. Seible (1991). "Design of Retrofit Measure for Concrete Bridges," in *Seismic Assessment and Retrofit of Bridges* , University of California, San Diego, Structural Systems Research Project Report No. SSRP 91/03, July 1991, 197-250.

ADVANCED COMPOSITE MATERIALS IN BRIDGES AND STRUCTURES
K.W. Neale and P. Labossière, Editors; Canadian Society for Civil Engineering, 1992

Matériaux composites d'avant-garde pour ponts et charpentes
K.W. Neale et P. Labossière, éditeurs; Société canadienne de génie civil, 1992

ADVANCED COMPOSITE CONFINEMENT OF CONCRETE

T.G. Harmon and **K.T. Slattery**
Washington University
St. Louis, Missouri, USA

ABSTRACT

The results of testing to demonstrate the effectiveness of using advanced composite reinforcement on high strength concrete cylinders to create compression members with both high strength and high ductility are reported. Potential applications for these members are in columns or piers, or as the compression flange in an advanced composite beam or truss structure. Circumferential fibre-reinforcement of concrete cylinders yields a more economical and reliable composite structure because the fibres are loaded in tension and their strength is used more efficiently. Tests were conducted on both moderate- and high-strength concrete cylinders with various reinforcement ratios of AS4 carbon fibre to concrete by volume. The most heavily reinforced, high strength concrete cylinders have a maximum compressive strength of 300 MPa, a maximum strain of 0.035, and the energy required to fail this specimen was 40 times that of the unreinforced concrete.

RÉSUMÉ

On présente des résultats de tests démontrant l'efficacité des composites pour le renforcement de cylindres de béton à haute résistance et grande ductilité. Les applications potentielles de ces sections sont dans des colonnes ou des piliers, ou comme semelle comprimée d'une poutre ou treillis composite. Les renforcements en fibres autour des cylindres de béton permettent une structure composite plus économique et fiable parce que les fibres sont chargées en tension et que leur résistance est utilisée avec plus d'efficacité. Des tests ont été faits sur des cylindres à résistance modérée ou élevée, avec différents rapports de renforcement de fibre de carbone AS4. Les cylindres le plus renforcés ont une résistance en compression maximum de 300 MPa, une déformation maximum de 0,035 et l'énergie nécessaire pour produire la rupture du spécimen est 40 fois celle d'un béton sans renforcement.

INTRODUCTION

Advanced composite materials have been used successfully to reinforce concrete as both prestressed and non-prestressed longitudinal reinforcement (e.g. Iyer et al., 1991 and Bank et al., 1991). In addition use of glass and graphite fiber reinforcement as confinement for columns retrofitted for seismic loads has been suggested (Dauksys, 1992). The purpose of this paper is to explore the idea of using advanced composite materials as confinement for concrete, particularly for high strength concretes which tend to be very brittle. Existing concrete failure theories suggest that small amounts of confinement will dramatically increase the strength and ductility of high strength concrete resulting in a material with many interesting applications such as corrosion-resistant, lightweight bridge girders and piers. In order to investigate the behavior of concrete confined with advanced composites, a pilot test program has been started at Washington University. Some preliminary results will be reported here.

BACKGROUND

If advanced composite materials are to be used effectively in civil engineering structures, issues relating to performance and economy must be addressed. Simple replacement technology such as using beam cross section designs borrowed from steel construction may not optimize the cost or the performance of composite structural systems. Advanced composites, with their highly directional properties, should not be expected to perform efficiently in a configuration which was developed for isotropic materials. Because of the greater specific cost of advanced composites, hybrid structural elements where advanced composites are used to reinforce less costly materials and at the same time form a "composite" section with such materials may provide a much more efficient use of all materials involved. The resulting structural elements would also possess the important properties of corrosion resistance, light weight and long fatigue life, while maintaining cost competitiveness with conventional structural materials.

The basic objective of this approach is to produce a structural element in which the composite primarily acts in tension. Concrete confined with advanced composite material is used to resist compression while the composite is used alone to resist tension and shear. A high strength, ductile compression member can be fabricated from cylinders of concrete confined in the circumferential direction with carbon fibers in an epoxy matrix. This approach is related to the use of spiral reinforcement in steel reinforced concrete columns. The spiral reinforcement provides no additional strength, but a great deal of ductility. For this reason, the ACI code permits a small increase in the resistance factor for spiral reinforced columns as compared to tied columns. Since the concrete which covers the spiral spalls before failure is reached, little increase in strength occurs. Any strength increase comes after very high deflections and, therefore, cannot be considered in design. Carbon/epoxy composite on the outside of a column, for example, would require no cover and would be corrosion resistant. Therefore, the loss of strength due to spalling would not occur.

Concrete failure theory suggests that confinement reinforcement can be significantly more efficient in resisting compressive force than longitudinal reinforcement. Therefore, the relatively expensive composite material can be used most efficiently as confinement reinforcement, not only to increase strength, but also to increase ductility. Circumferentially reinforced cylinders provide a compression member where the advanced composite is loaded in tension. Composites tend to be less reliable under compressive stress. Thus this configuration has some significant advantages over pure composite structural members. The compressive strength and modulus are generally less than the tensile properties. The compressive properties are also much more

300

sensitive to manufacturing flaws, and more strict processing controls are required to ensure good compressive properties. It is expected that the manufacturing process for confined cylinders would be relatively simple and insensitive to minor flaws.

The principle expected use of confined cylinders of concrete would be as compression flanges of "composite" beams. Basically, an advanced composite "Tee" section and a confined cylinder of concrete would form the composite beam. The composite section together with confined cylinders might also form a box section or truss. Manufacturing methods must be developed if such sections are to become economically feasible.

TEST PROGRAM

A pilot test program is currently underway to establish the feasibility of confining concrete cylinders with carbon/epoxy composite and to determine basic behavior. The experimental program involves testing 51 mm (2 in) diameter by 102 mm (4 in) long cylinders in uniaxial compression. The cylinders are confined by wrapping them with carbon fibers coated with epoxy using manual placement procedures. The epoxy was cured at room temperature for several days. AS4 carbon fibers with a tensile strength, based on the manufacturer's data, of 3500 MPa (510 ksi) and elastic modulus of 235 GPa (34,000 ksi) were used to wrap the cylinders with varying volumetric reinforcement ratios. The cylinders had smooth ends, but no attempt was made to reduce friction between the concrete and the steel bearing platen.

Two concrete mixes were used, one with a compressive strength of about 41 MPa (6 ksi), and one with a strength of about 103 MPa (15 ksi). Composite reinforcement ratios ranged from 0% to about 5%. The cylinders were tested on a Baldwin testing machine with 300,000 pounds capacity. Instrumentation included a load cell to measure axial force and LVDTs and strain gages to measure axial and circumferential strain. Results of a total of ten separate tests are reported here.

Axial Stress vs. Axial Strain

Figures 1 and 2 show the axial strain versus axial stress results for the low and high strength concretes, respectively. The relationships are given for each value of the confinement reinforcement ratio, ρ. The stress-strain curves are bilinear with a "yield stress" somewhat higher than the failure stress of the unreinforced cylinders, depending on the confinement reinforcement ratio. Increasing the reinforcement ratio has only a small effect on the slope of the initial portion of the stress-strain relationship, but has a fairly significant effect on the slope of the second portion. Also, increasing the reinforcement ratio increases the final failure stress significantly, but has only a minor effect on the yield stress. Increasing the concrete strength increases both the yield stress and failure stress by a value roughly equal to the increase in concrete strength.

Axial Stress vs. Circumferential Strain

Figures 3 and 4 show the transverse strains for the low and high strength concretes, respectively. LVDTs were used to determine the strains for the low strength concrete and strain gages were used to determine the strains for the high strength concrete. Difficulty was experienced in both methods because of the rough surface of the wrapped cylinders. Therefore, the results should be viewed from a qualitative stand point rather than a quantitative stand point. Two conclusions can be drawn from this data. The first is that the transverse strains increase dramatically at some point after the failure stress of the unreinforced cylinder is reached. Second, the transverse strains decrease as the circumferential reinforcement is increased, as would be expected. Note that the horizontal scale is much longer in Fig. 3 due to the relatively ductile behavior of the low strength concrete.

Failure Stress vs. Reinforcement Ratio

Figure 5 shows the failure stress versus the reinforcement ratio for both concretes. The benefit of the confinement is roughly independent of the concrete strength. The increase in failure stress is approximately 39 MPa (5.7 ksi) per each percent increase in confinement reinforcement ratio. The stress equivalent to the uniaxial tensile strength of the confinement reinforcement is 35 MPa (5.1 ksi) per percent reinforcement. Thus the confinement has a strength efficiency of 1.12. It is expected that this strength efficiency could be increased with better fabrication methods. It would also be greater if compared with the uniaxial compressive strength of the composite. The "stiffness efficiency" depends on the reinforcement ratio. The strain to failure of the carbon fibers is approximately 1.5%. The strain at failure for the confined cylinders ranges from .004 for $\rho = 0\%$ to .035 for $\rho = 5.4\%$. The stiffness efficiency ratio is about 1.0 for $\rho = 1.5\%$, although the higher strength concrete tends to improve this ratio slightly.

Effect of Cyclic Loading

Figure 6 shows results of cyclic load testing for a cylinder made of the low strength concrete with $\rho = 2.7\%$. The results suggest that the cylinders can be subjected to cyclic loading with little degradation of properties, although considerably more testing is required.

CONCLUSIONS

Confining concrete with high strength and high stiffness fibers is a very effective and efficient method for improving the strength and ductility of high strength concrete. The properties of these structural sections can be tailored to provide an economical, ductile, highly corrosion resistant compression member for a variety of civil engineering applications. Considerable work is required to determine optimum concrete mix designs, optimum choice of composite material and reinforcement ratios, and effective cross-sections designs and fabricating techniques.

REFERENCES

Bank, L.C., Xi, Z. and Mosallam, A.S. (1991). Experimental Study of FRP Grating Reinforced Concrete Slabs. *Advanced Composites Materials in Civil Engineering Structures*, ASCE, 111-122.

Dauksys, R.J. (1992). Composites in Industry Overview. *Proceedings Workshop on Use of Composites in Construction*, Constructed Facilities Center, Morgantown, West Virginia, VII.9-VII.19.

Iyer, S.I., Khubchandani, A. and Feng, J. (1991). Fiberglass and Graphite Cables for Bridge Decks. *Advanced Composites Materials in Civil Engineering Structures*, ASCE, 371-382.

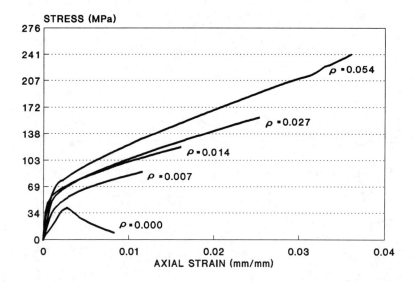

Figure 1. Stress vs. Axial Strain for Mix I Concrete

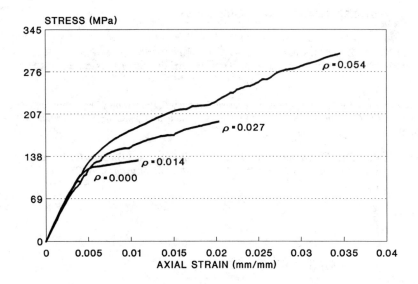

Figure 2. Stress vs. Axial Strain for Mix II Concrete

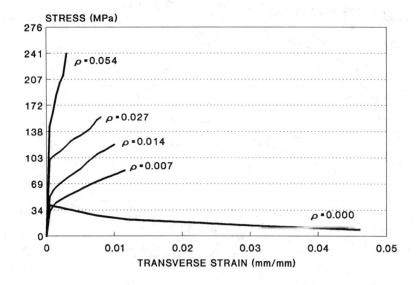

Figure 3. Stress vs. Transverse Strain for Mix I Concrete (LVDT)

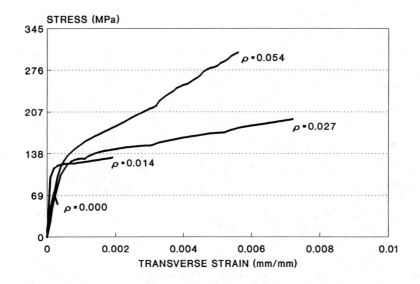

Figure 4. Stress vs. Transverse Strain for Mix II Concrete (Strain Gauge)

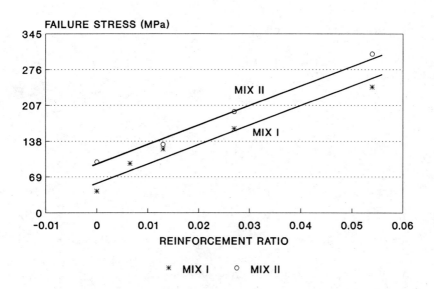

Figure 5. Failure Stress vs. Fiber/Concrete Reinforcement Ratio

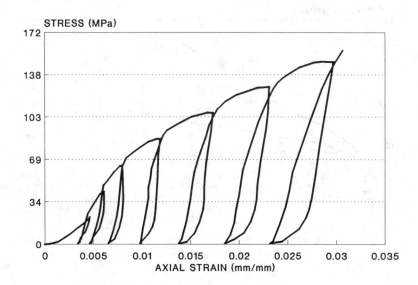

Figure 6. Stress vs. Axial Strain under Cyclic Loading (ρ =0.0027)

Pultruded Sections and Grids

Sections pultrudées et maillages

ADVANCED COMPOSITE MATERIALS IN BRIDGES AND STRUCTURES
K.W. Neale and P. Labossière, Editors; Canadian Society for Civil Engineering, 1992

Matériaux composites d'avant-garde pour ponts et charpentes
K.W. Neale et P. Labossière, éditeurs; Société canadienne de génie civil, 1992

AN EXPERIMENTAL INVESTIGATION OF THE BEHAVIOUR OF CONCENTRICALLY LOADED PULTRUDED COLUMNS

S.J. Yoon, D.W. Scott and **A. Zureick**
Georgia Institute of Technology
Atlanta, Georgia, USA

ABSTRACT

The determination of the design strength of concentrically loaded pultruded fibreglass reinforced composite members is governed not only by the strength limit states but also by serviceability requirements. Due to this material's low mechanical properties, serviceability criteria such as deformation and vibration often dominate in the structural design. Therefore, an understanding of the behaviour of pultruded shapes under axial compressive loads is essential. This paper describes the experimental investigation pertaining to the behaviour of concentrically loaded fibre-reinforced pultruded columns. These experiments involve testing full scale doubly-symmetric sections of varying lengths to determine both local and global buckling loads. The load-deformation curve for each of the tested specimens is also presented.

RÉSUMÉ

Le calcul de la résistance de poteaux composites, renforcés par des fibres de verre et soumis à un effort normal de compression simple, est gouverné à la fois par les exigences des états limites sur les contraintes et les critères de service à la déformation. Tant que les fibres de verre présentent des propriétés mécaniques faibles, les déformations et vibrations dominent souvent le calcul. L'étude du comportement de ces poteaux sous l'action des efforts normaux de compression est donc essentiel. Dans cet article, on décrit des résultats expérimentaux sur le comportement des poteaux composites soumis à un effort normal de compression simple. Ces essais ont été limités aux profilés doublement symétriques pour étudier leur flambement. La relation charge-déplacement pour chaque poteau est également présentée.

INTRODUCTION

The use of alternative materials in civil engineering structures is becoming much more frequent as the demands of modern design make traditional materials such as concrete and steel less attractive. In particular, pultruded fiber reinforced materials are becoming much more prevalent in modern construction. Pultrusion is a manufacturing process in which continuous fibers are pulled through a resin bath, formed into a useable shape, and drawn through a heated die in which polymerization of the material takes place. The formed cross section is then cut to the appropriate length.

Structural members manufactured using the pultrusion process can be formed into practically any cross section desired. A few of the commonly used shapes are shown as Figure 1. Pultruded materials have several advantages: light weight, high specific strength, electromagnetic transparency, corrosion resistance, and taliorability to a wide variety of applications. However, the behavior of the material under various loading conditions is not well understood. Therefore, a comprehensive investigation of the behavior of pultruded materials is necessary for reliable design criteria to be developed for use by the engineering community. To that end, an extensive research program has been underway at The Georgia Institute of Technology for the past few years. This program involves both analytical and experimental studies of pultruded structural shapes in a variety of loading combinations. The overall objective of this research is to understand the behavior of the material so that the aforementioned design criteria can be formulated.

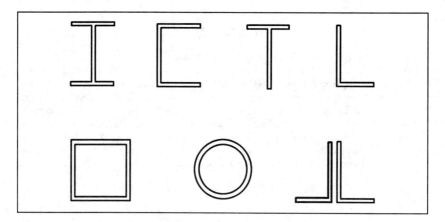

Figure 1. Typical Cross Sections

BEHAVIOR OF PULTRUDED STRUCTURAL MEMBERS IN COMPRESSION

When a pultruded fiber reinforced structural shape is subjected to axial compressive loads, the design strength is normally controlled by either the strength or serviceability limit states. The strength limit state includes material strength as well as local and global instability. The serviceability limit state may involve excessive deformation or vibration of the member. Due to low mechanical properties, the design of pultruded shapes will often be dominated by the serviceability limit state. Therefore, a thorough understanding of the behavior of pultruded members in axial compression is essential.

A literature review revealed very little published work on the behavior of pultruded materials in compression. Previous experimental work has been done by Hewson (1978) and Lee and Hewson (1979). These investigations involved glass fiber reinforced channels. Related works have also been presented by Zureick et al. (1992) and Scott et al. (1992).

EXPERIMENTAL INVESTIGATION

Tested Sections

The experiments reported here were performed on vinylester fiberglass reinforced doubly symmetric wide flange and box column members. These specimens were manufactured by Morrison Molded Fiberglass Company (MMFG, 1989). The wide flange shapes were utilized in local buckling experiments, while the box sections were used in the global bucking investigation. The dimensions of the cross sections as well as the slenderness ratios (L/r) for the wide flange and box sections are shown in Tables 1 and 2, respectively.

Table 1. Specimens used in Stub Column Experimental Program

Specimen Designation	Dimension (mm)					Slenderness Ratio
	L	b_f	h_w	t_f	t_w	
W305x12.7-2743-V-2	2743	305	292	12.7	12.7	37.5
W203x12.7-1524-V-1	1524	203	191	12.7	12.7	31.1
W152x9.5-892-V-1	892	152	148	9.5	9.5	24.2

L: Length, b_f: Flange Width, h_w: Web Depth, t_f: Flange Thickness, t_w: Web Thickness

Table 2. Specimens used in Slender Column Experimental Program

Specimen Designation	Dimension (mm)					Slenderness Ratio
	KL	b	t	A	r	
BOX 76x6.35-2489-V-14	2489	76	6.35	1768	28.7	86.7
BOX 76x6.35-2184-V-15	2184	76	6.35	1768	28.7	76.1
BOX 76x6.35-1880-V-16	1880	76	6.35	1768	28.7	65.5

KL: Effective Length, b: Wall Width, t: Wall Thickness, A: Area, r: Radius of Gyration

Experimental Setup

The experiments were performed using a screw-type load machine and computer controlled data acquisition system. A schematic outlining the test setup is shown in Figure 2. The stub column experiments used steel plates to distribute the axial load from the test machine. The slender column experiments used steel knife edges to replicate pinned ends. A single knife edge was used rather than a double knife edge so that the plane of rotation for the box sections would be known. Data was taken during the experiments using strain gages and LVDTs. These devices were placed at the flange tips and web center for the stub column experiments. The slender column experiments used the LVDTs at the quarterpoints of the specimen. In each experiment, an LVDT was used to measure the axial shortening of the member. The specimens were loaded at a uniform 0.635 mm/minute.

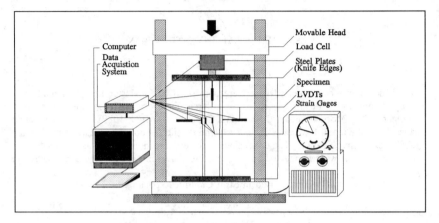

Figure 2. Experimental Setup

Results

Stub Column Test Results

Typical strain, lateral deflection, and axial shortening curves for the stub column experiments are presented as Figures 3, 4, and 5, respectively. Table 3 summarizes the results from 3 stub column tests representative of the overall local buckling investigation. In addition to providing the experimentally determined buckling load, Table 3 also lists results from a finite element analysis of the sections. The material properties used in the finite element analysis were obtained from material tests on coupons taken from the tested specimens. The analysis performed was based on the work done by Vakiener, et al. (1991). The material properties, as well the deformed shape for the each of the sections, is shown in Figures 6, 7, and 8.

Table 3. Summary of Stub Column Test Results

Specimen Designation	Finite Element Method		Experiment	
	No. Half Sine waves	P_{FEM} (kN)	No. Half Sine waves	P_{EXP} (kN)
W305x12.7 2743-V-2	5	553	5	516
W203x12.7-1524-V-1	4	844	4	814
W152x9.5-892-V-1	3	403	3	465

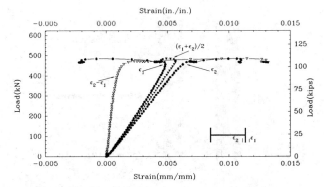

Figure 3. Load-Strain Curves - W 152 x 9.5 - 892 - V - 1

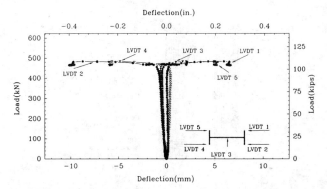

Figure 4. Load-Deflection Curves - W 152 x 9.5 - 892 - V - 1

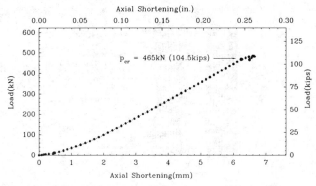

Figure 5. Load-Axial Shortening Curve - W 152 x 9.5 - 892 - V - 1

313

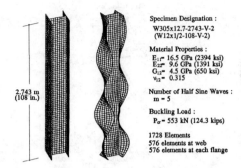

Specimen Designation :
W305x12.7-2743-V-2
(W12x1/2-108-V-2)

Material Properties :
E_{11}= 16.5 GPa (2394 ksi)
E_{22}= 9.6 GPa (1391 ksi)
G_{12}= 4.5 GPa (650 ksi)
v_{12}= 0.315

Number of Half Sine Waves :
m = 5

Buckling Load :
P_{cr}= 553 kN (124.3 kips)

1728 Elements
576 elements at web
576 elements at each flange

2.743 m
(108 in.)

Figure 6. Finite Element Analysis Results - W 305 x 12.7 - 2743 - V - 2

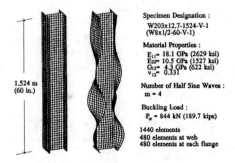

Specimen Designation :
W203x12.7-1524-V-1
(W8x1/2-60-V-1)

Material Properties :
E_{11}= 18.1 GPa (2629 ksi)
E_{22}= 10.5 GPa (1527 ksi)
G_{12}= 4.3 GPa (622 ksi)
v_{12}= 0.331

Number of Half Sine Waves :
m = 4

Buckling Load :
P_{cr} = 844 kN (189.7 kips)

1440 elements
480 elements at web
480 elements at each flange

1.524 m
(60 in.)

Figure 7. Finite Element Analysis Results - W 203 x 12.7 - 1524 - V - 1

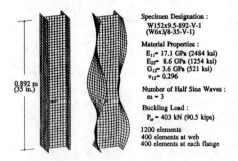

Specimen Designation :
W152x9.5-892-V-1
(W6x3/8-35-V-1)

Material Properties :
E_{11}= 17.1 GPa (2484 ksi)
E_{22}= 8.6 GPa (1254 ksi)
G_{12}= 3.6 GPa (521 ksi)
v_{12}= 0.296

Number of Half Sine Waves :
m = 3

Buckling Load :
P_{cr} = 403 kN (90.5 kips)

1200 elements
400 elements at web
400 elements at each flange

0.892 m
(35 in.)

Figure 8. Finite Element Analysis Results - W 152 x 9.5 - 892 - V - 1

Slender Column Test Results

A typical midpoint lateral deflection curve for the slender column experiments is shown in Figure 9. Also shown is a Southwell Plot based on the midpoint lateral deflection. Figure 10 shows a typical axial shortening curve. The results from 3 slender column tests representative of the overall global buckling investigation are shown in Table 4. In addition, estimated buckling loads based on Euler's approach are listed. These estimates were determined using the equation

$$P_{cr} = \frac{\pi^2 E^* A}{\left(\frac{KL}{r}\right)^2}$$

where E^* was estimated as 22.1 GPa. This estimate was obtained from the average of the values for the major Young's modulus E taken from the linear portion of each of the axial deflection curves.

Table 4. Summary of Slender Column Test Results

Specimen Designation	Experiment			Euler
	P_{EXP} (kN)	P_{SWP}* (kN)	P_{EUL} (kN)	$\dfrac{P_{EXP}}{P_{EUL}}$
BOX 76x6.35-2489-V-1	54.7	55.2	51.2	1.07
BOX 76x6.35-2184-V-15	75.6	75.6	66.3	1.14
BOX 76x6.35-1880-V-16	95.2	101.0	89.9	1.06

* P_{SWP} denotes values obtained from the slopes of the Southwell Plots.

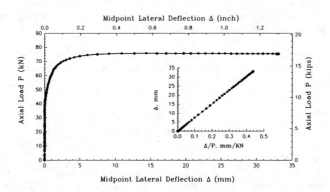

Figure 9. Load - Midpoint Lateral Deflection Curves - BOX 76 x 6.35 - 2184 - V -15

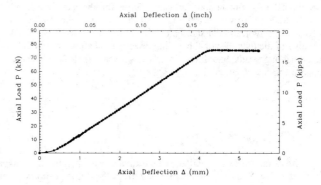

Figure 10. Load-Axial Shortening Curve - BOX 76 x 6.35 - 2184 - V - 15

CONCLUDING REMARKS

1) The discussion in this paper is limited to short term behavior only.

2) In all of the experiments the specimens were observed to behave linearly for the majority of the prebuckling stage. Near buckling, and in the postbuckling regime, nonlinear behavior was apparent. Elastic behavior was exhibited by the specimens for the duration of the test.

3) The behavior of the specimens was consistent in that for both the local and global buckling investigations specimens with varying cross sections and lengths tended to act in a similar fashion under loading.

4) In the estimation of the slender column buckling load, the use of E^* obtained from the load-axial shortening curve in the Euler equation appears reasonable for the box sections.

ACKNOWLEDGEMENT

This work is being supported in part by the National Science Foundation (NSF) under Grant No. MSM-8909140. Morrison Molded Fiberglass Company (MMFG) has also provided support including the test specimens. The Georgia Institute of Technology has provided additional support for this research. The support by each of these institutions is greatly appreciated.

REFERENCES

Hewson, P., 1978, "Buckling of Pultruded Glass Fibre-Reinforced Channel Sections," *Composites*, January, pp 56 - 60.

Lee, D. J., and Hewson, P., 1979, "The Use of Fibre-Reinforced Plastics in Thin-walled Structures," *Stability Problems in Engineering Structures and Components*, Richards, T.H., and Stanley, P. (Editors), Applied Science Publisher, pp 23-55.

MMFG, 1989, *Extren Fiberglass Structural Shapes Design Manual*, Morrison Molded Fiber Glass Company, Bristol, Va.

Scott, D. W., Yoon, S.J., and Zureick, A., 1992, "Full Scale Tests on Concentrically Loaded Fiber Reinforced Pultruded Columns," *Proceedings of the American Society of Civil Engineers Material Engineering Congress*, August 10 - 12, Atlanta, Georgia.

Vakiener, A.R., Zureick, A., and Will, K.M., 1991, "Prediction of Local Buckling in Pultruded Shapes by Finite Element Analysis," *Proceedings of the ASCE Specialty Conference on Advanced Composites Materials in Civil Engineering Structures*, Edited by Srinivasa L. Iyer and Rajan Sen, Las Vegas, Nevada, Jan 31 - Feb 1, pp 302-312.

Zureick, A., Yoon, S.J., and Scott, D.W., 1992, "Experimental Investigation on Concentrically Loaded Pultruded Columns," *Proceedings of the Second International Symposium, Textile Composites in Building Construction*, June 23-25, Lyon, France.

ADVANCED COMPOSITE MATERIALS IN BRIDGES AND STRUCTURES
K.W. Neale and P. Labossière, Editors; Canadian Society for Civil Engineering, 1992

Matériaux composites d'avant-garde pour ponts et charpentes
K.W. Neale et P. Labossière, éditeurs; Société canadienne de génie civil, 1992

TESTS ON PULTRUDED GRP POSTS FOR HANDRAIL/BARRIER STRUCTURES

G.J. Turvey and **R.C. Slater**
Lancaster University
Lancaster, Lancashire, England

ABSTRACT

Details of a series of tests on two sizes of pultruded GRP post are presented. The smaller section posts had either GRP or mild steel bases and the larger had steel bases. The posts were loaded up to both service and ultimate loads. Load versus post tip deflection data are presented for the service load tests. Ultimate loads are tabulated and the failure modes are described. The tests show that the posts are potentially suitable for handrail/barrier applications.

RÉSUMÉ

Les détails d'une série de tests sur deux formats de poteaux en plastique renforcé de fibres de verre (GRP) sont présentés. Les poteaux avec la plus petite section ont une base soit en GRP soit en acier doux, et ceux avec la plus grande section ont une base en acier. Les poteaux ont été chargés jusqu'à la charge limite en service et à la charge ultime. Les charges ultimes sont présentées dans des tableaux et les modes de rupture sont décrits. Les tests démontrent que les poteaux sont potentiellement utilisables dans des barrières ou des rampes.

INTRODUCTION

GRP pultrusions have been used in structural applications for many years in the USA, where their development was pioneered. Over the past five or more years they have begun to be used in various kinds of civil engineering structures in the UK. The use of structural grade GRP pultrusions is particularly appropriate where, in addition to meeting structural requirements, advantage may also be taken of their low mass and high corrosion resistance characteristics. Thus, these materials are finding increasing application in barrier and walkway structures associated with water and sewage purification installations and chemical plant.

Factors which continue to inhibit the rate of increase in the use of pultruded GRP structural materials are the lack of design codes and the paucity of independently derived data on the performance of full-scale structures. The lack of codes of practice has motivated manufacturers of GRP structural pultrusions to provide interim guidance in the form of design handbooks (see, for example, Anon, 1989). However, the scarcity of test data remains an obstacle to the development of designer confidence in the use of structural pultrusions. As far as the authors are aware, and despite the fact that many tens of metres of pultruded GRP handrailing/barriers have been installed, no independent data on their structural response characteristics have been reported. Thus, the primary purpose of this paper is to present some of the data obtained from a series of tests associated with the development of a post and rail structure typical of that presently used in handrail/barrier systems. Although a complete structure was tested to failure, the present paper only reports data derived from tests carried out on free-standing single posts. The data obtained from the post and rail tests will be reported in a future paper.

POST GEOMETRY AND MATERIAL PROPERTIES

Two types of post were tested for use in the post and rail structure. The smaller section post was intended for use in "light duty" (LD) structures and the larger in "heavy duty" (HD) structures. Because of the limited range of pultruded structural sections readily available in the UK at the time of testing (July 1990) square cross-section posts had to be used even though rectangular cross-section posts would have been more efficient. The LD posts were made of two square tubular sections chosen from the standard range of structural pultrusions manufactured by Fibreforce Composites Ltd. The inner section (nominally 44mm x 44mm x 6mm) was bonded throughout its length to the outer section (nominally 50mm x 50mm x 3mm) using a two part epoxy adhesive. A cast polyester resin block 140mm long was bonded into each end of the LD posts with the same epoxy adhesive to provide local stiffening. The HD posts (nominally 75mm x 75mm x 6mm) were chosen from the EXTREN 525 series of structural pultrusions manufactured by MMFG Co. Inc.. 140mm long resin blocks were also bonded into the ends of these posts to provide local stiffening.

The E-glass reinforcement used in the laminated wall construction of the posts was of two kinds, viz. continuous filament mat (CFM) and uni-directional (UD) roving. The planar isotropic stiffness and strength properties of CFM ensured that the post walls had adequate transverse stiffness and strength. The matrix material of both the LD and HD posts was a mixture of polyester resin and filler. Glass fibre volume percentages of the smaller and larger tubular sections used in the LD posts were 47% and 43% respectively and the value for the HD posts was 45%.

POST BASE DETAILS

Two types of base were used in the tests on the LD posts. The first was a rectangular section (nominally 50mm x 30mm) pultruded GRP bar 160mm long comprising UD rovings in a polyester resin and filler matrix. The post was connected to the GRP base by means of four 12mm diameter pultruded GRP dowels. The dowels, which also comprised of UD rovings in a matrix of polyester resin and filler, were bonded with epoxy adhesive into pre-drilled holes in the base and the resin block in one end of the post. The GRP base was connected to the support by two 16mm diameter black bolts. The second type of base for the LD posts was a mild steel socket made from a 75mm long SHS (nominally 60mm x 60mm x 4mm) with one end fillet welded to a mild steel plate (nominally 160mm x 120mm x 12mm). The post was held in the SHS socket by means of two 16mm diameter black bolts and the base plate was fixed to the support by two similar bolts. Steel bases, similar in form to the LD bases, were used with the HD posts. Again, two 16mm diameter black bolts were used to connect the post to the 100mm long SHS socket (nominally 100mm x 100mm x 10mm), but four 16mm bolts were used to connect the plate (nominally 150mm x 130mm x 12mm) to the support. One of the LD posts was bolted into the SHS socket prior to testing. All of the other posts were bonded, with an epoxy adhesive, and bolted into the socket.

DESIGN CRITERIA FOR POST AND RAIL STRUCTURES

At the time this work was being planned, the authors were unaware of the existence of any codes of practice for the design of handrail/barrier structures made of GRP materials. Hence, prior to carrying out the LD and HD post tests, it was necessary to assess what use might be made of design criteria available in codes of practice for metallic handrail/barrier structures. Accordingly it was decided, where possible, to use criteria given in BS 6180 (Anon, 1982). This Code of Practice specifies design loads and their locations as well as minimum rail heights and limiting displacements. This information was adapted for a post spacing of 1.65m to give a serviceability limit state (SLS) test load of 297N for the LD posts and 594N for the HD posts. In each case this load was to be applied at a height of 1100mm above the underside of the base of the post. The SLS deflection limit, which applies at the mid-span of the top rail in a handrail/barrier structure, is equal to (rail span)/125, or 13.2mm for both LD and HD structures. Of course, this deflection may only be used as a guide to an acceptable value for the post tip deflection, since it represents the combined post and rail deflection.

TEST PROCEDURE

The basic test procedure was similar for both LD and HD posts. The posts were tested as horizontal tip loaded cantilevers with their bases bolted to a stiff vertical mild steel channel section support which was rigidly clamped to the strong floor of the structures laboratory. For the SLS load tests weights were applied at the free end of the cantilever and for the ULS tests the end load was applied upwards by means of a jack reacted against the strong floor. In the SLS series of tests the posts were loaded in both planes of symmetry and through several load - unload cycles, whereas in the ULS tests the posts were tested in the plane of symmetry normal to the longer dimension of the base. Post end or tip deflections were measured by means of two dial gauges symmetrically disposed about the plane of bending. The readings from these gauges confirmed that there was no discernable twist due to inadvertent eccentricites in the articulated loading hanger and jack. The SLS and ULS loading arrangements are shown in Figs. 1 and 2 respectively.

TEST RESULTS AND DISCUSSION

It is convenient to present and discuss the SLS and ULS test data separately. Hence, the SLS results are considered first.

SLS Tests

LD Posts with GRP Bases

The first series of SLS tests carried out were on two LD posts with pultruded GRP bases. In the first of these tests the load was applied in the plane of symmetry normal to the line joining the two bolts in the GRP base. The intention was to apply the load in increments up to a maximum load of 301.2N (i.e. just above the SLS load of 294N). Unfortunately, when the load reached just over 200N the post began to show an apparent sign of reduction in flexural stiffness - often the first indication of impending failure. Nevertheless, it was decided to continue with the test in order to see if the SLS load could be reached. However, at a load of just over 250N the tip deflection began to increase very rapidly and it appeared doubtful that the SLS load could be achieved. Therefore, a decision was taken to unload the post and record the residual deflection. The load versus tip deflection plot for this test is shown in Fig.3(a). Visual examination of the post and base after the conclusion of the test showed that the post was undamaged. However, the pultruded GRP base had failed by longitudinal splitting as shown in Fig.3(c) and this was the primary reason for the LD post being unable to meet the SLS load and deflection criteria. In the light of this first test result, it was decided to reduce the maximum end load applied in the second LD post test to 125N. Two load - unload cycles were applied in the same plane of symmetry as in the first post test and deflection readings were recorded immediately after applying/removing the load and again three minutes later. A three minute time interval was found sufficient to allow deflections to stabilise or "settle" and was subsequently adopted for nearly all of the other post tests. The load versus "settled" tip deflection results for the second test are shown in Fig.3(b). The response is essentially linear and there is evidence of a residual post tip deflection of the order of 1mm on unloading.

LD Posts with Steel Bases

Because of the unsatisfactory performance of the GRP bases, it was decided to proceed with caution in testing the LD posts with steel bases. Therefore, for the first test the maximum load applied to the post was 163.8N, i.e. just over half the SLS load. The load was first applied in the plane of symmetry normal to the line joining the two bolts in the base plate. Three load - unload cycles were applied and the five minute "settled" tip deflections are shown in Fig.4(a). The response is linear and maximum residual tip deflections on unloading appear to be of the order of 2mm. On completion of this test, the post was rotated through 90° about its longitudinal axis and re-clamped to the support to allow a test to be carried out with the load applied in the other plane of symmetry. The five minute "settled" tip deflections for this case are shown in Fig.4(b). Comparison of Figs.4(a) and 4(b) suggests that the post is slightly less stiff when bending takes place in the plane of symmetry normal to the line joining the bolts in the base plate. After the completion of the second loading test on the first steel base LD post a visual inspection was carried out for signs of damage, but none was evident. It was, therefore, decided to load the second post to a maximum load slightly in excess of the SLS load. Again, the second post was tested in both planes of symmetry. The deflections measured during three load - unload cycles applied in each of the two loading planes are shown in Figs. 5(a) and 5(b) respectively. These results show: that the post stiffness is constant and identical for both loading planes, the tip deflection is about 11mm at the maximum load of 301.2N and the residual tip deflection is of the order of 0.5mm to 0.75mm. It is also of interest to note that in the case of the second post test the maximum load in the second loading cycle remained on overnight before unloading and the maximum load in the third cycle was applied for one hour before unloading commenced.

Using the geometric and material data given in (Mottram, 1991) the tip deflection under an end load of 301.2N was calculated as 8.67mm (neglecting shear deformation) and 8.78mm (including shear deformation). Examination of Figs.5(a)-(b) shows that the measured deflection is about 11mm. Thus, the measured deflection is about 25% - 27% greater than the theoretical values. This is probably due to the lack of rigidity in the steel base - only two bolts were used to connect the base plate to the support.

HD Posts with Steel Bases

Two HD posts with steel bases were tested. The maximum load applied was 693.6N (somewhat greater than the SLS load) in each case. Three load - unload cycles were applied to the first HD post in the plane of symmetry normal to the longer base dimension. The three minute "settled" tip deflections for this case are shown plotted in Fig.6(a). During the second load cycle the maximum load was applied for thirty minutes and during the third load cycle the maximum load remained on overnight before unloading commenced. The results obtained when the post was rotated through 90°, re-clamped to the support and then loaded through three cycles in the other plane of symmetry are shown in Fig.6(b). These two sets of results indicate that the post and base assembly is equally stiff in both planes of bending and that the maximum deflection is about 14mm with a residual tip deflection of nearly 3mm on final unloading. The second steel base HD post test results (for only one bending plane) are shown in Fig.6(c). These three minute "settled" results show a similar maximum tip deflection, though the residual deflection is much smaller amounting to less than 1mm.

Using the geometric and material property data given in (Anon, 1989) the tip deflection under an end load of 693.6N was calculated as 11.77mm (neglecting shear deformation) and 12.16mm (including shear deformation). Examination of Figs.6(a)-(c) shows that the measured tip deflection varies from about 12mm to 14mm depending on the loading cycle and the loading plane of symmetry. The good correlation between the observed and calculated deflections suggests that the steel base provides a reasonably rigid support.

ULS Tests

Here the ultimate load tests on the steel base LD and HD posts are discussed. The failure of one of the GRP base LD posts has already been discussed under SLS Tests and the second post was not tested to failure. Although tip deflections were recorded in the initial stages of the ULS post tests, the deflections at failure greatly exceeded the travel of the dial gauges and, therefore, estimates of deflections at failure were made on the basis of jack extension. These varied from about 170mm for the LD posts to about 185mm for the HD posts. The ultimate loads are listed in Table 1. As expected failure was confined to the length of the post in the socket and immediately above. Because the first steel base LD post tested was only bolted into the SHS socket, it was possible to separate the post from the steel base after completion of the ULS test in order to examine the extent of cracking in the end of the post. A view of the damage to the LD post wall is shown in Fig.7(a). The other steel base LD post and the two steel base HD posts could not be inspected in this manner, because they were both bonded and bolted into their SHS sockets. A view of the plastic deformation of the baseplate of the LD post, which was bonded and bolted into the SHS socket, is shown in Fig.7(b). Finally, the visible damage near the end of one of the HD posts is shown in Fig.7(c).

CONCLUSIONS

The test results on free-standing LD posts with GRP bases indicate that they would not be satisfactory because of the poor performance of the base plate. However, the bonded and bolted steel base LD and HD posts could be expected to meet the SLS criteria, because they would form part of a structure and their tip deflections would be less than those recorded in the tip loaded cantilever tests. The post failure loads greatly exceed the ULS loads, but, unfortunately, very large deflections are required to produce failure. Accurate measurement of these large deflections during the ULS tests caused difficulties and this is an area which requires further development.

ACKNOWLEDGEMENTS

The work described in this paper was partially funded by the Engineering Department, Lancaster University and Fibreforce Composites Ltd. The pultruded GRP posts, bases, dowels and cast resin blocks were provided by Fibreforce Composites Ltd and the steel bases were fabricated and supplied by Mark Rainer International Ltd. The authors wish to record their appreciation to all parties for their support in this project and acknowledge the contribution made by Mr. Paul Fox who carried out the tests under the authors' guidance.

REFERENCES

Anon. (1989). Design Manual. Morrison Molded Fiber Glass Company, Bristol, Virginia.

Anon. (1982). British Standard Code of Practice for Protective Barriers in and Around Buildings (BS 6180: 1982). British Standards Institution, London.

Mottram, J.T. (1991). Evaluation of Design Analysis for Pultruded Fibre-Reinforced Polymer Box Beams. *Structural Engineer*, **69**, 211-220.

Table 1

Post Type	Test Number	Failure Load (kN)
LD	1	4.0
LD	2	5.0
HD	1	9.2
HD	2	8.8

Fig.1 SLS test arrangement

Fig.2 ULS test arrangement

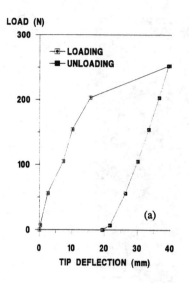

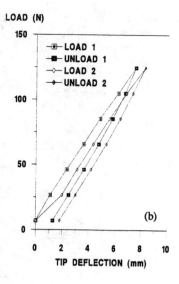

Fig.3 GRP base LD post SLS test results: (a) first post, (b) second post and (c) base failure mode in first post test

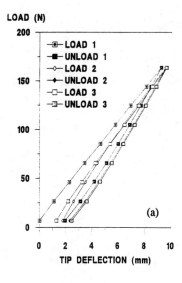
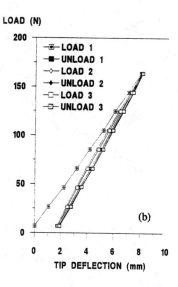

Fig.4 First steel base LD post test results (163.8N maximum load): (a) load acting in plane of symmetry normal to the line joining the two bolts in the base plate and (b) load applied at 90° to the previous case

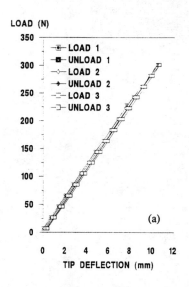
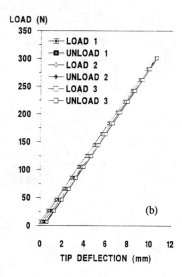

Fig.5 Second steel base LD post SLS test results: (a) load applied in plane of symmetry normal to line joining the two bolts in the base plate and (b) load applied in the plane of symmetry at 90° to the previous case.

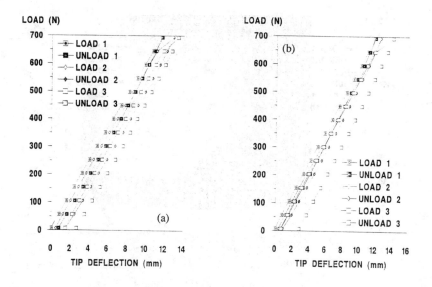

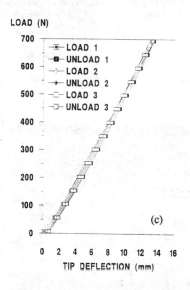

Fig.6 Steel base HD post SLS test results: (a) first post - load applied in plane of symmetry normal to the longer base dimension, (b) first post - load applied in plane of symmetry normal to shorter base dimension and (c) second post - loading direction as for (a).

328

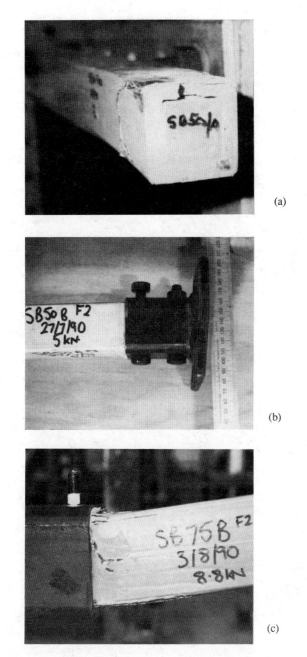

(a)

(b)

(c)

Fig.7 Visual damage to posts and bases after ULS tests: (a) steel base LD post, (b) plastic deformation in base plate (LD post) and (c) steel base HD post.

ADVANCED COMPOSITE MATERIALS IN BRIDGES AND STRUCTURES
K.W. Neale and P. Labossière, Editors; Canadian Society for Civil Engineering, 1992

Matériaux composites d'avant-garde pour ponts et charpentes
K.W. Neale et P. Labossière, éditeurs; Société canadienne de génie civil, 1992

APPLICATIONS OF FRP GRID REINFORCEMENT TO
PRECAST CONCRETE PANELS

M. Sugita, T. Nakatsuji, K. Sekijima and T. Fujisaki
Shimizu Corporation
Tokyo, Japan

ABSTRACT

First an outline of the development of the FRP grid reinforcement "NEFMAC" is described. Experiments on a concrete panel reinforced with NEFMAC and a prestressed concrete panel with NEFMAC, for the purpose of applying NEFMAC for precast concrete panels, are presented. Finally, examples of application are introduced.

RÉSUMÉ

L'article présente d'abord le processus de développement d'un renforcement en plastique renforcé de fibres nommé NEFMAC. Ces explications seront suivies par une description des essais effectués sur un panneau de béton renforcé de NEFMAC, et un panneau en béton précontraint avec NEFMAC, afin de montrer les applications de ce produit sur les panneaux en béton prémoulé. Des exemples d'application sont présentés.

INTRODUCTION

FRP grid reinforcement "NEFMAC" is a new composite material for concrete reinforcement. NEFMAC is made from high-strength continuous fibers (carbon, glass, and/or others) impregnated with resin and formed into grids. It is very lightweight, stronger than steel reinforcement, free from rust and corrosion, and highly salt resistant; these are only some of its many useful features.

This paper first provides an overview of developments of NEFMAC for practical use, and describes demonstrative experiment for applying which NEFMAC was applied to precast concrete panels, and introduces application examples.

OVERVIEW OF NEFMAC DEVELOPMENT

Table 1 is an overview of NEFMAC research and development (R&D) to the present. R&D was begun in 1984. In the beginning, fundamental R&D was done for our technological development project; later, joint R&D was done with universities.

As fundamental R&D for our technological development project, we clarified NEFMAC's tensile strength and conducted studies related to the method of lapped joint, which confirmed that NEFMAC is effective as concrete reinforcement.

In joint R&D did with universities, we first clarified shear and compressive strength -- NEFMAC's fundamental mechanical characteristics -- and then determined the mechanism by which it anchors to concrete. Additionally, to determine behavior during earthquakes, the cyclic loading characteristics of compression and tension were also studied. Moreover, tests on chemical resistance under constant tensile deformation confirmed NEFMAC's durability. To determine the behavior of concrete reinforced with NEFMAC in fires and at high temperatures, NEFMAC's heat resistance was also clarified.

We then test in cooperation with universities to verify applicability to concrete structures. For wall panel development, in-plane bending-shear tests under reversed cyclic lateral loading and bending tests under out-of-plane loading were done and structural characteristics clarified. For slab panel development, beam-anchoring methods, flexural behavior, and long-term deflection were confirmed. To improve flexural strength, we studied the possibility of using the pretension prestress method. Also, wall and slab panel fire resistance were studied and the applicability of NEFMAC was verified. Furthermore, for applications to columns and beams, we confirmed flexural, shear, and fatigue strength, and flexural strength after long-term exposure.

FLEXURAL BEHAVIOR AND LONG-TERMDEFLECTION
OF
NEFMAC-REINFORCED CONCRETE PANEL

Flexural Behavior
To be able to apply NEFMAC-reinforced concrete panels to curtain walls and the fender plates for small ships, we conducted bending tests to clarify flexural behavior. Table 2 shows the physical properties of NEFMAC and the concrete used in testing.

To develop curtain walls, we confirmed the wind resistance of the precast concrete panels by bending tests. Shapes of specimen are shown in Fig. 1 and load-deflection relationship of specimen in Fig. 2. Incidentally, bending tests were also done on specimens undergoing fire resistance test according to JIS; Fig. 2 shows test results.

The aforementioned tests clarified that the flexural cracking load exceeds the design load and that maximum strength of the precast concrete panels declines little, even after fire resistance test. We also learned that the existing bending theory for reinforced concrete can be applied to calculated initial stiffness (Ig), post-cracking stiffness (Icr) and maximum strength (Pu). Additionally, we clarified through both experiments and analysis that allowable crack width under the design load is 0.3mm or less, even when there is flexural cracking.

Fender plates for small ships were originally designed with epoxy coated steel reinforcing bars. However, comparison of flexural behavior (exhibited in bending tests) of two precast concrete panel specimens -- one with epoxy coated steel reinforcing bars and the other with NEFMAC reinforcement -- led us to use NEFMAC in some of the panels. The dimensions of the specimens are shown in Fig. 3, physical properties of the materials used in Table 2, and the load-deflection relationship of the specimen in Fig. 4. As NEFMAC has a small Young's modulus, the bending stiffness of the specimen dropped after flexural cracking, causing the deflection approximately 5 times larger below the yield (i.e., within the elastic range) for the epoxy coated steel reinforcing bars. However, we understood from this result NEFMAC-reinforced specimen has a large capacity of absorbing energy -- an advantage for a fender plate function.

Long-Term Deflection

To clarify long-term deflection of concrete panels reinforced with NEFMAC, long-term loading tests were done on unidirectional slabs with both ends fixated (see Fig. 5). The two types of loads -- below and above flexural cracking load -- were uniformly distributed. Physical properties of NEFMAC and the reinforcing bars and concrete used in testing are shown in Table 3.

Fig. 6 shows secular change in deflection at slab center and Fig. 7 the increase ratio of deflection. While long-term deflection of concrete reinforced with NEFMAC(N1) is similar to that of ordinary concrete slabs (S1) below the flexural cracking load, which is normally adopted for the design load, deflection(N2) is larger than for the ordinary reinforced concrete slabs (S2) above the flexural cracking load (N2), owing to NEFMAC's low Young's modulus. However, comparison with the increase ratio of deflection revealed that the values of specimens N1, N2, S1, and S2 came to nearly equal one another, as the increase ratio of deflection is governed by the characteristics of the concrete on the compression side.

To improve long-term deflection beyond the flexural cracking load, the presstressing method is effective to reduce the burden of the concrete on the compression side.

TRANFER LENGTH AND FLEXURAL BEHAVIOR
OF
NEFMAC PRESTRESSED CONCRETE

Transfer Length of NEFMAC

As shown in Fig. 8, specimens were pre tensioning prestressed concrete slabs with NEFMAC arranged as tendons at the upper and lower locations. Three sizes of stretching force were applied. Table 4 shows the physical properties of the materials used in testing. The NEFMAC pre-stressing method, as shown in Photo 1) concrete was placed at both ends of NEFMAC; 2) tensile force was applied to NEFMAC by expanding the concrete blocks through jacking; 3) concrete was placed at the specimen portion; and 4) jacks were released after the concrete had hardened. NEFMAC strain distribution before and after prestressing is shown in Fig. 9. As NEFMAC secures bond mainly at cross points of grids, grid strain was assumed to be constant. Over 90% of the tensile force on the center of the specimen were retained by the grids at both ends, and tensile force was almost 100% at the second grids. Transfer length was thus the distance from each end to the second reinforcement, meaning that it was extremely short.

Flexural Behavior

Bending tests were performed with prestressed specimens and their flexural behavior studied. Test results of the relationships between strain at the midspan of NEFMAC at the lower portion and load are shown in Fig. 10. They mostly agreed with the elastic theory calculations assuming the total cross-sectional area before flexural cracking. After flexural cracking, values gradually became closer to those calculated with the elastic theory, neglecting tensile stress of the concrete. It was thus clarified that the conventional flexure theory is applicable to prestressed concrete members when NEFMAC is used as a prestressing tendon.

NEFMAC Applications

Precast concrete panels reinforced with NEFMAC were applied to practical structures after it was verified by the experiments described above that the structural characteristics are enough to use.

Photo 2 shows the application to reinforcing a curtain wall by NEFMAC of a building in Yokohama. Photo 3 is of NEFMAC applied to reinforce fender plates. In Japan, applications of ACM, such as NEFMAC, to curtain walls require the approval of the Minister of Construction; this example is the first for which such approval was obtained.

Photo 4 is an example of applying concrete panels prestressed with NEFMAC to a pedestrian bridge. The introduced axial force is approximately 40% of the maximum load.

Three to five years have passed since these structures were built, with no problems resulting thus far.

Conclusion

The above was an overview of FRP grid reinforcement NEFMAC, which the authors developed, a description of experiments for application to precast panels, and an explanation of actual application to practical structures.

Requirements for increased durability and function in concrete structures will continue to boost the need for materials like NEFMAC in future. The authors hope that this report will be the trigger that increases such need.

Acknowledgments

Research and development were done jointly with Asahi Glass Matex Co., Ltd.; the authors deeply appreciate the valuable instructions and attentive cooperation.

Table 1 Research and Development Items of FRP Grid Reinforcement

Aim		Practice
Clarification of Fundamental Properties of FRP Reinforcement	Clarification of Tensile Strength of Fibers	Relationship of Tensile Strength between Fibers and FRP
		Tensile Strength, Hybrid Effect
	Clarification of Mechanical Properties	Compressive Strength
		Shear Strength
	Clarification of Behavior under Reversed Cyclic Load	Reversed Cyclic Loading (Tension and Compression)
	Clarification of Anchorage Mechanism	Anchorage to Concrete (by Bending or Grid-shaping)
		Lapped Joint
	Clarification of Durability	Deterioration of Tensile Strength under Spa Atmoshere
		Creep Strength
		Chemical Resistance under Constant Tensile Deformation
	Clarification of Heat Resistance	Tensile Strength under/after Heating/Cooling
Proof of the Applicability to Concrete Structures	Application to Earthquake Resisting Wall	Behavior under Reversed Cyclic Lateral Loading
	Application to Precast Wall Structure	Shear Resistance of Vertical Joint
	Application to Wall Panel	Bending Ultimate Strength
		Fire Resistance
	Application to Slab Panel	Anchorage to Beam
		Time-Dependent Deflection
		Bending Ultimate Strength
		Fire Resistance
		Effectiveness of Prestressing
	Application to Beam and Column	Effectiveness of Main and Shear Reinforcement
		Confined Effect by Lateral Reinforcement
		Fatigue Strength
		Bending Ultimate Strength after Sustained Loading
		Bending Ultimate Strength, Reinforced with Exposed FRP in Air
		Effectiveness of Chemical Prestressing

Table.2 Material Properties of Bending Test

Applications	Materials	Type	Max.(Yield)Load(ton)	Stiffness(ton)
Curtain Wall	NEFMAC	H8	3.79	224
		G8	3.10	155
	Light Weight Concrete	Fc=303kgf/ cm²	——	——
Fender Plate	NEFMAC	G19	17.6	886
	Reinforcing Bar	D19 (SD295A)	Yield=10.3	5,707
	Concrete	Fc=161kgf/ cm²	——	——

Table.3 Material Properties of Long-Term Loading Test

Materials	Type	Max.(Yield)Load(ton)	Stiffness(ton)
NEFMAC	H10	5.76	361
Reinforcing Bar	D10 (SD295A)	Yield=2.66	1,349
Concrete	Fc=270kgf/ cm²	——	——

Table.4 Material Properties of Prestressing Test

Materials	Type	Max.(Yield)Load(ton)	Stiffness(ton)
NEFMAC	H8	3.45	163
Concrete	Fc=458kgf/ cm²	——	——

336

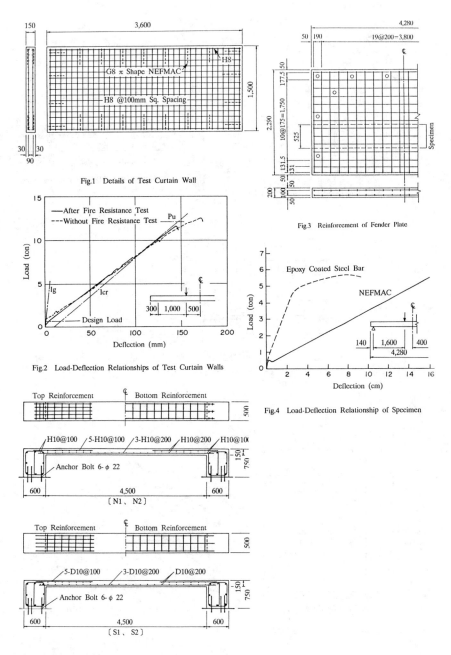

Fig.1 Details of Test Curtain Wall

Fig.2 Load-Deflection Relationships of Test Curtain Walls

Fig.3 Reinforcement of Fender Plate

Fig.4 Load-Deflection Relationship of Specimen

Fig.5 Details of Test Slabs

337

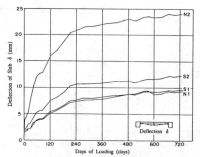

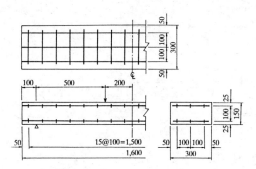

Fig.6 Time-Dependent Deflections of Test Slabs

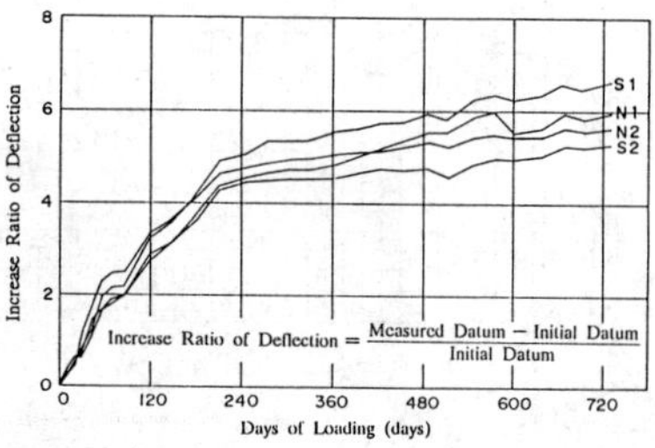

Fig.7 Increase Ratio of Deflection for Test Slabs

Fig.8 Prestressed Concrete Slab

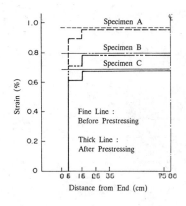

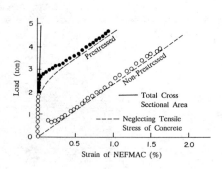

Fig.10 Relationship Between Load and Strain of Lower NEFMAC

Fig.9 Strain Distribution of NEFMAC

Photo 1 Prestressing Method of NEFMAC

Photo 2 Application of NEFMAC to Curtain Walls

Photo 3 Application of NEFMAC to Fender Plates

Photo 4 Application of Prestressed NEFMAC to a Pedestrian Bridge

340

ADVANCED COMPOSITE MATERIALS IN BRIDGES AND STRUCTURES
K.W. Neale and P. Labossière, Editors; Canadian Society for Civil Engineering, 1992

Matériaux composites d'avant-garde pour ponts et charpentes
K.W. Neale et P. Labossière, éditeurs; Société canadienne de génie civil, 1992

CONTINUOUS ARAMID MESH REINFORCED CEMENT PANELS FOR CONCRETE FORMS IN BUILDING CONSTRUCTION

S. Ohno and **K. Tanaka**
Takenaka Corporation,
Osaka, Japan

H. Mori
Takenaka Civil Engineering and Construction Co. Ltd.
Nagoya, Japan

J. Ida
Tokai Concrete Industrial Co. Ltd.
Nagoya, Japan

ABSTRACT

High-strength fibres and their composites have lately attracted considerable attention as the subjects of research work because of their mechanical properties and durability. The authors have developed a thin cement-based panel for concrete forms. The panel is 2000 x 1000 x 15 mm and is reinforced with a three-dimensional aramid fibre mesh. This paper describes the mechanical properties of the form and the various experimental work related to the selection of reinforcement, the manufacturing method, and the performance of the panel. In addition, full-scale experiments during the placing of concrete are reported.

RÉSUMÉ

Les fibres à haute résistance et leurs composites ont attiré récemment une attention considérable comme sujets de travaux de recherche du point de vue des propriétés mécaniques et de la durabilité. Un panneau mince à base de ciment fut développé comme coffrage. Ce panneau de 2000 x 1000 x 15 mm est renforcé avec un treillis en fibres d'aramide tridimensionnel. Cet article décrit les propriétés mécaniques du coffrage et les divers travaux expérimentaux relatifs à la sélection de l'armature, la méthode de fabrication et les performances du panneau. On présente aussi des essais de mise en place du béton.

INTRODUCTION

High-strength fibers such as carbon and aramid, for reinforcing concrete members became interesting in as the subjects of research work. Especially, FRP reinforcement and continuous fibers are considered to be attractive alternatives to conventional steel reinforcement from the viewpoint of their excellent mechanical properties and durability (JSCE, 1992) These fiber reinforcement methods are suitable not only for the main structure, but also for thin structural components, such as concrete forms.

At the same time, much attention has recently been paid in Japan to streamlining construction work and to the search for environmentally benign technologies. The development of lighter and thinner permanent forms has been of particular concern.

FEM ANALYSIS OF THE FORM

The developed permanent form was intended to have the following three features;
(i) To be lighter and thinner than conventional forms.
(ii) To be supported only by at it's edges and separator-bolts, without external supports (Fig. 1)
(iii) To be reinforced with continuous fiber meshes

Considering above points, the form's shape and dimensions have to be chosen, but these factors are also closely related to the load (support) conditions and the flexural properties of the composite. In order to determine the dimensions of the form and location of separators, FEM analysis was carried out. In the analysis, it was assumed that a form would be supported by three edges and the separator bolts resist the liquid pressure of the concrete.

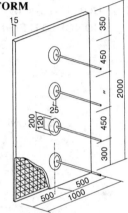

Figure 1 Shape of the permanent form

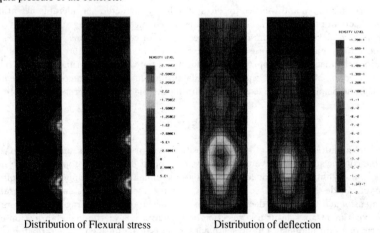

Distribution of Flexural stress   Distribution of deflection

Figure 2 One of results obtained by FEM analysis

The analysis was designed to determine the shape and thickness of the panel in the vicinity of the separator bolts, the location of the support (separator), and the boundary conditions. As a result, the following conclusions have been reached.

(1) As shown in Figure 2, the stress is greater towards the bottom while it is concentrated on the separator bolts. The stress is shown to be greatly affected by the fixing condition at the boundary and at the separator bolts.

(2) Rib reinforcement is less effective in reducing maximum stress than expected, although it does have some stiffening effect. To reduce the maximum stress, the panel thickness should be varied in proportion to the stress distribution over the panel. If the area near the separators, where a particularly high stress is concentrated, is thickened, this should be effective in not only reducing flexural stress but also in enhancing the punching shear strength at that point.

(3) The results suggest that the form shown in Figure 1 is good fo the stress level (about 10MPa) just below the limit of proportionality of the composite. The panel is 2000x1000x15mm(l·w·t), and is thickened to 40mm in an area of 200 to 250mm in diameter around the separators. The spacing of the separator bolts is 450mm. It was also confirmed that even with this thin panel, the deformation limit required of the form will be satisfied under the service load.

These results may not be an accurate evaluation, particularly as regards the boundary conditions of the actual form, but they are quite useful in determining the shape and support arrangement.

MATRIX PROPERTIES

Mix Proportion of the Matrix in the Experiment

According to FEM analysis, there are some local areas where relatively high flexural stresses of about 8-10MPa works. It is possible to produce cement composites which are able to withstand this level of stress. However, if cracking occurs in the matrix, it causes a reduction in stiffness and the deformation may then exceed the limit. To avoid this, it is recommended that the cracking strength of the matrix should exceed 10 MPa in flexure.

Table 1. Test program and results of matrix mix proportions

Name	Mix proportion (weight %)					silica sand (#)	de-watering method	Flexural strength (MPa)		Compressive strength (MPa)	
	w/c (%)	s/c (%)	Water reduce agent	shrinkage reduce agent	silica fume			7 days	28 days	7 days	28 days
				(% to cement weight)							
25-35	25	35	3%			7	--	14.3	18.8	82.0	91.7
27-35		35						13.7	15.0	82.8	92.4
27-35A	27					5		12.8	13.5	76.5	88.2
27-35B						6		12.6	13.6	78.5	84.3
27-50C			2%					11.0	12.6	78.5	85.5
27-50D		50		3%				11.1	13.0	70.9	81.6
27-50E			---	15%	7	--	12.7	15.2	85.6	90.2
27-50F			3%	15%			11.2	12.9	74.6	84.1
30-35		35	1.5%					11.9	13.3	76.4	90.6
30-70		70	2%					11.2	12.3	70.6	73.4
30-70A	30	70	1.5%	---	---	6	O	12.3	13.5	--	--
30-70B							--	11.3	12.2	66.1	80.4
35-80	35	80	2%	---	---	6	--	7.6	8.0	69.3	78.5
45-70A	45	70	—	---	---	5	O	12.1	13.2	--	--
45-70B							--	4.0	5.1	33.6	40.5

The matrix also needs to have excellent fluidity to satisfy production requirements. Since the form is 15mm thick; very thin compared with the conventional designs, shrinkage of the matrix should be as small as possible to avoid distortion during curing. Flexural strength tests and drying shrinkage tests for various mix proportions were carried out as shown in Table 1 in order to select the best mix proportion for this composite. Specimens of 250 x 50 x 15mm (length · width · thickness) were loaded in three-point bending tests with a span of 200mm.

Flexural strength of the matrix

The water-cement ratio (w/c) was main experimental parameter and it was varied from 25% to 45% with no vacuum dewatering. The sand cement ratio (S/C) and the amount of water reduceing agent were also varied to obtain the required workability. The results show that flexural strength was in the range 5 to 15 MPa and that strengths higher than 10 MPa were achieved with a water cement ratio of less than 30%.

When the vacuum dewatering process was applied to mortar of 45% water cement ratio, the flexural strength was the same as that of mortar with a 30% w/c. However, the effects of dewatering became less significant in the case of lower water cement ratios (30%).

On the other hand, if reinforcing fiber meshes exist in the mortar, dewatering is likely to be obstructed by the fiber meshes. Eventually this results in poorer strength than with unreinforced specimens (see Table 3). Therefore, even if vacuum dewatering is used, a smaller water-cement ratio is recommended to obtain the high cracking strength.

Drying Shrinkage

Figure 3 shows the drying shrinkage of mortar with a water-cement ratio of 30% and a sand-cement ratio of 70%, where (a) contains no reinforcing fiber meshes, while (b) contains fiber mesh. These results reveal that when the drying shrinkage of a mortar is high, the shrinkage is likely to be restricted by the presence of reinforcing fiber mesh. The use of steam curing or a shrinkage reducing agent effectively reduces drying shrinkage, with the effectiveness of both being almost equivalent. It was also confirmed that less shrinkage occurs as the size of the aggregate particles is increased.

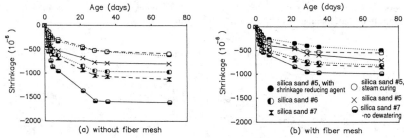

Figure 3   Drying Shrinkage of matrix mortar with different mix proportions

REINFORCING FIBER MESH

Reinforcing materials selected for consideration during the development stage were continuous fibers of carbon, aramid, polyvinyl-alcohol, and glass, all of which were manufactured into a mesh form. There are various types of mesh treatment available. If, however, a mesh of extremely closely spaced fibers is used in the panels such as fibrillated polypropylene fibers, special equipment is required for composite production. In order to produce a variety of components in relatively small number without large-scale mechanized equipment, a reinforcing

Table 2 Type of fibre meshes

Note	Type of fibers	Tensile strength of fibers (MPa)	Number of fillament	Diameter of fillament (μm)	Cross sectional (mm²)	Spacing of strand	Mesh Type
2A21	Aramid	3100	2000	8	0.151	12.5	2-drectional woven polymer impregnated
3A31			3000	12	0.226	12.5	3-drectional bonded
3A32						18	
3A33						25	
2V11	Poly-vinyl alcohol	1400	1000	14	0.154	10	2-drectional bonded
3V21			1875		0.288	18	3-drectional bonded
2G11	AR-Glass	2500	2880	12	0.326	8	2-drectional woven polymer impregnated
2G12					0.326	8	

mesh with coarsely spaced fibers is appropriate. Considering the technological production problems and the characteristics of the fibers, a two-directional mesh and a three-directional mesh were chosen, since these can be handled by current production technology. Since the type of fiber and the manufacturing method of mesh are closely related, the same mesh manufacturing method cannot always be applied to all fibers. In the experiment, three types of fibers - aramid, polyvinyl-alcohol, and glass - were chosen as shown in Table 2.

Photograph 1 shows the three-directional mesh which comprises three fibrous strands oriented at 60 degrees to each other and bonded with adhesive.

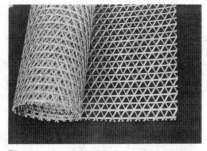

Photograph 1   Three directional mesh of Aramid fibers

The three-directional mesh can be manufactured at low cost, and is easily handled on the composite production line. Since the fiber strands of the mesh are bonded only at their intersections by a weak resin, no mechanical anchoring effect can be expected at the intersections.

There are two types of two-directional mesh. One is a mesh formed by bonding fiber strands, and the other is made by weaving the fiber strands and impregnating polymer into the strands. The two-directional polyvinylalcohol fiber mesh is the former type and the two-directional glass and aramid meshes were of the latter type, hardened by impregnation with epoxy resin.

MANUFACTURE OF CEMENT COMPOSITE SHEET

Adoption of an efficient production process for thin-panel forms is an important factor in reducing production costs and controlling the quality. For structural members such as parmanent forms and curtain walls, the use of continuous fibers is an effective way to obtain sufficient strength and toughness with relatively small fiber content. However, the manufacture of the cement composites may be made more complicated than the conventional mixing process for short fiber cement composites. Although a mechanized process for the continuously production of cement components using continuous fibers has been reported (Vittone, 1983), this process is designed for the mass production of such products as corrugated sheets at a plant. On the other hand, in building construction, there are many situations where a variety of products in small numbers have to be manufactured. From this point of view, we have investigated a suitable production method for the cement composites reinforced with continuous fiber meshes and adopted a vacuum dewatering method - as commonly used in the production of GRC components.

It is well known that this method allows water to be extracted from the cement matrix and this leads to minimal shrinkage and to enhance matrix strength. Furthermore, it also makes it easy to accurately place the reinforcing fiber meshes in the cement matrix. Accurate placement of the reinforcing fiber meshes is crucial to ensuring the ultimate flexural strength of the composite, because, as will be discussed latter, the flexural strength of a composite reinforced with fiber meshes is influenced by their depth distribution. However, synthetic fibers are normally lighter than the mortar matrix, and therefore tend to float or to be irregularly brnt during production.

To prevent this, reinforcing fiber mesh is first laid onto mortar of the designated thickness, and then fixed onto the matrix by vacuum dewatering. This operation is repeated until the desired compound is completed. The reinforcing fiber mesh is placed about 2 to 3mm from the faces of the panel, as shown in Photograph 2.

This method can be implemented using a relatively simple set of production equipment. It also this enables immediate removal of the form after dewatering, thus improving production efficiency.

Photo. 2   Cross section of the composite reinforced with Aramid fiber mesh

MECHANICAL PROPERTIES OF THE COMPOSITE

In order to select a reinforcing material, flexural tests of composites reinforced with the various fiber meshes listed in Table 3 were carried out. The specimens used were 250 x 50 x 15mm($l \cdot w \cdot t$) and each was tested in three-point loading with a span of 200mm. The load-deflection curve was measured.

Flexural Behavior

Table 3 shows the results of the flexural strength tests; the limit of proportionality (LOP: corresponds to the matrix cracking strength) and the ultimate flexural strength.

First cracking strength (limit of proportionality)

Since each composite specimen was manufactured by vacuum dewatering, the effects of water content on first cracking strength were considered to be relatively small. However the first cracking strength decreased with increasing the water cement ratio, while the water-cement ratio had almost no effect on the flexural strength of the plain mortar after vacuum dewatering.

This implies that the presence of fiber mesh in the composites prevents the extraction of excess water from the mortar. In particular, it is llkely that full dewatering cannot be achieved within the normal dewatering time, when there is a great excess of free water. It is also thought that excess water remained at the upper side of the fiber meshes after dewatering, eventually leading to poor bonding properties between the fiber mesh and matrix. Therefore, even when vacuum dewatering is employed, the minimum possible water content is desirable to achieve a high first cracking strength.

First cracking strength seems to be affected by the type of fiber mesh. The cracking strength of the two-directional woven meshes (of glass and aramid) , which were hardened after impregnation with resin, is lower than that of panels reinforced with the other meshes (see Table 3). These hard two-directional meshes may cause high stress concentrations around the strand intersections, as a result of their anchoring effect at the intersections.

Ultimate flexural strength and failure mode

The ultimate flexural strength increases with increasing fiber volume content. The failure mode and reinforcing efficiency vary slightly according to the properties of the fiber, the mesh type, and the bonding properties between the fibers and the matrix.

Table 3. Flexural test program and the results

Test No.	Matrix mix proportion	Type of reinforcing fibre		Fiber content		LOP (MPa)	MOR (MPa)
				No.of Mesh	volume (%)		
1	w/c=27% s/c=50%	plain		---	---	13.0	--
2		3-directional Aramid mesh	3A2	1	0.14	14.4	14.3
3				2	0.27	14.4	25.5
4		plain		--	---	13.2	--
5			3A31	2	0.42	11.8	39.0
6				4	0.84	11.8	39.0
7				2	0.31	11.8	24.0
8		Aramid mesh 3 directional	3A32	3	0.47	12.1	34.6
9	w/c=30% s/c=70%			4	0.62	13.4	42.3
10				6	0.94	13.0	39.4
11			3A33	8	0.42	11.7	33.8
12				2	0.27	11.3	12.0
13		PVA mesh 3-directional	3V21	3	0.40	11.4	18.7
14				4	0.54	11.6	24.0
15				6	0.80	10.8	23.6
16		2 directional Glass mesh	2G11	4	1.22	9.1	44.9
17			2G12	4	1.22	11.5	23.9
18		2 directional Aramid mesh	2A21	3	0.47	9.5	32.5
19				4	0.62	8.7	38.5
20	w/c=45% s/c=70%	plain		---	---	13.2	--
21		Aramid mesh	3A21	2	0.27	10.5	25.7
22		PVA mesh	2V11	2	0.20	10.7	10.7

Figure 4, 5 and 6 show the stress-deflection curves for the aramid, polyvinylalcohol and glass fiber cement composites, respectively. The aramid fiber cement achieves a higher flexural strength with the same fiber content and has a higher rigidity in the post-cracking region than polyvinylalcohol fiber cement. This is due to the aramid fiber's higher strength and modulus of elasticity. These results are considered to be important elements in designing thin panels which have a safety factor for a given displacement under service loads.

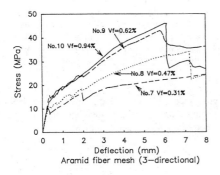

Figure 4 Stress-deflection curves
in Flexural loading
(Aramid fiber mesh)

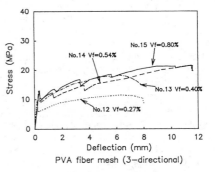

Figure 5 Stress-deflection curves
in Flexural loading
(Polyvinylalcohol fiber mesh)

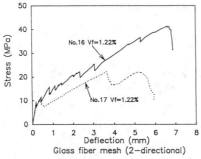

Figure 6 Stress-deflection curves
in Flexural loading
(Glass fiber mesh)

Photograph 3
Flexural loading test of the panel

High modulus fibers can satisfy the required limit of deformation under service conditions with a lower fiber content, and this leads to a simpler manufacturing process for the composites. From this point of view, high modulus fibers such as carbon may be suitable if bond between the fiber meshes and the matrix is maintained. However, carbon fibers composites tend to lose toughness because of the low strain capacity of the fibers. Since no reasonable product of carbon fiber mesh existed at that time, carbon mesh was not examined in this experiment except at the preliminary stage, but it might be considered in future.

Two-directional glass fiber mesh with epoxy resin impregnation and three-directional aramid fiber mesh yield almost the same level of ultimate flexural strength. The former has a modulus of elasticity slightly higher than the latter in the post-cracking region.This is probably because, in the aramid fiber cement, debonding between the three-directional aramid mesh and the mortar takes place in the region close to the ultimate strength, which a fact revealed as a sudden increase in deformation. Since, in this flexural test, the specimens were not very wide (50mm), the fiber strands with angled at 60 degrees to the main direction may not effectively transfer the stress, thus debonding may take place. Therefore, in an actual panel form, the effect of the fiber strands at that an angle is expected to be somewhat higher.

The ultimate failure mode in flexural tests is due to compressive failure of the mortar in most of the specimens. However, since the panels are very thin at 15mm, they are capable of considereble deformation. As shown in Photograph 3, an actual-size three-directional aramid mesh panel can deform by an especially large amount, and this behavior will assure adequate safety even under accidental excess loading conditions.

In terms of prediction of flexural strength, since the cement composite used in these experiments is reinforced with several meshes, the conventional calculation methods for reinforced concrete member can be applied rather than the method for the fiber-cement composites.

Effect of mesh type
The difference between the two-directional mesh and three-directional mesh is the effect of the fiber orientation on composite behavior. When the fibers are incorporated into a composite, the flexural behavior is influenced by the orientation of the main fibers to the working stress. Figure 7 shows the flexural strength of specimens with various main strand orientations (the specimens

348

were cut from a large panel at different angles). In figure 7, the test results are shown as the ratio of the flexural strength of the specimens with angled fibers to those without an angle. The figure indicates that the three-directional mesh loses less strength than the two-directional mesh according to the orientation, and that the former is affected by such losses over a smaller range of orientations than the latter. These characteristics are especially important for panel forms which are point-supported at the separators, because the stress is distributed concentrically around the support points.

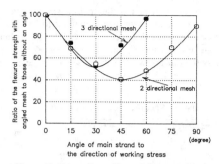

Figure 7 Orientation effect of fiber mesh on flexural strength

Also the other experiments on the shear strength around the separators and their reinforcing methods for them were also carried out separately. Based on these experimental results, the specifications shown in Table 4 were adopted from the viewpoints of mechanical properties, workability, and economy, etc.

FULL-SCALE MODEL EXPERIMENT

Life-size permanent forms were manufactured according to the specification given in Table 5. Full-scale model tests were carried out using these forms to checked their performance and to clarify those issues such as support conditions for the forms and stress distribution during casting concrete, etc. which remained unresolved by the earlier analysis. In this experiment, two forms were used to partition the space in a concrete box, as shown in Figure 8, and concrete was placed from above in free fall. The strain on both sides of the forms, the strain on the separator bolts, and the displacement of the forms were measured. The concrete used for casting had a slump value of 23cm to give a fluid pressure as close as possible to the analyzed condition. Although this method of placement caused problems with the measuring intermittent strain increases due to the impact of free-falling concrete, the results were considered reasonable.

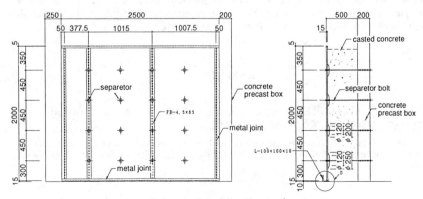

Figure 8 Set-up of the full scale experiment for the permanent form

349

The measurements indicate that the stress at the mid-points between separators was higher than predicted. This difference is thought to be caused by the difficulties in evaluating boundary conditions and support conditions of the forms. In the experiments, considerably worse conditions than those encountered in practical concrete placement were tested, but the maximum deformation was 0.7mm and within the target value, while the predicted value is 1.2 mm. As shown in Photograph 4, it was confirmed that the forms performed excellently after concrete placement.

Table 4 Specification of panel forms

Compornents	Specification		
Panel	size	2000 x 1000 x 15mm	
	cement matrix	w/c=30%, s/c=70% Ad.1.5%	
	Reinforce-ment	Aramid fiber 3-directional mesh	
	Manu-facturing	vacuum dewatering after placing mortar	
Reinforcing separetor head	spacing	@450x500mm	
	size	ϕ 120x ϕ 200x25mm (uppeer x bottom x thickness)	
	cement matrix	w/c=45%, s/c=70%	
	Reinforce-ment	glass fiber, Vf=5%	
	Manu-facturing	spray-up method, components were pasted with epoxy resin on the panel	

Photograph 4

Condition after placing concrete

CONCLUSION

Various experiments were carried out to develop a new concrete form which is lighter and thinner than conventional designs by using high-strength fibers. Since the forms are supported by their edges and the separator bolts, separators were placed at appropriate positions on the form and the part of the form around them was thickened. High-strength mortar with a low water cement ratio was used as a matrix and the fibers were fixed by vacuum dewatering to enhance strength and improve productivity. In terms of the reinforcing materials, three-directional aramid mesh was thought to be most effective as regards the reinforcing effect and the failure mode. Life-size thin-panel forms were tested using actual concrete and proved to be effective as permanent forms.

REFERENCES

The Japan Society of Civil Engineering, Proceeding of Symposium ' Application of FRP reinforcement for Concrete Structure', Apr. 1992.

Vittone, A. Netlike products in polypropylene fibrillated films - Production and Applications, Third International Conference of Polypropylene Fibers and Textiles, University of York, Oct., 1983.

ADVANCED COMPOSITE MATERIALS IN BRIDGES AND STRUCTURES
K.W. Neale and P. Labossière, Editors; Canadian Society for Civil Engineering, 1992

Matériaux composites d'avant-garde pour ponts et charpentes
K.W. Neale et P. Labossière, éditeurs; Société canadienne de génie civil, 1992

PERFORMANCE OF DOUBLY-REINFORCED PULTRUDED
GRATING/CONCRETE SLABS

L.C. Bank and **Z. Xi**
The Catholic University of America
Washington, D.C., USA

E. Munley
Turner-Fairbank Highway Research Center
McLean, Virginia, USA

ABSTRACT

The performance of full-scale concrete slabs reinforced with commercially produced pultruded fibre-reinforced-plastic (FRP) grating is described. Results of tests of slabs measuring 6.1 m x 1.2 m x 21.6 cm (20 ft. x 4 ft. x 8.5 in.) and tested as continuous beams over two spans of 2.44 m (8 ft.) are presented. The slabs were doubly-reinforced (top and bottom of the slab) with 5.1 cm (2 in.) deep pultruded gratings having longitudinal bar spacings of 7.62 cm (3 in.) and 5.1 cm (2 in.) on-centre, respectively. Quasi-static monotonic loading tests to failure were conducted. The results of tests on 5 slabs are presented. Load versus deflection and load versus strain data at critical locations are reported. The failure mechanisms of the slabs are described.

RÉSUMÉ

La performance de dalles de béton, armées de grilles de plastique renforcé de fibres (FRP), est décrite. On présente les résultats d'essais sur des dalles et des poutres continues sur deux portées. Les dalles sont renforcées sur deux faces. On a exécuté des tests quasi-statiques monotones menant à la rupture. Les résultats des essais sur cinq dalles sont présentés ainsi que les comportements charge-déflexion et charge-déformation aux points critiques. Les modes de rupture des dalles sont également décrits.

INTRODUCTION

The life expectancy of bridge decks, particularly steel reinforced concrete bridge decks, has been an issue of growing concern over the past decade (Bettigole, 1990). New technologies are being explored by the transportation industry for the construction of new bridge decks and the replacement of deteriorated bridge decks on existing bridges. Various bridge deck systems using conventional materials are currently being proposed, evaluated and tested. These include, cast-in-place concrete (conventional removable formwork or stay-in-place steel deck), precast concrete panels, open steel grid, concrete-filled steel grid, exodermic and steel orthotropic (Montgomery et al, 1992). The steel industry is promoting the use of a variety of steel decking systems and also the use of a Bridge Deck Rating System to evaluate and compare different alternatives (Bettigole, 1990; Montgomery et al, 1992). Of particular interest are bridge decks for shortspan bridges which comprise 90% of the highway bridges in the U.S. (Montgomery et al, 1992).

In addition to conventional material systems for bridge decks the use of non-conventional composite material systems have begun to be considered as potential replacements for steel, timber and concrete. Glass/epoxy composite material bridge deck panels (Plecnik et al, 1990) and hybrid composite material systems (Bakeri and Sunder, 1990) have been proposed. Alternatively, the use of non-metallic reinforcements (generally referred to as fiber-reinforced plastics (FRP) or advanced composite materials (ACM)) for cast-in-place, precast or prestressed concrete slabs have been proposed. A number of different composite material reinforcing systems are being considered. Recent studies on concrete reinforced with FRP bars (Faza and GangaRao, 1991; Saadatmanesh and Ehsani, 1991; Pleimann, 1991), with FRP composite grids (Nakatsuji et al, 1990; Goodspeed et al, 1991), with FRP molded grating (Bank et al, 1991; Larralde and Zerva, 1991), with pultruded FRP grating (Bank et al, 1991, Bank et al, 1992), and with FRP prestressing tendons (Iyer et al, 1991; Sen et al, 1991; Kakihara et al, 1991; Gerritse and Werner, 1991; Nanni et al, 1992) have been reported.

The use of pultruded fiber-reinforced plastic grating as a reinforcement for concrete slabs is discussed in this paper. The pultruded grating is used as an alternative to conventional steel reinforcing bars to create a "composite" load bearing structural slab. The advantages of using FRP materials to reinforce concrete include their resistance to corrosion and their electromagnetic transparency. Additional advantages of using *pultruded FRP grating* to reinforce concrete include the ease of construction delivered by a grating panel, the ability of the grating to create a reliable mechanical interlock with the concrete due to the geometry of its longitudinal and transverse bars, its ability to contribute to the shear strength of the unreinforced concrete, and its high modulus relative to molded grating.

Results of tests of full-size concrete bridge deck slabs, conducted at the Turner-Fairbank Highway Research Center of the Federal Highway Administration (FHWA) in McLean, VA, are reported in this paper. Results are presented for tests of continuous doubly-reinforced slabs subjected to quasi-static monotonic loads. The work described in this paper forms the early part of a comprehensive research investigation into the testing, analysis and design of bridge deck slabs reinforced with pultruded FRP gratings. The study is being conducted in parallel with an identical study which is utilizing Nefmac[1] composite material grids in place of the pultruded grating (Schmeckpeper et al, 1992). The whole research program will consist of static, cyclic and dynamic (fatigue and impact) tests and will investigate flexural, flexural shear and punching shear failure modes. A concurrent study

[1]Manufactured by Nefcom Corporation.

to investigate the durability of pultruded FRP grating reinforced concrete
slabs will begin in the fall of 1992. Results of tests of small-scale
specimens (Bank et al, 1991) and of full-scale simply-supported singly-
reinforced slabs (Bank et al, 1992) have been reported elsewhere. The work
described in this paper is a continuation of that described in Bank et al
(1992). Following the success of the tests conducted on the simply-supported
spans (single curvature), tests of continuous slabs having both positive and
negative curvatures and doubly-reinforced with pultruded FRP gratings were
conducted. The performance of the doubly-reinforced continuous slabs is
described in detail in this paper.

This paper concentrates on a detailed description of the results of the
tests. Issues relating to material selection, design constraints and
assumptions, and slab fabrication, discussed in detail in Bank et al (1992),
are only briefly reviewed. The test set-up for the continuous tests is
described and locations of displacement and strain gages are detailed.
Results of tests of 4 slabs reinforced with pultruded FRP grating and one slab
reinforced with steel rebars are presented. Results of identical tests
conducted by Goodspeed and co-workers describing the performance of the Nefmac
composite grid reinforced slabs will be reported independently.

MATERIALS AND FABRICATION

Slabs measuring 6.1 m x 1.2 m x 21.6 cm (20 ft x 4 ft x 8.5 in)[2] were
fabricated. Except for a control slab reinforced with steel rebars the slabs
were reinforced with commercially produced pultruded FRP grating. Pultruded
FRP grating is produced by a number of U.S. manufacturers and is primarily
used in the construction of platforms and walkways in corrosive environments.
Pultruded grating is an orthogonal grid constructed of longitudinal and
transverse glass/polyester or glass/vinylester pultruded members (bars). The
longitudinal bars typically have miniature I or T cross-sectional profiles and
range from 1.27 to 2.54 cm (0.5 to 2.0 in) in height. The transverse bars (or
cross-rods) are typically of a circular shape and much smaller in cross-
section than the longitudinal bars (or bearing bars). The longitudinal bars
are typically spaced at 2.54 to 7.62 cm (1.0 to 3.0 in) on center depending on
grating type and the transverse bars are typically spaced at 15.24 to 30.48 cm
(6.0 or 12.0 in) on center. The longitudinal and transverse bars are
connected by proprietary mechanical interlocking systems.

Based on the results of previous tests (Bank et al, 1991; Bank et al,
1992) two different commercially available gratings[3] were selected:
Safe-T-Grate[™][4] and Duradek[™][5]. The grates chosen were both from the "T" series
having 5.08 cm (2 in) high longitudinal T bars. For the bottom reinforcement
a grating having the longitudinal T bars at 5.08 cm (2 in) on center was used,
while for the top reinforcement a grating having longitudinal T bars at 7.62
cm (3 in) on center was used. Both top and bottom gratings had transverse
bars at 15.24 cm (6 in) on center. A photograph of small samples of the top
reinforcement gratings are shown in Fig. 1. The "T" shape of the longitudinal
bars can be seen. The approximate cross-sectional area of the "T" bars was
measured as 3.48 cm[2] (0.54 in[2]). The approximate centroidal second moment of

---

[2]All original dimensions were in U.S. customary units and have been converted
to SI equivalents.

[3]Trade names of the FRP gratings used are given to enable identification of
the products used. It does not imply any endorsement of these particular
products or the manufacturer's cited.

[4]Manufactured by Seasafe, Inc.

[5]Manufactured by Aligned Fiber Composites, Inc.

Fig. 1   Photograph of Safe-T-Grate (left) and Duradek (right)FRP Grating

area (moment of inertia) of the T bar was calculated as 11.63 cm^4 (0.28 in^4).
In the analysis of concrete slabs reinforced with FRP grating the shape of the
T bar must be accounted for; it is inappropriate to assume that the bar area
is the only governing geometric parameter as in the case of a circular steel
rebar. For example in calculating the effective stiffness of the slab the
moment of inertia of the T bar must be considered (Bank et al, 1991).

The gratings were placed in wooden plywood forms with allowance for 2.54
cm (1 in) of concrete cover, both top and bottom. Since the assumption is
that FRP reinforcement is corrosion resistant a cover is theoretically not
actually required. A 2.54 cm (1 in) cover was however deemed necessary for a
variety of other reasons including protection of the grating during "real-
life" service from expose to fire and UV radiation, complete embedment of the
grating to ensure mechanical interlocking with the concrete, and finish of the
top "riding" surface. The gratings were placed in the forms with the
longitudinal bars of the top grating off-set from the longitudinal bars of the
bottom grating to allow concrete infiltration and vibration with pencil
vibrators. The steel control slab was isotropically reinforced with #5[6] bars
@ 11.43 cm (4.5 in), on center (top and bottom) with a 2.54 cm (1 in) cover.

Transit mixed normal weight portland cement concrete that was required to
meet the Virginia Department of Transportation (Virginia, 1987) standard A4
Posts and Rails mix specification (with high range super plasticizer) was
obtained from a local vendor. The specification calls for a 27.5 MPa (4000
psi) nominal strength, nominal maximum aggregate size of 1.27 cm (0.5 in),
minimum cement content of 3.691 kN/m^3 (635 lbs/yd^3), maximum water content of
0.45 (weight water/weight cement), slump of 5.08 - 12.92 cm (2 - 5 in) and air
content of 7 ± 2 %. In addition the specification states that "the slump
shall not exceed 17.78 cm (7 in) when high-range water reducer is used". The
Posts and Rails mix was chosen because of its small maximum aggregate size
which was needed to allow for infiltration of the concrete between the closely
spaced grating bars. The super plasticizer was used to improve the
workability of the concrete. A total of 7 slabs were cast (3 Duradek, 3
Safe-T-Grate, 1 steel). Two castings were done, on different days, with
concrete from the same vendor. Cylinders were cast from each batch and 7 and
28 day tests were performed. No problems were encountered with fabrication of
the slabs, including infiltration of the concrete through the grating. Forms
were stripped after 7 days. Testing was performed after 28 days and was
completed (all slabs) in approximately 4 weeks.

Mechanical properties of the pultruded material used in the gratings are
not easy to establish. Mechanical tests were performed on the gratings and
will be reported elsewhere. From manufacturers data the following nominal
values can be assumed: Longitudinal stiffness, E = 34.5 GPa (5 x 10^6 psi);
longitudinal tensile strength, σ > 413 MPa (60 ksi).

---

[6]deformed grade 60 bars,; ϕ = 1.58 cm (5/8 in), A = 2.0 cm^2 (0.31 in^2)

TEST SET-UP AND INSTRUMENTATION

The concrete slabs were supported on three roller supports spaced 2.44 m (8 ft) apart. Load was applied with two 1,334 kN (300 kip) hydraulic rams which were driven by an electric pump and controlled by a manually operated load accumulator. A photograph of a slab in the test fixture is shown in Fig. 2. Equal loads of magnitude P, placed at 1.03 m (3.38 ft) from the center support, were applied simultaneously to each span. This position of the loads was selected in order to develop maximum negative moment over the middle support. The middle support reaction for this loading configuration was 1.54 P. Loads were applied over a 0.25 m x 0.64 m (10 in x 25 in) contact area (AASHTO (1989) Art. 3.30) through a 5.08 cm (2 in) thick steel bearing plate and rubber pad. Load cells were used to measure load magnitudes.

Deflection transducers and strain gages were placed on the slab transverse center-line and 7.62 cm (3 in) from one edge. Deflection transducers were placed at four locations along the length; under the two load points and at 1.43 m (4.69 ft) from the middle support in each span. Strain gages were bonded (before casting) to both the top and bottom FRP gratings on their top flanges closest to the slab surfaces at two locations along the length; at the midpoint of the left-hand span (positive moment) and at the middle support (maximum negative moment). Strain gages were bonded to the concrete surfaces (top and bottom) at the same locations as the gages in the gratings. Data were recorded on a MEGADAC 2000 data acquisition system.

PERFORMANCE EVALUATION CRITERIA

The performance of the slabs was evaluated with respect ultimate and serviceability limit state criteria. The performance of the FRP grating reinforced slabs was compared with that of the steel rebar reinforced slab which was designed according to AASHTO (1989) specifications Art. 3.24.3.1 *Case A - Main Reinforcement Perpendicular to Traffic*. The slab was designed for a live load moment given by Art. 3.24.3.1 using a nominal MS-22.5 (HS-25)

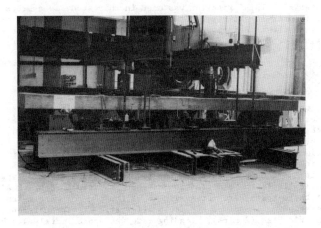

Fig. 2 Slab test set-up

loading. MS-22.5 (HS-25) is defined *in the spirit of* current AASHTO (1989)
loadings (Appendix E - Metric Equivalents, 1991 Interim) and it used to
designate a loading 25% greater than the standard MS-18 (HS-20) with a wheel
load $P_{22.5}$ = 89 kN (P_{25} = 20,000 lbs). The higher loading than the AASHTO
standard MS-18 (HS-20) was used to anticipate future specifications and
provide for a more rigorous test program. The design live load moment was
taken following Art. 3.24.3.1 as,

$$\left(\frac{S + 0.61}{9.74} \right) P_{22.5} \ (kN\text{-}m/m) \quad \left[\ \left(\frac{S + 2}{32} \right) P_{25} \ (ft\text{-}lb/ft) \ \right] \quad (1)$$

where S is the effective span length in meters (feet). (The 0.8 continuity
factor for slabs continuous over three or more supports was not applied.) The
maximum live load impact factor of 30% according to AASHTO (1989) Art. 3.8.2.1
was applied to the nominal load bringing the nominal service load to 115.7 kN
(26,000 lbs). This load was used to determine the serviceability limit state
of the slab.

    The serviceability limit state criterion for concrete bridge decks
reinforced with non-metallic (non-corrosive) reinforcement is subject to some
interpretation. A deflection limit for bridge deck slabs spanning in the
transverse direction is not given clearly in the current AASHTO code (1989).
Art. 8.9 - *Control of Deflections*, states that: "Flexural members of bridge
structures shall be designed to have adequate stiffness to limit deflections
or any deformations that may adversely affect the strength or serviceability
of the structure at service load plus impact." In the Ontario code (Ontario,
1983) the serviceability deflection criterion is controlled by a limiting
crack width. This is presumably applicable to concrete slabs reinforced with
steel rebars which are susceptible to corrosion. In the absence of corrosion
(assuming that FRP materials do not corrode in the conventional sense) it is
not clear how to set the deflection limit for the serviceability limit state.
A recent AASHTO draft specification (June 6, 1991) has proposed a service
limit state criterion which would limit the local slab radius of curvature to

$$\rho = \frac{EI}{M} > 152.4 \ m \ (6000 \ in) \quad (2)$$

This criterion is intended to limit deck deformations to prevent rider
discomfort, excessive rotations of supporting components and break up of
surface material. This criterion was used in this study as a means of
evaluating the serviceability limit state. Since accurate strain data was
available from the experiments local curvatures could be calculated at
critical slab locations and compared with Eq. (2).

SLAB TEST PROGRAM

    Slabs were tested to failure. All slabs reported in this paper were
tested under monotonically increasing load to 116 kN (26 kips) (service load),
then subjected to 10 loading-unloading cycles 0 - 116 kN (26 kips), and then
loaded monotonically to failure. These slabs were tested in this fashion to
obtain ultimate strength data but nevertheless to allow for some effect of
"settling-in" at the service load. These slabs are referred to as being
subjected to "monotonic" load. The two remaining slabs of each type were
tested cyclically in the same fashion as that reported in Bank et al (1992).
Results of these tests were not available at the time of writing and will be
reported elsewhere. Load was applied quasi-statically in increments or
decrements of 8.9 kN (2 kips). Loading rate was approximately 4.5 kN per
minute (1 kip per minute). Data were recorded at each increment. Loading was
halted at periodic intervals to record crack patterns and take photographs.

SLAB TEST RESULTS

For each slab tested a total of 26 channels of data were recorded.
Selective data is presented in graphical and tabular form. A description of
the slab response and failure modes is first given. This is followed by the
data. The slabs are identified according to the following identification
scheme: Reinforcement type; S - Safe-T-Grate; D - Duradek; ST - Steel:
Concrete batch; 1, 2 or 3. Slabs from concrete batches 1 and 2 were cast on
the same day. Slabs from batch 3 were cast 2 weeks later. All concrete was
ordered to the same specification. 28 day cylinder tests on batches 1, 2 and
3 gave average (of 5 cylinders) compressive strength values of 24.1 MPa (3500
psi), 21.4 MPa (3100 psi), and 35.9 MPa (5200 psi), respectively. The low
strengths of batches 1 and 2 was a source of concern and could not be easily
explained. It is possible that the cylinder strengths are not representative
of the actual concrete strengths. Slabs were tested in the following order;
S1, D1, S3, D3, ST3.

The behavior of all of the FRP grating reinforced slabs under load was
similar. Flexural cracks developed early on in the loading history in both
the positive and negative moment regions. These flexural cracks lined up with
the locations of the transverse bars in the grating. As loading increased
crack depths and widths increased. A photograph of the central region of slab
S1 at a load of P = 347 kN (78 kips) is shown in Fig. 3. Note the depth of
the flexural cracks (neutral axis location) and the visible midspan
deflections. (Fig. 2 shows the same slab after the 10 cycles at service load,
P = 116 kN (26 kips)). The slabs all failed in a shear failure mode in the
short shear span between the middle support and one of the load points. No
evidence of shear cracks was seen prior to the failure. However, audible
cracking noises could be heard from the slabs when loads reached approximately
80% of ultimate. The noises are characteristic of FRP failure and suggest
localized transverse matrix cracking in the pultruded grating material. At
failure a series of diagonal shear cracks developed in the concrete confined
between the two gratings as shown for slab S1 in Fig. 4. These cracks tended
to propagate horizontally along the top and bottom interfaces between the
gratings and the concrete at the mid-height of the slab. Load was removed
immediately following failure of slab S1. For slabs D1, S3 and D3 the load
was maintained following first load drop-off in a attempt to measure the
post-peak capacity of the grating reinforced slabs. Wherever possible this

Fig. 3 Flexural cracks in slab S1 at P = 347 kN (78 kips)

357

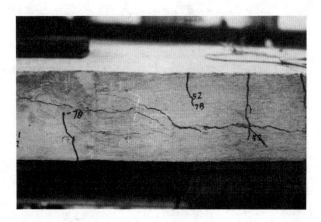

Fig. 4 Close-up of failure mode of slab S1

post-peak data was recorded. It was not always possible to record this post-peak data on the data acquisition system that was used and absence of data does not mean that post-peak carrying capacity was not obtained. Significant post-peak capacity was observed. The slabs continued to carry load as the individual grating members failed progressively in a longitudinal shear mode. In contrast to the FRP grating reinforced slabs the steel rebar reinforced slab failed in shear with no prior warning and could support no post-peak load.

In Table 1 data are given for the slabs at the service load of 116 kN (26 kips) after the tenth cycle and at the ultimate failure load. Maximum tensile strain in the FRP and maximum compressive strain in the concrete at midspan (positive curvature) and over the middle support (negative curvature) are given. Local radii of curvature (at the service load) at these two locations are given. Maximum slab deflections in the left hand and right hand span are also given. The load versus deflection for all slabs is shown is Fig. 5. The maximum deflection of the two spans is shown with its corresponding load. The post-peak loads and deflections are also shown where recorded. The load versus strains in the concrete and the FRP for slab S1 are shown in Fig. 6.

TABLE 1 Test Data at Service and Ultimate Loads

Slab	P (kN)	δ_{left} (mm)	δ_{rght} (mm)	ϵ_{conc}^{top} (μstr)	ϵ_{FRP}^{top} (μstr)	$\epsilon_{FRP}^{bot.}$ (μstr)	ρ^{+} (m)	$\epsilon_{conc}^{bot.}$ (μstr)	$\epsilon_{FRP}^{bot.}$ (μstr)	ϵ_{FRP}^{top} (μstr)	ρ^{-} (m)
S1	116	2.8	2.5	-491	-310	768	151	-607	-143	1403	95
	494	22.8	20.8	-3152	-1356	4876	--	-2436	-2805	6030	--
D1	116	2.6	3.4	-475	-252	755	155	-424	-312	1392	104
	451	18.7	16.8	-2730	-1000	4800	--	-1995	-1496	5848	--
S3	116	3.2	2.1	-639	-219	179	233	-346	-256	1246	120
	484	21.5	16.7	-2222	-690	2839	--	-1392	-2133	5611	--
D3	116	2.8	2.8	-260	-122	200	414	-238	-211	1336	121
	483	16.4	19.0	-1597	-543	3451	--	-1230	-1501	6933	--
ST3	116	1.7	1.0	-314	-148	470	243	-201	-176	738	203
	387	7.6	5.3	-969	-444	2126	--	-597	-254	2379	--

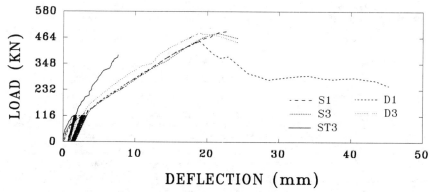

Fig. 5 Load versus maximum deflection for all slabs

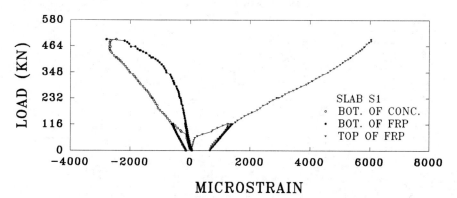

Fig. 6 Load versus strains for slab S1

DISCUSSION AND CONCLUSIONS

From the test results it can be seen that the FRP grating reinforced slabs all carried more load than the steel reinforced slab, albeit at larger deflections. This is attributed to the contribution of the pultruded grating to the shear strength of the slab. Tensile strains in the FRP and compressive strains in the concrete were generally below their failure strains (indicating no flexural failure of the slabs). The non-linear compressive strain in the FRP grating at higher loads (see Fig. 6) was seen in all the grating reinforced slabs and may be an indication of localized compressive failure in the grating material. The local radii of curvature in the positive moment region generally satisfied Eq. (2), however in the negative moment region (higher moment) Eq. (2) was only satisfied by the steel slab. Deflections in the spans at the service load were well below a L/500 limit of 4.9 mm (0.19 in). The load versus deflection of the FRP slabs was approximately linear to failure. Strains in the slabs from batch 3 tended to be lower than those from batch 1. Overall the performance of the grating reinforced slabs was satisfactory both from a strength and a stiffness perspective. Further testing is needed to investigate punching shear failure and response to dynamic loads. Based on the results to date is seems likely that the punching shear strength of grating reinforced slabs will be satisfactory.

ACKNOWLEDGEMENTS

Support from the National Science Foundation (grants MSM-9003867 and MSS-9114188, Dr. J. Scalzi, Program Director) and the Federal Highway Administration under the Grants for Research Fellowships (GRF) program is acknowledged. The assistance of Mr. Lloyd Cayes and Ms. Susan Lane is appreciated. Donations of FRP gratings are gratefully acknowledged.

REFERENCES

AASHTO, 1989, (1990, 1991 Interim) Standard Specifications for Highway Bridges , 14th ed, Washington.

Bakeri, P.A., and Sunder, S.S., 1990, "Concepts for Hybrid FRP Bridge Deck Systems," Serviceability and Durability of Construction Materials, ASCE, 1006-1015.

Bank, L.C., Xi, Z., and Mosallam, A.S., 1991, "Experimental Study of FRP Grating Reinforced Concrete Slabs," Advanced Composites Materials in Civil Engineering Structures, ASCE, 111-122.

Bank, L.C., Xi, Z., and Munley, E., 1992, "Tests of Full-Size Pultruded FRP Grating Concrete Bridge Decks," proceedings of the 1992 Materials Engineering Congress, ASCE, Atlanta, GA, August 10-12.

Bettigole, N.H., 1990, "Designing Bridge Decks to Match Bridge Life Expectancy," in Extending the Life of Bridges, ASTM STP 1100, American Society for Testing and Materials, Philadelphia, PA, 70-80.

Faza, S.S. and GangaRao, H.V.S., 1991, "Bending and Bond Behavior of Concrete Beams Reinforced with Plastic Rebars," Transportation Research Record 1290, TRB, 185-193.

Gerritse, A. and Werner, J., 1991, "ARAPREE - A Non-metallic Tendon - Performance and Design Requirements," Advanced Composites Materials in Civil Engineering Structures, ASCE, 143-154.

Goodspeed, C., Schmeckpeper, E., Gross, T., Henry, R., Yost, J., Zhang, M., 1991, "Cyclical Testing of Concrete Beams Reinforced with Fiber Reinforced Plastic (FRP) Grids," Advanced Composites Materials in Civil Engineering Structures, ASCE, 278-287.

Iyer, S.L., Khubuchandani, A., and Feng, J., 1991, "Fiberglass and Graphite Cables for Bridge Decks," Advanced Composites Materials in Civil Engineering Structures, ASCE, 371-382.

Kakihara, R., Kamiyoshi, M., Kumagai, S., and Noritake, K., 1991, "A New Aramid Rod for Reinforcement of Prestressed Concrete Structures," Advanced Composites Materials in Civil Engineering Structures, ASCE, 132-143.

Larralde, J. and Zerva, A., 1991, "Load-Deflection Performance of FRP Grating-Concrete Composites," Advanced Composites Materials in Civil Engineering Structures, ASCE, 271-277.

Montgomery, J.M., Gorman, C.D., and Alpago, R.P., 1992, "Shortspan Bridge Design in the 1990s," Modern Steel Construction, 32(6), 32-36.

Nakatsuji, T., Sugita, M., and Fujimori, T., 1990, "FRP Grid Reinforcement for Concrete and Soil," Preprint No. 89-CP057, 69th TRB Annual Meeting, Jan 7-11, Washington, DC.

Nanni, A., Utsunomiya, T., Yonekura, H., and Tanigaki, M., 1992, "Transmission of Prestressing Force to Concrete by Bonded Fiber Reinforced Plastic Tendons," ACI Structural Journal, 89(3), 335-344.

Ontario Highway Bridge Design Code, 1983, Ontario.

Plecnik, J., Azar, W., and Kabbara, B., 1990, "Composite Applications in Highway Bridges," Serviceability and Durability of Construction Materials, ASCE, 986-995.

Pleimann, L.G., 1991, "Strength, Modulus of Elasticity, and Bond of Deformed FRP Rods," Advanced Composites Materials in Civil Engineering Structures, ASCE, pp. 99-110.

Saadatmanesh, H. and Ehsani, M.R., 1991, "Fiber Composite Bar for Reinforced Concrete Construction," Journal of Composite Materials, 25, 188-203.

Schmeckpeper, E.R., Zhang, M., and Goodspeed., C., and E. Munley, 1992, "Full-scale Testing of FRP Composite Grid Reinforced Concrete Bridge Deck Slabs," proceedings of the 1992 Materials Engineering Congress, ASCE, Atlanta, GA, August 10-12.

Sen, R., Iyer, S., Issa, M., and Shahawy, M., 1991, "Fiberglass Pretensioned Piles for the Marine Environment," Advanced Composites Materials in Civil Engineering Structures, ASCE, 348-359.

Virginia Department of Transportation, 1987, Road and Bridge Specifications, Richmond, VA.

Anchorages and Connections

Ancrages et assemblages

ADVANCED COMPOSITE MATERIALS IN BRIDGES AND STRUCTURES
K.W. Neale and P. Labossière, Editors; Canadian Society for Civil Engineering, 1992

Matériaux composites d'avant-garde pour ponts et charpentes
K.W. Neale et P. Labossière, éditeurs; Société canadienne de génie civil, 1992

DESIGN, TESTING AND MODELING OF AN ANCHORAGE SYSTEM FOR RESIN BONDED FIBREGLASS RODS USED AS PRESTRESSING TENDONS

T.M. Sippel
Universität Stuttgart
Stuttgart, Germany

ABSTRACT

This investigation concerns the behaviour of an anchorage system for resin bonded fibre-glass rods used as prestressing tendons. Taking as a starting point the action of a segmented clamping sleeve anchorage for single rods, an anchoring system has been developed for bundles of eight prestressing rods. The bearing behaviour of this system mechanism has been investigated under short-term, long-term and cyclic tension loading. The results of finite element analysis are used to describe the transfer of transverse clamping forces. Anchoring relationships previously developed for single rods are applied to bundles of rods.

RÉSUMÉ

Ce rapport présente le comportement d'un système d'ancrage pour des tiges en fibres de verre imprégnées de résine et utilisées comme tendons de précontrainte. En partant de l'examen d'un ancrage pour des tiges individuelles dans une gaine, un mécanisme d'ancrage a été développé pour des assemblages de huit tiges de précontrainte. Le comportement de ce mécanisme d'ancrage a été étudié sous des charges de tension à court terme, long terme, et cycliques. Une analyse par éléments finis est utilisée pour décrire le transfert des forces transversales d'agrippement. Les relations d'ancrage développées précédemment pour des tiges individuelles sont appliquées aux assemblages de tiges.

INTRODUCTION

The economy and reliability of a prestressing system with glass fiber tendons depends in large measure on the function and construction of the anchoring device, which should resist short-term, long-term and cyclic loadings in a safe, durable and loss-free manner. In the anchorage system investigated here (Fig. 1), the fiberglass rods are anchored in a resin-sand matrix, surrounded by a segmented copper sleeve, which is in turn surround by clamping blocks.

Anchors developed up to now did not permit the use of the ultimate strength of the fiberglass, especially under sustained or cyclic loading. The anchoring system developed at the IWB for single rod, based on the principle of both injection and clamping, facilitates a zero-loss transfer of forces (Faoro, 1988). Force transfer can be controlled by variation of the mean parameters of influence, such as transverse pressure, surface quality, and geometry of the clamping blocks.

This theoretical and experimental work investigates whether the principle of segmented clamping sleeves could be applied to anchorages for bundles of prestressing tendons.

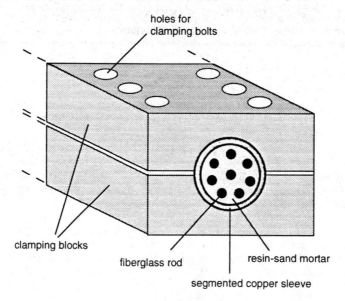

Fig. 1: Anchorage system

MATERIAL PROPERTIES

The composite material used in these tests has been manufactured industrially for almost 12 years. It consists of parallel-laid E-glass strands, pulled through unsaturated polyester resin and afterwards tempered thermally. Each rod has a nominal diameter of 7.5 mm and consists of 32 strands; each strand consists of approximately 2000 single fibers (Sippel, 1991).

The main material properties of single rods under short-term, sustained, and cyclic loadings are listed in Table 1. Under uniaxial tensile loading up to failure, the material shows an almost linear stress-strain behaviour. At a stress level of about 80% of the uniaxial tensile strength the behavior becomes slightly non-linear.

Table 1: Material properties of single rods (mean values, after Sippel, 1989)

uniaxial tensile strength f_t	1578 N/mm^2
ultimate strain at failure ε_u	33%
interlaminar shear stress τ_u	40 N/mm^2
transverse compressive strength f_{qc}	140 N/mm^2
transverse tensile strength f_{qt}	20 N/mm^2
modulus of elasticity E	52000 N/mm^2
endurance at $\sigma_{sust} = 0.8\ f_t$	5.1 hours
cycles to failure under pulsating tension (upper stress level $\sigma_o = 0.5\ f_t$)	
stress amplitude = 60 N/mm^2	1.75 x 10^6
stress amplitude = 80 N/mm^2	0.25 x 10^6

The function of an anchoring system working by injection and clamping is highly dependent on the bond stress-slip relationship of single rods. The bond stress-slip relationship is normally determined with pull-out tests using cylindrical specimens with short embedment lengths, about four diameters. Because the anchoring system works by transverse and friction force, the dependence of the bond stress-slip relationship on the transverse force must be investigated. Detailed analysis shows a linear increase of bond stress τ and slip s with increasing transverse force p (Faoro, 1988).

ANCHORING SYSTEM FOR BUNDLES OF GLASS FIBER RODS

General

The most important parameter used to describe the performance of an anchoring system is the so-called "mechanical degree of effectiveness", η_A, which is the ratio between the actual and the theoretical capacities of the prestressing rod ($\eta_A = P_u/cal\ P_u$). According to Sippel (1989), the following material properties of fiberglass rods complicate the designing zero-loss anchorages:

- comparatively low modulus of elasticity: this leads to large strain differences between the rod and the anchor

- high sensitivity to peak stresses: this requires a long embedment of the rods and an even distribution of the transverse force

- low shear load bearing capacity: this requires a longer embedment length

- low transverse compressive strength: transverse compression must be limited

- sensitivity to fretting fatigue: relative displacement at the rod surface must be avoided or limited

Promising solutions are anchoring systems based on injection or combinations of injection and clamping systems (Sippel, 1989). These systems are described briefly in the following sections.

Clamping sleeve anchor

Construction of the bundle of rods and the anchoring system

The bundle consists of 8 single rods, each with a nominal diameter of 7.5 mm. Seven rods are arranged in a circle around the central rod. The single rods are embedded in clamping sleeves of copper, filled with resin mortar consisting of unsaturated polyester resin mixed with 1 mm diameter sand particles. Each copper sleeve has a diameter of 42 mm, a wall thickness of 1.5 mm, and an internal thread to assure a stiff transfer of shear forces between the mortar and the sleeve.

This sleeve geometry gives a compact arrangement of the rods, and also enough mortar surrounding each rod to transfer the bond stresses and provide a more uniform distribution of the transverse stresses. The structure and the geometry of the clamping sleeve and the anchor are shown in Fig. 2.

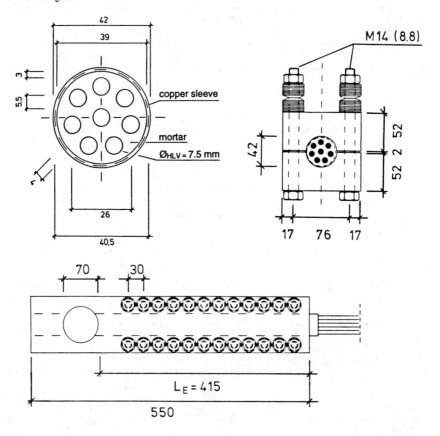

Fig. 2: Structure and geometry of the clamping sleeve and the anchoring system (Sippel, 1989)

366

<u>Function of the anchoring system</u>

Along the embedment length the force in the rod is transferred in the copper sleeve by bond between the glass fiber rod and the injection mortar. The copper sleeve transfers the load by friction or bond into the clamping plates. It is obvious from this that the force transfer can be controlled by the stiffness and bond relationship of the anchorage.

This principle of anchorage for resin bonded glass fibers was developed and investigated by Faoro (1988) for single rods. It was shown that the bond behaviour between single fiber rods and mortar could be controlled by applying transverse stresses, and that the bond behaviour between the clamping sleeve and the anchor plates could be controlled in a similar way. Furthermore, it was found that the surface of the clamping blocks, and therefore the friction or bond behaviour, could be changed by sandblasting or greasing.

The axial stiffness of the clamping sleeve can be decreased by segmenting (subdividing the sleeve into sections or segments). In this manner, the strain differences and the relative slip between the surface of the glass fiber rods and the mortar will be decreased. The principle of the segmented clamping sleeve is shown in Fig. 3.

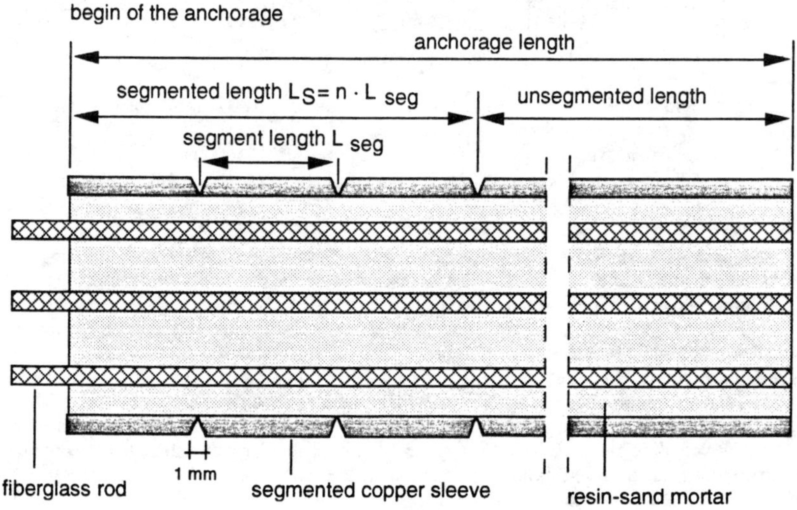

Fig 3: Principle of the segmented clamping sleeve

Element Behavior under Transverse Clamping Pressure

Due to the relatively low transverse compressive stiffness of the glass fiber rods, the transverse clamping pressure produces local variations in the transverse stress around the rods. To investigate this, a cross section of the clamping sleeve was modelled and analysed with a finite element program (ANSYS). The finite element mesh is shown in Fig. 4.

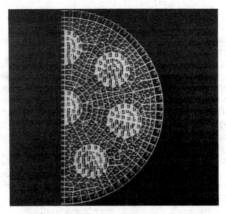

Fig. 4: Analytical model (Sippel, 1989)

The system was loaded with a uniform radial load q = 100 N/mm. In the analysis the following characteristic material moduli were assumed:

copper sleeve:	E_{Cu} =	110000 N/mm^2
injection mortar:	E_M =	5000 N/mm^2
fiber rod (transverse direction):	E_Q =	18000 N/mm^2

Because the complete analysis was made without axial forces, the axial shortening of the rods was not included in the analysis. Also, transverse stresses caused by Poisson effects and by radial splitting forces were not taken into account.

With the finite element analysis, the transfer of forces and the distribution of transverse principal stresses could be described. The principal transverse compressive stresses acting on the rods in both directions were between 66% and 70% of the nominal transverse compressive stress that would have been produced in a uniform cylinder under the same conditions. Essentially, the copper sleeve, which is stiffer, reduces the transverse stresses within the mortar. The mortar itself is relatively flexible, and does not appreciably affect the force transfer. This reduction in transverse stress on the rods implies a reduction in the frictional force that can be developed between the rods and the mortar.

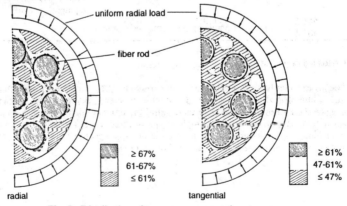

Fig. 5: Distribution of transverse compressive stresses

EXPERIMENTAL TESTS WITH BUNDLES OF EIGHT PRESTRESSING RODS

General

As described in more detail below, anchoring tests were carried out under short-term loading to determine the effectiveness factor, η_A, and also to evaluate the global load-slip behaviour of the anchors.

Long-term loading tests were carried out at about 80% of the ultimate capacity, implying severe demand on the anchorage. An anchorage that functions without any losses at this load level will generally show a loss-free behaviour at lower load levels.

Pulsating tension tests were carried out with stress amplitude of 60 and 80 N/mm² to a maximum working stress level of one-half the ultimate capacity. This stress amplitude is higher than the stress amplitudes which usually occur in structures prestressed with glass fiber rods. This stress amplitude also places high demands on the anchoring system.

Altogether, 12 tests were carried out: 6 short-term tests; 3 long-term tests; and 3 cyclic loading tests. In 4 of the short-term load tests, an embedment length of 350 mm was used. All other tests were carried out with an embedment length of 415 mm (Sippel, 1989). Each test series will now be described in more detail.

Short-Term Load Tests

The copper sleeves of the specimens used in these tests had 8 segments, each 20 mm long. In each test, the relative displacement between the copper sleeve and the clamping blocks was measured. The results are summarized in Table 2. The last column of that table refers only to failures of the anchorage system itself. In those tests for which no anchorage failure mode is indicated, failure occurred in the free length of the fiberglass rods themselves, and is obviously independent of the anchorage.

Table 2: Results of short-term load tests

Test	Observed Failure Load, kN	Calculated Failure Load, kN	Effectiveness Factor η_A	Failure Mode of Anchorage
1	517.0	534.6	0.97	
2	514.1	534.6	0.96	
3	547.1	557.6	0.98	
4	470.0	557.6	-	anchorage failure (bond failure between mortar and clamping sleeve)
5	551.6	557.6	0.99	
6	503.4 *	557.6	-	

*   not loaded as planned

The mean value of the effectiveness factor is about 0.98. Figure 6 shows a bundle at the moment of failure, and also after rupture. It can clearly be seen that all fibres failed in the free length between the anchors, and therefore the level of the ultimate load was not influenced by the anchoring system. This also shows the high degree of effectiveness indicated in Table 2. The values of anchorage slip measured during the tests at the upper anchor of the tendon are shown in Fig. 7. The measured values are quite consistent from test to test.

369

Fig. 6: Eight-rod bundle at the moment of failure and after rupture

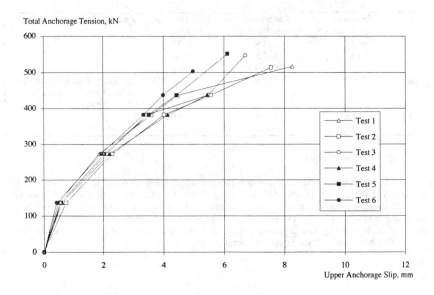

Fig. 7: Anchorage slip at different load steps

370

Long-Term Load Tests

The three long-term load tests were carried out using 80% of the calculated mean load at failure under short-term loading, reduced by the average observed effectiveness factor. This leads to a sustained load 437.2 kN, equivalent to a nominal stress in the rod of 1237 N/mm^2.

On an average basis the long-term load tests resulted in an endurance of 5.7 hours, 10% longer than that for single rods (Table 1). In all three tests, failure occurred in the free length between the anchors, implying no influence of the anchoring system. No increase in anchorage slip was detected over the loading time. The mean value of all slip (including initial slip) was about 6.5 mm.

Pulsating Tension Load Tests

Pulsating tension load tests ended prematively by fatigue failure of the rods. This failure was a result of the following sequence of events:

1) The clamping blocks had been machined with a rough edge where the two halves joined.

2) This rough edge cut into the segmented copper sleeve along a longitudinal line, preventing relative axial deformations among the segments.

3) Because the surrounding resin-sand matrix was now axially stiff compared with the fiberglass rods, deformation was concentrated in the matrix itself, and a fretting fatigue failure occurred in the rods within the matrix (Fig. 8).

Fig. 8: Fiber rod failure inside the anchorage under pulsating tension load

SUMMARY

Taking as a starting point the action of a segmented clamping sleeve anchorage for single rods, an anchoring system has been developed for bundles of eight prestressing rods. The bearing behaviour of this anchoring system has been investigated under short-term, long-term and pulsating tension loading.

The short-term load tests showed an almost zero-loss transfer of forces, with a degree of effectiveness η_A equal to 0.98 up to rod failure. On an average, the load tests to 80% of the rod failure load gave a 10% longer endurance compared to long-term single rods. The pulsating tension tests, however gave far fewer cycles to failure than for single rods. This premature failure can be attributed to production inaccuracies of the clamping blocks which caused a fretting fatigue failure in the rods. The results of finite element analysis made it possible to describe, qualitatively and quantitatively, the transfer of transverse forces due to clamping.

REFERENCES

Faoro, M. (1988): "Zum Tragverhalten kunstharzgebundener Glasfaserstäbe im Bereich von Endverankerungen und Rissen im Beton" ("Bearing Behaviour of Resin Bonded Glass Fiber Rods in Anchor Regions and in Cracked Concrete Regions" - in German). PhD Thesis, Institut für Werkstoffe im Bauwesen, Universität Stuttgart, IWB-Mitteilungen 1988/1, 189 pp.

Sippel, T.M. (1989): "Untersuchungen zum Tragverhalten von Verankerungen für Spannglieder aus kunstharzgebundenen Glasfaserstäben" ("Investigations on the Bearing Behaviour of Anchors for Prestressing Tendons of Resin Bonded Glass Fiber Rods" - in German). Diploma Thesis, Institut für Werkstoffe im Bauwesen, Universität Stuttgart, 84 pp.

Sippel, T.M. (1991): "Neue Werkstoffe: HLV-Elemente" ("New Materials: Heavy Duty Composite Bars" - in German and English). Institut für Werkstoffe im Bauwesen, Universität Stuttgart, IWB-Mitteilungen 1991/2, pp. 26-29.

Sippel, T.M. (1991): "Zum Materialverhalten von kunstharzgebundenen Glasfaserstäben" ("On the Material Behaviour of Resin Bonded Glass Fiber Rods" - in German) in Beiträge zum Forschungskolloqiuim "Faserverbundwerkstoffe im Betonbau und Lichtwellenleitersensorik für die Bauwerksüberwachung" (in Proceedings of Research Colloquium "Fiber Composite Materials in Concrete Structures and Monitoring Systems for the Control of Structures" - in German). Institut für Werkstoffe im Bauwesen, Universität Stuttgart, 3 pp.

ADVANCED COMPOSITE MATERIALS IN BRIDGES AND STRUCTURES
K.W. Neale and P. Labossière, Editors; Canadian Society for Civil Engineering, 1992

Matériaux composites d'avant-garde pour ponts et charpentes
K.W. Neale et P. Labossière, éditeurs; Société canadienne de génie civil, 1992

DESIGN OF BOLTED CONNECTIONS FOR ORTHOTROPIC FIBRE-REINFORCED COMPOSITE STRUCTURAL MEMBERS

C.N. Rosner and S.H. Rizkalla
University of Manitoba
Winnipeg, Manitoba, Canada

ABSTRACT

A comprehensive experimental and analytical investigation was conducted at the University of Manitoba to study and to determine the behaviour of bolted connections in composite materials used for civil engineering applications. Based on the research findings a design procedure is introduced which accounts for material orthotropy, pseudo-yielding capability, and other factors that influence bolted connection behaviour. The proposed model is capable of predicting the ultimate capacity and the mode of failure of the connections. Because of the generic nature of the model, the design guidelines can be applied to a multitude of composite material systems. Due to the model's simplicity, the proposed design procedure is ideal for implementation in design codes.

RÉSUMÉ

Un programme expérimental et analytique a été entrepris à l'Université du Manitoba pour déterminer le comportement de connexions boulonnées dans des matériaux composites utilisés en génie civil. En se basant sur les résultats de ces recherches, une méthode de design est présentée. Celle-ci tient compte de l'orthotropie du matériau, de la capacité en quasi-écoulement, et d'autres facteurs qui influencent le comportement de connexions boulonnées. Le modèle proposé est capable de prédire la capacité ultime et le mode de rupture des connexions. À cause de la nature générique du modèle, la méthode peut être appliquée à une multitude de systèmes en matériaux composites. À cause de la simplicité du modèle, la méthode proposée est idéale pour les codes de design.

INTRODUCTION

The high strength-to-weight ratio of fibre-reinforced composite materials makes them extremely attractive as a building material to the civil engineer. Although much research has been conducted on the behaviour of this material for the aeronautical and automotive industries, there has been very little research conducted for the civil engineering field, especially in the area of bolted connections. Bolted connections, which are the most practical connection for civil applications, not only sever the reinforcing fibres and thus reduce the overall strength of the composite, but also introduce high stress concentrations which promote fracture. This is complicated by the fact that the behaviour of fibre-reinforced composites lies somewhere between that of perfectly elastic behaviour and fully plastic behaviour and therefore cannot be characterized by either.

A comprehensive experimental and analytical investigation was conducted at the University of Manitoba to study and to determine the behaviour of bolted connections in composite materials for civil engineering applications. Based on the research findings, a design procedure was developed. The proposed methodology is capable of predicting the ultimate capacity and failure mode of single-bolt double-shear connections.

EXPERIMENTAL PROGRAM

A total of 102 single-bolt double-shear lap joints made of glass fibre reinforced composite material (GFRP) were tested. The various parameters considered in the investigation were the member width to hole diameter ratio (w/d), the edge distance to hole diameter ratio (e/d), the thickness of the members (t) and the direction of the fibres with respect to the applied load as given in Table 1.

The configuration of the single-bolt double-shear connection tested in this investigation is shown in Fig. 1 with the basic geometric parameters given in Fig. 2. The two plate double-shear configuration was selected, to subject the composite GFRP members to concentrically applied loading and to eliminate bending effects. The test set-up simplified strain and displacement measurements and allowed direct observation of the various modes of failure. A 19 mm (3/4 in) high strength bolt was used in all the tested connections. A hole diameter of 20.6 mm (13/16 in) provided a 1.6 mm (1/16 in) clearance for the bolt in all connections. The bolts were tightened by a torque wrench to a constant torque of 32.5 N-m (24 ft-lbs) for all connections.

The members tested were fabricated from EXTREN Flat Sheet/ Series 500, a pultruded glass fibre sheet produced by Morrison Molded Fiber Glass Company (MMFG). Three different thicknesses were used for this investigation, 9.525 mm (3/8 in), 12.7 mm (1/2 in) and 19.05 mm (3/4 in). The composite material is orthotropic, consisting of symmetrically stacked, alternating layers of identically oriented unidirectional E-glass roving and randomly-oriented E-glass continuous strand mat in a polyester matrix.

To determine the material properties, 80 tension tests, 75 compression tests, and 60 shear tests were tested according to ASTM standards D638, D695, and D3846 respectively. The tests were conducted for all three thicknesses and at various angles of the fibres with respect to the loading direction.

TEST RESULTS AND DISCUSSION

The measured material properties for the principal material directions are summarized in Table 2. The given coefficients of variation reflect the large material variability.

The various modes of failure observed in this investigation are illustrated in Fig. 3. These consisted of three basic modes including net-tension failure as shown in Fig. 3a, cleavage failure as shown in Fig. 3b, and bearing failure as shown in Fig. 3c. Two

374

combined modes of failure were also observed: bearing-net tension failure as shown in Fig. 3d and bearing-cleavage failure as shown in Fig. 3e. Net tension failure was characterized by typical fracture through the net section. Cleavage failure was characterized by a crack parallel to the applied load propagating from the end of the plate towards the bolt hole leading to the initiation of other cracks near the net section due to the formation of in plane bending stresses. Bearing failure was characterized by crushing of the material in the vicinity of the bolt-to-hole interface. The two combined modes were a combination of the various basic modes.

Typical load-displacement relationships for the three basic modes of failure are shown in Fig. 4. The displacement is the average of two LVDT readings, one on each side of the connection, and the load is the resistance of the two plates combined. The behaviour indicated that there was little friction resistance for the specified applied torque, since slipping of the connections occurred at the initial loading stage. Once the bolt slipped into bearing all the connections behaved linearly. Fig. 4 illustrates that for the connections that failed in a sudden manner such as in the case of net-tension or cleavage, there was a considerable drop in load carrying capacity as each plate in the connection failed. The sudden drop in the load occurred in fractions of a second as was confirmed by the load and displacement response recorded by a storage oscilloscope at a rate of 16,000 samples per second. For connections that failed in bearing, the load reduction occurred gradually as the bolt pulled through the composite plates and the overall behaviour was much more ductile than the other modes of failure.

The influence of fibre orientation on the modes of failure is shown in Fig. 5 for connections of the same dimensions. Due to the presence of the unidirectional fibres at 45 and 90 degrees to the applied load, the typical cleavage failure that had occurred in the connections with the fibres at 0 degrees to the applied load, was suppressed for the corresponding connections that had the fibres at 45 and 90 degrees to the applied load.

PROPOSED DESIGN PROCEDURE

The proposed design procedure is semi-empirical and semi-analytical, using a modified version of the theory presented by (Hart-Smith, 1978) which accounts for the elastic stress concentrations at a loaded bolt hole in brittle isotropic materials. The correlation factors for the three fibre directions used in this investigation were evaluated based on the experimental results. The correlation factors account for the composite's orthotropy, pseudo-yielding capability, and other factors which influence bolted connection behaviour. Since the basis of the theory is for elastic isotropic materials, the theory could be applied to many material systems using limited test data to determine the corresponding correlation factor for the specific composite material.

The proposed design procedure provides an overall failure envelope. The envelope includes criteria for net tension failure and bearing/cleavage failure. For a given geometrical configuration of a connection, the envelope is capable of predicting the ultimate strength and the mode of failure.

Net Tension Failure

The maximum stress adjacent to a bolt hole along a net section of a plate, σ_{max}, for a given applied load, P, perpendicular to the net section can be determined as follows:

$$\sigma_{max} = k_{te} \frac{P}{t(w-d)} \qquad (1)$$

where t, w, and d are the thickness, width, and hole diameter of the connection respectively, as shown in Fig. 2. The elastic tensile stress concentration factor k_{te} could be estimated using the expression proposed by Hart-Smith for an isotropic, perfectly elastic material as follows:

$$k_{te} = 2+(w/d-1)-1.5\frac{(w/d-1)}{(w/d+1)}\theta \qquad (2)$$

where, θ is a non-dimensional factor and is a function of the edge distance to width ratio (e/w) and is given by:

$$\theta = 1.5-\frac{0.5}{e/w} \qquad (3)$$

It should be noted that the θ expression is a modified version of the one presented by Hart-Smith to include practical values of the (e/w) range.

It should be reiterated that the stress concentration factor given in Eq.(2) is for isotropic elastic materials and not fibre-reinforced composites which exhibit different behaviour. To correlate the two materials, it has been reasonably shown that the stress concentrations in isotropic elastic materials k_{te}, and those in fibre composites k_{tc}, could be linearly related and could be expressed by the following equation (Hart-Smith, 1978):

$$(k_{tc}-1) = C(k_{te}-1) \qquad (4)$$

where:

$$k_{tc} = F_{tu}\frac{t(w-d)}{P_{ult}} \qquad (5)$$

The correlation factor C can be determined via a regression analysis of a limited number of experimental observations and thus can be easily determined for any given composite material system with a certain fibre direction. The correlation factor accounts for the composite's orthotropy, pseudo-yielding capability, clearance effects, and other factors which affect bolted connection behaviour. This linear relationship is valid only for the net tension mode of failure and therefore experimental results for connections that failed in net tension should be used only. In Eq.(5) F_{tu} is the ultimate tensile strength of the composite material in the loaded direction and P_{ult} is the ultimate load.

Through algebraic manipulation of Eq.(1), (2), and (4), the expression for the ultimate load of a single bolted composite material connection that fails in net tension is:

$$P_{ult} = \frac{t \cdot w \cdot F_{tu}}{C(k_{te}-1)+1}(1-d/w) \qquad (6)$$

Given the correlation factor "C" and the properties of a composite material, the design engineer can predict the ultimate "net tension failure" load of a single bolt connection, of any geometry, using Eq.(6). The above equation can be used to produce a family of failure envelopes and is shown in Fig. 6 in terms of the connection efficiency $(P_{ult}/(t \cdot w \cdot F_{tu}))$ and the ratio (d/w). Each envelope given in Fig. 6 is given for a constant (e/d) value. Included in Fig. 6 is the experimental data for the 0-degree-fibre-angle connections that failed in net tension with C=0.33. As can be seen, the failure envelopes predict the test results extremely well. Reported data (Rosner, et.al., 1992) indicated that connection strengths increased with increasing edge-distance up to a maximum value of (e/d)=5. Therefore, the failure envelope corresponding to (e/d)=5 is set as the outermost failure envelope.

Bearing/Cleavage Failure

As the (d/w) ratio becomes small, net tension failure is normally preceded by bearing failure for connections with large edge distances and by cleavage or shearout failure for connections with small edge distances. It was found in this investigation that cleavage failure is related to pure bearing failure by a simple quadratic expression in terms of the ratio (d/2e), (Rosner, 1992). This finding was used to introduce an expression for the ultimate load of a connection that fails in bearing or cleavage as follows:

$$P_{ult} = t \cdot w \cdot F_{tu} \frac{F_{br}}{F_{tu}} \frac{d_{bolt}}{d} \left(\frac{10}{9} - \frac{5}{9} \frac{d}{e} \right)^2 \frac{d}{w} \qquad (7)$$

where F_{br} is the ultimate bearing strength of the fibre composite material and d_{bolt} is the diameter of the bolt. Eq.(7) was used to produce a family of non-dimensional failure envelopes in terms of the ratio (d/w) and the structural efficiency ($P_{ult}/(t \cdot w \cdot F_{tu})$), as shown in Fig. 7. The various envelopes are given for a constant (e/d) ratio.

The average bearing strength of the material was determined to be 1.9 times the ultimate tensile strength for the material used in the experimental program. Using a value of $F_{br}=1.9 F_{tu}$, Eq.(7) was used to predict the behaviour of all the 0-degree-fibre-angle connections that failed in bearing or cleavage as given in Fig. 7. The experimental data including the cases of cleavage failure are in excellent agreement with the proposed model.

In this investigation it was found that connections with (e/d)≥5 failed predominantly in bearing. Therefore as a limiting case when (e/d) approaches 5, the squared term in Eq.(7) becomes unity and the expression reduces to one characterizing pure bearing failure. Therefore the expression for pure bearing, accounting for the difference in bolt and hole diameters, is simply the product of the ratio of the material's bearing strength to tensile strength and the ratio (d/w). Test results also indicated that for (e/d)<5 the mode of failure was predominantly cleavage.

The shearout mode of failure was not observed in this experimental investigation due to the presence of a high volume of random fibres in the material used. However, since shearout and cleavage can be considered types of bearing failures with inadequate edge distances, it is reasonable to assume that the behaviour for cleavage failure discussed here could be applicable to shearout failure which would occur in other composite materials.

Design Procedure

Using the failure envelopes of the two failure criteria described above, one family of design envelopes were developed as shown in Fig. 8. For a given geometrical configuration, material properties, and correlation coefficient, the proposed overall failure envelope can be used to determine the ultimate load and the mode of failure of a connection.

Using the proposed design procedure, the predicted and experimental ultimate loads for all the 0-degree-fibre-angle connections tested in this investigation are given in Fig. 9. The comparison indicates that most of the data fall close to the 1:1 correspondence line or are on the conservative side.

It should be noted that the correlation coefficient is not only dependent on the material system used but also on the angle of the principal material directions. Obviously connections that were tested with the principal fibre direction at 45 and 90 degrees to the applied load had lower ultimate loads than their "0 degree" counterparts. However, due to even lower values of F_{tu} in these directions their efficiencies were actually higher than their "0 degree" counterparts. This means that the failure envelopes for the "0 degree" case can be used to predict conservatively the loads of angled-fibre cases.

Practical Application

Given a connection with the dimensions w=130 mm, e=40 mm, t=12 mm, d=21 mm, d_{bolt}=19 mm and the material property F_{tu}=166 MPa, the structural efficiency can be determined from the envelopes in Fig. 8 for (d/w)=0.16 and (e/d)≈2 and is equal to 0.185.

Consequently the ultimate load P_{ult}=Efficiency·t·w·F_{tu} is equal to 47.9 kN. Since the failure is located within the straight line portion of the envelope, the failure is a bearing or cleavage failure. In this case the failure is cleavage, since (e/d)<5. If a similar connection is used except with w=40 mm and thus (d/w)=0.53, the efficiency is found to be 0.32 and hence the ultimate load is 25.5 kN with the governing mode of failure being net tension. These results can also be achieved mathematically using Eq.(6) and Eq.(7) with a correlation factor of C=0.33 and F_{br}=1.9 F_{tu}, as determined experimentally for this type of material.

CONCLUSIONS

The proposed design procedure predicts the ultimate load and failure mode of the tested connections with an adequate degree of accuracy. Because the procedure is based on isotropic theory and uses empirical data to correlate the failure criteria it could be used for a variety of different composite material systems.

The correlation coefficient which relates the isotropic theory to composite materials accounts for material orthotropy, pseudo-yielding capability, hole size and clearance effects. In some respects the coefficient can be thought of as a "catch all" factor accounting for all those effects which complicate the stress analysis of a loaded bolt-hole. It is therefore reasonable to expect that as the material systems and connection configurations used by civil engineers become more standardized, a data base of test results could be developed to allow the design engineer to "pick and choose" the appropriate "C" value from a design code without ever doing a single test.

Considering the versatility and simplicity of this design procedure it is ideal for implementation in future design codes.

REFERENCES

Hart-Smith, L.J. (1978). Mechanically-Fastened Joints for Advanced Composites - Phenomenological Considerations and Simple Analyses. Proceedings of the Fourth Conference on Fibrous Composites in Structural Design,San Diego, California, November 14-17 1978, New York, Plenum Press 1980, pp.543-574

Rosner, C.N., Rizkalla S.H., and Erki, M. (1992). Bolted Connections for Fibre-Reinforced Composite Structural Members. Proceedings of the 1992 Canadian Society of Civil Engineering Annual Conference. Quebec, May 27-29, 1992. Vol. 3, pp.305-314.

Rosner, C.N. (1992), Single-Bolted Connections for Orthotropic Fibre-Reinforced Composite Structural Members. MSc. Thesis, Department of Civil Engineering, University of Manitoba, Winnipeg, Manitoba, August, 1992.

Table 1   Experimental Parameters

Parameter:	Dimensions:
Thickness "t" (mm)	9.5 , 12.7 , 19.0
Width "w" (mm)	254 , 152.4 , 101.6 , 50.8 , 38.1 , 25.4
Edge Distance "e" (mm)	203.2 , 101.6 , 63.5 , 38.1 , 19.0
Fibre Angle (deg.)	0 , 45 , 90

Table 2   Material Properties

Thickness	Fibre Angle	Tensile Modulus	Elongation	Tensile Strength	Comp. Strength	Shear Strength
(mm)	(deg.)	(GPa)	(%)	(MPa)	(MPa)	(MPa)
9.525	0	15.2	1.6	198	213	32.3
	90	9.8	1.2	101	145	37.2
12.7	0	12.7	1.6	166	175	27.8
	90	10.5	1.4	110	145	24.0
19.05	0	13.1	1.6	166	157	27.6
	90	11.1	1.4	103	139	27.9
Coefficient of Variation for each Property:		5.3 to 16.4%	3.8 to 14.0%	5.3 to 16.4%	4.0 to 9.7%	7.4 to 26.1%

Shear Modulus = 4.3 GPa
Major Poisson's Ratio = 0.29

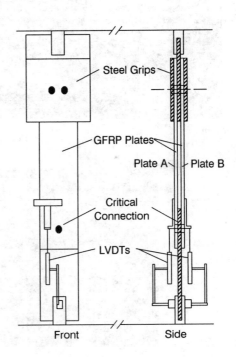

Figure 1   Test Set-up

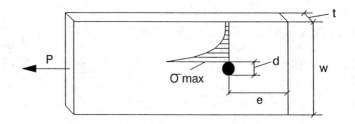

Figure 2 Connection Parameters

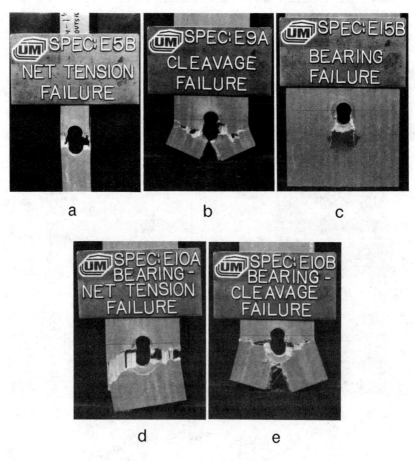

a   b   c

d   e

Figure 3 Failure Modes

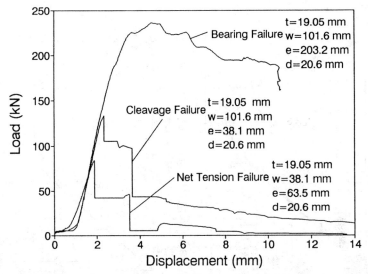

Figure 4 Typical Load-Displacement Curves

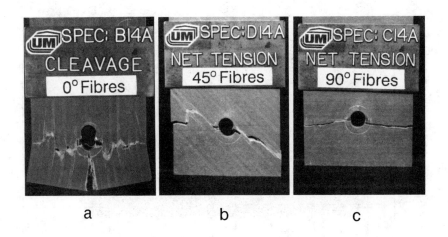

a   b   c

Figure 5 Effect of Fibre Orientation on Failure

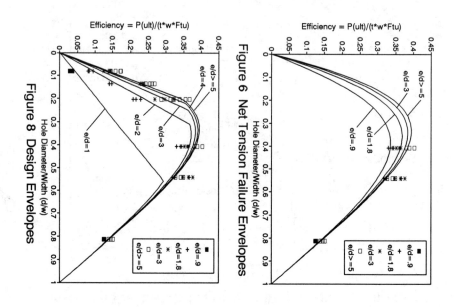

Figure 6 Net Tension Failure Envelopes

Figure 7 Bearing/Cleavage Envelopes

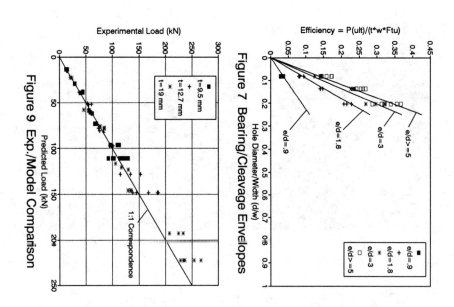

Figure 8 Design Envelopes

Figure 9 Exp./Model Comparison

ADVANCED COMPOSITE MATERIALS IN BRIDGES AND STRUCTURES
K.W. Neale and P. Labossière, Editors; Canadian Society for Civil Engineering, 1992

Matériaux composites d'avant-garde pour ponts et charpentes
K.W. Neale et P. Labossière, éditeurs; Société canadienne de génie civil, 1992

ÉTUDE D'UN ASSEMBLAGE EN BOIS LAMELLÉ-COLLÉ RENFORCÉ PAR FIBRE DE VERRE

C.A. Szücs
Universidade Federal de Santa Catarina
Florianópolis, Sta Catarina, Brazil

P. Jodin and **G. Pluvinage**
Université de Metz
Metz, France

RÉSUMÉ

Un assemblage de deux poutres en bois lamellé-collé a été effectué par l'intermédiaire d'une pièce fabriquée en bois lamellé-collé renforcée par de la fibre de verre. Cela, pour rendre possible la conception d'un élément d'assemblage où les pièces métalliques sont absentes. De cette façon, on privilégie la bonne tenue du bois au feu. L'encastrement des poutres à la pièce d'assemblage est assuré par des entures multiples usinées d'un côté et de l'autre de l'aboutage. Les essais qui ont été réalisés sur des prototypes à l'échelle peu réduite ont montré que cette pièce d'assemblage renforcée élimine le problème de rupture prématurée qui apparaît sur les pièces d'assemblages non renforcées.

ABSTRACT

Two glued laminated wood beams were joined by a composite of fibreglass reinforced glued laminated wood. A better fire resistance of the wood was obtained due to the absence of metallic joints. The beams were fixed to the connection by means of finger joints. The tests conducted with almost full-size specimens showed that the utilization of fibre-reinforced connections eliminated problems of premature failure which normally occur in unreinforced connections.

INTRODUCTION

En tenant compte de la bonne tenue du bois au feu on peut dire qu'il s'agit d'un matériaux très favorable du point de vue sécurité au moment d'un sauvetage et évacuation d'un bâtiment en incendie. Cela, parce qu'un matériaux ne doit pas être analysé seulement par sa réaction au feu mais aussi par sa résistance au feu.

Cela dit, on trouve par exemple chez les éléments métalliques, très souvent utilisés dans les assemblages des structures en bois, un comportement dont la réaction est non inflammable mais la résistance mécanique est très basse pour des températures élevées. Par contre, le matériaux bois qui présente une réaction inflammable peu être résistant longtemps durant un incendie (CTBA-114). Cela, parce que le feu qui brûle rapidement la partie périphérique de la pièce de bois produit une couche de charbon empêchant la propagation de celui-ci vers l'intérieur de la pièce à la même vitesse initiale. Pourtant, en tenant compte de la vitesse de propagation du feu (en moyenne 0,7mm/min pour le bois / CTBA-93)on peut même évaluer le temps de sécurité pour le service de sauvetage.

Compte tenue la bonne tenue du bois au feu ainsi que sa bonne résistance dans des milieux corrosifs, on présente dans ce travail l'étude d'une pièce d'assemblage composée en bois lamellé-collé. Cette pièce encastrée aux éléments qui composent une structure en bois par des entures multiples, fait qu'il n'y a pas d'éléments métalliques dans l'assemblage.

L'ENCASTREMENT PAR ENTURES MULTIPLES

On peut faire un encastrement direct entre deux pièces de bois en usinant des entures multiples d'un côté et de l'autre du plan d'aboutage. En employant une pression de serrage sur ces entures collées avec de la résorcine-phénol-formol on arrive à un assemblage de bonne résistance aux efforts élevés.

La géométrie des entures joue un rôle très important pour la résistance de l'assemblage. On trouve donc, dans la littérature (Götz and Möhler), des spécifications concernant la géométrie des entures et la pression de serrage comme par exemple dans la norme DIN 68 140 (Deutsche Normen). Les paramètres qui caractérisent ces entailles sont présentés par la figure 01.

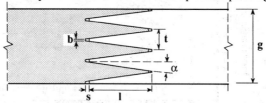

Fig. 01 - Assemblage par entures multiples.

où :

- l → longeur des entures.
- g → largeur totale de l'assemblage.
- t → pas des entures.
- b → épaisseur d'extrémité d'enture.

- s → jeu en fond d'enture.
- α → pente du plan collé.
- $e = \dfrac{s}{l}$ → jeu relatif de l'enture
- $v = \dfrac{b}{t}$ → degré d'affaiblissement.

La possibilité d'effectuer l'encastrement direct d'une pièce dans l'autre permet la conception d'un assemblage en angle (CTBA-93, Götz and Natterer) comme le montre la figure 02(a). D'autre part on peut concevoir d'une autre manière un assemblage par pièce de coin comme ceux de la figure 02(b)(c) où l'angle entre la direction des contrainte au plan d'aboutage et la direction des fibres du bois peut être divisé par deux ou même annulé. Cela veut dire que les composantes de contraintes perpendiculaires aux fibres du bois seront d'intensité plus petite en comparaison avec celles de la figure 02(a).

Le présent travail prend en compte la possibilité d'assemblage par pièce de coin comme ce de la figure 02(b).

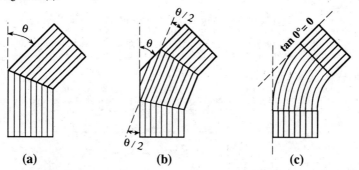

(a)   **(b)**   **(c)**

Fig. 02 - Assemblage d'angle de bois sur bois. a) aboutage directe d'une pièce sur l'autre. b) assemblage par pièce de coin. c) assemblage par pièce courbe.

Concernant la pression de serrage au niveau de l'encastrement par entures multiples collées une étude a été menée au CTBA-Centre Technique du Bois et Ameublement (CTBA-92) basé sur ce que préconise la norme DIN 68 140. La représentation graphique de cette étude est présentée par la figure 03 qui donne la pression de serrage en fonction de la longueur des entures.

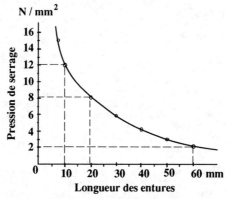

Fig. 03 - Graphique indiquant les pressions de serrage en fonction de la longueur des entures.

Pour la partie expérimentale du présent travail des entures multiples avec les caractéristiques géométriques indiquées ci-dessous ont été utilisées au niveau de l'aboutage entre les pièces de bois (Szücs, 1991).

$$\sigma' = \frac{\sigma_{tp+ent} \cdot 3,1}{2,1}$$

où : σ_{tp+ent} ⇒ contrainte en traction parallèle au plan des entures.

              σ' ⇒ contrainte de traction concentrée sur les flancs des dents.

CARACTÉRISTIQUES DES MATÉRIAUX

Le bois

L'essence choisie pour la fabrication des éprouvettes était l'une des plus utilisée dans la construction en bois lamellé-collé, c'est-à-dire, l'**épicéa**.

Ce bois de nom scientifique "*Picea abies*" est connu sous les noms de "Spruce" dans les pays anglo-saxons, "Épicéa" dans les pays francophones et "Fichte" dans les pays germaniques.

Une évaluation préliminaire sur le lot de bois disponible pour la partie expérimentale du travail a indiquée un bois à **12%** d'humidité et **0,44 g/cm³** de masse volumique.

Une série d'échantillons a été préparée pour la caractérisation mécanique du bois. Les résultats les plus importants sont présentés par une analyse statistique au tableau 01.

Essais		quan-tité	valeur moyenne	écart-type	valeur minimale	valeur maximale	coef. de variation (%)
taux d'humidité	(%)	18	11,74	0,46	11,06	12,65	3,96
masse volumique	(g/cm³)	18	0,436	0,04	0,37	0,51	9,26
FLEXION PURE							
module d'Young	(MPa)	35	13442	2063	8749	16463	15,35
limite élastique	(MPa)	35	61,37	9,17	39	73	14,93
contrainte de rupture	(MPa)	35	92,31	15,60	45	112	16,90
TRACTION PARALLÈLE							
contrainte de rupture	(MPa)	3	81,65	8,11	72,77	88,66	9,93
TRACTION TRANSVERSALE							
module d'Young	(MPa)	10	57,58	7,57	39	69	13,14
contrainte de rupture	(MPa)	10	2,12	0,39	1,20	2,78	18,56
CISAILLEMENT PARALLÈLE							
contrainte de rupture	(MPa)	4	3,03	0,25	2,71	3,29	8,34

Tableau 01 - Caractéristiques physico-mécaniques de l'épicéa.

Des échantillons ont été également préparés pour les essais de traction inclinée par rapport aux fibres du bois. Pour cela, cinq échantillons de chaque inclinaison indiqué sur le graphique de la figure 04 ont été rompus et on a constaté une très bonne corrélation entre les résultats expérimentaux et l'expression de Hankinson avec "n=1,5" (Bodig / Kollmann).

Afin de connaître le comportement du bois assemblé par des entures multiples, une série d'échantillons pour la traction sur ces entures ont été préparés avec les caractéristiques géométriques indiqués sur la figure 05.

De ces essais on a déduit que l'assemblage par enture multiple entraîne un affaiblissement d'environ 20% (65,40MPa) si on les compare aux résultats des essais des échantillons de traction parallèle sans l'assemblage par enture multiple (81,65MPa). Voir tableaux 02 et 01 respectivement.

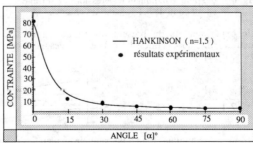

Fig. 04 - Corrélation entre les résultats expérimentaux et l'expression de Hankinson.

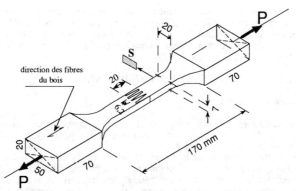

Fig. 05 - Échantillon utilisé pour les essais de traction sur l'assemblage par entures.

Essais	quan- tité	valeur moyenne (MPa)	écart- type (MPa)	valeur minimale (MPa)	valeur maximale (MPa)	coef. de variation (%)
TRACTION ⊥ RENFORCÉ contrainte de rupture	6	12,39	1,85	9,76	14,85	14,92
TRACTION / ENTURES contrainte de rupture.	3	65,40	9,24	55,71	74,11	14,12
composante de cisaillement sur les flancs des dents	3	10,03	1,41	8,55	11,37	14,12
composante de traction ⊥ aux flancs des dents	3	1,06	0,15	0,90	1,20	14,12

Tableau 02 - Caractéristiques mécaniques de l'assemblage par entures et du bois renforcé.

Le bois renforcé par fibre de verre

Dans le but de renforcer le matériau bois dans la direction transversale à ces fibres, on a étudié la possibilité de combiner des lamelles de bois et un tissu de fibre de verre de façon à obtenir un composite à fibres croisées.

Cela a été possible en employant un tissu de fibre de verre de fils orientés. Ce tissu, de la société Sotiver (Lyon-France) a été étudié auparavant au Laboratoire de Fiabilité Mécanique-Université de Metz (MOULIN). Il s'agit d'un tissu unidirectionnel identifié par UC 420-791. Les essais réalisés par MOULIN ont donné les résultats suivants:

• module d'Young → 40200 MPa	• contrainte de rupture → 920 MPa

Par la combinaison du tissu de fibre de verre de fils orientés et la technique du bois lamellé-collé, on a préparé des échantillons suivant la figure 06. Des essais ont donc été réalisés sur ces échantillons de traction transversale aux fibre du bois mais renforcé par fibre de verre.

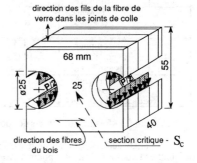

Fig. 06 -Échantillon de traction transversale aux fibres du bois renforcé par fibre de verre.

387

L'analyse des résultats obtenus à partir de six échantillons montre que pour ce rapport entre la masse de bois et de fibre de verre, la contrainte de rupture vaut 12,39MPa (voir tableau 02). Cela représente une contrainte de rupture 485% plus élevée que celle des échantillons soumis à la traction transversale du bois sans renfort, c'est-à-dire (2,12MPa - voir tableau 01).

ÉTUDE EXPÉRIMENTALE

Poutres sous assemblage droite

Initialement on a préparé six poutres droites en bois lamellé-collé qui ont été utilisées pour la composition des éprouvettes avec assemblage droite, pourtant, sans changement de direction entre les deux poutres assemblées.

Ces éprouvettes, montrés sur la figure 07 sont composées par des lamelles d'épicéa choisies parmi 261 qui ont été préparées au préalable. Un programme informatique a été conçu de façon à choisir les lamelles à module d'Young plus élevé et les placer en position plus éloignée de l'axe neutre de chacune des six poutres. De plus le programme choisit les lamelles de tel sorte que les modules d'Young des poutres se ressemblent. De cette façon on a une composition telle que l'ensemble des éprouvettes aient des caractéristiques bien homogènes.

Parmi les six éprouvettes ainsi composées on en a choisit trois pour rester comme poutres droites sans assemblage (témoins) tandis que les trois autres on été interrompues au milieu où on a prélevé un morceau de 10cm qui a été préparé comme pièce d'assemblage. Voir figure 07.

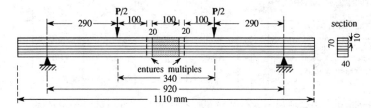

Fig. 07 - Géométrie et schéma d'essai des poutres droites sous assemblage aligné.

Les résultats de ces essais sont présentés au tableau 03 où on fait la comparaison entre le comportement des poutres assemblées et celui des poutres qui sont restées comme témoins, c'est-à-dire sans la pièce d'assemblage (Szücs,1991).

Poutre nº	Observation	Module d'Young (MPa)	Contrainte limite élastique (MPa)	Contrainte de rupture (MPa)
01	- témoins -	15346	52	82
03	sans pièce	15123	55	84
05	d'assemblage	14601	50	82
	moyenne...	15023	52,33	82,67
	écart-type...	382,37	2,52	1,15
	coefficient de variation...	2,55 %	4,8 %	1,4 %
02	- interrompues -	14579	57	61
04	avec pièce	14251	61	78
06	d'assemblage	14956	56	58
	moyenne...	14595	58,00	65,67
	écart-type...	352,78	2,65	10,79
	coefficient de variation...	2,42 %	4,56 %	16,43 %

Tableau 03 - Résultat des essais des poutres droites avec et sans la pièce d'assemblage.

En analysant ces résultats on remarque une parfaite cohérence entre le module d'élasticité des poutres témoins et ceux des poutres assemblées. Cela veut dire que l'assemble ne change pas le comportement élastique des poutres ni la limite d'élasticité car on remarque des valeurs très proches entre les deux séries d'éprouvettes. Par contre on constate que les poutres assemblées ont eu un niveau de résistance à la rupture 20% plus bas que celui des poutres sans assemblage. Cela représente un affaiblissement occasioné par l'aboutage à entures multiples. D'ailleurs le même niveau de réduction a été constaté lors des essais des échantillons de traction parallèle comportant un assemblage. Voir tableaux 01 et 02.

Poutres sous assemblage d'angle en bois lamellé-collé sans renfort

Pour la vérification du comportement de l'assemblage non aligné on a préparé six éprouvettes en bois lamellé-collé montré par la figure 08.

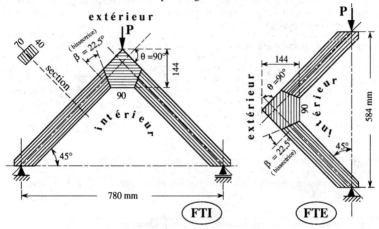

Fig. 08 - Géométrie et schéma statique des éprouvettes "FTI" et "FTE" pour les assemblages par **pièce de coin en bois lamellé-collé ordinaire**.

Ces éprouvettes de poutres droites assemblées par l'intermédiaire d'une pièce de coin présentent un changement de direction de 90°. Ils ont été groupés en deux séries de trois éprouvettes dont l'une pour l'application d'une charge au sommet ce qui donne la sollicitation FTI-Fibres Tendues à l'**Intérieur** et l'autre pour l'application d'une charge à l'extrémité ce qui donne la sollicitation FTE-Fibres Tendues à l'**Extérieur** (Szücs,1991). Une analyse de ce qui se passe au niveau du plan d'aboutage par entures multiples est montrée sur la figure 09.

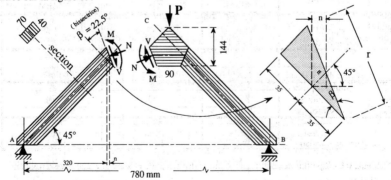

Fig. 09 - Schéma statique pour la détermination des efforts au niveau de l'assemblage.

L'analyse du comportement de l'assemblage par pièce de coin a été réalisée au niveau du plan d'aboutage par enture multiple où on a une zone d'affaiblissement occasionné par l'usinage des entures. Cette analyse considère en plus un plan d'aboutage réalisé selon l'angle bissectrice. Cet angle donne une inclinaison identique soit entre la direction des efforts et la direction des fibres du bois de la pièce de coin, soit entre la direction des efforts et la direction des fibres du bois de la poutre droite.

La moyenne des résultat des essais qui ont été vérifié au moment de la rupture des éprouvettes FTI est présentée sur la figure 10.

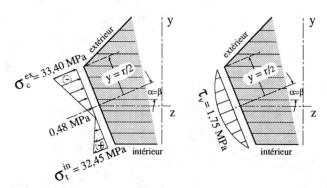

Fig. 10 - Les contraintes de rupture au niveau du plan d'aboutage des éprouvette FTI.

De manière analogue les essais et analyses des éprouvettes FTE ont été réalisés dont les résultats sont présentés au tableau 04 (Szücs,1991).

Essai	Contrainte normale sur le bord extérieur (MPa)	Contrainte normale sur le bord intérieur (MPa)	Contrainte de cisaillement (MPa)	Notes
FTI	- 33,40	+ 32,45	1,75	rupture de la pièce de coin
FTE	+ 36,58	- 40,45	1,20	rupture de la pièce de coin

Tableau 04 - Résumé des contraintes de rupture **au niveau du plan d'aboutage** des éprouvettes FTI et FTE.

On a remarqué que les essais des six éprouvettes FTI et FTE ont présenté une rupture au niveau de la pièce de coin sans aucun cas de rupture au niveau du plan d'aboutage. Or, si on fait une analyse de l'intensité des contraintes suivant les directions orthotropes du bois de la pièce de coin, on peut comprendre pourquoi le matériau bois est rompu avant de céder au niveau du plan des entures. Voir le résumé de l'analyse faite par le cercle de Mohr au tableau 05.

Essai	Traction parallèle (MPa)	Traction transversale (MPa)	Cisaillement parallèle (MPa)
FTI	27,70	4,75	11,50
FTE	31,22	5,36	12,93
limite de résistance	81,65 (tableau 01)	2,12 (tableau 01)	3,03 (tableau 01)
Notes	FTI-avant lim. rupture FTE-avant lim. rupture	FTI-au-delà lim. rupture FTE-au-delà lim. rupture	FTI-au delà lim. rupture FTE-au delà lim. rupture

Tableau 05 - Résumé des contraintes sur les directions orthotropes du bois de la pièce de coin des éprouvettes FTI et FTE.

On voit donc que les composantes de contraintes de traction transversale et de cisaillement parallèle aux fibres du bois atteint des valeurs supérieures à la limite de rupture du matériau.

Dans le but de neutraliser cette rupture prématurée on a mis au point une pièce de coin en bois lamellé-collé renforcé par fibre de verre.

Poutres sous assemblage d'angle en bois lamellé-collé renforcé par fibre de verre

En employant la technique du bois lamellé-collé on a étudié la possibilité d'assembler le matériau bois avec la fibre de verre de fils orientés. On a donc un composite à fils croisés représenté par la figure 11. De cette manière le produit final, résistant parallèlement aux fibres du bois devient également résistant dans la direction transversale à ces fibres (Szücs,1991).

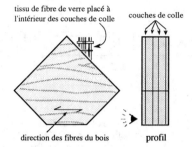

Fig. 11 - Schéma de la composition de la pièce de coin renforcée.

Une nouvelle série d'éprouvettes FTI et FTE a été préparée mais cette fois-ci avec un assemblage par pièce de coin en bois lamellé-collé renforcé par fibre de verre.

Le schéma d'essai de ces éprouvettes suit exactement ce qui a été fait pour la série présentée précédemment. Voir représentation de la figure 12.

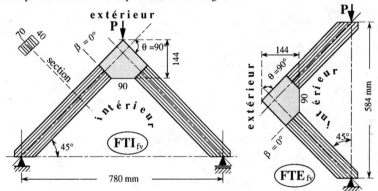

Fig. 12 - Schéma statique des éprouvettes "FTI$_{fv}$" et "FTE$_{fv}$" pour les assemblages par **pièces de coin en bois lamellé-collé renforcé" par fibres de verre.**

Dans le tableau 06 sont présentés les moyennes des résultats des contraintes au niveau du plan de l'aboutage par entures multiples (Szücs,1991).

Essai	Contrainte normale sur le bord extérieur (MPa)	Contrainte normale sur le bord intérieur (MPa)	Contrainte de cisaillement (MPa)	Notes
FTI$_{fv}$	- 45,98	+ 43,67	1,73	rupture au niveau des entures multiples
FTE$_{fv}$	+ 39,93	- 43,00	2.31	rupture au niveau des entures multiples

Tableau 06 - Résumé des contraintes de rupture **au niveau du plan d'aboutage.**

391

En comparant les contraintes de rupture des éprouvettes renforcées avec les précédentes (tableau 04) on remarque un gain de **35%** pour FTI_{fv} et **9%** pour FTE_{fv} (Szücs,1991). Concernant les contraintes orthotropes le résultat est présenté au tableau 07.

Essai	Traction parallèle (MPa)	Traction transversale (MPa)	Cisaillement parallèle (MPa)
FTI_{fv}	21,84	21,84	21,84
FTE_{fv}	19,97	19,97	19,97
limite de résistance	81,65 (tableau 01)	12,39 (tableau 02)	inconnu
Notes	FTI-avant lim. rupture FTE-avant lim. rupture	FTI-au-delà lim. rupture FTE-au-delà lim. rupture	- x -

Tableau 07 - Résumé des contraintes sur les directions orthotropes du bois de la pièce de coin des éprouvettes FTI_{fv} e FTE_{fv}.

CONSIDÉRATIONS FINALES

On a démontré que l'assemblage entre deux poutres en bois sans l'utilisation des éléments métalliques peut être réalisé en employant une pièce de coin également en bois.

Néanmoins, dans les assemblages par pièce de coin sans renfort on constate l'apparition des micro-fissures prématurement bien avant la rupture finale du matériau. Cela compromet donc la sécurité d'une structure ainsi constituée.

De toute façon, même si on tient en compte la rupture finale, on a toujours le problème de rupture dû à la faible résistance du bois aux efforts transversaux par rapport à ses fibres. Cela, sans l'apparition de ruptures au niveau des entures multiples où on a théoriquement un plan d'affaiblissement.

Par contre, on a constaté qu'on peut bien contourner le problème de rupture prématurée du bois en employant le composite de bois lamellé-collé renforcé par de la fibre de verre. Cette solution qui présente quand même une rupture fragile donne par ailleurs des valeurs de rupture bien supérieures à celles de l'assemblage non renforcé. Cela, sans offrir des altérations du côté du module d'Young et de la limite élastique.

La solution de renforcer le bois dans le sens transversal à ses fibres nous fait penser en plus à des très nombreux cas de structures en bois qui pourront bénéficier de renforts localisés. On peut citer comme exemples, les zones d'assemblage par boulons, clous...; les assemblages entre les barres d'un treillis; les rotules d'une poutre Gerber et bien d'autres exemples.

RÉFÉRENCES BIBLIOGRAPHIQUES

Bodig J. and Jayne B.A. (1982). Mechanics of Wood and Wood Composites. New York (USA). Van Nostrand Reinhold Company. 310-311

Cahier du centre technique du bois - cahier nº 114. (1979). Le comportement du bois au feu. CTBA. Paris (França). 7-8.

Cahier du centre technique du bois - cahier nº 92. (1973). Étude technico-économique de l'aboutage. CTBA. Paris (França). 48 p.

Cahier du centre technique du bois - cahier nº 93. (1979). Les structures en bois lamellé-collé. CTBA. Paris (França). 6-8 et 27.

Deutsch Normen - DIN 68 140. (1971). Wood Finger-Jointing. DIN, Berlin. Allemagne. 3 p.

Götz, Karl-Heinz and Hoor, D. and Möhler, K. and Natterer, J. (1987). Construire en bois / Choisir, concevoir et réaliser. Lausanne (Suisse). Presses Polytechnique Romandes. 71 et 133.

Kollmann, F.F.P. and Côté, W.A.Jr. (1984). Principles of Wood Science and Technology / Solid Wood. New York (USA). Springer - Verlag. v.1 / 326-328.

Moulin, J.M. and Jodin Ph. and Pluvinage G. (1990). Comportement d'un nouveau composite: Le LCR (Lamellé-Collé Renforcé). Textil Composites in Building Construction. Pluralis Éd.

Szücs, C.A. (1991). Étude d'un assemblage par pièce de coin en bois lamellé-collé renforcé par fibres de verre. Metz (France). LFM (thèse de doctorat). 200 p.

ADVANCED COMPOSITE MATERIALS IN BRIDGES AND STRUCTURES
K.W. Neale and P. Labossière, Editors; Canadian Society for Civil Engineering, 1992

Matériaux composites d'avant-garde pour ponts et charpentes
K.W. Neale et P. Labossière, éditeurs; Société canadienne de génie civil, 1992

THE DEVELOPMENT AND APPLICATION OF A GROUND
ANCHOR USING NEW MATERIALS

S. Mochida
Kajima Corporation
Tokyo, Japan

T. Tanaka and **K. Yagi**
Mitsubishi Kasei Corporation
Yokohama, Japan

ABSTRACT

This paper presents the development and application of ground anchors using CFRP rods, instead of prestressed steel. CFRP does not corrode, is lighter than steel and has the same tensile failure strength as a steel strand. Thus it is well-suited for use as permanent ground anchors. After studying various anchoring methods, a procedure of injecting mortar into a steel sleeve containing a CFRP rod was adopted. The new materials have been utilized in a new stress-ribbon bridge construction. Sixteen anchors were installed in each abutment. The tensioning force was 400 kN after initial prestressing. The long-term behaviour of the anchors has been monitored to assure safety.

RÉSUMÉ

Cet article présente le développement et l'application d'ancrages de fondation en utilisant des barres renforcées de carbone (CFRP) plutôt que de l'acier précontraint. Le CFRP ne rouille pas, est plus léger que l'acier et a la même résistance en tension qu'un fil d'acier. Ainsi, il est adéquat pour utilisation comme ancrage permanent. Après avoir étudié plusieurs méthodes d'ancrage, une technique d'injection de mortier dans un manchon en acier, contenant la barre en CFRP, a été adoptée. La technique a été utilisée lors de la construction d'un nouveau pont-ruban. Seize ancrages ont été installés dans chaque appui. La force de tension était de 400 kN après la précontrainte initiale. Le comportement à long terme des ancrages a été surveillé pour en assurer la sécurité.

INTRODUCTION

Carbon Fiber Reinforced Plastics (hereafter referred to as CFRP) are a new material comprising a plastic matrix such as thermosetting resin or thermoplastic resin reinforced with carbon fibres. The specific gravity of CFRP is about one fifth that of steel, but its tensile strength is almost equivalent to that of strand. Moreover, its excellent durability in any environments has enabled it to be widely used as a construction material, for example, as a substitute for re-bars or prestressing strands (hereafter referred to as PC strands).

The authors carefully studied the properties of CFRP in particular its durability, and started research and development (R & D) to determine its applicability to tensile rod ground anchoring systems, as shown in Fig. 1. This paper describes the R & D and practical utilization of CFRP rods for ground anchors.

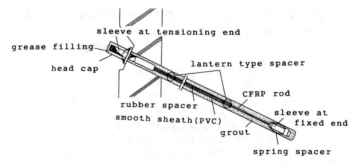

Fig.1 Ground Anchor Using CFRP Rods

PRINCIPAL CHARACTERISTICS OF CFRP RODS

The CFRP rods studied are of a composite material with a comparatively high Young's Modulus. The fibers are made of coaltar pitch and the matrix is a thermosetting epoxy resin. The rods are about 8 mm in diameter. The tensile strength of the fiber itself is 2940 MPa and the fiber volume fraction of the composite material is about 65%. All of the continuous fibers are arranged parallel to the longitudinal direction and a uniform tensile force is applied to each fiber. They are then impregnated with thermosetting epoxy resin to form a rod. Thus, the rod is circular and its surface is quite smooth. Table 1 shows the rod property. The tensile strength of the rod is the same as that of a PC strand, but it has no yielding point and the rupture elongation percentage is 1.3%. Since fibers are arranged longitudinally, the rod has a smaller compressive strength in the transverse direction: about 1/6 to 1/7 that in the longitudinal direction.

When this material is used for tensile ground anchors, it has the following advantages:
a) Because the rods are small and light, they are easy to handle, thus making work easier and safer even under bad environmental conditions, and also saving energy.
b) As the tensile elastic rigidity of the CFRP rod can be decreased below that of normal PC strand, it is less sensitive to load variations than a PC strand, thus reducing tension loss after prestressing and anchoring.
c) The CFRP rod is not corroded or weathered by alkali, acid, salt or bacteria in the soil, and is thus maintenance free.
d) As the rod surface is smooth, friction loss is smaller.

Table 1   CFRP Rod Specification

Item	Specification
Nominal diameter	8.0 mm
Fiber volume fraction	65 %
Tensile strength	1.8 GPa
Young's modulus	147 GPa
Specific gravity	1.6

R & D OF ANCHORING SYSTEM AT ROD END

General Concept of Anchoring System

The problems to be solved in utilizing CFRP rods as tensile members is how to apply the tensile force at the rod ends and how to fasten the rod end to the structural elements. The most common system now used for PC strands is the wedge-anchoring system, or a similar method based on this principle. The problem with this system is that it reduces the rod's load carrying capacity: the full (100%) tensile capacity of the rod can not be reached or transmitted at the rod ends. With this system, the tensile force produces lateral or transverse compression at the rod ends, which generates rupture. The ideal anchoring system is one which produces little lateral compression at the rod ends and which can produce a higher friction force to anchor the rod. Therefore, most wedge-anchoring systems are designed with a small taper angle in order to minimize the transverse compression.

To meet the above requirements, a new anchoring system has been developed. As shown in Fig. 2, this new system consists of a steel sleeve with mortar fillers on its inside to fix the rod ends such that no large lateral compression is imparted to the rod. The anchorage zone of the rod is deformed and embedded in the sleeve with non-shrink cement mortar so as to increase the fixing friction between the rods and mortar against the pull-out force of the rods. Thus, the sleeve prevents swelling and splitting of the filled mortar and also works as a device for fastening the rod to the structures.

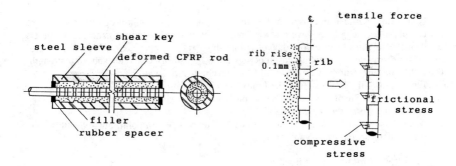

Fig.2   New Anchoring System
        for CFRP Rod

Fig.3   Stress Transmission
        Mechanism of Anchorage

Factors Affecting Anchorage System

The following parameters affect the anchoring capacity of the CFRP rods.
a) Strength of the material injected into the sleeve
b) Confinement provided by the sleeve
c) Rod anchorage length
d) Type of deformed rod (rise, width and pitch of deformed ribs)
e) Sand content of the fillers
f) Coefficient of expansion of the fillers

Of these parameters, item b) has been reported by other researchers (Forsyth and Tebbett, 1988). These studies have shown that the thickness of the sleeve is not a major factor and even a thin sleeve can provide enough confinement of the fillers. In this study, a stocky sleeve was adopted which was thick enough to transmit the tensile force in the rods. Thus, item b) was omitted from the following basic tests of anchorage system.

In modelling the stress transmission mechanism of anchorage system, compression forces are distributed to each rib as shown in Fig. 3. It is thought that the rod anchoring capacity is carried out by the compressive frictional resistance. This compression causes the rod and ribs to shrink in the transverse direction, because the elasticity of the rod and rib is relatively small. Thus, the tensile force applied to the rod may squeeze the ribs into the wide filler zone (neck of rod) between the sleeve and rod portion where there are no ribs. However, this is less likely to occur if the rib rise is large, but in this case failure may be governed by the longitudinal shear of the ribs or the injected mortar. Thus, the deformed configuration of the ribs is an important parameter affecting both rib shear and filler shear. Rod tensile force is balanced by the frictional resistance of the injected filler, so the sand content becomes important in maximizing the frictional coefficient of the mortar filling.

The preliminary tests on the type of deformed rod have clarified the following three points:
a) Parallel rib deformation type is found to be the best shape to resist the pulling-out force.
b) Even a small rib rise, as shown in Fig. 3, can prevent pulling-out failure.
c) The mortar filling should have a non-shrink character to afford good bond.

Based on the results of these preliminary tests, the following anchorage tests were carried out.

Rod-Filler Bond Experiments

Required Characteristics of the Filler

Non-shrink mortar was chosen for the filler material. Various mix proportions were tried and compressive strength tests were carried out to determine their performance. Parameters tested included flow value for rheology, bleeding ratio, coefficient of expansion and compressive strength. The required properties are a non-shrink character and high strength. Thus, the mix proportions were designed to achieve non-shrinkage.

Fig. 4 shows the test results. The following were clarified.
a) The investigation of flow value based on workability, showed that the higher the sand content the worse the injectability.
b) The mortar strength increases with sand content up to a certain point, but above this point the strength decreases.

The Best Rod Deformation for Bond

To determine the best rod deformation type, various kinds were tested by pull-out tests. Five types (A, B, C, D, E) were tested, as shown in Fig. 5, with various widths and pitches of ribs. The rib rise was kept constant, as determined from the preliminary tests. Rod anchorage lengths of 100 and 150 mm were tested. The rod anchorage zone was covered with a sleeve and the inside of the sleeve was filled and anchored with injected non-shrink mortar. The sleeve was 30 mm in diameter, 5.5 mm thick and its tensile capacity was 147 kN.

Fig. 6 shows the results of the tensile tests for a rod anchorage length of 150 mm rod deformation types. Types A, B and C maintained their capacity up to rod rupture, but type D caused slip rupture and was pulled out below the rod's tensile capacity. With type E, rod's tensile capacity was decreased. Thus, only types A, B and C were chosen for further pull-out tests, with the rod anchorage length changed to 100 mm to confirm the bond strength. Test results showed that type A was the best deformation to shorten the rod anchorage length.

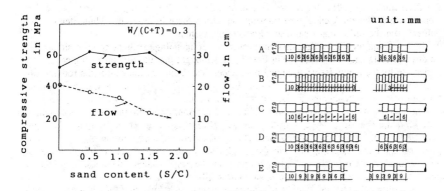

Fig.4　Relation between Sand Content and Filler's Properties

Fig.5　Deformation Types of CFRP Rods

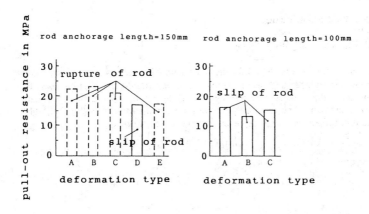

Fig.6　Results of Tensile Tests for Rod Deformation Types

Proportioning of the Filler Constituents

The above pull-out tests were conducted to determine the effects of the proportions of filler constituents in the sleeve. Type A rods were used and pull-out tests were carried out for a rod anchorage length of 100 mm. The mix parameters of sand content and water/cement ratio are compared and discussed from the view point of average bond strength.

Fig. 7 shows the test results. Fig. 7 (a) shows the relation between sand content (S/C) and pull-out resistance for a water/cement ratio of 0.3. There is a scatter of pull-out resistances at S/C=0 and the resistance decreases at S/C=2.0, clearly showing the decreasing injectability. Therefore, a suitable sand content is thought to be 0.5 ~ 1.5. Fig. 7 (b) shows the relation between water/cement (including inflating agent: T) ratio [=W/(C+T)] and pull-out resistance at a sand content of 1.0. It can be seen that the smaller the water/cement ratio, the higher the pull-out resistance. It may be said that the pull-out resistance increases linearly with compressive strength, because the compressive strength largely depends on the water/cement ratio. Therefore, the proportioning in Table 2 is adopted taking into account the better workability of the fillers and the better bond effects.

Table 2 Specification of Fillers

W/(C+T)	T/C	S/C	W:water,C:cement
(%)	(%)	(%)	T:inflating agent
30	12	100	S:sand

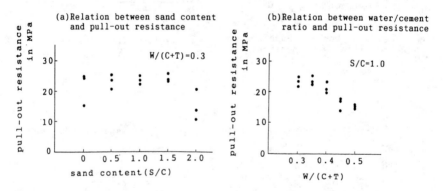

Fig.7 Results of Tensile Tests for Filler Constituents

Development of Anchorage for Multi-Tendons

Based on the optimum conditions described in the previous sections, the authors tried to develop a multi-tendon system using several rods together, of deformation type A. So far four kinds of multi-tendons have been developed and studied. These multi-tendons comprise 3 ϕ8 mm dia rods, 5 ϕ8 mm dia rods, 7 ϕ8 dia rods and 9 ϕ8 mm dia rods. Photo 1 shows the nine-rod-type grip, which is affirmed by pull-out test to fail in rod rupture without slip or pulling-out of the CFRP rods from the grip. Further, the view of the failed nine rods is shown in Photo 2, which shows simultaneous and instantaneous broom type rupture. To check the rod

398

arrangement effects, two arrangements, bundled bars and distributed bars, were carried out for three and five rods as shown in Fig. 8.

It may be concluded from the "one deformed rod" pull-out test that the average tensile capacity is 88 kN and the theoretically calculated value from the non-deformed sectional area of a rod is 94 kN. Therefore, the anchoring system can transmit 94 percents of the rod tensile capacity. This is called "effective gripping ratio".

The relationship between the rod anchorage length obtained from the multi-tendon pull-out test and the maximum tensile load of the rod-arrangement test is shown in Fig. 8. Here, the so called "effective gripping ratio of 100%" is based on the reduced cross section. The tests for seven- and nine-rod groups were conducted with a distributed rod arrangement, because it became clear from the arrangement test of three and five rods that the necessary rod anchorage length could be shortened in the distributed arrangement type compared with that of the bundle type. Table 3 shows the rod tensile capacity, necessary rod anchorage length for gripping ability higher than rod tensile capacity obtained from the multi-tendon test results. It must be noted that Table 3 shows the results for distributed rod arrangements.

Photo 1   Nine-rod-type Grip   Photo 2   View of Failed Nine-Rods

Table 3   Anchorage Capacity of Multi-Tendon Grips

Rod component	Anchorage length (mm)	Tensile capacity (kN)
3- 8mm dia	300	245
5- 8mm dia	500	412
7- 8mm dia	600	598
9- 8mm dia	600	745

Discussion of Rod End Anchoring Mechanism

To clarify the rod end anchoring mechanism, pull-out displacement of rods from the grip was measured in three specimens of nine-rod type. The test was done by applying multi-cyclic tensile loads. Fig. 9 shows the residual displacement at each loading cycle step on condition that the initial load was 50 kN and the cyclic load increment was 50 kN. This residual

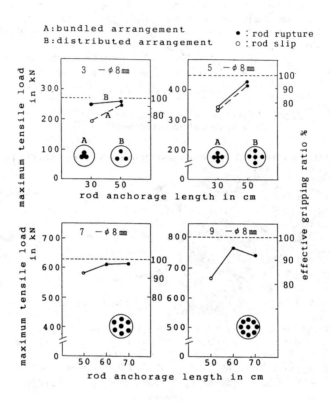

Fig.8 Test Results of Multi-Tendon Grips

displacement is rod pull-out slip after the peak load of each cycle. It can be seen that residual displacements occur after each cyclic peak load step and the displacement increases linearly with load. In other words, the gripping ability of this kind of end anchoring mechanism is given by the relative displacement between rod and filler.

The authors have suggested the model of the stress transmission mechanism of anchorage system shown already in the section entitled "Factors Affecting Anchorage System". To affirm this suggestion, the residual displacement of the rod was measured. The rib width was 3 mm, and the measured residual displacement was more than 3 mm beyond 450 ~ 500 kN, as shown in Fig. 9. Thus, the rib at the front part of the grip might have crossed over the wide portion of the filler by the pulling force of 450 ~ 500 kN, and this phenomenon might successively spread the rear part of the grip until rod rupture occurred. This proves that the cross-over occurred in the grip as the authors predicted.

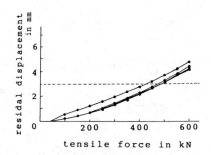

Fig.9 Relation between Tensile Force
and Residual Displacement

APPLIED EXAMPLE OF GROUND ANCHOR USING NEW MATERIAL

Generalities

A stress-ribbon bridge has been constructed as a pedestrian bridge for a golf course in Japan, using various new materials. A ground anchor system has been adopted to control the large horizontal forces occurring at the abutments. A tuff layer two meters beneath the ground surface was used as the fixing layer.

Bridge Specification

Fig. 10 shows a sectional view of the bridge. Main specifications are as follows:

bridge type	: pedestrian bridge		
structural type	: stress-ribbon bridge		
bridge length	: 54.5 m	span length	: 46.5 m
width of footway	: 1.7 mm	construction period	:1990.5 ~ 9
numbers of anchors	: 32	sleeve length	: 600 mm
rod rib deformation	: type A	proportioning	: Table 2

Sixteen ground anchors were used at each abutment. 9 ϕ8 mm-diameter tendons were adopted and their anchorage length was 15 ~ 20 meters. The tension force just after prestressing was 392 kN. Tension loss caused by rock creep and by other factors was estimated to be 20% and so the effective tensioning load was 314 kN. The CFRP rod length used was 5400 meters in total.

Long Term Measurement for Maintenance

The working load is assessed to maintain the stability of the abutment after prestressing and gripping the ground anchor. Fig. 11 shows the measurement locations. The measurements were conducted with wire-strain-gage type center-hole load cells at five points in each abutment. Fig. 12 shows the working load change with time after anchoring.

Tension loss just after anchoring the sleeve grip with nuts was less than 10 kN excluding temperature change effect. The deviation after creep loss and at a stable stage was less than 10 kN. One and a half years after completion of the ground anchors, the working load remains stable, although a slight change is observed, caused by changes in atmospheric temperature.

401

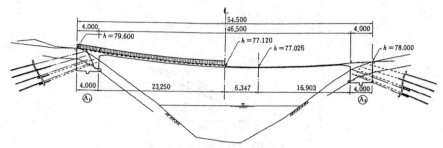

Fig.10   Sectional View of Bridge

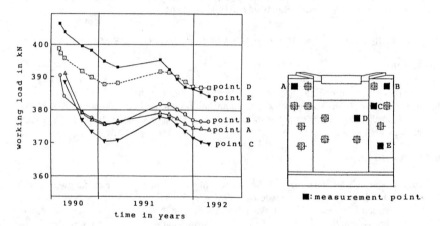

Fig.12   Working Load Change with Time

Fig.11   Measurement Loacations of Anchor Load

CONCLUDING REMARKS

It has been demonstrated that the CFRP rods may successfully be applied to the prestressing tendons of permanent ground anchors owing to the new anchorage system developed by the authors. There is a need for further study with the choice of the proper tensioning stress.

REFERENCES

UK Department of Energy (1984). Offshore Installations: Guidance on Design and Construction, HMSO, London, 4,84-88.

Forsyth, P. and Tebbett, I.E. (1988). New Test Data on the Strength of Grouted Connection with Closely Spaced Weld Beads. Proc. Annu. Offshore Technol. Conf., Texas, 237-245.

Kubota, M., Yamamoto, T. and Murayama, Y. (1990). Design and Construction of Stress-Ribbon Bridge Reinforced with New Materials, Intnl. Symp. Innov. Applic. Preca. Prestr., Singapore, 31-38.

Bridge Applications

Applications aux ponts

ADVANCED COMPOSITE MATERIALS IN BRIDGES AND STRUCTURES
K.W. Neale and P. Labossière, Editors; Canadian Society for Civil Engineering, 1992

Matériaux composites d'avant-garde pour ponts et charpentes
K.W. Neale et P. Labossière, éditeurs; Société canadienne de génie civil, 1992

APPLICATION OF A TENDON MADE OF CFRP RODS TO A POST-TENSIONED PRESTRESSED CONCRETE BRIDGE

M. Koga and **M. Okano**
Obayashi Corporation
Tokyo, Japan

H. Sakai
Mitsubishi Kasei Corporation
Kitakyushu-city, Japan

Y. Kawamoto
P.S. Corporation
Tokyo, Japan

K. Yagi
Mitsubishi Kasei Corporation
Tokyo, Japan

ABSTRACT

The slab type prestressed concrete roadway bridge "Bachigawa-Minami-Bashi" was constructed in 1989. In the outer girder, 8 tendons, which consisted of 8 carbon fibre-reinforced plastic (CFRP) rods 8 mm in diameter, were applied to transfer the prestressing force to the concrete girder by post-tensioning. During the construction, various investigations were carried out: tensioning tests of the tendons, cyclic loading tests of the manufactured girders, traffic loading tests of the complete bridge and measurements of the long-term changes of prestressing forces in the girders. The outer girder behaves well as an element of the total bridge system as designed, thus the CFRP tendon is applicable to post-tensioned prestressed concrete systems.

RÉSUMÉ

Le pont routier "Bachigawa-Minami-Bashi", formé d'une dalle en béton précontraint a été construit en 1989. Le long des poutres extérieures, 8 tendons constitués de 8 barres de CFRP de 8 mm de diamètre ont été installés pour appliquer la force de précontrainte par post-tension. Durant la construction, des observations variées ont été faites : tests en tension des tendons, chargement cyclique des poutres, chargement du pont sous des charges de traffic, mesure des pertes de précontrainte. Les poutres extérieures se comportent bien comme et confirment que le tendon fabriqué de barres de CFRP est applicable dans des systèmes de béton précontraint en post-tension.

1. INTRODUCTION

The application of the tendon made of Carbon Fiber Reinforced Plastics (CFRP) Rod to the prestressed concrete bridge was started a few years ago.   And now, not to mention pre-tensioned girder, post-tensioned girders are constructed on trial.   The data for design and construction of the post-tensioned concrete girder and bridge are accumulated.

In this situation, the Tendon made of CFRP Rods, which were made from coaltar-pitch based Carbon Fiber and Epoxy Resin, had an opportunity to be applied to an outer girder of roadway bridge by the post-tensioning method.

This report explains the outlines of design and construction of "Bachigawa-Minami-Bashi" bridge and the results about various investigations carried out during the construction (1).

2. OUTLINE OF CONSTRUCTION

2.1 Outline of the Project

Name of Bridge   :   Bachigawa-Minami-Bashi Bridge
Scale of Bridge   :   Simply supported 2 spanned roadway bridge with 18 to 19 m in length respectively, and with 12.3 m in width as shown in Fig. 1
Type of Bridge   :   Prestressed concrete slab type bridge consists of 32 pre-tensioned girders and 2 post-tensioned girders
Design Standard :   the Specifications for Highway Bridges provided by Japan Road Association
Design Load   :   Japanese 1st class traffic loads : TL-20
Construct. Period :   November 1988 ~ September 1989
Construct. Place :   Yahata-Nishi-ku Kitakyushu-city, Japan
Owner   :   Mitsubishi Kasei Corp., Kurosaki Plant

Fig. 1 and Table 1 show the general plan and main material quantities of this bridge, respectively.

2.2 Outline of the Construction

(1) the Schedule of the Construction

The bridge construction schedule from the preparation work to the completion is shown in Table 2.

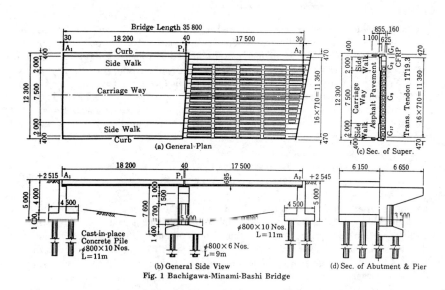

(a) General Plan

(c) Sec. of Super.

(b) General Side View

(d) Sec. of Abutment & Pier

Fig. 1 Bachigawa-Minami-Bashi Bridge

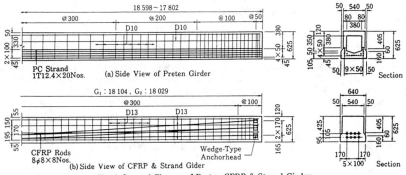

PC Strand
1T12.4×20Nos.　(a) Side View of Preten Girder

G_1 : 18 104 , G_2 : 18 029

CFRP Rods
8φ8×8Nos.　　　　　Wedge-Type Anchorhead
(b) Side View of CFRP & Strand Gider

Fig. 2 General Figures of Preten, CFRP & Strand Girder

Table 1 Main Material Quantities

Super Struc.	Sum (Nos.)	Tendon	
		Kind	Total Length
Preten Girder	32	1T12.4	11 415 (m)
CFRP Girder	1	8φ 8.0	1 265
Strand Girder	1	1T21.8	157
Trans.Tendon	1	1T19.8	432

Table 2 Practical Schedule

Item	1988			1989								
	10	11	12	1	2	3	4	5	6	7	8	9
Preparation												
Bridge Removal												
Drainage Change												
Temporary Jetty												
Abutment A_1												
Pier P_1												
Abutment A_2												
Bank Protection												
Preten Girders												
CFRP Girder												
Erection												
Superimpose												

Table 3 Design Condition of Girders

		Manu. Method	Pre-Ten.	Post-Ten.	Post-Ten.
		Kind of Girder	Preten G.	CFRP G.	Strand G.
		Figure of Girder	Hollow Rec.	Solid Rec.	Solid Rec.
Concrete	Strength (kgf/cm²)		500	400	400
	Young's Modulus (kgf/cm²)		4.0×10⁵	3.5×10⁵	3.5×10⁵
	Section Area (m2)		0.2444	0.3565	0.3565
Tendon	Japan Indus. Standard (Diameter, mm) (Numbers)		SWPR 7A 1T12.4 20	CFRP 8φ8.0 8	SWPR 19 1T21.8 8
	Permissibles (tons)		9.75	40.00	35.05
	Young's Modulus (kgf/cm²)		1.98×10⁶	1.42×10⁶	1.95×10⁶
	Coefficient of Frictionloss		—	0.3 0.004	0.3 0.004

(2) the Manufacture of the Precast - concrete Girders

The precast concrete girders, which consist of 32 girders made by pre-tensioning method and 2 girders made by post-tensioning method, were manufactured in a precast concrete manufacturing factory located 90 km far from the bridge construction site.

The pre-tensioned girders were prestressed by 20 sevenwired high strength steel strands with 12.4 mm in diameter as shown in Fig. 2. One of the post-tensioned girders, which was No. 1 girder used as the outer girder at the down stream side of bridge in P1-A2 span, was prestressed by 8 tendons. The tendon was consisted of 8 CFRP Rods with round section, 8 mm in diameter and smooth surface as shown in Fig. 2 and 5. And the other one, which was No.2 girder used close to No.1 girder, was prestressed by 8 multi-twisted high strength steel strands with 21.8 mm in diameter. In order to compare the behaviours between both girders, they had same dimensions of girder section and the same arrangements of tendon as shown in Fig. 2.

In this report, these girders are called as "the Preten Girder", "the CFRP Girder" and "the Strand Girder" and these tendons are called as "the CFRP Tendon" and "the Steel Tendon", respectively

(3) the Transportation into the Site, Erection of Girders and the Transverse Prestressing

All the precast girders were carried into the bridge construction site by trailers, two girders were loaded in each trailer. Considering a traffic condition, the transportation was done at night. All the precast girders were erected and installed at designed places by a hydraulic crane respectively and prestressed transversly to connect these girders after concrete had been poured into the spaces between the installed girders.

3. DESIGN OF THE GIRDERS AND
THE MANUFACTURE OF THE CFRP GIRDER

3.1 Design of the Superstructure
(1) the Selection for the Type of the Superstructure

The superstructure of this bridge was required to minimize the girder height because the clearance between the top of embankment at the both sides of river and the highest water level of river is very small.　The slab type superstructure, consists of pre-tensioned hollow rectangular concrete girders, was adopted after the various comparisons.　This type could economically satisfy the 650 mm of girder height limitation to span the length of 18 m to 19 m.

(2) the Employment of the CFRP Girder

Various problems listed below shall be studied or confirmed by investigations against the actual-scale structure in order to design and construct the prestressed concrete bridge, which consists of the post-tensioned girders using the CFRP Tendon.　Two girders out of the 34 girders used in this bridge were manufactured by post-tensioning method in oder to investigate these problems.

①The coiling a long size CFRP Rod around a reel vessel with 2.5 m in diameter for transportation.

②The draw-out of long size CFRP Rod from the transportation reel vessel and the proper cutting to make a CFRP Tendon.

③The method to insert the CFRP Tendon into a duct formed in the girder concrete.

④The method of tensioning and anchoring for the CFRP Tendon and the comparison with the conventional methods.

⑤The protection against the damages to CFRP Rods during the works of items ① to ④.

⑥The differences among the tensile forces transfered to each Rod at the anchoring works.

⑦The reliabilities of the anchorsystem for a short and long period.

⑧The efficiency of the cement grout around the CFRP Rods.

⑨The elastic behaviour of the CFRP Tendon in the girder under the load.

⑩The change of girder characteristic for a long period.

⑪The evaluation of accumulated data in oder to construct the post-tensioned concrete girders by the CFRP Tendon.

(3) the Condition and Result of the Superstructure Design

The design conditions for the Preten Girder, the CFRP Girder and the Strand Girder are shown in Table 3 and the result of design is shown in Fig. 2, respectively.

In design, following items were considered :

①The section figure for the CFRP Girder and the Strand Girder, instead of the hollow rectangle for the Preten Girders, was solid rectangle because of the tendon bent-up arrangement.

②The concrete strength was changed between post- and pre-tensioned girders to equal the bending stiffness of these in order to apply an anisotropic plate theory analysis.

③The values about the CFRP Tendon were employed as follows :

The permissible tensile force of the CFRP Tendon

$= 0.65 \times$ Breaking force of the CFRP Tendon

The coefficient of friction between the CFRP Tendon and the duct

$=$ coefficient of friction of the Steel Tendon

④The analyzing formula considering the bond between the CFRP Tendon and concrete was employed in calculation of the fiber stresses of the girder section.

⑤The ultimate limit state conditions against the bending and shearing forces working in the girders were checked with the following load conditions:

$1.30 \times Wd + 2.50 \times Wl$　　and $1.70 (Wd + Wl)$

where, Wd : dead loads including superimposed dead load

Wl : live loads by traffic and pedestrian load

(4) the Inspection Plan for the Behaviour of Girders

Concrete strain gauges, concrete effectivestress gauges, concrete nonstress gauges and thermometers were embedded in the CFRP Girder, paper strain gauges were pasted at the surface of girder and CFRP Rods and loadcells were installed at the both ends of a CFRP Tendon as shown in Fig. 3.　Differences among the each rod tensile forces, reliabilities of anchorsystem, elastic

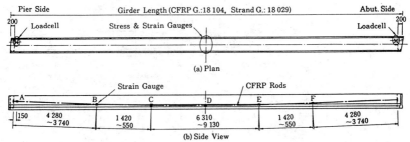

Fig. 3 Plan of Gauges

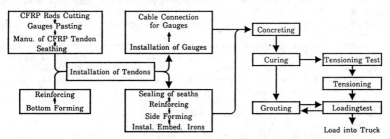

Fig. 4 Manufacturing Flow of CFRP Girder

Table 4 Characteristic Value of Tendons (kgf/cm²)

kinds	Dia. (mm)	Area (mm²)	Yield Stress Tested	Yield Stress Permi.	Breaking Stress Tested	Breaking Stress Permi.	Young's Modulus	Elongation (%)
CFRP Rods	8±0.05	49.0	—	—	184	157	1.42×10^4	1.21
SWPR 19	21.8	312.9	169	161	189	187	1.95×10^4	6.5

Table 5 Concrete Mix

Max. of Coarse Ag.	Slamp (cm)	Air Contents(%)	Water-Cement Ratio(%)	Fine.Aggregate Percentage(%)
20(mm)	7.0±1.5	2.0±1.0	36.4	40.5

Weight Mix (kgf/m³)

Water	Cement	Aggregate	Coarse Aggregate	Water Reducing Admixture
151	415	708	1 248	4.150

Table 6 Characteristic Value of Concrete

Characters Testing Time	Compres. Strength (kgf/cm²)	Young's Modulus Ec (×10⁵ kgf/cm²) Tangent 1	Young's Modulus Ec (×10⁵ kgf/cm²) Tangent 2	Age (days)
Prestressing	433	2.90	——	5
Loadingtest Before Grout	524	3.20	3.22	18
Loadingtest After Grout	554	3.17	3.34	26

Tangent 1 : Tangent at point of 1/3×Compressive Strength
Tangent 2 : Tangent at point of Compressive Strength 100kgf/cm²

behaviour of the CFRP Tendon and behaviour of CFRP Girder in the complete total bridge system under working loads would be investigated.

The same gauges were also set at the same points of Strand Girder to compare the data with the CFRP Girder's.   In addition, the deflection of girders was inspected by sensors installed at the center and the both ends of girder.

3.2 Manufacture of the CFRP Girder
(1) the Manufacturing flow of the CFRP Girder and the Manufacture of the CFRP Tendon
The general manufacturing flow of the CFRP Girder is shown in Fig. 4.

The long size CFRP Rod with 8 mm in diameter, which was drawn out from transportation reel vessel with 2.5 m in diameter, showed completely straight linear shape.   The workability for the manufacture of CFRP Tendon, such as cutting and binding properties, was as good as or better than the Steel Tendon.   The characteristic values about CFRP Rod and multi-twisted high strength Steel Strand are shown in Table 4, comparatively.

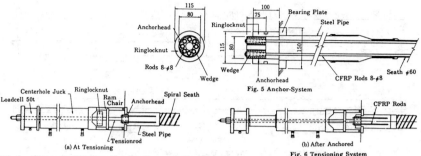

Fig. 5 Anchor-System

(a) At Tensioning

(b) After Anchored

Fig. 6 Tensioning System

(2) the Concrete Placing, the Curing and the Grouting

A plan of concrete mix, satisfied the compressive strength 400 kgf/cm² at 28 days age by cylindrical test piece, was shown in Table 5.

The wet steam curing for girder was increased for 2 hours, kept at 60 degrees centigrade for further 2 hours and after that left free from the temperature control under a cover sheet. The test results of concrete characteristic is shown in Table 6.

After prestressing and loadingtest as written later, the grout, with the mix of ordinary portland cement, super waterreducing admixture Pozzolith GF-600.and water-cement ratio 42 %, was injected into the duct by the initial injecting pressure 2 kgf/cm² and kept at the last pressure 4 kgf/cm² for total 7 minutes for each duct.

3.3 Method of the Tensioningtest for the CFRP Tendon

(1) the Characteristics of the Anchorsystem

A multi-Rods type anchorsystem using wedges shown in Fig. 5 was adopted in this project, which had been developed for the post-tensioning method with the CFRP Tendon, and been already evaluated its reliability for 3 years.   This system is composed of 8 wedges to hold 8 CFRP Rods, an anchorhead to hold 8 wedges in its 8 drilled tapering anchorholes respectively and a ringlocknut to transfer the tensile force exactly by adjusting the distance between the anchorhead and a bearing plate embedded in concrete.

The wedge, separated in 2 pieces, was specially developed to hold the CFRP Rod softly and surely, without the stress concentration because of its low bearing capacity against the shearing stress (2).   When the tendon consisted of 8 CFRP Rods is tensioned under the use of the multi-Rods type anchorsystem, differences appear among moving distances occured between the wedge and the anchorhole in anchorhead until the wedge is holded by the anchorhead perfectly, because of the manufacturing gaps and the installation gaps of these by human work.

If these differences are large, the Rod will be broken by the excessive tensile force concentration on the earliest holded Rod.

It is indispensable to investigate these differences of tensile force concentration on each Rod in order to keep the safe tensioning work, improve the anchorsystem and determine the permissible tensile force for the multi-Rods type tendon system.

(2) the Installation of the Anchorsystem

The 8 Rods in the CFRP Tendon were inserted into 8 anchorholes in anchorhead respectively and the 8 wedges covered with vinyl films were pushed in between Rods and anchorholes by hands until the marking line, which shows the designed correct point on the Rods to be stopped.

A retaining plate was installed at the back of the anchorhead by set-bolts to push the head of wedges, which has two significant purposes : fixing the wedges at the correct point on the Rods during the installation work and pulling the anchorhead toward the wedges to minimize the moving distances occured between wedge and anchorhole in anchorhead during tensioning.

(3) the Installation Achievement-test of the Anchorsystem

After centerhole-jacks and loadcells were installed by tension-rods behind the anchorheads of both ends of tendon, the anchorheads were tensioned up to tensile force 1.5 tons by jack systems. At this tensioning process, the investigation whether the two values were within permissible ranges : the wedge movement surveyed by the eyewitness and the tensile force concentration on each Rod measured by the strain gauges pasted on each Rod surface.

410

Table 7 Estimated Coefficient of Frictionloss

Assumptive Value μ		0.0	0.1	0.2
λ	CFRP Tendon	0.001	0.0005	0.0002
	Steel Tendon	0.003	0.002	0.0015

Table 8 Apparent Young's Modulus & Frictionloss

Kinds of Tendon	Young'sModulus Ep (kgf/cm²)	Coefficient of Frictionloss μ
CFRP Tendon	1.39×10^6	0.07
Steel Tendon	1.89×10^6	0.11

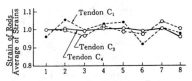

Fig. 7 Difference of Tensile Force of Rods

(4) the Tensioningtest up to the Designed Tensile Force

After the initial investigation as mentioned above, the tensile force was increased with the steps by 1.5 to 3.5 tons up to the designed tensile force 40 tons and the tensioned anchorheads were surely fastened with the ringlocknut.   All the data from every gauges and sensors were continuously recorded all through the tensioning process.

3.4 Result of the Tensioningtest

(1) the Stability of the Anchorsystem

The anchorsystem could hold the Rods as tightly as the laboratory test and the data for analysis about the ability of anchorsystem were stored.

(2) the Coefficients of the Friction Loss along the Tendons

The coefficients of friction loss along the tendons were estimated by applying a following formula to the data about the tensile forces recorded by the loadcells installed at the both ends of tendon during the 4 times test-tensioning and 8 times complete tensioningtest (3,4).

P fixed side = P tension side $\times$ exp $\{-(\mu \alpha + \lambda \ell)\}$

Where, P : Tensile forces at the ends of tendon

μ : Coefficient of the friction loss along the α

α : Change the angle of tendon

λ : Coefficient of the friction loss along the ℓ

ℓ : Length of the tendon

The coefficient λ was estimated using the values of (P fixed side) / (P tension side) under the assumptive values 0.0, 0.1 and 0.2 of μ.   The results of λ about the CFRP Girder and the Strand Girder are shown in Table 7.

Table 7 shows that the coefficient of friction loss along the CFRP Tendons was much smaller than that of the Steel Tendon.   This fact indicates that the CFRP Tendon for the post-tensioning system works more effectively than the Steel Tendon, but it should be noted that this result comes from the CFRP Tendon surface is smoother than the Steel Tendon.

(3) the Deviation among the CFRP Rod Tensile Forces

Fig. 7 shows the ratio of the deviated tensile force to the average tensile force of 8 Rods in each CFRP Tendon measured by the strain gauges pasted on the Rod surfaces during the tensioningtest.   As shown in Fig. 7, the above mentioned ratios are within about 5 %, which must be considered to decide the permissible tensile force for the multi-Rods type CFRP Tendon.

4. LOADINGTEST ON THE CFRP GIRDER AND THE STRAND GIRDER

4.1 Outline of the Loadingtest

It should be investigated whether The CFRP Girder and Strand Girder have a load bearing capacity as designed, and whether the installed gauges work properly with the aim for the traffic loadingtest after the bridge completion and for the measurement for long period.

By these reason, the CFRP Girder and the Strand Girder were tested in the elastic range under the static cyclic loading (4).   The testload was applied by the bending test method as shown in Fig. 8 : to the CFRP Girder before and after grouting and to the Strand Girder after grouting.

The testload was applied cyclicly 3 or 4 times : the load equal to superimposed deadload was once and the load equal to total design load was twice or 3 times.   The applied load value, the concrete stress and strain and the deflection at the center of girder were recorded continuously during the test.   Table 9 shows maximum designed moment for the girders and applied testload values.

411

Table 9 Design Load & Testing Load

Load	Designed Momemt(tf·m)	Testing Load(tf)
Own Weight	34.12	0.0
Superimp.Dead Load	16.66	4.1
Live Load	19.40	5.1
Total	70.18	9.2

Table 10 Elastic Rigidity (tf/cm)

Girders	Grouting	Tested Value	Calcu.Value	Ratio
CFRP Girder	Before	3.43	3.47	0.99
	After	3.83	3.66	1.05
Strand Girder	After	3.90	3.69	1.06

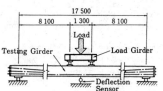

Fig. 8 Loadingtest System

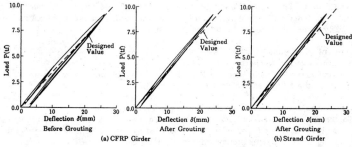

Fig. 9 Relationship of Load & Deflection

(a) CFRP Girder

(b) Strand Girder

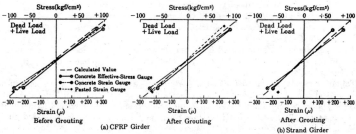

Fug. 10 Distribution of Bending Stress & Strain

(a) CFRP Girder

(b) Strand Girder

4.2 Result of the Test

The elastic stiffnesses of the girders are shown in Table 10 comparatively for designed and tested, in which the tested result was calculated from the applied maximum load divided by the deflection under that load, while the designed deflection value was calculated using the Moment of Inertia of Area and the material test result. As shown in Table 10, the test result was very close to the designed value, the value before grouting was close to the value after grouting and the value of CFRP Girder was also close to the value of Strand Girder.

Fig. 9 shows the relationship between the applied load and the deflection at the centers of two tested girders and in which the calculated design elastic stiffness is plotted with dashed line. Fig. 10 shows the bending stress and strain at the center of girder under the maximum load in the last loading cycle, in which all values at the load starting are zeros, the concrete effective-stress values and the concrete strain values are the gauge data and the concrete surface strain values are the average values from the data measured at the front and back side of girder, respectively.

All the data in each loading condition were close to the designed values.

4.3 Conclusion of the Test

The loadingtest result against the post-tensioned girders showed that the CFRP Girder had the same elastic stiffness and sectional stress distribution as designed value and that the CFRP Girder behaved similarly to the Strand Girder.

5. TRAFFIC LOADINGTEST AGAINST THE COMPLETE BRIDGE

5.1 Outline of the Test

It is necessary to inspect that the CFRP Girder works as designed as an element of the complete bridge with sufficient property.   So, the inspection for the CFRP Girder under the traffic loading against complete bridge was carried out in order to confirm the reliability of CFRP Girder by comparing the deflection and increased bending moment at the center of girder with the analyzed values.

The load by dumptruck shown in Fig. 11 was applied on the bridge with 36 patterns loading combination using 1 to 4 trucks.   Fig.12 shows the example of 4 trucks loading.

5.2 Test Result

(1) the Deflection and the Bending Moment

Fig. 13 shows the deflection values from the test result and the analyzed result at the span center comparativey, in which the analyzed value was calculated by the simplified concentrated loading on the gridpoint in the gridwork modeled.   Fig. 13 shows :

①The tendency for the transverse distribution of deflection at the bridge center was similar to the analyzed result.   So, the CFRP Girder works completely as the one of girders.

②The deflection under the full loading was about 50 % of the analyzed values.

The reason for ② is as follows : the portion of neutral axis of the girder section, calculated from the measured concrete stress and strain, is nearly equal to the neutral axis of the section including the sidewalk concrete paving and curb on the bridge, but inspite of this, these surfacings were excluded in the analyzed result.

Fig. 14 shows the bending moment calculated from the concrete strain and effectivestress under the traffic loadingtest, compared with the analyzed result.   Fig. 14 also shows that bending moments of the CFRP Girder and the Strand Girder are close to those of the analyzed result.

(2) the Relationship between the Deflection and the Bending Moment

Fig. 15 shows the relationship between the deflection and the bending moment at the center of the CFRP Girder and Strand Girder under the 36 loading patterns.   The increment of the deflection has direct proportion to that of the bending moment, though little deviation is recognized.

(3) the Conclusion of the Traffic Loadingtest

It can be concluded, based on the behaviour about the deflection, the concrete stress and the bending moment for the CFRP Girder and for the Strand Girder under the traffic loading, that the two post-tensioned girders have the same property as the other pre-tensioned girders for the deflection distribution and work satisfactorily as designed as a part of the complete bridge.

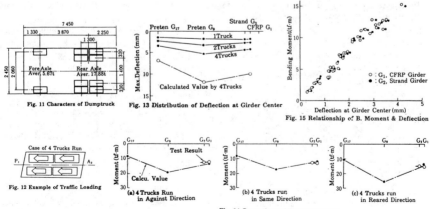

Fig. 11 Characters of Dumptruck

Fig. 13 Distribution of Deflection at Girder Center

Fig. 15 Relationship of B. Moment & Deflection

Fig. 12 Example of Traffic Loading

(a) 4 Trucks Run in Against Direction

(b) 4 Trucks run in Same Direction

(c) 4 Trucks run in Reared Direction

Fig. 14 Comparison of Bending Moment

413

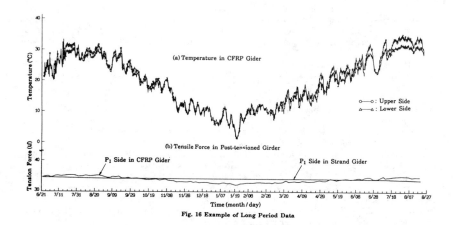

Fig. 16 Example of Long Period Data

6. CHANGES OF THE CHARACTERISTICS OF THE GIRDERS FOR THE LONG PERIOD

The mechanical characteristic behaviours of the CFRP Girder and the Strand Girder have been continuously measured for the long period, since the girder manufacture, including the girder cyclic loadingtest, the girder erection, until the complete bridge traffic loadingtest.
And the behaviours of the post-tensioned girders are and will be measured under natural traffic condition. Fig. 16 shows the temperature inside the post-tensioned girders and the tensile forces measured by the loadcells installed at the both ends of the tendons free from the concrete bond in the girders respectively.

In general, the tensile force of high strength steel tendon used in the prestressed concrete girder is gradually reduced by the reason of the longterm concrete creep and shrinkage.
In Fig. 16, the tensile force for the Steel Tendon in the Strand Girder are slightly decreased for longterm without the effect of the seasonal temperature change.

On the other hand, the tensile force for the CFRP Tendon in the CFRP Girder varies i.e. increase in hot season and decrease in cold season.   This was caused by the difference of the thermal expansion coefficient between the negligibly small coefficient of CFRP Rod and the comparatively large coefficient of concrete.

This phenomenon is successively analyzed and its result will be announced in the congress.

REFERENCES

1. Sakai, Yagi, Koga, Kawamoto : The Application of the Tendons made of CFRP Rods with Post-Tensioning Method to Outer Girder of the Slab Type Bridge – Construction of the Road Bridge " Bachigawa-Minami-Bashi " –, Concrete Journal, Japan, Vol.28, No.11, pp.14-24, Nov. 1990
2. Inukai : The research on the application of the tendons made of carbon fiber reinforced plastics, Journal of Prestressed Concrete, Vol.30, No.5, pp.41-46, 1988
3. Kitta, Saito : The design and construction of the stressing for the prestressed concrete bridge, Gendai Rikougaku Publication, pp.120-199, 1977
4. F.K.K Japan : The standard specification of the Freyssinet Method, 1989
5. Okano, Kobatake, Kimura : The bending test of the prestressed concrete girder used the tendon made of CFRP Rods,
Preceedings of the Japan Concrete Institute, Vol.12, No.1, pp.1111-1116, 1990

ADVANCED COMPOSITE MATERIALS IN BRIDGES AND STRUCTURES
K.W. Neale and P. Labossière, Editors; Canadian Society for Civil Engineering, 1992

Matériaux composites d'avant-garde pour ponts et charpentes
K.W. Neale et P. Labossière, éditeurs; Société canadienne de génie civil, 1992

DEVELOPMENT AND CONVERSION OF THE PROPERTIES OF ACM INTO PRESTRESSING TENDONS FOR BRIDGES AND STRUCTURES

M. Faoro
SICOM GmbH
Cologne, Germany

ABSTRACT

Due to some of their excellent material properties, high performance glass fibre composite materials are used in an increasing degree in the field of civil engineering as a corrosion resistant alternative to conventional prestressing steels. During the development and realization of useful prestressing systems, the specific properties of the material have to be considered. The directional strength properties lead to expected problems during the anchoring of the prestressing bundles and also in the field of curvatures of tensile forces (saddles). In the present contribution these difficulties are discussed on the basis of an appraisal of the essential material properties. Moreover, possibilities to resolve these problems are shown.

RÉSUMÉ

Les matériaux composites de haute performance – grâce à quelques-unes de leurs propriétés mécaniques excellentes – sont utilisés de plus en plus dans le secteur du génie civil comme alternative résistante à la corrosion au lieu des aciers précontraints conventionnels. Lors du développement et de la réalisation de systèmes de précontrainte, il faut tenir compte des propriétés spécifiques du matériau. À cause de leurs caractéristiques mécaniques directionnelles, on peut prévoir des difficultés non seulement lors de l'ancrage de câbles de précontrainte mais également dans les sections des courbes des forces de traction (selles). Dans cet article, ces problèmes sont discutés sur la base d'une évaluation des propriétés essentielles du matériau. En outre, on explique des possibilités de résolution de ces problèmes.

INTRODUCTION

Owing to some of the excellent properties of glass fiber composite materials, application of this new material has experienced a dramatic development in almost all fields of technology during the last few years.

First investigations into the application possibilities of high-perfromance resin bonded glass fiber bars in construction were carried out over 30 years ago. On the basis of the information then gained and following a series of comprehensive research projects to determine the main characteristic values and properties of the material, the basic applicability of synthetic resin bonded glass fiber bars for use as prestressing reinforcement could be established. But during the development of a capable and economical prestressing system some significant differences with regard to the material behaviour of glass fiber composite bars and conventional prestressing steels had to be considered. This led to special constructions for the end anchoring of the bar bundles and to certain material combinations in case of the cable ducts, especially in the area of the saddles.

All material and component development is now so far advanced that a corresponding prestressing system will receive general approval from the building authorities in the present year.

MATERIAL PROPERTIES OF RESIN BONDED GLASS FIBER COMPOSITE BARS

Structure and Composition of the Material

The strengthening fibers provide the actual strength and ductility in the fiber composite material for loads parallel to the fibers.

The binding agent, the so-called matrix, is intended to achieve a shear resistant combination of the fibers and to protect them against mechanical loads. The matrix also serves to retain the inherent stability of the composite material. Polyester and epoxy resins are the most suitable binding agents for the glass fiber composite materials dealt within this paper.

Through objective selection and design of the individual components, fiber composite materials basically offer the possibility of producing a composite material with purpose-designed characteristics.

Uni-directional glass fiber composite material, which has now been manufactured on an industrial basis for roughly 12 years, is produced in a continuous pultrusion process from numerous, parallel running, continuous glass fibers and a binding matrix comprising unsaturated polyester resin. In this process, glass fiber rovings are arranged parallel, impregnated with fluid resin, and drawn through a shaping bed for thermal curing. With the material currently available, a bar comprises approx. 64.000 individual fibers. With a bar diameter of 7.5 mm (nom.-dia.) and individual fiber diameters of roughly 25 μm, a glass content of approximately 69 vol.-% results (see fig. 1).

The bond behaviour of the composite bars in both concrete and the injection and grouting mortars for the end anchorages is of decisive importance for the application of prestressing force on the bars. On technical production reasons the glass fiber reinforced composite (GFRC)-bars are wound with chemical fibers which provide the bars with a certain surface roughness and ripple (fig. 2a) which in turn have a favourable effect on the bonding behaviour in concrete and injection mortar.

To increase the resistance to aggressive media, for example alkaline residual moisture from the concrete, and as a protection against defects resulting from mechanical loads and handling on the site, the GFRC-bars are usually also extruded with an approx. 0.5 mm thick sheathing comprising a high-filled polyamide (PA 6). As a result the surface of the sheathed bars (see fig. 2b), and thereby the bonding behaviour in concrete or injection mortar, can be specifically controlled.

416

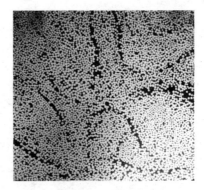
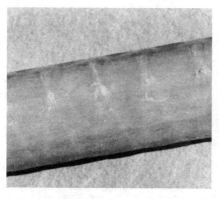

Fig. 1: Cross-section images of resin bonded glass fiber bars (electron scan microscope; Faoro, 1988)

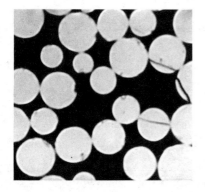
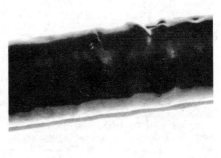

a.)   b.)

Fig.2: GFRC-bar with (fig. 2b) and without (fig. 2a) polyamide sheathing (Faoro, 1988)

Relevant Properties of the GFRC-Material

The tensile strength and stress/strain behaviour are of prior interest for the short-term load. With this material the relation between stress and strain can be considered as mainly linear (fig. 3), i.e. the behaviour of the GFRC-elements is almost completely elastic.

As can be seen from fig. 3, failure occurs at an ultimate strain of approx. $\epsilon = 3.3$ %. In the working load range, the experimentally found modulus of elasticity of the GRFC-bars amounts to approx. 51.000 N/mm². The transverse contraction ratio determined in the tests is roughly $\mu = 0.27$ and confirms the data in previous investigations (Rehm and Franke, 1974). Particularly in the bar anchorage area, it is usually necessary for comparatively high shear forces to be applied to the glass fiber bars. The behaviour of the material is hereby mainly influenced by the strength and deformation behaviour of the matrix resin and the bonding capacity and bonding characteristic between the glass fibers and the resin. A further significant material characteristic is therefore the so-called interlaminary shear strength τ_u. Numerous punch-through tests were carried out in order to determine this characteristic value and the data obtained coincides well with earlier investigations.

417

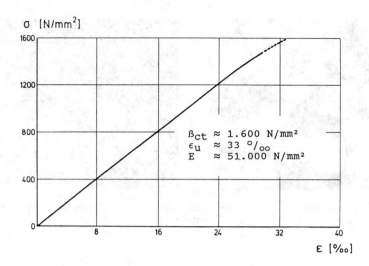

σ [N/mm^2]

$\beta_{ct} \approx 1.600$ N/mm²
$\epsilon_u \approx 33$ °/$_{oo}$
$E \approx 51.000$ N/mm²

ϵ [‰]

Fig. 3: Experimentally determined stress/strain curve of GFRC-bars

A further criterium for assessment of the workability and applicability of the uni-directional glass fiber composite material is the effect of load duration of the tensile strength. The long term strength of the material comes to approx. 70 % of the short term tensile strength ßc. Caused by the specific structure of the material a very low loss of stress due to relaxation can be recognized under permanent load. During a period of about 50 years the loss of stress amounts only to 3 % of the used initial tensile stress.

Significant effects on the strength are also to be expected if the material is subjected to non-static load. The test data given (Schlottke and Faoro, 1985) show clearly that the behaviour differs fundamentally from that of comparable steel tension elements. Whereas with prestressing steel the usual and sufficiently accurate stress amplitude at 2×10^6 load cycles can be defined as fatigue strength for a certain average stress, this is apparently not permittable for the present GFRC-bars as material failure can also occur with considerably higher load cycles. The question of whether any true fatigue strength value exists for the glass fiber composite bars cannot be conclusively answered on the basis of the available test results.

Unidirectiol glass fiber composite bars - in comparison with conventional prestressing steels - do have the same tensile strength but a significantly higher corrosion resistance and a lot of other advantageous properties as follows:

*   low own weight
*   due to the low modulus of elasticity they have a considerably lower decrease of
        tension in case of components shortenings due to creep or shrinkage
*   high corrosion and chemical resistance
*   electromagnetic neutrality

Fracture Behaviour of the Composite Material in Case of Combined Stresses

The anisotropic composition of the material of the glass fiber bars conditions directional strengths and determines therefore especially in the area of anchoring the loadbearing capacity in case of combined stresses out of longitudinal tension σ_{ct}, compressive stress σ_{cnc} and shear τ.

According to recent studies (Herrmann, 1982) it can be assumed that the bearing capacity of a glass fiber composite material is not affected or reduced by a combination of transverse pressures and shear stresses when loaded simultaneously in the direction of the fibers.

418

The effects on the material have to be found out in arithmetical or experimental studies and to be faced to a failure hypothesis which has to be as precise as possible before the anchorages are dimensioned. For the practical use of anchorages it has to be taken into account that not only stresses due to short term loads have to be considered but that the combined stresses having a long term effect have to be compared with the respective failure criteria for long term stresses. Therefore a failure line (Rehm et al. 1979) in the long term strength range is indicated or estimated on the basis of stress-rupture tests with unidirectional GFRC-material. Fig. 4 gives an impression of the range of the short term and long term stress combinations and of proposed usable stress ranges for GFRC-bar anchorages.

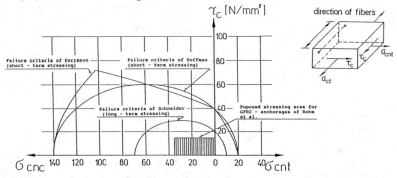

Fig. 4: Failure criteria for short term and long term stresses and a proposal for admissible stresses for glass fiber bar anchorages

ANCHORING SYSTEMS FOR GFRC-BARS

General reflections

During the application of prestress on the GFRC-bars the following material specific properties have to be considered:

* Due to the anisotropic composition the material has only a relatively low transverse compression strength ß $_{cnc}$. It amounts to approx. 10 % of the tensile strength in the direction of the fibers.
* Because of the lack of plastification capacity the material is sensible to peak and locally concentrated transverse pressures.
* The interlaminar shear strength and the shear strength of the sections placed near to the surface is limited and clearly inferior to that of metallic materials.
* The abrasion resistance of the material allows only limited stresses on friction.
* The low modulus of elasticity leads in between stiff anchoring constructions to comparatively great relative displacements (slips).

Design Criteria for Anchorages

In most of the cases when ACM is used, conventional anchoring methods such as clamping anchorings or the cutting of threads and the jumping of heads do not lead to satisfactory results. Due to the a.m. relationships it would be favourable to embed the bars in the anchoring section in appropriate intermediate layers or grouted mortar and to bundle them in an appropriate way. Concerning the systems for the application of prestressing of GFRC-bars known until today (see also Rehm et al., 1979; Faoro, 1988) in general the following types can be distinguished:

* grouted anchorages - using grouted mortar, the bars are fixed in appropriate anchoring elements which - according to their constructive design - are able to exert transverse pressures (e.g. cone sleeve) on the material
* clamping block anchorings - the bars are clamped over special intermediate layers - the transverse pressures being constantly or increasing - according to the increasing tensile force
* grouted-/clamping anchorings - the bars are grouted with appropriate end sleeves and these end sleeves are clamped, e.g. by wedges

The use of clamping block anchorages is problematic due to the required long term stability of the necessary intermediate layers and due to the high friction abrasion of the bars within the anchor elements. Grouted-/Clamping anchorages do not have these disadvantages. In case of an appropriate construction they can guarantee an anchoring without any loss (Faoro, 1989) and this under short term, long term and non-static load. But these kind of anchoring systems require a very high expenditure on the manufacture. Therefore the possibilities of application - useful from the economical point of view - are very limited.

But grouted anchorages can be produced in a very economical way - grouting the bar bundle in a profiled sleeve with a special resin mortar. This process can be controlled very easily and does not demand high technical requiremtents from the manufacturer.

Extensive studies concerning the bond bearing behaviour of GFRC-bars processed with mortar (Faoro, 1989) show that in case of high bond stresses and/or relative displacements the glass fiber bars can be damaged. The ESM-photograph in fig. 5 shows a test specimen which has been removed from the pull-out-test body after having beared bond stresses in the level of the bond strength. It can be recognized that the bond failure does not take place on the boundary surface between bar surface and resin mortar, but only in the section of the GFRC-elements near to the surface between resin cover and wrapping on the one hand and the "glass core" on the other hand. The ranges of failure are characterized through the fact that resin cover and wrappings are sheared off the glass core and that many of the bare fibers do have cracks. The breaking and delamination of small fiber bundles could also be oberserved.

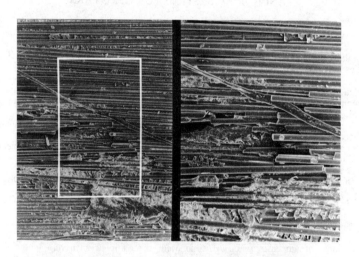

Fig. 5: Surfaces of glass fiber bars grouted with resin mortar after bond stress of
approx. $\tau = 30$ N/mm² (ESM-photographs)

In order to avoid these kind of damages which always lead to early failures within the anchorages the relative displacements and the bond stresses of the bars have to be limited. This can be realized through a so-called segmentation of the anchoring length (see Sippel, 1989; Faoro, 1988) or through special protective measures regarding the bar surfaces.

Therefore in the present case each bar is provided in the beginning of the anchoring length with a glass fiber sock. This excellent abrasion protection leads to significant improvements of the efficacy of grouted anchorages and especially in case of non-static loads. Fig. 6 shows schematically a grouted anchorage in prestressed condition and fig. 7 shows the installation of a tendon comprising 19 individual bars and the corresponding anchorage.

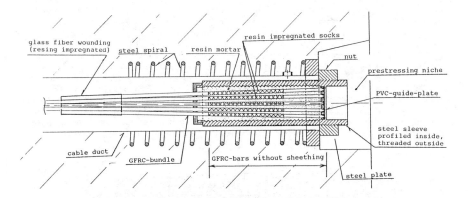

Fig. 6: Grouted anchorage of a bar bundle comprising 19 individual bars in prestressed condition (section)

Fig. 7:   Installtation of a prestressing element with grouted anchoring in the formwork

CURVATURE OF TENSILE FORCES OF GFRC-TENDONS IN THE AREA OF SADDLES

Curvature pressures, friction and abrasion

In case of curvature of tensile forces of prestressing tendons transverse or curvature pressures occur in dependency on the radius of the saddle, the prestressing force and the dimensions of the prestressing element. Even locally they must not exceed the permanently bearable transverse pressure strength. The level of the locally appearing transverse pressures and the related abrasion stress of the bars is decisively influenced by the shape of the cable ducts and the meaningful combination of the friction partners.

In order to clarify this question extensive friction tests with simulated friction lengths of more than 2.0 m have been executed. These tests could be realized with the aid of a saddle test stand and a curvature radius of R = 8.0 m and a contact length of L = 5.0 m. Prestressing elements comprising 19 individual bars (working load 600 kN) and two different types of cable ducts have been used (see fig. 8).

cable duct type HYDRA

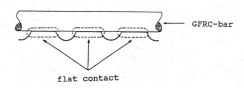

flat contact

cable duct type SUSPA

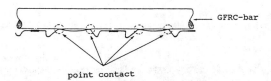

point contact

Fig. 8: Longitudinal section through the examined steel cable ducts and comparison of the contact surfaces

It turned out that the cable ducts with a point contact surface - in case of long friction lengths - can cause considerable abrasion damages (abrasion of PA-sheathing). Therefore cable ducts welded longitudinally with flat contact characteristics have been used in the present prestressing procedure. Even after extreme friction stresses no damages occured on the prestressing elements in case of these cable ducts (type HYDRA). The coefficient of friction between prestressing elements and cable ducts has been determined with a sufficient accuracy of $\mu = 0.18$ on the basis of numerous tests and measurements during prestressing on up to 60 m long bridges. This value is situated in the same range as that of conventional steel prestressing elements.

Minimum saddle radius

Moreover it has to be considered that in the curvature area applied tensile stresses and bending stresses do overly. The following is valid:

$$\max \sigma_{ct,c} = \sigma_{ct} + E \times d_{bar} / (2 \times R) \qquad (1)$$

where

$\max \sigma_{ct,c}$	- max. tensile force in the lateral fibers [N/mm²]
σ_{ct}	- applied tensile force in the GFRC-material [N/mm²]
E	- modulus of elasticity of the material [N/mm²]
d_{bar}	- bar diameter [m]
R	- saddle or curvature radius [m]

Due to the fact that the material does not have a plastification capacity, a limitation of the tensions in the lateral fibers is required. It has been determined for the discussed prestressing procedures as follows:

$$\sigma_{ct,c} = 1.03 \times \sigma_{ct} \qquad (2)$$

With an admissible working load of $\sigma_{ct} = 715$ N/mm² and equation (1) the following is valid after rearrangement:

$$\min R = E \times d_{bar} / (0.06 \times \sigma_{ct}) \qquad (3)$$

If for construction reasons the value falls below this minimum radius of $R = 8.92$ m the tensile force in the area of saddles has to be reduced.

SUMMARY

Starting from a description and a discussion of the essential material properties of GFRC-bars, conclusions with regard to the anchoring technologie, to the choose of appropriate material and to the shape of the curvature of tensile forces (saddles) are drawn.

It turns out that it is possible to anchor the material without almost any losses when the bars are protected in an appropriate way against damaging relative displacements.

In the area of the curvature of tensile forces (saddles) too small saddle radius and local peak pressures have to be avoided. In case of the use of cable ducts with flat contact zones between the GFRC-bars and the ducts even very extreme friction abrasion has no negative effects on the durability of the prestressing elements.

REFERENCES

Faoro, M (1988): Tragverhalten kunstharzgebundener Glasfaserstäbe im Bereich von Endverankerungen und Rissen im Beton (Bearing Behaviour of Resin Bonded Glass Fiber Bars in Anchor Zones and in Cracked Concrete Regions). PhD Thesis, Institut für Werkstoffe im Bauwesen, Universität Stuttgart, IWB-Mitteilungen 1988/1

Faoro, M. (1989): Über die Beanspruchungen kunstharzgebundener Glasfaserstäbe im Krafteinleitungsbereich (On the Stressing of Resin Bonded Glass Fiber Bars in the Anchorage Zone). In: Werkstoff und Konstruktion II. Prof.Dr.-Ing.Dr.-Ing. e.h. Gallus Rehm zum 65. Geburtstag. Institut für Werkstoffe im Bauwesen, Universität Stuttgart, pp. 49

Rehm, G. and Franke, L. (1974): Verhalten von kunstharzgebundenen Glasfaserstäben bei unterschiedlichen Beanspruchungszuständen (Behaviour of Resin Bonded Glass Fiber Bars during various Stressing States). Die Bautechnik, Vol. 4, pp. 132-138

Rehm, G.; Franke, L. and Patzak, M. (1979): Zur Frage der Krafteinleitung in kunstharzgebundene Glasfaserstäbe (On the Question of Application of Prestress in Resin Bonded Glass Fiber Bars). Deutscher Ausschuß für Stahlbeton (DAfStb), Vol. 304, Publisher Wilhem Ernst & Sohn, Berlin

Schlottke, B and Faoro, M. (1985): Materialverhalten bei langzeitiger Beanspruchung (Material Behaviour in Case of Long Term Load). Technischer Bericht des Instituts für Werkstoffe im Bauwesen, Universität Stuttgart

Sippel, T.N. (1989): Untersuchungen zum Tragverhalten von Verankerungen für Spannglieder aus kunstharzgebundenen Glasfaserstäben (Investigations on the Bearing Behaviour of Anchors for Prestressing Tendons for Resin Bonded Glass Fiber Bars). Diploma Thesis, Institut für Werkstoffe im Bauwesen, Universität Stuttgart

ADVANCED COMPOSITE MATERIALS IN BRIDGES AND STRUCTURES
K.W. Neale and P. Labossière, Editors; Canadian Society for Civil Engineering, 1992

Matériaux composites d'avant-garde pour ponts et charpentes
K.W. Neale et P. Labossière, éditeurs; Société canadienne de génie civil, 1992

EXPERIENCE WITH GLASSFIBRE PRESTRESSING ELEMENTS
FOR CONCRETE BRIDGES

R. Wolff and **H.-J. Miesseler**
SICOM GmbH
Cologne, Germany

ABSTRACT

High performance glass fibre composite materials – until now nearly exclusively used in the field of aerospace or car industry – are now also applied in the construction industry. The choice of different kinds of fibres, such as carbon, glass or aramid fibres, and of different kinds of resins, e.g. polyester, epoxy or vinyl, offers the possibility to produce fibre composite materials for a large range of applications. Glass fibre composite materials – especially used in the construction industry as prestressing elements, distinguish themselves by their tensile strength which is equal or higher than that of high tensile steel. They have a high elasticity, an excellent corrosion resistance and there is the possibility to integrate optical fibre sensors for a permanent monitoring of fibre composite materials and the concrete structures themselves.

RÉSUMÉ

Les matériaux composites en fibres de verre, jusqu'à présent presque uniquement utilisés dans le domaine des industries aéronautiques et automobiles, sont utilisés aujourd'hui également dans l'industrie de la construction. En choisissant des fibres différentes comme des fibres de carbon, de verre et d'aramide, et des résines différentes comme celles de polyester, d'époxy ou de vinyle, il est possible de produire des matériaux composites pour des applications très diverses. Les fibres de verre utilisées dans l'industrie de la construction – surtout comme éléments de précontrainte – sont caractérisées par une résistance au moins égale à celle des aciers précontraints. Elles ont une élasticité très élevée et sont très résistantes à la corrosion. En outre, il est possible d'y intégrer des fibres optiques afin de surveiller les structures composites d'une manière permanente.

INTRODUCTION

Work is being done to continue to develop fiber composite materials into an intelligent high-tech product with tensile strength and media resistance.

The first construction concerning the development of a prestressing system on the basis of glass fiber composite materials was the Bridge Ulenbergstrasse in Düsseldorf. It was the first bridge world-wide for heavy road traffic, which was prestressed with glass fiber prestressing elements. In the meantime other bidges, for example the Bridge Berlin-Marienfelde - the first bridge with external prestressing without bond - , the Bridge Schiessbergstrasse in Leverkusen and the Bridge Nötsch in Kärnten (Austria) were prestressed with glass fiber composite material in combination with a permanent monitoring system based on optical fiber sensors.

The combination of fiber composite prestressing elements and sensor technology for permanent monitoring of structural elements is the future of modern construction technology

THE PRESTRESSING TENDON

The fundamental appropriateness of glass fiber tendons as material in the field of structural engineering has already been proved by Prof. Rehm , Technical University of Stuttgart, in fundamental research studies. Glass fiber bars are not suitable as ordinary reinforcement in concrete due to their low modulus of elasticity, however they are a potentially interesting alternative to prestressing steel, particularly for concrete structures endangered by corrosion, such as bridges.

The main differences between the glass fiber prestressing tendons (HLV-tendons) in comparison to prestressing steel are:

- The modulus of elasticity for HLV-tendons amounts at 51.000 N/mm² to only one fourth of that of steel prestressing tendons. Tension force losses from creep and shrinkage of the concrete are reduced correspondingly to one-fourth of the initial value
- The prestressing tendons show linear stress/strain behaviour until failure.
- The long-term strength amounts to 70 % of the short-term strength.
- The glass fiber composite material shows the same behaviour at high temperatures as prestressing steel.
- The low specific weight of 2.0 g/cm³ compared with 7.85 g/cm³ for prestressing steel.
- Electro-magnetic neutrality.
- Possibility to integrate sensors to create intelligent prestressing systems.

	Reinforcing steel BSt 500	Prestressing steel St 1470/1670	(R) Polystal (68% Glass-fibers)	Arapree (R) (Aramid-fibers)	Carbon fiber composite material
Tensile strength (N/mm²)	> 550	> 1670	1670	1610	1700
Yield strength (N/mm²)	> 500	> 1470	-	-	-
Ultimate strain (%)	10	6	3,3	2,5	1,1
Modulus of elasticity (N/mm²)	210.000	205.000	51.000	64.000	146.000
Specific weight (g/cm³)	7,85	7,85	2,0	1,3	1,5
Fields of application	Reinforced concrete structures	Prestressed structures			Stay cables, bracings

Table 1: Materialcharacteristics and -comparison

Being composite anisotropic material, these composite glass fiber materials only tolerate transverse pressure up to 10 % of their longitudinal tensile strength. For this reason, completely new solutions had to be found in the field of ancorage engineering. Thus, the absence of cold workability prevents the utilization of upset heads, rolled-on threads or even the utilization of steel wedges which "bite" directly into the "soft" composite glass fiber bar material.

The development of a tubular grouted anchor at SICOM is a breakthrough for the anchorage of high performance glass fiber composite tendons The composite tendon is grouted in a profiled steel tube with a synthetic resin specially developped for this purpose. The use of these grouted prestressing tendons covers the entire spectrum of prestressing tendons from 600 kN (up to 1000 kN working load) and the entire sphere of soil and rock anchoring. Their applications to date and the general approval given by the "Institut für Bautechnik" (Institute for Civil Engineering) in Berlin together with the expertises by Professor König, Rehm and Rostasy , show that this problem could be solved. The types of anchors developped up to the point of application maturity will be employed for the anchorage of prestressing tendons in prestressed concrete structures, and also for the airside anchorage with soil and rock anchors.

THE BUILDINGS

Bridge Schiessbergstrasse

Fig. 1: Schiessbergstrasse Bridge

The Bridge Schiessbergstrasse is a triple-span road bridge (load class 60/30) with span widths of 2 x 16.30 m and 20.40 m and a thickness of 1.10 m. The bridge is designed with limited prestressing comprising 27 glass fiber prestressing tendons (working load 600 kN) and post-bonding. Three glass fiber bars per tendon are provided with sensors and there are four additional optical fiber sensors integrated directly into the concrete on the upper and four on the lower side of the slab.

Bridge Nötsch in Kärnten, Austria

Fig.2: Nötsch Bridge

The Nötsch Bridge is the first bridge in Austria with glass fiber prestressing tendons. The triple-span road bridge (Bridge class I, Austrian Standard B 4002) with two spans widths of 13.00 m and one of 18.00 m and a slab thickness of 0.75 m, was furnished with limited prestressing comprising 41 glass fiber prestressing tendons, with post-bond.

The design of the bridges regarding the prestress did not show significant differences in comparison with conventional prestressing. An especially developped synthetic resin-mortar with low shrinkage features was used for the injection of the prestressing elements.
An one-off approval formed the basis of the execution of the bridges.

SENSOR TECHNOLOGY

In order to monitor buildings in a useful way it is necessary to develop appropriate sensors which are able to guarantee reliable measurements during a long period of time. Nowadays the intelligent processing of the high quantity of measured values is no problem due to the available and efficient personal computers.

The sensor technology is - regarding to the monitoring of buildings - only in the beginning of its development. The application of strain gauges on the prestressing steel or the measurement of the prestressing forces with the aid of load cells is not possible in case of prestressing with post-bond. Moreover it is not a durable solution in case of prestressing without bond.

Sensors for the monitoring of the prestressing elements and the stress/strain behaviour of the concrete

Only the application of fiber composite materials facilitates a permanent control of the prestressing element over its entire length due to the integration of copper wire sensors or optical fiber sensors. Even the monitoring of each individual bar is possible. The senors are already integrated into the tendon during its fabrication. The sensors indicate the integrity of the tendon or they locate the damage. In the Schießbergstraße bridge 3 tendons, each prestressing tendon comprising 19 individual bars, are equiped with copper wire sensors, in the Nötsch Bridge 3 bars of each prestressing element consisting of 19 bars are equiped with an optical fiber sensor and additionally as redundance with copper wire sensors.

Besides the monitoring of the prestressing elements the observation of the stress/strain behaviour of the concrete in the zone subject to tensile forces is very important. Therefore the tensile zone above the piers and the spans are monitored permanently with integrated optical fiber sensors with a accuracy of $\pm 0,15$ mm.

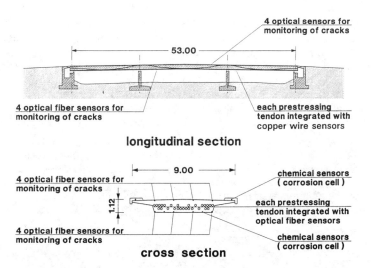

Fig. 3: Arrangement of the optical fiber sensors and chemical sensors
on the Schiessbergstrasse Bridge

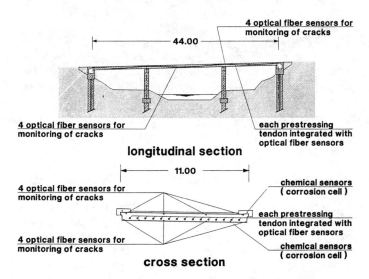

Fig. 4: Arrangement of the optical fiber sensors and chemical sensors
on the Nötsch Bridge Austria

Chemical sensors (Corrosion cell)

Due to the increase of enviromental damages (acid rain and de-icing salts) the influence of chemicals becomes bigger an bigger. For that reason the Institut für Bauforschung (Institute for construction research) in Aachen developped so-called corrosion cells. In the Schießbergstraße bridge in total 9 corrosion cells have been integrated into the superstructure and in the moulding cap. In the Bridge Nötsch in total 5 corrosion cells are integrated in the moulding cap. These cells indicate the progression of carbonation and an eventual penetration of chlorides. Here all parameters having a decisive influence on the chemical changes of the concrete and consequently on the reinforcing steel are measured.

Fig. 5: Chemical sensors for the bridge

Data processing

The measured values are processed by a personal computer in a measuring chamber with a special developped software.

A phone line from the measurement chamber to the office of the client allows an inquiry and a storage of the measured values. Comparing the measured values with the theoretical values it is possible to indicate immediately considerable divergences by so-called alert indications.

This automatic processing and control of all data which - important for all changes in the building structures - facilitates a significant reduction of the maintenance costs of the buildings. This permanent observation allows at any time to recognize changes in the building structures and to start at an early stage with countermeasures. It is known that the costs for maintenance can be reduced considerably when they are done in good time.

PROSPECTS

In the meantime the Schießbergstraße bridge and Nötsch bidge are the fourth and fifth bridge which have been prestressed with glass fiber tendons. Due to the numerous applications which already have been executed, it is now possible to manufacture the prestressing tendons in series which supersedes the manual way of production. Moreover an other rationalization of the manufacturing process will lead to the fact that glass fiber composite materials will have the same price as conventional prestressing elements comprising steel with a respective corrosion protection. But fiber composite materials have the great advantage that it is possible to monitor them over their entire length.

Also the "General Approval" which has been given in the meantime by the Institut für Bautechnik (Institute for Constructional Technique) in Berlin will lead to an international acceptance of this new prestressing method.

An other important characteristic for this buildings is the sensor conception for the data processing of all relevant datas. For the first time this conception offers the client a complete storage of measured values indicating very early the changes of the building so that it is possible for him to undertake the required maintenance steps.

REFERENCES

Miesseler, H.-J.; Preis, L.: High Performance Glass Fiber Composite Bars as Reinforcement in Concrete and Foundation Structures. Bauen mit Kunststoffe, Heft 2/1988, Seiten 4 - 14.

Miesseler, H.-J.; Lessing, R.: Experiences in monitoring of load bearing structures with optical fiber sensors. IABSE-Kongreß, Lissabon 1989.

Miesseler, H.-J.; Wolff, R.: Experience with the monitoring of structures using optical fiber sensors. FIP XIth International Congress on Prestressed Concrete, Hamburg, 4 - 9 Juni 1990.

Schiessl, P.; Raupach, M.: Chloridinduzierte Korrosion von Stahl in Beton. Betoninformation (1988), Nr.3/4, S. 33-45.

Schiessl, P.; Raupach, M.: Chloride-induced corrosion of steel in concrete-investigations with a concrete corrosion cell. Institute for Building Research, Technical University of Aachen, F.R. Germany. The life of structures 24 to 26 April 1989, Brigthon, England.

Wolff, R.; Miesseler, H.-J.: Prestressing tendons of glass fiber composite material in practical applications. "beton" 2\89 Pages 47-51.

Wolff, R.; Miesseler, H.-J.: Application and experience with intelligent prestressing systems based on fiber composite materials. FIP XIth International Congress on Prestressed Concrete, Hamburg, 4-9 Juni 1990.

ADVANCED COMPOSITE MATERIALS IN BRIDGES AND STRUCTURES
K.W. Neale and P. Labossière, Editors; Canadian Society for Civil Engineering, 1992

Matériaux composites d'avant-garde pour ponts et charpentes
K.W. Neale et P. Labossière, éditeurs; Société canadienne de génie civil, 1992

SPANNING 'DEVIL'S POOL' WITH A PRESTRESSED CABLE/ FRP TUBE STRUCTURAL SYSTEM

G.E. Johansen, R. Wilson, D.A. Pope
G. Goss, P. Ritchie and J. Mellen
E.T. Techtonics
Philadelphia, Pennsylvania, USA

ABSTRACT

The construction of three bridges of varying span lengths (6.1 m, 9.75 m, and 15.24 m) recently constructed in Fairmount Park, Philadelphia, PA, using a new lightweight composite structural system (PRESTEK) has been investigated in this study. The PRESTEK system is constructed of fibreglass reinforced plastic (FRP) tubes and kevlar or steel cables. It derives its unique structural properties by prestressing a beam-truss geometry. This case study will address the difficult problems posed by the inaccessibility of the site, the aesthetic issues in the development of the final design solution and the advantages derived in using the PRESTEK system in comparison to alternative structural systems.

RÉSUMÉ

La construction de trois ponts à Philadelphie, dont les portées varient de 6,1 à 15,24 m, et fabriqués d'un système structural en composites légers (PRESTEK), est décrite dans cet article. Le système PRESTEK comprend des tubes de FRP et des câbles de kevlar ou d'acier. Les propriétés structurales découlent de la prétension appliquée au système poutre-treillis. On discute ici des problèmes causés par l'inaccessibilité du site, de l'esthétique de la solution retenue, et des avantages du système PRESTEK en comparaison avec d'autres alternatives.

Photograph #1 - Proposed Site of the 3 Bridges

INTRODUCTION

In the fall of 1989, E.T. Techtonics was approached by the Friends of the Wissahickon (a volunteer group in Philadelphia involved in the maintenance and conservation of Fairmount Park) concerning the reconstruction of 3 bridges in the Devil's Pool area of Fairmount Park, Philadelphia, PA. A strong wind storm in the early 1970's had done major damage to the existing wooden bridges (constructed in the 1920's) in this area requiring the Park to remove the structures. This resulted in a major break in the foot trail. Due to the inaccessibility of the site, the cost of the reconstruction of the 3 bridges using conventional materials and construction techniques was estimated at over $100,000 excluding any additional site work. The Friends of the Wissahickon had an estimated budget of $35,000 which included completion of all necessary site work. Further complicating the project were the approvals required from the Fairmount Park Commission concerning the siting of the proposed bridges due to potential legal problems. Also, the overall design had to be approved by the Philadelphia Art Commission due to the aesthetic implications of the proposed project.

E.T. Techtonics was in the process of developing a new lightweight structural system (PRESTEK) constructed of fiberglass shapes and kevlar cables which had great potential to solve the above design problems (Johansen and Roll 1986-87, Johansen and Roll

1988, and Johansen and Roll 1989). The system achieved its unique strength/stiffness characteristics by prestressing a beam-truss configuration. Historically, kingpost, queenpost, and bowstring trusses were structural geometries typically found in this category. It is interesting to note that the wooden bridges previously on the site were kingpost type structures.

The initial design proposed 3 new fiberglass and kevlar cable bridges in the same locations as the previous 3 bridges, i.e., a 6.1 m (20'-0") span next to the Shakespeare Rock (left in Photograph #1), a 9.75 m (32'-0") span on the opposite side of Devil's Pool (right in Photograph #1) and a 15.24 m (50'-0") span over Devil's Pool (tape measure line in Photograph #1). The proposed design was as follows: 6.1 m span - kingpost truss, 9.75 m span - queenpost truss, and 15.24 m truss - bowstring truss. E.T. Techtonics had successfully constructed bridges up to 9.14 m (30'-0") at that time, but needed further testing to determine the characteristics of the bowstring truss as well as the structural problems of a lightweight 15.24 m span of this nature. After much debate concerning liability issues approval was received from the Fairmount Park Commission for the proposed project in May 1990. The project received preliminary approval from the Art Commission in June 1990 based on submission of final handrail details and choice of color for the beams and cables.

DESCRIPTION OF TEST STRUCTURES

A 12.19 m (40'-0") span bowstring truss test structure was constructed at the University of Pennsylvania in August 1990 to determine the feasibility of the proposed main bridge span. The structure consisted of the following components, 50.8 mm x 152.4 mm x 3.2 mm FRP beams, 50.8 mm x 50.8 mm x 6.4 mm FRP posts, 9.5 mm FRP plates, pressure treated wood decking, 19 mm A307 steel bolts, and 15.9 mm kevlar 149 cables (Creative Pultrusions 1987, United Ropeworks 1987, and Dupont 1986). It was estimated that the structure weighed approximately 6.7 kN. The structure was loaded with 30 people, but was found to be too flexible for the proposed use. It was determined that bracing should be added to the system to stiffen the structure.

Connection plates were redesigned and fabricated with the 8 50.8 mm x 50.8 mm x 6.4 mm braces that were added to the system. The modified structure was erected in October 1990 to determine the new characteristics of the system. The structure's stiffness was significantly improved, but the visual "lightness" of the previous design was dramatically compromised (Johansen and Roll 1990 and Johansen and Roll 1991). E.T. Techtonics was not satisfied with the visual quality of the proposed structure therefore a new design for the main span was required. At this time it was decided that the 6.1 m bridge should be erected on the site as soon as possible to determine possible construction problems as well as vandalism problems while redesign was progressing.

437

Photograph #2 - 6.1 m (20'-0") Span Bridge

6.1 m SPAN BRIDGE AT THE SHAKESPEARE ROCK

On March 31, 1991, the 6.1 m (20'-0") span bridge was constructed at Devil's Pool. Total erection time including carrying the components to the site (approximately 1.3 km) was 3 hours. The beam-truss geometry chosen for the first bridge was a kingpost truss. The bridge was constructed from the following components: 50.8 mm x 152.4 mm x 3.2 mm beams, 3.2 mm x 3.2 mm x 6.4 mm posts and handrail, pressure treated wood decking, 19 mm dia. A307 galvanized steel bolts and 9.5 mm steel cable. It was decided by the client to replace kevlar cable with steel cable due to the potential vandalism problem. Total weight of the bridge was approximately 3.6 kN (800 lbs.).

The bridge performed well during the 6 month trial test. Its estimated use was approximately 300 people each day during the spring and summer months. The only apparent problem during this period was the recurrence of graffiti on the bridge. This was easily removed by wiping the beams and handrails with acetone which completely removed marker and paint from the FRP surfaces.

Photograph #3 - 9.75 m (32'-0") Span Bridge

9.75 m SPAN BRIDGE ON LIVEZEY LANE SIDE

On November 3, 1991, the 9.75 m (32'-0") span bridge was erected on the Livezey Lane side of Devil's Pool. Construction time including carrying the components to the site (approximately 1 km) was 4 hours. As shown in the photograph, the site was much more inaccessible than that of the first bridge. Bridge #2 was constructed from the same components as Bridge #1 except the steel cable was 15.9 mm diameter. The beam-truss geometry used on this bridge was a queenpost configuration. Due to the difficulties in saw cutting the existing rock ledge at the north end of the bridge, it was necessary to use different length queenpost trusses to clear the rock. Total weight of the bridge was estimated at 5.8 kN (1300 lbs.).

Bridge #2 has performed well to date. Graffiti has also been a problem even though the structure is somewhat more isolated than Bridge #1. Estimated usage is approximately 200 people per day during the spring and summer months.

Photograph #4 - 15.24 m (50'-0") Span Bridge

15.24 M (50'-0") SPAN BRIDGE CONSTRUCTED OVER CRESHEIM CREEK

On June 13, 1992, the 15.24 m (50'-0") span bridge was constructed over Cresheim Creek near Devil's Pool. 15.24 m FRP beams (see Photograph #5), weighing approximately .4 kN (90 lbs.) each, were carried approximately 1.3 km to the site over an access trail and a foot path. Wood decking, FRP handrail, steel cable assemblies, and bolts were driven down the access trail in a small pickup truck to the foot path where they were unloaded and then carried to the site. This operation was completed in approximately 2-1/2 hours.

Construction of the bridge was begun with the connection of the 15.24 m beams to the foundations. Temporary wood supports were used to facilitate erection of the wood deck, handrail and cable assemblies (see Photograph #6). Construction time was estimated at approximately 4 hours after components arrived on the site.

Bridge #3 was constructed from the same components as Bridge #2. The beam-truss geometry used on this bridge was a combined queenpost and kingpost configuration. This provided increased strength and stiffness for the long span structure as well as relating to the aesthetic nature of the other two bridges. Total weight of the bridge was estimated at 11 kN (2500 lbs.).

Photograph #5 - 15.24 m (50'-0") FRP Main Members

Photograph #6 - Bridge #3 Under Construction

Saw cutting of the existing rock ledge was necessary on the north side of the bridge before pouring of the concrete pad. The foundation on the south side was sited on the river bank on a sand and clay type soil. Due to the difficulty in carrying heavy materials to the site, it was decided to use FRP as part of the substructure.

Bridge #3 was subjected to a heavy load test the following week after construction of the structure. U.S. Senator Harris Wofford (Pennsylvania) led a clean-up day in the Devil's Pool area of Fairmount Park. Approximately 200 people participated in the event. The Senator held a press conference at the bridge. It was estimated that over 60 people were on the bridge at one time (see Photographs #7 and #8). The structure performed well during this loading condition. Estimated usage per day is approximately 300 people per day during the spring and summer months.

CONCLUSIONS

The above case study demonstrates the feasibility of constructing long span FRP/steel cable pedestrian bridges on difficult sites. The unique strength/stiffness characteristics of the PRESTEK System combined with its lightweight nature provide distinct advantages over traditional construction systems in wood, concrete or steel. Besides being easier to erect, PRESTEK is aesthetically pleasing as well as low maintenance. It is particularly cost effective in those applications which have difficult site constraints.

This investigation is limited to span lengths up to 15.24 m (50'-0"). Based on laboratory tests, computer analysis, and field observations, it is believed that pedestrian bridges up to 23 m (approximately 75'-0") can be constructed with the same components. A structure of this type would weight approximately 18kN (4000 lbs.).

ACKNOWLEDGEMENTS

This investigation is based on the work of Robert LeRicolais, a pioneer in the development of minimum weight/volume structural configurations. The authors also express their thanks to Dr. Frederic Roll, Ben Derosa, Kevin Driscoll, Varisara Gerjarusak, Donna Sanker, Diana Torelli, Steve Butler, Ken Marran, Don Sleeth, Erik Graber, Glen Engle, and Frank Brown for their help in the successful completion of the above project.

Photograph #7 - Bridge #3 Subjected to Heavy Pedestrian Loading

Photograph #8 - U.S. Senator (Pennsylvania) Harris Wofford and
State Senator (Pennsylvania) Allyson Schwartz
Inspecting Bridge #3 During Clean-up Day

443

REFERENCES

1.   "Minimizing Weight and Maintenance by Using a Prestressed Kevlar Structural System," Johansen, G. Eric, and Roll, Dr. Frederic, Pennsylvania's Ben Franklin Partnership Seed Grant Program Phase I, 1986-87.

2.   "A Prestressed Kevlar Stiffening System: A new Approach to Rehabilitation of Large Structures," Johansen, G. Eric, and Roll, Dr. Frederic, National Science Foundation SBIR Program Phase Report, 1988.

3.   "A Prestressed Kevlar/E-glass Structural System: Lightweight, Maintenance-free and Adjustable," Johansen, G. Eric, and Roll, Dr. Frederic, National Science Foundation SBIR Program Phase I Report, 1989.

4.   "A Prestressed Kevlar/FRP Structural System," Proceedings of the First Materials Engineering Congress, ASCE, 1990, Johansen, G. Eric, and Roll, Dr. Frederic, pp. 640-48.

5.   "A Prestressed Kevlar/FRP Structural System: Effects of Cable, Post and Main Member Stiffness," The Specialty Conference on Advanced Composites in Civil Engineering Structures, ASCE, 1991, Johansen, G. Eric, and Roll, Dr. Frederic, pp. 383-393.

6.   Creative Pultrusion Design Guide, CPI, 1987.

7.   Phillystran Data Manual, United Ropeworks, 1987.

8.   Data Manual for Kevlar 49 Aramid, Du Pont, 1986.

ADVANCED COMPOSITE MATERIALS IN BRIDGES AND STRUCTURES
K.W. Neale and P. Labossière, Editors; Canadian Society for Civil Engineering, 1992

Matériaux composites d'avant-garde pour ponts et charpentes
K.W. Neale et P. Labossière, éditeurs; Société canadienne de génie civil, 1992

CREEP RELAXATION CHARACTERISTICS OF A PRESTRESSED KEVLAR CABLE/FRP TUBE STRUCTURAL SYSTEM

M.-A. Erki
Royal Military College of Canada
Kingston, Ontario, Canada

G.E. Johansen, F. Roll, K. Marran and **D. Sleeth**
E.T. Techtonics
Philadelphia, Pennsylvania, USA

ABSTRACT

The time-dependent characteristics of a new lightweight composite structural system have been investigated experimentally in this study. The proposed system is constructed of fibreglass reinforced plastic (FRP) tubes and either kevlar 49 or 149 cable. It derives its unique structural properties by prestressing a beam-truss geometry. Research conducted in this study has evaluated the time-dependent characteristics of the structural system under laboratory conditions (relatively constant temperature conditions) and the outside environment in Kingston (fluctuating temperature conditions).

RÉSUMÉ

Le comportement d'un système structural faisant usage de matériaux composites a fait l'objet de cette étude. Ce système est constitué de tubes de FRP et de câbles, en kevlar 49 ou 149. Ses propriétés découlent de l'application de la précontrainte au système. On a évalué le comportement à long terme du système structural en laboratoire (à température à peu près constante) et sous les conditions climatiques extérieures de Kingston.

Series

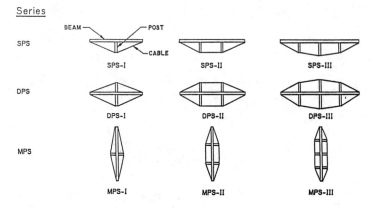

Fig. 1 PRESTEK System

INTRODUCTION

There has been an increasing demand for fiberglass reinforced plastic (FRP) structural components for use in special construction applications such as corrosive environments and non-magnetic and electrically non-conductive environments. These components, usually constructed of E-glass and either polyester or vinylester resins, provide distinct advantages over traditional steel and concrete members.

While improvements in the pultrusion process have dramatically lowered fabrication costs of FRP components, thereby making these members cost competitive in certain situations with traditional materials, for most building applications, FRP structural systems are not economical. This has been attributed to problems such as time dependent behavior. FRP material exhibits creep and relaxation under sustained loading conditions and changes in temperature, therefore FRP components must be designed for lower allowable stresses to minimize the time dependent effects.

Since 1985, E.T. Techtonics has been involved in the research and development of a prestressed kevlar cable/FRP tube structural system (PRESTEK) which has great potential to solve the above problems, while being cost competitive with traditional materials (Johansen and Roll, 1986; Johansen and Roll, 1988; Johansen and Roll, 1989; Johansen and Roll, 1990; Johansen and Roll, 1991). PRESTEK achieves its unique lightweight, high strength and high stiffness characteristics by prestressing a class of structural forms known as beam-trusses. Figure 1 shows the different configurations of the PRESTEK system. In this paper, the time dependent characteristics of the PRESTEK System under laboratory conditions versus the outside environment are investigated.

446

Photograph #1 - DPS II Under Sustained Load Condition

INVESTIGATION OF TIME DEPENDENT CHARACTERISTICS

In this research program, full-scale model testing was conducted on the SPS and DPS Series of the PRESTEK System. This paper will evaluate the test results from two of these tests; a laboratory test presently being conducted on a double queenpost (DPS-II) type at the University of Pennsylvania in Philadelphia, PA (see Photograph #1) and an outside environment test being run on a double bowstring (DPS-III) type at the Royal Military College in Kingston, Ontario Canada. Initial model tests were conducted at the ATLSS Center at Lehigh University by Phil Ritchie, a graduate student in Civil Engineering under the supervision of Dr. David A. Thomas, Professor of Materials Science and Engineering and Dr. Le-Wu Lu, Professor of Civil Engineering. Also assisting on the project was Guy M. Connelly, a materials specialist.

Description of Laboratory and Outdoor Structural Models

Both the laboratory and outdoor full-scale models consisted of pultruded FRP (E-glass/isophthalic polyester resin) 50.8 mm x 152.4 mm x 3.2 mm (2 in x 6 in x 1/8 in) FRP main beams, 50.8 mm x 50.8 mm x 6.4 mm (2 in x 2 in x 1/4 in) FRP posts, 9.5 mm (3/8 in) FRP plates, pressure treated wood decking, 19 mm (3/4 in) FRP bolts, and 15.9 mm (5/8 in) diameter kevlar 149 cables (Du Pont, 1986). The DPS-II (double queenpost) laboratory model had a nominal 9.14 m (30 ft) overall length. The DPS-III (double bowstring) outdoor model had a nominal 12.2 m (40 ft.) overall length. The FRP components were produced by Creative Pultrusions Inc., Alumbank, PA. (Creative Pultrusions, 1987), and the kevlar cables were supplied by United Ropeworks, Inc., Montgomeryville, PA (United Ropeworks, 1987).

Instrumentation of the DPS-II model was as follows; top and bottom strain gages (Micro-Measurement type CEA-06-500UW-350) on the main members at midspan, deflection gages on the main member at midspan and the quarter points, and load cells at the end of each cable assembly. The DPS-III model had the same instrumentation, except that no deflection gages were used. The DPS-II model was supported on concrete blocks at each end, whereas the DPS-III model was supported on timber sawhorses.

Description of Testing Procedures

The DPS-II laboratory model was initially prestressed to approximately 15.1 kN (3400 lbs) in the bottom cable and 13.8 kN (3100 lbs) in the top cable, with a 63.5 mm (2.5 in) camber in the system. The simply supported structure was then loaded with approximately 11 kN (2500 lbs) of sustained load applied uniformly throughout the system, resulting in approximately 0.58 N/m (40 lbs/ft). An initial set of readings from strain gages, deflection gages, and load cells was taken without any load on the test structure. A second set of readings was taken immediately after the models were prestressed. A third set of readings was taken after the loads were applied. Several readings per day were taken during the first week, a minimum of one reading per day for the next 3 months, and a minimum of 3 readings per week for the remaining test period. At the time of writing, the laboratory test had been conducted for approximately 10,000 hours.

The DPS-III outdoor model was initially prestressed to approximately 11.1 kN (2488 lbs) in the bottom cable and 7.7 kN (1729 lbs) in the top cable. The prestressing was conducted at an ambient temperature of approximately 5°C (41°F). The camber of the system was not recorded. The model was orientated in the East-West direction, such that the entire length of one of the main members had a southerly exposure, and the other a northerly exposure. This orientation had an influence on the observed response of the structure. The DPS-III model remained unloaded for the duration of the test. Readings were taken daily for the first 3,000 hours of testing. Thereafter readings were taken twice a week. At the time of writing, the test had been conducted for almost 6,000 hours.

Experimental Results of the Laboratory Model

The top and bottom cables of the DPS-II laboratory model were initially prestressed at different levels, namely 13.8 kN (3400 lbs) and 15.1 kN (3100 lbs), respectively, to introduce a camber of 63.5 mm (2.5 in) to the system. Under an applied load of approximately 11 kN (2500 lbs), the system deflected 10.77 mm (0.424 in) from the initial camber point leaving approximately 52 mm (2.08 in) of camber in the structure with a top cable tension of 9.4 kN (2125 lbs), bottom cable tension of 19.2 kN (4325 lbs) and main member midspan strains of -245 μmm/mm (μin/in) at the top and -1194 μmm/mm (μin/in) at the bottom. Initial main member midspan stresses were determined to be 6.34 MPa (919 psi) compression at the top and 30.87 MPa (4478 psi) compression at the bottom. This was based on an initial modulus of elasticity of the 50.8 mm x 152.4 mm x 3.2 mm (2 in x 6 in x 1/8 in) FRP tube of 24.132×10^3 MPa (3,500 ksi).

The DPS-II structure exhibited some creep and relaxation during the first 5,000 hours of the test, but after this initial behavior it showed little change except that due to temperature variations in the laboratory environment. After 10,000 hours, the system had deflected an additional 5.99 mm (.236 in) leaving a camber of approximately 46.7 mm (1.84 in) in the structure, as shown in Fig. 2. The top cable tension had decreased to 5.2 kN (1200 lbs), which is a relaxation loss of 4.2 kN (925 lbs). The bottom cable tension had decreased to 16 kN (3600 lbs.) which is a relaxation loss of 3.2 kN (725 lbs), as shown in Fig. 3. Main member midspan strains had decreased to -59 (top) and -947 (bottom), indicating a decrease in overall stress level. Approximately 67% of the creep behavior and 40% of the relaxation losses occurred in the first week. The description of an equation which fits the data in Fig. 2 is given later in this paper.

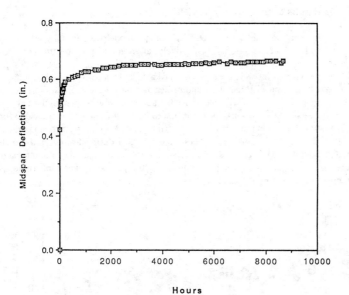

Fig. 2 Midspan Deflection of the DPS-II Laboratory Model

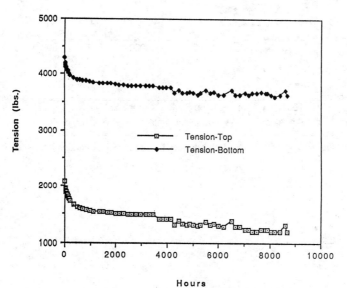

Fig. 3 Top and Bottom Cable Tensions in the DPS-II Laboratory Model

449

Experimental Results of the Outdoor Model

The top and bottom cables of the DPS-III outdoor model were initially prestressed at 7.7 kN (1729 lbs) and 11.1 kN (2488 lbs), respectively, at an ambient temperature of 5°C (41°F). The temperature influenced the stresses in the structure, because, for FRP the sign of the coefficient of thermal expansion is positive and for kevlar it is negative, which results in greater decreases of stresses in the FRP members and cables as temperature drops and greater increases in stresses as temperature rises. Temperature variations combined with inherent creep and relaxation of the model to give, what appear at first to be erratic, changes in the cable forces and main member strains, as shown in Figs. 4 and 5. Ambient and bridge surface temperature of the south facing and north facing main members were recorded during testing, and are shown as broken and solid lines on Figs. 4 and 5. It should be noted that the ambient and bridge temperatures are the same up until approximately 1,300 hours, after which instrumentation for surface temperature monitoring was installed.

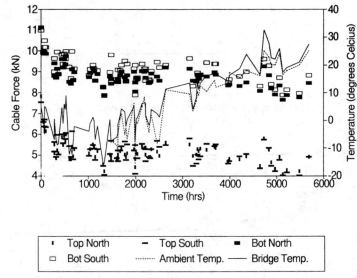

Fig. 4 Top and Bottom Cable Forces for the DPS-III Outdoor Model

450

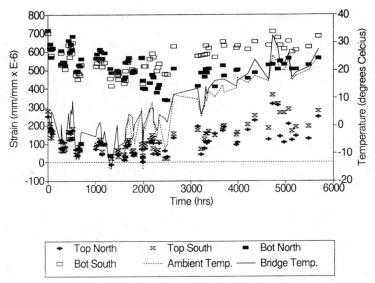

Fig. 5 South Facing and North Facing Top and Bottom Main Member Strains

On sunny days, readings of the instrumentation were generally taken at dusk when the difference in temperature between the south facing and north facing main members would be at a minimum. However, the average surface temperature difference between these members on sunny days was generally three to four degrees. The maximum difference in surface temperature readings was 6.25°C, at 1,992 hours, which corresponded to the coldest ambient temperature reading recorded during the first 6,000 hours of testing, namely -15.7°C (3.74°F). This resulted in a difference between the forces carried by the south facing and north facing top cables of 681 N (153 lbs). That is to say that the north facing top cable had 12% less load than the south facing top cable. Similarly, the forces carried by the south facing bottom cable and north facing bottom cable differed by 831 N (187 lbs), which was an 9% decrease in load carried by the north facing bottom cable. Also, compared to initial prestressing levels, the load carried by the top cables had decreased to 5.151 kN (1,158 lbs), a drop of 33%, and the load carried by the bottom cables had decreased to 8.9 kN (2,001 lbs), a drop of 20%. The portion of these drastic losses attributable to the temperature drop were recovered when the temperature subsequently increased. The difficulty in interpreting the outdoor test results arises, because the influence of temperature fluctuations compared to those of creep and relaxation are not readily apparent. A mathematical model is developed in the next section with a view to separating these factors in the results.

Referring to Fig. 5, the initial main member midspan strains were -729 μmm/mm (μin/in) at the top and -1042 μmm/mm (μin/in) at the bottom. Initial main member midspan stresses were calculated to be 17.59 MPa (2.55 ksi) compression at the top and 25.15 MPa (3.65 ksi) compression at the bottom. This was based on an initial modulus of elasticity of the 50.8 mm x 152.4 mm x 3.2 mm (2 in x 6 in x 1/8 in) FRP tube of 24.132×10^3 MPa (3,500 ksi). Further observations of the DPS-III outdoor model will be made in the following section, which describes an equation for the creep and relaxation of the DPS-II and DPS-III models.

Creep and Relaxation Equation for the DPS-II and DPS-III Test Results

Figures 2 and 4 show the losses in cable tensions for the DPS-II and DPS-III models. The creep and relaxation behavior in Fig. 4 is difficult to interpret, because of the fluctuations in stresses due to temperature variations. However, an estimate of the creep and relaxation behavior may be attempted by fitting the following equation to each of the curves in Fig. 2.

$$p = (a+bt)(e^{(-tc/a)}-1)+p_o \tag{1}$$

where c is the initial slope of the tangent to the curve at time $t=0$, b is the
slope of the linear portion of the curve after $t \approx 1,000\ hours$, a is the numerical difference between the intercept of this line with the vertical axis and the initial value of the tension load p_o at $t=0$, and p is the tension load. From Fig. 2, for the tension in the top cables, the values of these constants are

$$c = 14.19\ N/hr\ (3.19\ lbs/hr) \quad b = 0.17\ N/hr\ (0.037\ lbs/hr)$$
$$a = 2.4\ N\ (550\ lbs)$$

For the tension in the bottom cables the values are the same except that

$$a = 2.0\ N\ (440\ lbs)$$

These equations for the tension load in the top and bottom cable of the DPS-II laboratory model are plotted on the graph of the cable forces for the DPS-III outdoor model, with the only change that p_o is equal to the initial tension load of the cables in the DPS-III test. The result is shown in Fig. 6.

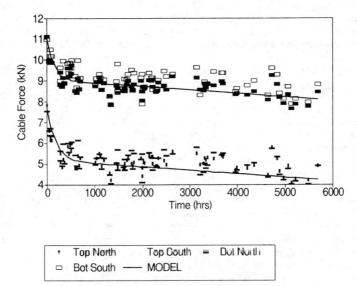

Fig. 6 Superposition of the Creep and Relaxation Curves of the DPS-II Model onto the DPS-II Model Results

Although the DPS-II and DPS-III models differ in geometry and loading conditions, which would result in different creep and relaxation behaviors, the models are sufficiently similar such that the trends in creep and relaxation behavior seem to be well predicted in Fig. 6. It would be expected that cable forces would fall below the creep and relaxation curve when the temperature fell below the initial temperature of 5° (41°F) at which the structure was prestressed, and would be above the curve when the temperature was higher than the initial temperature at prestressing. Comparing Fig. 6 with Fig. 4 confirms this observation. After 2,500 hours, when temperatures were consistently above 5° (41°F), the cable forces are mostly above the predicted curve. Work is underway to quantify the constants of Eq. (1) with respect to geometry and loading to permit prediction of the general creep and relaxation behavior of the PRESTEK Systems.

CONCLUSIONS

Two prestressed kevlar cable/FRP tube structural systems were investigated to determine their time dependent characteristics. The DPS-II model was tested in a laboratory environment, and the DPS-III model was tested in an outdoor environment. For the DPS-II model, approximately 67% of the creep behavior and 40% of the relaxation losses occurred in the first week. The outdoor environment did not appear to adversely affect the creep and relaxation behavior of the DPS-III model. Variations in cable forces due to temperature fluctuations were transitory, and may be considered negligible with respect to the overall time dependent behavior of the system. In fact, the time dependent behavior of the DPS-II and the DPS-III models appeared to be virtually identical.

ACKNOWLEDGEMENTS

This investigation is based on the work of Robert LeRicolais, a pioneer in the development of minimum weight/volume structural configurations. The authors also express their thanks to Diana Torelli, Steve Butler, Mark Lefkon, and Frank Brown for their help in the successful completion of the above project.

REFERENCES

Johansen, G. Eric, and Roll, Dr. Frederic (1986). *Minimizing Weight and Maintenance by Using a Prestressed Kevlar Structural System*. Pennsylvania's Ben Franklin Partnership Seed Grant Program Phase I, 1986-87.

Johansen, G. Eric, and Roll, Dr. Frederic (1988). *A Prestressed Kevlar Stiffening System: A New Approach to Rehabilitation of Large Structures*. National Science Foundation SBIR Program Phase Report.

Johansen, G. Eric, and Roll, Dr. Frederic (1989). *A Prestressed Kevlar/E-glass Structural System: Lightweight, Maintenance-free and Adjustable*. National Science Foundation SBIR Program Phase I Report.

Johansen, G. Eric, and Roll, Dr. Frederic (1990). *A Prestressed Kevlar/FRP Structural System*. Proceedings of the First Materials Engineering Congress, ASCE. pp. 640-48.

Johansen, G. Eric, and Roll, Dr. Frederic (1991). *A Prestressed Kevlar/FRP Structural System: Effects of Cable, Post and Main Member Stiffness*. The Specialty Conference on Advanced Composites in Civil Engineering Structures, ASCE. pp. 383-393.

Creative Pultrusions (1987). *Design Guide, CPI*.

United Ropeworks (1987). *Phillystran Data Manual*.

Du Pont (1986). *Data Manual for Kevlar 49 Aramid*.

454

ADVANCED COMPOSITE MATERIALS IN BRIDGES AND STRUCTURES
K.W. Neale and P. Labossière, Editors; Canadian Society for Civil Engineering, 1992

Matériaux composites d'avant-garde pour ponts et charpentes
K.W. Neale et P. Labossière, éditeurs; Société canadienne de génie civil, 1992

GLULAM-GFRP COMPOSITE BEAMS FOR STRESS-LAMINATED T-SYSTEM BRIDGES

J.F. Davalos, H.A. Salim and **U. Munipalle**
West Virginia University
Morgantown, West Virginia, USA

ABSTRACT

Based on interface bond shear strength, a resorcinol formaldehyde wood adhesive is identified as satisfactory to bond E-glass-polyester/vinylester pultruded composites to yellow poplar wood. The modeling of Glulam-GFRP beams is discussed, and the response predictions are correlated with experimental results. The analysis and design of T-system bridges with Glulam-GFRP stringers is discussed and examples are presented.

RÉSUMÉ

En se basant sur l'adhérence de l'interface, un adhésif resorcinol formaldehyde pour le bois est jugé satisfaisant pour lier des composites pultrudés de verre-E-polyester/vinylester à du bois de peuplier jaune. La modélisation des poutres de Glulam-GFRP est discutée, et les prédictions de comportement sont comparées avec des résultats expérimentaux. L'analyse et le dimensionnement de ponts 'Système-T' avec des sections en Glulam-GFRP sont discutés, et des exemples sont présentés.

INTRODUCTION

Stress-laminated timber decks were developed in Canada for rehabilitation of nail-laminated timber bridges (Taylor and Csagoli 1979, Taylor et al. 1983). In the United States, a national timber bridge initiative program funded by Congress in 1989 fostered research, development, and construction of demonstration stress-laminated timber bridges. Under this program, which includes 41 states, approximately 130 bridges were constructed by the end of 1991 (Crist 1990). In West Virginia, 46 of these bridges will be constructed by 1992, following design specifications developed at the Constructed Facilities Center (CFC) of West Virginia University (WVU). The designs will include at least 16 T-system bridges.

Stress-laminated T-system bridges consist of laminated timber deck sections and glued-laminated timber (Glulam) beams post-tensioned transversely by high-strength steel bars that pass through holes predrilled on the wide-face of the deck and beam components. The Glulam stringers used in these systems offer several advantages: light weight, economical production of curved members, excellent energy absorption characteristics (seismic, damping, and acoustical responses), high chemical and corrosion resistance, and better fire resistance than steel. One disadvantage of Glulam is its relatively low stiffness and strength. For this reason, the construction of large-span T-system timber bridges [18.3 to 30.5 m (60 to 100 ft)] require Glulam members of large depths [122 to 152 cm (48 to 60 inches)]. To significantly increase the stiffness and strength of Glulam, the members can be reinforced with pultruded E-glass fiber-reinforced Polyester or Vinylester plastics (GFRP). The GFRP reinforcement reduces the required depth of a glulam member, which in turn reduces its weight, and the necessity of bracing the member to prevent lateral buckling. However, to promote the use of Glulam-GFRP in bridge construction, the following three fundamental issues must be addressed: (1) identification of a commercially available wood adhesive that can develop an adequate bond between wood and GFRP under exposed environments; (2) development of practical, computationally feasible, and sufficiently accurate models to predict the response of Glulam-GFRP beams; and (3) development of simple design procedures for bridges using Glulam-GFRP stringers.

In this paper we present an experimental program which identifies a modified resorcinol formaldehyde adhesive as satisfactory for providing bond strength between yellow-poplar wood and E-glass-polyester/vinylester pultruded composites. Subsequently, we briefly discuss the modeling of composite Glulam-GFRP beams, and the prediction equations are correlated with limited experimental results for yellow-poplar Glulam beams reinforced with pultruded GFRP. The ultimate goal is to develop tabulated design properties for standard Glulam-GFRP combinations approved by the American Institute of Timber Construction. This paper also discusses briefly the analysis and design of stress-laminated T-system bridges with Glulam-GFRP stringers. The analysis methods include an orthotropic finite element (FE) modeling accounting for shear effects, a Macro-Approach analytical solution (GangaRao 1975), and the simplified WVU design method, which reduces the problem to a "T-beam" section by defining an effective flange-width through a parametric FE study. The paper presents a summary of design examples for two-lane bridges of three span-lengths, which demonstrate the advantages of using GFRP reinforcement for the stringers.

456

COMMERCIAL ADHESIVES FOR WOOD-GFRP BONDING

The bond shear strength of the adhesive interface of yellow poplar (*Liriodendron tulipifera*) wood and pultruded E-glass fiber-reinforced polyester/vinylester composite samples were experimentally evaluated. A screening of possible commercial adhesive types identified the following three: resorcinol-formaldehyde (RF), cross-linked polyvinyl acetate (PVA) emulsion, and epoxy. The RF and PVA adhesives have been used to bond wood/wood and wood/plastic, respectively, and the epoxy is used to bond pultruded composites. The three adhesive types were used to bond wood-wood, wood-composite, and composite-composite samples. The wood samples included sapwood and heartwood. The shear-test specimens were prepared following ASTM D-905 specifications. Twenty replications were used for each test, with a total of 600 specimens. Dry and vacuum-pressure-soak samples were tested for each adhesive and materials combination (e.g., RF adhesive for heartwood to composite). The dry bond shear strengths were evaluated from compression loading tests (ASTM D 905); the vacuum-pressure-soak bond shear strengths were evaluated by saturating the samples with water (ASTM D1101) and testing them in shear (ASTM D905); the integrity of the bond interface was established from 5-cycle vacuum-pressure-soak tests (ASTM D1101). The comparative bond shear strength mean values of the wood-wood and wood-vinylester samples for the three adhesives are shown in Fig. 1. Based on a minimum allowable bond shear strength of 7.4 MPa for dry wood samples (AITC 1987), the RF adhesive provided adequate dry bond strength for wood-polyester/vinylester samples (Fig. 2). Similarly, based on the solid wood shear strength of 5.4 MPa for wet yellow poplar (Wood Handbook 1987), the RF adhesive provided adequate wet bond strength for wood-polyester samples (Fig.2). The wet bond strength of the wood-vinylester samples are below the wet solid wood strength; however, to use the wet solid wood strength for this comparison is too conservative.

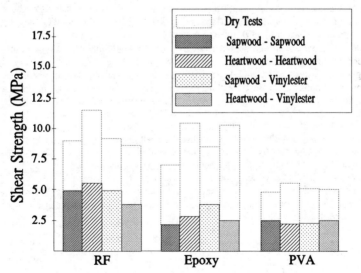

Fig. 1. Comparative bond shear strength mean values

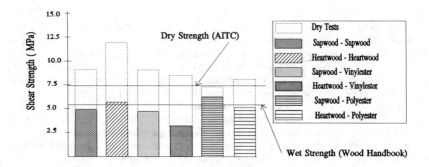

Fig. 2. Shear Strength With RF

MODELING OF GLULAM-GFRP BEAMS

Wood is often modeled as an orthotropic material. A practical and valid approach is to model Glulam beams as transversely isotropic (Davalos et al. 1991). Similarly, pultruded composite members of rectangular cross sections with uniformly distributed fibers can be modeled as transversely isotropic. Based on lamination beam theory (LBT), which includes shear deformation (Barbero 1990), the expressions for the axial (A), bending with respect to the neutral axis (D), and shear (F) stiffnesses of transversely isotropic laminated composite beams are (Davalos and Barbero 1991):

$$A - b\sum_{i-1}^{n} E_i t_i \quad ; \quad D - b\sum_{i-1}^{n} E_i\left(t_i \bar{y}_i^2 + \frac{t_i^3}{12}\right) \quad ; \quad F - \frac{1}{\kappa} b\sum_{i-1}^{n} G_i t_i \tag{1}$$

where, E_i and G_i are the elastic and shear moduli of the laminae; b, t_i, and y_i are the geometric constants shown in Fig. 3; and κ is the shear correction factor. Using Eqs. (1), the normal stress at a layer i^{th} and shear stress at an interface k^{th} can be computed as

$$\sigma_i - \frac{MyE_i}{D} + \frac{NE_i}{A} \tag{2}$$

$$\tau^k - \frac{V}{D}\sum_{i-k}^{n} t_i \bar{y}_i E_i \tag{3}$$

where, M is the bending moment, N is the axial force, and V is the shear force at the section of interest.

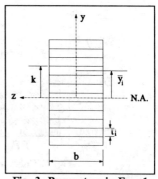

Fig. 3. Parameters in Eqs. 1

Response Verification of Glulam-GFRP Beams

The response of four yellow poplar Glulam-GFRP beams are presented. The longitudinal and shear moduli of the constituent laminae were obtained from bending and torsion tests. The beams were tested in bending with and without the glass fiber composite. Each beam consisted of six wood layers and one GFRP tension layer. The approximate dimensions and properties of each wood layer were: 5.2 x 1.94 cm, moisture content = 10%, $E_{av} = 13.6$ GPa, $G_{av} = 732$ MPa. The approximate dimensions and properties of each GFRP-vinylester layer were: 5.2x0.94 cm, E=19.65 GPa, G = 4752 MPa. As shown in Table 1, the LBT theory predicts quite well the bending stiffness of the test beams. It is significant that the addition of 9.4 mm thick composite increases the bending stiffness by 30% (predicted increase is 32%). The LBT analysis also predicts average increases of 43% shear stiffness and 11% axial stiffness. The strains in the Glulam and Glulam-GFRP beams were measured at the midspan with clip-gage transducers (Loferski and Davalos 1989). The measured strains were converted to stresses and compared to the LBT predictions computed from Eq. 2. The experimental and analytical values were in close agreement.

Table 1. Analytical vs Experimental Displacements For Shear-free Span (Bending Deflection Only) of 1.22 m / 3 = 0.41 m

Beam #	Experimental (cm)	Analytical (cm)	diff (%)
Glulam1	0.053	0.051	3.8
Glulam2	0.06	0.053	11.7
Glulam3	0.063	0.051	19.1
Glulam4	0.06	0.056	6.7
Glu-GFRP1	0.038	0.039	2.6
Glu-GFRP2	0.039	0.04	2.6
Glu-GFRP3	0.045	0.039	13.3
Glu-GFRP4	0.042	0.042	0.0

ANALYSIS AND DESIGN OF T-SYSTEM COMPOSITE BRIDGES

A generalized deflection function of a simply supported orthotropic plate stiffened by edge beams (Fig. 4) is given by a macro solution derived by GangaRao (1975), which is summarized as follows: (1) obtain the solution of a plate with only edge beams, and (2) through compatibility of deflections along the stringer lines, determine the unknown interactive forces and deflections of an interior stringer. Details of the solution are given by Davalos and Salim (1991).

In the WVU design method, once the interactive forces are obtained, a transverse wheel load distribution factor W_f is defined (Raju 1989), from which, the maximum live load moment and deflection for an interior T-beam section are computed from

459

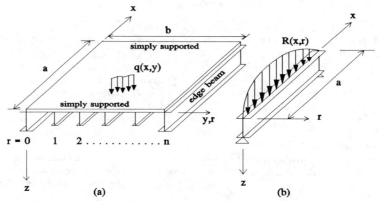

Fig. 4. (a) T-system model; (b) Interactive forces on an interior stringer

$$M_{LL+I} - \frac{P_d L}{4}(1 + DLA) \quad ; \quad \delta_{LL} - \frac{P_d L^3}{48 E_s I_c}(1 + DLA) \tag{4}$$

where,

$$P_d - (AASHTO\ lane\ moment)\left(\frac{4}{L}\right)(N_L)(W_f) \tag{5}$$

DLA = Dynamic load allowance, and N_L = number of lanes.
The design procedure described in this section apply to single-span, simply-supported, T-system bridges under AASHTO HS-25 (AASHTO 1989) truck loading, and it is described in detail by Davalos and Salim (1991).

For a trial deck thickness, the center-to-center spacing of the stringers S (Fig. 5) is designed by computing the maximum transverse local deflection δ_{max} and stress σ_{max} directly under a wheel load applied at midspan of the deck section between stringers:

$$\delta_{max} - \frac{P S^3}{4\ \alpha\ E_T t^4} \quad ; \quad \sigma_{max} - \frac{3 P S}{2\ \beta\ t^3} \tag{6}$$

where,

$$\alpha - -10.9 + 7.8\left(\frac{S}{t}\right) + 0.27\left(\frac{E_L}{E_T}\right)$$

$$\beta - 3.0 + 3.1\left(\frac{S}{t}\right) + 0.152\left(\frac{E_L}{E_T}\right)$$

E_L, E_T = longitudinal and transverse elastic moduli of the deck

P = the resultant of a wheel load of an AASHTO truck = 89 kN (20 kips)

t = thickness of the deck

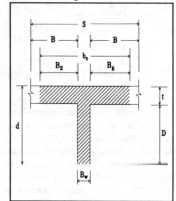

Figure 5. Isolated T-beam

460

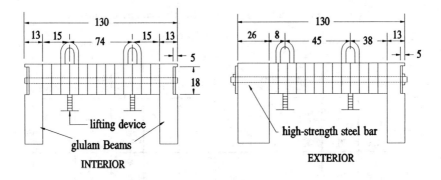

INTERIOR   EXTERIOR

Fig. 6. Detail of modular sections (Dims. in cm)

A T-beam section (Fig. 5) is loaded at the center by an equivalent concentrated load P_d (Eq. 5). The composite moment of inertia I_c of the isolated T-beam is computed by defining the effective over-hanging flange-width from:

$$\frac{B_E}{B} = 0.4586 + \frac{1}{198}\left(\frac{L}{B}\right)\left(\frac{D}{t}\right)\left(\frac{E_s}{E_L}\right) \qquad (7)$$

where, L is the bridge span, E_s is the longitudinal elastic modulus of the stringer, and D and t are defined in Fig. 5. The maximum live load moment and deflection (including impact) are computed from Eqs. 4. Design examples are presented next.

The design is for modular two-lane bridges of 7.2 m (23.5 ft) clear width between curb blocks and spans of 18.3, 24.4, and 30.5 m (60, 80, and 100 ft). Each bridge consists of six modules of 1.3 m (51 in) out-to-out (Fig. 6). The deck is built with 5.1×23 cm (2×9 in) Red Maple (No. 2, Joist & Plank, NDS 1988), and the stringers are either Glulam 24F-V3-SP/SP (NDS 1988) or a Glulam-GFRP combination. Based on a cost assessment, the Glulam-GFRP combination shown in Fig. 7 was selected for the design of these bridges. The equivalent elastic modulus E and the allowable bending strength F_b were obtained using ASTM D-3737. Based on the WVU method and a

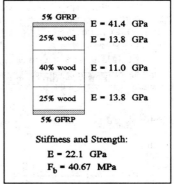

Fig. 7. Selected Glulam-GFRP Combination

deflection limit of L/400, the required stringer depths are computed as shown in Table 2. The design examples are analyzed by a finite element method (Davalos and Salim 1991), a plate macro solution (GangaRao et al. 1975), and the WVU design method. The maximum deflection and bending stresses of the most loaded stringer and deck section between stringers for the 30.5 m (100 ft) bridge are summarized in Tables 3 and 4.

Table 2. Required Stringer Depths for Glulam and Glulam-GFRP

	Bridge Span (m)								
	18.3 (60 ft)			24.4 (80 ft)			30.5 (100 ft)		
	G	GF	diff (%)	G	GF	diff (%)	G	GF	diff (%)
Depth (cm)	129	95	26.4	172	118	31.4	210	141	32.8
$L/\Delta \geq 400$	703	423	-	775	415	-	839	427	-
Design Controlled by	BS	S	-	BS	S	-	BS	S	-

Note: G: Glulam alone. GF: Glulam-GFRP composite beam
BS: Beam Strength S: Beam Stiffness

Table 3. Maximum Deflection and Stresses for Design Example of 30.5 m (100 ft) Bridge with Glulam Stringers

			FE method	Macro solution	WVU method
maximum deflection (cm)	local (live)*		0.2032	-	0.2082
	global	live	3.400	3.223	3.635
		total	6.232	6.134	6.452
maximum stress (MPa)	stringer		10.323	9.045	10.558
	deck	local*	0.809	-	0.832
		global	-5.30	-5.07	-6.12

* In transverse direction of deck section between stringers.
Note: 1 in = 2.54 cm; 1 psi = 6.894 kPa

Table 4. Maximum Deflection and Stresses for Design Example of 30.5 m (100 ft) Bridge with Glulam-GFRP Stringers

			FE method	Macro solution	WVU method
maximum deflection (cm)	local (live)*		0.2032	-	0.2082
	global	live	6.878	6.363	7.138
		total	11.274	11.046	11.811
maximum stress (MPa)	stringer		21.370	18.752	22.440
	deck	local*	0.809	-	0.832
		global	-7.335	-6.780	-8.115

* In transverse direction of deck section between stringers.
Note: 1 in = 2.54 cm; 1 psi = 6.894 kPa

CONCLUSIONS

Bonding pultruded fiber-reinforced plastics (FRP) to Glulam beams with commercial wood adhesives is a promising approach for the commercial production of reinforced Glulam beams in existing laminating plants. The following conclusions are presented:

(1) A modified resorcinol formaldehyde wood adhesive is shown to provide adequate bond strength between yellow poplar wood and E-glass-polyester/vinylester pultruded composites (see Figs. 1 and 2).

(2) The response of Glulam-GFRP beams can be accurately modeled using Beam Lamination Theory, which includes shear effects, as verified experimentally in this paper (see Table 1).

(3) A small amount of FRP reinforcement (e.g., 10%, see Fig. 7) can significantly increase the stiffness and strength of Glulam stringers for bridges (see Table 2). The design examples presented in this paper show a 30% decrease in stringer depth by adding a 10% reinforcement.

(4) The WVU design method outlined in this paper can be efficiently used for the design of stress-laminated T-system timber bridges with Glulam-GFRP stringers (see Tables 3 and 4).

The commercial implementation of Glulam reinforced with FRP appears feasible. However, optimal lay-up combinations must be developed, tested, and AITC approved. The cost-assessment of Glulam-GFRP beams should be based on cost-comparisons with other materials, such as reinforced concrete; these comparisons should be expressed as capacity (e.g., moment, stiffness) per one dollar cost.

REFERENCES

AITC Inspection Manual 200-83. (1987). American Institute of Timber Construction. Englewood, CO.

Annual Book of ASTM Standards. (1989). Vol. 04.09. American Society for Testing and Materials. Philadelphia, PA.

Barbero, E. J. (1990). Pultruded Structural Shapes: From the Constituents to the Structural Behavior. *SAMPE Journal,* 27(1), 25-30.

Crist, J.P. (1990). The National Timber Bridge Initiative. *Wood Design Focus.* Wood Products Information Center, 1(3), 11-12.

Davalos, J.F., and Barbero, E.J. (1991). Modeling of Glass-Fiber Reinforced Glulam Beams. *1991 Int. Timber Engrg. Conf., TRADA*. London, U.K., 3, 3.234-3.241.

Davalos, J.F., Loferski, J.R., Holzer, S.M., and Yadama, V. (1991). Transverse Isotropy Modeling of 3-D Glulam Beams. *ASCE Journal of Materials in Civil Engineering*, 3(2), 125-139.

Davalos, J.F., and Salim, H.A. 1991. Analysis and Design of Stress-Laminated T-system Timber Bridges. *Report CFC-91-153*. Constructed Facilities Center. West Virginia University, Morgantown, WV 26506-6101, USA.

GangaRao, H.V.S., Elmeged, A.A., and Chaudhry, V.K. (1975). Macroapproach for Ribbed and Grid Plate Systems. *ASCE Journal of the Engineering Mechanics Division*, 101 (EM1), 25-43.

Loferski, J.R., Davalos, J.F., and Yadama, V. (1989). A Laboratory-Built Clip-On Strain Gage Transducer for Testing Wood. *Forest Products Journal*, 39(9), 45-48.

National Design Specifications for Wood Construction. (1988). National Forest Products Association. Washington, D.C.

Raju, P.R. (1989). Wheel Load Distribution on Highway Bridges. *M.S. Thesis in Civ. Engrg*. West Virginia University, Morgantown, WV 26506-6101, USA.

Standard Specifications for Highway Bridges. (1989). 14th Ed. Am. Assoc. of State Highway and Transp. Officials. Washington, D.C.

Taylor, R.J., and Csagoli, P.F. (1978). Transverse Post-tensioning of Longitudinally Laminated Timber Bridge Decks. Ministry of Transportation and Communications. Downsview, Ontario, Canada, 236-244.

Taylor, R.J., Batchelor, B. DeV., and Dalen, K.V. (1983). Prestressed Wood Bridges. *Structural Research Report SRR-83-01*. Ministry of Transportation and Communications, Downsview, Ontario, Canada.

Wood Handbook: Wood as an Engineering Material. (1987). Agriculture Handbook No. 79. USDA-FS-Forest Products Laboratory. U.S. Government Printing Office, Washington, D.C.

ADVANCED COMPOSITE MATERIALS IN BRIDGES AND STRUCTURES
K.W. Neale and P. Labossière, Editors; Canadian Society for Civil Engineering, 1992

Matériaux composites d'avant-garde pour ponts et charpentes
K.W. Neale et P. Labossière, éditeurs; Société canadienne de génie civil, 1992

DYNAMIC VIBRATION OF CABLE-STAYED BRIDGES USING CARBON FIBRE COMPOSITE CABLES

M.A. Khalifa
University of Nebraska-Lincoln
Lincoln, Nebraska, USA

ABSTRACT

Due to its light weight, high strength, and corrosion resistance, fibre-reinforced plastic (FRP) is becoming more popular in cable-stayed bridge construction. In this investigation, the dynamic behaviour of carbon fibre composite cable (CFCC) in cable-stayed bridges was studied. Vibrational characteristics of the stay cable from two similar cable-stayed models, one CFCC and the other conventional style cable, have been compared using modal analysis. A finite element discretization was used for the cable elements and the three-dimensionality of the bridge was considered. Preliminary findings include vibrational models and numerous cable-deck-tower modes, as well as pure cable vibration modes. However, the sequence of the modes on each model was found to be distinct and the participation factors used in earthquake-response analysis, calculated from both models, showed significant disagreement.

RÉSUMÉ

Avec leur faible poids, leur haute résistance, et leur résistance à la corrosion, les FRP pourraient servir à la construction de ponts haubanés. Ici, le comportement dynamique de câbles en composites renforcés de carbone (CFCC) a été étudié. On a comparé le comportement en vibration de haubans pour deux modèles similaires, l'un en CFCC et l'autre en acier, par une analyse modale. Une discrétisation par éléments finis a été utilisée pour les éléments du câble et les effets tri-dimensionnels du pont ont été considérés. Les résultats incluent les modèles de vibrations et plusieurs modes câble-tablier-tour de même que des modes de vibration des câbles seuls. Cependant, la séquence des modes sur chaque modèle est différente, et les facteurs de participation utilisés dans l'analyse de réponse aux séismes, calculés selon les deux modèles, montrent des différences significatives.

INTRODUCTION

Cable-stayed bridges are increasing not only in number and popularity worldwide, but also in center (or effective) span length. In his proposal for building a bridge across the Strait of Gibraltar, Meier (1987) suggested the use of carbon fiber reinforced plastic (CFRP) in the construction of a cable-stayed bridge as the most economical solution for a super-long span (span of more than 4,000 m, or 13,000 ft). Constructing super-long spans is becoming more feasible because of the wide-spread development of light weight composite materials and advances in construction technology (Meier, 1987; Lin, 1991). While span lengths are getting longer, bridge decks are getting shallower, and using high strength composite materials in construction is becoming increasingly more feasible. For all of these reasons, cable-stayed bridges are becoming more flexible and lighter, with inherently very low structural damping. Furthermore, due to a steadily increasing number of heavier and higher-powered vehicles and trains, cable-stayed bridges are subjected to vibrational stress fluctuations and reversals (Nazmy and Abdel-Ghaffar, 1990; Khalifa, 1991). Thus, with the use of light composite materials in cable-stayed bridges, traffic-induced vibrations play a significant role and should receive attention equal to that given to environmental loadings such as wind, rain, and earthquakes.

The importance of including the cable vibration in the overall dynamic analysis of cable-stayed bridges has been demonstrated by Khalifa (1991), Khalifa and Abdel-Ghaffar (1991), and Abdel-Ghaffar and Khalifa (1991). Discretization of each stay cable into small elements yields numerous pure cable vibration modes, deck-cable modes, as well as deck-tower bridge modes. The coupled deck-cable modes involve complex lateral bending and torsional motions of the deck as well as vertical and swinging cable motions. These vibration modes can not be predicted if cables were modeled as one straight element (i.e. disregard cable vibration in the overall) or even if linearized frequencies are used for individual cables. When the vibrational characteristics of the stay cables are taken into consideration, the sequence of the complex modes depends on the characteristics of the stay cables. The effect of these modes on the participation factors of any dynamic-response calculation is significant.

This investigation gives deeper insight into the differences of the dynamic characteristics of two similar cable-stayed bridges; carbon fiber composite cables (CFCC) were used in one bridge, and conventional steel cables (CSC) were used in the second. Finite element discretization was used for the cable elements to include the vibrational characteristics of the stay cable. The three-dimensionality of the bridge was also considered. Comparisons drawn between the two sets of vibrational modes and the effects of the differences in the overall dynamics of cable-stayed bridges was also studied. Understanding these differences is necessary for realistic predictions of dynamic response.

BACKGROUND

The development of advanced composite materials (ACM) began more than four decades ago. The aerospace, automobile, and sports industries have lead by incorporating fiber reinforced plastic (FRP) technology into their products. There are many different composite materials on the market today. CFCC is a new product, developed in Japan and has been introduced to several European countries. The unit weight for CFCC is 1.5 g/cm³ (.0936 k/ft³) (Zoch et al.,1991) while the unit weight of CSC is 8.49 g/cm³ (0.53 k/ft³) that is almost 1:5. Tensile strength and tensile modulus for carbon composites are as high as those for steel strands and CFCC does not experience residual stresses due the release of tension forces (Tokyo Rope Manufacturing Company, 1989). However, tension failure of CFCC is brittle while CSC undergoes plastic deformation before failure. Although the flexibility of a carbon composite is much lower than steel flexibility, it is in an acceptable range. Manufacturers claim that the flexibility of carbon composites relative to steel is about 1:4. The importance of flexibility, however, extends itself to more than structural performance; it is necessary so that the relatively long cables can be manually coiled and easily transported.

Bedard (1992) provided a comprehensive survey of composite reinforcing bars, covering the strengths and weaknesses of their mechanical properties. He presented an interesting cost comparison between steel and composite bars, taking into account the differences in weight, strength, application, and maintenance costs. Due to their light weight, high tensile strength, excellent corrosion resistance and flexibility, applications for ACM, cover a wide range of structures and components.

Several pedestrian bridges have been constructed for research purposes using ACM. The Virginia glass fiber reinforced plastic (GFRP) pedestrian bridge was developed in 1976 with 4.9 m (16 ft) girders (Meier, 1991). Other pedestrian bridges are the Chongqing cable-stayed bridge which contained a GFRP box girder, and the Guanyinqiao bridge which was completed in 1988, both are in China (Bruce, 1989). In Germany, the Lünen'sche Gasse experimental bridge in Düsseldorf was built in 1980 using GFRP strands for the first time (Mufti, Erki and Jaeger, 1991; Meier, 1991; Bedard, 1992) and the Adolf Kiepert bridge built most recently in Berlin with two spans of 27.61 and 22.98 m (90 and 75 ft) (Bedard, 1992).

Some of the most important GFRP highway bridges have been built in Germany. The Ulenbergstrasse bridge was completed in 1986, the first roadway built using GFRP prestressing tendons (Mufti, Erki and Jaeger, 1991; Meier, 1991; Bedard, 1992; Ballinger, 1990). Carbon composites were also used, a total of 80 m (262.5 ft) length, prestressed bridge in Ludwigshafen, Germany as well as the Shinmyabashi bridge in Japan with a 6 m (19.7 ft) span were built using CFRP tendons (Zoch et al.,1991).

One of the most pronounced applications of carbon composites is their use as tension cables in the long-span suspension and cable-stayed bridges. Meier (1987) provided graphs showing the difference in the limiting span (spans at which a structural system will just support itself) for suspension bridges versus the specific design load for steel and CFRP as well as GFRP. He also showed the price differences between composite materials and steel for different spans concluding that for spans more than 4,000 m (13,000 ft) carbon composites are more economical. In this category of bridges the use of the unidirectionally reinforced carbon composites cables, with their high resistance of corrosion and fatigue, will be optimized. Such composite cables are being developed and tested for possible use as a replacement for conventional steel cables (Plenck, et al., 1990; Kim and Meier, 1991; Iyer, et al., 1991).

For this research emphasis was placed on the dynamic behavior of cable-stayed bridges and the effect of using CFCC as stay cables, because recent trends show an increasing interest of using carbon composites in these designs. To the knowledge of the author no such elaborated study is provided in the literature.

THREE-DIMENSIONAL MODELING AND ANALYSIS

The effect on the dynamic response of cable-stayed bridges due to wind, rain, earthquake, and moving loads has gained attention in the literature over the last two decades. These loads contain a broad spectrum of excitation frequencies and cause large dynamic amplification of the structural response, particularly in these low-damped structures. Most vulnerable to such vibrations are the high strength cables which can vibrate with the deck and the tower or independently from the main bridge. Vibrations of these bridges become harmful when a predominant excitation frequency is in the vicinity of a natural frequency of the structural system or structural members such as stay cables.

In order to study the effect of stay cable vibration on the overall dynamic characteristics of the bridge, two similar systems were considered. In the first, conventional steel cables were used, while in the second, carbon fiber composite cables were used. The nodal points and the elements of the model are shown in Fig. 1 along with the discretization system of cable elements. The multi-element cable system model, which has previously been used (Khalifa, 1991), has a center-span of 670.56 m (2,200 ft) and two side spans of 292.61 m (960 ft) each. In terms of span length, this model represents the near-future design trend. The two main girders and the cross-beams were assumed to be steel for both CFCC and CSC systems. Carbon fiber composite deck was not considered in this study. A harp system cable arrangement was chosen from an aesthetic viewpoint and because anchoring at the tower end is easier.

In this study each stay cable is modeled by eight truss elements. The effect of cable sag was accounted for by the reduced modulus of elasticity of the cables. In the static analysis, different sources of nonlinearity were included using the large deflection theory. Nonlinearities can be caused by changes in the geometry of the cables due to tension changes, axial force and bending moment interaction in the bridge tower and in the deck elements, and changes in the geometry of the whole bridge due to large deflections.

Modal Analysis

The eigenvalue problem of each system was solved using the tangent stiffness matrix of the bridge in the dead-load deformed state which was obtained from the geometry of the bridge under gravity load conditions as shown in Fig. 2 (Nazmy and Abdel-Ghaffar, 1990). Irvine (1981) discussed analytical expressions for the linearized natural frequencies of inclined cables. A comparison of natural frequencies for the in-plane modes, the X-Z plane of Fig. 1, as well as the out-of-plane or swinging motion (the Y direction of Fig. 1) of cables no. 1, 3, and 5 are shown in Tables 1 and 2, respectively. These frequencies were calculated from the analytical expressions as well as by using finite element analysis of the whole bridge for both the CFCC and CSC systems. It is important to point out that in this comparison the frequencies and associated mode shapes selected from the finite element results are the pure cable modes and have similar modal configurations as those resulting from the analytical methods.

Although there is reasonably good agreement for the vibration of individual cables, in no way will the calculation predict the combination of these individual cables as viewed on the bridge, nor will it predict the dynamic interaction between the vibrating cables and the vibrating deck-tower system. Thus, it is misleading to rely solely on these frequency expressions to provide a complete picture of the three dimensional vibrating bridge.

Analysis of the Results

A comparative study of the vibrational characteristics of the two systems, with the modes of the CFCC system and the corresponding modes of the CSC system covering the same frequency band, are presented in Fig. 3. The first 18 bridge modes of each system are compared in Table 3. In the CSC system many pure cable modes are of the same level of bridge frequencies, thus, clusters of cable modes are present early in the mode sequence, while for the CFCC systems pure cable modes are mainly grouped together, dominating modes no 23 through mode no. 81.

For each system the first four computed three-dimensional mode shapes are shown in Figs. 4 and 5. It is evident that cable interaction with the bridge vibration occurs only in modes no. 3 and 4 of the CSC system. Whereas, the first distinct interaction motion between the cables and the bridge in the CFCC system is in mode no. 22. As many as 32 first order pure cable modes were retrieved in the frequency range of 0.28 Hz to 0.64 Hz in the CSC system, while for the CFCC system a total of 50 pure cable modes were retrieved, 24 in-plane modes, 23 out-of-plane modes, and three modes involving three-dimensional pure cable motion. These modes are within the frequency range of 0.73 Hz to 1.06 Hz.

Figures 4 through 7 as well as Tables 1, 2, and 3 show that the first four modes of each system are of similar modal configuration with prominent swinging cable and vertical cable motions in modes no. 3 and 4 of the CSC system. The associated frequencies are within comparable values. The corresponding equivalent for mode no. 5 through mode no. 15 of the CFCC system, fall within mode no. 37 and mode no. 79 of the CSC system with different sequences for some modes, see Table 3 and Fig. 6 which shows some selected corresponding pairs of modes from the two systems. Although modes no. 16, 17, and 18 in the CFCC system are bridge modes and have frequencies less than 0.64 Hz (the highest frequency retrieved in the CSC system), these modes have no match in the CSC system. Because modes 19-22, 39-42, 60-63, 73, and 82-90 in the CFCC system are higher bridge modes, they are not covered in the first 90 modes of the CSC system. These modes include a variety of three-dimensional modes composed of different combinations of cable, tower, and deck motions. Some of the unique modes are shown in Fig. 7. Modes 23-38, 43-59, 64-72, and 74-81 of the CFCC system are pure cable modes; similar mode shapes for the CSC system are obtained but at different levels of frequencies. In the CSC system there are 32 first order pure cable modes in addition to many other modes which involve either tainted or distinctive cable motions while some involve different features of coupled deck-cable motions. Modes no. 19, 20, 27 and 28 have no match in the CFCC system. Finally, in this frequency range, modes no. 80 to 90 are pure cable modes involving two-half sine waves.

Earthquake-response Analysis

When a bridge is subjected to different ground motions with three components at the anchor piers and the two tower piers, the earthquake participation factors are given by

$$
\alpha_{ni} = \frac{-(\phi_n)^T (M_{ss} M_{sg})(g_{psi} g_{pgi})^T}{(g_{psi} g_{pgi})^T (M_{ss})(\phi_n)} \qquad (i = 1, 2, ..., 12; \; n = 1, 2, 3, ...) \qquad (1)
$$

where ϕ_n = the
to unity with all its other elements being zero; g_{psi} is the ith quasi-static function that results from unit displacement in the ith degree of freedom at a supporting point (where an earthquake input is expected at this point in that particular degree of freedom); M_{sg} is a rectangular mass matrix where M = the mass matrix, the subscript "g" designates the degree of freedom corresponding to the points of application and direction of ground motions, and the subscript "s" corresponds to all other structural degrees of freedom of the bridge.

The participation factors for the uniform ground motion inputs for the CSC and the CFCC systems were calculated by

$$
\beta_n = - \frac{\phi_n^T M I}{\phi_n^T M \phi_n} \qquad (n = 1, 2, 3, ...) \qquad (2)
$$

where I = the unit vector. The results are shown in Fig. 8, while those for nonuniform ground motion are shown in Fig. 9 for the CFCC system. It is apparent from these figures that the CFCC system would significantly result in a different set of earthquake response

469

characteristics as compared with those from the CSC system. For example many higher modes (order of 60 or more) showed substantial high participation factors, see Fig. 9. Furthermore, when the generalized forces were factored in, substantial differences were obtained when CFCC was compared with CSC for the two ground motion inputs.

CONCLUSION

Dynamic vibration of cable-stayed bridges involve numerous pure cable vibration modes, in addition to deck-tower bridge modes. These pure cable motions involve the vibration of the longest, intermediate and short cables of both the center and side spans, and a complicated combination of in-plane vertical and longitudinal motions as well as out-of-plane swinging or lateral motion configurations. However, the modal sequence and the frequency levels depend heavily on the characteristics of the cable material.

The dynamic characteristics of CFCC can not be completely identified using expressions of linearized natural frequencies for individual vibrating cables. Numerous additional cable modes and associated frequencies were obtained by applying the finite element discretization, along with the three dimensionality of the bridge. Moreover, with the use of light composite materials, cable-stayed bridges are becoming more flexible and more susceptible to dynamic loads, thus, the dynamic behavior of a CFCC system can be significantly different from that of a CSC system. Modal participation factors showed substantial differences between the two systems. Higher modes from the CFCC system are contributing significantly to the dynamic response. An elaborated, complete dynamic analysis, considering cable vibration interactions must be conducted in order to better verify characteristics of the CFCC system.

The different CFCC system characteristics provided a profound insight into the tools of the dynamic analysis of such bridges and opened the door for further investigations toward mastering the design task of super-span cable-stayed bridges. Future research will include an investigation of dynamic characteristics of a cable-stayed bridge model using CFCC as well as carbon composites for the deck.

REFERENCES

Abdel-Ghaffar, A. and Khalifa, M. (1991). Importance of Cable Vibration in the Dynamics of Cable-Stayed Bridges. *J. of Engrg. Mech. ASCE*, **117** (11), 2571-2589.

Bakht, B., Gilkie, R.C., and Jaeger, L.G. (1991). Advanced Composite Materials with Applications to Bridges. *State-of-the-Art Report, Technical Committee on Advanced Composite Materials in Bridges and Structures*, CSCE, 217-230.

Ballinger, C.V. (1990). Structural FRP Composites. *Civil Engineering*, ASCE, **60** (7), 63-65.

Bedard, C. (1992). Composite Reinforcing Bars: Assessing Their Use in Construction. *Concrete International, ACI*, **14** (1), 55-59.

Bruce, R.N., Jr. (1989). Fiber Reinforced Plastic Bridges in Chongqing 1983-1988. *68th Annual TRB Meeting*, Washington, D.C.

Dean, D.L. (1961). Static and Dynamic Analysis of Guy Cables. *J. of Struct. Div.*, ASCE, **87**, 1-21.

Ehsan, F. and Scanlan, R.H. (1989). Damping Stay Cables with Ties. *Proc. of the 5th U.S.-Japan Workshop On Bridge Engrg.*, Public Work Research Institute, Tsukuba, Japan, 203-217.

Hikami, Y. (1986). Rain Vibration of Cables in Cable-Stayed Bridges. *J. of Wind Engrg.*, (27).

Irvine, H.M. (1981). Cable Structures. The MIT Press Series in Structure Mechanics, Cambridge, Massachusetts.

Iyer, S.L., Khubchandani, A. and Feng, J. (1991). Fiberglass and Graphite For Bridge Decks. Advanced Composite Materials in Civ. Engrg. Struct. *Proc. of the Specialty Conference*, ASCE, Las Vegas, Nevada, 371-383.

Khalifa, M. and Abdel-Ghaffar, A. (1991). Traffic Induced Vibration and Fatigue of Cable-Stayed Bridges. *Report No. CRECE-5,* Civ. Engrg. Dept., Univ. of Southern California, Los Angeles, Calif.

Khalifa, M.A. (1991). Analysis of Traffic-induced Vibration and Fatigue of Cable-Stayed Bridges. A dissertation submitted in partial fulfillment of the requirements for the degree of Doctor of Philosophy, Civil Engineering Department, University of Southern California, Los Angeles, Calif.

Kim, P. and Meier, U. (1991). CFRP Cables for Large Structures. Advanced Composites Materials in Civ. Engrg. Struct. *Proc. for the Specialty Conference, ASCE*, Las Vegas, Nevada, 233-245.

Lin, T.Y. and Chow, P. (1991). Gibraltar Strait Crossing - A Challenge to Bridge and Structural Engineers. *Struct. Engrg. International*, **1** (2).

Meier, U. (1987). Proposal for Carbon Fiber Reinforced Composite Bridge Across the Strait of Gibraltar at its Narrowest Site. *Proc. of the Institute of Mech. Engineers*, **201** (B2), 73-78.

Meier, U. (1991). Advanced Composite Materials with Application to Bridges. *State-of-the-Art Report, Technical Committee on Advanced Composite Materials in Bridges and Structures*, CSCE, 274-284.

Mufti, A.A., Erki, M-A., and Jaeger L.G. (1991). Advanced Composite Materials with Applications to Bridges. *State-of-the-Art Report, Technical Committee on Advanced Composite Materials in Bridges and Structures*, CSCE, 1-20.

Nazmy, A.S. and Abdel-Ghaffar, A.M. (1987). Seismic Response Analysis of Cable-Stayed Bridges Subjected to Uniform and Multiple-Support Excitation. *Report No. 87-SM-1*, Dept. of Civ. Engrg., Princeton Univ.

Ohshima, K. and Nanjo, M. (1987). Aerodynamic Stability of the Cables of A Cable-Stayed Bridge Subject to Rain. A Case Study of Ajigawa Bridge. *Proc. of the 3rd U.S.-Japan Bridge Workshop*, Public Works Research Institute, Tsukuba, Japan, 324-335.

Plecnik, J., Sanchez, V.F., Munley, E., Plecnik, J.M., and Ahmad, S.H. (1990). Development of High Strength Composite Cables. *Proc. of First Materials Engrg. Congress*, ASCE, Denver, CO, 1016-1025.

Tokyo Rope Manufacturing Company, Ltd. (1989). *Carbon Fiber Composite Cable Technical Data.*

Zoch, P., Kimura, H., Iwasaki, T., and Heym, H. (1991). *Carbon Fiber Composite Cables A New Class of Prestressing Members.* TRB, Washington, DC.

471

Table 1 Comparison between First Vertical Cable Frequency for CSC and CFCC
Systems
Resulting from Finite Element Analysis and Analytical Methods

Vibrating cable	CSC System (Hz)		CFCC System (Hz)	
	FEM	Analytical	FEM	Analytical
1	0.3244	0.3508	0.7360	0.7426
3	0.3892	0.4114	0.8778	0.8914
5	0.4635	0.4856	1.0588	1.0690

Table 2 Comparison between First Swinging Cable Frequency for CSC and CFCC
Systems
Resulting from Finite Element Analysis and Analytical Methods

Vibrating cable	CSC System (Hz)		CFCC System (Hz)	
	FEM	Analytical	FEM	Analytical
1	0.3244	0.3508	0.7361	0.7411
3	0.3892	0.4114	0.8840	0.8902
5	0.4635	0.4856	1.0604	1.0680

Table 3 Comparison between similar vibrational modes resulting from CSC and
CFCC systems.

CSC		CFCC	
Mode	Frequency	Mode	Frequency
1	0.20224	1	0.18617
2	0.26026	2	0.24503
3	0.28844	3	0.30384
4	0.31321	4	0.32222
19	0.33887	no match	
20	0.35735	no match	
27	0.37887	no match	
28	0.38319	no match	
37	0.41940	7	0.42113
38	0.42684	5	0.38585
39	0.42725	9	0.43539
40	0.42868	6	0.40082
57	0.48912	8	0.42680
58	0.49614	10	0.44775
59	0.52007	11	0.46400
60	0.52020	12	0.46468
61	0.54657	13	0.49975
78	0.60978	14	0.55514
79	0.63371	15	0.60253
no match		16	0.60438
no match		17	0.61659
no match		18	0.64058

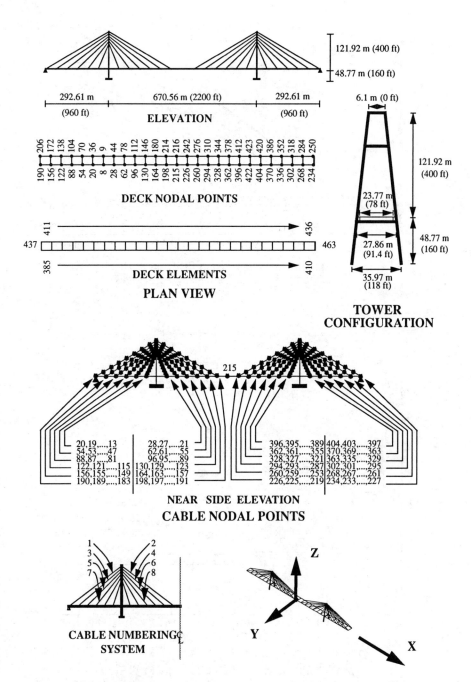

121.92 m (400 ft)

48.77 m (160 ft)

292.61 m
(960 ft)

670.56 m (2200 ft)

292.61 m
(960 ft)

ELEVATION

6.1 m (0 ft)

121.92 m
(400 ft)

23.77 m
(78 ft)

48.77 m
(160 ft)

27.86 m
(91.4 ft)

35.97 m
(118 ft)

DECK NODAL POINTS

**TOWER
CONFIGURATION**

411   436
437   463
385   410

DECK ELEMENTS
PLAN VIEW

215

20,19,...,13	28,27,...21	396,395,...,389	404,403,...,397
54,53,...,47	62,61,...,55	362,361,...,355	370,369,...,363
88,87,...,81	96,95,...,89	328,327,...,321	363,335,...,329
122,121,...,115	130,129,...,123	294,293,...,287	302,301,...,295
156,155,...,149	164,163,...,157	260,259,...,253	268,267,...,261
190,189,...,183	198,197,...,191	226,225,...,219	234,233,...,227

NEAR SIDE ELEVATION
CABLE NODAL POINTS

1 2
3 4
5 6
7 8

Z

Y

X

CABLE NUMBERING
SYSTEM

Figure 1.   3-D Cable-Stayed Bridge Model Used in the Investigation

473

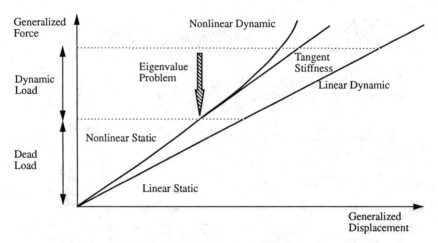

**Figure 2 Diagram Showing Tangent Stiffness at Dead-Load
Deformed Position of Cable-Stayed Bridges**

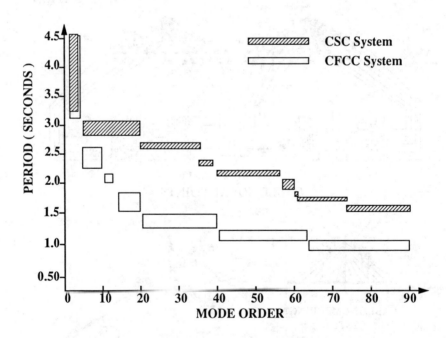

Figure 3 Vibrational Modes for CSC and CFCC Systems

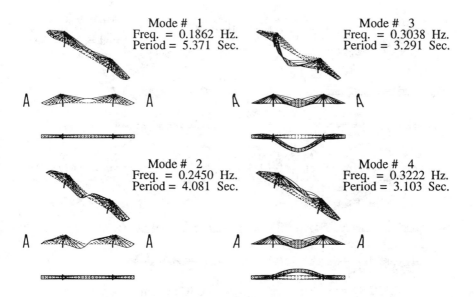

Figure 4 First Four Computed Mode Shapes for CFCC System

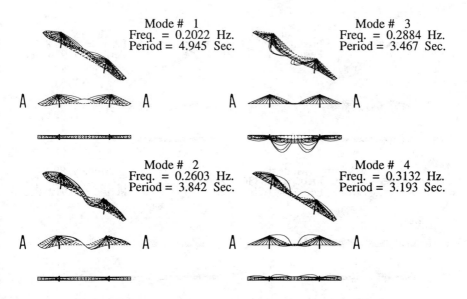

Figure 5 First Four Computed Mode Shapes for CSC System

475

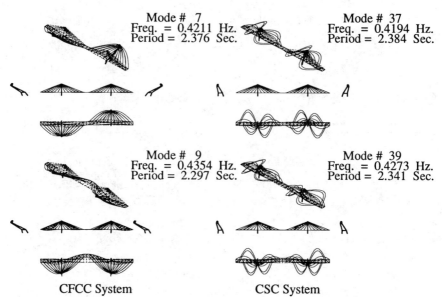

CFCC System   CSC System

Figure 6 Selected Corresponding Higer Modes for CFCC and CSC Systems

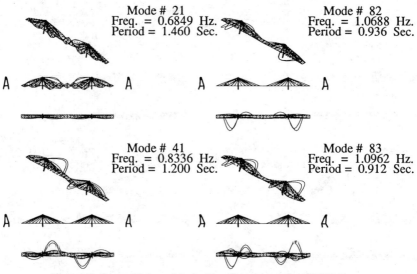

Figure 7 Some Unique Mode Configurations for CFCC System

476

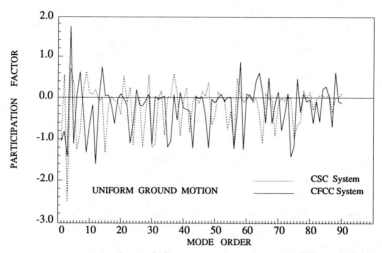

Figure 8 Earthquake-Response Participation Factors for Uniform Ground-Motion

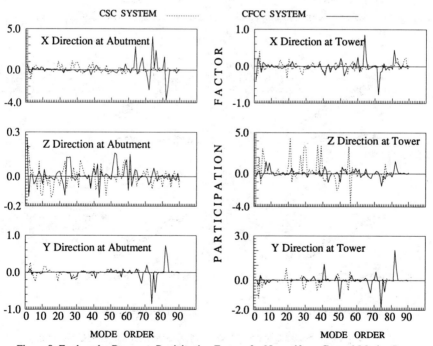

Figure 9 Earthquake-Response Participation Factors for Nonuniform Ground-Motion Inputs

ADVANCED COMPOSITE MATERIALS IN BRIDGES AND STRUCTURES
K.W. Neale and P. Labossière, Editors; Canadian Society for Civil Engineering, 1992

Matériaux composites d'avant-garde pour ponts et charpentes
K.W. Neale et P. Labossière, éditeurs; Société canadienne de génie civil, 1992

NEW BRIDGES FOR HIGH-SPEED TRAINS

G. König and **M. Zink**
Technical University Darmstadt
Darmstadt, Germany

ABSTRACT

Building new bridges for high-speed trains will be an important task for structural engineering in the coming years. The bridges of the new German lines built in the eighties still leave possibilities for improvements. The appearance of the single-cell box girders is determined by the slenderness ratio of L/h = 11. A new type of composite structure emanating from France offers a chance to improve aesthetics and to obtain a significant decrease in dead load. Corrugated steel webs are used to carry shear. Using high-strength concrete for the top and bottom slabs, the depth of the girder can be decreased to less than 75 percent compared to the current girders. Concrete with a strength up to 85 MPa (12 300 psi) is suitable for the box girders.

RÉSUMÉ

La construction de nouveaux ponts pour des trains à grande vitesse sera une importante tâche de génie civil dans les prochaines années. Les ponts des nouvelles lignes allemandes construites durant les années 1980 pourraient encore être améliorées. L'apparence des poutres-caissons simples est régie par un rapport d'élancement L/h=11. Un nouveau genre de structures composites français offre la possibilité d'améliorer l'esthétique et de diminuer significativement la charge permanente. Des tôles d'acier reprennent le cisaillement. En utilisant du béton à haute résistance pour les hourdis supérieurs et inférieurs, la hauteur de la poutre peut être réduite à moins de 75 pour cent des poutres courantes. Du béton avec une résistance de 85 MPa (12 300 psi) est approprié pour les poutres caissons.

INTRODUCTION

The devolopment of a European high-speed network is a necessity to solve the problems caused by the enormous increase in transportation. On the other hand, building railway bridges has been a main task of structural engineering since it's beginning in the late 19 th century. Many bridges have reached an age of 80 years or more. Due to this fact, the rehabilitation and maintenance of old bridges is another reason to stress the importance of the topic.

Requirements as for new high-speed railway lines have never been known up to now. A route selection compatible to the topography of the highlands is excluded by the design speed of 300 km/h, which requires a maximum grade of 40.0 °/oo and a standard radius of 7,000 m. About 9 % of the two new lines in Germany are bridges. To be able to build so many bridges with equal demands in a high quality, the German Federal Railway published the General Design, the so-called 'Rahmenplanung'.

The General Design introduces two different distances of pier-axis, 44.00 m and 58.00 m. The corresponding construction heights are 4.00 m and 5.00 m for the single-span superstructures. Examples are shown in Fig. 1 to Fig. 3. There are two main reasons to choose this kind of standard system. A track structure without any rail expansion joint is possible. With continuously welded rails there is no difference between bridge and open track, and problems caused by the expansion joints are avoided. Another advantage is the possibility of easy lateral shifting. Generally, the renewal of superstructures is facilitated by a limited length. Using any temporary structures to carry track is unthinkable due to the design criterea, the high share of tunnels and an average bridge length of about 1,000 m. However, the break-down of traffic during interchange of girders is limited to only one night.

The feasibility of a new type of bridge has to be verified at the two standard systems, the 44.00 m and the 58.00 m single-span girder. The results may be transferred to any related structure, for example continuous girder bridges or bridges with special systems for the longitudinal loads.

Fig. 1: Leinach Valley-Bridge near Würzburg - 44.00 m Single-span Girder

480

Fig. 2: Bartelsgraben Valley Bridge
58.00 m Continuous Girder

Fig. 3: Rombach Valley Bridge
near Fulda

Fig. 4: Rail Expansion Joint

481

DESIGN

Requirements

The main task for the valley bridges is to provide maximum railway transportation. The classical principale 'form follows function' has to be realized. Some important aspects are:

- durability
- convenient equipment
- maintenance
- aesthetics
- economical efficiency
- simplicity of construction

Some main features of the new bridges are taken from the General Design:

- distances of pier-axis are 44.00 and 58.00 m.

- elements and structure of carriageway
  the track ballast is increased by 10 cm for the new design speed of 300 km/h. There are no slab tracks used.

- section of edge caps with standard equipment adjusted to the modified track ballast

- system of single-cell box girder superstructures with two tracks and possibility of access

- piers and abutments
  pier heads may be improved by use of high-strength concrete

Deformation limits

The deformation limits are taken from the German standard for bridges with a design speed of 250 km/h. The new European standard including tracks for 300 km/h is still in preparation.

The midspan deformation limit for the girder is length divided by 2700 for bridges with more than one span. For bridges with a ballast track structure, the deformation is caused only by live load and temperature variations. The minimum stiffness of the girder is determined by the deformation limit, which is the starting point for the improvement of the superstucture. The basic idea is to start the design with a girder which fulfills the demands of minimum stiffness. This girder will be light and must withstand higher stresses. To overcome these stresses high-strength concrete (h.s.c.) is used. Using improved materials as h.s.c. and steel in a composite structure is the second approach.

Shear deformation has been neglected in this study. Its share is smaller than 20 % of total deformation if shear stiffness is only calculated from the web area. The stiffness of the edge caps has been neglected also. Additional research on this topic is necessary regarding the durability of bond between the edge caps and the cantilevering plates.

Cross Section of the box girder

A new composite structure mixed with improved materials is used for the superstructure. It is a composite bridge with corrugated steel webs and high-strength concrete. In the report of the IABSE Symposium Brussels 1990 (Cheyrezy and Combault) the main features of this new type of bridges are listed.

Compared to the current girders of new high-speed tracks in Germany, the advantages of corrugated steel webs are:

- Self-weight is decreased in the webs

- Steel is used to carry shear

- The inner lever arm is nearly increased up to the total girder height

- Difficulties linked with the casting of the 4.00 to 5.00 m deep concrete webs are avoided Serious problems like screening of aggregate by tendons occurred at many bridges

- Web stiffeners, as used for conventional steel webs are avoided

- Buckling is no critical criterion for the webs because they are only used to carry shear

- Prestressing forces are not dissipated by the steel webs

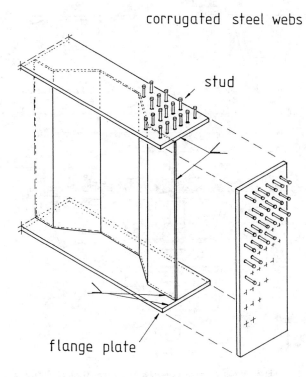

Fig. 5: Corrugated steel webs (sketch)

44.00 M SINGLE-SPAN GIRDER

The 44.00 m distance of pier axis is the standard case for bridges on the new German lines. The following specific results are achieved when using corrugated steel webs:

- Girder height is reduced from 4.00 m to 3.20 m
  A further reduction to 3.00 m is possible.

- Corrugated steel webs have a thickness of 30 mm
  To guarantee a sufficient safety against fatigue, steel ST 52 with an ultimate yield point of 520 MPa is used.

- High-strength concrete B 75 with a compressive strength of 75 MPa is used

- Longitudinal prestressing of the bottom slab with a force of 57.970 MN -
  30 cables of SUSPA 0.6"-15 wire system with 1.932 MN/cable are used.

The limit for the reduction in girder height is set by the shear area of steel webs and the requirement of an accessible girder. In the calculated example a profiled underside view is proposed to improve aesthetics. Without this detail a further decrease of girder height of 0.2 m is possible without reaching the deformation limits.

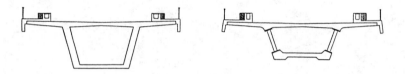

Fig. 6: General Design Section   Fig. 7: Proposed Section

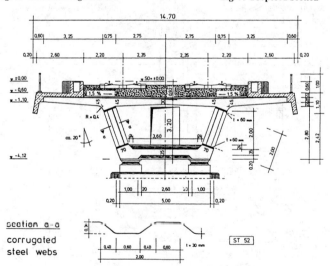

Fig. 8: Midspan Section of 44.00 m Single-span Girder

484

58.00 M SINGLE-SPAN GIRDER

The 58.00 m distance of pier axis is the system for high bridges crossing valleys without rivers. The following specific results are achieved when using corrugated steel webs:

- Girder height is reduced from 5.00 m to 3.50 m

- Deformation limits are met exactly

- Corrugated steel webs have a thickness of 30 mm
  To guarantee a sufficient safety against fatigue, steel ST 52 with a 520 MPa yield point is used.

- High-strength concrete B 85 with a compressive strength of 85 MPa is used

- Longitudinal prestressing of the bottom slab with a force of 83.944 MN -
  28 cables of SUSPA 0.6"-22 wire system with 2.998 MN/cable are used.

The limit for the reduction in girder height is set by the deformation requirements and the possible number of prestressing cables in the bottom slab. The shear stresses in the dowelled composite joint are also at a high level.

Fig. 9: General Design Section   Fig. 10: Proposed Section

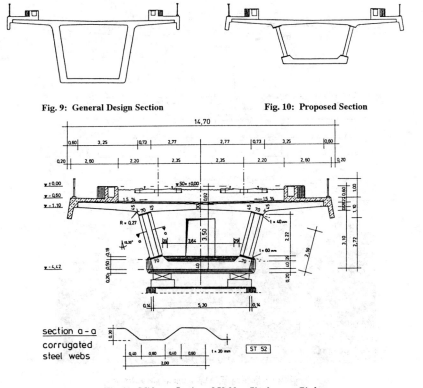

Fig. 11: Midspan Section of 58.00 m Single-span Girder

485

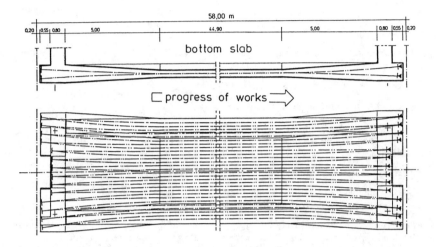

Fig. 12: Longitudinal Prestressing

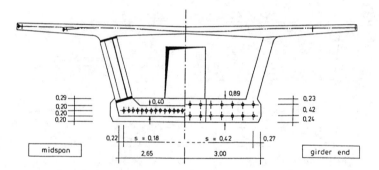

Fig. 13: Tendons in Section

Fig. 14: Improved Slenderness in Side View

486

Fig. 15: Train passing the bridge   Fig. 16:   Corrugated Web Structure

Fig. 17:   Web Structure From Below

CONCLUSIONS

The use of improved materials, like high-strength concrete and steel mixed with the new corrugated web structure, enables a significant reduction in girder depth. As the study shows, the chosen system is able to meet the requirements of the German General Design. No important technical problems prevent the testing of such a structure in full-size. The study may even be an impulse for more detailed analysis, particularly concerning the behaviour of webs under torsion and lateral forces. Finally, one may assume that the classic engineering topic railway bridge has not lost its fascination today. To use new techniques and materials is a challenge for the age of high-speed traffic.

REFERENCES

[1]   Cheyrezy M. and Combault J., Composite Bridges with Corrugated Steel Webs - Achievements and Prospects, Proceedings of IABSE SYMPOSIUM BRUSSELS 1990 International Association for Bridge and Structural Engineering

[2]   German Federal Railway, DS 899/59
Special Requirements for Bridges of New High-Speed Lines,
BZA Munich, 01/01/85

[3]   German Federal Railway, General Design, Series 1a,
Valley Bridges, Box Girder, two Tracks, single Cell, P.C.
state of 1991

[4]   Prommersberger G., DB Neubaustrecke Mannheim-Stuttgart · Talbrücken
Engineering Structures ibw Nr. 4, Elite Trust Reg. Vaduz ·03/87

[5]   Siebke H. and Schacknies O., Bedarfgerechte Eisenbahnbrücken -
ein Beitrag zum wirtschaftlichen Schienenverkehr
Railway Bridges due to Request - Contribution to Economic Railroading
Die Bundesbahn (magazine), Vol. 6/1987

Pictures are taken from the high-speed track bridges of Germany and from an 1:87 scale modell of the new 58.00 m bridge structure in spring 1992.

Innovative Applications of Composite Materials

Applications novatrices des matériaux composites

490

ADVANCED COMPOSITE MATERIALS IN BRIDGES AND STRUCTURES
K.W. Neale and P. Labossière, Editors; Canadian Society for Civil Engineering, 1992

Matériaux composites d'avant-garde pour ponts et charpentes
K.W. Neale et P. Labossière, éditeurs; Société canadienne de génie civil, 1992

INNOVATIVE DESIGN OF FRP COMBINED WITH CONCRETE

T.C. Triantafillou
Massachusetts Institute of Technology
Cambridge, Massachusetts, USA

U. Meier
Swiss Federal Laboratories for Materials Testing and Research (EMPA)
Dübendorf, Switzerland

ABSTRACT

Developments in the area of composite material systems linked to innovative designs of components using fibre-reinforced plastics (FRP) in combination with concrete can enable more efficient, reliable and cost effective structures to be produced. This study presents the basic mechanics of the short term behaviour of hybrid glass fibre-reinforced plastic (GFRP) box beams, combined with a layer of concrete in the compression zone and a unidirectional carbon (CFRP) laminate in the tension zone. The concept results in low cost elements with pseudo-ductile characteristics, possessing at the same time high stiffness and strength properties, and can be thought of as a better way of producing structural members based on pultruded elements. A design methodology for the hybrid sections is also presented, based on a complete set of stiffness, strength and ductility design requirements.

RÉSUMÉ

L'évolution des systèmes de matériaux composites, combiné à des designs innovateurs de pièces structurales utilisant des FRP et du béton peut mener à la production de structures plus efficaces, fiables, et économiques. Cette étude présente la mécanique du comportement à court terme de poutres-caissons hybrides en plastique renforcé de fibres de verre (GFRP), liées à une couche de béton dans la région en compression et à un stratifié unidirectionnel en carbone (CFRP) dans la zone en tension. Le concept produit des éléments économiques avec des caractéristiques pseudo-ductiles, possédant à la fois une haute rigidité et une haute résistance. Une méthodologie de design pour sections hybrides, basée sur des exigences relatives à la rigidité, la résistance et la ductilité, est présentée.

INTRODUCTION

Substantial progress has been made in the use of fiber reinforced plastics (FRP) in specialized market sectors of the construction industry over the last years, with the introduction of mass produced composite structural members into civil engineering structures. Composite materials consist of continuous fibers of glass, aramid or carbon embedded in a polymer resin matrix. Typical applications of composites in civil engineering include: (a) lightweight structural components such as framing and bridges; (b) high-strength lightweight cables for cable-supported bridges and tendons in prestressed elements; (c) composite rods as reinforcement in concrete structures, offering corrosion immunity and providing non-conductive/magnetic fields; (d) strengthening of existing structural members and reinforcement of new ones with nonprestressed or prestressed epoxy-bonded FRP sheets; and (e) other applications such as storage tanks, pipes and stabilization of soils as well as retaining walls.

Manufacture of composite materials by automated processes can produce today high quality components at a relatively low labor cost. One such process is pultrusion, in which fibers are pulled through a heated die into which resin is injected, and a fully cured member is produced with good dimensional stability. Pultrusion is a fast-growing process for manufacturing FRP structural members, and a great awareness among engineers of how the features of pultruded products can be translated into cost saving benefits has made the method quite popular. However, until significant further developments take place in manufacturing technology linked to *innovative designs* to enable more efficient, reliable and cost effective structures to be produced, composite materials will hardly take their place in construction alongside traditional materials such as concrete, steel and wood.

This paper presents in detail how composite materials can be combined with a low-cost construction material, concrete, to result in new concepts for the design of lightweight, corrosion immune and yet inexpensive beams with excellent damping and fatigue properties. The proposed concept lends itself to low cost prefabrication of high performance structural elements,with a high potential of use in both today's construction of specialized composite structures and tomorrow's buildings and bridges formed out of modular systems.

NEW DESIGN CONCEPTS

Consider for instance the case of a glass fiber reinforced plastic (GFRP) pultruded beam section. Thin walled box sections are the most efficient for beams (e.g., Ashby, 1991), and are, in fact, very commonly used in structural applications for pultruded profiles. However, they suffer from some disadvantages, including the following: (a) the compressive flange is considerably weaker than the tensile flange, because GFRP has a compressive strength about half its tensile strength and because of local buckling phenomena (Banks and Rhodes, 1983; Holmes and Just, 1983); (b) failure is usually catastrophic without warning, as composite materials are linear elastic to failure; and (c) the design is usually governed by stiffness (because of the relatively low stiffness of GFRP), resulting in a need for excessive use of composite material to satisfy certain displacement requirements. In view of the above, a novel and more efficient design of composite box sections is possible, driven by the following considerations:

(i) The compression stresses in the section should be carried by a material with the highest compressive strength and stiffness to cost ratio, and hence, the GFRP flange could be eliminated and substituted by a layer of concrete.

(ii) Another composite material with a failure strain less than that of GFRP could be added to the section's tension zone, so that it will be the first element to fail giving some warning of an imminent collapse (pseudo-ductility). Since this element will be part of a flange, it should preferably possess a high stiffness, too, to increase the section's rigidity. An externally epoxy-bonded thin layer of unidirectional carbon fiber reinforced plastic (CFRP) appears to be the best candidate material for this purpose. Selection of this material will also enhance the member's fatigue and creep behavior, given that unidirectional CFRP has an excellent response to fatigue loading and is practically creep-free.

(iii) Since the proposed design involves casting of concrete, part of the cross section should be used as formwork for the wet concrete, to minimize fabrication costs.

492

A schematic illustration of a hybrid FRP-concrete cross section for beams is given in Fig. 1. Note that the top concrete layer is encased in a GFRP channel with wall thickness just equal to that required to carry the wet concrete. Furthermore, a very good bond between the concrete and the GFRP can be achieved either by the use of epoxy adhesives or by providing the GFRP-concrete surface with mechanical deformations, or, finally, by a combination of the two.

The flexural response of a 1.5 m long hybrid FRP-concrete beam (and of the same beam without the concrete layer and the CFRP laminate) subjected to three-point bending is shown in Fig. 2. CFRP fracture gives warning of failure at a load corresponding to a certain percentage of the ultimate load, while ultimate collapse is defined when the concrete crushes in the compression zone. A better insight into the basic mechanical behavior of the proposed scheme and highlights of a design methodology for the new concept are given in the following sections.

MECHANICAL BEHAVIOR OF HYBRID FRP-CONCRETE ELEMENTS

A description of the proposed cross section for hybrid FRP-concrete beam elements is given in Fig. 1. The webs have a depth d and a thickness t_w; the bottom GFRP flange has a thickness t_1; the concrete layer has a thickness c; the CFRP laminate has a width b_2 and a thickness t_2; and the section has a width b. Furthermore, it is assumed that the elements supporting the concrete layer are very thin and do not affect the behavior of the section. The properties of the different materials constituting the cross section are as follows: E_c=Young's modulus of concrete; f'_c=compressive strength of concrete; ε^c_u=ultimate compressive strain of concrete; E_w=longitudinal Young's modulus of webs; E_{wT}=tranverse Young's modulus of webs; G_w=shear modulus of webs; ν_L=longitudinal Poisson's ratio of webs; ν_T=transverse Poisson's ratio of webs; τ^*_{fw}=web shear fracture strength; E_1=Young's modulus of GFRP bottom flange; ε^*_1=tensile failure strain of GFRP; E_2=Young's modulus of CFRP laminate; and ε^*_2=tensile failure strain of CFRP.

Stiffness

The flexural rigidity D of the hybrid FRP-concrete section is given by

$$D=E_w\left[\frac{n_cbc^3}{12}+n_cbc\left(y+\frac{c}{2}\right)^2+n_1bt_1(d-y)^2+n_2bt_2(d-y)^2+\frac{t_wd^3}{6}+2t_wd\left(\frac{d}{2}-y\right)^2\right] \tag{1}$$

where $n_c=E_c/E_w$, $n_1=E_1/E_w$, $n_2=E_2b_2/E_wb$ and y is the depth of the centroidal axis from the concrete bottom fiber given as

$$y=\frac{-\frac{1}{2}n_cbc^2+n_1bdt_1+n_2bdt_2+t_wd^2}{n_cbc+n_1bt_1+n_2bt_2+2t_wd} \tag{2}$$

In thin walled box sections under a vertical shear force most of the shear load is carried by the webs. Hence, a simple approximate formula for the shear rigidity Q gives

$$Q=2G_wt_wd \tag{3}$$

Failure Analysis

The hybrid section loaded in bending can fail in a number of possible ways. The webs may fracture or buckle due to shear stresses, resulting in shear failure; one or more of the beam's elements may fail due to normal stresses, resulting in flexural failure; the beam may buckle laterally (lateral torsional buckling); and it can be argued that the bond at the FRP-concrete interface may fail

493

causing debonding. Debonding is not examined in this study because it is believed that it is not of crucial importance. Epoxy adhesives for instance (and/or surface deformations) can result in high performance interfaces with shear strengths higher than that of concrete (e.g., Kaiser, 1989; Triantafillou et al., 1992). The remaining failure mechanisms are discussed next.

Web Shear Fracture

As an approximation, the maximum shear stress τ_{max} in the web may be taken to be equal to 1.5 times the average shear stress in the web, thus:

$$\tau_{max} = \frac{3}{2} \frac{V_u}{2t_w d} \tag{4}$$

where V_u is the section's ultimate shear strength. Shear fracture occurs when the maximum shear stress equals the in-plane fracture shear strength of the webs τ^*_{fw}, giving

$$V_u = \frac{4}{3} t_w d \tau^*_{fw} \tag{5}$$

Web Shear Buckling

The average web shear buckling stress τ^*_{bw} can be determined theoretically as follows (Timoshenko and Gere, 1961; Holmes and Just, 1983):

$$\tau^*_{bw} = \frac{4K \sqrt[4]{D_L D_T^3}}{t_w d^2} \qquad \text{for} \quad \theta > 1 \tag{6a}$$

or

$$\tau^*_{bw} = \frac{4K \sqrt{D_T H}}{t_w d^2} \qquad \text{for} \quad \theta < 1 \tag{6b}$$

where

$$D_L = \frac{E_w t_w^3}{12(1 - \nu_L \nu_T)} \tag{7a}$$

$$D_T = \frac{E_{wT} t_w^3}{12(1 - \nu_L \nu_T)} \tag{7b}$$

$$H = \frac{1}{2}(\nu_L D_T + \nu_T D_L) + \frac{G_w t_w^3}{6(1 - \nu_L \nu_T)} \tag{7c}$$

$$\theta = \frac{\sqrt{D_L D_T}}{H} \tag{7d}$$

and the value of K depends on θ as shown in Table 1. Shear buckling occurs when the average shear stress equals the shear buckling stress:

$$V_u = 2t_w d \tau^*_{bw} \tag{8}$$

Flexural Failure

In a well designed hybrid FRP-concrete section the CFRP laminate fails first (thus giving a warning of collapse) at a moment M_2. The stresses are then redistributed and the section has a

494

moment carrying capacity until the concrete crushes in compression when the maximum compressive strain equals the ultimate failure strain of concrete $\varepsilon^c{}_u$. Crushing of concrete defines flexural collapse of the cross section at a moment M_u which is higher than M_2.

The normal strain and stress distributions corresponding to M_2 are given in Fig. 3. Assuming that when the CFRP laminate fails the concrete is still linear elastic, the depth of the neutral axis is given by Eq.(2) and M_2 is calculated as

$$M_2 = n_c \varepsilon_2^* E_w bcy \frac{\left(d+\frac{c}{2}\right)}{(d-y)} + n_c \varepsilon_2^* E_w bc^2 \frac{\left(d+\frac{2}{3}c\right)}{2(d-y)} + \varepsilon_2^* E_w t_w y^2 \frac{\left(d-\frac{y}{3}\right)}{(d-y)} - \frac{1}{3}\varepsilon_2^* E_w t_w (d-y)^2 \qquad (9)$$

under the condition that the strain at the concrete top fiber is less than $\varepsilon^c{}_u$, that is

$$y < \frac{d\varepsilon_c^u - c\varepsilon_2^*}{\varepsilon_c^u + \varepsilon_2^*} \qquad (10)$$

The normal strain and stress distributions corresponding to the ultimate flexural capacity of the cross section are illustrated in Fig. 4. The stresses in the concrete layer are calculated here based on the equivalent rectangular stress block approach (e.g., Park and Paulay, 1975). The depth of the neutral axis y_u is established from internal force equilibrium

$$y_u = \frac{-\dfrac{\beta_1 f_c' bc^2}{\varepsilon_c^u E_w} + n_1 bdt_1 + t_w d^2}{\dfrac{\beta_1 f_c' bc}{\varepsilon_c^u E_w} + n_1 bt_1 + 2t_w d} \qquad (11)$$

and, finally, moment equilibrium gives the flexural capacity of the cross section

$$M_u = \beta_1 f_c' bc \left(d + \frac{c}{2}\right) + \varepsilon_c^u E_w t_w y_u^2 \frac{\left(d - \dfrac{y_u}{3}\right)}{(c+y_u)} - \varepsilon_c^u E_w t_w \frac{(d-y_u)^3}{3(c+y_u)} \qquad (12)$$

under the constraint that the GFRP flange has not fractured ($\varepsilon_1 < \varepsilon^*_1$), that is

$$y_u > \frac{d\varepsilon_c^u - c\varepsilon_1^*}{\varepsilon_c^u + \varepsilon_1^*} \qquad (13)$$

Lateral Instability

Although box sections have a high resistance to lateral torsional buckling in general, limits to a section's height to width ratio are often imposed to prevent lateral instability and satisfy other practical design requirements. Hence, a constraint inequality of the form

$$\frac{c+d}{b} < k_1 \qquad (14)$$

is adopted in this study, where k_1 is a constant to be chosen by the designer. Practical experience with composite material sections and with thin walled hybrid sections made of other materials indicates that a number around 3 is a reasonable conservative estimate for k_1.

495

Ductility Considerations

At the cross section level, ductility can be defined as the ratio of the curvature at failure (ϕ^u) to that at the deviation from the linear elastic response, that is when the CFRP laminate fractures (ϕ^*). From Fig. 3 and 4 the curvature ductility is calculated as

$$\frac{\phi^u}{\phi^*} = \frac{\varepsilon_c^u}{\varepsilon_2^*} \frac{(d-y)}{(c+y_u)} \tag{15}$$

DESIGN METHODOLOGY

The problem under consideration here is the selection of the cross section's geometric variables (d, t_w, c, b, t_1 and t_2) in terms of the given material properties, so that a given set of design requirements is satisfied at the minimum cost. A typical set of design constraints could consist of a bending moment and a shear force to be carried safely by the cross section (strength constraints), as well as a maximum displacement limit (stiffness constraint). Some essential concepts towards the development of an appropriate design procedure are discussed next: (a) the proposed hybrid section does not offer a shear strength considerably higher than that of a geometrically similar GFRP section without the concrete and the CFRP layers; (b) the webs are designed optimally when they fail simultaneously according to all their associated failure modes; (c) CFRP is an expensive material and the primary purpose of its application should be to provide a pseudo-ductile response in bending; (d) the ductility increases when the thickness of the CFRP laminate decreases; (e) if the area fraction of CFRP used is extremely low, the CFRP laminate will fail prematurely at a low load; (f) if the load at failure of the CFRP is a high fraction of the ultimate load and given that the jump of either the load or the displacement at CFRP failure should not be too high (see Fig. 3a), warning of an imminent collapse comes too late; and (g) concrete is a very cheap material and its use in the cross section should be maximized.

Item (b) above suggests that Eq.(5)-(8) should all be satisfied, indicating that d and t_w can be obtained in terms of the material properties and the ultimate shear force:

$$d = \sqrt{\frac{3V_u}{4\tau_{fw}^*}} \sqrt{\frac{K \sqrt[4]{E_w E_{wT}^3}}{2(1-\nu_L \nu_T)\tau_{fw}^*}} \qquad \text{for } \theta > 1 \tag{16a}$$

$$d = \sqrt{\frac{3V_u}{4\tau_{fw}^*}} \sqrt{\frac{K \sqrt{E_{wT}\left[\frac{1}{2}(\nu_L E_{wT} + \nu_T E_w) + 2G_w\right]}}{2(1-\nu_L \nu_T)\tau_{fw}^*}} \qquad \text{for } \theta < 1 \tag{16b}$$

$$t_w = \frac{3V_u}{4\tau_{fw}^* d} \tag{17}$$

In addition, items (e) and (f) suggest that the designer should specify a certain ratio of the moment at CFRP fracture to the ultimate moment, say

$$M_2 = k_2 M_u \tag{18}$$

Finally, from (g) we may conclude that inequality (14) should be used in the form of an equation:

$$\frac{c+d}{b} = k_1 \tag{19}$$

496

Given the above considerations, the proposed design methodology (omitting here for simplicity the application of material and load uncertainty factors) for hybrid FRP-concrete sections is summarized as follows:

1. Design the cross section for shear by solving Eq.(16) and (17) for d and t_w.
2. Select a very low CFRP thickness t_2.
3. Solve the nonlinear system of Eq.(12), (18) and (19) for c, b and t_1.
4. Calculate the flexural and shear rigidities and hence the deflection at a given load.
5. If the stiffness requirement is not met, increase d and possibly t_2 and repeat steps 3-4 until the stiffness constraint is satisfied.

It must be noted that box-type sections are inherently stiff. Furthermore, separation of the stiff concrete and CFRP layers is expected to increase the rigidity of the cross section considerably, and it is believed that the stiffness constraint will rarely be activated.

CONCLUDING REMARKS

Combination of different fiber reinforced plastic materials with concrete appears to be a feasible way of producing efficient and cost effective hybrid members. These members possess many desirable mechanical behavior characteristics, such as ductility, high stiffness and strength, while maintaining a low weight. The main features of the proposed concept for hybrid sections can be summarized as follows: a concrete layer substitutes the GFRP compressive flange of traditional pultruded box sections, thus reducing the materials cost and increasing the stiffness; and the bottom flange is made by a combination of two composites (GFRP and CFRP), one failing in tension earlier than the other (and, possibly, in a gradual manner), serving the role of a "sensor" which indicates an imminent collapse (pseudo-ductile response).

The design of hybrid FRP-concrete components is a relatively straightforward task once all the possible failure mechanisms have been identified and the design requirements and constraints have been set up. One can either employ a nonlinear optimization algorithm to minimize a certain function (e.g., materials cost) based on a certain set of constraints (e.g., stifness, strength), or follow the simple design methodology outlined above to select the cross section dimensions.

The proposed concept for hybrid FRP-concrete elements can be thought of as a better way of designing composite profiles using materials by combination and placing them exactly where they perform best. Optimum combination of materials in structural design is increasingly becoming a necessity as well as an indispensible part of the structural engineer's response to the pressure for more durable and lightweight premanufactured components.

Finally, ongoing research contacted by the authors will address both analytically and experimentally the issue of bond between GFRP and concrete, the insulation of the top GFRP part from the alkaline environment of the concrete (e.g., via the use of an epoxy layer and/or a gelcoat at the interface), and the role of long-term phenomena such as creep (and shrinkage of concrete), fatigue and durability (including temperature effects) in the performance of the hybrid members.

REFERENCES

Ashby, M. F. (1991). Materials and Shape. *Acta metall. mater.* **39**(6), 1025-1039.

Banks, W. M. and Rhodes, J. (1983). The Instability of Composite Channel Sections. In Composite Structures 2, *Proc., 2nd Intern. Conf. on Comp. Struct.*, 443-452.

Holmes, M. and Just, D. J. (1983). GRP in Structural Engineering. Applied Science Publishers Ltd., England.

Hull, D.(1981). An Introduction to Composite Materials. Cambridge University Press, Cambridge, England.

Kaiser, H. (1989). Strengthening of Reinforced Concrete with Epoxy-bonded Carbon-fiber Plastics. Doctoral thesis, ETH, Zurich, Switzerland (in German).

Park, R. and Paulay, T. (1975). Reinforced Concrete Structures. John Wiley & Sons, New York.

Timoshenko, S. P. and Gere, J. M. (1961). Theory of Elastic Stability. McGraw-Hill Co., New York.

Triantafillou, T. C., Deskovic, N. and Deuring, M. (1992). Strengthening of Concrete Structures with Prestressed FRP Sheets. To appear in *ACI Struct. J.*.

TABLE 1. Values of θ Against K in Web

θ	0	0.2	0.5	1.0	2.0	3.0	5.0	10.0	20.0	40.0
K	18.6	18.9	19.9	22.2	18.8	17.6	16.6	15.9	15.5	15.3

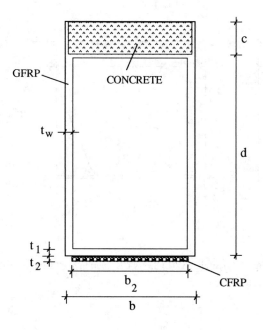

Fig. 1 Beam Section Made of FRP and Concrete Materials by Combination.

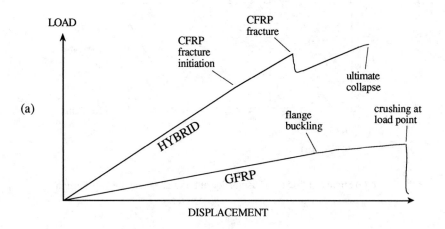

Fig. 2 Load Versus Displacement Behavior of Hybrid FRP-Concrete Beam
and GFRP Beam Subjected to Three-Point Bending.

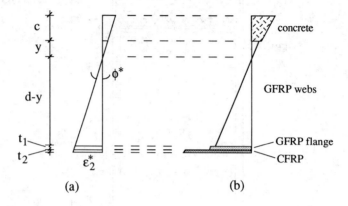

Fig. 3 (a) Strain and (b) Stress Distribution at CFRP Fracture.

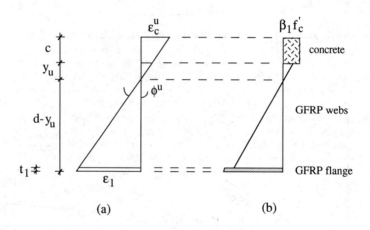

Fig. 4 (a) Strain and (b) Stress Distribution at Flexural Failure of Cross Section.

ADVANCED COMPOSITE MATERIALS IN BRIDGES AND STRUCTURES
K.W. Neale and P. Labossière, Editors; Canadian Society for Civil Engineering, 1992

Matériaux composites d'avant-garde pour ponts et charpentes
K.W. Neale et P. Labossière, éditeurs; Société canadienne de génie civil, 1992

DESIGN OF A COMPOSITE BOX BEAM FOR
BUILDING APPLICATIONS

S.V. Hoa
Concordia University
Montréal, Québec, Canada

ABSTRACT

Due to their light weight, high stiffness and high strength, composites have been used in many applications in aircraft and aerospace structures. From the success of these applications, there are possibilities that composites can also be successfully applied to building structures. This paper examines considerations on the mechanical performance of composite box beams as building support structures. Taking into account that material cost needs to be low, fibreglass reinforced polyester is preferred over graphite fibre composites. Since fibreglass materials have low stiffness, design of structures made of these materials is governed by limit on deflection. Results from this preliminary work show that it is possible to support a floor of 3.3m x 3.3m (10 ft x 10 ft) having a load requirement of 3 kPa (150 lbs/sq ft) using two beams made from unidirectionally reinforced glass fibre vinylester having reasonable dimensions.

RÉSUMÉ

Cet article étudie la possibilité d'utiliser des poutres caissons en matériaux composites dans des structures de génie civil. Le choix d'un polyester renforcé de fibres de verre (GRP) est justifié par son coût inférieur à la fibre de carbone. À cause de leur faible rigidité, le design de structures de GRP est contrôlé par la déflexion. On montre qu'il est possible, en utilisant des poutres de GRP de dimensions raisonnables, de supporter un plancher de 3.3m x 3.3m (10 pi x 10 pi) devant reprendre une charge uniformément répartie de 3 kPa (150 lb/pi. ca.)

Introduction:

The recent trend in pushing composite applications to commercial sectors has spurred a lot of interest in building applications. Composites have been used in a few applications in building structures [1,2]. There are many attractive features in using composites in building applications. These are:

- Light weight. The relative light weight of composites (as compared to steels) would facilitate transportation and handling.

- Good corrosion resistance. This is particularly useful in corrsosive environments such as in chemical processing plants, in marine environments or in outdoor atmosphere.

- Applications where non-metallic environment is necessary.

However, to introduce new materials to new applications, many considerations need to be taken into account. These considerations are numerous and should include the following:

- Strength requirements.

- Deformation requirements.

- Flammability .

- Cost.

The more common composites in use in the industry at the present time are graphite fiber composites, kevlar fiber composites and glass fiber composites. From cost considerations, graphite and kevlar fibers are still expensive. Their use in building applications therefore may not yield structural elements where large volume is possible. Most composites in building applications therefore have been restricted to glass fiber composites.

Common techniques of production of composite structures are hand-lay-up, filament winding, pultrusion, resin transfer molding, braiding etc. Most structural composites used in building applications up to the present have been pultruded. Companies such

502

as Morrison Molded Fiberglass, Creative Pultrusions etc. provide structural elements of different cross section shapes. These structural elements have been used mainly in frames such as roof, wall or grating.
Most structural elements for building applications have been made using vinyl ester resins [3]. In terms of fire resistance, these resins will need additives to enhance their fire retardancy. Resins such as phenolics or modar have better fire resistance. Once the large volume manufacturing techniques such as pultrusion can be used to manufacture composites of these resins successfully, composite structural elements with better fire resistance can be obtained.

As mentioned earlier, most work on composites in building applications have been in light structures such as roofs, side walls or gratings . No investigation has been made on the use of composites in making beams for supporting structures such as floors in buildings. In this paper the concept of using composite beams for supporting a floor structure is investigated. Both the deflection under static loading and the long term creep performance of the beams are examined.

Static loading:

If a fiberglass box beam is to be used to support the floor deck of a building as shown in Figure 1, the load on that beam can be assumed to be uniformly distributed.

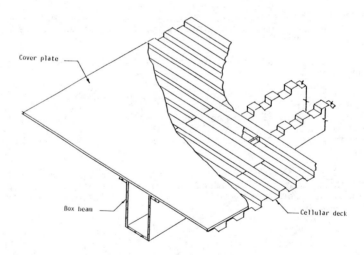

Figure 1: Fiber Reinforced Plastic Floor/Roof System

For a simply supported beam subjected to uniformly distributed load as shown in Figure 2, the deflection at the midlength of the beam is given by [4]:

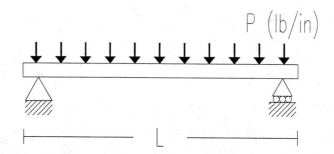

Figure 2: Simply supported beam under uniform load

$$y = (5\ p\ l^4)/(384\ E\ I) \qquad\qquad (1)$$

where
    y: deflection at mid length.
    p: uniformly distributed load.
    l: length of beam.
    E: Young modulus of material.
    I: cross section inertia.

In order to get a realistic estimate on the magnitude of the deflection, some consideration on the beam dimensions and material properties need to be considered.

For a standard office of 10 ft x 10 ft, a beam length l = 10 ft is considered.

Assuming the allowable load on the floor be 150 lb/ft^2 , the total load on that floor would be 15,000 lbs. If two beams are to be used to support the floor, the total load on each beam is 7,500 lbs. If this load is uniformly distributed over a length of 10 ft, the magnitude of the uniform load is p = 7,500/10 = 750 lbs/ft or 62.5 lbs/in.

Consider a beam cross section shown in Figure 3. The cross section of this beam is designed to be fabricated using pultrusion technique. The cross section inertia of this beam is calculated to be I = 230.3 in^4.

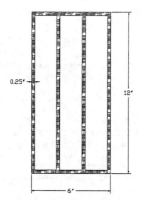

Figure 3: Beam cross section

For the material properties, two different materials can be considered. If the beam is made of hand-lay-up layers which consist of Mats and Woven Rovings, the Yound modulus can be taken to be [5]:
$E = 1.23 \times 10^6$ psi. If the beam is made of tensioned unidirectional materials produced by pultrusion or by filament winding, the Young modulus can be taken to be [6]: $E = 5.12 \times 10^6$ psi.

Using the above values in equation (1), one has:

* For hand-lay-up glass/vinyl ester materials:

$$y = (5 \times 62.5 \times 120^4)/(384 \times 1.23 \times 10^6 \times 230.3)$$

$$y = 0.596 \text{ in.} \tag{2}$$

The ratio of deflection over length is:

$$y/l = 0.596/120 = 1/201 \tag{3}$$

The ratio of the total load of 7500 lbs over the deflection is:

$$P/y = 7500/0.596 = 12,584 \text{ lbs/in.} \tag{4}$$

* For tensioned unidirectional materials:

$$y = (5 \times 62.5 \times 120^4)/(384 \times 5.12 \times 10^6 \times 230.3)$$

$$y = 0.143 \text{ in.} \tag{5}$$

The ratio of deflection over length is:

$$y/l = 0.143/120 = 1/839 \tag{6}$$

The ratio of the total load of 7500 lbs over deflection is:

$$P/y = 7500/0.143 = 52,448 \text{ lbs/in.} \qquad (7)$$

Using a deflection criterion of $(y/l) < (1/320)$ [7], comparing this with the ratios in equations (3) and (6), it can be seen that beams made by tensioned unidirectional fibers meet the deflection requirements while beams made by hand-lay-up materials do not.

Experiment on static loading:

Experiment was performed on static loading of one box beam . The experimental set-up is as shown in Figure 4. For the test, a four point bending is used. Due to the unavailability of pultruded box beams of dimensions shown in Figure 3, box beams made by hand-lay-up were used. Length of the beam between supports is 117 in. and the distance between the support and the loading point is 39 in.

The box beam tested has an overall length of 125.5 in., a height of 11.875 in. and a width of 5.875 in (Figure 5). There are seven baffles equally spaced along the length of the beam. The distance from the end of the beam to the outer baffle is 3.77 in. Baffles also contain ribs for stiffening purpose. Baffles and ribs are incorporated into the beam by hand-lay-up technique. Thicknesses of different sides are as follows:

The **top flange** (side 1) has the lay-up sequence of MMMRMRM (7 layers, 5 Mat (M) and 2 Woven Roving (R) layers). The total thickness of this side is $t_1 = 0.268$ in. The orientation of the woven roving layers are 0 and 90 degrees with respect to the axis of the beam. Woven Roving layers are of 24 oz/sq.ft (ounce per square feet) type. The **webs** (side 2 and side 4) have the lay-up sequence of MMMRM (5 layers, 4 Mat layers and 1 Woven Roving layer). The thickness of these two sides are $t_2 = t_4 = 0.193$ in.

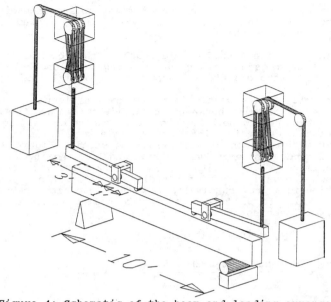

Figure 4: Schematic of the beam and loading arrangement

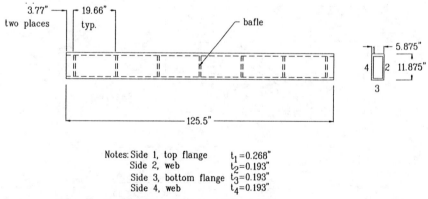

Notes: Side 1, top flange $t_1 = 0.268"$
Side 2, web $t_2 = 0.193"$
Side 3, bottom flange $t_3 = 0.193"$
Side 4, web $t_4 = 0.193"$

Figure 5: Configuration of beam 1

The woven roving layers are oriented at 45 and -45 degrees to the axis of the beam. Woven Roving layers on these two sides are of 18 oz/sq.ft. type. The **bottom flange** (side 3) has the same lay-up sequence as side 2 and side 4. Its thickness is $t_3 = 0.193$ in. However, the orientation of the woven roving layers are at 0 and 90 degrees to the axis of the beam. Also, woven roving layers for the bottom flange is of the 24 oz/sq.ft. type.

The baffles inside the beam have the lay-up sequence of MMMRMRM (7 layers). These baffles have ribs which have the same composition and thickness as the baffles.

Strain gages are placed at midlength on the top and bottom of the beam. Strain gages are oriented along the length of the beam. Deflection at midlength is measure using a dial indicator.

The results of the static test is shown in Figures 6 to 8. Figure 6 shows the relation between the tensile strain and the load at one application point. Both loading and unloading curves are shown. The relation between the load and tensile strain is approximately linear with a slope of 18182 lbs / % strain. Figure 7 shows the relation between compressive strain and load. Again the relation is approximately linear with a slope of 27273 lbs / % strain. Figure 8 shows the variation of the midlength deformation with load. The relation is approximately linear with a load/displacement ratio of 8219 lbs/in. If the total load at two loading points is considered, the ratio becomes:

$$P/y = 16,438 \text{ lbs/in.} \qquad\qquad (8)$$

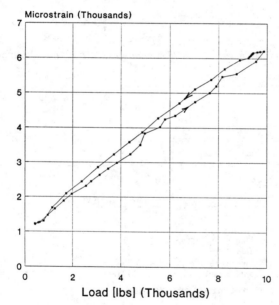

Figure 6: Tensile strain vs. load.

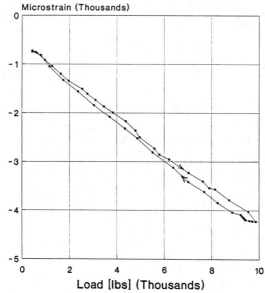

Figure 7: *Compressive strain vs. load.*

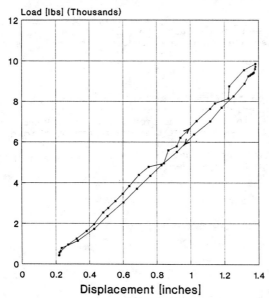

Figure 8: *Midlength deflection vs. load.*

To compare the experimental deflection with calculated values, the formula in Roark and Young [4] is used. For a beam under four point loading, the equation is:

$$EI\ y = -(W/6) < (l/2) - a>^3$$

$$+ (W/12)\ (\ l-a)\ [(l^2 /4) + a^2 - 2a\ l] \qquad (9)$$

where   y: midlength deflection.
         W : load applied at one loading point.
         a : distance from support point to load point.

When a = 1/3 which is the case for the test set-up here, one has

$$y = 0.0178\ Wl^3/EI \qquad (10)$$

The ratio of load at one point over displacement is:

$$W/y = EI/(0.0178\ l^3) \qquad (11)$$

Using $E = 1.23 \times 10^6$ psi, $l = 125.5$ in. and $I = 99.66$ in.^{4}, one has:

$$W/y = 3484\ lbs/in.$$

The ratio of total load over displacement is:

$$P/y = 3484\ lbs/in. \qquad (12)$$

Comparing between equation (8) and (12), there is a significant difference between the calculated value and the experimental value. This is because the calculation does not take the reinforcing baffles into account.

Creep tests:

Creep tests have been performed on three composite box beams of similar configurations as the one shown in Figure 5. Figure 9 shows the change in midlength deformation for beam 2. Beam 2 has similar configuration as Beam 1 except beam 2 has larger thickness. The top flange of Beam 2 has 6 Mats and 3 Woven Roving layers. The bottom flange has 5 Mats and 2 Woven Roving layers. The two webs have 5 Mats and 2 Woven Roving layers.

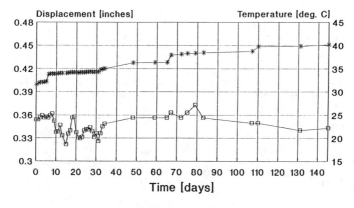

Figure 9. Displacement and Temperature vs. time for beam 2

According to Holmes and Rahman [8] who performed creep tests on composite box beams over a period of about 20 months, most of the creep deflection occurs within the first 1000 hours (42 days). For beam 2, not taken the fluctuation in temperature into account, over a period of 140 days (3360 hours), the deflection increases by 0.05 in. from 0.40 in to 0.45 in. giving an average creep deflection of 0.000357 in./day.

Discussion:

Even though beams of different cross sections have been examined, the following synthesis can be made.

Figure 9 shows that the increase in midlength deflection of beam 2 over a period of 140 days is 0.05 in. Assuming that this accounts for the majority of creep deflection as concluded by Holmes and Rahman, this amount can be added to the static deflection for the design of the beam. Since beam 2 is made by hand-lay-up materials, use of 0.05 in. for beams made by tensioned unidirectional fibers would be conservative. For a beam having the cross section of Figure 3, equation (5) gives a midlength deflection of 0.143 in. Adding 0.05 in. to this gives 0.193 in. The ratio of deflection over length now is:

$$y/l = 0.193/120 = 1/621 \qquad (13)$$

This ratio is still less than the ratio 1/320 as required by the code.

Conclusion:

The above considerations show that from the mechanical performance point of view, it is possible to use box beams made of fiberglass reinforced vinyl ester materials to support office floors of a significant floor load. It is assumed that pultruded beams are used. Further work needs to be done on actual testing of the pultruded beams themselves and also on the flammability resistance of the beams.

Ackowledgement:

The financial supports from the Natural Sciences and Engineering Research Council Canada through grant No. OGP0000413 and from the Formation des Chercheurs et l'Aide a la Recherche (Quebec) are appreciated.

References:

1. Liskey K. " Structural Applications of Pultruded Composite Products", Proceedings of the Conference on <u>Advanced Composites Materials in Civil Engineering Structures</u> ed. S.L. Iyer and R. Sen, Las Vegas, Jan./Feb. 1991.

2. Grace N.F., Bagchi D.K., and Kennedy J.B. " Use of Composites for Vibration Control of Buildings", Proceedings of the Conference on <u>Advanced Composites Materials in Civil Engineering Structures</u> ed. S.L. Iyer and R. Sen, Las Vegas, Jan./Feb. 1991.

3. Anonymous, "Design Manual, Extren Fiberglass Structural Shapes" Morrison Molded Fiberglass Company, Virginia, 1989.

4. Roark R.J. and Young W.C. " Formulas for Stress and Strain" 5th ed., McGraw Hill, 1975.

5. Hoa S.V., Sankar T.S. and Bargiora R. "Tensile Behavior of Laminates used for making Fiber Reinforced Plastic Vessels", Journal of Reinforced Plastics and Composites, Vol. 2, April 1983.

6. Hoa S.V., <u>Analysis for Design of Fiber Reinforced Plastic Vessels and Pipings</u>, Technomic Publishing Co., 1991.

7. Anonymous, National Building Code, 1990.

8. Holmes M. and Rahman T.A. "Creep behaviour of glass reinforced plastic box beams", Composites, April 1980, p.79.

ADVANCED COMPOSITE MATERIALS IN BRIDGES AND STRUCTURES
K.W. Neale and P. Labossière, Editors; Canadian Society for Civil Engineering, 1992

Matériaux composites d'avant-garde pour ponts et charpentes
K.W. Neale et P. Labossière, éditeurs; Société canadienne de génie civil, 1992

HAUTE TECHNOLOGIE COMPOSITE DANS LA
CONCEPTION ARCHITECTURALE

P. Spanek
École d'architecture de Bordeaux
Talence, France

RÉSUMÉ

La conception architecturale se situe dans le contexte des logiques de la créativité. Les méthodes conceptuelles basées sur des logiques créatives peuvent apporter des solutions innovantes du point de vue technique, technologique et esthétique au projet architectural orienté vers l'utilisation des matériaux nouveaux. Nous pouvons parler de l'enchaînement "créativité - conception - projet" car le projet n'est que le résultat du processus conceptuel, qui à son tour n'est que l'application de la démarche créative. La pédagogie du projet architectural est étroitement liée à la recherche des méthodes conceptuelles basées sur la "créatique" (pédagogie de la créativité).

ABSTRACT

Architectural conception is part of the logics of creativity. Conceptual methods based on creative logics may bring about innovative technical, technological or aesthetic solutions to architectural projects which experiment with new materials. One may speak of the sequence "creativity - design - project", because the project is the result of the conceptual process, which is an application of the creative approach. The pedagogy of an architectural project is closely connected with the search for conceptual methods based on "créatique" that is to say the teaching of creativity.

1. LES MATERIAUX NOUVEAUX, LA CONCEPTION ET LA CREATIVITE.

Il y a deux sortes d'approches conceptuelles dans l'architecture et dans le design de produit qui utilisent de nouveaux matériaux .

L'approche "traditionaliste" considère un nouveau matériau comme matériau de "substitution" sans chercher le changement structurel, formel, fonctionnel et esthétique qu'il induit et ne prend en compte que le concept "d'amélioration" en vue d'un meilleur comportement du produit sur le marché existant.

L'approche "novatrice" utilise le nouveau matériau comme matériau "innovant". La création du produit nouveau, non existant, dépend directement du changement technique, technologique et esthétique provoqué par l'utilisation du nouveau matériau.

Ces deux types d'approches se développent parallèlement et indépendamment, même si le "remplacement" semble à tort être la première phase de "l'innovation".

L'histoire de l'architecture en offre une multitude d'exemples. Le système "poteau-poutre" peut être réalisé en bois, en pierre, en béton ou en matériaux composites sans changer ni le système constructif, ni l'esthétique architecturale. L'architecture grecque a reproduit la tectonique du bois en pierre et R. Bofill reproduit l'architecture grecque en béton armé préfabriqué. Mais G. A. Eiffel ne pouvait pas réaliser ses constructions sans l'acier, comme P. L. Nervi sans béton armé ou Frei Otto sans les composites souples.

Il est clair que la démarche "traditionaliste" de la conception, cherchant une nouvelle esthétique, ne peut produire qu'un "pastiche culturel" et que la nouvelle esthétique, exprimant une nouvelle technologie, ne peut être le résultat que de la démarche "novatrice", fondée sur la créativité et l'invention.

J.P. Guilford, psychologue américain, a mis en évidence que l'aptitude à créer, à inventer des idées nouvelles, existe à l'état potentiel chez tous les être humains. La capacité à créer est mesurée par quatre facteurs: l'originalité (idées inédites), la flexibilité (idées différentes), la fluidité (variantes d'idée) et l'élaboration (formalisation et réalisation).

R. Leclercq travaillait sur les logiques de la découverte. Tandis que la logique déductive est efficace pour gérer l'existant et pour traiter des problèmes connus, l'invention s'appuie sur la logique combinatoire (décomposition et recomposition d'un objet), sur la logique associative (le transfert technologique, l'analogie bionique et la synectique) et sur la logique onirique (le domaine de l'inconscient et du subconscient).

Dans le processus créatif, il y a deux mouvements et cinq phases. Le mouvement divergent permet la production d'un maximum d'idées tandis que le mouvement convergent permet l'évaluation des propositions. Les cinq phases - perception, analyse, production, sélection et application - constituent une méthode d'innovation et assurent l'introduction des nouveaux matériaux et des nouveaux produits sur le marché.

2. THEME "CREATIVITE - CONCEPTION - PROJET".

Pour un enseignant de la conception architecturale, structurelle et du design, orientée vers une pratique professionnelle, il n'est pas facile de séparer les trois thèmes du séminaire sur les processus de conception.

Les théories et les pratiques de la conception architecturale font partie de la problématique plus générale de la créativité et influencent directement les pratiques professionnelles du projet.

Pour cette raison, il est préférable de parler de l'enchaînement "créativité - conception - projet" car le projet n'est que résultat du processus conceptuel, qui n'est que l'application de la démarche créative.

Il est vrai que pour des raisons analytiques il faut séparer des éléments dans l'enchaînement "l'enseignement de la conception architecturale dans la pratique professionnelle du projet", surtout lorsqu'il s'agit de la conception orientée vers l'innovation technique, technologique et esthétique.

Les logiques de l'innovation diffèrent de la logique déductive dans le processus de conception. Pour aborder la pratique du projet comme résultat de la conception orientée vers l'innovation, il faudra examiner les logiques de la créativité.

3. CREATIVITE.

L'homme ne peut créer au sens absolu du terme, qui signifie faire quelque choseà partir de rien. Les produits de son génie ne sont jamais que des combinaisons nouvelles d'éléments préexistants basées sur une idée nouvelle. L'idée nouvelle qui donne la naissance à l'invention, est le fruit des fonctions mentales inter-hémisphériques du cerveau humain.

Le professeur Sperry, prix Nobel de médecine en 1981, a mis en évidence la dissymétrie fonctionnelle des hémisphères cérébraux et mis l'accent sur les rôles complémentaires des deux cerveaux. Le cerveau gauche, "la rigueur scientifique et technique", a la capacité du raisonnement analytique basé sur les logiques déductives et mathématiques et fonctionne d'une manière linéaire et progressive. Le cerveau droit, "l'imagination artistique", a la capacité de la synthèse basée sur des logiques intuitives et sensorielles et fonctionne d'une manière globaliste et instantanée.

Suivant notre bagage intellectuel dû à notre formation préalable scientifique ou artistique, la rigueur du cerveau gauche bloque l'imagination du cerveau droit ou vice-versa.

Les techniques de créativité essaient de rétablir le dialogue entre le scientifique et l'artiste qui sont en nous en développant l'aptitude à créer, à inventer des solutions nouvelles.

4. PROJETS D'ARCHITECTURE.

La région d'Aquitaine, où siège, notamment, l'industrie Aérospatiale, a fait depuis une décennie un effort considérable dans le développement de la technologie de pointe, spécialement dans le domaine de la mise au point et de la réalisation de matériaux composites performants. Pour soutenir et faire reconnaître cette activité majeure de la région, le Conseil Régional a créé le Comité pour le Développement des Matériaux Composites (CODEMAC).

Pour promouvoir l'utilisation de matériaux composites dans l'architecture et la construction , le CODEMAC a organisé une conférence d'information et d'échange entre les industriels, les organismes de développement économique, les architectes et les ingénieurs-conseil. Les architectes invités n'ont pas été d'emblée séduits par les matériaux composites qui peuvent pourtant par leurs qualités exceptionnelles apporter une contribution essentielle à l'architecture, tant sur le plan technologique qu'artistique. Les architectes n'étaient pas préparés par leur formation initiale à concevoir des structures spatiales avec un poids nul. Pour eux, le bâtiment a été rattaché au sol par son poids et l'architecture s'exprime par sa masse. C'est ce qui nous a conduit à proposer un enseignement de l'Architecture des structures spatiales et légères à l'Ecole d'Architecture de Bordeaux en 1983.

La participation de l'Institut des Matériaux Composites d'Aquitaine à cet enseignement a introduit une réflexion complexe sur les technologies et les matériaux contemporains. Elle a permis dès le lancement de cet enseignement d'élargir l'éventail des matériaux utilisables pour les structures réticulées, tendues, suspendues et gonflables destinées à la construction et à l'expression architecturale.

Les projets étudiants, présentés dans cet article, illustrent l'approche et la démarche créatives pour l'utilisation du textile et des composites dans l'expression plastique et architecturale :

- Trois projets d'étudiants de l'école d'architecture de Bordeaux de l'année universitaire 1989-90, qui remportaient les deux premiers prix et une mention au concours international d'architecture "Un bâtiment tout textile", matériaux composites à renforts textiles appliqués à la construction pour un Centre international des technologies du textile, organisé par le FITAT (Forum International des Technologies Appliquées du Textile) avec le concours de la Cité des Sciences et de l'Industrie et du Plan Construction et Architecture à l'occasion du Symposium International des Matériaux Composites à Renfort Textiles Appliqués à la Construction à Lyon 1990.

- Trois projets d'étudiants de l'école d'architecture de Bordeaux de l'année universitaire 1990-91 qui remportaient les quatre premiers prix et le prix du public au concours d'architecture "Un centre régional d'innovation et de promotion de la science et de la technologie", organisé par le Comité d'Expansion Aquitaine avec CODEMAC à l'occasion des Journées d'études et des rencontres sur le thème "Composites et nouveaux matériaux dans l'architecture, l'architecture intérieure et le design" à Bordeaux 1991.

4.1. Un bâtiment tout textile
1er prix - Olivier Lehmans, Pierre-Yves Portier

L'enveloppe est constituée de panneaux reliés par une résille en profilés, reposant sur une trame de poteaux. Des volumes modulaires (3x 3x 3 m) sont reliés par des passerelles, des escaliers et des ascenseurs. Les fonctions se répartissent sur quatre niveaux évoluant du premier, ouvert au public, au dernier, privé. Elles sont différenciées grâce aux jeux de lumière, de couleurs et de transparence dans une ambiance tamisée.

On accède côté route par un grand escalier donnant sur deux amphithéâtres. Une "rue suspendue", large de 6 mètres, traverse le hall d'exposition et dessert, en bas, les espaces publics de découverte et de travail, la cafétéria ouverte sur la "forêt de bambous". En haut, on distingue le centre de ressources.

Les poteaux donnent une dimension verticale à cet espace tramé mais libre, protégé mais ouvert. Le bâtiment est en lui-même une expression de la technologie des matériaux composites. Chaque élément, du plus petit au plus grand, du tissu à l'enveloppe, participe à la démonstration.

4.2. Un bâtiment tout textile
2e prix - François Nogué, Gérard Marre, Frédéric Autier, Denis Lecat

Le centre international des technologies du textile véhicule l'image d'un lac qui s'étend au devant, d'un hectare recouvert avec une toile qui semble flotter au ras du sol.

Après un plongeon dans le lac, une baignade dans une lumière diffusée par la toile, le visiteur découvrira des formes inattendues, trouvera des expositions et de l'exploitation des matériaux nouveaux.

La toile en polyester enduit de PVC est supportée par un maillage en câbles de Kevlar mis en tension avec des tendeurs.

4.3. Un bâtiment tout textile
Mention - Sandrine Ducoloner, Isabelle Pendariès

L'espace est modulé entre le coeur et l'enveloppe. Le coeur, la sphère évidée, est le centre de l'exposition vers lequel tous les espaces convergent. Un parcours qui s'organise autour de ce centre dans un mouvement en spirale dessert les différents services pour aboutir à un espace de découverte et de communication.

L'enveloppe en matériaux composites, une succession d'arcs de dimensions variables, joue avec la transparence et la légèreté et facilite ainsi les rapports visuels entre les services ou interdit l'accès par l'opacité. La fibre de verre et de carbone traduit l'opposition du vide et du plein.

4.4. Centre régional d'innovation
1er prix - Jean-Christophe Masnada

L'enveloppe en matériaux composites emprunt des courbes aux formes naturelles, se pose le long du quai remodelé, tutoie la Garonne de manière sensuelle, largement ouverte sur la ville.

A l'intérieur de la coque porteuse, le hall d'exposition court derrière une grande baie vitrée et les passerelles parcourent la cinquième façade pour découvrir des vitrines d'expositions qui apparaissent comme des bulles d'air à la surface de la peau.

L'administration et le restaurant sont des cabanes de pêcheurs qui ponctuent les rives de la Garonne. Seuls l'amphithéâtre et l'entrée, qui montrent du doigt la fontaine des Trois Grâces, viennent perturber l'épiderme en strates des matériaux composites.

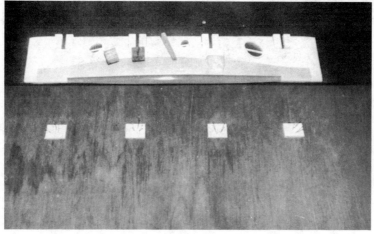

4.5. Centre régional d'innovation
2e prix et prix du public - Bénedicte Huot-Marchand, Pascal Carrère

Une coque monolithique translucide en matériau composite, dont la plus grande partie se trouve sur la Garonne et se déplace en suivant les courants et les marées, pivote autour d'une rotule et repose sur un flottant.

La rotule fixe abrite l'accueil, l'espace formation, ressources et affaires, l'administration et des locaux techniques. dans la partie mobile se trouvent des salles d'expositions, de conférences et la cafétéria.

La coque (longueur 160 m, largeur 40 m, hauteur 25 m) est constituée d'un sandwich nid d'abeille de fibre de verre et de résine phénolique autour d'une ossature en composites. Les planchers en nid d'abeille aluminium - résine époxy sont repris par l'ossature de la coque.

La partie fixe repose sur un double cylindre en béton (d'un diamètre de 30 m) le long et autour duquel coulisse l'anneau de guidage en acier (45 m de haut) de la partie mobile.

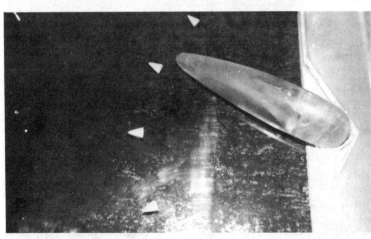

4.6. Centre régional d'innovation
3e prix - Jean-Christophe Perrodo, Pierre-Alain Gongora, Hamide Jaghouar

La conception architecturale est le résultat du "brain-storming" comme la technique créative, à partir des mots contenus dans le titre "centre régional d'innovation et de promotion de la science et de la technologie".
- Innovation - aller de l'avant
promotion - communication
science, technologie - matériaux nouveaux
* aller de l'avant - dynamisme des formes, source d'énergie, mouvement, catalyseur, futur, renouer avec son passé
* communication - liaison, repère, public, commerce, information, sensibiliser, savoir, rassurer
* matériaux nouveaux - éduquer, futuriste, oser, lisse, translucide, brillant

L'environnement du centre, le projet de Riccardo Bofill pour la Bastide de Bordeaux donnait une autre série de mots clefs:
tracé urbain - alignement, rupture, futur, composé

La forme et l'intégration dans l'environnement urbain du centre est la synthèse pratiquée sur les mots découverts par le "brain-storming".

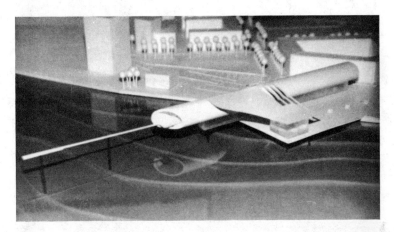

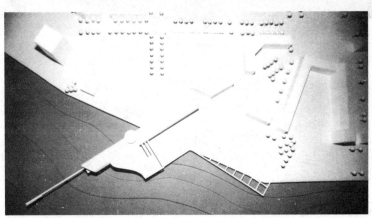

ADVANCED COMPOSITE MATERIALS IN BRIDGES AND STRUCTURES
K.W. Neale and P. Labossière, Editors; Canadian Society for Civil Engineering, 1992

Matériaux composites d'avant-garde pour ponts et charpentes
K.W. Neale et P. Labossière, éditeurs; Société canadienne de génie civil, 1992

DESCRIPTION ET ANALYSE DES PROPRIÉTÉS MÉCANIQUES ET THERMIQUES DES STRUCTURES SANDWICH FABRIQUÉES EN MATÉRIAUX COMPOSITES

G. Bélanger
Centre d'étude des matériaux plastiques Bélanger Ltée
St-Germain-de-Grantham, Québec, Canada

RÉSUMÉ

Les matériaux composites sont de plus en plus utilisés dans les secteurs industriels de la construction, du transport, de la corrosion et de l'aéronautique. Ils possèdent les propriétés mécaniques les plus appropriées, surtout lorsqu'ils sont utilisés sous forme de structure sandwich. Le moulage par contact et par enroulement filamentaire sont les procédés de fabrication les plus courants et les plus performants. Cet article décrit les propriétés et caractéristiques des structures sandwich composites qui en font un matériau de choix pour des réalisations structurales. Six applications illustrent les concepts exposés.

ABSTRACT

Composite materials are now commonly used in the transportation, corrosion, construction and aeronautical sectors of industry. When combined with lightweight materials, in the form of a sandwich structure, composite materials offer the maximum mechanical properties under flexural and impact loads. Filament winding and hand lay-up are the two moulding processes which facilitate the fabrication of the required finished products. The major characteristics and properties of sandwich structures are demonstrated for six applications.

INTRODUCTION

Depuis quelques années, l'utilisation des matériaux composites a augmenté à un rythme rapide et constant malgré le manque d'informations techniques sur ces matériaux. On les a surtout utilisés sous forme d'habillage ou de coquille de revêtement, puisqu'ils peuvent prendre d'innombrables formes et que la reproduction dimensionnelle est facile. De plus, dans certains cas on s'en est servi pour imiter ou simuler un produit traditionnel (bois incrusté, composante de meubles).

Grâce à cette première introduction qui a montré la performance des matériaux composites, il a été possible d'envisager la réalisation de composantes particulièrement complexes comme celles qui entrent dans la formation de certaines structures. Cependant, le potentiel de ces matériaux n'a été qu'effleuré.

Puisque le matériau composite offre un module d'élasticité de flexion faible en comparaison de l'acier (10 fois moins), ce dernier sera souvent associé à d'autres matériaux pour former des laminés sandwich. Les applications décrites dans cet article exploitent les propriétés des composés laminaires en sandwich avec divers matériaux.

DÉFINITIONS

Une structure sandwich en matériau composite consiste en un assemblage de deux plaques minces et d'un noyau léger. L'assemblage est obtenu par collage, de façon à rigidifier l'ensemble et transmettre les contraintes de cisaillement entre les deux plaques minces.

PRINCIPES DE FONCTIONNEMENT

Lorsque la structure sandwich est soumise à des charges transversales et/ou axiales, les deux parois extérieures (plaques minces) offrent toute la résistance nécessaire aux contraintes induites sous forme de compression, tension, cisaillement et moments. Le noyau a pour fonction de garder espacé les deux parois et de transmettre les contraintes de cisaillement entre elles, de façon à ce qu'elles soient fonctionnelles par rapport à un axe neutre. Il a aussi pour fonction d'apporter au panneau sandwich la rigidité en cisaillement.

En résumé, un choix judicieux de la composition des parois et du noyau permet de générer une structure sandwich qui, lorsque soumise à des contraintes de flexion, offre un très haut rapport rigidité versus poids.

Le concept de base est donc d'espacer au maximum deux parois de très haute résistance mécanique et de les stabiliser au moyen d'un adhésif ou d'un collage, de façon à obtenir une structure monocoque qui réagit uniformément lorsque mise sous charge en flexion.

Une analogie parfaite existe entre le panneau sandwich et la poutre en I.

Les contraintes de compression et de tension sont encaissées par les parois extérieures ou les ailes. Les contraintes de cisaillement sont encaissées par le noyau ou l'âme.

LES COMPOSANTES

Les deux principales composantes d'une structure sandwich composite sont: les parois extérieures et le noyau.

Les parois extérieures

De par leur fonction, les parois extérieures se doivent d'être constituées d'un laminé relativement de haute performance, c'est-à-dire qui offre des propriétés mécaniques élevées. En général, les parois extérieures seront composées de:
- tissu de fibres orientées orthotropiquement ou isotropiquement,
- résine thermodurcissable dont les propriétés mécaniques et chimiques sont compatibles avec l'application visée.

Les tissus les plus utilisés sont: toiles ou tissus croisés ou tissus unidirectionnels à base de fibres de verre, carbone, kevlar...

Les résines thermodurcissables les plus utilisées sont: polyester, époxie, phénolique, etc...

Dans certains cas où une haute résistance spécifique est recherchée <u>(résistance mécanique)</u>, les tissés "prepreg" seront utilisés poids

Les tissés "prepreg" sont constitués essentiellement d'un tissé qui a été préimprégné de résine thermodurcissable, type époxie, généralement à partir d'un appareil mécanisé qui permet de contrôler judicieusement le rapport fibre/résine. Ces tissés "prepreg" offrent donc la possibilité de fabriquer sous contrôle, des laminés ou plaques dont l'épaisseur sera précise, dont le rapport fibre/résine sera constant et dont les propriétés mécaniques seront de très haut niveau dans le cas où l'orientation des fibres lors du laminage aura été établi en fonction de l'orientation des efforts ou contraintes principales.

Le noyau

Le noyau dont la fonction est de relier les deux parois extérieures et de les retenir solidement doit être constitué d'un matériau dont la densité se doit d'être faible à cause de l'épaisseur importante requise.

Les matériaux homogènes qui sont utilisés couramment sont le bois de balsa et les mousses synthétiques. Ceux qui offrent le minimum de poids sont les noyaux alvéolaires genre nid d'abeille. Disponibles sous forme métallique ou synthétique, ils permettent d'obtenir des réductions de poids très importantes tout en sacrifiant certaines propriétés mécaniques. De plus, de par leur géométrie, ils sont excessivement difficiles à lier ou coller aux parois extérieures du panneau ou de la structure sandwich.

Malgré sa fonction secondaire, le noyau se doit de posséder un minimum de propriétés mécaniques et thermiques.

POURQUOI UTILISER UNE STRUCTURE SANDWICH

A quel moment le designer ou l'ingénieur se doit d'utiliser une structure sandwich? La réponse la plus simple est dans le cas où l'on recherche le maximum de rigidité pour le minimum de poids. Aucun autre type de structure existant ne présente un potentiel de compétition avec la structure sandwich.

Habituellement la rigidité étant recherchée dans les cas où des phénomènes de flexion existent, il en résulte que le facteur moment d'inertie devient un facteur important. Par définition, le moment d'inertie est la résultante de deux dimensions: épaisseur et largeur.

Dans le cas d'une plaque simple soumise a une charge en flexion, le moment d'inertie est:

$$\frac{bh^3}{12}$$ b = largeur
  h = épaisseur

Considérant le fait que l'épaisseur est traitée à la puissance 3 ou cube, il devient donc important et intéressant de l'exploiter au maximum. Par exemple, si l'on double l'épaisseur d'une plaque, on constate que le moment d'inertie augmente de 800% sans que l'on ait modifié la largeur (b):

$$1^3 = 1$$

$$2^3 = 8$$

Un autre exemple très visuel et commun pour nous tous est celui du fameux 2" x 4" en bois. Si l'on place le 2" x 4" à plat, son moment d'inertie est de 2.67 po^4. Si l'on tourne le 2" x 4" de 90° et qu'on le positionne verticalement, son moment d'inertie devient 10.67. On constate donc une augmentation de rigidité de près de 5 pour la même quantité de matière utilisée.

Si l'on se réfère à l'ensemble des équations de flexion applicables à différents types de structures soumises à des charges de flexion, on note que le moment d'inertie I apparaît toujours au dénominateur. On conclut donc que l'augmentation d'épaisseur d'une plaque demeure le facteur le plus important pour varier la rigidité ou la résistance à la déflection. A la limite, on note que le fait de doubler l'épaisseur d'une plaque d'un matériau est 4 fois plus efficace que le fait de doubler la résistance en tension ou compression ou flexion du même matériau lorsque cette plaque est mise sous charge en flexion.

Donc, il devient intéressant de concevoir des pièces qui sont soumises à des contraintes de flexion en recherchant le maximum d'épaisseur sans toutefois collecter la pénalité "poids". La solution ultime demeure donc d'utiliser un "espaceur" inter-plaques de faible densité, solution acceptable si l'on considère le fait que les propriétés mécaniques requises du noyau sont nettement inférieures à celles des parois extérieures.

L'origine des poutres en I résulte essentiellement de ce concept et il est tout à fait compatible de l'utiliser dans le cas des structures sandwich. A la limite, on pourrait définir une structure sandwich comme étant la résultante d'un ensemble de poutres en I placées côte à côte. Il faut cependant garder en mémoire que la limite de l'épaisseur permise est directement reliée à la qualité et aux propriétés individuelles des composantes de la structure sandwich. Il serait insensé d'anticiper un comportement équivalent entre un noyau de bois de balsa et un noyau de mousse d'uréthane. Plus les propriétés mécaniques du noyau seront élevées, plus la densité sera élevée: ce fait demeure une réalité de la vie avec laquelle l'ingénieur se doit de vivre.

APPLICATIONS

Application 1: Semi-remorque autoportante.

Application: Transport de produits laitiers et chimiques sur route. (Capacité: 25,000 litres).
Semi-remorque autoportante sans chassis métallique avec isolation thermique intégrée.

Objectifs recherchés: - Poids minimum.
                      - Capacité maximale.
                      - Fini extérieur intégré.
                      - Rigidité maximale.
                      - Comportement routier amélioré.

Construction: Paroi sandwich (7.5 cm total)
                  (Bois balsa, mousse d'uréthane, fibre de verre,
                  résine vinyl ester).

Procédé de moulage: Enroulement filamentaire .

Application 2: Pale d'éolienne.

Application: Pale pour l'éolienne de Cap-Chat (Hydro-Québec et
                  Conseil National de Recherche CNRC).
                  Fabrication du recouvrement de la structure de
                  l'éolienne selon un profil NACA aérodynamique.

Objectifs recherchés: - Stabilité dimensionnelle.
                      - Conservation du profil NACA.
                      - Résistance à la pression du vent($5000kg/m^2$).
                      - Assemblage mécanique rapide.
                      - Résistance à la foudre
                        (conductivité électrique intégrée).

Construction: Paroi sandwich (20 mm total).
                  (Bois balsa, tissu de verre, résine vinyl ester,
                  grillage métallique).

Procédé de moulage: Moulage contact.

Outillage: 2 moules: - Section parabolique
                             - Section conique.

Application 3: Plancher mobile de piscine.

Application: Fabrication modulaire de plancher mobile de piscine
                  de type autoportant et flottant.

Objectifs recherchés: - Résistance à la corrosion.
                      - Assemblage flottant (poids spécifique <1)
                      - Coloration et surface antidérapante intégrées
                      - Résistance mécanique aux charges vives (poids
                        des baigneurs et forces de levage: montée-
                        descente).
                      - Installation rapide sans enlèvement de l'eau.
                      - Surface moyenne à couvrir: 500-600 mètres^2
                      - Dimensions maximales des composantes.

Construction: Type 1:   Panneaux sandwich doubles.
                  Type 2:   Panneaux sandwich simples sur poutres
                            portantes.
                            (Bois balsa, tissu de verre et résine
                            vinyl ester).

Procédé de moulage: Type 1:   Moulage contact.
                     Type 2:   Moulage contact et enroulement
                               filamentaire.

Application 4: Tuyauterie de ventilation.

Application: Système de tuyauterie de ventilation du stade
olympique de Montréal.
Système à trois compartiments intégrés à l'intérieur
d'un seul module).

Objectifs recherchés: – Intégration des 3 compartiments
(aller, retour, mélange).
– Poids minimal
(système de suspension simplifié).
– Isolation thermique intégrée
(air climatisé).
– Variété de formes géométriques courbes.
– Recherche d'un esthétique d'ensemble.

Construction: Type 1:   Paroi sandwich (20 mm total).
(Bois balsa, fibre de verre et résine
polyester).
               Type 2:   Paroi simple (5 mm total).
(Résistance thermique satisfaisante pour
éviter la condensation).

Procédés de moulage: – Enroulement filamentaire.
– Moulage contact.

Application 5: Hutte monocoque.

Application: Bâtiment modulaire monocoque et autoportant pour
transport et installation rapide.

Objectifs recherchés: – Manutention par treuil de levage.
– Poids minimum.
– Aucune ossature métallique.
– Haute charge concentrée sur le plancher.
– Forme géométrique courbe.
– Résistance aux intempéries.
– Haute résistance thermique.

Construction: Paroi sandwich (65 mm total).
(Mousse d'uréthane et laminé de verre-polyester).

Procédé de moulage: Moulage contact assisté de projection de
fibres-résine par pistolet.

Application 6: Toit de bâtiment.

Application: Module de toit autoportant et monocoque de géométrie
elliptique.

Objectifs recherchés: – Poids minimum.
– Rigidité maximale.
– Fabrication de série.
– Respect des normes applicables.
– Isolation thermique intégrée.

Construction: Paroi sandwich (50 mm total).
(Bois balsa et laminé de verre-polyester).

Procédé de moulage: Enroulement filamentaire.

Outillage: Mandrin elliptique permettant la fabrication de 2 modules en un seul bobinage.

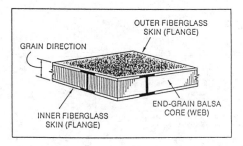

Fig. 1

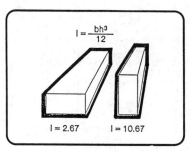

Fig. 2

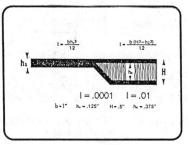

Fig. 3

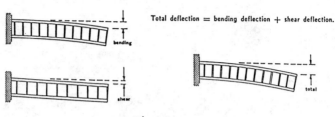

Total deflection = bending deflection + shear deflection.

Fig. 4

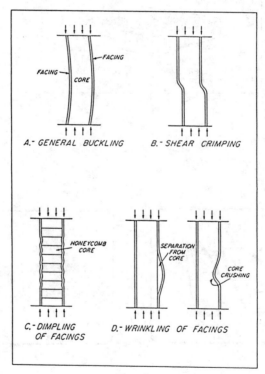

A.- GENERAL BUCKLING

B.- SHEAR CRIMPING

C.- DIMPLING OF FACINGS

D.- WRINKLING OF FACINGS

Fig. 5

BASIC CONSIDERATIONS FOR SANDWICH STRESS ANALYSIS

1	Facings to take tensile and compressive stresses.	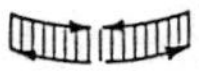
2	Honeycomb to take shear stresses.	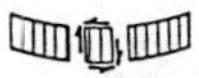
3	Sufficient rigidity to minimize deflection.	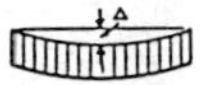
4	Core to have sufficient compressive strength.	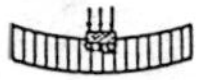
5	Sandwich to take edge-wise compressive stresses.	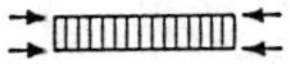
6	Adhesive to take tensile, shear and peel stresses.	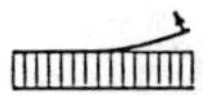
7	Close outs and fasteners to tie core and facings to substructure.	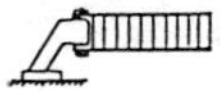

Fig. 6

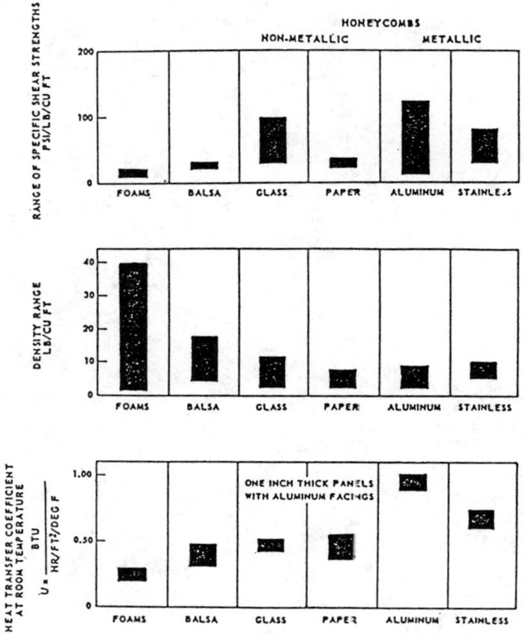
HONEYCOMBS
NON-METALLIC
METALLIC
RANGE OF SPECIFIC SHEAR STRENGTHS PSI/LB/CU FT
200
100
0
FOAMS
BALSA
GLASS
PAPER
ALUMINUM
STAINLESS
DENSITY RANGE LB/CU FT
40
30
20
10
0
FOAMS
BALSA
GLASS
PAPER
ALUMINUM
STAINLESS
HEAT TRANSFER COEFFICIENT AT ROOM TEMPERATURE
U = BTU / HR/FT²/DEG F
1.00
0.50
0
ONE INCH THICK PANELS WITH ALUMINUM FACINGS
FOAMS
BALSA
GLASS
PAPER
ALUMINUM
STAINLESS

Fig. 7

(Courtesy, Messrs Oleesky and Mohr, and Reinhold Book Corp)

Properties of Various Core Materials at Room Temperature.

ADVANCED COMPOSITE MATERIALS IN BRIDGES AND STRUCTURES
K.W. Neale and P. Labossière, Editors; Canadian Society for Civil Engineering, 1992

Matériaux composites d'avant-garde pour ponts et charpentes
K.W. Neale et P. Labossière, éditeurs; Société canadienne de génie civil, 1992

CONSTRUCTION OF A PRESTRESSED CONCRETE BARGE
USING ARAMID FRP RODS

K. Noritake, S. Kumagai, J. Mizutani and **K. Mukae**
Sumitomo Construction
Tokyo, Japan

ABSTRACT

The composite materials FRP (fibre-reinforced plastics) which are free from corrosion
have been gaining attention as PC tendons and studies for practical uses are being made
in various countries. Several concrete structures using FRP have been already constructed
in the world as well as in Japan. Although there are several kinds of FRP, aramid FRP
has excellent characteristics as PC tendons. This paper discusses the characteristics of
aramid FRP and an example of the application of aramid FRP to a marine structure PC
barge.

RÉSUMÉ

Les plastiques renforcés de fibres (FRP) qui sont exempts de corrosion gagnent de l'importance comme tendons, et des projets d'utilisation pratique sont prévus dans plusieurs
pays. Plusieurs structures de béton armé de FRP ont déjà été construites au Japon et
ailleurs dans le monde. De toutes les formes de FRP, les FRP à fibres d'aramide ont
d'excellentes caractéristiques comme tendons de précontrainte. Cet article présente un
exemple d'application dans une structure marine flottante.

INTRODUCTION

In recent years, FRP (Fiber Reinforced Plastics), which are continuous fiber composite materials consisting of fibers with high tensile strength hardened with resin, have been receiving much attention as a construction material. FRP rods have the characteristics of being light and rustproof. In particular, aramid FRP (hereinafter referred to as 'AFRP'), which have aramid fibers as reinforcement material, have a high tensile strength, and it is hoped they may be used as PC tensioning material in place of the traditional PC tendons.

Reports have already been published on the use of AFRP as tensioning material in PC road bridges (pre-tension and post-tension bridges.) This paper discusses the characteristics of AFRP rods and the construction of a PC barge using AFRP as tensioning material, to serve as an example of the application of AFRP to a marine structure.

CHARACTERISTICS OF AFRP RODS

AFRP rods which were made as PC tendons were developed jointly with Teijin Co., Ltd. by using aramid fiber (brand name: Technora®). This rod is manufactured into a specified shape by the 'pultrusion' method. The performance of a rod is highly influenced by the type of resin used as the matrix material. Hence, vinylester resin which has a good moldability, adhesive property and resistance to chemicals is used.

PC tendons must have a high bond performance with grout or concrete to transmit the stress. In order to improve the bonding performance, a spiral wound rod as shown in Fig. 1 was developed. As a result, the AFRP spiral wound rod can be used practically. Table 1 shows the physical properties of 6mm diameter AFRP rod.

PC tendons must have a high bonding performance to transmit the stress. In order to examine the bonding performance of the AFRP spiral wound rod, a pull-out test was carried out and similar tests of the existing PC tendons were carried out for comparison. Table 2 shows the bond stress of each tendon.

The application to pre-tensioning was tested by making pre-tensioned simple beam specimens of which dimensions were 2000mm length and (100mm x 200mm) cross section. A static loading test and a bending fatigue test were carried out, and also a bond length of AFRP spiral wound rod was obtained by measuring the strain of the concrete at the time of prestressing. The strain of the concrete caused by prestressing is shown in Fig. 2.

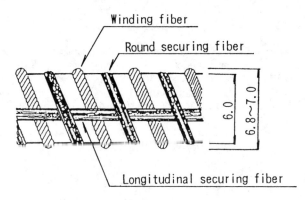

Winding fiber

Round securing fiber

Longitudinal securing fiber

Figure 1 Spiral wound rod (φ6mm)

Table 1 Physical properties of AFRP rod (ϕ6mm)

Volume of fiber	65%
Specific gravity	1.3
Tensile strength	1.9 KN/mm^2
Tensile modules	53 KN/mm^2
Elongation at breaking point	3.7%

Table 2 Bond stress of PC tendons

Tendon	CFRP strand	Steel Strand	AFRP rod (bundled)	AFRP rod (dispersed)
Maximum average bond stress (N/mm^2)	6.5	5.8	9.2	7.6
Shape				
Surface area (300mm length)	15800 mm^2	15400 mm^2	14100 mm^2	17000 mm^2

$$\text{Average bond stress} = \frac{\text{Tensile load}}{\text{Surface area}} \ (\text{N/mm}^2)$$

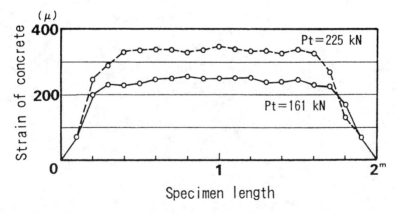

Figure 2 Strain distribution of pre-tensioned specimen

OUTLINE OF THE PROJECT

Cargo handling barge within the Ehime plant of Sumitomo Chemical Co., Ltd. at Niihama City in Japan, constructed over 30 years ago, had deteriorated and become due for reconstruction. The new barge was planned as a PC slab bridge with simple hollow girders, consisting of five spans and a total length of 61m. In one 9m span, PC girders using AFRP as tensioning material were employed as shown in Fig. 3. The other spans were constructed using girders prestressed with steel strands (T12.4).

The portion of the barge using girders with AFRP tensioning consisted of a total of 17 pretensioned hollow girders, with the general design conditions as set out in Table 3. Fig. 4 shows the cross-section of the barge, and the dimensions of the girders are shown in Fig. 5. In addition to the TL-20 based on Japanese Specification for Highway Bridges, a 50-tonne cargo-handling truck-crane and a 35-tonne power shovel were used as a design live load.

AFRP is a material with superb corrosion resistance, and thus is suitable as reinforcement for structures with the highly corrosive environment of a barge. This being

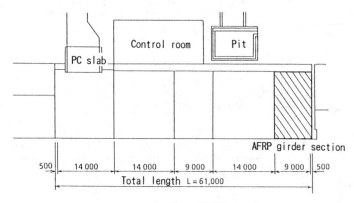

Figure 3 Outline of PC barge

Table 3 General design conditions

Type of structure	Pretensioned PC simple hollow girders
Length of (AFRP) pier section	8.760m
Girder length	8.760m
Effective span	8.320m
Effective width	13.800m
Live load	TL-20, Truck crane, Power shovel
Impact coefficient	$\dfrac{10}{25+L}$, $\dfrac{20}{50+L}$
Design seismic coefficient	Kh = 0.24

536

the first ever instance of the use of AFRP in a marine structure, stress meters were installed in selected girders with the aim of measuring over time the stress changes occurring in the prestressing.

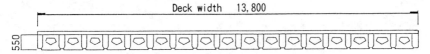

Figure 4 Cross-section of Aramid-PC slab

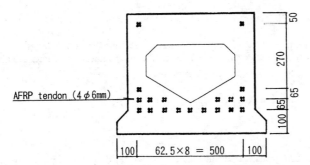

Figure 5 Cross-section of girder

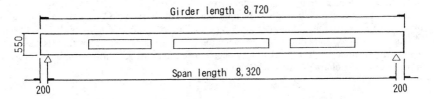

Figure 6 Dimensions of Aramid-PC girder (side elevation)

THE APPLICATION OF AFRP RODS

AFRP tensioning material consists of Aramid fibers hardened with resin, and possesses a high tensile strength. There are several different varieties of Aramid fiber, and AFRP tensioning materials exist employing each one of these. In the present work, two types of AFRP tensioning materials were used: one using the 'Technora®', Aramid fiber produced by Teijin Co., Ltd., and another named 'Arapree' using the 'Twaron®' Aramid fiber produced by Akzo Co., Ltd. Both AFRP were fabricated by drawing-out, using the pultrusion method. In addition to its high tensile strength, AFRP tensioning material also has the properties of high chemical stability ensuring resistance to corrosion, and of absence of magnetism. Moreover, its weight is around 1/6 of that of steel members, and its elastic modulus between 1/3 and 1/4 that of steel members. The physical properties of the AFRP material used this time are listed in Table 4. This paper will describe 'Technora®' AFRP mainly. The positioning of the 'Technora®' AFRP tensioning material is shown in Fig. 5.

537

Table 4 The physical properties of AFRP tensioning materials

Tensioning material	'Technora®' AFRP	'Araapree' AFRP
Shape of rod	Deformed (ϕ6mm)	Plane rod (20x5mm)
Rod area (mm^2)	28.3	88.0
Modulus of tensile elasticity (KN/mm^2)	53	59
Matrix material	Vinyl ester resin	Epoxy resin
Specific gravity	1.30	1.25
Composed tendon	Bundle of 4 ϕ6mm rods	2 rods of 20mm x 5mm
Tensile strength (KN)	204	201

THE CONSTRUCTION OF THE PC BARGE

Anchoring

Bonded anchoring was used to anchor the AFRP tensioning material. The bonded anchoring consisted of an outer steel tube into which the rod was inserted, this being held in place by the adhesion arising between the rod and the mortar introduced as a filler. The outer tube is traversed by an external screw, anchored by a nut. The outline of the anchoring used is shown in Fig. 7. In the case of 'Technora®' AFRP, 4 ϕ6mm rods in a bundle were inserted into the outer steel tube to form a tendon. When bonded anchoring of this type is used to anchor FRP members, the bonding characteristics of the FRP assume a great importance, but it has previously been verified that AFRP spiral would rods possess superior bonding characteristics with mortar.

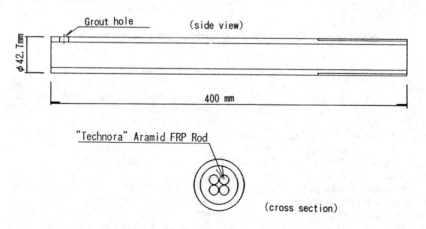

Figure 7 Outline of anchoring

Construction of the Girders

The girders were constructed in the same way as normal pretensioned girders, using factory girder construction beds. The length of these beds was from 60m to 100m, but the tensioning instrument was designed for use with steel strands. Since AFRP rods have an elastic coefficient of 1/4 that of steel, their elongation is greater than that of steel. If AFRP rods are tensioned along the entire length of the bed, the elongation is more than 1400mm, more than the length allowed for by the tensioning instrument, and thus tensioning by this means is impossible. The solution found to this problem was to determine the total length of the portion of the tensioning instrument occupied by the girder at the time of maximum elongation, placing AFRP tendons along the section taken up by the girder only (2 girder lengths: L=20m), while taking up the remaining length of the bed with PC steel stands (T15.2). A special connector was used to connect the steel strands and the AFRP anchoring. Each AFRP tendon was anchored to a movable cotter plate by a nut, and force applied to the cotter plates using a tensioning jack allowed the entire tendon to be tensioned at once. The total number of girders constructed, including test girders, was 18.

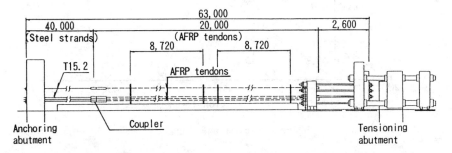

Figure 8 Diagram of construction bed used for main girders

Photo 1 Construction (tensioning work)   Photo 2 Construction (stirrup assembly)

Tension Monitoring

Since no friction acts on the AFRP tendon, tension monitoring during construction of the girders relied on measurement of the elongation and tension load of the tendons. In consideration of possible variations in measurements due to a variety of factors, tension monitoring was carried out allowing a margin of error of ±5% with regard to the elongation of the AFRP tendon. Fig. 9 shows one example of tension monitoring.

The tensioning target was set at 0.7 Pu (Pu being the guaranteed tensile strength). The target tension load, the point at which tensioning was halted, was set at the target load while the elongation was checked in the allowable limit. The elongation of a 20m tendon of AFRP was around 450mm.

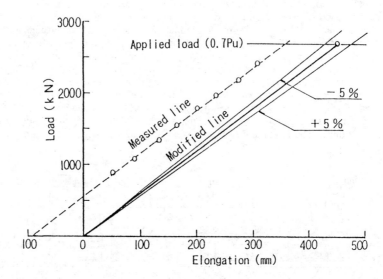

Figure 9 Tension monitoring

Long-term Monitoring

The PC barge under discussion is the first ever instance of AFRP tensioning material being applied to a marine structure. In order to observe the long-term variations in the prestressing of the girders containing AFRP tensioning material used in the PC barge, stress meters were installed in selected girders in order to measure the prestress acting on the concrete. Further, a comparison with the AFRP girders was obtained by installing stress meters also in girders of equivalent length contained in the spans constructed using PC steel strands (T12.4). The prestress acting on the concrete was measured by installing a strain gauge on the upper side of each of the selected girders, and an effective stress meter as well as a strain gauge on the lower side.

The measurements of the prestress on the concrete obtained from the effective stress meter are shown in Fig. 10. The graph obtained here indicates that the AFRP girders functioned normally competitively with the PC steel girders. Measurements continue to be taken.

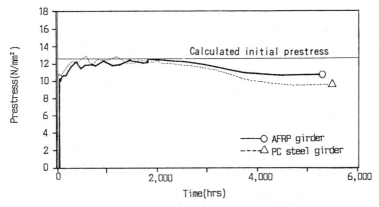

Figure 10 The results of measurements of stress levels in the concrete girders

Photo 3 Erection of Aramid-PC girder   Photo 4 View of completed

CONCLUSION

The application of continuous fiber composite materials, including AFRP rods, to concrete structures is still in its infancy, and as yet there are few examples of their application to working structures. It is hoped that the accumulation of examples of use of AFRP in working structures such as the PC barge discussed in this paper will result in widespread recognition of the practicality of AFRP, and that developments of the technology involved, including cost reductions, will continue in the future.

REFERENCES

Kakihara, K. et al. (1991). A New Aramid Rod for the Reinforcement of Prestressed Concrete Structures. Specialty Conference on Advanced Composite in Civil Engineering Structures. ASCE,
Minosaku, K. (1991). Application of FRP in the Field of Civil Engineering. Concrete Journal. Vol.29, No.11, 56-63.
Mizutani, J. et al. (1991). Application of AFRP Tendons for Prestressed Concrete Road Bridge. Proc. of JCI Symposium on Extensive Utilization of Prestressing Technology, 185-192.

ADVANCED COMPOSITE MATERIALS IN BRIDGES AND STRUCTURES
K.W. Neale and P. Labossière, Editors; Canadian Society for Civil Engineering, 1992

Matériaux composites d'avant-garde pour ponts et charpentes
K.W. Neale et P. Labossière, éditeurs; Société canadienne de génie civil, 1992

APPLICATIONS OF ADVANCED COMPOSITE MATERIALS
IN OVERHEAD POWER LINES AND
TELECOMMUNICATIONS STRUCTURES

G. McClure
McGill University
Montréal, Québec, Canada

L. Boire
Bell Canada
Varennes, Québec, Canada

J.-C. Carrière
Hydro-Québec
Montréal, Québec, Canada

ABSTRACT

Structural components made of advanced composite materials offer several properties advantageous to applications in overhead power line and telecommunications structures. Their light weight and high strength-to-weight ratio contribute to reduce transportation and construction costs, and make them interesting alternatives to more traditional materials for the maintenance and refurbishment of existing facilities, or for the erection of new installations in remote areas. Moreover, their electromagnetic transparency and low electrical conductivity are essential assets that can be fully exploited in power line and telecommunications structures. A few examples of applications and investigations of the structural use of ACM in these utility industries are presented, which illustrate that advanced composite materials make it possible to optimize the design of structures beyond strictly mechanical performance.

RÉSUMÉ

L'utilisation des matériaux composites d'avant-garde dans la fabrication d'éléments structuraux ouvre la voie à plusieurs applications intéressantes dans les supports de lignes de transmission d'électricité et dans les supports d'antennes de télécommunications. Ces matériaux à la fois légers et résistants peuvent remplacer les matériaux plus traditionnels comme le bois ou l'acier pour la maintenance et la reconstruction d'installations difficiles d'accès. De plus, leur transparence aux ondes électromagnétiques et leur faible conductivité électrique peuvent être pleinement exploitées dans ces domaines d'application. Les auteurs présentent quelques exemples d'études et de projets qui illustrent que les matériaux composites d'avant-garde permettent d'optimiser la conception structurale au-delà des strictes performances mécaniques.

INTRODUCTION

When the secret technology behind the so-called "stealth" military aircraft was disclosed, it became clear that advanced composite materials would have many potential applications in antenna supporting structures. Up to recent years, however, it was puzzling to observe that the telecommunications industry was not using these materials more widely. Advanced composites are also increasingly popular in electrical applications and current investigations on ceramic fibres indicate that their use will continue to grow.

Due to the combined efforts of researchers, engineers and entrepreneurs, it is now possible for advanced composites to compete in strength with the more traditional structural materials like steel, concrete and timber. This paper presents examples of applications in antenna supports and power line structures. It shows how many engineering properties of advanced composites - large strength-to-weight ratio, electromagnetic transparency, low electrical conductivity, and resistance to corrosion - can be fully integrated in the design.

REPLACEMENT OF WOOD UTILITY POLES

Motivation

In Canada, Bell uses a yearly average of 40 000 new telephone wood poles for the construction and the maintenance of its aerial network. In Quebec, Bell shares over 90% of its utility poles with Hydro-Québec for low-voltage distribution purposes. Other Hydro-Québec needs include 69 to 161 kV line supports, ranging from single poles to H-frames.

Environmental concerns and a shortage in long and large capacity wood poles have motivated a search for alternatives. It was recognized that manufactured poles were already widely used in the United States (Gart and Krambule 1983) and in Europe, but under less severe climatic conditions. A stronger replacement candidate is a glued-laminated wood utility pole now being developed by Forintek Canada and sponsored by the Canadian Electrical Association until 1993.

In 1988, Bell initiated its own investigation of the potential use of fibre-reinforced resin poles. The objectives of the project were threefold: i) To assess the mechanical behaviour of these poles, ii) To evaluate their compatibility with existing network components, and iii) To evaluate their compatibility with existing maintenance and operating practices.

Mechanical Testing

Tests were carried out at Bell's Centre de Recherche du Réseau Extérieur (CERRE) - Outside Plant Research Centre - in Varennes, Québec in November 1988 (Boire and Papa, 1988). The prototype tested was an Italian product supplied by TPR Sicilia spa. It was a truncated hollow circular cone made of fibre glass reinforced polyester unsaturated resin and fabricated by centrifugal casting. The reinforcement was a 40 weight% fabric woven with mono-directional roving. Mechanical tests on six specimens have shown that the product could safely resist efforts comparable to wood poles in the same conditions, and that its behaviour was truly elastic even for very large deflections. Stiffness proved insufficient, however, but its increase poses no difficulty. Failure of the poles was mainly caused by ovalization of the cross-section, degenerating in local instability in the compression zone.

Compatibility with Existing Network Components

A major constraint imposed by the pole manufacturer was that the cross section could not be perforated. A special pole clamp was designed, similar to those used with concrete poles, and tests proved its good performance and ease of assembly. This pole clamp can fit a variety of existing attachments and network components.

Compatibility with Existing Maintenance and Operating Procedures

This aspect of the feasability study was crucial. Current maintenance procedures require service personnel to climb wood poles with special climbering irons that are strictly forbidden with composite poles. It is acceptable to use insulated ladders where access by bucket trucks is impossible, but for structures requiring frequent access, the investigators developed a special climber's gaff hook to be strapped to the pole on a stainless steel band. This solution is costly, however.

Obstacles and Research Needs

As already mentioned, over 90% of Bell telephone poles in Québec are jointly used with Hydro-Québec, and accessibility is a major obstacle. The systematic use of ladders is almost impossible for Hydro-Québec because of the large heights to accommodate. Nevertheless, Bell is now preparing a performance specification for a synthetic pole of its own. The document is not restricted to any specific material, however, and is aimed at providing some guidance to the manufacturers interested in developing an innovative utility pole that would suit Bell's needs or joint use capabilities.

Another concern is the uncertainty surrounding the long-term behaviour of advanced composites utility poles. A minimum life-span of 40 years is required to make this alternative competitive with wood poles treated with chromated copper arsenate. Resistance of composite poles to ultra-violet light needs to be improved and much research remains to be done in the development of resistant protective coatings, since mechanical performances are considerably reduced by photodegradation.

REPLACEMENT OF CROSSARMS IN WOOD H-FRAMES

Motivation

As mentioned above, Hydro-Québec is reluctant to use advanced composite poles on its distribution and low-voltage transmission aerial networks, mainly because of accessibility constraints. Current efforts in the search for natural wood pole alternatives are directed to composite glued-laminated wood products that retain the advantages of lumber and have improved mechanical properties.

Advanced composites remain good candidates for crossarms applications, however, since these members are not climbed in maintenance operations. In typical wood H-frames used for 69, 120 and 161 kV lines, the conductors are suspended to horizontal wood crossarms that are prone to rot despite the use of preservatives. Checks and cracks inevitably develop at the surface due to drying-wetting cycles, and accumulate rainwater. In most new projects, wooden crossarms are replaced by a round tubular galvanized steel crossarm that is fully compatible with existing hardware attachments.

The investigation of pultruded structural shapes as a lighter alternative is motivated by significant potential savings in transportation, construction and maintenance costs, especially in remote areas. Ideally, the composite crossarms should also be entirely compatible with existing wood connectors: A round tubular shape could satisfy that criterion. For new structures, however, this limitation is unduly restrictive and can be relaxed.

Mechanical Evaluation and Further Investigation Needs

In view of this potential application, an experimental project is now ongoing at McGill University to evaluate the mechanical performance of pultruded beams under large concentrated loads that represent the effect of suspended conductors. Three cross-sectional shapes are studied: a wide flange I section, and round and rectangular tubular sections. Tests are aimed at characterizing the lateral instability at the cantilever ends of the wide flange open section, and the ovalization of highly stressed tubular sections.

Biaxial bending behaviour will also need to be investigated later since longitudinal imbalanced loads may be combined to gravity, ice and wind effects. Heavy vertical loads are maximum when the conductors are fully covered with ice, and that condition can prevail for several weeks: creep studies are necessary.

As for the fibre glass utility poles, line designers are not yet convinced of the long-term mechanical reliability of these components when exposed to ultra-violet light and more research is needed in this area. It is recognized that UV protective coatings are effective but in practice, the surface of these components will likely be scratched or damaged, either during transportation or construction. Simple techniques for effective coating repair will have to be developed for a wide range of temperature and humidity conditions.

USE OF ACM CANTILEVER INSULATION RODS IN COMPACT LINE SUPPORTS

Motivation

In low-voltage distribution lines, line post insulators are rigid cantilever beams connecting the conductors to the pole or crossarm. A typical unit consists of an inner core rod (glass fibre reinforced resin) embedded in a flexible rubber covering (silicone or epoxy resin molded by high pressure injection) and ended by a metal fitting that can fit various types of support connections. The main advantage of using advanced composite line post insulators over traditional glass or porcelain units is their better resilience. Sometimes, their improved pollution performance is also an important factor.

In higher voltage lines, however, larger electrical clearances are necessary and traditional rigid posts can no longer be used. They are replaced by flexible porcelain or glass insulator strings that are connected to a supporting crossarm or tower. Since these flexible suspension strings are forced to sway in the transverse direction due to wind effects on the line, long crossarms are necessary to ensure proper clearances under various wind conditions. Longer crossarms imply the need for a larger rigth-of-way, larger resulting moments at the base, larger strength demand and higher direct and maintenance costs.

Advanced composite line posts allow the construction of more compact lines, with reduced rigth-of-way, or conversely, can be used for upgrading voltage levels on existing structures. The mechanical flexibility of composite posts, as compared to rigid ceramic posts, is an important factor in the reduction of line load imbalances, both static and dynamic. Elimination of the crossarms also results in reduced visual impact. (Schneider *et al.* 1989)

Although advanced composite line posts were first introduced for low-voltage distribution applications, they are now available for voltages as large as 400 kV. (Sediver

546

1990) However for voltages of 230 kV and more, they cannot be used as cantilevers because of larger electrical clearance requirements.

Mechanical Investigations

Development of advanced composite line posts has required extensive research (Dumora *et al.* 1990), considering the complex interaction between its mechanical and electrical requirements. Mechanical investigations have focused on resistance to fatigue and cyclic loads, temperature effects, long term performance under sustained line loads, and failure modes under combined bending and compression. Tests have shown that below a certain load level, defined as the limit of damage, apparent creep is almost elastic and time-dependent deformations are fully recoverable. Above that stress level, however, the composite material experiences permanent cumulative damages until failure. Damage limits are established through extensive controlled testing programs but a satisfying theoretical model for long term performance has yet to be proposed. Such a model should be validated by microscopic observations (using X-rays or ultrasonic techniques) of the spatial distribution of broken fibres and localized delaminations.

USE OF ADVANCED COMPOSITES IN ANTENNA SUPPORTING STRUCTURES

Design of Electromagnetically Transparent Supports

FM and omni-directional antenna supports are applications where interferences to electromagnetic signals have to be prevented inasmuch as possible. This problem can be solved by advanced composites in the design of transparent structures where pultruded shapes can replace metal members on the portion of the support that interferes. In the same manner, kevlar cables with polyethylen coatings have also been successfully used as guyed cables in FM antenna towers, to replace interfering steel guy wires. Because of the high costs of these composite cables, a compromising solution consists of using the kevlar cable only on the partial length of the guy where interference is to be prevented. The composite cable is coupled with a regular galvanized steel guy wire on the remaining length that is anchored to the ground.

Antenna Enclosures

Another special application to antenna supporting structures is the use of composite cladding to enclose antennas and telecommunications equipment - An example is the torus (donut-shaped) structure near the top of the Toronto CN tower. This practice can be necessary to protect equipment or for strictly aesthetical reasons, but it can also result in true structural benefits.

In heavy icing zones, for instance, or in high altitude terrain prone to in-cloud icing, ice accretion on antennas and equipment mounts can be very severe and damage the telecommunication equipement and its attachments to the tower. Reliability can be improved by enclosing the strategic equipment in composite boxes attached to the main support. This results in larger projected areas exposed to wind but the total drag effect may yield smaller wind loads, especially if the geometric design is optimized with aerodynamics constraints. Considering the resulting reduction in vertical loads, the net effect on the support can be less than in the unprotected structure. It may even prove economical to enclose the complete antenna tower in composite cladding, especially in high altitude locations where icing

547

conditions can be so severe that accumulations almost fill up the voids between the members of traditional latticed supports.

Obstacles and Research Needs

The main reasons mentioned by structural designers for not using advanced composite material shapes more widely in antenna supporting structures are prohibitive costs and, again, lack of confidence in their long-term mechanical behaviour. This negative perception seems even more acute for commercially available pultruded shapes. As for utility poles, it is felt that aging characteristics and mechanical integrity of exposed components need more validation.

Ongoing Study on Creep of Pultruded Angle Sections

Designer's concerns about creep and time-dependent distortion of latticed structures made of pultruded shapes have motivated an experimental project at McGill University. The objectives of the project are: i) To observe the creep behaviour of angle stubs both in tension and in compression, ii) To correlate these observations with creep measurements on coupons, and finally iii) To verify whether or not these results can be extrapolated to predict the time-dependent distortions in light trusses under sustained gravity loads. Experimental work is still in the initial stage of creep measurements on angle stubs and coupons, and results should be reported in 1993.

CONCLUSIONS

Advanced composite materials are slowly becoming used for load-bearing components in various structural applications. The examples presented here indicate that overhead power line structures and antenna supports are applications with promising potential. Multidisciplinary research is still needed, however, to assess the long-term mechanical reliability of advanced composites, especially in exposed structures. Coordinated efforts in experimental research will contribute to the development of improved quality control techniques for fabrication, and will continue to support the development of theoretical failure-prediction models. These efforts, combined to actual observations of case studies, should evolve towards design code specifications essential for wider acceptance of advanced composites in structural engineering.

REFERENCES

Boire, L. and Papa, M.D. (1988). Ultimate Strength Test on Fiberglass Poles. Bell Outside Technology Research Report # LR88-0008, 20 p.

Dumora, D., Feldmann D. and Gaudry M. (1990) Mechanical Behavior of Flexurally Stressed Composite Insulators. *IEEE Transactions on Power Delivery*, 5(2), 1066-1073.

Gart, M. and Krambule, G. (1983). Backyard pole replacement using fiberglass poles. *Transmission and Distribution*, Nov. 1983, 57-60.

Schneider, H.M., Hall, J.F., Karady, G. and Rendowden, J. (1989) Nonceramic Insulators for Transmission Lines. *IEEE Transactions on Power Delivery*, **4**(4), 2214-2221.

Sediver. (1990). Mechanical Application Guide for Composite Line Post Insulators. Commercial documentation. 36 p.

ACKNOWLEDGEMENTS

Thanks are due to Mr. Richard Martin, Eng., of Hydro-Québec's vice-présidence Équipements de transport (Department of Transmission Equipment) and formerly of Sediver, for providing information on composite line posts. The contribution of Mr. Ciro Martoni, Eng., of Martoni, Cyr et associés, inc., Montréal (Québec), through discussion of applications in the telecommunications industry, is also acknowledged. Experimental projects at McGill University are funded by the McGill Faculty of Graduate Studies and Research.

ADVANCED COMPOSITE MATERIALS IN BRIDGES AND STRUCTURES
K.W. Neale and P. Labossière, Editors; Canadian Society for Civil Engineering, 1992

Matériaux composites d'avant-garde pour ponts et charpentes
K.W. Neale et P. Labossière, éditeurs; Société canadienne de génie civil, 1992

CARBON FIBRE TUBES FOR BRACKETS NEAR THE TOP OF LATTICED MASTS

D.A. Owens and **J.S. Ellis**
Royal Military College of Canada
Kingston, Ontario, Canada

ABSTRACT

Carbon fibre tubes are examined for possible use in naval latticed masts. Using three carbon fibre composite tubes, beam flexural tests were shown to be an accurate predictor for determining the longitudinal Young's modulus of a compression member. This longitudinal Young's modulus value and the Euler buckling equation provide a good prediction of the buckling load. Column buckling tests on the tubes verified these predictions.

RÉSUMÉ

On examine l'utilisation possible de tubes en fibres de carbone dans des mâts de navires. En utilisant trois tubes en composite de fibres de carbone, des tests de flexion ont permis de prédire avec précision le module longitudinal de Young d'une pièce en compression. Cette valeur du module de Young et l'équation de flambement d'Euler permettent une bonne prédiction de la charge de flambement. Les tests expérimentaux confirment les prédictions.

Introduction

The purpose of this research was to improve the latticed masts on warships. Its corollary is the improvement of latticed structures in general. Improvement means the reduction of weight and the increase of the fatigue performance of such structures. It was appreciated that the key component in latticed structures is the compression member.

Specifically then, the objective became that of reducing the weight of such compression members and an arbitrary slenderness of 150 was considered. For this slenderness, and using the results of the most efficient tube tested, the ratios of buckling load to material density are given in the Table 1, where CFRC stands for carbon fibre reinforced composite.

Table 1 – Buckling Load / Density Comparison

Aluminum Alloy 6061–T6	Steel	CFRC NCT–301
1.0	0.98	1.47

Because of the weight saving shown here by carbon fibre composite members over similar aluminum or steel members, three CFRC tubes were fabricated for testing purposes. It should be noted at this time that carbon fibre composites are the best of the above three materials for fatigue performance. [1]

Tube Construction

The hollow, square tubes tested were fabricated in the Department of Mechanical Engineering of Concordia University and were measured at the Royal Military College as recorded in Table 2.

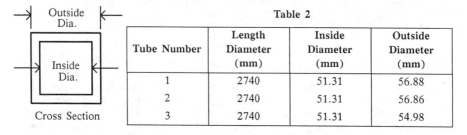

Table 2

Tube Number	Length Diameter (mm)	Inside Diameter (mm)	Outside Diameter (mm)
1	2740	51.31	56.88
2	2740	51.31	56.86
3	2740	51.31	54.98

The tubes were constructed using sheets of 309 mm wide unidirectional prepreg tape designated NCT–301, supplied to Concordia University by Newport Composites in Santa Ana, California. The tubes were cured at 120° and under a pressure of 3 atmospheres. The tube layup data is provided in Table 3, in which 0° describes a ply orientation along the length of the tube, and 90° describes a ply orientation transverse to the tube length.

Table 3 - Tube layup

Layer	Tube #1	Tube #2	Tube #3
1 (inside)	0°	0°	0°
2	+45°	+45°	+45°
3	−45°	−45°	−45°
4	90°	90°	0°
5	0°	0°	0°
6	+45°	+45°	0°
7	−45°	−45°	0°
8	90°	0°	0°
9	0°	0°	0°
10	+45°	+45°	0°
11	−45°	−45°	+45°
12	90°	0°	−45°
13	0°	0°	90°
14	+45°	+45°	
15	−45°	−45°	
16	90°	0°	
17	0°	0°	
18	+45°	+45°	
19	−45°	−45°	
20 (outside)	90°	90°	

The following material properties were determined at Concordia University:

$E_{11} =$	113.9 Gpa	$v_{21} =$	v_{31} (assumed)
$E_{22} =$	7.971 Gpa	$G_{12} =$	3.113 (suspected to be low)
$E_{33} =$	E_{22} (assumed)	$G_{23} =$	2.8 Gpa
$v_{1.} =$	0.286	$G_{31} =$	2.851 Gpa
$v_{23} =$	0.4 (assumed)	$G_{21} =$	G_{31} (assumed)
$v_{31} =$	0.012	$\rho =$	1480 kg/m^3

Where v is the Poisson's ratio, G is the shear modulus, and ρ is the material's density.

The cross sectional dimensions of the hollow square tubes came from the dimensions of the top bracket of an actual warship's mast, as can be seen in Figure 1.

Figure 1
Typical Warship Mast

Beam Test Experiment

For the selected slenderness value of 150, failures of compression members in a latticed mast structure were deemed to be due to overall member buckling. Euler's equation gives the critical load for any column in compression as $P_{cr} = \pi^2 EI /(KL)^2$, where P_{cr} is the critical buckling load, E is Young's Modulus, I is the moment of inertia of the cross section about its axis of buckling, and (KL) is the column's effective length.

With different orientations and layups possible for a built up carbon fibre composite member, the determination of E for each tube tested became vital. The approach followed in obtaining Young's Modulus was similar to a method commonly used in the lumber industry. In testing board strengths, the lumber industry uses a machine called a Continuous Lumber Tester. In it, the boards are subjected to a series of automated loads, creating deflections of the wooden beam. The values of these deflections are then used to give the strength and its Young's Modulus of the lumber tested.

Treating the carbon fibre columns as beams then, they were loaded transversely in their elastic range and their deflections were recorded with every 500 gram increment of load. Each tube was loaded on each of its four sides in the configuration shown in Figure 2 below, with three deflection gauges installed along the tubes' lengths.

Each tube was loaded so that no longitudinal constraints were introduced, with a pinned joint at one end, and a roller at the other. The loads were applied at the 1/3 points along the beam, subjecting the center portion of the tubes to pure moment. The loads consisted of standard masses on load hangers which were in turn hung from wires

Figure 2

Experimental Setup Beam Flexure Tests

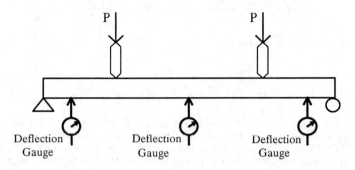

looped over the top of the tube. At all points of concentrated load (i.e. under the loads and over the bearings) two 1.5 mm thick, 25 X 50 mm rubber pads were placed in contact with the tube and an 8 mm thick, 25 X 50 mm block of aluminum was placed between the rubber and either the bearing or the wire hanger. This padding of the load was done to prevent any localized damage to the fibre composite at these locations due to the point loads (up to P=215 N) and to allow for the irregular outer surface of the tube. Although the loads applied were acting as very short uniformly distributed loads, point loads and reactions were assumed for the purposes of all calculations.

Using the readings from the three gauges (located 60 mm from each bearing and at the midspan) and the second theorem of the moment–area method, $E_{predicted}$ was found, using Figure 3 and the following expression, equation (1).

Figure 3

Moment Area Method

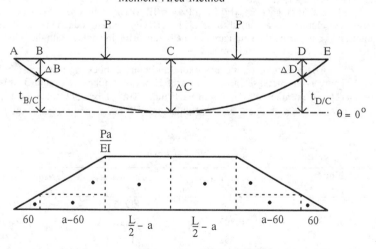

E calculated with the left gauge reading:

$$E = \frac{1}{\Delta C - \Delta B} \; [\; (a-60)(\frac{P\;60}{I})(\frac{a-60}{2}) \; + \; 0.5(a-60)(\frac{P\;a}{I} - \frac{P\;60}{I})(\frac{2}{3})(a-60)$$

$$+ \; (\frac{L}{2} - a)(\frac{P\;a}{I})(\frac{\frac{L}{2} - a}{2} + a - 60) \;] \qquad\qquad \text{... (1)}$$

Column Buckling Experiment

An aluminum alloy, 6061–T6, was used to fabricate six end fittings which were each grooved to receive the ends of the carbon fibre tubes, see Figure 4. An epoxy resin called Hysol Epoxy was used as a glue to bind the tube and end fittings together. A spherical cavity was provided in the end fittings for a one inch diameter steel ball bearing at each end of the tube. These 1 inch diameter ball bearings were held in place but were free to rotate in 1.25 inch diameter semi–spherical sockets in the piston and end bracket face.

Loads were introduced to the horizontally loaded column through the ball bearings. A manually operated hydraulic jack was used to apply the load, and a load cell was installed to measure the pressure applied. As can be seen in Figure 4, the midspan horizontal and vertical deformations were measured as the load was applied, through the use of two mounted LVDT's. Load and midspan deflection data were measured approximately every 3 seconds during the tests.

Experimental Results

All three tubes exhibited similar sudden buckling failures when loaded. As an example, both the horizontal and vertical load/mid–span deflection curves from the tube 3 buckling test are shown below in Figures 5 and 6. From these graphs, the P_{cr} value was determined which then gave $E_{buckling}$ from $P_{cr} = \pi^2 EI /(KL)^2$, where E is $E_{buckling}$ and K=1.0 because the column was assumed to act with perfectly pinned ends. This is a reasonable assumption , considering the small area of the ball bearing in contact with the oiled bearing surfaces of the piston and end bracket.

The results of the beam flexure and column buckling tests are tabulated in Table 4. There is an increase in the values of E between tubes 1, 2, and 3; this is due to the increasing number of $0°$ plies in each tube. Tube 1 has 5/20 plies at $0°$, tube 2 has 8/20 plies at $0°$, and tube 3 has 8/13 plies at $0°$. From a comparison of the $E_{predicted}$/

Table 4 – Results

Tube Number	$E_{prediction}$ (MPa)	$E_{buckling\;test}$ (MPa)	$E_{pred.} / E_{buckling}$
1	39019	42936	1.10
2	48807	51696	1.06
3	58332	61146	1.05

Figure 4 - Column Buckling Experiment

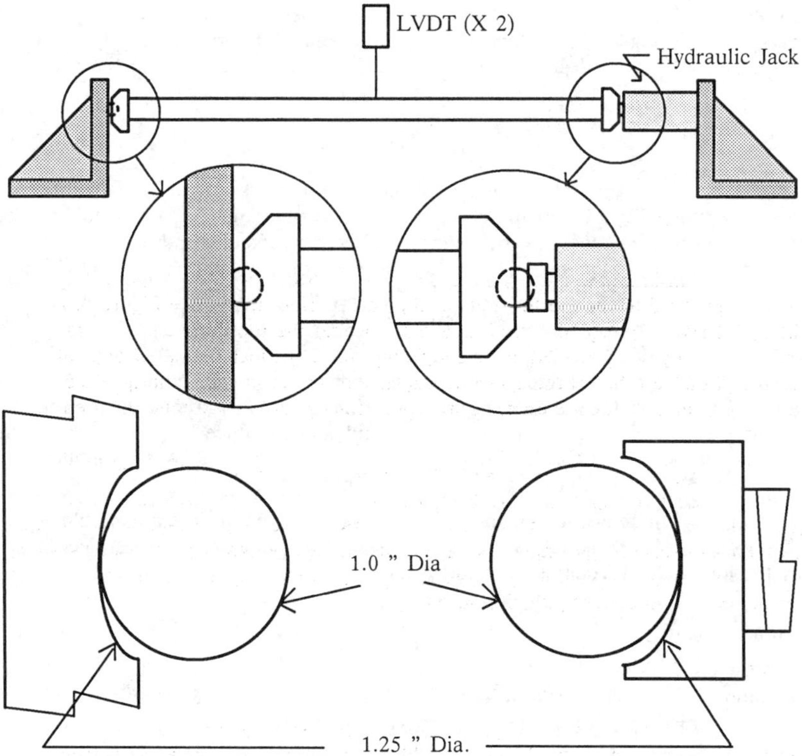
LVDT (X 2)
Hydraulic Jack
1.0 " Dia
1.25 " Dia.

Figure 5

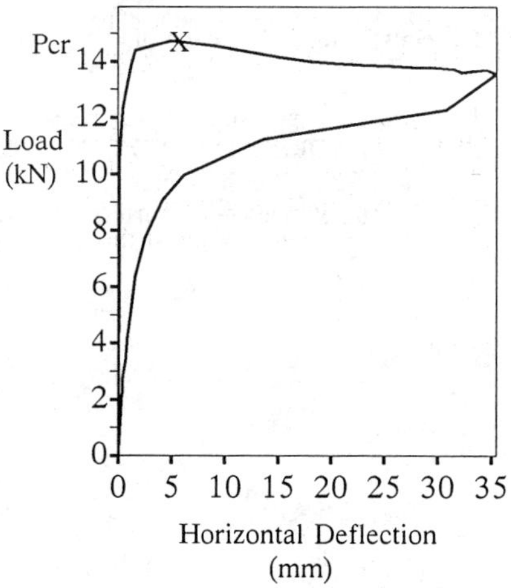
Pcr
X
Load
(kN)
0
2
4
6
8
10
12
14
0 5 10 15 20 25 30 35
Horizontal Deflection
(mm)

Figure 6

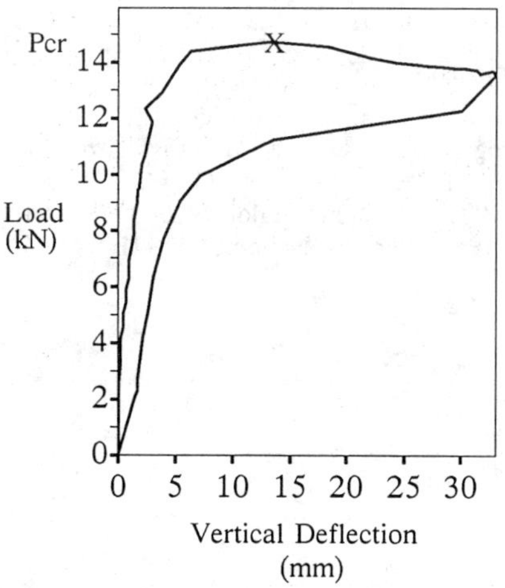
Pcr
X
Load
(kN)
0
2
4
6
8
10
12
14
0 5 10 15 20 25 30
Vertical Deflection
(mm)

$E_{buckling}$ ratios, it was apparent that the flexure testing of the composite columns gave fairly accurate predictions of Young's Modulus to use in Euler's equation. It appears, then, that the method of using $E_{prediction}$, a quantity obtained from the non destructive flexural tests, is justified as a way to design slender compression members of carbon fibre tubes.

Conclusions

The main difficulty experienced with this work was in the fabrication stage with the extraction of the mandrel from the completed tube. In order to have mass production of these composite tubes, a more efficient means of mandrel extraction should be examined. In the immediate future, however, of first importance should be the non–destructive testing of the carbon fibre tubes for inter–layer delaminations. Here, acoustic emission procedures hold promise. To this end, the Physics Department at RMC will carry out work on these three tubes as they do not appear to have been fractured.

Looking ahead to practical applications, a machine similar to the Continuous Lumber Testing machine is seen as being an effective way to predict the longitudinal E of compression members. For the design of rigid–jointed latticed frames of carbon fibre members, possibly using aluminum joints, the program DREAM available in the Department of Civil Engineering at RMC could be used. [2]

If finite element methods were to be used, then the lateral E would also have to be evaluated. Work would have to be undertaken in this area, as this project looked at only the longitudinal Young's Modulus.

Acknowledgements

The authors would like to acknowledge Dr. Hoa, Department of Mechanical Engineering, Concordia University, for his cooperation with this work.

References

[1] Broutman, L.J. & Krock, R.H., **Composite Materials Volume 5**, Academic Press, Inc., New York, NY: 1974.

[2] Srinivasan, J., Shyu, C.T., Ellis, J.S. 1991. "DREAM Package: Manuals for Users and Programmers; Source Code Listing of Computer Programs (DREAM1 and DREAM2) for APOLLO and SILICON Graphics Versions", Director Scientific Information Services (DSIS) Accession Catalog #9104320 to #9104323, National Defence Headquarters, Ottawa, Ontario, Canada, November 1991.

ADVANCED COMPOSITE MATERIALS IN BRIDGES AND STRUCTURES
K.W. Neale and P. Labossière, Editors; Canadian Society for Civil Engineering, 1992

Matériaux composites d'avant-garde pour ponts et charpentes
K.W. Neale et P. Labossière, éditeurs; Société canadienne de génie civil, 1992

IMPACT PERFORMANCE OF GLASS FIBRE COMPOSITE MATERIALS FOR ROADSIDE SAFETY STRUCTURES

A.L. Svenson and **M.W. Hargrave**
Turner-Fairbank Highway Research Center
McLean, Virginia, USA

L.C. Bank
The Catholic University of America
Washington, D.C., USA

ABSTRACT

This investigation focuses on the understanding of the impact behaviour of glass fibre-reinforced composite materials when subjected to dynamic loading. Some of the pertinent literature from the past two decades related to impact testing is briefly highlighted. Results from drop tower testing of pultruded composite material samples are presented. The critical parameters for comparing impact damage response are determined and discussed.

RÉSUMÉ

Cette recherche se concentre sur la compréhension du comportement sous impact de matériaux composites renforcés de fibres de verre soumis à un chargement dynamique. Après une brève revue de la littérature des deux dernières décennies, les résultats de tests, où des échantillons pultrudés sont soumis à un impact, sont présentés. Les paramètres critiques de l'endommagement suite à l'impact sont déterminés et discutés.

INTRODUCTION

The Federal Highway Administration (FHWA) is actively studying new structural applications for fiber reinforced composite materials. Potential applications are roadside safety structures. Examples include: roadside barriers, crash cushions, signs and lighting supports. These structures perform specific transportation functions and, at the same time, must be "safe" or "crashworthy" to vehicle occupants when impacted by an errant, out-of-control motor vehicle.

In the case of a roadside barrier, a primary goal is to maintain the integrity of the barrier (i.e., to prevent the impacting vehicle from penetrating through) while at the same time maximizing the energy absorbed by the barrier. The latter parameter, in effect, reduces the velocity of the impacting vehicle by converting the vehicle's kinetic energy into deformation energy absorbed by the barrier. In addition, for an oblique impact, some additional vehicle kinetic energy is dissipated through friction (coulomb) losses as the vehicle scrapes along the barrier without penetrating. This loss also reduces the vehicle velocity while redirecting the vehicle roughly parallel to the roadway. For a roadside barrier to be considered crashworthy, the velocity of the impacting vehicle must also be reduced in a controlled manner such that the probability of occupant injury is minimized (Michie, 1981). Thus, an optimal barrier design must maximize the load carrying ability of the barrier (i.e., contain the vehicle) while at the same time maximize the energy absorbed by the barrier (i.e., minimize the vehicle's forward velocity). The material testing outlined in this paper is a preliminary step in the design of an acceptable composite barrier.

This investigation focuses on the understanding of the dynamic impact response of glass fiber reinforced plastic composite specimens when subjected to impacts similar to vehicles impacting roadside structures. The impact testing in this study was conducted at the FHWA Turner-Fairbank Highway Research Center located in McLean, Virginia. The testing apparatus used was a drop weight test machine combined with a computerized data acquisition system. Test specimens were simply supported and were dynamically loaded with a striker impacting at the center of the span. The acceleration history of the impacting striker was obtained using an accelerometer mounted on the drop weight. From this information velocity, load and absorbed energy were calculated.

THEORETICAL AND PRACTICAL CONSIDERATIONS

Over a time period of approximately two decades, numerous instrumented impact studies have concluded that the fracture initiation load, the initiation energy, the maximum load, the energy at the maximum load, and the total energy absorbed by the impacted specimen are important parameters for comparison of materials (Ireland, 1974; Saxton, et al., 1974; Roche and Kakarala, 1987; Gause and Buckley, 1987; Agarwal and Broutman, 1990). During the initial phase of dynamic loading up to the initiation load, P_i, (see fig. 1) initiation energy (primarily elastic strain energy), E_i, is accumulated in the specimen during bending. During this phase, no gross failures occur although failures on a micro scale, micro buckling of fibers on the compression side and/or micro debonding of the fiber-matrix interface on either the compression or the tension side, may occur (Agarwal and Broutman, 1990). When the initiation load is reached, the specimen begins to fail in a gross manner either by tensile (fiber) failure or shear (interlaminar) failure. At this point, the fracture propagates either in a catastrophic (brittle-like) manner or in a non-catastrophic (ductile-like) manner. In the case of the catastrophic failures, the failure mode is very sudden such that the initiation load point, P_i, and the maximum load point, P_m, are often coincident. In the case of non-catastrophic failures, the fiber breakage is characterized by load oscillations which can remain essentially steady or can drift up or down (Roche and Kakarala, 1987). This latter failure mode is more gradual and the initiation load point, P_i, and the maximum load point, P_m, are often distinct. Frequently, the failure is such that a combination of the two modes occurs with the initiation load point followed by load oscillations until an abrupt failure results. This combined mode of failure is illustrated in Fig. 1. In this example, the

560

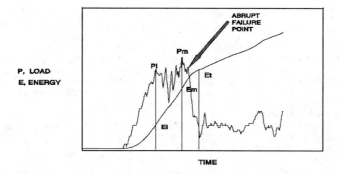

Figure 1 Typical load and energy versus time plots
indicating important data points

initiation load and the maximum load are discrete points as in the non-catastrophic failure mentioned previously. The total energy, E_t, is defined, for this study, as the point in time on the energy curve when the impact event is essentially over. In this manner, effects outside the impact event (specimen falling off the supports, friction forces, etc.) are neglected in the determination of E_t.

To account for variations in the cross-sectional dimensions of the specimens, previous studies have normalized the load and energy responses by dividing by the cross-sectional area at the point of impact (Adams, 1977). Because the mode of failure tends to change as the thickness-to-span ratio increases (predominately flexure failures change to shear failures), judgement must be applied when comparing specimens which have differing cross-sectional areas. In aircraft applications, where weight is a primary concern, load and energy responses are often normalized by the weight of the specimen (Wardle and Zahr, 1987). However, irrespective of the normalization technique employed, glass fiber reinforced material exhibits a relatively high impact energy absorbing capability. When normalized by cross-sectional area, this composite can rival the best of the metals. Typical energy values include: S-glass/epoxy or Kevlar 49/epoxy 694 kJ/m², 4130 steel alloy 593 kJ/m², and 431 stainless steel 509 kJ/m² (Adams, 1977). Also, on a cost per unit weight basis, the energy absorbing characteristics of glass fiber composites exceed that of a myriad of other composite materials.

As previously stated, the drop weight is instrumented with a linear accelerometer. Immediately after release of the weight, until impact with the specimen, the striker's acceleration is constant and equal to the acceleration due to gravity (friction and air resistance losses are neglected). Thus, the velocity of the striker increases at a uniform, linear rate during free-fall. At impact, the striker's velocity can be expressed by the relationship,

$$v_o = g t_o = [2 g h_o]^{1/2} \qquad (1)$$

where v_o is the striker velocity at impact, g is the acceleration of gravity, 9.8 m/s² (32.2 ft/sec²), t_o is the time between release and impact, and h_o is the drop height.

During the impact event, the instantaneous velocity of the striker becomes non-linear and is initially reduced due to the resistance of the specimen. This velocity is the area under the striker's instantaneous acceleration trace (determined from the output of the accelerometer) and is computed from the relationship,

$$v = g \int a \, dt \cong g \sum a \Delta t \qquad (2)$$

where a is the instantaneous acceleration of striker expressed in g's, and dt (or Δt) is a time step increment expressed in seconds. Typical velocity versus time plots are depicted in Fig. 2 for both a primarily longitudinal (LV2) and a primarily transverse (TP3) fiber specimen.

561

As shown in the figure, the striker's velocity approaches a local maximum as the resistance of the specimen increases and, subsequently, a local minimum as the resistance decreases. A comparison of Fig. 2-a with Fig. 3a-1, the specimen's corresponding force versus time history, indicates that this velocity minimum corresponds with the end of the impact event (i.e., the point at which the specimen's resistance has diminished to near zero). As such, this local minimum in striker velocity has been arbitrarily defined as the end of the impact event for computational purposes. Further, it should also be noted that the resistance load does not return to zero at this point in time because of some remaining bending resistance in the specimen and friction resistance as the specimen falls off of its supports and its ends come in contact with the support sides.

The linear accelerometer is also used to determine the instantaneous resistance load of the specimen during impact. Because a translating rigid body's acceleration is proportional to the resultant force acting on the body, the expression,

$$P = w_w a \qquad (3)$$

is used to determine the instantaneous resistance of the specimen where w_w is the weight of the striker (also, the constant of proportionality) and a is the instantaneous acceleration of the striker expressed in g's. To compute the instantaneous energy absorbed by the specimen at any time during the impact event, the relationship,

$$E = \int P v dt \cong \sum P v_\Delta t \qquad (4)$$

is used. Plots of specimen resistance load, P, and absorbed energy, E, for all specimens tested are shown in Figs. 3a through 3g.

TEST PROCEDURES

Test Specimens

The test specimens were designated by a five character nomenclature. The first character was a letter which was either an 'L' for 0° (the majority of fibers in the longitudinal direction) or 'T' for 90° (the majority of fibers in the transverse direction). The second letter referred to the matrix type, either vinyl ester ,'V', or polyester, 'P'. The third character was a number referring to the specimen thickness given in eighths of an inch. For example, a '2' refers to 2/8 inch. The thicknesses in SI units were as follows: 2 - 6.35 mm, 3 - 9.56 mm, and 4 - 12.7 mm. The last two digits refer to the sequential specimen number, 01, 02, 03, etc. All of the specimens had dimensions of 25.4 mm (1.0 in) nominal width and ranged in nominal length from 159 to 210 mm (6.25 to 8.25 in). The test specimens were cut from three standard types of pultruded sections made by Creative Pultrusions, Inc. in Alum Bank, Pennsylvania. These were: channels (LV2, LP3, TP3 - all of which were cut from the web), I-beams (TV3-web, LV3-flange) and plates (LV4, TV4). All of the material tested contained alternating layers of unidirectional fibers and layers of continuous strand mat. In addition, there was a polymeric surface veil on the top and bottom layers which provided a smooth outer surface.

Test Apparatus

An MTS Vertical Drop Weight Test Machine, Model 850.02A-01 was used for the impact tests. The drop weight and striker assembly was 82 kg (181 lb). Using a drop height of 0.457 m (1.5 ft) for all tests, an initial impact energy of 380 J (271.5 ft-lb) was obtained. An accelerometer mounted on the drop weight provided a complete acceleration versus time history of the impact event. The accelerometer output was collected at a sampling frequency of 37878.78 samples per second by a computer and data acquisition system. The data acquisition system was triggered by a microswitch as the weight fell. The switch was tripped just prior to impacting the specimen. The specimen was struck by a cylindrical striker head 63 mm long by 13 mm wide (2.5 by 0.5 in) perpendicular to the surface at the center of a 152 mm (6 in) simply supported span. The specimen was placed on its supports with the veil layer facing outward (i.e., the thickness was the vertical dimension). After data was collected from a test, it was filtered by a lowpass filter at 600 Hz. Then, it was imported into a spreadsheet for velocity, load, and energy calculations. These were calculated using Eqs. (2-4) with a Δt of 2.6399×10^{-5} seconds. Also, one of each type of specimen tested was filmed by a high speed camera (1000 frames per second) to aid in the analysis of data and to determine failure mechanisms.

DISCUSSION

The experimental results are presented in Table 1. The five important points from the load and energy plots are considered for further examination. For each of these points, the resulting values of the five test specimens (four in the case of LV4) are listed followed by the average and standard deviation values. The last line in each row is a value normalized by the cross-sectional area of the specimen. The normalized load is given in units of

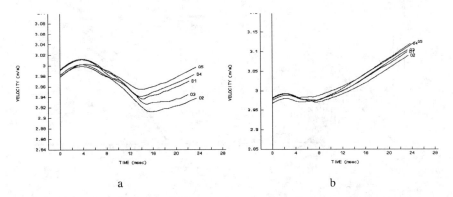

a   b

Figure 2 Typical velocity versus time plots: (a) LV2, (b) TP3 (Filtered at 600Hz.)

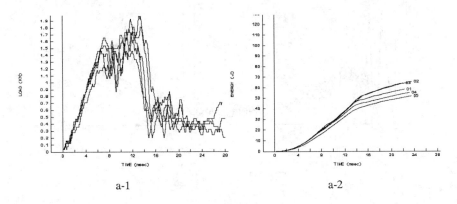

a-1   a-2

Figure 3 (1) Load versus time, (2) energy versus time (Filtered at 600 Hz.)
(a) LV2

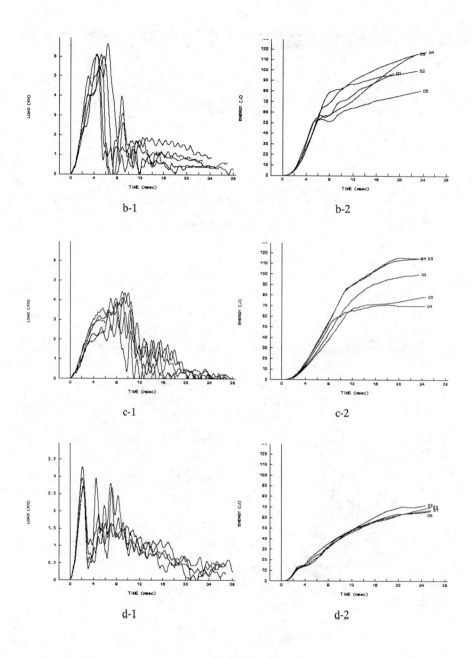

Figure 3 cont. (Filtered at 600 Hz.)
(b) LV3, (c) LP3, (d) LV4

564

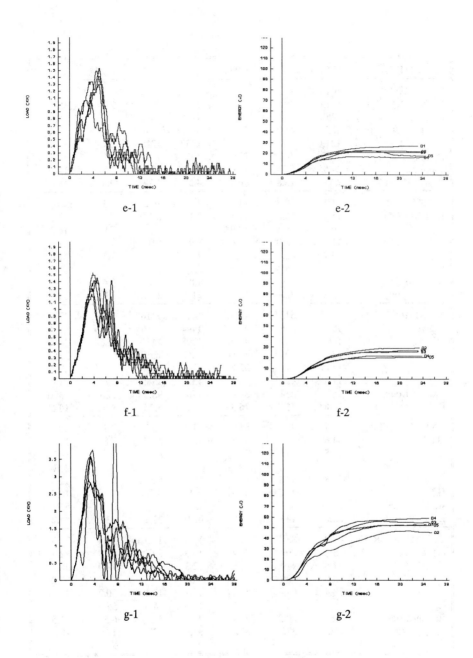

Figure 3 cont. (Filtered at 600 Hz.)
(e) TV3, (f) TP3, (g) TV4

Table 1-Experimental Results

SPECIMEN	LV2	LV3	LP3	TV3	TP3	LV4	TV4
INITIATION	1415	4522	2713	786.6	1376	2714	3776
LOAD (N), P_i	1415	3991	2399	904.0	1258	2950	3540
	1258	3878	2870	1179	1494	3264	3580
	1258	4168	2870	983.0	1146		3350
	1219	2596	1927	1337	1219	2714	2832
P_{iav}	1313	3830	2556	1038	1299	2911	3416
standard dev.	84.5	654	358	196	122	225	1481
P_{iavN} (MN/m^2)	**8.1**	**15.8**	**10.6**	**4.29**	**5.37**	**9.02**	**10.6**
INITIATION	11.1	30.9	11.4	4.1	10.2	7.1	20.4
ENERGY (J), E_i	15.4	16.2	11.5	2.1	8.1	7.8	12.1
	10.7	15.5	12.9	6.0	7.6	7.9	16.2
	11.5	18.0	13.6	5.9	5.0		27.0
	13.7	12.4	12.8	7.4	4.4	7.1	11.6
E_{iav}	12.5	18.4	12.5	5.1	7.1	7.5	17.5
standard dev.	1.8	6.5	0.9	1.8	2.1	0.4	5.7
E_{iavN} (kJ/m^2)	**77.5**	**76.1**	**51.7**	**21.1**	**29.4**	**23.2**	**54.2**
MAXIMUM	1927	6135	4444	1416	1416	2714	3776
LOAD	1809	6665	4129	1494	1455	2950	3540
(N), P_m	1966	6075	4366	1298	1496	3264	3850
	1731	6017	3894	1062	1219		3350
	1456	6135	3500	1534	1337	2714	2910
P_{mav}	1778	6205	4067	1361	1385	2911	3431
standard dev.	181	234	343	170	98.0	226	1370
P_{mavN} (MN/m^2)	**11.0**	**25.7**	**16.8**	**5.63**	**5.73**	**9.02**	**10.6**
ENERGY AT P_m	35.7	38.4	64.5	11.4	10.8	7.1	20.4
(J), E_m	44.6	58.2	53.5	10.1	10.7	7.8	12.1
	45.5	37.7	70.0	10.1	8.3	7.9	16.2
	34.7	32.7	49.1	7.3	6.2		27.0
	26.8	44.1	58.5	10.7	6.5	7.1	11.6
E_{mav}	37.5	44.2	59.1	9.9	8.5	7.5	17.5
standard dev.	6.9	8.8	7.5	1.4	2.0	0.4	5.7
E_{mavN} (kJ/m^2)	**232**	**183**	**241**	**40.9**	**35.1**	**23.2**	**54.2**
TOTAL ENERGY	47.0	83.1	110	15.9	19.5	57.5	30.9
(J), E_t	53.6	80.5	90.4	15.9	20.2	65.9	22.7
	51.8	119	115	12.3	20.2	49.9	38.1
	43.0	106	65.5	9.0	9.5		33.2
	38.4	61.7	68.1	16.8	12.1	50.2	45.5
E_{tav}	46.8	90.1	89.7	14.0	16.3	55.9	34.1
standard dev.	5.6	20.2	20.4	2.9	4.6	6.5	11.5
E_{tavN} (kJ/m^2)	**290**	**372**	**371**	**57.9**	**67.4**	**173**	**106**

Note: All data obtained from accelerometer was filtered at 600 Hz.

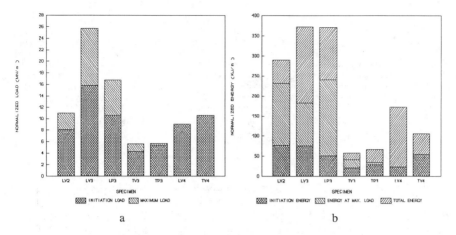

a   b

Figure 4 (a) Normalized load, (b) normalized energy

MN/m². The normalized energy is given in units of kJ/m². These values are presented graphically in Fig. 4.

As mentioned previously, normalizing by the cross-sectional area has been established as a precedent to compare specimens of varying widths and thicknesses. However, this technique may result in misleading or inaccurate conclusions. This is the case since the stress state introduced is bending rather than tension or compression. For example, when normalized by area, given two identical specimens except that the width of one is twice that of the other, both should fail at the same load and have the same absorbed energy. But, the thicker specimen actually has one-half the normalized load and energy of the thinner specimen. Because of this deceptive result, normalizing by a bending parameter, such as, the area moment of inertia or section modulus, may be more appropriate. Since all specimens in this investigation have the same nominal width, normalizing by cross-sectional area is equivalent to normalizing by specimen thickness. However, for the reasons presented here, the use of this approach, in future investigations, requires further examination and review.

From Fig. 4, two observations are selected for discussion. First, the LV3 vinyl ester and the LP3 polyester specimens have nearly identical normalized total energies but, the LV3 specimens have substantially higher normalized initiation and maximum load levels. This indicates that the vinyl ester matrix specimens failed in the abrupt, catastrophic failure mode. On the other hand, the polyester specimens (LP3) failed in the more ductile-like, non-catastrophic manner. This result seems reasonable when one considers that vinyl ester matrix materials permit a higher strain-to-failure ratio (i.e., a higher deformation prior to failure) than polyester matrix materials. A hypothesis can be stated as follows. The more deformable vinyl ester resin material carries the dynamic applied load longer and together with the glass fibers; subsequently fails abruptly and transfers all of the load to the glass fibers; at which point most of these fibers fail in unison in a catastrophic manner. The less deformable polyester material fails earlier in the loading sequence and at lower values of applied load; the load that is transferred to the individual glass fibers is lower and less of an impulsive type; resulting in the fibers failing individually after the matrix fails. In this case, more of a non-catastrophic failure mode occurs. This result raises the question of which material is more suitable for a roadside barrier, the high strength brittle-like material or the lower strength ductile-like material (considering total absorbed energy is the same)? For a given design configuration, the former provides greater vehicle containment ability while the latter provides greater velocity reduction ability. The second observation, the primarily transverse specimens (TV3, TP3 and TV4) all have relatively low normalized load and energy absorption. This result empirically demonstrates that, in the absence of other design considerations, the fibers in the composite should be oriented in the longitudinal or primary load carrying direction of the rail.

With regard to the energy versus time traces (see Fig. 3), all specimen types exhibit

567

consistent, repeatable results. This is the case even though variations in the magnitude of applied load during impact, typical of dynamic loading, are present. The exception to this is the LV3 and LP3 specimens and, the reasons for the scatter in energy levels of these types is not readily obvious. Also, the load traces are all consistent with respect to failure mechanism (catastrophic or non-catastrophic). An exception to this is the TV4-04 trace which exhibits a very large negative load spike followed by an equally large positive load spike about the true material response curve. This rapid load oscillation is thought to be a product of the test environment rather than a true material response and, for this one test, the maximum load point reported is not the maximum load recorded. Rather, the maximum reported in Table 1 occurs earlier (at approximately 3 msec after impact), is coincident with the initiation load point and subsequent to initiation, fractures at a decreasing load level until failure (if the rapid load oscillation is ignored).

CONCLUSION

The purpose of the testing conducted in this study was to lay the foundation for future research in the area of composite materials for roadside structural applications. The results presented here are by no means a termination point. Rather, the information assimilated as a result of this study is an invaluable tool in furthering the development of testing methods and identifying the parameters necessary for this objective. Several investigations of this type are essential before a full scale prototype can be developed.

REFERENCES

Adams, D.F., (1977), "Impact Response of Polymer-Matrix Composite Materials," *Composite Materials: Testing and Design (Fourth Conference), ASTM STP 617,* American Society for Testing and Materials, p. 409-26.

Agarwal, B.D. and Broutman, L.J., (1990), *Analysis And Performance of Fiber Composites,* Second Edition, John Wiley and Sons, New York, p. 314-39.

Gause, L.W. and Buckley, L.J., (1987), "Impact Characterization of New Composite Materials," *Instrumented Impact Testing of Plastics And Composite Materials, ASTM STP 936,* American Society for Testing and Materials, p. 248-61.

Ireland, D.R., (1974), "Procedures and Problems Associated with Reliable Control of the Instrumented Impact Test," *Instrumented Impact Testing, ASTM STP 563,* American Society for Testing and Materials, p. 3-29.

Michie, J.D., (1981), "NCHRP Report 230, Recommended Procedures For The Safety Performance Evaluation Of Highway Appurtenances," Transportation Research Board, Washington, D.C.

Roche J.L., and Kakarala, S.N., (1987) "Methodology for Selecting Impact Tests of Composite Materials in Automotive Applications," *Instrumented Impact Testing of Plastics and Composite Materials, ASTM STP 936,* American Society for Testing and Materials, p. 24-43.

Saxton, H.J., Ireland, D.R., and Server, W.L., (1974), "Analysis and Control of Inertial Effects During Instrumented Impact Testing," *Instrumented Impact Testing, ASTM STP 563,* American Society for Testing and Materials, p. 50-73.

Wardle, M.W. and Zahr, G.E., (1987), "Instrumented Impact Testing of Aramid-Reinforced Composite Materials," *Instrumented Impact Testing of Plastics and Composite Materials, ASTM STP 936,* American Society for Testing and Materials, p. 219-35.

ADVANCED COMPOSITE MATERIALS IN BRIDGES AND STRUCTURES
K.W. Neale and P. Labossière, Editors; Canadian Society for Civil Engineering, 1992

Matériaux composites d'avant-garde pour ponts et charpentes
K.W. Neale et P. Labossière, éditeurs; Société canadienne de génie civil, 1992

CRASHWORTHINESS DESIGN OF LAMINATED PLATE STRUCTURES WITH MULTIPLE DELAMINATIONS

T. Yoda
Waseda University
Tokyo, Japan

T. Aoki
University of Tsukuba
Tsukuba-shi, Japan

K. Ando
ESI Asia
Tokyo, Japan

ABSTRACT

The concept of an energy-absorbing laminated plate structure with artificially introduced multiple delaminations is proposed for use in crashworthiness design. Numerical and experimental studies are conducted through delaminated laminates subjected to axial compression, where achieving a high energy absorption performance is investigated by using failure initiation technique. As a result, buckling load decreases with the introduction of delamination, and the postbuckling behaviour is altered to more desirable energy-absorbing characteristics. Delamination can thus be used for increasing the energy-absorbing ability of laminated plate structures made of advanced composite materials.

RÉSUMÉ

Le concept d'une structure plane stratifiée absorbant l'énergie par l'intermédiaire de délaminages multiples est proposé pour le design contre les chocs par impact. Des études numériques et expérimentales sont menées sur des plaques stratifiées délaminées soumises à de la compression axiale, où l'obtention d'une grande absorption d'énergie est étudiée en appliquant la technique de l'initiation de la rupture. En conséquence, la charge de flambement diminue avec l'introduction du délaminage, et le comportement après flambement devient plus favorable à l'absorption d'énergie. Le délaminage peut donc être utilisé pour accroître la capacité d'absorption d'énergie de structures stratifiées planes en matériaux composites.

INTRODUCTION

Advanced composite materials have recently been widely used in aerospace and other structures in which structural efficiency is greatly required. These materials have advantages for tailoring and laminating to fit the specific design requirements. A common failure mode in laminated structures is delamination which usually results in the reduction of structural load capacity. A considerable number of investigations have been made concerning delamination initiation and growth (Kim and Soni,1984;O'Brien, 1982).

Many investigators have also studied problems dealing with delamination buckling and growth in composite laminates. Chai et al. (1981) studied both the delamination buckling load using a one-dimensional model and the delamination growth by employing the fracture energy of the system. Simitses et al. (1985) also developed a one-dimensional model and evaluated the effects of delamination size and location on the buckling loads in detail. In their subsequent work, Yin et al. (1986) conducted a postbuckling analysis. Wang et al. (1985) have utilized the Rayleigh-Ritz method and the finite element method for the buckling and postbuckling analyses of a plate with through-width delamination. Two-dimensional delamination has also been analyzed by some investigators. For example, Whitcomb and Shivakumar (1989) studied the square and rectangular delaminations, and calculated the energy release rate distribution along the delamination front using a newly developed virtual crack closure technique. For the beam-plate with multiple region of delamination, Kapania and Wolfe (1989) used a simple beam-column element in the finite element analysis to obtain the buckling load and postbuckling behavior. In all the foregoing studies, delamination has been an undesirable defect which results in degradation of structural capacity.

In the case of applications of advanced composite materials, high specific moduli and specific strengths of composite materials play a key role up to failure. However, from the view point of crashworthiness design, the relatively brittle nature of advanced composite materials causes difficulties in meeting the required safety performance. The methods of achieving a high energy absorption performance have been studied by many investigators. For example, Hanagud et al. (1989) used a corrugated web for the energy-absorbing device under axial compressive load. They also showed the importance of the failure initiator.

In the present study, an energy-absorbing laminated structure with artificially introduced multiple delaminations is considered. Existing investigations have revealed that the delamination reduces the buckling load of the laminate. Hence, by introducing sufficient initial delaminations, the buckling load and the load-deflection curve are shown to be controlled as desired. The prebuckling behavior of the delaminated plate is identical with the non-delaminated plate, which results in the merit that the stiffness of the structure is not affected before the buckling occurs. This is shown schematically in Fig. 1.

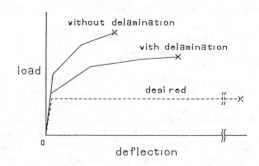

Fig. 1   Ideal behavior of delaminated plate

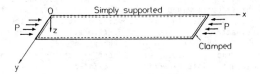

Fig. 2 Plate under uniform compressive load

NUMERICAL ANALYSIS

Calculation Model

Consider a homogeneous plate of thickness 1.125mm containing three parallel plane delaminations at a depth 0.375mm from the surface of the plate. The plate has a constant width between two lateral edges and it is subjected to uniform compressive axial load at the clamped ends(Fig. 2). As shown in Fig. 3, each initial delamination extends over the length 50mm and runs across the entire width of the plate.

The assumptions of this modelling include:
1) The laminate is composed of uni-directional carbon-fiber/PEEK prepreg.
2) The material behavior is linearly elastic.
3) Delaminations exist before compressive load is applied, but they do not grow.

Hence, calculation model is assumed to have three delaminations which separate the plate into eight regions as indicated by solid lines(neutral planes) in Fig. 4. Each delaminated region is modelled by 8-node parabolic shell elements located on the neutral plane of each of the regions. The rigid element in Fig. 4 signifies a rigid link between two nodes, namely the master node and the slave node.

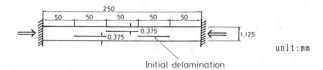

Fig. 3 Schematic diagram of plate with multiple delaminations

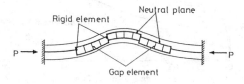

Fig. 4 Representation of delaminated plate

In this study, the master node is taken at the midpoint of the whole thickness of the plate. As the nodes displace due to deformation, the slave node in the neutral plane of each plate element is constrained to translate and rotate such that the distance between the master node and the slave node remains constant and the rotations at the slave node are the same as the corresponding rotations at the master node, which satisfies Kirchhoff-Love's hypothesis of plate theory.

In order to avoid the overlapping of adjacent plates, a gap element is introduced between the two adjacent plate elements. The existence of a gap (which indicates delamination) affects the calculation of appropriate buckling mode. The gap element has the characteristics that, when a gap element is in tension, axial stress becomes zero, on the contrary, a gap element in compression transmits axial compressive stress.

The symmetry condition with respect to the midpoint yields the continuity of deflection and slope at the other lines, and only a quarter model is considered for the finite element analysis. The validity of the symmetric displacement mode is verified beforehand by linear buckling analysis. Throughout the present analyses, the current version of ADINA is employed.

NUMERICAL RESULTS AND DISCUSSION

In order to evaluate the postbuckling behavior of non-delaminated and delaminated plates, large displacement analyses were performed on the basis of the above-mentioned finite element model. As for the nonlinear numerical procedure, the displacement incremental solution method is used, and then the load versus displacement relations are obtained. In the present analysis, it is assumed that the fracture toughness of the material is sufficient enough to resist the growth of the delamination even if finite deformation occurs. Moreover, the initial imperfection given by the linear buckling analysis is applied to initiate out-of-plane displacement of the plate.

Figure 5 shows axial reaction versus displacements relation of the non-delaminated plate. Here, the axial displacement at the node where the incremental displacement is prescribed and the lateral displacement at the midpoint are plotted as indicated in this figure. As shown in Fig. 5, the behavior of the non-delaminated plate is divided into three categories of displacement mode. The first displacement mode, namely prebuckling mode, indicates the increase of the axial displacement in linear manner with no lateral

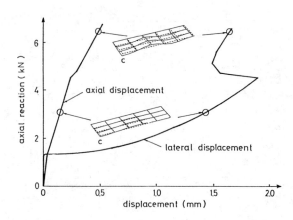

Fig. 5 Postbuckling behavior of non-delaminated plate

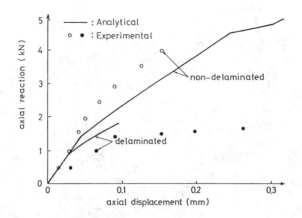

Fig. 6 End shortening of non-delaminated and delaminated plates

displacement. The second mode, which appears when the axial reaction reaches the bifurcation point of the structure (approximately 1.4 kN), yields the sudden increase of the lateral displacement and the slight decrease of the axial rigidity which may be observed as the slope of axial displacement-reaction curve. With further increase of the prescribed displacement, the second displacement mode is transformed to the third one, and this transformation of the mode is observed as the sudden decrease of the lateral displacement and the slight but rapid decrease of the axial rigidity.

In Fig. 6, the comparison between the non-delaminated and delaminated plates is shown. As mentioned before, it is observed that the presence of artificial delamination in the plate reduces the buckling load although the prebuckling behavior is identical. The axial rigidity of the delaminated plate is smaller than that of the non-delaminated plate in the realm of the postbuckling behavior, and this may be considered to produce a preferable effect within an energy-absorbing structure.

EXPERIMENT

Test Procedure and Results

Test specimens with Young's modulus 153 GPa are composed of unidirectional carbon fiber/Polyether-ether-ketone(PEEK). Each test plate has 1 cm of margin at both sides and ends. The test plates were supported by rods on both sides where steel bars of circular cylinder were used for fixing the plate. The upper and lower ends were firmly fixed to the rigid frame by using bolts as shown in Fig. 7. Adjustments in the upper end fixtures were made before loading to assure uniform compression. A dial-gage was fabricated to measure the end shortening. Strain gages were used on both surfaces of the test plate to check deformation (buckling modes) of the plate during loading. Initial imperfection was not measured beforehand.

The static energy absorption tests in which specimens were placed in a universal testing machine and loaded in a static manner were conducted on non-delaminated and delaminated plates. One of the typical experimental results for delaminated plate and non-delaminated plates are shown in Fig. 6, in which the circles represent the results of non-delaminated plate, and the filled circles represent those of delaminated plate.

Fig. 7 Overall View of Test Setup

Discussion

The objective of model tests was to examine the actual energy absorption behavior of delaminated plates and to study the effect of artificially introduced delaminations. A total of 6 specimens were tested with one pattern of initial delaminations as shown in Fig. 3. Qualitative agreement between the theoretical and experimental values seems to indicate energy absorption capability of delaminated plates. The load-end shortening curves demonstrated in Fig. 6 are the typical results from tests on six speciments. Fig. 8 shows the corresponding displacement modes of the test plate. These results show that the delaminated plates exibit preferrable energy absorption capability by showing the increase of deformation capacity.

Although there were no visible evidence whether initial delaminations grow or not, it is believed that the delamination growth will produce a preferrable effect on the energy absorption so long as the layer bondage is assured. It should be emphasized, however, that problem of energy absorption efficiency requires further study because a knowledge of stress distribution at the delamination front is still lacking.

U.I kN   I kN   4 kN

0.1 kN   0.9 kN   1.2 kN

(a) Non-delaminated plate   (b) Delaminated plate

Fig. 8 Displacement Modes of Test Plate

CONCLUDING REMARKS

Numerical and experimental studies are conducted to evaluate the energy absorption behavior of laminated plates with multiple delaminations loaded in axial compression.
The results of the present studies may be summarized as follows:
1) The concept of energy-absorbing laminated structures with multiple delaminations is proposed for the possible application in crashworthiness design.
2) Laminates with multiple delaminations are successfully analyzed through a simple finite element discretization.
3) The preferable characteristics of energy-absorbing laminated structures is confirmed both numerically and experimentally.
4) Energy absorption behavior may be controlled intentionally, but further parametric studies will be required in the practical design procedure for advanced composite materials.

REFERENCES

Chai, H., Babcock, C. D. and Knauss, W. G. (1981). One Dimensional Modelling of Failure in Laminated Plate by Delamination Buckling. Int. J. Solids & Structures, 17, 1069-1083.

Hanagud, S., Craig, J. I., and Zhou, W. (1989). Energy Absorption Behavior of Graphite Epoxy Composite Sine Webs. J. Composite Materials, 23, 448-459.

Kapania, R. K. and Wolfe, D. R. (1989). Buckling of Axially Loaded Beam-Plate with Multiple Delaminations. J. Pressure Vessel Technology, 111, 151-158.

Kim, R. Y. and Soni, S. R. (1984). Experimental and Analytical Studies on the Onset of Delamination in Laminated Composites. J. Composite Materials, 18, 70-80.

O'Brien, T. K. (1982). Characterization of Delamination Onset and Growth in a Composite Laminate. Damage in Composite Materials. ASTM STP 755, K. L. Reifsnider, Ed. American Society for Testing and Materials, 140-169.

Simitses, G. J., Sallam, S. N. and Yin, W. L. (1985). Effect of Dimension of Axially Loaded Homogeneous Laminated Plates. AIAA J., 23, 1437-1444.

Wang, S. S., Zahlan, N. M. and Suemasu, H. (1985). Compressive Stability of Delaminated Random Short-Fiber Composites, Part I-Modelling and Methods of Analysis. J. Composite Materials, 19, 296-316.

Whitcomb, J. D. and Shivakumar, K. N. (1989). Strain-Energy Release Rate Analysis cf Plate with Postbuckled Delaminations. J. Composite Materials, 23, 714-734.

Yin, W. L., Sallam, S. N. and Simitses, G. J. (1986). Ultimate Axial Load Capacity of a Delaminated Beam-Plate. AIAA J., 24, 123-128.

ADVANCED COMPOSITE MATERIALS IN BRIDGES AND STRUCTURES
K.W. Neale and P. Labossière, Editors; Canadian Society for Civil Engineering, 1992

Matériaux composites d'avant-garde pour ponts et charpentes
K.W. Neale et P. Labossière, éditeurs; Société canadienne de génie civil, 1992

THE USE OF A POLYPROPYLENE BITUMINOUS COMPOSITE OVERLAY TO RETARD REFLECTIVE CRACKING ON THE SURFACE OF A HIGHWAY

A.R. Woodside, B. Currie and **W.D.H. Woodward**
University of Ulster
Newtonabbey, Antrim, Northern Ireland

ABSTRACT

For many years reflective cracking has been a problem in the maintenance of a road infrastructure. Various options have been tried in the past. However, these systems have necessitated other ancillary works. Consequently, the authors have developed a composite material consisting of a polypropylene mat sandwiched in a thick slurry bituminous matrix. A laboratory testing programme and road trials are outlined, indicating how the life of the road pavement may be enhanced and the reflective cracking deferred. The paper discusses the additional advantages of such a system and concludes by indicating how this composite mat may affect the "life-time" costing of a pavement.

RÉSUMÉ

Depuis plusieurs années, la fissuration constitue un problème pour l'entretien des routes. Les auteurs ont développé un matériau composite consistant en un protecteur de polypropylène en sandwich dans une matrice bitumineuse. Un programme d'essais en laboratoire et des essais sur route sont décrits, indiquant comment la durée de vie du pavage peut être améliorée et la fissuration être retardée. L'article discute des avantages additionnels d'un tel système et indique comment ce composite affecte le coût total à long terme du pavage.

INTRODUCTION

Surface cracking and reflective cracking cause considerable maintenance problems on much of the world's infrastructure. This is particularly evident on the heavily trafficked routes. The simplest solution available has been to scarify the old bituminous surface, treat the joints and then resurface with a superior material such as Hot Rolled Asphalt or Asphaltic Concrete. However, this method frequently is often only a temporary solution with the old problem reappearing with time.

An alternative solution adopted by several road authorities has been the use of a structural layer as the most viable solution. This method, however, necessitates alteration of pavement surface ironwork such as gullies and manhole covers, and the raising of kerbs which in many cases causes surface water drainage problems. One can argue in favour of either system but the authors would suggest that there are valid reasons against their selection, the main one being the cost of the replacement/overlay and the associated remedial work.

The cheapest form of remedial action carried out in the United Kingdom is to simply surface dress or "chip-seal" the road surface and trust that its life may be extended for a number of years before the cracking/crazing becomes visible once more. This method has proved most successful when a polymer binder has been used as the binding agent. For example, the use of bitumen with Ethylene-Vinyl-Acetate or Styrene-Butadiene-Styrene co-polymers provide a degree of elasticity to overcome the movement due to surface cracking.

However, if an overlay was provided which instead consisted of a thin structural layer and possessing a tensile strength characteristic it might prove to be a feasible solution to this problem. The authors decided to examine the use of woven membranes laid in conjunction with a bituminous material could enhance its properties and so provide a viable, cheap and long-term solution to the problem of surface cracking.

In an attempt to itemise what properties would be required from such a surfacing, the authors list the following as being necessary:

(a)   Absorb crack movement by the elasticity of the new surfacing material.
(b)   Provide an adequate bond to the existing road surface.
(c)   Compatible bonding of individual materials.
(d)   Cost effective.
(e)   Simple to lay.
(f)   Regulate the original surface.
(g)   Non-susceptible to temperature changes.
(h)   Conserve energy.
(i)   Environmentally acceptable.
(j)   High skid resistant surface.

Consequently, the authors have developed a composite material known as Ralumat. This consists of a stress absorbing polypropylene mat sandwiched in the micro asphalt surfacing known as Ralumac. This new process was developed by the Highway Engineering Research Team at the University of Ulster's Technology Unit in conjunction with Colas (Northern Ireland) Limited.

RALUMAC / RALUMAT

Ralumac is a polymer modified, cold applied micro asphalt which is German in origin and has been used extensively in the United Kingdom and in Ireland by Colas Limited. Based on a two layer thick slurry system it has proven to be a cost efficient and

578

environmentally acceptable material which is successfully used to fill ruts, restore profiles, treat cracked and porous surfaces, and provide a stable and long-lasting skid-resistant surface.

Because of these reasons it was decided by the authors to further develop this already successful surfacing by incorporating a stress absorbing membrane or mat to see if its performance could be enhanced.

This involved a range of comparative performance test methods to be devised at the University of Ulster.

TESTING PROGRAMME

The following groups of tests were carried out:

(a)   Tensile testing of membranes
(b)   Component material compatibility assessment
(c)   Skid resistance assessment
(d)   Comparative point load testing
(e)   Tensile testing
(f)   Retardation of reflective cracking assessment

Each of these will now be briefly discussed and some of the main findings outlined.

Tensile Testing of Membranes

A wide range of potentially suitable membranes were initially considered. Of these, a large number were deemed unsuitable or not viable due to its intended use and financial constraints. However, polypropylene matting appeared to be a feasible option as it was found to bond to a bituminous mixture and have the ability to stretch or be elongated for a reasonable amount without breaking. Ideally this should be a distance greater than the sum of the widths of the cracks over which it is to be laid.

To assess the suitability of possible types a large number were tested using an Instron machine under direct tension. Samples of 50 mm length were assessed with a cross-head separation speed of 20 mm/min. Typical average breaking load and percentage elongation values for a selection of materials are shown in Table 1.

Component material compatibility

It is essential that the individual components of any bituminous mix are compatible and behave in a prescribed manner. Laboratory testing showed that polypropylene membranes provided an excellent bond with all types of bituminous mixtures providing the binder content was adequate. However, not all aggregate and binder combinations were successful. For example, binder was observed to strip from quartzite aggregates. Consequently, tests were carried out to assess the compatibility of the chosen materials. This had been carried out by Colas (Northern Ireland) Limited and indicated, which of a number of sources of aggregate, could combine with the bituminous content to give the required Ralumac properties of Marshal Stability $> 10kN$ and Flow Value of $< 4mm$.

To assess performance comparative wheel tracking trials were carried out using Ralumac, Ralumat, Hot Rolled Asphalt and Close Graded Macadam.

The polypropylene membrane still requires an overlay to seal the surface, provide skid resistance and prevent the ingress of water. Further testing was carried out on surface dressed/membrane and Ralumac/membrane combinations. These were wheel-tracked using a modified wheel-tracking machine with a locked wheel on every return passage. This test quickly caused the surface dressed/membrane combination to fail whilst the Ralumac did not.

Skid Resistance Assessment

Typically, thin overlays such as slurry seals do not have high levels of skid-resistance due to the type and size of aggregate used. But, because of the high skid resistant coarse aggregate ($<$8mm) used in Ralumac the resulting skid resistance values are comparable to other skid-resistant types of surfacing. Figure 1 shows results obtained using the British Pendulum Tester which indicate that Ralumac has an average Skid Resistance Value of 103 compared with 79 for Close Graded Macadam. In this test a higher result indicates a more skid resistant surface.

Comparative Point Load Testing

A point load test was developed to assess the loading characteristics of the Ralumat material. This consisted of placing prepared slabs between two supports 200mm apart and applying a gradually increasing central point load. Deflection of the sample was measured as the sample was tested to destruction. All testing was carried out at a standardised temperature of 22^{0}C. For comparative purposes a number of different types of bituminous mix were tested. Figure 2 is a summary of some of the results produced.

It can be seen that the commonly used 14mm Close Graded Macadam mixes failed under a load of 0.028kN, Ralumac at 0.014kN and 0.070kN for Ralumat.

Tensile Testing

Tensile testing was carried out using an Instron machine to compare the following:

(i)   Mat on its own (17 strands).
(ii) Ralumac on its own.
(iii) Ralumat (Ralumac and 17 strands of polypropylene mesh).

Some of the results are shown in Figure 3. From the test results obtained, average values for failure were as follows:

(i)	Mat on its own	1.72kN
(ii)	Ralumac	0.14kN
(iii)	Ralumat (mesh in bottom)	1.95kN
(iv)	Ralumat (mesh middle and bottom)	3.85kN

They indicate how the mat has contributed to the tensile strength of the overall material. Ralumac on its own had a relatively small value of 0.14kN. This compares to 1.95kN when the mat is used. This would indicate that the warp in the mesh is being used to increase the tensile strength of the material by assisting in bonding the polypropylene to the slurry. Furthermore, it is evident that two layers of mat on their own ie 3.44kN, is less than two layers used in conjunction with Ralumac - 3.85kN. Again, This suggests that the two materials are bonding to form a composite which is of higher tensile strength than the sum of the individual members. It was also noted that the composite material failed at a definite peak which was reached in a reasonably uniform manner showing no indication of slippage (bond-breaking) between the two components. Thus the point of failure can easily be predicted.

Retardation of Reflective Cracking Assessment

Modifications to a wheel-tracking machine enabled reflective cracking to be simulated in the laboratory. Various combinations of reinforced and non-reinforced Ralumac were assessed under differing test conditions such as loading and width of crack separation. Some of the results are shown in Figure 4 where the number of passes required to produce a cracked test specimen are shown for different crack widths and degree of reinforcement.
The results show how the Ralumat reinforced material can delay the formation of reflective cracking.

Road Trials

A small scale road trial has been carried out on a lightly trafficked residential road. Areas were selected which displayed signs of reflective cracking and using small sections of fabric these areas were reinforced while adjacent areas were surfaced in the normal manner with a thick slurry. The result, after two years, is that the reflective cracking has reappeared in the surrounding areas adjacent to the Ralumat. Thus the life of the reinforced overlay appears to be much greater than that of the unreinforced.

However, problems were experienced in the laying process and research is now underway to design a mechanism whereby the fabric may be laid together as an integrated part of the mix.

Furthermore, a two stage operation, ie fabric laying followed by slurry laying increases the overall cost of the operation and thus makes it unattractive when compared with a hot mix overlay such as Hot Rolled Asphalt. The approximate cost of a Ralumat system would appear to be approximately £1.55 compared to £1.85 for a Hot Rolled Asphalt.

The authors believe that this process has greatest potential in some of the hot climate developing countries where labour is relatively inexpensive.

CONCLUSIONS

The simplicity of the Ralumac cold applied micro asphalt system is an attraction in itself especially to the experienced contractor. The system provides the same element of waterproofing and restoration of skid resistance as surface dressing without the need to worry about binder spread rates, chipping size, rates of spread, or the adverse affects of temperature and rainfall.

However, neither surface dressing nor surfacing such as Ralumac offer a satisfactory long-term solution to the problem of reflective cracking.

The results obtained from the authors investigation using polypropylene matting to enhance the Ralumac micro asphalt performance would indicate that additional tensile strength and overall performance could be achieved by the inclusion of such a membrane and appears to be a step closer to overcoming the problem of reflective cracking.

ACKNOWLEDGEMENTS

The authors wish to acknowledge the help and co-operation they have received in the implementation of this research by The Department of Civil Engineering & Transport at The University of Ulster and Colas (NI) Ltd.

Table 1   Testing of Polypropylene Mats

Fabric	Construction	Warp			Weft		
		Tex	Breaking Load (kN)	% Elongation	Tex	Breaking Load (kN)	% Elongation
A	24 x 10	44	0.214	23.7	111	27.7	15.5
B	24 x 16	44	0.171	29.0	111	30.6	24.0
C	16 x 12	44	0.187	29.5	111	28.1	25.0

Note: Construction is number of warp tapes per 10cms by number of weft tapes per 10cms.

Tex is the mass in grammes per 1.00m length of tape.

Figure 1 Skid Resistance Results

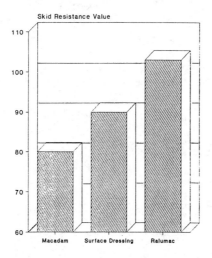

Figure 2 Load v Deflection for
Different Surfacing Treatments

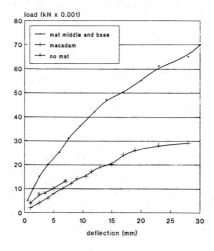

Figure 3 Tensile Test
Graph of Load v Extension

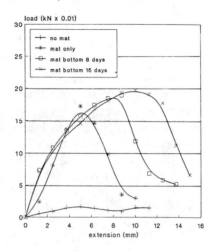

Figure 4 Reflective Cracking -
Number of Passes to Form a Crack

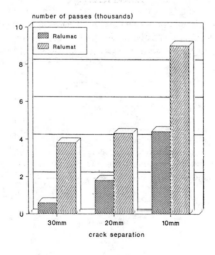

ADVANCED COMPOSITE MATERIALS IN BRIDGES AND STRUCTURES
K.W. Neale and P. Labossière, Editors; Canadian Society for Civil Engineering, 1992

Matériaux composites d'avant-garde pour ponts et charpentes
K.W. Neale et P. Labossière, éditeurs; Société canadienne de génie civil, 1992

USE OF POLYMER MORTAR COMPOSITES CONTAINING RECYCLED PLASTICS IN THE REPAIR AND OVERLAY OF PAVEMENTS, BRIDGES AND OTHER STRUCTURES

K.S. Rebeiz
Lafayette College
Easton, Pennsylvania, USA

D.W. Fowler and **D.R. Paul**
University of Texas
Austin, Texas, USA

ABSTRACT

The properties and behaviour of polymer mortars (PM) using unsaturated polyester resins based on recycled plastics are discussed in this paper. The properties obtained show that the material may efficiently be used in the repair and overlay of pavements, bridges, and other structures.

RÉSUMÉ

Les propriétés et le comportement des polymères de mortier (PM) utilisant des résines de polyester insaturé à base de plastique recyclé sont discutés dans cet article. Les propriétés obtenues montrent que le matériau peut être efficacement utilisé pour la réparation et le recouvrement des routes, des ponts, et d'autres structures.

INTRODUCTION

Polymer mortar (PM) is a composite material formed from a resin binder and inorganic aggregates. The resulting product is a very strong and durable material that can efficiently be used in the repair and overlay of pavements, bridges, and other structures. Another important advantage of PM is its fast curing time (PM cures in a few minutes or hours while cement-based materials cure in a few days or weeks). The main disadvantage of PM, however, is the relatively high cost of the material coming from its resin component. If resins based on recycled plastics can be used in the production of good quality PM materials at a lower cost, their use will be important to the PM industry.

Recycled poly(ethylene terephthalate), PET, mainly recovered from used beverage bottles, can be used to produce unsaturated polyester resins. These resins can then be mixed with sand and fly ash to produce PM. It should be noted that the term unsaturated polyester refers to a broad class of materials and that a very large number of variations in formulation or performance are possible depending on the intended use of the material. The objective of this paper was to study the properties and behavior of PM using resins based on recycled PET that are important in the structural use of the material. Resins based on recycled PET can help reduce the cost of PM-based products. The recycling of PET in PM would also help alleviate an environmental problem and save energy.

EXPERIMENTAL

Materials

Recycled PET, obtained from used plastic bottles, was chemically modified to produce unsaturated polyester resins. The PET chemical conversion was not done at the University of Texas laboratories because the necessary facilities were not available. Two different unsaturated polyester resins based on recycled PET, resin 1 and resin 2, were used in this study. The two resins varied in their formulations and physical properties. The physical properties of resins 1 and 2 are shown in Table 1. The tensile properties of the neat resin (cured resin or plastic without the use of aggregates) were evaluated according to ASTM D638 procedures.

Resin 1 is a rigid resin with high modulus and low elongation at break, while resin 2 is a flexible resin with low modulus and high elongation at break. Resin 1 was dark in color and the recycled PET used in its production was not purified to the same extent as the recycled PET used in the production of resin 2. In most PM applications, the purity of the recycled PET is not very important, which should minimize the cost of resins based on recycled PET. Both resins were prepolymers with relatively high viscosity. They were therefore diluted with styrene to reduce their viscosity and allow their cure to a solid upon the addition of suitable initiators and promoters. Resin 1 and resin 2 used 40 percent and 30 percent by weight, respectively, of recycled PET in the alkyd portion of their formulations, i.e., before the addition of styrene.

The following inorganic fine aggregates were used: River siliceous sand with a fineness modulus of 3.26, and type F fly ash. The fine and spherical particles of fly ash provided the fresh mix with good lubricating properties, thus improving its plasticity and cohesiveness. The sand was oven-dried for a minimum of 24 hours at 125 °C to reduce its moisture content to less than 0.5 percent by weight, thus ensuring good bond between the polymer matrix and the sand (Nutt and Staynes, 1987). Fly ash was already obtained dry from the supplier and therefore did not need to be oven-dried.

Mix Design

The mix design was optimized for workability, strength, and economy. PM mix proportioned by weight consisted of the following: 20 percent resin, 60 percent oven-dried sand, and 20 percent type F fly ash. One percent (by weight of resin) of methyl ethyl ketone peroxide (MEKP) initiator and 0.1 percent (by weight of resin) of a 12 percent solution cobalt naphthenate (CoNp) promoter were added to the resin immediately prior to its mixing with inorganic aggregates.

PM1 refers to the PM material that used resin 1 as a binder while PM2 refers to the PM material that used resin 2 as a binder. Mixing was done using a conventional concrete mixer for a period of about three minutes. The low viscosity and good wetting properties of resin 1 resulted in a fresh PM1 mix with excellent workability. The workability of the fresh PM2 mix was not as good as the workability of the fresh PM1 mix because of the relatively high viscosity of resin 2. Specimens were then cast in molds and allowed to cure at room temperature.

Testing

There are no standard tests that are directly applicable to PM specimens. ASTM standards applicable to cement-based materials were therefore used as guidelines.

Compression tests were performed on 76-mm x 152-mm cylinders. Electrical strain gages, bonded to the specimens and connected to a data acquisition system, were used to read strains. Flexure specimens were 50-mm x 50-mm x 305-mm beams. A dial gage was used to read the midspan deflection of the beam.

The water absorption and chemical resistance test used 50-mm cubes cut from the flexure specimens. The sandblast abrasion test was performed on 150-mm x 150-mm x 15-mm specimens. The test was conducted in a sandblasting cabinet using No. 20 to 30 Ottawa sand and an air pressure of 415 kPa. Each of the specimens was sandblasted for a period of one minute on a 25-mm diameter area at eight different locations.

Bond strength between PM overlays and portland cement concrete substrate was measured using the pull-out test method (ACI Committee 503, 1979). Specimens were thin overlays, about 12-mm thick, cast directly on sand-blasted portland cement concrete slabs. Circular grooves (100-mm diameter) were cored through the overlays and into the portland cement concrete substrate. Circular steel disks were then bonded to the sand-blasted overlay at the cored locations using a strong epoxy. The disks were then pulled out in direct tension to determine the type and magnitude of the bond failure.

The thermal expansion test used 76-mm x 152-mm cylinders. Longitudinal electrical strain gages were bonded to the specimens using a special epoxy system insensitive to high temperatures. The strain gages were then connected to a switch and balance unit in a full-bridge configuration. Strain and temperature readings were taken in increments of $6°C$. The specimens were left at a constant temperature for a minimum of eight hours to ensure thermal stabilization before recording strains and temperatures.

The Dupont®'s method was used to measure shrinkage strains (Rebeiz 1992). Specimens consisted of 76-mm x 76-mm x 305-mm beams cast inside Teflon®-lined molds. The molds were wrapped in a plastic sheet to reduce the effect of ambient temperature changes on the plastic shrinkage readings. Immediately after mixing and placing the materials in the molds, the shrinkage measuring device was carefully inserted into the fresh PM mix. The peak exotherm was measured by inserting thermocouples into the fresh mix and connecting them to a digital temperature indicator.

Thermal cycling testing was done on 6-mm, 12-mm, and 24-mm thick PM overlays cast directly on sand-blasted portland cement concrete slabs. The specimens were put in an environmental chamber and subjected to thermal cycles. In each cycle, the temperature varied from $-25°C$ to $70°C$ over a 24 hour period of time. The temperature was gradually increased and decreased to avoid thermal shock. Thermocouples, inserted inside the overlays and at different depths, were used to ensure that all specimens had the same temperature. At different thermal cycles, specimens were removed and the PM overlay was tested for its tensile bond strength to portland cement concrete using the pull-out test method.

RESULTS AND DISCUSSION

Fundamental Properties

The mechanical properties and the dimensional stability of PM materials using resins 1 and 2 are shown in Table 2. It can be observed that excellent mechanical properties can be obtained from PM materials using resins based on recycled plastics. The bond strength between the PM and the portland cement concrete is also very good. These properties are comparable to those obtained from PM using virgin materials and tested for the same conditions at the University of Texas.

The shrinkage strains of PM1 and PM2 during curing were continuously monitored. Most of the shrinkage strains took place within the first eight hours after mixing and stopped after 24 hours. The shrinkage mechanism in PM is different than in cement-based materials. PM only experiences short term shrinkage (plastic shrinkage) due to resin polymerization, whereas cement-based materials experience both short term shrinkage (plastic shrinkage) and long term shrinkage (drying shrinkage) due to water evaporation from the cement paste.

Relatively low shrinkage is important in PM applications because studies have reported that excessive shrinkage can cause delamination between the overlay and the portland cement concrete substrate (Al-Negheimish, 1988, Letsch, 1987).

Both polymer mortars show significant bilinear changes in thermal expansion characteristics in the temperature range 10°C to 20°C. Others have noted similar behavior with PM using virgin materials (Letsch, 1984). The thermal expansion is important because PM is used in conjunction with portland cement concrete. If the coefficient of thermal expansions of PM is much higher to the one corresponding to cement concrete, then repeated changes in temperature in the composite structure will create shear stresses at the interface between the two materials that may eventually cause deterioration in the structure.

PM1 and PM2 showed good chemical resistance with the exception of acetone. When immersed in acetone, both PM1 and PM2 specimens disintegrated in one day and discolored into dark green. The weight change of PM1 and PM2 was less than one percent when immersed in 10 percent sulfuric acid and hydrochloric acid solutions, and less than 4 percent when immersed in 10 percent sodium hydroperoxide solution. Both PM1 and PM2 specimens discolored into yellow bright colors when immersed in acid solutions. Good chemical resistance is important when PM overlays are used to protect industrial floors, tanks, pipes or containers from aggressive liquids or radiation from nuclear wastes. In very aggressive environments, specially formulated polyester resins are used in making PM to provide the necessary resistance against the action of heat and flame, strong chemicals, or other aggressive agents.

Both PM1 and PM2 had a very good abrasion resistance. A good abrasion resistance helps PM overlays against the action of traffic in pavements, floors, and bridges, and against erosion in dams and other hydraulic structures.

The PM specimens had a very low water absorption (much less than one percent by weight). The water absorption property is important when, for example, PM is used to overlay pavements and bridges. Overlays with low water absorption prevent the intrusion of water and salts that could cause corrosion of the reinforcing steel or freeze-thaw attacks in the portland cement concrete substrate.

Thermal Cycling of PM Overlays

Variations in temperature in PM overlays can result in high shearing stresses because the coefficient of thermal expansion of unsaturated polyester composites is high compared to cement-based materials. The repeated changes in temperature, or thermal cycles, may cause thermal fatigue and eventual bond failure at the interface of the PM overlay and the portland cement concrete substrate. Bond strength failures are to be avoided in pavements and bridges because they cause delamination between the PM overlay and the portland cement concrete substrate and they increase the permeability of the overlay to water and chloride ions (Krauss, 1988, Sprinkel, 1988, and Sprinkel 1982).

The tensile bond strengths of PM1 and PM2 overlays on portland cement concrete slabs as a function of number of thermal cycles are shown in Figs. 1 and 2, respectively. It should be remembered that PM1 was made with a rigid resin binder while PM2 was produced with a flexible resin binder. Before thermal cycling, the bond strength of PM1 and PM2 overlays to the portland cement concrete substrate was good. After thermal cycling, a reduction in bond strength occurred between PM1 and PM2 overlays and the portland cement concrete substrate. The loss in bond was very substantial for PM1 and the overlays delaminated completely after 80 thermal cycles. Conversely, the loss in bond was not as substantial for PM2 and the bond strength of the overlays was relatively still good after 80 thermal cycles. The use of flexible resin binders with low modulus and high elongation at break is therefore important to prevent thermal cycling failure of overlays. Low modulus resin binders are desirable because they produce low modulus PM overlays, offsetting the effect of the higher coefficient of thermal expansion. Also, the use of PM materials made with resins with high elongation at break, capable of stretching during thermal movements, are desirable. The same kind of behavior was observed in PM overlays using virgin polyester resins (Sprinkel, 1986).

A visual observation of the specimens after the application of 21 thermal cycles is provided in Table 3. It was observed that all PM overlays were in good conditions. The concrete bases of the 24-mm PM1 and PM2 overlays cracked severely while the concrete bases of the 6-mm and 12-mm PM1 and PM2 overlays were in good conditions. The portland cement concrete subbases of PM1 specimens severely disintegrated while the portland cement concrete subbases of PM2 specimens were in good conditions, especially for the 6-mm and 12-mm overlays.

The failure types of the materials due to thermal cycling are presented in Table 4. After the application of thermal cycling, most of the PM overlays failed at the interface between the PM and the portland cement concrete. However, some of the PM2 overlays did have a partial failure (5 to 20 percent) occurring in the portland cement concrete substrate, even after the application of 80 thermal cycles.

CONCLUSIONS

The main objective of this study was to determine if unsaturated polyester resins based on recycled PET can be used to produce good quality PM materials for structural applications. The analyses of the results clearly indicated that the properties and behavior of PM using resins based on recycled PET are comparable to those obtained from PM using virgin resins. A large waste stream of PET plastic, mainly recovered from used beverage bottles, is available for recycling applications. The main advantage of recycling PET in PM is that it helps decrease the cost of these polymer composite products. Other advantages include the long term disposal of plastic wastes, the conservation of raw petrochemical products, and energy savings. Field applications and continuous monitoring of PM materials using resins based on recycled PET would really determine the long term behavior of these materials under field conditions.

ACKNOWLEDGEMENT

The authors acknowledge the support for this research from the Advanced Research Program of the Texas Higher Education Coordinating Board.

REFERENCES

ACI Committee 503 Report (1979). Appendix A.

Al-Negheimish, A. (1988). Bond Strength, Long Term Performance and Temperature Induced Stresses in Polymer Concrete-Portland Cement Concrete Composite Members. Ph.D. Dissertation, The University of Texas.

Krauss, P. D. (1988). Status of Polyester-Styrene Resin Concrete Bridge Deck and Highway Overlays in California. Proceedings of the 43rd Annual Conference of the Composites Institute, 16D/1-16D/7.

Letsch, R. (1987). Polymer Mortar Overlays - Measurement of Stresses. Proceedings of the Fifth International Congress on Polymers in Concrete, 119-123.

Nutt, W. O., and Staynes, B. W. (1987). The Next Twenty Five Years. Proceedings of the Fifth International Congress on Polymers in Concrete, 413-416.

Rebeiz, K. S., (1992). Structural Use of Polymer Composites Using Unsaturated Polyester Resins Based On Recycled Poly(ethylene Terephthalate). Ph.D. Dissertation, The University of Texas.

Sprinkel, M. M. (1986). Polymer Concrete Overlay on the Big Swan Creek Bridge. Virginia Highway and Transportation Research Council, Report 37.

Sprinkel, M. M. (1982). Thermal Compatibility of the Polymer Concrete Overlays. Transportation Research Record, No. 899, 64-73.

TABLE 1. Physical Properties of Resins 1 and 2

Properties	Resin 1	Resin 2
Percent by weight of recycled PET	40	30
Percent by weight of styrene monomer	40	30
Viscosity at 25°C (cps)	110	700
Specific gravity	1.09	1.16
Appearance	Dark green	Clear amber
Tensile strength (MPa)	21.1	13.3
Young's modulus (GPa)	1.24	0.30
Elongation at break (%)	2.4	53.5

TABLE 2. Mechanical Properties and Dimensional Stability of PM1 and PM2

Properties	PM1	PM2
Compressive strength (MPa)	90.2	72.2
Compressive modulus (GPa))	16.7	6.7
Flexural strength (MPa)	18.0	14.6
Flexural modulus (GPa)	10.6	4.4
Tensile bond strength to cement concrete (MPa)	2.7	2.6
Thermal coefficient: 20°C to 70°C (10^{-6} mm/mm/°C)	38.8	41.7
Poisson's ratio	0.28	0.32
Shrinkage (10^{-3} mm/mm) at 24 hours	7.5	4.9
Peak exotherm (°C) at 2 hours	42	40

TABLE 3. Visual Inspection of PM1 and PM2 Overlays after 21 Thermal Cycles

Location	Overlay Thickness (mm)	PM1 Overlay	PM2 Overlay
Cement	6	good	good
Concrete	12	good	good
Base	24	severe cracking	severe cracking
Cement	6	disintegration	good
Concrete	12	disintegration	good
Substrate	24	disintegration	microcracking
PM	6	good	good
Overlay	12	good	good
	24	good	good

TABLE 4. Failure Types of PM Overlays

Thermal Cycles Number	Overlay Thickness (mm)	Failure Type	Failure Type
	6	substrate	interface
0	12	interface	10% substrate
	24	substrate/interface	interface
	6	interface	interface
25	12	interface	interface
	24	interface	interface
	6	interface	interface
60	12	a	20% substrate
	24	interface	interface
	6	a	10% substrate
80	12	a	5% substrate
	24	a	a

a. Specimens severely deteriorated

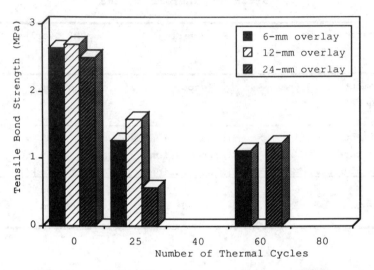

FIG. 1. Thermal Cycling of PM1 Overlays

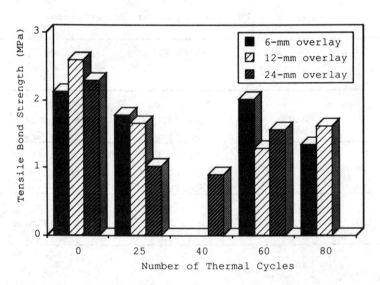

FIG. 2. Thermal Cycling of PM2 Overlays

Analytical and Design Methods

Méthodes analytiques et de design

ADVANCED COMPOSITE MATERIALS IN BRIDGES AND STRUCTURES
K.W. Neale and P. Labossière, Editors; Canadian Society for Civil Engineering, 1992

Matériaux composites d'avant-garde pour ponts et charpentes
K.W. Neale et P. Labossière, éditeurs; Société canadienne de génie civil, 1992

NONLINEAR ANALYSIS OF FIBRE-REINFORCED
CONCRETE STRUCTURES

A.G. Razaqpur and **M. Nofal**
Carleton University
Ottawa, Ontario, Canada

ABSTRACT

Micromechanical damage mechanics, in conjunction with the *rule of mixtures*, is applied in a nonlinear finite element scheme to trace the full deformation response of a number of fibre-reinforced concrete beams and slabs tested by others. In addition to either steel fibre or carbon fibre reinforcement, some of the test specimens also contained conventional mild steel reinforcement. In the present numerical model full bond was assumed between the fibres and the matrix throughout the deformation process. Comparison of the results in the range of zero to maximum load shows good agreement between all the available measured data and the corresponding numerically calculated values. The current finite element scheme is, however, unable to predict the softening portion of the load-deformation response. It is significant that in the cases investigated herein fibre pull-out did not appear to appreciably affect the strength and stiffness of the specimens.

RÉSUMÉ

La mécanique de l'endommagement micromécanique et la règle des mélanges sont appliquées dans une analyse par éléments finis non linéaires afin de déterminer les déformations de poutres et dalles de béton renforcées de fibres d'acier ou de carbone. En plus de ces fibres, quelques échantillons contenaient de l'acier conventionnel doux. La présente modélisation numérique est basée sur un lien parfait entre les fibres et la matrice pendant toute la procédure. La comparaison des résultats entre zéro et la charge maximum démontre la compatibilité des mesures expérimentales disponibles et des résultats numériques. La méthode est cependant incapable de prévoir la portion post-pic de la courbe charge-déformation. Il est significatif que, dans les cas étudiés ici, l'arrachement des fibres ne semble pas affecter la résistance ni la rigidité des échantillons.

INTRODUCTION

Due to the opening and propagation of microcracks, the load-deformation response of concrete structures becomes nonlinear at a relatively low level of load. The presence of moderate to high percentage of fibres in fibre-reinforced concrete seems to retard this aspect of concrete behaviour but does not completely eliminate it. Whereas linear elastic fracture mechanics can be used to trace the displacements and propagation of macrocracks in a material, the random distribution and sizes of microcracks in concrete cannot be dealt with by direct application of classical linear fracture mechanics. On the other hand, micromechanical damage mechanics can be used to deal with the effects of dilute distributed cracks on the load-deformation response of a material.

The concept of damage mechanics was initially proposed by Kachanov (1958) which has been rigorously developed by others (Krajcinovic and Sumarac 1989) to deal with the effects of voids and defects on material nonlinearity, creep response, load-induced anisotropy, etc. Two distinct modelling approaches have evolved in damage mechanics: the phenomenological models and the micromechanical models (Krajcinovic 1989). In the present paper we shall use the "rule of mixture" in conjunction with micromechanical damage mechanics to develop the basic constitutive relations for fibre-reinforced concrete. These relations will then be utilized in a nonlinear finite element scheme to analyze a series of fibre-reinforced concrete beams and slabs in order to trace their full response under increasing load. The fibres will be either steel or carbon, and the concrete may also contain conventional steel reinforcement. It will be shown that in all the cases presently investigated good agreement exists between the experimentally measured data and the numerically calculated results up to the maximum load or *bend over point* (BOP). The prediction of softening, however, is not easy by numerical methods. From the design point of view, the softening part has no impact on the maximum load carrying capacity of a structure, but it is important in determining its energy absorption capacity and ductility. The focus of the present study is mainly on strength and stiffness.

FINITE ELEMENT PROCEDURES

The nonlinear finite element program NONLACS (Razaqpur and Nofal 1990) was used in the present study. The program can analyze over the full loading range any reinforced/pre-stressed concrete, steel, fibre-reinforced concrete, or composite concrete-steel structures composed of assemblages of thin plates and panels. It has a library of plane stress (strain), plate bending, flat shell, three dimensional bar and shear connector elements.

For plates and shells, layered elements are utilized to capture the change in material properties and deformations through the thickness. Each layer is assumed to be in a state of plane stress, and increments of stress $\{\Delta\sigma\}$ are related to the corresponding increments of strain $\{\Delta\epsilon\}$ at a given material point by

$$\{\Delta\sigma\} = [D]\{\Delta\epsilon\} \tag{1}$$

where $[D]$ is the constitutive matrix. For steel structures, the classical theory of plasticity is employed, assuming the normality condition and an associated flow rule. Various yield criteria are allowed although generally the von-Mises criterion is actually used.

Steel reinforcing bars or prestressing tendons may be modelled as individual bars or they may be smeared into a layer possessing strength and stiffness in the direction of the axis of the bars only. For concrete, the concept of equivalent strain (Darwin and Pecknold 1977) or constitutive relations based on micromechanical damage mechanics (Krajcinovic 1989) may be employed. In the present analyses, the constitutive relations for plain and fibre-reinforced concrete are based on damage mechanics. Since this aspect of the constitutive modelling is new in the program, its salient features will be briefly discussed.

DAMAGE-BASED CONSTITUTIVE MODEL

In micromechanics defects, such as cracks, are treated as material property. Thus fibre-reinforced concrete is assumed to consist of the matrix (cement-paste and aggregates), the fibres and the microcracks. The fibres and the cracks are assumed to be randomly distributed within the matrix. The cracks are assumed to be dilute, i.e. there is no interaction among them.

In the present study the effect of the fibres on the matrix was accounted for by determining the fibre-matrix composite properties via the "rule of mixture". In other words

$$
\begin{aligned}
E_{fc} &= \mathcal{V}_c E_c + \mathcal{V}_f E_f \\
\nu_{fc} &= \mathcal{V}_c \nu_c + \mathcal{V}_f \nu_f
\end{aligned}
\tag{2}
$$

where E, ν, and $\mathcal{V}$ are the initial elastic modulus, the initial Poisson's ratio, and the volume fraction, respectively, and the subscripts c, f, and fc denote concrete, fibre, and fibre-concrete. In considering the effect of fibres in the above manner, fibre pull-out and fracture are not explicitly considered. Thus full bond is assumed between the fibres and the matrix throughout the deformation process. To account for the presence of microcracks, we use the principles of micromechanics as follows.

Fibre-reinforced Concrete Compliance

The total current strain vector, $\{\epsilon\}$, and the total current stress vector, $\{\sigma\}$, at any point in a structure may be related by

$$
\{\epsilon\} = [C]\{\sigma\}
\tag{3}
$$

where $[C]$ is the current compliance matrix which is related to the constitutive matrix $[D]$ in Eq. (1) by

$$
[D] = [C]^{-1}
\tag{4}
$$

It can be shown (Razaqpur and Nofal 1992) that

$$
[C] = [C_{fc}] + [C_{cr}]
\tag{5a}
$$

$$
[C_{cr}] = [C_{cr}]^g + [C_{cr}]^a
\tag{5b}
$$

where the subscript cr refers to the crack and the superscripts a and g signify arrested and growing cracks, respectively. Arrested and growing cracks can be distinguished by comparing their stresses to those needed to propagate a crack. The latter stresses are related to the stress intensity factors which can be obtained by fracture mechanics considerations (Ashby 1979). The compliance of fibre-matrix composite, $[C_{cf}]$, is assumed to remain constant throughout the deformation process until the BOP and is given by its initial elastic value

$$
[C_{fc}] = \frac{1}{E_{fc}}
\begin{bmatrix}
1 & -\nu_{fc} & 0 \\
-\nu_{fc} & 1 & 0 \\
0 & 0 & 2(1+\nu_{fc})
\end{bmatrix}
\tag{6}
$$

The compliance $[C_{cr}]$ depends on the stress level and it can be calculated by integrating the current crack displacements (Horii and Nemat-Nasser 1983). For a single penny shaped crack embedded in a homogeneous and isotropic elastic material and subjected to a given stress field, the crack displacements can be obtained using the solution given by Lekhnitskii (1950). By integrating those displacements around the crack, its compliance can be obtained as

$$
[C_{cr}] = \frac{\pi a^2}{A}
\begin{bmatrix}
0 & 0 & 0 \\
0 & & \\
& B_{22} & B_{21} \\
0 & B_{12} & B_{11}
\end{bmatrix}
\tag{7}
$$

in which a is the radius of the crack and A is its area. The elements of B_{ij}, $(i = j = 1, 2)$ are obtained from the roots of the characteristic equation of the problem of an embedded crack (Krajcinovic and Sumarac 1989). Equation (7) is valid for a crack that both opens and slides. For non-opening cracks which can slide, it needs to be modified as shown elsewhere (Razaqpur and Nofal 1992; Ju 1990).

599

For an ensemble of cracks, we assume a joint probability density function $p(\theta, a)$ for the cracks size and orientation, and then integrate the compliance of the cracks over the domain of interest to obtain the compliance of the crack ensemble. That is

$$[C_{cr}] = \int_{\theta_i} \int_{a_i} [C_{cr}]_i \, p(\theta, a) \, da \, d\theta \qquad (8)$$

where θ_i indicates the orientation of crack i. Th joint probability density function is commonly assumed to be Gaussian $\left(\frac{1}{\pi}\right)$.

By using the above procedures, Razaqpur and Nofal (1992) showed that it was possible to determine the stress-strain characteristics and strength of fibre-reinforced concrete under various plane stress conditions, including uniaxial and biaxial tension, or compression, and combined tension-compression. In the next section, we will show that the suggested procedure equally applies to the analysis of fibre-reinforced concrete structures.

EXPERIMENTAL VERIFICATION

It was mentioned earlier that the proposed model was used to rather accurately predict the response of fibre-reinforced concrete subjected to different stress regimes (Razaqpur and Nofal 1992). In this section, we will show the results of numerical analyses of a series of structural elements, based on the preceding model, and compare those results with the corresponding experimental data. It will be observed that the agreement is favourable.

CFRC Beams

Ohama *et al.* (1985); Banthia and Sheng (1990) and Banthia (1992) constructed a number of rectangular concrete beams reinforced with pitch-based carbon fibres. Fibre contents of 1%, 3%, and 5% were used, while some control beams had no fibres. The beams were simply supported and tested under a central point load. Their dimensions and loading are shown in Fig. 1, while Table 1 shows their properties. Using symmetry, half of each beam was modelled by sixteen 4−node plane stress elements, eight along the span and two through the height. Each element had three nodal degrees of freedom, two inplane displacements and a drilling rotation. The material properties, as input in the numerical model, are given in Table 1.

Table:1 Material properties used in the numerical analysis

Material	Test Specimens / Property		CFRC Beams				SFRC Beams			SFRC Slabs		
			0.0%	1.0%	3.0%	5.0%	0.0%	1.0%	2.0%	0.0%	0.5%	1.0%
Concrete matrix	Initial Elastic Modulus, E_c (GPa)		16.67				18.94			17.35		
	Poisson's Ratio, ν_c		0.20*				0.20*			0.15*		
	Interface Mode I Fracture, K_{IC}^{if} (N/mm$^{3/2}$)		8.7[#]	11.3	22.6	26.3	18.2[#]	32.0	50.1	13.4[#]	19.0	20.5
	Interface Mode II Fracture, K_{IIC}^{if} (N/mm$^{3/2}$)		34.6[#]	39.0	48.0	54.0	49.5[#]	52.0	60.7	47.0[#]	45.0	47.4
	Cement-Paste Mode I Fracture, K_{IC}^{c} (N/mm$^{3/2}$)		40.0[#]	44.3	55.4	63.0	71.4[#]	75.0	83.5	67.8[#]	65.2	68.4
	Initial Crack Diameter, a_o (mm)		5.4	4.0	3.0	2.0	7.5	5.0	3.0	7.0	5.0	3.0
	Final Crack Diameter, a_f (mm)		9[!]				15[!]			14[!]		
	Coefficient of Friction, μ_c		0.6*				0.6*			0.6*		
Fibres	Fibre Young's Modulus, E_f (GPa)		38				200			200*		
	Poisson's Ratio, ν_f		0.15				0.30			0.30		
	Tensile Strength, σ_f (MPa)		800				1303			460		
Steel Rft.	Young's Modulus, E_s (GPa)		N/A				200			200*		
	Strain Hardening Modulus, E_{sh} (GPa)		N/A				20			20		
	Poisson's Ratio, ν_s		N/A				0.30			0.30		
	Yield Stress, σ_s (MPa)		N/A				420			460		

* Assumed
! Based on the maximum aggregate size (Krajcinovic 1989)
Calculated as a function of a_f and maximum tensile and compressive strengths (Razaqpur and Nofal 1992)

The results of the analyses are compared with the available experimental data in Fig. 1. We notice that except for one of the beams with 3% fibre, Fig. 1(b), the numerical and experimental results agree well in the other cases. As mentioned earlier, the proposed method does not consider strain softening. In the case of the one beam, for which the agreement is not as good, the experimental results appear to be anomalous, for the beam with 3% fibre content appears to be stiffer than the one with 5% fibre. The same is not revealed by the experimental data of Ohama *et al.* in Fig. 1(a). Because there was no repeat specimens for those beams, we ascribe the above lack of agreement to experimental variabilities rather than the shortcoming of the model.

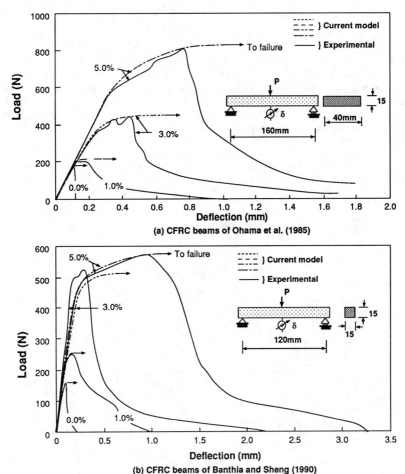

Fig. 1: **Load-deflection curves for carbon fibre-reinforced concrete beams**

SFRC Beams

Oh *et al.* (1989) tested a number of rectangular beams simply supported and loaded with third point loads. The beams were either singly or doubly reinforced with conventional mild steel bars in addition to up to 2% steel fibres. The fibres were 40 mm long and 0.7 mm in diameter. Diagonal

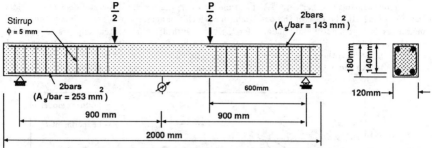

Fig. 2: Typical details of steel fibre-reinforced concrete beams

tension reinforcement was also provided within the shear span. Typical details are shown in Fig. 2.

Due to symmetry, half of each beam was divided into 10 finite elements along the span and three along the depth. The longitudinal reinforcement was modelled as bar elements while the shear reinforcement was smeared into a layer.

The load midspan deflection curves of the singly reinforced beams are shown in Fig. 3. We observe the close agreement between the experimental and numerical results. Due to lack of experimental data, we are unable to compare other quantities of interest, such as strain and curvature. The results for the doubly reinforced beams compared equally well.

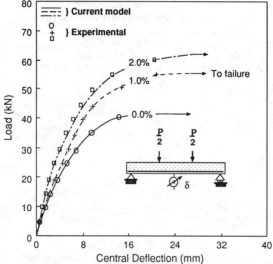

Fig. 3: Load-deflection curve of steel fibre-reinforced concrete beams

SFRC Slabs

Theodorakopoulos and Swamy (1989) tested a number of square slabs built monolithically with a central stub column and simply supported around the periphery. The slabs were made of lightweight concrete and were reinforced with an orthogonal mesh of mild steel reinforcement near the top and bottom faces. The stub columns also had steel reinforcement. The slabs were loaded

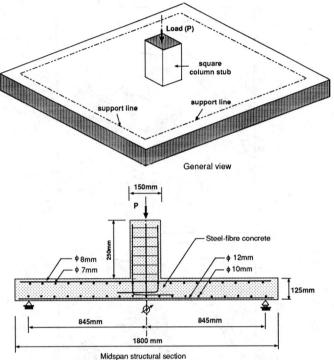

Fig. 4: Steel fibre-reinforced concrete slabs

with a central point load over the column. Figure 4 shows the complete details of a typical test specimen, including its dimensions and reinforcement arrangement.

The concrete mix comprised cement, fly ash, sand, and lightweight aggregates known by the trade name *Lytag*. These ingredients were mixed in the ratio 287 : 123 : 560 : 696 kg/m^3, respectively, with a water/binder ratio of 0.40. The maximum aggregate size was 14 mm. The mix also contained steel fibres (length = 50 mm, diameter = 0.5 mm) with fibre contents of 0%, 0.5%, and 1%.

Due to symmetry one quarter of the slab was modelled by an 8 × 8 mesh of flat shell elements. The inplane component of the shell element was the same as the plane stress element described earlier. The bending part is a 4−node quadrilateral element with three degrees of freedom per node. The element is based on the discrete Kirchoff theory of plate bending (Razaqpur and Nofal 1990). Because the purpose of the stub column was to transfer loads to the slab without causing punching shear, the column was not modelled by finite elements. The load was applied uniformly over an area at the center of the slab equal to the column cross-section. The slab reinforcement was modelled as smeared layers while the slab was divided into 5 concrete layers through its thickness. The material properties, as used in the analysis, are shown in Table 1.

Results of the analysis are compared in Figs, 5, 6, and 7. Figure 5(a) shows the load-central deflection of the slabs while Fig. 5(b) depicts the load versus the edge rotations. Figure 6 shows the concrete strain in the top surface of the slab at a point halfway between the center and the edge of the slab. Figures 7(a) and 7(b) show, respectively, the load versus strain variation in the bottom and top steel layers directly below the applied load.

Generally there is good agreement between the calculated and the measured values for the various quantities. There appears to be some discrepancy between the two sets of results for the

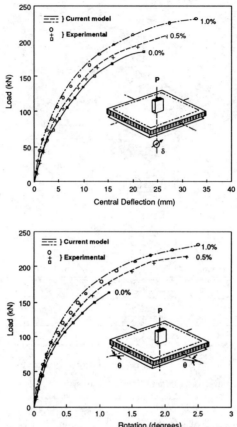

Fig. 5: Deflections and rotations of steel fibre-reinforced concrete slabs

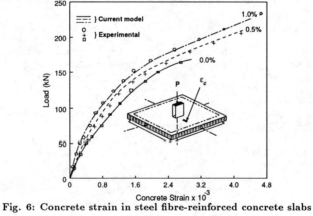

Fig. 6: Concrete strain in steel fibre-reinforced concrete slabs

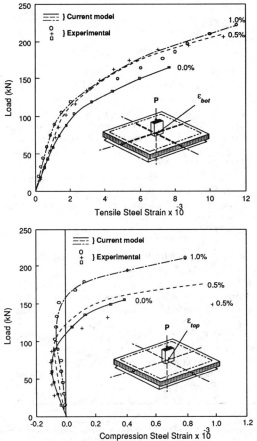

Fig. 7: Steel Strain in steel fibre-reinforced concrete slabs

strains in the top steel layer in the slab with 0.5% fibre content. Since all other strains compare favourably, we speculate that the above difference may be due to some punching. The finite element program utilized in the current study does not consider through thickness deformations in the slab, and is consequently incapable of accounting for punching shear.

CONCLUSIONS

The results in this investigation show that:

(1) Micromechanical damage mechanics in conjunction with the the "rule of mixture" can be used to capture the full response of fibre-reinforced concrete beams and slabs, with or without conventional mild steel reinforcement.

(2) The nonlinear finite element approach is capable of producing results that agree well with experimental data for fibre-reinforced concrete beams and slabs.

(3) The assumption of full bond between the concrete and the fibre within the range of zero to maximum load appears to be reasonable. In other words, for the fibre types and contents investigated herein, fibre pull-out seems to have no effect on the strength of the structures analyzed.

ACKNOWLEDGMENTS

This research was supported by the Natural Sciences and Engineering Research Council of Canada which is gratefully acknowledged.

REFERENCES

Ashby, M. F., (1979). Micromechanisms of fracture in static and cyclic failure. In Fracture Mechanics, current status, future, prospects. Smith, R. A., (Eds.) Pergamon, Oxford, 1, 1-27.

Banthia, N. (1992). Pitch-based fibre-reinforced cements: structure, performance, applications, and research needs. *Can. J. Civ. Engrg.*, **19**(1), 26-38.

Banthia, N., Sheng, J. (1990). Micro-reinforced cementitious materials. Materials Research Society Symposium Proceedings, **211**, Mindess, S., and Skalny, J., (Eds.), Boston, Mass., 25-32.

Darwin, D., and Pecknold, D. A., (1977). Nonlinear biaxial stress-strain law for concrete. *J. Engrg. Mech.*, ASCE, **103**(EM4) 229-241.

Horii, H., and Nemat-Nasser, S. (1983). Overall moduli of solids with microcracks: load induced anisotropy. *J. of Mech. of Phys. and solids*, **31**(2), 155-171.

Ju, J. W., (1990). On two-dimensional self-consistent micromechanical damage models for brittle solids. *Int. J. of Solids and Struct.* **27**(2), 227-258.

Kachanov, L. M., (1958). Time of the rupture process under creep conditions. *IVZ Akad Nauk, S.S.R., Otd Tech Nauk*, **8**, 26-31.

Krajcinovic, D., and Sumarac, D., (1989). A mesomechanical model for brittle deformation process: Part I. *J. of Applied Mech.*, ASME, **56**(3), 51-56.

Krajcinovic, D., (1989). Damage Mechanics. *Mechanics of Materials*, **8**(9), 117-197.

Lekhnitskii, S. G. (1950). Theory of elasticity of an anisotropic elastic body. The Government Publishing House for Technical-Theoretical Works, Moscow and Leningrad, 1950; Holden-Day, San Francisco, 1963.

Ohama, Y., Amano, M., and Endo, M., (1985). Properties of carbon fibre-reinforced cement with silica fume *Conc. Int.*, ACI, (3), 58-62.

Oh, B. H., Lee, H. J., and Lee, S., (1989). Deformation characteristics of reinforced concrete beams containing steel fibres. In Fibre-reinforced cements and concretes, Recent developments. Swamy, R. N., and Barr, B., (Eds.) Elsevier Applied Science, London, U.K., 444-453.

Razaqpur, A. G., and Nofal, M., (1990). Analytical modelling of nonlinear behaviour of composite bridges. *J. Stuct. Engrg.,* ASCE, **116**(6) 1715-1733.

Razaqpur, A. G., and Nofal, M., (1992). Micromechanical damage-based model For fibre-reinforced concrete materials. Proc. of the Annual Conf. of Canadian Soc. for Civ. Engrg. Vol III, 283 -292

Theodorakopoulos, D. D., and Swamy, R. N., (1989). Punching behavior of lightweight concrete slabs with steel fibres. In Fibre-reinforced cements and concretes, Recent developments. Swamy, R. N., and Barr, B., (Eds.) Elsevier Applied Science, London, U.K., 640-650.

ADVANCED COMPOSITE MATERIALS IN BRIDGES AND STRUCTURES
K.W. Neale and P. Labossière, Editors; Canadian Society for Civil Engineering, 1992

Matériaux composites d'avant-garde pour ponts et charpentes
K.W. Neale et P. Labossière, éditeurs; Société canadienne de génie civil, 1992

DEFLECTIONS OF FRP-REINFORCED SLABS : A FINITE ELEMENT STUDY

A.H. Rahman and **D.A. Taylor**
National Research Council Canada
Ottawa, Ontario, Canada

ABSTRACT

Deflections of concrete slabs reinforced with fibre-reinforced plastic (FRP) were examined by the finite element (FE) method, which yielded results in good agreement with experimental data for one-way slabs. With the same FE method, two-way flat plates reinforced with FRP and with steel were analyzed to compute service load deflections and to compare the results. It is shown that the typical slab, which deflects within acceptable limits when reinforced with steel, would suffer large deflections if reinforced with a FRP having a modulus of elasticity of about 20 percent of that of steel. Adding drop panels was found to reduce the deflections of the FRP-reinforced slab significantly. In addition to drop panels, it is necessary to use FRP of a higher modulus, about 40 percent of that of steel or higher, to have deflections comparable to those of a steel-reinforced slab without drop panels.

RÉSUMÉ

Les déflexions de dalles de béton renforcées de FRP ont été étudiées par éléments finis (EF). Cette méthode a donné de bons résultats pour des dalles unidirectionnelles. Avec la même méthode EF, des dalles bi-directionnelles renforcées de FRP et d'acier ont été analysées pour calculer les déflexions sous chargement et comparer les résultats. On montre qu'une dalle typique, dont les déflexions sont acceptables avec une armature en acier, subirait des déflexions importantes si l'armature en FRP avait un module d'élasticité d'environ 20 pour cent de celui de l'acier. L'ajout de ressauts réduit considérablement la déflexion des dalles renforcées de FRP. En plus des ressauts, il est toutefois nécessaire d'utiliser des FRP avec un module de 40 pour cent ou plus de celui de l'acier pour obtenir des déflexions comparables à celles d'une dalle renforcée d'acier et sans ressaut.

607

INTRODUCTION

In many parts of the world, corrosion of steel reinforcement leading to premature deterioration of concrete structures has become a major problem. The economic losses arising are very substantial.

The principal cause of steel corrosion lies in the structure's environment, about which very little can be done. While good design details, quality of concrete and construction workmanship play significant roles in reducing corrosion, they are not enough to prevent damage. Consequently, various protective measures, such as waterproofing membranes, epoxy-coated steel, and cathodic protection, have been developed to help prevent, delay, or reduce the corrosion of steel reinforcement. These measures have so far had varying degrees of success.

An effective solution may lie in using an alternative to steel reinforcement that does not corrode. Being highly resistant to corrosion, fibre-reinforced plastic (FRP) has the potential to be such an alternative. Researchers, including the authors, are investigating the technical effectiveness of FRP in reinforcing concrete. Since the modulus of elasticity of FRP is significantly lower than that of steel, FRP-reinforced structures will tend to deflect more than steel-reinforced ones. Deflection is therefore an important aspect of the investigation of FRP as a suitable reinforcement for concrete.

This paper presents a finite element study of the deflection of a typical building slab reinforced with FRP.

BACKGROUND

Building slabs are required to satisfy serviceability limit states of cracking and deflection. Crack width in FRP-reinforced slabs may not be as important as in steel-reinforced slabs with respect to corrosion but may still have to be limited in parking garages to prevent leakage through the slab. Excessive deflection of slabs is to be prevented to protect items, such as partitions, from being damaged, and to avoid ponding and unsightly appearance.

The modulus of elasticity of typical FRPs range between 30 000 and 80 000 MPa, depending mainly on the type of fibres used. These values of the moduli are rather low compared to 200 000 MPa of steel. Consequently, FRP-reinforced beams and slabs are expected to deflect more than steel-reinforced ones. Flat plate slabs of moderate to large span, such as those in office buildings and parking garages, will be most vulnerable.

OBJECTIVE AND METHOD

The primary objectives of this study are to estimate the service load deflections of a typical building slab reinforced with FRP, to compare the deflections with those of a similar steel-reinforced slab, and to explore ways of controlling deflections in the FRP-reinforced slab. The finite element (FE) method was used for this purpose. Depending principally on the fineness of discretization, choice of constitutive relations, and techniques used to model special phenomena such as shear friction and bond slip, the finite element method has proven to be a reasonably accurate tool for tracing the load-deflection behaviour of many reinforced concrete structures (Bangash 1989).

608

FINITE ELEMENT ANALYSIS

The Computer Program

The FE computer program, FELARC, used in this study was developed by Ghoneim (1978). It can trace the nonlinear behaviour of reinforced and prestressed concrete structures subjected to monotonic or cyclic loading including the time-dependant effects of creep and shrinkage. The theoretical aspects of the program relevant to this study are briefly treated below; a more comprehensive treatment is available in the original work (Ghoneim 1978).

The program uses the equations originally proposed by Saenz (1964), and by Smith and Young (1955), to define the stress-strain curve for concrete under uniaxial compression. For concrete under uniaxial tension, it uses a linear relationship between stress and strain with the same modulus of elasticity as in compression. Under a biaxial state of stress, the concept of equivalent uniaxial strain introduced by Darwin and Pecknold (1977) is used to account for stress-induced orthotropy. To determine the ultimate strength under biaxial stress conditions, the modified biaxial failure envelope proposed by Kupfer and Gerstle (1973) is used.

For steel, the program employs a bilinear stress-strain relationship identical in tension and compression. The relationship is defined by four parameters, viz., yield strength, elastic modulus, strain-hardening modulus, and ultimate strain.

A smeared cracking approach is used as opposed to discrete cracking. A crack is assumed to occur perpendicular to the principal stress direction whenever that stress exceeds the uniaxial tensile strength of concrete. After cracks occur in both principal directions, all the coefficients of the constitutive matrix except the shear modulus become zero. A shear retention factor accounts for dowel action of reinforcement and aggregate interlock across the cracks. The tension carried by uncracked portions of concrete between cracks, referred to as tension-stiffening, is also considered. The program can predict a flexural type of failure, caused either by crushing of concrete or by tensile failure of reinforcement or concrete, but not a shear failure. Geometric nonlinearity, bond slip between concrete and reinforcement, and fatigue are not considered.

For modelling slabs, the program uses a multilayered quadrilateral thin shell element with 24 degrees of freedom. Thus membrane forces in the slab are accounted for. The multiple-layer formulation allows the stiffness of the individual layers to vary according to their states of stress. Distributed steel reinforcement is modelled by a smeared layer of steel of an equivalent thickness.

The program uses an incremental iterative tangent stiffness procedure to solve the nonlinear problem. Either a force or a displacement criterion can be used for convergence and divergence of the solution.

Comparison with Experimental Results

To verify the accuracy of computations, it is desirable to compare analytical results with experimental ones. Experimental data on the load-deflection behaviour of two-way flat plates reinforced with FRP were not available to the authors. However, data were available from experiments carried out on one-way strips of slabs reinforced with two types of FRP as well as ordinary reinforcing steel (Schmeckpeper 1992). One type of the FRP reinforcement, FRP-CG, is made of a mixture of carbon and glass fibres while the other, FRP-C, of only carbon fibres. Both types are of a grid construction developing bond in any direction through direct concrete bearing on transverse bars.

Finite element analyses were carried out on these slab strips for comparison. While the key properties of concrete were available, some properties such as ultimate tensile strength and initial tangent modulus were derived by using code recommendations and well-established formulae.

609

The FRP-reinforced strips in the experiments failed in shear, a failure mode which cannot be predicted by the finite element program used. For the FRP-reinforced strips, higher than experimental ultimate loads were thus predicted by the FE analysis. The load-deflection behaviour obtained from the FE analysis is compared in Fig. 1 with that obtained by Schmeckpeper. It is seen that the FE analysis can trace the load-deflection behaviour in the post-cracking range reasonably well. The larger discrepancy between FE and experimental results for the FRP-reinforced slabs compared to the steel-reinforced one is believed to be caused by higher bond slip along FRP bars. Note that the FE analysis assumes perfect bond between concrete and reinforcement.

The FE Model

The number and size of panels in the slabs of real-life buildings vary widely. Here, a flat plate slab with 3 panels of 7.5 m x 7.5 m size in each direction was selected for analysis. To satisfy punching shear provisions of the code (Canadian Standards Association 1984), a slab thickness of 250 mm was selected. Although a smaller thickness for the interior panels would be permissible, the same thickness was assumed for the entire slab since slabs are usually constructed with uniform thickness for ease of formwork and placement of reinforcement.

Taking advantage of symmetry, only a quarter of the slab was modelled. The FE mesh for the slab, consisting of 225 shell elements, is shown in Fig. 2. The 250 mm thick shell elements were divided into 10 layers. Each column, one storey high, was modelled by three spring elements of appropriate axial and torsional stiffnesses to represent the actual column stiffnesses corresponding to the degrees of freedom common to the slab and the column. The flexural stiffnesses of the 300 mm square columns with 4-#35M bars were calculated assuming cracked sections. All column stiffnesses were assumed to remain constant for the entire range of loading relevant to this study.

The area and distribution of reinforcement in the FE model were determined to satisfy code requirements for steel reinforcement, except for minor adjustments made to conform to the FE mesh and to keep data input simple. The only difference between the slabs reinforced with steel and FRP was in the reinforcement material properties; area and distribution of reinforcement were exactly the same. An average effective depth of 225 mm was assumed for both FRP and steel reinforcement. For the same amount of clear cover, this assumption makes the steel-reinforced slab slightly stiffer than actual since steel reinforcement at each plane consists of two layers whereas the FRP reinforcement is a single-plane grid.

Properties of Concrete

Tensile strength and initial tangent modulus are the most significant concrete properties that govern the load-deflection behaviour of slabs under service loads. Ultimate tensile strain and the cracked shear constant play relatively minor roles. Values of all concrete properties input for the FE analysis are given below.

Ultimate compressive strength	25.0 MPa
Ultimate tensile strength	2.2 MPa
Strain at ultimate compressive strength	0.0018
Ultimate strain in compression	0.0035
Ultimate strain in tension	0.0004
Initial tangent modulus	25 000 MPa
Poisson's ratio	0.15
Shear retention factor	0.5

Properties of Reinforcement

Two types of FRP reinforcement were used. Values of all reinforcement properties required as input for the FE analysis are given below.

Property	FRP-CG	FRP-C	Steel
Modulus of elasticity, MPa	42 000	85 000	200 000
Strain-hardening modulus, MPa	200	200	2000
Yield strength, MPa	800	1200	400
Ultimate strain	0.022	0.022	0.05

Note that the modulus of elasticity is the most significant property of the reinforcement that governs the load-deflection behaviour in the service load range. The yield strength, strain-hardening modulus and ultimate strain govern the ultimate load.

Loads and Other Data

The weight of the slab amounts to a uniformly distributed load of 6.0 kPa. The live load was assumed as 2.4 kPa, stipulated by the code for parking garages. In general, the load was applied in increments of 1.2 kPa, up to a total of 12.0 kPa, well beyond the factored load of 11.1 kPa; in the analyses with unloading and reloading, the live load was applied in smaller steps of 0.6 kPa. A displacement criterion was used for convergence with a tolerance of one percent.

Effects of creep, shrinkage and temperature were not included in these analyses.

RESULTS AND DISCUSSION

The computed deflections at selected locations of the slab reinforced with FRP-CG are plotted against the uniformly distributed load in Fig. 3. It is seen that under service load (DL+LL), the mid-panel deflection varies from 16 mm in the interior panel (location 5) to as large as 110 mm in the corner panel (location 4). Deflections at other locations are also quite large, about 65 mm at the middle of the edge panel and about 63 mm at the edges of the corner panel. For comparison, deflections at the same locations of the steel-reinforced slab are shown in Fig. 4.

The effect of adding drop panels in reducing deflections was investigated. The drop panels, shown shaded in Fig. 2(b), are 75 mm thick and extend to a distance of 20% of the span length from the column centre in each direction. The reinforcement distribution was kept the same as in the slab without drop panels. The deflections in the slab with drop panels are plotted in Fig. 5. When compared to Fig. 3, a large improvement in the deflections can be observed. For example, the largest service-load deflection occurring in the middle of the corner panel is reduced from 110 mm in the uniform slab to only 9 mm in the slab with drop panels.

However, as is apparent from the sharp bends in the load-deflection curves of Fig. 5, the slab starts to crack under the full service load. Indeed, the slab may already be cracked due to shrinkage and temperature effects before reaching the full service load. To obtain an improved estimate of the deflections in recognition of this precracking, a FE analysis was carried out by loading the slab above the service load, unloading to dead load only, and reloading up to the factored load. This procedure cracks the slab wherever concrete stress exceeds the tensile strength, leading to a cracking that is likely to be more extensive than that due to shrinkage and temperature effects. Therefore, the reloading segments of the load-deflection curves from this analysis are expected to

611

give upper bounds of the deflections. Fig. 6 shows these curves. It is seen that the mid-panel deflection in the corner panel of the precracked slab is about 59 mm under service load.

To estimate further improvement of deflections that would be provided by a FRP with a higher modulus of elasticity, the above analysis was repeated for the FRP-C type of reinforcement. Since the steel-reinforced slab without drop panel also starts to crack under the full service load (Fig. 4), the analysis for that slab was repeated following the load-unload-reload procedure.

The computed short-term deflections under service load for both steel and FRP-reinforced slabs are shown in Table 1. Except for the case FRP-CG (without drop panel), the deflections are from the analyses following the load-unload-reload procedure

Table 1 shows that the computed short-term deflections under service load are quite large in a slab without drop panels and reinforced with FRP-CG; compared with those of a steel-reinforced slab, they are about 3 to 6 times larger depending on the location. When drop panels are added, these deflections decrease significantly, by more than 50% in the key locations. If the FRP-C type reinforcement is used in addition to drop panels, these deflections are further reduced by about 50%; the largest deflection in that case is about 10 mm larger than that of the steel-reinforced slab.

Due to creep, shrinkage and temperature effects, slabs undergo significant additional deflection in the long term. A finite element estimate of this additional deflection was beyond the scope of this study. A simplified approach is followed here to estimate the additional deflection. For the same concrete and construction conditions, the shrinkage and temperature effects are independent of the reinforcement, and creep of concrete depends mainly on the compressive stress level. An examination of the computed stresses in concrete showed no significant difference in the slabs reinforced with steel and FRP. Thus it can be reasonably assumed that the additional deflection due to creep, shrinkage and temperature effects will be the same for FRP as for steel reinforcement. For steel, this additional deflection is about two times the short-term deflection neglecting compression reinforcement, according to the code (Canadian Stds. Assoc. 1984).

The long-term deflections were thus calculated by multiplying the computed short-term deflections of the steel-reinforced slab by two and adding these to the computed short-term deflections of all slabs; Table 1 shows these long-term deflections. The largest long-term deflections in the slabs with drop panels are seen to be 97 mm for FRP-CG and 67 mm for FRP-C, compared to 57 mm in the steel-reinforced slab.

Various other options are available to the designer for controlling deflections in FRP-reinforced flat plates. Since corner and edge panel deflections are the largest, an edge beam will improve deflections. Increasing the area of reinforcement and the slab thickness in the corner panel may also be considered.

CONCLUSIONS

1.   The finite element analysis used in this study has been shown to predict load-deflection behaviour of one-way FRP-reinforced strips with reasonable accuracy.

2.   By extending this finite element analysis to a two-way slab, short-term deflections of a flat plate on a 7.5 m x 7.5 m column spacing, and reinforced with a FRP having a modulus of elasticity of about 20% of that of steel, were computed. These deflections vary from 16 mm at the middle of the interior panel to 110 mm at the middle of the corner panel, and are 3 to 6 times greater than the corresponding deflections of a steel-reinforced slab.

3.   Adding drop panels to the slab but keeping everything else same reduces the deflection by at least 50%.

4.   Using a FRP with a higher modulus of elasticity, 40% of that of steel, a further reduction of 50% in the deflections can be achieved.

5.   A slab using the higher modulus FRP and with drop panels will have deflections comparable to those of a steel-reinforced slab without drop panel.

ACKNOWLEDGEMENTS

The authors wish to thank Dr. Edwin Schmeckpeper of the University of New Hampshire for providing results of his one-way slab tests for comparison with the results of this finite element study.

REFERENCES

Bangash, M. Y. H. (1989), Concrete and Concrete Structures: Numerical Modelling and Applications, Elsevier Applied Science, London and New York, 668p.

Canadian Standards Association (1984), Design of Concrete Structures for Buildings, *CAN3-A23.3-M84*.

Darwin, D. and Pecknold, D. A. (1977), Nonlinear Biaxial Stress-Strain Law for Concrete, *ASCE Journal of the Engineering Mechanics Division*, **103**, No. EM2, 229-242.

Ghoneim, G. A. M. (1978), Nonlinear Finite Element Analysis of Concrete Structures, *Ph.D. Thesis*, Civil Engineering Department, The University of Calgary, Calgary, Alberta, Canada.

Kupfer, H. B. and Gerstle, K. H. (1973), Behaviour of Concrete under Biaxial Stresses, *ASCE Journal of the Engineering Mechanics Division*, **99**, No. EM4, 852-866.

Saenz, L. P. (1964), Discussion of Equation for the Stress-Strain Curve of Concrete by Desai and Krishnan, *ACI Journal*, **61**, No. 9, 1229-1235.

Schmeckpeper, E. (1992), Performance of Concrete Beams and Slabs Reinforced with FRP Grids, *Ph.D. Thesis*, University of New Hampshire, USA.

Smith, G. M. and Young, L. E. (1955), Ultimate Theory in Flexure by Exponential Function, *ACI Journal*, **52**, No. 3, 349-359.

Table 1 Computed short-term and estimated long-term deflections

Location[1]	Computed short-term deflection, mm				Estimated long-term deflection, mm			
on slab	Steel	FRP-CG	FRP-CG.dp[2]	FRP-C.dp	Steel	FRP-CG	FRP-CG.dp	FRP-C.dp
1	3	16	6	3	9	22	12	9
2	10	63	32	14	30	83	52	34
3	13	68	33	17	39	94	59	43
4	19	110	59	29	57	148	97	67
5	5	16	3	1	15	26	13	11

[1]Location numbers given in key plans in Figs. 3 to 6.   [2]dp indicates drop panel

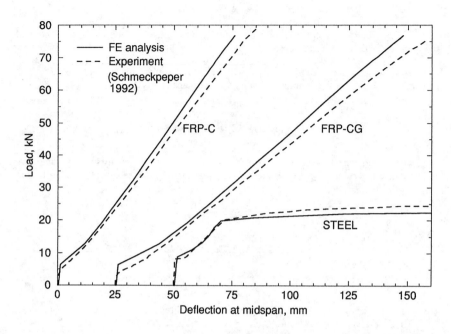

Fig. 1 Comparison of finite element analysis with experimental results for a slab strip. The strips are 300 mm wide, 200 mm deep, and 3.6 m in span loaded at the third points. For clarity, zero of deflection axis is shifted by 25 mm for FRP-CG and steel.

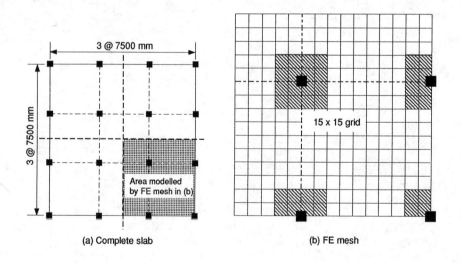

Fig. 2 Slab layout and finite element model

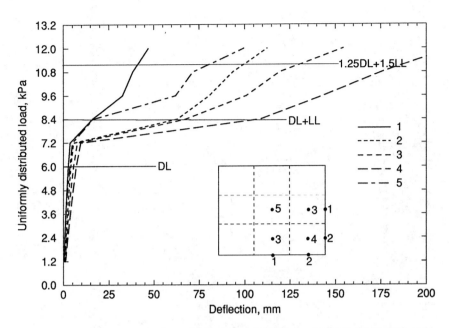

Fig.3 Load-deflection behaviour of slab without drop panel and reinforced with FRP-CG

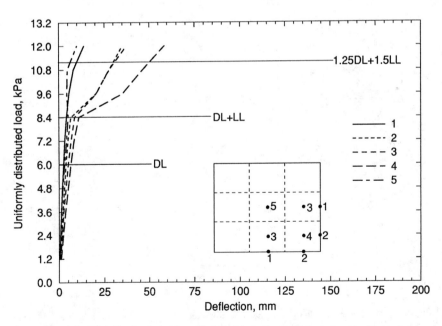

Fig. 4 Load-deflection behaviour of slab without drop panel reinforced with steel

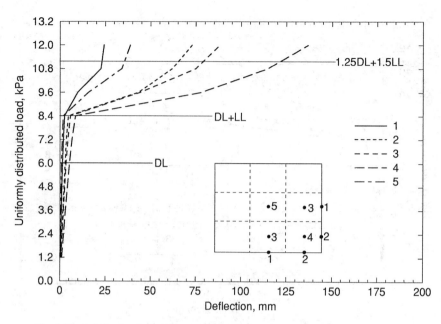

Fig. 5 Load-deflection behaviour of slab with drop panel and reinforced with FRP-CG

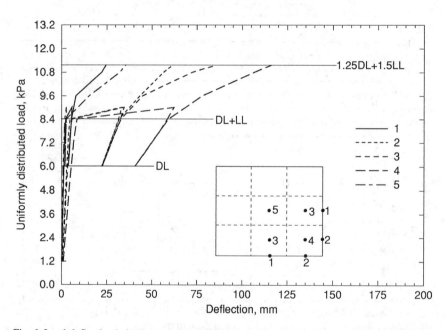

Fig. 6 Load-deflection behaviour of slab with drop panel and reinforced with FRP-CG following load-unload-reload procedure

ADVANCED COMPOSITE MATERIALS IN BRIDGES AND STRUCTURES
K.W. Neale and P. Labossière, Editors; Canadian Society for Civil Engineering, 1992

Matériaux composites d'avant-garde pour ponts et charpentes
K.W. Neale et P. Labossière, éditeurs; Société canadienne de génie civil, 1992

FINITE ELEMENT MODELLING OF FIBRE-REINFORCED CONCRETE BRIDGE DECKS ON STEEL GIRDERS

L.D. Wegner and **A.A. Mufti**
Technical University of Nova Scotia
Halifax, Nova Scotia, Canada

ABSTRACT

Experimental tests on half-scale models have demonstrated that polypropylene-fibre-reinforced concrete (PFRC) bridge deck slabs completely devoid of conventional steel reinforcement will fail by punching shear at loads considerably greater than those specified for design. Similar models were analyzed using nonlinear finite element techniques in order to reproduce experimentally observed load-deflection behaviours and failure loads. Commonly available concrete failure criteria for plain concrete were incorporated into the material model used or the PFRC deck slab. Results of the finite element analyses are presented. It is shown that while predicted load-deflection paths were less than satisfactory, accurate predictions of failure loads were achieved, but only after considerable tuning of various modelling parameters.

RÉSUMÉ

Des tests expérimentaux sur des modèles réduits ont démontré que des dalles en béton renforcé de fibres de polypropylène (PFRC), et sans autre armature conventionnelle, rupturent en cisaillement par perçage à des charges beaucoup plus grandes que celles spécifiées lors du design. Des modèles similaires ont été analysés par éléments finis non linéaires dans le but de reproduire les comportements charge-déflexion observés, et les charges de rupture. Les critères de rupture courants pour le béton non armé ont été incorporés dans le modèle du matériau utilisé pour la dalle de PFRC. Les résultats des analyses par éléments finis sont présentés. On montre que les cheminements charge-déflexion ne sont pas satisfaisants mais que des prédictions précises des charges de rupture ont été obtenues après plusieurs ajustements des paramètres de modélisation.

INTRODUCTION

Polypropylene fibres have been added to concrete for decades to improve crack control and create a tougher material. However, the low elastic modulus of polypropylene has rendered the fibres unsuitable for tensile reinforcement of concrete components of bridges and other structures. Therefore, polypropylene-fibre-reinforced concrete (PFRC) is not generally used in structural applications.

Recently, several half-scale models of PFRC bridge decks supported on steel girders and containing no steel reinforcement were tested to failure under concentrated loads (Mufti et al., 1992). It was established that PFRC bridge deck slabs will fail by punching shear at loads significantly greater than those required by the Ontario Highway Bridge Design Code (OHBDC, 1990) provided the top flanges of the steel girders are connected just below the deck by transverse steel straps and shear connectors are used. The low modulus of the polypropylene fibres is not of concern since arching action places the deck primarily into compression so that fibres are not called upon to resist tensile forces caused by primary structural actions such as flexure.

Alongside the experimental tests, nonlinear finite element (FE) analysis of the bridge deck slabs was undertaken to determine the ability of currently available models and techniques to recreate the load-deflection response to failure of a PFRC deck slab under a concentrated load. It was hoped that a reliable analytical tool could be found in nonlinear FE techniques so that the behaviour of experimentally untested configurations of deck slabs could be predicted with confidence. Such a tool would allow the efficient evaluation and optimization of such parameters as diaphragm configuration, concrete properties, and slab-to-depth ratio of PFRC deck slabs. This would lead to a reduction in the number of experimental tests required, and the ability to investigate many more configurations than are experimentally reasonable.

Failure criteria specific to fibre-reinforced concrete are not presently available for three-dimensional applications. Therefore, one of the objectives of this study was to determine whether material models available for plain concrete are suitable for modelling PFRC.

EXPERIMENTAL CONFIGURATION

The finite element models analyzed in this study represented two experimental slab-on-girder bridge configurations. The first, shown in Fig. 1 along with the test apparatus, was a two-girder system representing a single span bridge at half-scale. The deck slab was 100 mm thick and contained polypropylene fibres in the amount of 0.88% by volume. It was supported by two W460x82 steel girders spaced at 1067 mm centres and spanning approximately 3.5 m. The slab projected 530 mm beyond the centreline of each girder and was connected to the girders by shear studs. Three physical models of this type were tested, each with different diaphragm schemes. The girders of the first model were connected by three channel sections at mid-height of the girders. The second model added two channel sections at each end--one at mid-height and one at the lower flange. The decks of these two models failed in a flexural mode under centrally-located patch loads. Girders of the third model were connected to each other by five channels at mid-height, five channels at the lower flanges, and eight steel straps just below the upper flanges. The deck slab failed by punching shear under patch loads applied at mid-span and at quarter-

618

span. Finite element analyses corresponding to each of the four tests described were carried out.

The second system represented a three-girder, single span bridge at half-scale, and was similar in all respects to the third model except for the addition of a third girder and a corresponding increase in slab width. This model was tested to failure under a pair of rectangular patch loads straddling the centre girder and applied simultaneously. A test conducted at mid-span of the system was modelled numerically.

Results of the experimental tests have been reported by Mufti et al. (1992).

FINITE ELEMENT PROCEDURES

A PFRC deck slab subjected to a concentrated load develops a complex three-dimensional stress condition which is not fully understood. It was important that the FE package used be capable of modelling this behaviour and determining the particular state of stress leading to failure. The commercially available program ADINA (ADINA R&D, 1990) was chosen since it incorporated a sophisticated triaxial concrete material model, including state-of-the-art failure criteria. No attempt was made to modify the material model to account for the presence of fibres in the concrete.

ADINA's concrete model incorporates three basic features: 1) a nonlinear stress-strain relation allowing for the weakening of the material under increasing compressive stresses; 2) three-dimensional failure envelopes defining conditions which produce cracking in tension and crushing in compression; and 3) a strategy to model post cracking and crushing behaviour. Detailed descriptions of these features are found elsewhere (ADINA R&D, 1987; Bathe et al., 1989). Because of the use of default values for a number of input parameters, the definition of the concrete material model was reduced to providing only general material properties such as uniaxial compressive and tensile strengths and corresponding strains, Poisson's ratio, and initial tangent stiffness modulus.

A linear elastic uniaxial stress-strain material model was used for steel elements, with only Young's modulus and Poisson's ratio specified as input parameters.

Descriptions of the full-Newton iteration procedure used and element formulations are developed elsewhere and are not included here (ADINA R&D, 1987; Bathe, 1982; Bathe et al., 1989).

VERIFICATION MODELS

Prior to creating a detailed model of the slab and girder system, a study was undertaken to investigate the ability of a simplified model to reproduce general behaviours observed experimentally, in particular those of arching action caused by in-plane restraint at the boundaries of the deck slab, and punching shear failure.

The simplified model used in the preliminary study was a four element idealization of one quarter of a concrete slab supported along two sides and loaded at the centre, as shown in Fig. 2. The span and thickness of the model corresponded roughly to those of the experimental model, as did concrete material properties (i.e. Young's modulus, $E = 27600$ MPa; compressive strength, $\sigma_c = 27.6$ MPa; tensile strength, $\sigma_t = 2.76$ MPa; and Poisson's ratio, $v = 0.1$). Since the behaviour of the slab was neither a pure bending nor a plane stress problem, three-dimensional isoparametric elements were used with 20 nodes per element. Appropriate boundary conditions were applied along the planes of symmetry.

Arching Action

The model was first subjected to a series of tests designed to determine its ability to model the effect of arching action. Two of the simplified models were analyzed, one without any horizontal restraint at the supports (a roller support condition), and the other completely restrained from moving horizontally along the supported edge. Both models were subjected to concentrated loads of 17.8 kN applied in a single step at the centre.

The resulting deflections along the span through the point of load are shown in Fig. 3 for both the unrestrained and fully restrained cases. Clearly, horizontal restraint stiffened the model in the out-of-plane direction, evidenced by reduced deflections. Figure 4, which shows normal stresses at Gauss integration points nearest the top and bottom surfaces for the same load conditions, demonstrates that a net compressive stress, indicative of arching action, was developed throughout the slab as a result of edge restraint. The compression zone shifted from the top of the slab at mid-span to the bottom of the slab at the support. This also is consistent with arching action, which has been shown to require cracks to form at the bottom surface under the load and at the top surface close to supports. Load is then supported through compression "struts" extending from the top surface at the load to the bottom surface at supports. Thus, the ability of the model to represent the effects of arching action was verified.

Varying Lateral Restraint

The effect of varying the horizontal edge restraint--a condition realized experimentally--was next investigated. Using the same simplified model as above, truss elements extending from bottom surface nodes along the supported edge to bottom surface nodes along the mid-span line of symmetry were added to the model to act as horizontal spring supports. Varying the horizontal restraint at the support was achieved by varying the stiffness of these elements.

In this case, loads were applied incrementally in order to determine the entire load-deflection path to failure. The resulting load vs. load-point deflection curves for the various cases of edge restraint are shown in Fig. 5. The figure demonstrates that as the stiffness of the edge restraint was increased, the response of the slab to a vertical load became much stiffer and the failure load increased significantly.

This investigation demonstrated that increasing the lateral restraint and associated in-plane forces has a significant effect on the strength and stiffness of a concrete slab subjected to out-of-plane concentrated loads. Although the model used a simple and coarse finite element mesh, it was able to reproduce general trends which have been observed experimentally.

Punching Failure

ADINA's post-processing package is capable of producing plots which show location and orientation of cracks. This enables the analyst to determine the mode of failure predicted by the program. Despite the obvious effect of arching action on the stiffness and failure load, as noted in the previous section, the predicted failure mode was not definitively that of punching shear.

In an attempt to establish a clearer indication of the failure mode, various further changes were made to the fully restrained model. These included varying the tensile strength of the concrete model, altering the pattern of load increments, and modelling a different quadrant of the slab. Changes to each of these parameters produced unexpected and greatly varied outcomes, and resulted in some cases in numerical instabilities.

These variabilities point out the unstable nature of finite element analysis which incorporates the concrete material model. Such analyses are highly sensitive to the pattern of load application (i.e. size of load increments) as well as to the finite element description of the model itself, particularly when symmetry boundary conditions are used to reduce the size of the model. In the verification study, analytical failure loads did not always correspond to conditions which would produce a physical failure, but at times to an unrelated numerical instability. For these reasons was not possible to verify conclusively the program's ability to produce a punching failure with the simplified model.

FINITE ELEMENT MODEL DESCRIPTION

General Modelling Approach

Finite element analyses were performed corresponding to each of the experimental tests described earlier. The test at mid-span of the third experimental model was used as the standard to which to tune the FE model, since it was the first and simplest configuration for which a punching shear failure was achieved. Numerous analyses corresponding to this test were performed, each representing differences in a number of parameters. The combinations of parameters which produced the best results for this test were then used to analyze the remaining tests.

Although differences existed in the parameters for each individual FE run, the general modelling approach remained constant and can be demonstrated by the model shown in Fig. 6.

The deck slab, shown in plan in the upper frame of the figure, was represented by 20-node, three-dimensional isoparametric elements. The deck shown has been refined to allow the application of a pressure load over the two central elements, which correspond to the size of the experimental patch. For some runs, the load was applied at a single node, in which case the deck elements were of a more uniform size. The number of Gauss integration points per element varied.

The entire system is shown in an isometric view int eh lower frame of Fig. 6. The deck is shown only in outline so that the elements used to model the steel members below may be clearly seen. The girders were modelled using 2-node Hermitian beam elements located at the neutral axis of the girders. These beam elements were connected to the deck elements by means of vertically oriented rigid links (Hermitian beam elements with high section properties) which were capable of transferring both vertical forces and shear forces between the girder and concrete deck. Thus complete composite action was assumed. Channel section diaphragms were also modelled using beam elements and steel straps were modelled by truss elements capable of transmitting only axial forces. The figure shows diaphragms and straps located accurately. In some cases, upper channel diaphragms and straps were located at the underside of the slab, and lower diaphragms were located in the same plane as the neutral axes of the girders in order to reduce the computational effort required. Fig. 6 also shows the upper flanges of the girders modelled by beam elements.

For some runs these were omitted.

While Fig. 6 shows a model which represents an entire slab-on-girder system, some runs took advantage of conditions of symmetry and modelled only one-half or one-quarter of the system.

Material Properties

Four sets of concrete material properties were required for the analyses, one corresponding to each of the experimental slab systems. Concrete properties for models of each system are summarized in Table 1. Values for E_o, σ_t, and σ_c were determined experimentally, while values for ν, σ_u, ϵ_c, and ϵ_u have been estimated.

PRESENTATION OF RESULTS

Correlation between predicted and experimental values was based upon the maximum load-carrying capacities and the load-deflection curves from zero to ultimate load. Some account was also taken of predicted crack patterns, but these were difficult to interpret and are not included here.

Eleven FE runs were performed which corresponded to the mid-span test of the third experimental model. The modelling parameters and predicted failure loads are summarized in Table 2. Figures 7 and 8 show the correlation of predicted load-deflection curves to experimental results for each of the runs.

Results of all remaining analyses are summarized in Table 3, and corresponding load-deflections curves are shown in Figures 9 to 12. Parameters not listed in Table 3 were identical to those used for Run 8 shown in Table 2.

DISCUSSION

The best FE runs corresponding to each of the four mid-span tests predicted the

Table 1. Concrete material properties used for FE analyses.

Property	System 1	System 2	System 3	System 4
E_o (MPa)	26890	40890	43090	43440
ν	0.1	0.1	0.1	0.1
σ_t (MPa)	2.1	3.0	3.9	4.1
σ_c (MPa)	29.9	27.9	16.1	41.8
σ_u (MPa)	26.9	25.1	41.5	37.6
ϵ_c	0.002	0.002	0.002	0.002
ϵ_u	0.003	0.003	0.003	0.003

Run	Portion modelled	Diaphragm location	Integration order[1]	Deck thickness[2]	Flanges modelled?	Load applied	PU/EU[3]
1	quarter	not true	3x3x3	1	no	at node	0.80
2	half	not true	3x3x3	1	no	at node	0.49
3	half	true	3x3x3	1	no	at node	0.47
4	half	true	3x3x3	2	no	at node	0.34
5	full	true	3x3x3	1	no	at node	0.70
6	full	true	3x3x3	1	yes	at node	0.42
7	full	true	3x3x3	1	yes	pressure	0.91
8	full	true	2x2x3	1	yes	pressure	0.99
9	full	true	2x2x2	2	yes	pressure	0.51
10	full	true	2x2x3	1	yes	at node	0.25
11[4]	full	true	2x2x3	1	yes	pressure	>1.14

1. Refers to the number of Gauss integration points used for deck elements in x, y, and z directions respectively, where x and y are in the plane of the deck and z is out of plane.
2. Number of elements through thickness of deck.
3. Ratio of predicted ultimate load to experimental ultimate load.
4. Young's modulus was reduced for this run to 27580 MPa, 64% of that used for other runs.
Note:
   Load pattern for runs 1 to 6: 35.59 kN increments to 177.9 kN, then 8.9 kN increments to failure.
   Load pattern for runs 7 to 11: 35.59 kN increments to 249.1 kN, then 8.9 kN increments to failure.

experimental failure loads within 2%. This indicates that the ultimate load of a bridge deck of the configuration studied here can be predicted with some accuracy. However, the wide scatter of results produced by different runs shows that the FE models were very sensitive to a number of parameters.

In the tuning analyses corresponding to the mid-span test of the third system, the best predictions were achieved by models which incorporated the entire system without taking advantage of conditions of symmetry, and in which diaphragms were located accurately, girder flanges were present, and load was applied over a realistic area rather than at a single node. For all mid-span tests, the best results were achieved when a model as described above was used with an underintegrated (2x2x3 Gauss integration points) 3-D isoparametric element to model the concrete deck slab. In some cases, the choice of a load pattern to represent the monotonically increasing load was crucial to satisfactory results.

The sensitivity of the models to these various parameters means that, in general, nonlinear modelling of concrete deck slabs requires the use of the most sophisticated and costly modelling and numerical techniques available. Simplifying assumptions such as making use of symmetry boundary conditions, locating diaphragm members approximately, omitting flanges, and applying the load at a single node did not produce good results. Although not discussed above, it was also discovered early in the study that less costly iterative techniques than the full-Newton method were inadequate.

The sensitivity of the response of the model to the load pattern used implies that

Table 3. Summary of FE analyses corresponding to other systems.

System[1]	Run	Integration order[2]	Load function[3]	Ultimate load (kN)	PU/EU[4]
1	1	3x3x3	1	186.8	1.06
	2	2x2x3	1	151.2	.85
	3	2x2x3	2	115.7	.65
	4	2x2x3	3	173.5	.98
2	1	3x3x3	4	240.2	1.03
	2	2x2x3	4	231.3	.99
3 quarter-span	1	2x2x3	5	249.1	.76
	2	2x2x3	4	249.1	.76
4 mid-span	1	3x3x3	5	293.6	.70
	2	2x2x2	5	266.9	.64
	3	2x2x3	5	418.1	1.00

1. Refers to corresponding experimental slab-on-girder system.
2. Refers to the number of Gauss integration points used for deck elements in x, y, and z directions respectively.
3. Load patterns
   1: 35.6 kN steps to 142.3 kN, then 8.9 kN steps to failure.
   2: 35.6 kN steps to 106.8 kN, then 8.9 kN steps to failure.
   3: 22.2 kN steps to 155.7 kN, then 8.9 kN steps to failure.
   4: 35.6 kN steps to 177.9 kN, then 8.9 kN steps to failure.
   5: 35.6 kN steps to 249.1 kN, then 8.9 kN steps to failure.
4. Ratio of predicted ultimate load to experimental ultimate load.

one numerical analysis is inadequate, especially when using finite element techniques to analyze physically untested structural configurations.

Analytical predictions of the load-deflection path to failure were in every case too stiff. This has been noted elsewhere as a characteristic of the 20-node 3-D isoparametric element (Bathe, 1982; Gonzalez-Vidosa et al., 1991). Because of this, the ductile behaviour of experimental models which failed in flexure was not reproduced by analysis. The use of elements with fewer integration points (2x2x3) compensated somewhat for this overestimation of structural stiffness by calculating the numerical integration less accurately. However, the improvement was not significant when compared with the magnitude of the difference in stiffness between numerical and physical models.

Addressing the problem of an overly stiff element is particularly important when a structure such as a bridge deck is modelled. Although not a large deflection problem, the stress state within the deck is largely deflection-dependent. Compressive membrane forces develop only as the deck cracks and deflects, and in-plane stresses increase with out-of-plane deflections, provided the boundary conditions remain constant.

The successful prediction of failure loads for all mid-span tests indicates that the modelling procedures and parameters used for those tests can be employed to determine

624

failure loads for mid-span tests of some other configurations which have not been tested experimentally. However, the scope of untested configurations which may be modelled confidently is quite limited. Although different diaphragm configurations could be modelled with some confidence in the accuracy of the predicted ultimate loads, it is not clear, for example, that the same would be true for a slab of reduced thickness, since this was not tested as a variable during the numerical analyses, and the sensitivity of the model to changes of this nature is unknown.

In addition, load-deflection curves cannot be reliably predicted with the procedures used here. In addition, predicted and experimental failure loads for the quarter-span test on the third system did not correlate well. This demonstrates that the predicted behaviour of a slab-on-girder system loaded at a location other than mid-span is not reliable. Further tuning for this condition would be required to improve these predictions.

CONCLUSIONS

This study demonstrated that failure loads of PFRC deck slabs of slab-on-girder bridges subjected to concentrated loads can be accurately predicted using nonlinear FE analysis. However, the sensitivity of predicted behaviour to a number of modelling parameters meant that considerable tuning of the modelling scheme was required to produce good correlations. Because of this sensitivity, the scope of bridge deck configurations which may be confidently analyzed based upon this work is quite limited. Considerable modelling experience is required to extend nonlinear analysis techniques to experimentally untested configurations which differ substantially from those studied here.

The investigation also demonstrated that the material model which incorporated failure criteria for plain concrete was suitable for modelling concrete containing polypropylene fibres. The fibre volume ratio modelled was relatively low, and it is not known if similar material models would apply to concretes containing higher fibre ratios or other types of fibres. This should be investigated.

The three-dimensional isoparametric element used to model the deck slab produces overly stiff responses. For this reason, the load-deflection behaviour of a bridge deck modelled with the element cannot be reliably predicted, and poorer correlations are realized when the experimental system is more flexible. A reduction in the number of Gauss integration points improves the load-deflection correlation, but not significantly.

Based on these conclusions, it is evident that despite the advances in nonlinear FE analysis of concrete structures, considerable work is still required to improve numerical techniques.

ACKNOWLEDGEMENTS

The research on which this paper is based has been supported by the Natural Sciences and Engineering Research Council of Canada, whose support is gratefully acknowledged.

REFERENCES

ADINA R&D, Inc. (1990). ADINA: A Finite Element Program for Automatic Dynamic Incremental Nonlinear Analysis. 71 Elton Avenue, Watertown, MA.

ADINA R&D, Inc. (1987). ADINA Theory and Modeling Guide. 71 Elton Avenue, Watertown, MA.

Bathe, K.J., Walczak, J., Welch, A., and Mistry, N. (1989). Nonlinear Analysis of Concrete Structures. Computers and Structures, **32**, 563-590.

Bathe, K.J. (1982). Finite Element Procedures in Engineering Analysis. Prentice Hall, Inc., Englewood Cliffs, New Jersey.

Gonzalez Vidosa, F., Kotsovos, M.D., and Pavlovic, M.N. (1991). Three-dimensional Nonlinear Finite-element Model for Structural Concrete. Part 1: Main Features and Objectivity Study. Proceedings of the Institution of Civil Engineers, Part 2, **91**, 517-544.

Mufti, A.A., Jaeger, L.G., Bakht, B., and Wegner, L.D. (1992). Experimental Investigation of FRC Deck Slabs Without Internal Steel Reinforcement. Proceedings of the CSCE 1992 Annual Conference.

OHBDC (1990). Ontario Highway Bridge Design Code. Ministry of Transportation of Ontario, Downsview, Ontario.

Figure 1. Two-girder experimental model.

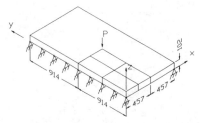

Figure 2. Verification model.

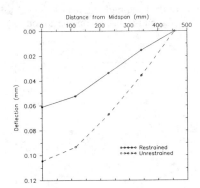

Figure 3. Mid-span deflections--
verification model.

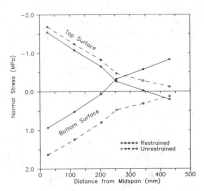

Figure 4. Normal stresses--verification
model.

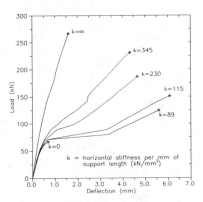

Figure 5. Load-deflection curves for
varying lateral restraint.

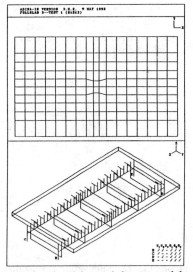

Figure 6. Slab-on-girder FE model.

627

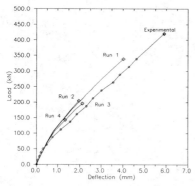

Figure 7. Load-defl. curves for runs 1 to 4 mid-span test on third model.

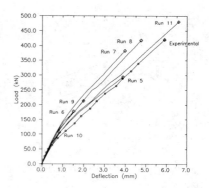

Figure 8. Load-defl. curves for runs 5 to 11 for mid-span test on third model.

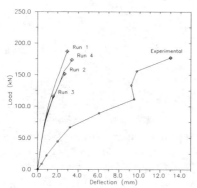

Figure 9. Load-deflection curves for mid-span test on first model.

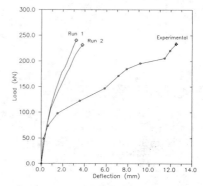

Figure 10. Load-deflection curves for mid-span test on second model.

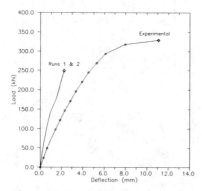

Figure 11. Load-deflection curves for quarter-span test on third model.

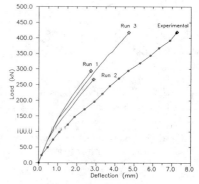

Figure 12. Load-deflection curves for mid-span test on fourth model.

ADVANCED COMPOSITE MATERIALS IN BRIDGES AND STRUCTURES
K.W. Neale and P. Labossière, Editors; Canadian Society for Civil Engineering, 1992

Matériaux composites d'avant-garde pour ponts et charpentes
K.W. Neale et P. Labossière, éditeurs; Société canadienne de génie civil, 1992

A SIMPLE METHOD OF OBTAINING 'EXACT' VALUES OF THE BUCKLING STRENGTH FOR SOME LAMINATED STRUCTURES FOR CIVIL CONSTRUCTION

D.H. Kim
Korea Composites
Seoul, Korea

ABSTRACT

Simple equations which can predict 'exact' values of the buckling strength for special orthotropic laminates are presented. Many laminates with certain orientations, including laminates with anti-symmetric configurations, can be solved using the same equation for special orthotropic laminates. If the quasi-isotropic constants are used, the equations for the isotropic plates can be used. Use of some coefficient can produce 'exact' values for laminates with such configurations. Most of the structures for civil construction require many layers of plies even though the ratio of the thickness to the length is small so that the effect of transverse shear deformation can be neglected.

RÉSUMÉ

Des équations simples servant à prévoir les valeurs 'exactes' de la résistance au flambement pour des stratifiés orthotropes spéciaux sont présentées. Plusieurs stratifiés avec certaines orientations, incluant ceux avec des configurations antisymétriques, peuvent être résolus par la même équation que les stratifiés orthotropes spéciaux. Si les constantes quasi-orthotropes sont utilisées, les équations pour des plaques isotropes peuvent être utilisées. L'usage de quelques coefficients peut produire des valeurs 'exactes' pour des stratifiés avec de telles configurations. La majorité des structures pour la construction en génie civil requièrent plusieurs couches de lamelles même si le rapport de l'épaisseur sur la longueur est petit, de telle sorte que l'effet de la déformation transversale en cisaillement peut être négligé.

In composite design, exact and accurate analysis is the must. One of the reasons is that, in general, the maximum yield strains of the composites are only a fraction of those of metals such as steel. This is one of the causes why any engineer with metal mentality may bring disastrous results in designing with composites. Analysis of composite structures is very much complicated. Many engineers are simply scared of using such materials from the beginning, even though the great advantages of composites are well known. In his recent book, the author(1992) proposes to use the quasi-isotropic constants by Tsai for the preliminary design of the composite primary structures for the civil construction. Such structures generally require a large number of laminae layers. This concept greatly simplifies the calculation effort at the early stage of design because

A. The classical mechanics and elasticity theories can be used.

B. There is no coupling between the bending and the mid-plane extension reducing the three simultaneous fourth order partial differential equations to one fourth order partial differential equation.

C. At the preliminary design stage, the orientations of laminae in a laminate are not known. This fact discourages the most of the engineers from the beginning. Use of the quasi-isotropic constants gives a guide-line toward a simple and accurate analysis.

In this paper, the simple formulas to obtain "exact" values of the buckling strengths of some laminates is presented. The Paper is the extension of the report made by the author in July 1992(2)

THEORIES AND FORMULAS USED

The author introduced methods useful in obtaining the critical buckling loads for one-dimensional beams and frames(1). He indicated that such method can be extended to the two dimensional composite laminated plates problems with arbitrary cross-sections and boundary conditions as he did with the vibration problems (Article 7-8-3 of Ref 1). However, for simplicity of discussion for this presentation, simple supported laminated plates with uniform cross- sections, for which closed form solutions are available, are considered for simple comparison.

The stiffnesses are given as

$$A_{ij} = \sum_{k=1}^{n} (\bar{Q}_{ij})_k (h_k - h_{k-1}) , \quad B_{ij} = \frac{1}{2} \sum_{k=1}^{n} (\bar{Q}_{ij})_k (h^2_k - h^2_{k-1})$$

$$D_{ij} = \frac{1}{3} \sum_{K=1}^{n} (\bar{Q}_{ij})_k (h^3_k - h^3_{k-1}),$$

(1)

where

$$\bar{Q}_{11} = Q_{11}m^4 + 2(Q_{12} + 2Q_{66})m^2n^2 + Q_{22}n^4$$

$$\bar{Q}_{12} = (Q_{11} + Q_{22} - 4Q_{66})m^2n^2 + Q_{12}(m^4 + n^4), \quad \bar{Q}_{13} = Q_{13}m^2 + Q_{23}n^2$$

$$\bar{Q}_{16} = -Q_{22} mn^3 + Q_{11}m^3n - (Q_{12} + 2Q_{66})mn(m^2 - n^2)$$

(2)

$$\bar{Q}_{22} = Q_{11}n^4 + 2(Q_{12} + 2Q_{66})m^2n^2 + Q_{22}m^4$$

$$\bar{Q}_{23} = Q_{13}n^2 + Q_{23} m^2$$

$$\bar{Q}_{26} = -Q_{22} m^3n + Q_{11}mn^3 + (Q_{12} + 2Q_{66})mn(m^2 - n^2)$$

$$\bar{Q}_{33} = Q_{33} , \quad \bar{Q}_{36} = (Q_{13} - Q_{23})mn$$

$$\bar{Q}_{44} = Q_{44}m^2 + Q_{55}n^2 , \quad \bar{Q}_{45} = (Q_{55} - Q_{44})mn$$

$$\bar{Q}_{55} = Q_{55}m^2 + Q_{44}n^2$$

$$\bar{Q}_{66} = (Q_{11} + Q_{22} - 2Q_{12})\, m^2 n^2 + Q_{66}(m^2 - n^2)^2$$

in which

$$Q_{11} = \frac{E_1}{1-\nu_{12}\nu_{21}} \quad, \quad Q_{12} = \frac{\nu_{12}E_2}{1-\nu_{12}\nu_{21}} = \frac{\nu_{21}E_1}{1-\nu_{12}\nu_{21}}$$

$$Q_{22} = \frac{E_2}{1-\nu_{12}\nu_{21}} \quad, \qquad\qquad Q_{66} = G_{12}$$

The quasi-isotropic constants are

$$[Q]^{iso} = \begin{vmatrix} U_1 & U_4 & 0 \\ U_4 & U_1 & 0 \\ 0 & 0 & U_5 \end{vmatrix} \tag{3}$$

in which

$$U_1 = \frac{1}{8}(3Q_{xx}+3Q_{yy}+2Q_{xy}+4Q_{ss}) \qquad U_4 = \frac{1}{8}(Q_{xx}+Q_{yy}+6Q_{xy}-4Q_{ss})=U_1-2U_5$$

$$U_5 = \frac{1}{8}(Q_{xx}+Q_{yy}-2Q_{xy}+4Q_{ss}) \tag{4}$$

The equations for the critical buckling load of the laminates with configurations studied in this report are as follows[1].

For specially orthotropic laminates,

$$Nx_{cr} = -\frac{\pi^2 a^2}{m^2}\left[D_1\left(\frac{m}{a}\right)^4 + 2D_3\left(\frac{m}{a}\right)^2\left(\frac{n}{b}\right)^2 + D_2\left(\frac{n}{b}\right)^4 \right]$$

$$= -\pi^2\left[D_1\left(\frac{m}{a}\right)^2 + 2D_3\left(\frac{n}{b}\right)^2 + D_2\left(\frac{n}{b}\right)^4\left(\frac{a}{m}\right)^2 \right] \tag{5}$$

in which $D_3 = D_{12} + 2D_{66}$

For anti-symmetric angle-ply laminates with boundary conditions,

at $x = 0$ and a,

$$w = 0$$

$$M_x = B_{16}\left(\frac{\partial v}{\partial x} + \frac{\partial u}{\partial y}\right) - D_{11}\frac{\partial^2 w}{\partial x^2} - D_{12}\frac{\partial^2 w}{\partial y^2} = 0$$

$$u = 0$$

$$N_{xy} = A_{66}\left(\frac{\partial v}{\partial x} + \frac{\partial u}{\partial y}\right) - B_{16}\frac{\partial^2 w}{\partial x^2} - B_{26}\frac{\partial^2 w}{\partial y^2} = 0$$

at $y = 0$ and b,

$$w = 0$$

$$M_y = B_{26}\left(\frac{\partial v}{\partial x} + \frac{\partial u}{\partial y}\right) - D_{12}\frac{\partial^2 w}{\partial x^2} - D_{22}\frac{\partial^2 w}{\partial y^2} = 0$$

$$v = 0$$

$$N_{xy} = A_{66}\left(\frac{\partial v}{\partial x} + \frac{\partial u}{\partial y}\right) - B_{16}\frac{\partial^2 w}{\partial x^2} - B_{26}\frac{\partial^2 w}{\partial y^2} = 0 \quad,$$

$$Nx_{cr} = -\left(\frac{a}{m\pi}\right)^2\left(T_{33} + \frac{2T_{12}T_{23}T_{13} - T_{22}T_{13}^2 - T_{11}T_{23}^2}{T_{11}T_{22} - T_{12}^2} \right) \tag{6}$$

where

$$T_{11} = A_{11}\left(\frac{m\pi}{a}\right)^2 + A_{66}\left(\frac{n\pi}{b}\right)^2$$

$$T_{12} = (A_{12} + A_{66})\left(\frac{m\pi}{a}\right)\left(\frac{n\pi}{b}\right)$$

$$T_{13} = -\left[3B_{16}\left(\frac{m\pi}{a}\right)^2 + B_{26}\left(\frac{n\pi}{b}\right)^2\right]\left(\frac{n\pi}{b}\right)$$

$$T_{22} = A_{22}\left(\frac{n\pi}{b}\right)^2 + A_{66}\left(\frac{m\pi}{a}\right)^2 \tag{7}$$

$$T_{23} = -\left[B_{16}\left(\frac{m\pi}{a}\right)^2 + 3B_{26}\left(\frac{n\pi}{b}\right)^2\right]\left(\frac{m\pi}{a}\right)$$

$$T_{33} = D_{11} \left(\frac{m\pi}{a}\right)^4 + 2(D_{12} + 2 D_{66}) \left(\frac{m\pi}{a}\right)^2 \left(\frac{n\pi}{b}\right)^2 + D_{22} \left(\frac{n\pi}{b}\right)^4$$

When the quasi-isotropic constants are used,

$D_{11} = D_{22} = D_{12} + 2D_{66} = D_3 = (h^3/12)Q_{11}{}^{iso}$

$B_{ij} = 0$

$A_{11} = A_{22} = A_{12} + 2A_{66} = hQ_{11}{}^{iso}$

and the Eq.(5) reduces to

$$N_{x_{cr}}{}^{iso} = -\pi^2 D_{11} \left[\left(\frac{m}{a}\right)^2 + 2\left(\frac{n}{b}\right)^2 + \left(\frac{n}{b}\right)^4 \left(\frac{a}{m}\right)^2 \right] \tag{8}$$

which is identical to the case of an isotropic plate.

Careful study of Eq.(6) and (7) gives the following results.

When $B_{ij} \rightarrow 0$,

$T_{13} \rightarrow 0$, and $T_{23} \rightarrow 0$,

and the Eq.(7) reduces to

$$N_{x_{cr}} = -(a/m\pi)^2 T_{33} \tag{9}$$

which is identical to Eq.(5). If quasi-isotropic constants are used this equation is exactly the same as the one for an isotropic plate.

When thick laminates are used for civil construction, considerable number of orientations will have rapidly decreasing quantities of B_{ij} and $D_{16} \rightarrow 0$, $D_{26} \rightarrow 0$, as the number of layers increases for which cases Eq.(5) can be used with good accuracy.

The relatively "exact" value of the buckling load can be obtained from the preliminary design stage by the use of the formulas proposed as follows.

$$N_{x_{cr}} = N_{x_{cr}}{}^{iso} \cdot FRC^2 \tag{10}$$

$$FRC^2 = \frac{D_1{}^* + 2D_3{}^* + D_2{}^* + 2D_3{}^*(R^2-1) + D_2{}^*(R^4-1)}{U_1[4 + 2(R^2-1) + (R^4-1)]} \tag{11}$$

where $R = \dfrac{na}{mb}$

If all plies have the same thicknesses and are of the same material, we may use

$$FRC^2 = [4(U_1 - U_3 \cdot CTH4) + 2(U_1 - 3U_3 \cdot CTH4)(R^2-1) + (U_1 - U_2 \cdot CTH2 + U_3 CTH4)$$
$$(R^4-1)] \times 1/\{U_1[4 + 2(R^2-1) + (R^4-1)]\} \tag{12}$$

where

$$CTH4 = \frac{h_o{}^3}{h^3} \sum_{i=1}^{N} \cos(4\theta_i)[i^3 - (i-1)^3]$$

$$CTH2 = \frac{h_o{}^3}{h^3} \sum_{i=1}^{N} \cos(2\theta_i)[i^3 - (i-1)^3] \tag{13}$$

in which h_o is the unit ply thickness.

If $R=1$,

$$FRC^2 = \frac{D_1{}^* + 2D_3{}^* + D_2{}^*}{4U_1} \qquad , \text{ or} \tag{14}$$

$$FRC^2 = \frac{U_1 - U_3 \cdot CTH4}{U_1} \tag{15}$$

If the laminate has the specially orthotropic orientation,

$$FRC^2 = \frac{U_1 - U_3}{U_1} \tag{16}$$

Eq. (16) is "exact" for specially orthotropic laminates with R=1. Eq. (11) and (12) are based on the equation for the specially orthotropic laminate. However, some laminates with certain orientations have $B_{16} \rightarrow 0$, $B_{26} \rightarrow 0$ as the number of plies increases, and for such laminates the Eq. (5) yields fairly good result.

We may use Eq. (8), (10) and (16) or (8), (10) and (14) to obtain "exact" values of the buckling loads of the laminate of any orientation at the planning stage.

The FRC is, in fact, the influence of anisotropy on the buckling strength of the laminate.

NUMERICAL EXAMPLES

The material properties used are as follows.

E_1 = 38.6 GPa

E_2 = 8.27 GPa

ν_{12} = 0.26

ν_{21} = 0.0557

h_o = 0.00125 m   and 0.000125m

G_{12} = 4.14 GPa, a=b=1m

The results of calculation are as shown in Tables 1 to 6.

Table 1. $[\pm\theta]_r$
θ = $\pm15°$ (Antisymmetric Angle-Ply), h_o = 0.00125 m

r(N)	6(12)	12(24)	18(36)	30(60)	42(84)	60(120)	72(144)
N_{xcr}(exact)	-207848	-1667169	-5629431	-26068650	-71537260	-208570900	-360414400
N_{xcr}(orth)	-208578	-1668628	-5631619	-26072300	-71542350	-208578200	-360423100
N_{xcr}(iso)	-227062	-1816498	-6130680	-28382770	-77882340	-227062200	-392363500
$B_{16}{}^*/D_{11}{}^*$	-0.0158	-0.0079	-0.00527	-0.003165	-0.002260	-0.0015825	-0.0013188
$B_{26}{}^*/D_{11}{}^*$	-0.0022	-0.0011	-0.00075	-0.000453	-0.000323	-0.0002265	-0.0001888
FRC^2(1)	0.8372	0.8372	0.8372	0.8372	0.8372	0.8372	0.8372
FRC^2(2)	0.9185	0.9185	0.9185	0.9185	0.9185	0.9185	0.9185
N_{xcr}^{iso}·FRC^2(1)	-190094	-1520753	-5132543	-23761770	-65202316	-190094203	-328482798
N_{xcr}^{iso}·FRC^2(2)	-208577	-1668616	-5631581	-2607212	-71541938	-208577066	-360421187
$\dfrac{N_{xcr}(exact)}{N_{xcr}(orth)}$	0.9965	0.9991	0.9996	0.9999	0.9999	0.9999	0.9999
$\dfrac{N_{xcr}(exact)}{N_{xcr}(iso)}$	0.9154	0.9178	0.9182	0.9185	0.9185	0.9186	0.9186

Table 2. [ABBAAB]_r
A=15° B=-15° , h_o = 0.00125 m

r(N)	2(12)	4(24)	6(36)	10(60)	14(84)	20(120)	24(144)
Nx_{cr}(exact)	-208497	-1668466	-5631376	-26071900	-71541800	-208577400	-360422100
Nx_{cr}(orth)	-208578	-1668628	-5631619	-26072300	-71542350	-208578200	-360423100
Nx_{cr}(iso)	-222062	-1816498	-6130680	-28382770	-77882340	-227062200	-392363500
B_{16}^*/D_{11}^*	-0.0052	-0.0026	-0.0017	-0.00105	-0.00075	-0.000527	-0.000439
B_{26}^*/D_{11}^*	-0.0007	-0.0003	-0.0002	-0.00015	-0.00010	-0.000075	-0.000063
$FRC^2(1)$	0.8372	0.8372	0.8372	0.8372	0.8372	0.8372	0.8372
$FRC^2(2)$	0.9185	0.9185	0.9185	0.9185	0.9185	0.9185	0.9185
$Nx_{cr}^{iso} \cdot FRC^2(1)$	-190094	-1520753	-5132543	-23761771	-65202316	-190054203	-328482798
$Nx_{cr}^{iso} \cdot FRC^2(2)$	-208577	-1668616	-5631581	-26072128	-71541938	-208577066	-360421187
$\dfrac{Nx_{cr}(exact)}{Nx_{cr}(orth)}$	0.9996	0.9999	0.9999	0.9999	0.9999	0.9999	0.9999
$\dfrac{Nx_{cr}(exact)}{Nx_{cr}(iso)}$	0.9182	0.9185	0.9186	0.9196	0.9196	0.9196	0.9196

Table 3. [ABCCAB]_r
A=15° B=-15° C=90° , h_o = 0.00125 m

r(N)	2(12)	4(24)	6(36)	10(60)	14(84)	20(120)	24(144)
Nx_{cr}(exact)	-203405	-1621315	-5468232	-25307090	-69435990	-202426900	-349788400
Nx_{cr}(orth)	-203787	-1622077	-5467375	-25309000	-69438660	-202430700	-349793000
Nx_{cr}(iso)	-227062	-1816498	-6130680	-28382770	-77882340	-227062200	-392363500
B_{16}^*/D_{11}^*	-0.0132	-0.00694	-0.00467	-0.002821	-0.002018	-0.0014139	-0.0011785
B_{26}^*/D_{11}^*	-0.0018	-0.00099	-0.00067	-0.000404	-0.000288	-0.0002024	-0.0001687
$FRC^2(1)$	0.8372	0.8372	0.8372	0.8372	0.8372	0.8372	0.8372
$FRC^2(2)$	0.8975	0.8975	0.8975	0.8975	0.8975	0.8975	0.8975
$Nx_{cr}^{iso} \cdot FRC^2(1)$	-190094	-1520753	-5132543	-23761771	-65202316	-190094203	-328482798
$Nx_{cr}^{iso} \cdot FRC^2(2)$	-208577	-1668616	-5631581	-2607212	-71541938	-208577066	-360421187
$\dfrac{Nx_{cr}(exact)}{Nx_{cr}(orth)}$	0.9981	0.9995	0.9998	0.9999	0.9999	0.9999	0.9999
$\dfrac{Nx_{cr}(exact)}{Nx_{cr}(iso)}$	0.8958	0.8925	0.8919	0.8916	0.8915	0.8915	0.8915

Table 4. $[\pm\theta]_r$

$\theta = \pm 15°$ (Antisymmetric Ang e-Ply), $h_o = 0.000125$ m

r(N)	6(12)	12(24)	18(36)	30(60)	42(84)	60(120)	72(144)
Nx_{cr}(exact)	-207.8	-1667.1	-5629.4	-26068.6	-71537.1	-208570.6	-360413.8
Nx_{cr}(orth)	-208.5	-1668.6	-5631.6	-26072.2	-71542.2	-208577.9	-360422.5
Nx_{cr}(iso)	-227.0	-1816.4	-6130.6	-28382.7	-77882.3	-227062.3	-392363.6
$B_{16}*/D_{11}*$	-0.015	-0.007	-0.005	-0.0031	-0.0022	-0.0015	-0.0013
$B_{26}*/D_{11}*$	-0.002	-0.0011	-0.0007	-0.0004	-0.0003	-0.0002	-0.0001
$FRC^2(1)$	0.8372	0.8372	0.8372	0.8372	0.8372	0.8372	0.8372
$FRC^2(2)$	0.9185	0.9185	0.9185	0.9185	0.9185	0.9185	0.9185
$Nx_{cr} \cdot FRC^2(1)$ iso	-190.0	-1520.7	-5132.5	-23761.7	-65202.3	-190094.28	-328482.8
$Nx_{cr} \cdot FRC^2(2)$ iso	-208.5	-1668.6	-5631.5	-26072.1	-71541.9	-208577.15	-360421.2
$\dfrac{Nx_{cr}(exact)}{Nx_{cr}(orth)}$	0.9965	0.9991	0.9996	0.9999	0.9999	0.9999	0.9999
$\dfrac{Nx_{cr}(exact)}{Nx_{cr}(iso)}$	0.9154	0.9178	0.9182	0.9185	0.9185	0.9186	0.9186

Table 5. $[ABCCAB]_r$

A=15° B=-15° C=90° , $h_o = 0.000125$m

r(N)	2(12)	4(24)	6(36)	10(60)	14(84)	20(120)	24(144)
Nx_{cr}(exact)	-208.49	-1668.46	-5631.37	-26071.89	-71541.72	-208577.10	-360421.60
Nx_{cr}(orth)	-208.57	-1668.62	-5634.62	-26072.29	-71542.28	-208577.90	-360422.50
Nx_{cr}(iso)	-227.06	-1816.49	-6130.68	-28382.79	-77882.36	-227062.30	-392363.60
$B_{16}*/D_{11}*$	-0.0053	-0.00264	-0.00176	-0.001055	-0.000754	-0.0005289	-0.0004395
$B_{26}*/D_{11}*$	-0.0007	-0.00038	-0.00025	-0.000151	-0.000108	-0.0000755	-0.0000629
$FRC^2(1)$	0.8372	0.8372	0.8372	0.8372	0.8372	0.8372	0.8372
$FRC^2(2)$	0.9185	0.9185	0.9185	0.9185	0.9185	0.9185	0.9185
$Nx_{cr} \cdot FRC^2(1)$ iso	-190.09	-1520.75	-5132.54	-23761.78	-65202.03	-190094.28	-328482.88
$Nx_{cr} \cdot FRC^2(2)$ iso	-208.57	-1668.61	-5631.58	-26072.1	-71534.95	-208577.15	-360421.27
$\dfrac{Nx_{cr}(exact)}{Nx_{cr}(orth)}$	0.9996	0.9999	0.9999	0.9999	0.9999	0.9999	0.9999
$\dfrac{Nx_{cr}(exact)}{Nx_{cr}(iso)}$	0.9182	0.9185	0.9186	0.9186	0.9186	0.9186	0.9186

Table 6. [ABCCAB]$_r$

A=15° B=-15° C=90° , h$_o$ = 0.00125 m

r(N)	2(12)	4(24)	6(36)	10(60)	14(84)	20(120)	24(144)
Nx$_{cr}$(exact)	-203405	-1621315	-5468232	-25307090	-69435990	-202426900	-349788400
Nx$_{cr}$(orth)	-203787	-1622077	-5467375	-25309000	-69438660	-202430700	-349793000
Nx$_{cr}$(iso)	-227062	-1816498	-6130680	-28382770	-77882340	-227062200	-392363500
B$_{16}$*/D$_{11}$*	-0.0132	-0.00694	-0.00467	-0.002821	-0.002018	-0.0014139	-0.0011785
B$_{26}$*/D$_{11}$*	-0.0018	-0.00099	-0.00067	-0.000404	-0.000288	-0.0002024	-0.0001687
FRC^2(1)	0.8372	0.8372	0.8372	0.8372	0.8372	0.8372	0.8372
FRC^2(2)	0.8975	0.8975	0.8975	0.8975	0.8975	0.8975	0.8975
iso Nx$_{cr}$·FRC^2(1)	-190094	-1520753	-5132543	-23761771	-65202316	-190094203	-328482798
iso Nx$_{cr}$·FRC^2(2)	-208577	-1668616	-5631581	-2607212	-71541938	-208577066	-360421187
$\dfrac{\text{Nx}_{cr}\text{(exact)}}{\text{Nx}_{cr}\text{(orth)}}$	0.9981	0.9995	0.9998	0.9999	0.9999	0.9999	0.9999
$\dfrac{\text{Nx}_{cr}\text{(exact)}}{\text{Nx}_{cr}\text{(iso)}}$	0.8958	0.8925	0.8919	0.8916	0.8915	0.8915	0.8915

FRC(1) : By Eq.(16)
FRC(2) : By Eq.(14)

CONCLUSION

Designing with composite materials is very much complicated. Not only the anisotropy of materials but the several kinds of coupling terms also make the analysis so much messed up. Even after obtaining the stresses and strains for each ply, the strength theory involves five equations for each ply. Thus, if both maximum stress and strain theories are used, each ply requires 10 equations. These has to be done for each lamina and a laminate with N laminae requires 10N equations for failure conditions. The real problem is that these equations do not express the real failure criteria. Use of quadratic equations especially for the strain space can reduce the number of equations significantly but use of "exact" theory for the preliminary design of large scale composite structures is too difficult if not impossible. The author(1992) proposed in his recent book to use quasi-isotropic constants for the preliminary design. This report proves that this concept is good for the critical buckling strength of the special orthotropic and antisymmetric angle ply laminates for which closed form solutions are available. This concept is good for many other laminates with different orientations especially when the increase of the number of laminae reduces the bending-extension coupling terms. The most of the structures used in civil construction are large in sizes and such structures require large number of plies even though the ratios of the thicknesses to the lengths are small so that the effects of shear deformation can be neglected.

It should be borne in mind that the "exact" analysis is the "must" at the stage of final analysis.   The maximun strains at failure of the most of the composites are much smaller than those of metals.   In case of advanced carbon fiber reinforcements, maximum elongation to failure reported to date is only 2%.

The use of proposed formulas to modify the result by the simple method, to obtain "exact" solution is proved to be effective.   The modification factor, FRC, is in fact, the influence of anisotropy on the buckling strength of the laminate.   Numerical Calculation is made for $h_o = 0.00125m$ (Tables 1 to 3) and $h_o = 0.000125m$ (Tables 4 to 6).   It is noted that the accuracy of this method is directly proportional to the number of plies regardless of the thickness of the individual ply.   The value of Nx_{cr} of the laminate with $h_o = 0.00125m$ is exactly 1000 times of that with $h_o = 0.000125m$.   This fact can be anticipated if it is recalled that Nx_{cr} is proportional to D_{ij} which are functions of $h_o{}^3$.

REFERENCE

Kim, D. H., Composite Structures for Civil and Architectural Engineers, Elsevier Science Publishers Ltd, to be published in 1992.

Kim, D. H., The Influence of Anisotropy on The Buckling Strength of Laminated Composite Structures for Civil Construction, Education Practice and Promotion of Computational Methods in Engineering Using Small Computers IV, Dalian, China, July 30, 1992.

ADVANCED COMPOSITE MATERIALS IN BRIDGES AND STRUCTURES
K.W. Neale and P. Labossière, Editors; Canadian Society for Civil Engineering, 1992

Matériaux composites d'avant-garde pour ponts et charpentes
K.W. Neale et P. Labossière, éditeurs; Société canadienne de génie civil, 1992

POSTBUCKLING AND OPTIMIZATION OF RECTANGULAR COMPOSITE LAMINATES

A.N. Sherbourne and M.D. Pandey
University of Waterloo
Waterloo, Ontario, Canada

ABSTRACT

A growing trend toward designing composite plates to function in postbuckling has motivated the tailoring of lamination parameters to improve this range of performance. This paper considers the effects of laminate optimization on the postbuckling behaviour of biaxially compressed, specially orthotropic laminated plates. The initial postbuckling stiffness, defined by the slope of the postbuckling load – end shortening relation at bifurcation, is adopted as a qualitative index to characterize postcritical behaviour. It has been found that unfavourable postbuckling performance usually follows optimization of the buckling load. Improved laminate designs are suggested that exhibit superior performance in both pre and postbuckling.

RÉSUMÉ

La fabrication de stratifiés taillés sur mesure permet d'améliorer le comportement de plaques composites après le flambement. Cet article porte sur les effets de l'optimisation des stratifiés sur leur comportement post-flambement. On considère des stratifiés spécialement orthotropes sollicités en compression biaxiale. La rigidité initiale post-flambement, définie par la pente de la relation charge-post-flambement en fonction du raccourcissement à la bifurcation, est adoptée comme indice qualitatif caractérisant le comportement post-critique. On a trouvé qu'un comportement défavorable après le flambement suit généralement l'optimisation de la charge de flambement. Des améliorations aux designs de stratifiés sont suggérées afin d'améliorer la performance pré- et post-flambement.

INTRODUCTION

Because of their thin walled, lightweight nature, the buckling load often becomes a critical design constraint for composite structural elements. Therefore, optimization of the lamina fiber orientation and thickness, in a preselected lamination sequence for maximizing the linear buckling load of plate and shell elements, is studied extensively. Besides optimizing the buckling load, the structural response in the postcritical range should also be carefully examined to establish its practical usefulness.

In structural optimization under linear stability constraints, two features are of special interest; firstly, the imperfection sensitivity, i.e., the drastic reduction in buckling load in the presence of imperfections as in the case of circular cylindrical shells and, secondly, the reduction in postbuckling stiffness of plate elements. Increased imperfection sensitivity of circular cylindrical shells, due to optimization of fiber orientation, has already been discussed by Pandey and Sherbourne (1991). As to the effects of optimizing the lamination parameters on the postbuckling stiffness of rectangular laminates, they are largely unknown and thus deserve exploration.

An interesting problem now arises as to how an optimal design, accounting for flexural action predominant in linear buckling only, will behave in postbuckling where membrane action becomes significant. It is logical, therefore, to suggest that such optimization would introduce significant changes in postbuckling stiffness, which, in general, may prove undesirable. This hypothesis is largely inspired by Frauenthal (1973) who reported a significant reduction in postbuckling stiffness of isotropic, circular plates due to optimization of the thickness distribution.

BACKGROUND

This paper studies the effects of lamination parameters on the linear and nonlinear stability of biaxially compressed, simply supported, symmetric laminates. In general, the postbuckling of laminated plates is analysed by formally tracing the nonlinear load - equilibrium path using various classical methods, namely, the Galerkin method (Zhang and Matthews 1984), direct energy minimization (Minguet et al 1989), dynamic relaxation (Turvey and Wittrick 1973) etc. The analytical and computational complexities of these formal approaches often preclude a more general understanding of the qualitative dependence of the postbuckling behaviour on the lamination parameters.

It is proposed to adopt a different approach where the initial postbuckling stiffness defined by the slope of the load - end shortening relation at bifurcation (Fig. 1b) is utilized as an indicator of postbuckling performance. That is, a laminate with a comparatively higher initial postbuckling stiffness is expected to exhibit superior behaviour and vice versa. This argument may be reasonably justified on the grounds that postbuckling deformations are generally monotonic until mode jumping at relatively higher loads is experienced. It is, therefore, appropriate to limit attention to the estimated initial stiffness and use it for measuring the effects of the optimization of lamination parameters.

The proposed approach involves the derivation of an accurate analytical expression for the initial postbuckling stiffness using a lemma proposed by Thompson (1964) which established that a nonlinear variational formulation employing the linear buckling mode will always yield the correct initial curvature for the postbuckling path of a symmetrical system like flat plates. Knowing the curvature, the postbuckling stiffness at bifurcation can be easily derived (Pope 1968). Using these analytical results, Harris (1975) presented a closed form expression for the initial postbuckling stiffness of simply-supported, anti-symmetric angle-ply laminates under biaxial compression which is slightly modified to address cases of symmetric angle-ply laminates.

ANALYSIS

The analytical solution for the initial postbuckling stiffness of a laminate, subjected to in-plane forces N_{xo} , N_{yo} (Fig.1), is briefly described. The non-linear equations of transverse equilibrium and compatibility in terms of the displacement, w, and force function, F, are given as (Harris 1975)

$$L_1 w = F,_{yy} w,_{xx} - 2 F,_{xy} w,_{xy} + F,_{xx} w,_{yy}$$
$$L_2 F = (w,_{xy})^2 - w,_{xx} w,_{yy}$$

(1)

The subscripts preceeded by a comma denote partial differentiation with respect to the corresponding coordinates. The differential operators are defined as

$$L_1 = D_{11} \frac{\partial^4}{\partial x^4} + 2(D_{12} + 2 D_{33}) \frac{\partial^4}{\partial x^2 \partial y^2} + D_{22} \frac{\partial^4}{\partial y^4}$$

$$L_2 = a_{22} \frac{\partial^4}{\partial x^4} + (2 a_{12} + a_{33}) \frac{\partial^4}{\partial x^2 \partial y^2} + a_{11} \frac{\partial^4}{\partial y^4}$$

and a_{ij} are in-plane flexibility coefficients obtained as $a_{ij} = A^{-1}{}_{ij}$. Note that in-plane and bending stiffness, A_{ij} , D_{ij}, respectively, are derived using classical laminate theory (Jones 1975). The buckling mode of a simply supported laminate can be approximated by

$$w = A_{mn} \sin\frac{m\pi x}{a} \sin\frac{n\pi y}{b}$$

(2)

where m and n are half sine waves in the X and Y directions, respectively. Force resultants are written in terms of the stress function

$$N_x = F,_{yy} , \quad N_y = F,_{xx} , \quad N_{xy} = - F,_{xy}$$

(3)

The principle of virtual displacement may then be applied (Harris 1975) using a virtual displacement of the form (2) in conjunction with the equation of transverse equilibrium that results in :

$$\int_0^a \int_0^b (L_1 w - F,_{yy} w,_{xx} + 2 F,_{xy} w,_{xy} - F,_{xx} w,_{yy}) \sin\frac{m\pi x}{a} \sin\frac{n\pi y}{b} \, dx \, dy = 0$$

(4)

Now, substituting for appropriate derivatives of w and F and following the procedure described by Pope (1968) and Harris (1975), the initial postbuckling stiffness can be derived, after considerable manipulation, as

$$\frac{dN_{xo}}{d\varepsilon} = \frac{(a_{22} + \alpha^4 a_{11})}{2 a_{11} a_{22} (1 + k \alpha^2) + (a_{22} + \alpha^4 a_{11}) (a_{11} + k a_{12})}$$

(5)

$$\text{where} \quad \alpha = \frac{n a}{m b} \quad \text{and} \quad k = \frac{N_{yo}}{N_{xo}}$$

The analytical details can be found elsewhere (Pandey and Sherbourne 1991). The effective prebuckling stiffness of a laminate under biaxial loading is simply

$$K_o = \frac{1}{a_{11} + k a_{12}}$$

(6)

In computation, firstly, the buckling load is obtained by minimizing the expression

$$N_{cr} = \frac{n^2 \pi^2}{b^2 (1 + k \alpha^2)} (D_{11} \alpha^{-2} + 2 (D_{12} + 2 D_{33}) + D_{22} \alpha^2]$$ (7)

with respect to wave numbers m and n. The critical wave numbers, so obtained, are used in calculating the initial postbuckling stiffness in eqn. (5).

A uniaxially compressed, square plate of equivalent isotropic material is taken as a reference and its buckling load and prebuckling stiffness,

$$N_{iso} = \frac{4 \pi^2 D_{iso}}{b^2} = \frac{\pi^2 U_1 t^3}{3 b^2}$$

$$K_{iso} = E_{iso} t$$ (8)

respectively, are used to normalize the corresponding quantities for the laminate. Note that $D_{iso} = E_s t^3 / 12(1 - v_s^2)$. The equivalent isotropic properties, elastic modulus, E_s, and Poisson's ratio, v_s, of an orthotropic material are defined (Tennyson 1987) in the following manner

$$E_s = (1 - v_s^2) U_1 \quad \text{and} \quad v_s = \frac{U_4}{U_1}$$ (9)

where

$$U_1 = \frac{1}{8} (3 Q_{11} + 3 Q_{22} + 2 Q_{12} + 4 Q_{33})$$

$$U_4 = \frac{1}{8} (Q_{11} + Q_{22} + 6 Q_{12} - 4 Q_{33})$$ (10)

Q_{ij} are orthotropic constants (Jones 1975)

$$Q_{11} = \frac{E_{xx}}{d}, \quad Q_{12} = \frac{v_{xy} E_{yy}}{d}, \quad Q_{22} = \frac{E_{yy}}{d}, \quad Q_{33} = G_{xy}$$ (11)

where $d = 1 - v_{xy} v_{yx}$.

POSTBUCKLING BEHAVIOUR

Bidirectional Laminates

A general group of symmetric, 16 - ply, bi-directional laminates of the configuration

$$\left[(\phi_1, -\phi_1, \phi_2, -\phi_2)_{sym} / (-\phi_1, \phi_1, -\phi_2, \phi_2)_{sym} \right]$$

is extensively studied because of its specially orthotropic nature (Caprino and Visconti 1982) in both plane stress and bending, i.e.

$$A_{13} = A_{23} = D_{13} = D_{23} = 0$$

which permits use of eqn. (5). The following nondimensionalized notation is adopted :
Buckling load, $\lambda_c = N_{cr} / N_{iso}$

Postbuckling stiffness, $K_P = \dfrac{1}{K_{iso}} \dfrac{dN}{d\varepsilon}$

Relative stiffness $K_r = \dfrac{1}{K_o} \dfrac{dN}{d\varepsilon}$

Results are computed for three biaxial load ratios, k = 0, 0.5, 1 by varying fiber angles, ϕ_1, ϕ_2 from 0° to 90° in steps of 5°. Typical surfaces of functions defining λ_C, K_P, K_r in the $\phi_1 - \phi_2$ space are plotted in Fig. 2 for k=0.5.

From eqns. (5) and (7), it is clear that the postbuckling stiffness and linear buckling load are described by completely different functions; the former depends on the in-plane flexibilities, a_{ij}, while the later is a function of bending stiffness, D_{ij}. In-plane flexibilities, a_{ij}, contrary to bending stiffnesses, are independent of the stacking sequence of constituent plies and any optimization of the linear buckling load that considers bending stiffnesses only would certainly introduce some changes in postbuckling which may lead to undesirable performance.

This philosophy is further reinforced by examining the λ_C and K_P surfaces, plotted in (ϕ_1, ϕ_2) space, which exhibit subtle qualitative differences. For example, in the case of uniaxially compressed rectangular plates (a/b = 2), the buckling load surface is convex with a maximum at (45°, 45°) whereas the K_P surface is concave with maximum near 0°. Peaks in buckling load variation are seen to be accompanied by depressions in postbuckling stiffness. In biaxial compression (Fig. 2), the K_P surface exhibits interesting variations marked by sharp peaks near 0° and 90° whereas the maximum buckling load is observed near 60° − 70°. It is seen that the variations of K_P and K_r are not consistent. In general, relative stiffness is higher when both the fiber angles, ϕ_1, ϕ_2, approach 90°.

Lamina fiber angles corresponding to maximum values of λ_C and K_P, respectively, are summarized in Tables 1 (a) and (b). For example, laminates having maximum buckling loads for three loading and two aspect ratios are presented in Table 1(a) and, at the same time, their postbuckling and relative stiffnesses are also shown for the sake of completeness. A study of these results suggests, in quantitative terms, that laminates optimal in linear buckling are most likely to exhibit inferior postbuckling behaviour marked by lower stiffness; to a certain degree, the reverse is also true e.g., for a uniaxially compressed laminate (a/b = 2), the optimal fiber angles are, $\phi_1 = \phi_2 = 45°$ in buckling and $\phi_1 = \phi_2 = 0°$ in postbuckling. Here, note that the postbuckling stiffness at optimal buckling (0.1798) is only about 15% of its optimal value (1.2691). Similarly, the buckling load at optimal stiffness (0.39) is about 30% of its maximum value (1.25).

Improved Designs:

In the previous section, it is seen that postbuckling stiffness is often maximum for fiber angles in the vicinity of (0°, 0°) or (0°, 90°). It should be stressed that postbuckling stiffness, a function of membrane stiffness, A_{ij}, only, is independent of ply stacking sequence. It is already known (Muc 1988) that optimal laminates in buckling always belong to the class of $(\pm \theta)_{sym}$ symmetric angle-ply laminates. It is logical to think of designs that combine the two optimal solutions which inherit superior performance in both buckling and postbuckling. Therefore, it is proposed to introduce a group of 0 and 90° plies in the core region of $(\pm \theta)_{sym}$ angle-ply and study the behaviour of the following three classes of laminates so obtained

Laminate 1 : $(\pm \theta / \pm \theta)_{sym}$
Laminate 2 : $(\pm \theta / 90 / 0)_{sym}$
Laminate 3 : $(\pm \theta / 0 / 0)_{sym}$

The buckling and postbuckling behaviour of improved designs 2 and 3 are compared typically with the reference design 1 in Fig. 3. In all the cases, laminate 3, i.e. $(\pm \theta / 0 / 0)_{sym}$, offers considerable improvement in postbuckling stiffness with a slight decrease in buckling loads. It is once again noted that the postbuckling stiffness of traditional angle-ply laminates is sharply reduced for fiber angles that are optimal in buckling. Yet, replacement of a set of ± θ plies by 0° plies in the core region results in a dramatic increase in the stiffness, K_p, for all fiber angles in the interval 0 to 90°. The behaviour of rectangular laminates of type 3 under biaxial compression (Fig. 3) is interesting due to the fact that optimal buckling and postbuckling solutions are coincidental, a truly desired feature. A quantitative description of the parametric study is summarised in Table 2 where optimal fiber angles for conventional angle-ply laminates (Type 1) are listed for all loading cases and corresponding buckling loads and postbuckling stiffness of the three laminate designs are also enumerated. Laminates of type 3 are characterized by very high stiffness, almost 3 to 5 times their conventional counterparts (Type 1). The relative stiffness, K_r, an indicator of loss of stiffness in the postbuckling compared to its pre-buckling state, is generally marked by abrupt variations especially in uniaxial compression. For biaxially compressed plates, its variation is more regular and peak values for laminate 1 are always higher compared to designs 2 and 3.

CONCLUSION

The slope of the postbuckling load versus end shortening curve at bifurcation is adopted as a qualitative index for studying the effects of laminate optimization on the postbuckling behaviour of biaxially compressed, specially orthotropic, symmetric laminates. An explicit analytical solution is described for simply supported laminates.

An extended parametric study based on specially orthotropic, bidirectional laminates demonstrate that laminates with optimal fiber angles with respect to linear buckling exhibit, in general, inferior postbuckling behaviour marked by lowered stiffness. It is realized that the buckling load is exclusively a function of bending stiffness and, similarly, initial stiffness depends only on the membrane stiffness which is known to be independent of the stacking sequence of the laminae. This has led to the idea of combining laminae with optimal fiber angles in buckling, as well as in postbuckling, to construct improved laminate designs. In this respect, it is reported that $(\pm \theta / 0 / 0)_{sym}$ laminates offer considerable improvement in postbuckling stiffness with only a slight decrease in buckling loads compared to their truly optimal value. Note that θ in this design is the optimal fiber angle with respect to buckling under the prescribed loading and aspect ratio. The proposed methodology is apparently useful in selecting final laminate designs from sets of multiple optimal solutions as encountered in ply-thickness optimization with prescribed fiber angles.

ACKNOWLEDGEMENTS

The writers are grateful for support of this work to NSERC of Canada through grant No. A-1582 to the primary author (ANS) and to the Province of Ontario through a fellowship (OGS) to the second author.

REFERENCES

Caprino, G. and Visconti, I.C. (1982). "A note on specially orthotropic laminates". J. Composite Material, 16, pp.395-399.

Frauenthal, J. C. (1973). "Initial Postbuckling Behaviour of Optimally Designed Columns and Plates". Int. J. Solids Struct., 9, pp.115-127.

Harris, G.Z. (1975). "The buckling of orthotropic rectangular plates, including the effect of lateral edge restraint". Int.J.Solids Strut., 11, pp.877-885.

Jones, R.M. (1975). *Mechanics of Composite Materials*, McGraw Hill Co. NY.

Minguet, P.J., Dogundji, J. and Lagace, P. (1989). "Postbuckling behavior of laminated plates using a direct energy-minimization technique". AIAA J., 27(12), pp.1785-1792.

Muc, A. (1988). "Optimal fiber orientation for simply supported, angle-ply plates under biaxial compression". Int.J. Composite Struct., 9, pp.161-172.

Pandey, M.D. and Sherbourne, A.N. (1991). "Imperfection Sensitivity of Optimized, Laminated Composite Shells : A Physical Approach". Int. J. Solids and Structures, 27(12), pp.1575-1595.

Pandey, M.D. and Sherbourne, A.N. (1991). "Postbuckling behaviour of optimized rectangular composite laminates". Submitted for publication.

Pope, G.G. (1968). "On the bifurcational buckling of elastic beams, plates and shallow shells". Aero. Quart., 19, pp.20-30.

Tennyson, R.C. (1987). "Buckling of composite cylinders under axial compression". in *Developments in Engineering Mechanics*, Selvadurai,A.P.S. (eds), pp.229-258.

Thompson, J.M.T. (1964). "Eigenvalue branching configuration and the Rayleigh-Ritz procedure". Quart.Appl.Math., 22, pp.244-251.

Turvey, G.J. and Wittrick W.H. (1973). "The large deflection and postbuckling behaviour of some laminated plates". Aero. Quart., 24(2), pp.77-86.

Zhang, Y. and Matthews F.L. (1984). "Postbuckling behaviour of anisotropic plates under pure shear and shear combined with compressive loading". AIAA J., 22(2), pp.281-286.

Table 1. Bidirectional laminates: Summary of results

(a) Fiber angles for maximum buckling load

No.	$\frac{a}{b}$	k	(ϕ_1, ϕ_2)	λ_c	K_P	K_r
1		0	45,45	1.2581	0.1798	0.5
2	1	0.5	45,45	0.8387	0.1691	0.2946
3		1	45,45	0.629	0.1596	0.1123
4		0	45,45	1.2581	0.1798	0.5
5	2	0.5	60,65	0.7298	0.1469	0.6627
6		1	70,70	0.4698	0.1791	0.9351

Table 1. Bidirectional laminates: Summary of results

(b) Fiber angles for maximum postbuckling stiffness

No.	$\frac{a}{b}$	k	(ϕ_1, ϕ_2)	K_P	λ_c	K_r
1		0	0,0	0.8982	0.7419	0.3457
2	1	0.5	0,0	0.7024	0.4946	0.2325
3		1	15,5	0.5867	0.4124	0.0624
4		0	0,0	1.2691	0.3971	0.4886
5	2	0.5	0,90	1.0298	0.4174	0.7362
6		1	0,90	0.8342	0.2504	0.6225

Table 2. Improved laminate design

$\frac{a}{b}$	k	θ	λ_c Laminates			K_P Laminates		
			1	2	3	1	2	3
	0	45	1.2581	1.1936	1.1936	0.1798	0.5	0.5826
1	0.5	45	0.8387	0.7957	0.7957	0.1691	0.4252	0.4697
	1	45	0.629	0.5967	0.5967	0.1596	0.3698	0.4328
	0	45	1.2581	1.1936	1.1936	0.1798	0.5	0.5826
2	0.5	60	0.715	0.7189	0.6422	0.2159	0.725	0.9762
	1	70	0.4698	0.4642	0.421	0.1791	0.3591	0.8718

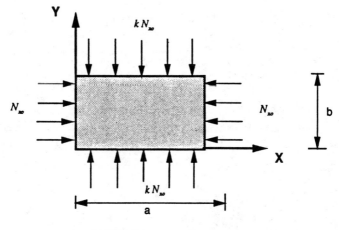

(a) Biaxially compressed plate

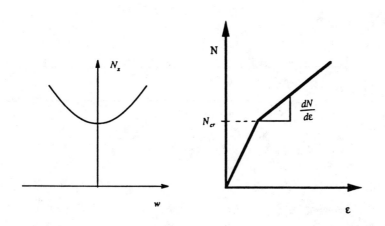

(b) Postbuckling

Figure 1. Postbuckling behaviour

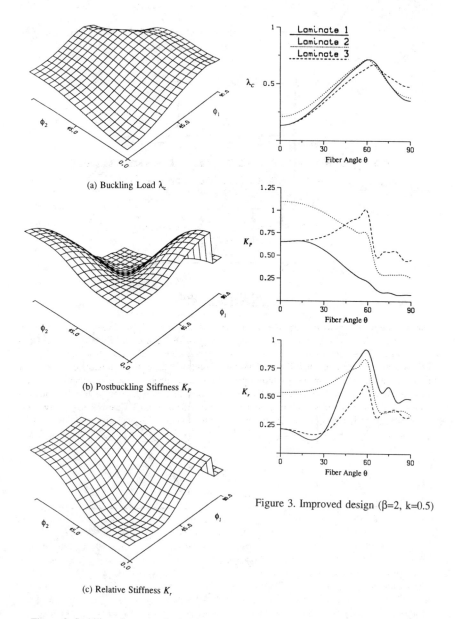

(a) Buckling Load λ_c

(b) Postbuckling Stiffness K_P

(c) Relative Stiffness K_r

Figure 3. Improved design ($\beta=2$, k=0.5)

Figure 2. Stability of rectangular laminates (k=0.5)

ADVANCED COMPOSITE MATERIALS IN BRIDGES AND STRUCTURES
K.W. Neale and P. Labossière, Editors; Canadian Society for Civil Engineering, 1992

Matériaux composites d'avant-garde pour ponts et charpentes
K.W. Neale et P. Labossière, éditeurs; Société canadienne de génie civil, 1992

POSTBUCKLING OF CYLINDRICALLY ORTHOTROPIC
CIRCULAR PLATES

A.N. Sherbourne and **M.D. Pandey**
University of Waterloo
Waterloo, Ontario, Canada

ABSTRACT

The postbuckling analysis of cylindrically orthotropic circular plates is characterized by singularities due to orthotropy and axisymmetry of deformations. In addition, geometric nonlinearities and strong coupling between the in-plane and transverse displacements make an explicit treatment difficult. However, circular delamination buckling is a critical failure mode in fibrous composite laminates. Here, a comprehensive initial-value formulation is presented introducing a transformation of problem variables to include cylindrical orthotropy. The resulting nonlinear, ordinary differential equations are numerically integrated using the Runge-Kutta-Merson method where general boundary conditions can be easily accommodated. It is shown that the buckling load, as well as postbuckling stiffness, can be improved by increasing the ratio of circumferential to radial elastic modulus.

RÉSUMÉ

L'analyse post-flambement de plaques circulairement orthotropes est caractérisée par des singularités qui dépendent de l'orthotropie et de l'axisymétrie des déformations. De plus, les non-linéarités géométriques et le couplage entre les déplacements, dans le plan et transversaux, compliquent le traitement explicite. Or, le flambement en délaminage circulaire est un mode de rupture critique pour les stratifiés de composites renforcés de fibres. Une formulation compréhensive est présentée en introduisant une transformation des variables du problème qui inclut l'orthotropie cylindrique. Les équations différentielles ordinaires résultantes sont intégrées numériquement en utilisant la méthode de Runge-Kutta-Merson, là où les conditions aux frontières le permettent. On démontre que la charge de flambement et la rigidité post-flambement peuvent être améliorées en augmentant le rapport des modules élastiques circonférentiels et radiaux.

INTRODUCTION

The axisymmetric buckling and postbuckling behaviour of circular plates has been a popular topic in the classical technical literature and numerous studies have been described a brief account of which has been given by Turvey and Drinali (1985), Huang (1975) and Uthgenannt and Brand (1973). Interest in this problem is also sustained by recent studies on circular delaminations in fibrous composite laminates (Yin and Jane 1989). The problem is theoretically challenging due to geometric nonlinearities and strong coupling between the in-plane and transverse displacements intrinsic to the von Karman equations. In an early study, Sherbourne (1961) analysed the behaviour of isotropic circular plates in greater depth. Later, with the introduction of composite materials in structural applications, many studies were published focusing on cylindrically orthotropic plates. But most of these studies were concerned with the postbuckling of annular orthotropic plates; a comprehensive treatment of fully circular orthotropic plates is barely mentioned. In fact, a finite element study by Raju and Rao (1983) is the only paper, to our knowledge, that deals explicitly with this problem. This somewhat surprising negligence of postbuckling analysis of circular orthotropic plates may not be coincidental as the problem is characterized by singularities due to orthotropy and axisymmetry of deformation thus contributing to mathematical complexity. Our study is an attempt to resolve some of these difficulties.

The plane stress solution for a circular orthotropic plate subjected to a uniform compressive stress, σ_R, (Fig.1) is characterized by a variable stress state along the radial coordinate (Lekhnitskii,1968) such that

$$\sigma_r = -\sigma_R \left(\frac{r}{R}\right)^{k-1}$$

$$\sigma_\theta = -\sigma_R k \left(\frac{r}{R}\right)^{k-1} \tag{1}$$

$$\sigma_{r\theta} = 0 \qquad \text{where} \quad k = \sqrt{E_\theta / E_r}$$

and E_r, E_θ are elastic moduli in the radial and circumferential directions, respectively. As seen from eqn. (1), when orthotropy ratio, $k > 1$, stresses decrease upon approaching the center and become zero at the pole; the reverse is true when $k < 1$ with the exception that the stresses become infinite at the plate center (Fig.2). It follows that a definite mathematical solution for the prebuckling stress state exists only if $k > 1$, implying that the circumferential direction is the principal material direction (Lekhnitskii 1968). This peculiar feature of the plane stress solution is tacitly recognized in the literature since most solutions of circular and annular plates are limited to cases of $k > 1$. The only exception is the study by Turvey and Drinali (1985) where numerical results are reported for cases including $k < 1$ using the dynamic relaxation method.

The second major concern is for singularities of the form 0/0 which occur in the nonlinear equilibrium equations governing the postbuckling problem because of radial symmetry of deformation which requires that slope and radial displacement to be zero at the plate center. This can be conveniently avoided by limiting the scope of the analysis to annular plates only which may explain the abundance of literature on this topic. To our knowledge, Sherbourne (1961) was the first to present an explicit mathematical treatment of this type of singularity using a suitable transformation of problem variables. Here, a new and suitable transformation of problem variables is devised to include cylindrical orthotropy.

It is noted that an accurate solution of nonlinear differential equations governing postbuckling of orthotropic circular plates is not available. In the literature, postbuckling analysis is often formulated as a two point boundary value problem and approximate solutions, from time to time, are reported using finite differences (Uthgenannt and Brand 1973), dynamic relaxation (Turvey and Drinali 1985), finite element (Raju and Rao 1983) and the Rayleigh-Ritz method (Yin and Jane 1989). Sherbourne (1961) suggested that the two-point boundary problem should be replaced with an initial value problem since it leads to a simpler, more straightforward yet very accurate formulation for numerical integration of the nonlinear differential equations based on the Runge - Kutta procedure. Based on a similar philosophy, an initial-value formulation is proposed for postbuckling analysis where a new and suitable transformation of problem variables is devised to include cylindrical orthotropy.

MATHEMATICAL FORMULATION

The scope of the present nonlinear analysis is limited to axisymmetric deformation incorporating the usual assumptions of the simple theory of bending. The nonlinear differential equations of postbuckling equilibrium are given as (Sherbourne and Pandey 1992)

$$r \frac{d^2u}{dr^2} = - \frac{du}{dr} - \frac{(1 - \nu_{\theta r})}{2} (\frac{dw}{dr})^2 + \frac{C\,u}{r} - r \frac{dw}{dr} \frac{d^2w}{dr^2} \qquad (2)$$

$$r \frac{d^3w}{dr^3} = - \frac{d^2w}{dr^2} + \frac{C}{r} \frac{dw}{dr} + 12\,r \frac{dw}{dr} \left\{ \frac{du}{dr} + \frac{1}{2} (\frac{dw}{dr})^2 + \nu_{\theta r} \frac{u}{r} \right\} \qquad (3)$$

Note that r, u and w are respectively normalized radius and in-plane and transverse displacements. $C = E_\theta / E_r$ is the orthotropy ratio and $\nu_{\theta r}$ denotes the major Poisson's ratio. The symmetry of deformation about the pole, r = 0, implies that

$$u\,(0) = (\frac{dw}{dr})_0 = 0 \qquad (4)$$

which leads to singularities of the form 0/0 in eqns. (2) and (3). These singularities can be avoided by redefining the problem in terms of a new set of variables obtained through the following transformations.

$$x = r^{k+1}$$
$$u = r^k U \qquad (5)$$
$$w = W \quad \text{where} \quad k = \sqrt{E_\theta / E_r}$$

The equations of equilibrium can now be reformulated as

$$U'' = - \frac{(3k+1)U'}{(k+1)x} - (1 - \nu_{\theta r} + 2k) \frac{(W')^2}{2x} - (k+1)\,W'W'' \qquad (6)$$

$$W''' = - \frac{(3k+1)}{(k+1)} \frac{W''}{x} + \frac{12(k + \nu_{\theta r})}{(k+1)^2} \frac{U\,W'}{x} + 6\,W' \left\{ \frac{2\,U'}{(k+1)} + (W')^2 \right\} \qquad (7)$$

where primes denote differentiation with respect to x.

Initial Conditions

Initial conditions related to the transformed equations of equilibrium are derived on the basis of physical arguments i.e. derivatives U'' and W''' at the origin (x = 0) should be bounded so that the deformed shape of the plate remains smooth at the origin (Sherbourne 1961, Huang and Sandman 1971). Since the plate center (x = 0) is also the origin of the cylindrical coordinate system, the first initial condition simply becomes

$$W_o = 0 \qquad (8)$$

Here, the subscript "o" refers to the origin or plate center, x = 0. For U'' and W''' to be finite at the origin, the coefficients of terms in 1/x from eqns. (6) and (7) should vanish, which furnishes the following expressions

$$U_o' = \frac{(\nu_{\theta r} - 2k - 1)\,(k + 1)}{2\,(3k + 1)} (W_o')^2 \qquad (9)$$

$$W_o'' = \frac{12\,(k + v_{\theta r})}{(3k + 1)\,(k + 1)}\, U_o\, W_o' \tag{10}$$

The initial values of U" and W"" may be determined by expanding U and W in Maclaurin series in the neighbourhood of the origin the details of which can be found elsewhere (Sherbourne and Pandey 1992).

$$U_o'' = -\,U_o\,(W_o')^2 \left\{ \frac{6\,(4k + 3 - v_{\theta r})\,(k + v_{\theta r})}{(4k + 2)\,(3k + 1)} \right\} \tag{11}$$

$$(4k + 2)\,W_o''' = \frac{12\,(2k + v_{\theta r} + 1)}{(k + 1)}\, U_o'\,W_o' + \frac{12\,(k + v_{\theta r})}{(k + 1)}\, U_o\,W_o'' + 6\,(k + 1)\,W_o'\,(W_o')^2 \tag{12}$$

For a given set of values of U_o and W_o', initial conditions for all remaining derivatives can be obtained from eqns. (8) - (12). It should be noted that sagging moments and tensile stresses are considered positive.

COMPUTATION

The nonlinear differential equations describing axisymmetric postbuckling behaviour can be solved by an initial value method based on the Runge-Kutta-Merson procedure. This approach requires a set of simultaneous first-order ordinary differential equations (ODEs) in which each derivative is expressed explicitly in terms of the dependent variables and is achieved by introducing the following new variables :

$$Y_1 = W \,,\ Y_2 = U \,,\ Y_3 = W' \,,\ Y_4 = U' \,,\ Y_5 = W'' \tag{13}$$

which allows one to write the following set of simultaneous five first order ODEs in explicit form :

$$\frac{dY_1}{dx} = W' = Y_3 \,, \qquad \frac{dY_2}{dx} = U' = Y_4$$

$$\frac{dY_3}{dx} = W'' = Y_5 \,, \qquad \frac{dY_4}{dx} = U'' \tag{14}$$

$$\frac{dY_5}{dx} = W'''$$

A computer program is developed that simulates the axisymmetric postbuckling behaviour of a simply supported or clamped circular plate of prescribed radius (r), thickness (h), orthotropy ratio (C). The essential steps are as follows :

1. Initial values of U_o and W_o' are assigned.

2. Initial values of other parameters, U_o', U_o'', W_o'' and W_o''' are evaluated using eqns. (9) - (12)

3. The set of first-order ODEs, eqn. (14) is numerically integrated using the NAG (Numerical Algorithm Group) subroutine D02BJF.

4. The terminal boundary condition (at r = R) is examined. If the B.C. cannot be satisfied in the first cycle, W_o' is systematically varied (keeping U_o constant) and the ODEs are numerically integrated until the prescribed B C is fulfilled.

5. Final results including postbuckling load, λ_{NL} , deflections, u, w, stresses, moments etc. are reported.

652

6. The complete postbuckling behaviour can be simulated by choosing various values of U_o and repeating steps (1) to (5).

The basic approach involves selecting some value of U_o and finding W_o' through a bisection method which not only satisfies the prescribed condition at the boundary but also results in reasonable values of postbuckling load and deflection.

Postbuckling Stiffness

The initial slope of the postbuckling load (λ_{NL}) vs. radial shortening (u) curve is often used as a convenient measure of the postbuckling stiffness. Presently, this slope is calculated by considering the portion of the λ_{NL} - u curve up to approximately twice the value of radial shortening at buckling (Turvey and Drinali 1985). As shown in Fig. 3, postbuckling as well as prebuckling stiffness, K_P and K_E, respectively, can be expressed as

$$K_P = \frac{\lambda_{NL} - \lambda_{cr}}{u_1 - u_{cr}} \quad \text{note that } u_1 \approx 2 u_{cr}$$

$$K_E = \frac{\lambda_{cr}}{u_{cr}}$$

(15)

such that their ratio can be written as

$$\frac{K_P}{K_E} = \left(\frac{\lambda_{NL}}{\lambda_{cr}} - 1\right)\left(\frac{u_1}{u_{cr}} - 1\right)^{-1}$$

(16)

The critical radial displacement, u_{cr}, is calculated corresponding to the prebuckling stress state defined by eqn. (1) (Sherbourne and Pandey 1992) and buckling loads are obtained using standard expressions (Swamidas and Kunukkasseril 1963).

RESULTS

The postbuckling behaviour of clamped and simply supported circular plates of constant nondimensional radius, R = 50, is studied for four orthotropy ratios, C = 1,2,5 and 8 and $\nu_{\theta r} = 0.3$. Postbuckling variations of transverse deflection, w, and radial shortening, u, with respect to the applied compressive load are shown in Figs. 4(a),(b). Here, the applied load is normalized by the buckling load of a similar isotropic, circular plate. As expected the load vs. w curve is parabolic. From these figures it is apparent that plates with higher orthotropy ratio, C, not only have proportionately higher buckling loads but also tend to be stiffer than their isotropic counterparts. Load ratio, $\Lambda = \lambda_{NL}/\lambda_{cr}$, is defined as the ratio of postbuckling to critical buckling load. It is interesting to note (Table 1) the significant increase in postbuckling stiffness with increasing orthotropy ratio which is in contrast to the previous study by Raju and Rao (1983). In comparison with isotropic plates, the variation of radial and circumferential moments in orthotropic plates is remarkably different (Sherbourne and Pandey 1992). In highly orthotropic plates ($C > 5$), the moment distribution is characterized by sharp peaks in the middle of the plate which is expected to affect, significantly, the nature of impact damage and delaminations.

CONCLUSION

A comprehensive initial-value formulation is presented for postbuckling analysis of cylindrically orthotropic, circular plates where nonlinear, ordinary differential equations are numerically integrated using the Runge-Kutta-Merson method. The genesis of the method is the modification of a previously proposed (Sherbourne 1961) initial value method to include material orthotropy by introducing new variable transformation techniques. The proposed approach is well justified by its remarkable simplicity and straightforward computational procedure. While numerical results are presented for simple and clamped edges, other boundary conditions can be easily handled.

It is shown that the buckling load, as well as postbuckling stiffness, can be improved by increasing the orthotropy ratio, the ratio of circumferential to radial elastic modulus. In circular plates, the circumferential direction is marked as the principal load carrying direction, and, therefore, increase in the elastic modulus, E_θ, is rightfully expected to increase prebuckling stiffness and, hence, the buckling load. The proposed method should find applications in studying delamination buckling problems in fibrous composite laminates.

ACKNOWLEDGEMENTS

The writers are grateful to NSERC of Canada for support of this work under grant A - 1582 to the first author (ANS) and to the Province of Ontario, Canada, for support of the second author (MDP) under an Ontario Graduate Scholarship.

REFERENCES

Huang, C. L. and Sandman, B.E. (1971). "Large amplitude vibrations of a rigidly clamped circular plate". Int. J. Nonlinear Mech., 6(4), pp.451-466.

Huang, C. L. (1975). "On postbuckling of orthotropic annular plates". Int. J. Nonlinear Mech., 10(1), pp.63-74.

Lekhnitski, S. G. (1968). Anisotropic Plates. Gordon and Breach Publishing Co., New York.

Raju, K.K. and Rao, G.V. (1983). "Finite-element analysis of post-buckling behaviour of cylindrically orthotropic circular plates". Fibre Science Tech., 19, pp.145-154.

Sherbourne, A.N. (1961). "Elastic, postbuckling behaviour of a simply supported circular plate". J. Mech. Engrg. Science, 3(2), pp.133-141.

Sherbourne, A.N. and Pandey, M.D. (1992). "Postbuckling of polar orthotropic circular plates - A retrospective". To appear in J. Engrg. Mechanics, ASCE.

Swamidas A.S. and Kunukkasseril, V.X. (1963). "Buckling of orthotropic circular plates". AIAA J., 11(12), pp.1633-1636.

Turvey, G.J. and Drinali, H. (1985). "Elastic postbuckling of circular and annular plates with imperfections". Proc. 3rd Int. Conf. Composite Struct., pp.315-335.

Uthgenannt, E.B. and Brand, R.S. (1973). "Postbuckling of orthotropic annular plates". J. Appl. Mech., pp.559-564.

Yin, W.L. and Jane, K.C. (1989). "Refined buckling and postbuckling of two dimensional delaminations". in Recent Developments in Buckling of Structures, Hui, D. et al (eds.), PVP vol.183, AD vol.18, ASME, pp.31-40.

Table 1: Postbuckling stiffness variation ($v_{\theta r} = 0.3$)

BC →	Clamped				Simple			
C	u_{cr}	u_1	$\lambda_{NL}/\lambda_{cr}$	K_P/K_E	u_{cr}	u_1	$\lambda_{NL}/\lambda_{cr}$	K_P/K_E
1	0.01882	0.034929	1.2766	0.3231	0.0053817	0.011049	1.1883	0.1788
2	0.02339	0.045704	1.3881	0.4068	0.0069983	0.01444	1.2061	0.1938
5	0.03246	0.065365	1.4877	0.4811	0.0102	0.021363	1.2381	0.2176
8	0.03899	0.075563	1.4811	0.5129	0.012505	0.023634	1.2053	0.2307

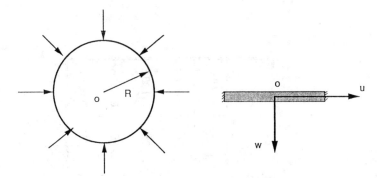

Figure 1: Circular plate under uniform compression

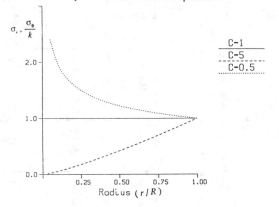

Figure 2: Plane stress solution

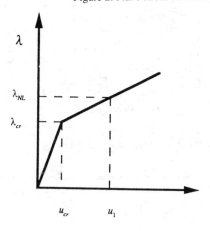

Figure 3: Postbuckling stiffness calculation

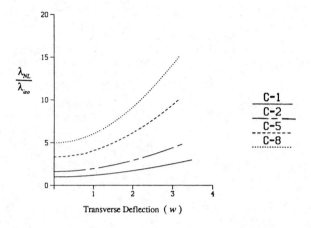

$\dfrac{\lambda_{NL}}{\lambda_{iso}}$

Transverse Deflection (w)

C-1
C-2
C-5
C-8

(a) : Load versus transverse deflection

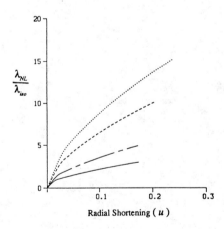

$\dfrac{\lambda_{NL}}{\lambda_{iso}}$

Radial Shortening (u)

(b) : Load versus radial displacement

Figure 4: Postbuckling behaviour of clamped plates

ADVANCED COMPOSITE MATERIALS IN BRIDGES AND STRUCTURES
K.W. Neale and P. Labossière, Editors; Canadian Society for Civil Engineering, 1992

Matériaux composites d'avant-garde pour ponts et charpentes
K.W. Neale et P. Labossière, éditeurs; Société canadienne de génie civil, 1992

OPTIMIZATION OF COMPOSITE MATERIALS WITH GENETIC ALGORITHMS AND NEURAL NETWORKS

P. Labossière
Université de Sherbrooke
Sherbrooke, Québec, Canada

N. Turkkan
Université de Moncton
Moncton, Nouveau-Brunswick, Canada

ABSTRACT

Due to the cumbersome calculations often required when dealing with advanced composite materials, innovative procedures are needed to facilitate optimization problems. Two new and efficient techniques will be demonstrated here for that purpose. Both are inspired from biological studies, and adapted respectively from genetic simulations and studies of neural systems. A failure criterion for a fibre-reinforced material will be defined by using these two methods.

RÉSUMÉ

En raison des calculs complexes requis pour les matériaux composites, des procédures innovatrices facilitant la résolution de problèmes d'optimisation sont nécessaires. Les deux techniques de calcul présentées ici, nouvelles et efficaces, sont inspirées de processus biologiques. Elles consistent à adapter des simulations génétiques ou à reproduire des réseaux de neurones. On les utilisera pour optimiser les critères de rupture d'un matériau renforcé de fibres unidirectionnelles.

INTRODUCTION

Because of their high strength-to-weight ratios and corrosion resistance, the use of fibre-reinforced composite materials is rapidly increasing in a variety of applications. In addition to the now classical ones in the aeronautical and transportations industries, many innovative applications in civil engineering are also being developed, some of them in bridges and structures. Interest in other materials showing natural anisotropy, such as wood and its derivatives, is also rapidly increasing.

Due to the cumbersome calculations often required when dealing with advanced composite materials, innovative procedures are needed to facilitate optimization problems. New and efficient techniques developed for that purpose will be demonstrated here. These methods are inspired from biological sciences, and adapted respectively from genetic simulations and neural networks.

A great variety of problems can be solved by using these techniques. In this article, they will be applied to predict the failure envelope of a typical fibre-reinforced anisotropic material. First, the parameters of the well-known tensor polynomial theory will be optimized by a genetic algorithm. Then the neural network solution will demonstrate an alternative method to predict failure when a great number of experimental data are available. It will be shown that both methods produce an improved correlation between experimental data and the analytical failure envelope for the example material.

GENERALITIES

Material Definition

The type of material considered here consists of thin, orthotropic, unidirectionally or bidirectionally fibre-reinforced, composite laminae. In most structural applications, laminae with different principal fibre orientations are glued together to form a laminate. Although a laminate can be subjected to bending and in-plane loading, the comprised laminae can generally be analyzed under the assumption of plane stress conditions; this is done by using the classical lamination theory.

Error Definition

To determine the strength properties of a particular lamina submitted to a combination of in-plane stresses σ_1, σ_2 and τ_{12}, failure theories are employed. In order to evaluate the capability of a given failure equation to represent accurately the experimental data, the total error E_t between series of experimental data points and the analytical curve will be defined as

$$E_t = \sum_{n=1}^{N} (L_*(\sigma_{1*},\sigma_{2*},\tau_{12*}) - L(\sigma_1,\sigma_2,\tau_{12}))^2 \tag{1}$$

Here N is the number of data points, and $L_*(\sigma_{1*}, \sigma_{2*}, \tau_{12*})$ is the length of the vector from the origin of the system of axis to the experimental failure point, given by

$$L_* = \sqrt{\sigma_{1*}^2 + \sigma_{2*}^2 + \tau_{12*}^2} \tag{2}$$

The other term, $L(\sigma_1, \sigma_2, \tau_{12})$, is the length of the strength vector from the origin of the system of axis to the failure point predicted by the chosen failure criterion.

Failure Criterion

Many criteria defining failure in the σ_1-σ_2-τ_{12} stress space have been proposed in the last twenty years. One of the most convenient and widely used is the tensor polynomial criterion. According to this approach (Tsai and Wu, 1971), failure occurs when the combination of in-plane stresses reaches the following:

$$F_i \sigma_i + F_{ij} \sigma_i \sigma_j + F_{ijk} \sigma_i \sigma_j \sigma_k + \ldots = 1 \qquad (i, j, k = 1,2,\ldots 6) \qquad (3)$$

Usually, only the quadratic terms are kept, and Eq.(3) becomes, in plane stress:

$$F_1 \sigma_1 + F_2 \sigma_2 + F_{11} \sigma_1^2 + F_{22} \sigma_2^2 + 2F_{12} \sigma_1 \sigma_2 + F_{66} \tau_{12}^2 = 1 \qquad (4)$$

where the F_i and F_{ij} parameters are related to the uniaxial strengths by

$$F_1 = \frac{1}{X} - \frac{1}{X'} \qquad F_{11} = \frac{1}{XX'}$$

$$F_2 = \frac{1}{Y} - \frac{1}{Y'} \qquad F_{22} = \frac{1}{YY'} \qquad (5)$$

$$F_{66} = \frac{1}{S^2}$$

Here, X and Y are respectively the tensile uniaxial strengths in the fibre direction and perpendicular to the fibre; X' and Y' are the corresponding compressive strengths, and S is the shear strength. To ensure that the failure surface is closed, the remaining interaction parameter, F_{12} in Eq.(4), must be selected in a range comprised within:

$$F_{11}F_{22} - F_{12}^2 \geq 0$$
$$F_{11}F_{66} \geq 0 \qquad (6)$$
$$F_{22}F_{66} \geq 0$$

This leads to a failure envelope which has the shape of an ellipsoid. This criterion reduces to the von Mises criterion for isotropic materials when provided with the appropriate strength properties.

Classical Optimization Procedures

Minimizing the value of the total error between the failure criterion, Eq.(3), and the N experimental points, involves the substitution of the experimental and analytical values of L and L_* into Eq.(1). When the relationships given by Eq.(5) are substituted into this equation, this leads to a relatively complex function which can be written in a simplified form as

$$E_t = f (F_1, F_2, F_{11}, F_{22}, F_{12}, F_{66}) = f (X, X', Y, Y', S, F_{12}) \qquad (7)$$

Various optimization methods can be used to find the combination of the six above parameters that would minimize the error between the data and the analytical equation (Labossière and Turkkan, 1992). In the next two sections, new types of optimization procedures will be shown to improve on the definition of the failure criterion for a fibre-reinforced composite material.

GENETIC ALGORITHMS

Description of the method

Genetic algorithms were developed after original work by Holland (1975). These algorithms are a class of optimization procedures based on principles inspired by natural evolution. Given a problem for which a closed-form solution is unknown, or almost impossible to find by using classical procedures, an initial random-generated "population" of possible solutions is gradually led to converge towards the best-possible solution by using a "darwinian" natural selection process. In our case, the function to optimize is Eq.(7).

The characteristics of the initial "population" are generated randomly. Each member of this group is assimilated to an individual who is characterized by a personal "string of genes". Each individual is evaluated, and classified in relation with its closeness to the "best", yet still unknown, solution to the initial problem. The first step consists in defining an evaluation function $g(x_1, x_2, ...x_T)$, also called objective function, which must be minimized. The x_i terms represent the parameters to select, or decision variables. The lowest the value of the objective function, the closer its parameters are to provide the solution to the problem. In our case, the objective function is given by

$$g (x_1, x_2, ...f_T) = E_t = f (X, X', Y, Y', S, F_{12}) \qquad (8)$$

Equation (8) is also called a "fitness" function.

The initial population is selected randomly in the space of possible solutions. In Eq.(8), this means creating np arbitrary values of X, X', Y, Y', S, and F_{12}. These parameters are coded into "genetic information" that will be used to transmit information to a future generation. This is done by allocating to each individual a "chromosome", or string, of length l, which will be coded in binary form. Specific portions of that chromosome represent one of the six parameters. After experimenting with many chromosome lengths, we have used here strings of length $l = 38$. Since these initial strings are generated randomly, there is no guarantee that a specific value is present in the initial population. In fact, the original population of $np = 120$ individuals is selected here among a possibility of 2^{38}, or 275×10^9 combinations.

Next, a new "population" is generated by recombination of parental genes. In a simulation of a biological system submitted to external constraints, the "fittest" members of the initial population are given better chances of reproducing and transmitting their genetic heritage to a next generation. It is expected that some members of this new population will inherit the best characteristics of both parents and, being better adapted to the "environmental conditions", will provide an improved solution to the problem. Additional constraints might be imposed, limiting the range of admissible solutions and, in effect, annihilating the reproductive capability of the most inefficient members of a generation. This younger population is submitted to the same evaluation procedure, and generates its own offsprings. The process is repeated until all members of a given generation share the same genetic heritage. From then on, there are virtually no differences between members of the population. The genetic information possessed by the members of the "final" generation, who can be very different from their "ancestors", is then decoded to identify the solution to the initial problem.

The probability of selecting an individual to generate a member of the following generation is taken here as "linear fitness with decrement 1". In this case, the individual with best performance is given a relative weight of $RW_j = np$; the second best gets a relative weight of $RW_j = np\text{-}1$; and so on down to the least fit member of the population who gets a relative weight $RW_j = 1$. The probability of reproduction PR_j of one member j of the population is taken as

$$PR_j = \frac{RW_j}{\sum\limits_{j=1}^{np} RW_j} \tag{9}$$

It has generally been found (Davies, 1991) that this weighing function permits to keep some "unfit" individuals who may nevertheless possess valuable genetic information for the next generation.

During the generation process, a certain number of parents will be reproduced without any changes. The percentage of new individuals issued from cross-over depends on the "cross-over rate", taken here as 0.80. In this case, pairs of "chromosomes" are recombined on a random basis to form new individuals. The recombination process implies the division and cross-over of the two parent chromosomes at one point along the string. The position of splitting is totally random. During the process, a possibility of "mutation", that is changing the genetic information from a "0" to a "1" (or vice-versa), is also considered for each bit on the string. This rate of mutation was taken here as 0.005.

Once a new generation has been created, the previous one is deleted. Evaluation of the new individuals is undertaken, and the entire procedure is repeated for a pre-determined number of generations, or until a strong individual has come to dominate the entire population. In order to find the best solution to the optimization problem, one has to experiment with various string lengths, cross-over and mutation rates, and number of generations. The genetic base of the first generation may also influence the rapidity of the convergence process.

Example of Application

Experimental data

The results used in this section were originally published by Rowlands et al. (1985) for a unidirectionally-reinforced material identified as a 100 per cent Lake State Softwood, unbleached paper craft, of basis weight 205 g/m^2 and mass density of 670 kg/m^3. Uniaxial coupons, cylinders, and cruciform specimens of this paperboard were subjected to various in-plane combinations of axial and shear stress. The results listed in the original reference, a total of 143 experimental points, cover a substantial portion of the failure envelope in the $\sigma_1 - \sigma_2 - \tau_{12}$ space. The data were obtained on planes of constant shear stress. The results show very good consistency along similar loading paths; a well-defined failure surface is obtained for all areas. Failure surfaces using various theories have already been proposed for this material (Rowlands et al., 1985; Suhling et al., 1985; Labossière and Neale, 1987, 1991), including various calculations of the F_i and F_{ij} parameters in the tensor polynomial failure theory.

Optimization Results

The genetic algorithm was applied to the above experimental data. It was assumed that the values of X, X', Y, Y', and S would be positive, as this physically implies failure in the direction of loading. The limits on the parameters were selected to leave enough room to pick the most appropriate values, knowing the uniaxial strengths that had been measured experimentally. The value of the interaction parameter was searched in the range $-0.00001 \leq F_{12} \leq 0.00001$ MPa^{-2}. The optimization procedure was stopped after 120 generations. In order to refine the results, a second-step optimization was performed in a more limited area centered around the previous results. For the set of parameters converging towards the best solution to the problem, Fig. 1 illustrates how the fitness of the "best-fit" chromosome of each generation has evolved from the beginning of the process until the end. The fast rate of convergence towards the final solution can be appreciated. The results are presented for three arbitrary initial populations. In the three cases, the final optimized solution after 40 generations was the same. The corresponding failure envelope is shown in Fig. 2, along with experimental data in the plane $\tau_{12}=0$. The total error between the experimental data and the analytical function thus obtained is 580 MPa^2; this compares favorably with total errors of 1243 MPa^2 for the solution proposed by Rowlands et al. (1985) and 928 MPa^2 for the solution of Labossière and Neale (1991). The calculated average discrepancy between the optimized failure envelope and each experimental point is in the order of 5%.

The results presented here demonstrate that the genetic algorithm optimization procedure was successful in identifying correctly the parameters of the tensor polynomial failure envelope in order to provide the best correlation with the available experimental data.

NEURAL NETWORKS

Description of the method

In the previous section, the best failure envelope was identified, through genetic alterations, in the form of combinations and mutations of the solutions in the admissible range. However, the form of the solution, in that case the second order tensor polynomial, had to be defined a priori. It will be shown here that neural networks can be used to calculate an appropriate failure envelope without restriction on the form of the function.

The method is based on a schematic representation of the neurons in the human brain, in which the neurons are part of a structured network. The neurons are organized in layers; some form of communication is established between the layers in order to find a relationship between the input data and the output result.

Each neuron receives a series of signals from neurons placed on the previous layer. This is the input function, of the following form

$$S_i = \sum W_{ij} O_j \tag{10}$$

where the O_i are the values of the signals transmitted by the j-neuron in the previous layer, and the W_{ij} are the weight of the connection between these neurons and the i-neuron in the current layer. A positive weight produces an excitation effect from the i-neuron to the j-neuron; to a negative weight corresponds an inhibiting effect. Once feeded by the input data, the i-neuron transforms it and produces a reaction, an output that will be transmitted to neurons on the following layer. Here, the input S_i and the output O_i are related by a transfer function, of a sigmoid form

$$O_i = f(S_i) = \frac{1}{1 + e^{-(S_i)}} \tag{11}$$

Each neuron within the layer emits an output related to the poundered weight of its connections.

The network evolves; originally, the weight values are generated randomly in the range -1.0 to 1.0. The evolution is characterized by a learning rule: it consists in modifying the relative weight of the connections until the network stabilizes, that means until the weight matrix of the connections does not change.

In this article, we are using a multilayered feedforward network with the back-propagation of the gradient method (Rumelhart et al., 1986). In this network, the learning is supervised, in the sense that the network is presented simultaneously with a series of input data and corresponding output. After each iteration t, the modification of the connection weights follows a function of the form

$$W_{ij}(t+1) = \Omega W_{ij}(t) + \mu \delta_j x_i \tag{12}$$

where Ω and μ are the momentum and learning parameters, and the δs are given by the following expressions

$$\delta_k = (S_k - x_k) x_k (1 - x_k)$$
$$\delta_j = x_j (1 - x_j) \sum \delta_k w_{kl} \tag{13}$$

for the output-layer and hidden-layer units respectively.

Identification of the Network

The network selected is presented in Fig. 3. It consists of an entry level of three neurons and one neuron at the exit level. The three neurons at the entry level represent the orientation of the stress vector in the failure surface; α, β, and Φ represent the orientation of the loading vector with respect to the σ_1-σ_2-τ_{12} axes, respectively. The single output neuron predicts the distance from the origin of the system of axes to the failure point for that loading combination. Between these input and output levels are inserted hidden layers of neurons. After experimenting with various neuronal configurations, two layers containing fifteen neurons each were selected.

Example of Application

The experimental results presented in the previous section were used to train the network. The program BrainMaker, available commercially from California Scientific Software, was used for the calculations, with the following parameters: a learning coefficient $\mu=1.0$, a momentum coefficient $\Omega=0.9$, and a convergence criterion of 6%. In this case, $\mu=1.0$ and $\Omega=0.9$ allow a high rate or learning with a high momentum. The 6% convergence criterion indicates that the algorithm will stop when the difference between the predicted failure and any of the 143 experimental data used to train the system is smaller or equal to 6%.

The correlation between the 143 experimental points and the predicted failure surface is excellent. The total error between the data points and the failure envelope predicted using the network is 411 MPa^2. The corresponding failure surface is shown, together with the experimental data in the plane $\tau_{12}=0$, in Fig. 4. This result is better than those obtained with optimization of the tensor polynomial failure theory. This is because the shape of the failure envelope is not defined a priori, but adapts to the local variations in the surface. The results presented here demonstrate that a neural network procedure can be quite successful in predicting failure. For the paperboard material, the technique has permitted to identify correctly a failure envelope providing an improved correlation with the available experimental data.

CONCLUSION

The genetic algorithm and neural network procedures described in this article can be applied to a variety of optimization problems. It was first shown here that genetic algorithms can succesfully optimize the parameters of the tensor polynomial failure criterion for fibre-reinforced composite materials. It was also demonstrated that, using neural networks, it may not be necessary to write an analytical failure criterion when enough experimental results are available. Error calculation shows that these two techniques produced improved results over solutions already proposed for the same material.

Acknowledgements

The authors thank the Natural Sciences and Engineering Research Council of Canada (NSERC) for its financial support.

REFERENCES

Davies, L. (1991). Handbook of Genetic Algorithms. Van Nostrand Reinhold, New York, 385pp.

Holland, J.H. (1975). Adaptation in Natural and Artificial Systems. The University of Michigan Press, Ann Arbor.

Labossière, P., Neale, K.W. (1987). On the Determination of the Strength Parameters in the Tensor Polynomial Failure Criterion. *Journal of Strain Analysis*, 22, 155-161.

Labossière, P., Neale, K.W. (1991). A Parametric Failure Criterion for Paperboard Material. *Journal of Strain Analysis*, 266, 461-466.

Labossière, P. and Turkkan, N. (1992). On the Optimization of the Tensor Polynomial Failure Theory with a Genetic Algorithm. Submitted to Transactions of the CSME.

Rowlands, R.E., Gunderson, D.E., Suhling, J.C., and Johnson, M.W. (1985). Biaxial Strength of Paperboard Predicted by Hill-Type Theories. *J.Strain Analysis*, 20, 121-127.

Rumelhart, D.E., Hinton, G.E., Williams, R.J. (1986). Learning Representations by Back-Propagating Errors. *Nature*, 323, oct.9, 533-536.

Suhling, J.C., Rowlands, R.E., Johnson, M.W., Gunderson, D.E. (1985). Tensorial Strength Analysis of Paperboard. *Experimental Mechanics*, 25, 75-84.

Tsai, S.W., Wu, E.M., (1971). A General Theory of Strength for Anisotropic Materials. *Journal of Composite Materials*, 5, 58-80.

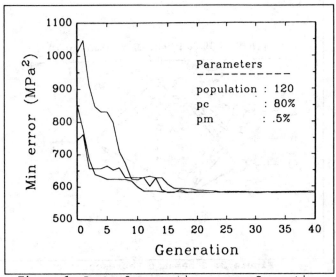

Figure 1: Best-of-generation versus Generation

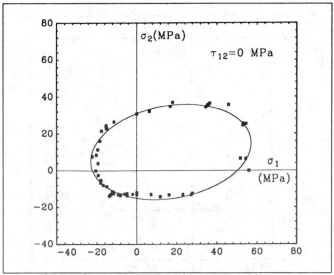

Figure 2: Optimized Failure Equation and
Experimental Data on the Plane $\tau_{12}=0$

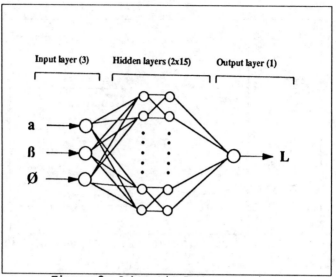

Figure 3: Schematic Representation
of a Neural Network

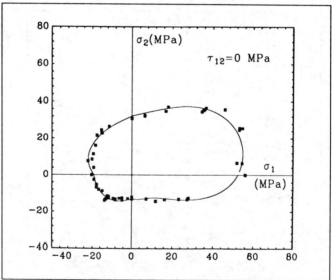

Figure 4: Experimental Data and Failure Enveloppe
Predicted Using the Neural Network for $\tau_{12}=0$

ADVANCED COMPOSITE MATERIALS IN BRIDGES AND STRUCTURES
K.W. Neale and P. Labossière, Editors; Canadian Society for Civil Engineering, 1992

Matériaux composites d'avant-garde pour ponts et charpentes
K.W. Neale et P. Labossière, éditeurs; Société canadienne de génie civil, 1992

PROPOSED SHEAR STRENGTH EQUATIONS FOR
STEEL–CONCRETE SANDWICH STRUCTURES

T. Ueda
Hokkaido University
Sapporo, Japan

ABSTRACT

This paper presents the shear strength equations recently specified in the proposed Japanese Code for Steel–Concrete Sandwich Structures, as well as the background where the equations are introduced. In the sandwich structure shear reinforcing steel plates are usually placed either parallel or normal to the member axis. With shear reinforcing steel plates truss-like mechanisms are formed to resist shear force. The shear strength equations conservatively predict the results reported in previous tests.

RÉSUMÉ

Cet article présente les équations de résistance au cisaillement développées récemment pour un éventuel Code japonais pour le dimensionnement des structures sandwich acier-béton. Dans une telle structure, des plaques d'acier sont placées parallèlement ou perpendiculairement à l'axe de la section. Avec les plaques d'acier, des mécanismes semblables à des treillis permettent de résister aux efforts de cisaillement. Les équations de résistance au cisaillement prédisent conservativement les résistances mesurées expérimentalement.

INTRODUCTION

The Japan Society of Civil Engineers specified the "Proposed Design Code of Steel-Concrete Sandwich Structure" in April 1992. Limit state design method is adopted in the code. One of the ultimate limit states is for shear force. In the code new equations for shear capacities as steel-concrete sandwich linear member are introduced. The shear capacities are estimated by assuming similar mechanical models to those for ordinary reinforced concrete linear members.

SHEAR CAPACITIES AS LINEAR MEMBER

Case without Shear Reinforcing Steel Plate

In the case without shear reinforcing steel plate, previous test results[1]-[5] indicate that shear capacity for slender beam or deep beam of ordinary reinforced concrete can predict the measured capacities for large and small shear span to effective depth ratios respectively. However, effect of shear connector on shear capacity should be considered in the case of diagonal tension failure because shear connector may reduce shear cracking strength[4][6][7]. The previous test result[8] shows that shear cracking strength is reduced to 85%. It is reported[9] that shear tension failure capacity can be increased to three times by locating no shear connector in a shear span.

Considering the above experimental facts, Eq.(1), derived from an equation for an ordinary reinforced concrete beam, is applied to predict the shear capacity for the case without shear reinforcing plate.

$$V_{uo} = f_{vc} b_w d \qquad (1)$$

where
- f_{vc} : the maximum of $0.191 f'_c{}^{1/3} \beta_d \beta_p \beta_n k$ and $0.188 f'_c{}^{1/2} \beta_d \beta_p \beta_s$
- b_w : member web width
- d : effective depth
- f'_c : concrete compressive strength, MPa
- $\beta_d = (1000/d)^{1/4}$ (d:mm) but ≤ 1.5
- $\beta_p = (100 A_s / b_w d)^{1/3}$ but ≤ 1.5
- $\beta_n = 1 + M_o / M_u$ (for N'$\geq$0) but ≤ 2
  - $= 1 + 2 M_o / M_u$ (for N'$<$0) but ≥ 0
- $\beta_s = 5/(1 + \cot^2 \theta)$
- k : reduction factor of shear cracking strength to that of an ordinary reinforced concrete linear member, 0.85
- A_s : cross-sectional area of tension reinforcing steel plate
- M_o : decompression moment for tension zone of ultimate flexural moment
- M_u : ultimate flexural moment
- N' : axial compressive force
- θ : angle between concrete diagonal compression strut and member axis, $\cot^{-1}(a/z)$
- a : distance from support to loading point (shear span)
- z : distance from position of resultant of compression stresses to that of tensile stresses

Case with Shear Reinforcing Steel Plate

For cases with shear reinforcing steel plates, truss-like mechanism is formed to resist shear forces as can be seen in an ordinary shear reinforced concrete linear member. Shear capacities, however, cannot be obtained by only applying prediction methods for ordinary reinforced concrete structures because shear reinforcement is plate instead of bar and may be placed with a large spacing, which is prohibited for ordinary reinforced concrete structures.

Case of Shear Reinforcing Steel Plate Located Parallel to Member Axis

The case of shear reinforcing steel plate located parallel to member axis as shown in Fig.1 is similar to the case of narrowly spaced shear reinforcing bars in an ordinary reinforced concrete linear member. Therefore, diagonal compression strut in truss mechanism is formed uniformly, and its angle to member axis is less than 45° but around 30° (see Fig.2). Observed angles in experiments and finite element analyses for ordinary reinforced concrete beams are also less than 45°. Difference from the shear reinforcing bar is shear resisting capacity of the shear reinforcing steel plate itself because steel plate is usually continuous in a shear span. For a small shear span to effective depth ratio, diagonal compression strut is formed in direction connecting loading point and support as seen in an ordinary reinforced concrete linear member, and its angle can be greater than 30° (see Fig.3).

Based on the experimental facts, it is considered that truss mechanism with diagonal compression strut of concrete, diagonal tension strut of shear reinforcing steel plate, lower chord of tension steel plate, and upper chord of concrete in compression zone and compression steel plate is a major part of shear resisting mechanism. This mechanism is expressed by the following equation.

$$V = \sin\alpha(\cot\theta+\cot\alpha)(z/s)A_w\sigma_w +V_o \qquad (2)$$

where
- V : applied shear force
- α : angle of tension force in shear reinforcing steel plate acting as diagonal tension strut to member axis, 60°
- θ : angle of diagonal compression strut of concrete to member axis, which is the maximum of 30° and $\cot^{-1}(a/z)$
- A_w : cross-sectional area of shear reinforcing steel plate in spacing of s, which is equal to $(t_w s)\sin\alpha$
- σ_w : principal tensile stress in shear reinforcing steel plate
- V_o : shear force carried by other than truss mechanism
- t_w : thickness of shear reinforcing steel plate

Substituting $(t_w s)\sin\alpha$ with A_w in Eq.(2), the following equation without spacing of s is derived.

$$V = \sin^2\alpha(\cot\theta+\cot\alpha)zt_w\sigma_w +V_o \qquad (3)$$

Previous test results[11][12][13] indicate that angles to member axis of the principal tensile strains in shear reinforcing steel plate range between 40° and 60° and are more or less normal to that of the principal compressive strains in core concrete. In general this angles become greater for a portion closer to the compression end. This implies that the principal strains contain flexural strains. Since many measuring points for strains are below the neutral axis, it is considered that the angles of the principal tensile strains excluding flexural strains would be greater. In Eq.(2), therefore, the angle is assumed to be 60°.

For prediction of the capacity of the truss mechanism, two cases of failure of concrete diagonal strut before and after yielding of shear reinforcing steel plate are considered separately. Since stress flow in core concrete is similar to that in an ordinary reinforced concrete linear member with narrowly and uniformly spaced shear reinforcement, it is considered that the ultimate capacity when concrete diagonal strut fails before yielding of shear reinforcing steel plate can be predicted by a similar way for an ordinary reinforced concrete member. However, shear stress component of the principal compressive stresses in shear reinforcing steel plate contributes additionally to the ultimate shear capacity, which can be expressed by Eq.(4).

$$V_{u1o} = f_{vu} b_w d + V_w \tag{4}$$

where f_{vu} : shear strength of diagonal compression strut of core concrete, which is the maximum of $1.25f'_c{}^{1/2}$ and $0.188f'_c{}^{1/2} \beta_d \beta_p \beta_s$
  V_w : shear force carried by shear reinforcing steel plate as other than diagonal tension strut in truss mechanism
  $\beta_s = 5/(1+\cot^2\theta)$
  θ : angle to member axis of concrete diagonal compression strut, which is the maximum of $30°$ and $\cot^{-1}(a/z)$

The shear strength of diagonal compression strut of core concrete is equal to that of an ordinary reinforced concrete linear member (diagonal compression strength), or may be taken as $0.188f'_c{}^{1/2} \beta_d \beta_p \beta_s$ which is the shear strength for a small shear span to effective depth ratio when the latter value is greater than the former.

Although shear failure both after and before yielding of shear reinforcing steel plate looks similar, shear failure with yielding of shear reinforcing steel plate occurs before shear force reaches the shear capacity obtained by Eq.(4). In some cases shear failure occurs soon after yielding of shear reinforcing steel plate, so that it is preferable to predict shear capacity conservatively by shear force when yielding of shear reinforcing steel plate. For the shear capacity in this case Eq.(5) is derived by substituting the yield strength of shear reinforcing steel plate, f_{wy} with σ_w in Eq.(3)

$$V_{u2} = \sin^2\alpha(\cot\theta+\cot\alpha)zt_w f_{wy} + V_o \tag{5}$$

where f_{wy} : yield strength of shear reinforcing steel plate, which is not greater than 392.3 MPa

Table 1 shows the measured shear capacity in previous tests[9][11][12][14] and the calculated capacities by Eqs.(4) and (5), where V_w and V_o are assumed to be zero, and the upper limit of 1.5 for β values is neglected. The shear forces at yielding of shear reinforcing steel plate predicted by Eq.(5) are greater than the shear capacities without yielding of shear reinforcing steel plate predicted by Eq.(4) only for specimen FW60 and TP60, where failure occurred in the same way as diagonal compression failure in an ordinary reinforced concrete linear member. The measured capacities are much greater than those predicted by Eq.(4). Specimen TP60 in reference 11 was reinforced with the same amount of shear reinforcing steel plate with slits (tie plate) as in specimen FW60. For specimen TP60, therefore, the value of V_w should be zero. The measured shear capacity of TP60 which is much greater than that predicted by Eq.(4) implies conservativeness of the value, $1.25f'_c{}^{1/2}$. Difference between the measured and predicted shear capacities of FW60 is even greater. It clearly indicates existence of V_w in Eq.(4). For the other specimens in Table 1, shear forces at yielding of shear reinforcing steel plate predicted by Eq.(4) are less than those by Eq.(5). Accordingly yieldings were observed in those specimens. Except specimen W-I, the measured shear capacities are greater than those predicted by Eq.(5). This fact implies existence of V_o in Eq.(5). In general shear force carried by other than truss mechanism increases as shear span to effective depth ratio decreases, amount of shear reinforcing, compression or tension steel plate increases, and concrete strength increases.

For cases of shear reinforcing steel plate located parallel to member axis, there are only few experimental results on shear failure reported. Especially test results on shear failure without yielding of shear reinforcing steel plate are very limited. Further study is needed on reasonable evaluation of V_o and V_w.

Spacing normal to member axis of shear reinforcing steel plate affects confinement of core concrete by shear reinforcing steel plate. It is expected that capacity per unit member width of diagonal compression strut of core concrete as well as value per unit member width of shear force carried by other than truss mechanism, V_o decreases as the spacing increases. Figure 4 shows the results of test[11] where member width varies. Failure of members was caused by diagonal compression failure of core concrete. The shear capacity per unit member width decreases as the member width increases. Solid line predicting conservatively the test results is expressed by Eq.(6).

$$V_{u1} = k_m (V_{u1o} - V_{ua}) + V_{ua} \tag{6}$$

where $k_m = 1/(b_w/d)^{1/2}$ but ≤ 1.0

Table 1 also gives the predicted values by Eq.(6). For specimen FW60 and TP60 Eq.(6) gives the predicted capacity because the values predicted by Eq.(6) are less than those by Eq.(5). It can be seen that Eq.(6) estimates the measured capacities conservatively. Further study on effect of spacing normal to member axis on shear capacity is needed because of lack of experimental data.

Case of Shear Reinforcing Steel Plate Located Normal to Member Axis

Figure 5 shows shear reinforcing steel plate located in direction normal to member axis. Core concrete is separated completely by the shear reinforcing steel plate and there is generally no shear connector mounted on shear reinforcing steel plate. Therefore, force in core concrete is not transferred through shear reinforcing steel plate. The truss mechanism in this case also consists of diagonal tension strut of shear reinforcing steel plate diagonal compression strut of core concrete and upper chords of flexural compression zone, and lower chord of tension steel plate as shown in Fig.6. In the truss mechanism diagonal compression struts are formed discretely. This fact is different from cases of a sandwich structure with shear reinforcing steel plate located in member axis direction and an ordinary reinforced concrete linear member with shear reinforcement in which diagonal strut is uniformly spread over a shear span as shown in Fig.2. Angle of diagonal compression strut, θ is expressed as $\cot^{-1}((s-z \cot\alpha)/z)$ by spacing of shear reinforcing steel plate, s, arm length of truss mechanism, z, and angle of shear reinforcing steel plate to member axis, α. In Fig.6 $\theta = \cot^{-1}(s/z)$ because $\alpha = 90°$. Diagonal struts in core concrete are formed in the same manner even for a small ratio of shear span to effective depth (see Fig.7). The fact that a diagonal compression strut is formed between adjacent shear reinforcing steel plates means that the tensile force in shear reinforcing steel plate does not depend on its spacing, while the tensile forces in shear reinforcing steel plate located in member axis direction and shear reinforcing bar in an ordinary reinforced concrete linear member depend on their spacings.

From the foregoing discussion, it can be said that Eq.(2) also represents the shear resisting mechanism in this case.

$$V = \sin\alpha(\cot\theta + \cot\alpha)(z/s)A_w \sigma_w + V_o \tag{2}$$

673

where α = angle of shear reinforcing steel plate to member axis
         θ = $\cot^{-1}((s-z\cot\alpha)/z)$
              : angle of concrete diagonal compression strut to member axis
         s : spacing of shear reinforcing steel plate
         A_w = $t_w b_w$
              : cross-sectional area of shear reinforcing steel plate

Usually shear reinforcing steel plate is located in a plane normal to member axis (α=90°), so that Eq.(2) becomes a simple equation as follows

$$V = A_w \sigma_w + V_o \qquad (7)$$

As in the case of shear reinforcing steel plate in direction of member axis, the capacity of this truss mechanism is determined by failure of strut in core concrete which takes place either before or after yielding of shear reinforcing steel plate as diagonal tension strut. When failure of diagonal compression strut takes place before yielding, sandwich structure between shear reinforcing steel plates fails as sandwich structure without shear reinforcing steel plate. The capacity can be predicted by assuming that the part between shear reinforcing steel plates is sandwich structure without shear reinforcing steel plate (see Fig.8). Thus Eq.(8) gives the capacity

$$V_{u1} = f_{vu} b_w d \qquad (8)$$

where f_{vu} = the maximum of $0.191 f'_c{}^{1/3} \beta_d \beta_p \beta_n k$ and $0.188 f'_c{}^{1/2} \beta_d \beta_p \beta_s$
         β_s = $5/(1+\cot^2\theta)$
         θ = $\cot^{-1}((s-z\cot\alpha)/z)$
              : angle of concrete diagonal compression strut to member axis

Failure of diagonal compression strut after yielding of shear reinforcing steel plate looks similar to that before yielding. However failure occurs at shear force less than the capacity predicted by Eq.(8) and may occur soon after yielding. Therefore, it is preferable to predict the shear capacity conservatively by shear force at yielding of shear reinforcing steel plate. Thus Eq.(9) is derived from Eq.(2) by substituting σ_w with f_{wy}.

$$V_{u2} = \sin\alpha(\cot\theta+\cot\alpha)(z/s)A_w f_{wy} + V_o \qquad (9)$$

When α = 90°, Eq.(9) is rewritten as follows

$$V_{u2} = A_w f_{wy} + V_o \qquad (10)$$

     Table 2 shows comparison between measured capacities in previous tests[9][10][15][16] and calculated ones by Eqs.(8) and (9), where V_o = 0 is assumed and upper limit of β(=1.5) is neglected. Since data[16] which are considered as flexural failure are eliminated, all the measured capacities in the table are less than predicted flexural capacities. In some specimens it was observed that tension steel plate yielded in flexure. Specimen MAR1-right is the case where diagonal compression strut in core concrete fails before any yielding of shear reinforcing or tension steel plate. This fact agrees with the fact that the shear force at yielding of shear reinforcing steel plate calculated by Eq.(9) (or Eq.(10)) is greater than the capacity of diagonal compression strut calculated by Eq.(8). The measured capacity of specimen MAR1-right is greater by about 10% than the capacity predicted by Eq.(8). For all other specimens the capacities predicted by Eq.(9)(or Eq.(10)) are less than those by Eq.(8), so that it is predicted that shear failure would take place after yielding of shear reinforcing steel plate. Actually yielding was observed except for specimen SDR. Except specimen CBSO-PC-3-1-1, the measured capacities which are much less than those

674

predicted by Eq.(8) indicate that Eq.(8) overestimates capacities when shear reinforcing steel plate yields. Since the measured capacities are much greater than capacities predicted by Eq.(9)(or Eq.(10)) where shear force carried by other than truss mechanism, V_o is neglected, it can be said that there is significant contribution of V_o. Although there is lack of data to quantify V_o at present, a value of V_o seems to be greater for a thicker tension and compression steel plate and a narrower spacing of shear reinforcing steel plate. A large ratio of shear span to effective depth and high concrete strength are considered to increase V_o as well. Specimen SDWR-right with 4% of tension steel plate ratio and 1.7 of spacing to member height is seemingly the case of the least contribution of V_o. Its measured capacity is greater by nearly 20% than the predicted one. Despite of yielding of shear reinforcing steel plate in specimen CBSO-PC-3-1-1, difference between the measured and predicted capacities is much greater than those for the other specimens. Thickness of tension and compression steel plate, 24.4 mm which is much greater than for the other specimens is considered to be the reason.

It can be said from the above comparison with the previous experimental results that Eqs.(8) and (9) (or Eq.(10)) can predict shear capacities reasonably and conservatively.

Shear Reinforcing Steel Plates Located Both Parallel to and Normal to Member Axis

When shear reinforcing steel plates are located both parallel to and normal to member axis, truss mechanism can be formed by either of the shear reinforcing steel plates. It can be considered that the shear capacity of member is equal to the maximum of capacities with the two truss mechanisms. Let us consider separately two cases: a large ratio of spacing of shear reinforcing steel plate to member height (Fig.9(a)) and a small ratio (Fig.9(b)). For a large ratio, diagonal compression strut in core concrete is inclined at around 30° and spread uniformly when the capacity of truss mechanism by shear reinforcing steel plate in member axis direction is greater (the upper in Fig.9(a)). When the capacity of truss mechanism by shear reinforcing steel plate normal to member axis is greater, diagonal strut is formed along a diagonal line between shear reinforcing steel plates (the lower in Fig.9(a)). For a small ratio of spacing of shear reinforcing steel plate to member axis as shown in Fig.9(b), diagonal strut is always formed along a diagonal line between shear reinforcing steel plates. The shear capacities in this case can be obtained by assuming that shear span is equal to spacing of shear reinforcing steel plate normal to member axis.

There has been no report on the shear capacity with shear reinforcing steel plates both parallel to and normal to member axis. It is necessary to conduct study on this urgently.

CONCLUDING REMARKS

It is observed that shear resisting mechanism in sandwich structure with shear reinforcing steel plates located parallel or normal to member axis is truss-like mechanism. Based on the observed truss mechanism prediction equations for shear capacities of sandwich structure as linear member are presented for both cases with and without shear reinforcing steel plates. The equations can predict the experimental results reasonably and conservatively, and are adopted in the JSCE Proposed Design Code of Steel-Concrete Sandwich Structure.

ACKNOWLEDGEMENT

The author wishes to express his gratitude to members of the JSCE Research Subcommittee on Steel-Concrete Sandwich Structures, particularly to Prof H. Okamura (Chairman), Prof Y. Kakuta (Vice-Chairman), Mr N. Masui and Dr T. Shioya for their valuable advices. Sincere thanks are also extended to Dr Taweep C. for his constructive comments.

REFERENCES

1) Hasegawa, T. et al: Development of Steel/Concrete Composite Members for Arctic Offshore Structures, Technical Research Report of Shimizu Corporation, No.45, April 1987, pp.15-25 (in Japanese).
2) Akiyama, H. et al: Strength of Steel/Concrete Composite Sandwich Member, Proc of the Japan Concrete Institute (JCI), Vol.8, 1986, pp.605-608 (in Japanese).
3) Ogawa, Y. et al: On the Strength of Composite Steel-Concrete Deep Beams of Sandwich System, Journal of the Society of Naval Architects of Japan, No. 160, November 1986, pp.415-423 (in Japanese).
4) Shioya, T. et al: Some Examinations on Shear Property of Steel/Concrete Composite Structures, Proc of The 2nd Symposium on Research and Application of Composite Constructions, JSCE, September 1989, pp.157-162 (in Japanese).
5) Akiyama, H. et al: Ultimate Strength of Steel/Concrete Composite Sandwich Structures, Proc of Symposium on Research and Application of Composite Constructions, JSCE, September 1986, pp.69-74 (in Japanese).
6) Ozawa, K. et al: Shear Resisting Mechanism of a Composite Member with Steel and Concrete, Transactions of JCI, Vol.8, 1986, pp.295-302.
7) Takeuchi, H. and Kato, K.: Shear Transfer between Steel and Concrete in Composite Structure, Proc of JCI, Vo. 9-2, 1987, pp.537-542 (in Japanese).
8) Yokota, H. and Kiyomiya, O.: Effect of Shear Reinforcement on the Ultimate Strength of Steel-Concrete Hybrid Beams, Proc of JCI, Vo.9-2, 1987, pp.531-536 (in Japanese).
9) Hasegawa, T. and Shioya, T.: Experimental Report, OS-SHEL Project, Experiment with Small Specimen, Phase II - Shear Test, Institute of Technology, Shimizu Corporation, September 1987 (in Japanese).
10) Ueda, T. et al: Ultimate Shear Strength of Sandwich Concrete-Steel Composite Beam, Proc of The 2nd Symposium on Research and Application of Composite Constructions, JSCE, September 1989, pp.143-148 (in Japanese).
11) Tasumi, Y. et al: Ultimate Shear Strength of Sandwich Concrete-Steel Beams, Proc of JSCE Hokkaido Branch, No.48, February 1992, pp.891-896 (in Japanese).
12) Ozawa, K.: Shear Resisting Mechanism of a Composite Member with Steel and Concrete, Master Thesis, University of Tokyo, 1986 (in Japanese).
13) Masui, N. et al: Experimental Data Analysis of Steel Plates in TYPE-1 and 2, Document for Research Subcommittee on Steel-Concrete Sandwich Structure, JSCE, December 1991 (in Japanese).
14) Shioya, T. et al: Experimental Data, Document for Research Subcommittee on Steel-Concrete Sandwich Structure, JSCE, December 1991 (in Japanese).
15) Kawamura, Y.: Shear Behavior of a Composite Member with Steel and Concrete, Master Thesis, University of Tokyo, 1988 (in Japanese).
16) Suhara, T. et al: On the Strength of Composite Steel-Concrete Structures of Sandwich System (1st-3rd Report), Journal of the Society of Naval Architects of Japan, No.141, May 1977, pp.205-216, No.142, November 1977, pp.312-322, No.145, May 1979, pp.164-175 (in Japanese).
17) Ueda, T. and Pantaratorn, N.: An Analytical Investigation of Sandwich Composite Beams in Shear, Proc of the Third International Conference on Steel-Concrete Composite Structures, September 1991, Fukuoka, Japan, pp.521-526.

Specimen	b_w	h	f'_c	A_s	f_{sy}	t_w	f_{wy}	a	$V_{u,exp}$ [1]	$V_{u1o,cal}$ [2]	$V_{u1,cal}$ [3]	$V_{u2,cal}$ [4]	Yield	Ref. [5]
	mm	mm	MPa	mm²	MPa	mm	MPa	mm	kN	kN	kN	kN		
A-I	1300	270	26.8	5759	372.7	3.12	274.6	862.5	652	2256.2	1203.0	390.8	F S	12)
A-II	1300	270	27.0	5754	372.7	3.12	274.6	862.5	593	2264.6	1207.2	390.8	F S	12)
S-I	1300	270	33.9	5109	337.3	2.7	409.0	862.5	530	2542.4	1340.6	505.1	F S	12)
W-I	1300	270	29.3	5109	337.3	5.6	329.8	862.5	652	2363.4	1250.4	844.8	F S	12)
CBS0-PZ-1-2-1	400	200	57.93	2600	438.5	6.16	321.5	200	1289.0	750.3	704.8	460.1	F S	9)
TYPE-1	1000	800	38.61	32000	316.8	6.0	296.0	2800	2972.9<	6102.2	5501.8	2312.9	F S	14)
TYPE-2	625	500	36.20	13750	329.9	4.5	326.5	1750	1233.2<	2303.1	2081.3	1188.3	F S	14)
FW60	600	150	12.0	7200	371.9	8.0	347.6	480	728<	374.3	246.8	635.9	F S	11)
TP60[6]	600	150	15.0	7200	371.9	16.0	347.6	480	578	419.1	273.8	635.9[7]	- S	11)

1) Calculated by Eq.(4) with V_w = 0. The upper limit of β, which is 1.5, is not considered.
2) Calculated by Eq.(6).
3) Calculated by Eq.(5) with V_o = 0.
4) F = flexural yielding
   S = shear yielding
5) Reference number
6) Shear reinforcing plate is with slits (tie-plate type).
7) Calculated by Eq.(9) with V_o = 0, θ = 30°, α = 90°, s = 80 mm and A_w = 640 mm².

Table 2 Shear capacity with shear reinforcing steel plate located
normal to member axis

Specimen	b_w	h	f'_c	A_s	f_{sy}	A_w	f_{wy}	s	a	$V_{u,exp}$ [1]	$V_{u1,cal}$ [2]	$V_{u2,cal}$ [3]	Yield	Ref. [4]
	mm	mm	MPa	mm²	MPa	mm²	MPa	mm	mm	kN	kN	kN		
SDR	100	300	33.7	1200	319.7	160	297.2	375	1500	70.1	125.7	47.6	- -	15)
SDW-right	100	300	32.4	1200	319.7	160	297.2	375	1500	72.6	125.0	47.6	- S	15)
SDWR-right	100	300	35.9	1200	319.7	160	297.2	500	1500	56.4	86.7	47.6	- S	15)
MAR1-right	100	200	34.6	900	273.6	320	274.0	350	700	67.4	59.7	87.7	- -	10)
MAR3-middle	100	200	31.9	900	273.6	230	274.0	200	400	102.0	120.7	63.1	- S	10)
NO.4-left	103	200	36.9	958	318.7	160	343.0	250	700	86.2	103.0	54.9	F S	10)
NO.4-right	103	200	36.9	958	318.7	160	343.0	100	700	86.2	225.5	54.9	F S	10)
CBS0-PC-3-1-1	200	200	51.24	4878	334.6	320	189.3	200	600	377.6	361.1	60.6	F S	9)

1) Calculated by Eq.(8). The upper limit of β, which is 1.5, is not considered.
2) Calculated by Eq.(9) (or Eq.(10)) with V_o = 0.
3) F : flexural yielding
   S : shear yielding
4) Reference number

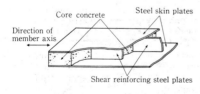

Fig.1 Shear reinforcing steel
plate located parallel to
member axis

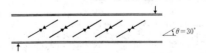

Fig.2 Shear resisting mechanism
with shear reinforcing steel
plate located parallel to
member axis

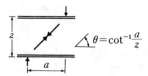

Fig.3　Shear resisting mechanism
with shear reinforcing steel
plate located parallel to
member axis (for a small ratio
of shear span to member height)

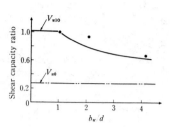

Fig.4　Influence of member width
on shear capacity

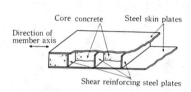

Fig.5　Shear reinforcing steel
plate located normal to
member axis

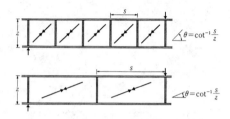

Fig.6　Shear resisting mechanism
with shear reinforcing steel
located normal to member axis

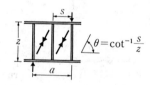

Fig.7　Shear resisting mechanism
with shear reinforcing steel
plate located normal to member
axis (for a small ratio of
shear span to member height)

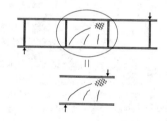

Fig.8　Shear failure with shear reinforcing steel plate located
normal to member axis

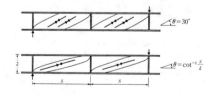

(a) Case for a large ratio of
spacing of shear reinforcing
steel plate to member height

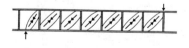

(b) Case for a small ratio of
spacing of shear reinforcing
steel plate to member height

Fig.9　Shear resisting mechanism with shear reinforcing steel plates
located both parallel to and normal to member axis

ADVANCED COMPOSITE MATERIALS IN BRIDGES AND STRUCTURES
K.W. Neale and P. Labossière, Editors; Canadian Society for Civil Engineering, 1992

Matériaux composites d'avant-garde pour ponts et charpentes
K.W. Neale et P. Labossière, éditeurs; Société canadienne de génie civil, 1992

PROPOSED JAPANESE DESIGN CODE FOR STEEL–CONCRETE SANDWICH STRUCTURES

H. Okamura
University of Tokyo
Tokyo, Japan

Y. Kakuta and **T. Ueda**
Hokkaido University
Sapporo, Japan

ABSTRACT

The proposed Design Code for Steel–Concrete Sandwich Structures, which was specified for the first time in Japan, is presented. This structure is defined as a composite structure in which core concrete is sandwiched by steel skin plates. The limit state design method is applied in the code. The ultimate member capacities for axial, flexural and shear forces are newly given.

RÉSUMÉ

On présente le Code japonais pour le dimensionnement des structures sandwich acier-béton, dans lesquelles le noyau de béton est compris entre des plaques d'acier. On emploie la méthode du calcul aux états limites pour calculer la résistance des sections sous des charges axiales, de flexion et de cisaillement.

INTRODUCTION

Recently various composite structures have been seen in Japan. One of them is steel-concrete sandwich structure, which has been applied to continuous underground wall, submerged tunnel, culvert, etc. No rational design method, however, had been developed for the sandwich structure. Previous studies indicate that the ultimate member capacities of the sandwich structure in flexure and shear cannot be predicted by the conventional methods for steel and concrete structures. Considering those circumstances, Japan Society of Civil Engineers (JSCE) established Research Subcommittee on Steel-Concrete Sandwich Structures in 1990, which was sponsored by Niju-Kokaku Kozo Kenkyukai (Association of Double Steel Skin Plate Structures) in Japan.

After intensive works in the Subcommittee for one and a half year to gather latest results of studies on the sandwich structures as well as to conduct its large scale tests, the Subcommittee presented "Proposed Design Code on Steel-Concrete Sandwich Structures" in April 1992.

PROPOSED DESIGN CODE

Proposed Design Code of Steel-Concrete Sandwich Structure contains the following chapters: 1. General, 2. General Requirements, 3. Design Values for Materials, 4. Loads, 5. Structural Analysis, 6. Limit States, and 7. Structural Details.

General

In this chapter, the steel-concrete sandwich structure is defined as a composite structure with full composite action in which core concrete is sandwiched by steel skin plates as shown in Fig.1. Although this design code is described considering the case in which the sandwich structural member is applied to submerged box structure as shown in Fig.2, the sandwich structure may be applied to other structures as well.

Design requirements other than specified in this code is to be based on JSCE Standard Specification for Design and Construction of Concrete Structures and Design Code for Steel Structures.

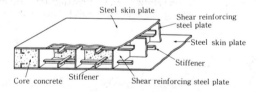

Fig.1 Steel-concrete sandwich structure

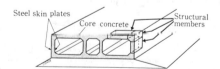

Fig.2 Steel-concrete sandwich structure applied to submerged box structure

Table 1 Standard values for safety factors

	Material factors		Member factors		Structural analysis factors	Load factors	Structural importance factors
	Concrete	Steel	Flexure	Shear			
During construction							
ULS[1] for S.S.[2]	—	1.05	1.1	1.1	1.0	1.0	1.0
SLS[1] for S.S.	—	1.0	1.0	1.0	1.0	1.0	1.0
ULS for C.S.[2]	1.3	1.05	1.15	1.15~1.3[3]	1.0	1.0~1.2[4]	1.0
SLS for C.S.	1.0	1.0	1.0	1.0	1.0	1.0	1.0
During service							
ULS	1.3	1.05	1.15	1.15~1.3[3]	1.0	1.0~1.2[4]	1.1
SLS	1.0	1.0	1.0	1.0	1.0	1.0	1.0

1) ULS : ultimate limit state, SLS : serviceability limit state
2) S.S.: steel structure (before composite action starts)
   C.S.: composite structure
3) Values are to be multiplied by 1.2 when effect of earthquake is considered.
4) Values are to be 1.0~1.2 for permanent loads, 1.1~1.2 for primary variable loads
   and 1.0 for secondary variable loads and accidental loads.

General Requirements

As prerequisite of design, it is noted that special attention to concreting is necessary because concrete is cast in a space enclosed by steel plates. At the same time it is pointed out that design details should be chosen so that the space enclosed by steel plates would be filled by concrete.

Standard values for safety factors are recommended as shown in Table 1.

Design Values for Materials

Design values for concrete and steel are specified in JSCE Standard Specification of Concrete Structures and Design Code for Steel Structures respectively.

Loads

Specifications for loads are based on JSCE Standard Specification of Concrete Structures. It is emphasized that loading actions during construction may be most severe for steel structure which has not been compounded with core concrete.

Structural Analysis

Structural analysis is said to follow JSCE Standard Specification of Concrete Structures.

Limit States

Ultimate Limit States during Construction

Ultimate limit states for steel structure, which has not been compounded with core concrete, can be examined in the same way as ordinary steel structure following JSCE Design Code for Steel Structures. After composite action starts, examinations of ultimate limit state will be the same as those during service.

Serviceability Limit States during Construction

Examinations for deflection of steel structure and sandwich structure are to be made according to JSCE Design Code for Steel Structures and the section concerning serviceability limit state during service in this code. Excessive deflections of steel plates may be harmful to sandwich structure during service.

Ultimate Limit States during Service

a) Flexural Moment and Axial Force

Ultimate capacity of member subjected to flexural moment and axial force can be calculated similarly to that of an ordinary reinforced concrete member. Strains of core concrete and steel plates are proportional to distances of considered points from neutral axis. Concrete stress in tension is neglected and rectangle stress block is assumed in compression. Stress-strain curves of steel skin plate in tension and compression are as shown in Fig.3. Considering local buckling of skin plate, stress limit in compression, f'_{ud} is given as follows

$$f'_{ud} = (t_f/b)(E_s f'_{yd})^{1/2} \qquad (1)$$

where f'_{ud} : design compressive strength of compression steel skin plate after local buckling
t_f : thickness of compression steel skin plate
b : spacing of stiffener parallel to member axis for compression steel skin plate (see Fig.4)
E_s : modulus of elasticity of compression steel skin plate
f'_{yd} : design yield strength in compression of steel skin plate

Stiffener for steel skin plate may be considered as tension or compression reinforcing steel. It can be considered, however, that buckling of stiffener would not take place. Shear reinforcing steel plate located in parallel to member axis may be also considered as tension or compression

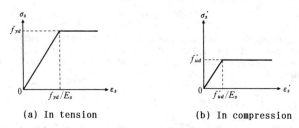

| (a) In tension | (b) In compression |

Fig.3 Stress-strain curves of steel skin plates

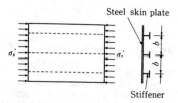

Fig.4 Spacing of stiffener

reinforcing steel plate. The yield strength of shear reinforcing steel plate as tension and compression reinforcing steel plate should be reduced by considering effect of stress as shear reinforcement.

$$f_{eyd} = f_{wyd}(1-\sigma_w/f_{wyd}) \tag{2}$$

$$f'_{eyd} = f'_{wyd}(1-\sigma_w/f_{wyd}) \tag{3}$$

where f_{eyd}, f'_{eyd} : design yield strengths in tension and compression of shear reinforcing steel plate used as tension and compression reinforcing steel plate

f_{wyd}, f'_{wyd} : design yield strengths in tension and compression of shear reinforcing steel plate, and not greater than 392.3 MPa

σ_w : tensile stress in shear reinforcing steel plate acting as shear reinforcing steel plate (≥ 0)

b) Shear Force

Shear capacities as a linear member are given for the following four cases:
(1) no shear reinforcing steel plate
(2) shear reinforcing steel plate located in direction of member axis
(3) shear reinforcing steel plate located in direction normal to member axis
(4) shear reinforcing steel plate located in both directions parallel and normal to member axis
The shear capacity in the case of no reinforcing steel plate can be calculated in a similar way to that of an ordinary reinforced linear member.

$$V_{u\theta d} = f_{vcd}\ b_w d/\gamma_{b1} \tag{4}$$

where f_{vcd} : design shear strength in the case of no shear reinforcing steel plate
b_w : member web width
d : effective depth
γ_{b1} : member factor (=1.3)

The design shear strength, f_{vcd} can be obtained by the formula for either slender or deep beam of ordinary reinforced concrete. Reduction of shear cracking strength due to shear connector on skin plate is only the point different from shear capacity of ordinary reinforced concrete.
In the case of shear reinforcing steel plate located only in direction of member axis (see Fig.5), the minimum of

$$V_{u1d} = k_m (V_{u1od}-V_{u\theta d})+V_{u\theta d} \tag{5}$$

or

$$V_{u2d} = \sin^2\alpha(\cot\theta+\cot\alpha)t_w z f_{wyd}/\gamma_{b2} +V_{od} \tag{6}$$

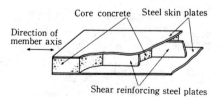

Fig.5 Shear reinforcing steel plate located
in direction of member axis

683

is to be shear capacity, where

$$V_{u1od} = f_{vud} \ b_w d/\gamma_{b1} \tag{7}$$

where k_m : coefficient for influence of spacing in direction normal to member axis of shear reinforcing steel plate on shear capacity

        $k_m = 1/(b_w/d)^{1/2}$ but <1.0

     f_{vud} : design shear strength at failure of diagonal compression strut in truss mechanism

       α : angle to member axis of diagonal tension strut in shear reinforcing steel plate for truss mechanism (=60°)

       θ : angle to member axis of diagonal compression concrete strut, the maximum of 30° and $\cot^{-1}(a/z)$

      t_w : thickness of shear reinforcing steel plate

      z : truss arm length

    γ_{b2} : member factor (=1.15)

    V_{od} : design shear capacity carried by other than truss mechanism at ultimate

    b_w : member web width, which is spacing of shear reinforcing steel plate

Eq.(5) gives shear capacity when diagonal compression concrete strut fails and Eq.(6) gives that when diagonal tension strut yields. Both of them indicate collapse of truss mechanism. The shear capacity given by Eq.(5) decreases as spacing of shear reinforcing steel plate increases. The shear strength, f_{vud} is equal to that when diagonal strut fails in an ordinary reinforced concrete linear member with heavy shear reinforcement.

    Similarly shear capacity in the case of shear reinforcing steel plate located only in direction normal to member axis (see Fig.6) can be obtained as the minimum of

$$V_{u1d} = f_{vud} b_w d/\gamma_{b1} \tag{8}$$

or

$$V_{u2d} = \sin\alpha(\cot\theta+\cot\alpha)A_w f_{wyd}(z/s)/\gamma_{b2}+V_{od} \tag{9}$$

where f_{vud} : design shear strength when diagonal compressive concrete strut fails

     A_w : cross-sectional area of shear reinforcing steel plate (=$t_w b_w$)

      θ : angle to member axis of diagonal compression concrete strut, the maximum of $\cot^{-1}((s-z \cot\alpha)/z)$ and $\cot^{-1}(a/z)$

    The shear strength, f_{vud} in this case is equivalent to that of an ordinary reinforced concrete linear member with a/d = $\cot\theta$ which is calculated in Eq.(9). Namely a part of sandwich structure between adjacent shear reinforcing steel plates is considered as sandwich structure without shear reinforcing steel plate.

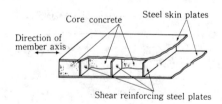

Fig.6 Shear reinforcing steel plate located in direction normal to member axis

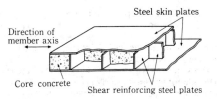

Direction of member axis

Steel skin plates

Core concrete

Shear reinforcing steel plates

Fig.7 Shear reinforcing steel plates located in both directions
parallel to and normal to member axis

When shear reinforcing steel plates are located in both directions
parallel to and normal to member axis (see Fig.7), shear capacity may be
obtained as the maximum of shear capacity calculated by considering only
shear reinforcing steel plate located in member axis direction and that by
considering only shear reinforcing steel plate in direction normal to member
axis.

c) Torsional Moment

Since there is no previous study on torsional capacity of sandwich
structure, the torsional capacity is conservatively evaluated to be equal to
torsional capacity of steel structure or that of core concrete.

Serviceability Limit States during Service

For examination of deflection limit state, reduction in cracking
strength due to shear connector should be considered.

Structural Details

Steel Plates

For steel plate except the parts directly touched with core concrete,
anti-corrosion measure should be taken.

Shear Reinforcing Steel Plate

Shear reinforcing steel plate should be anchored to steel skin plates
at its both ends.

Corner Connection

Steel skin plates and shear reinforcing steel plate in member axis
direction should be extended fully in corner connection, so that full member
capacities can be transferred at corner connection (see Fig.8).

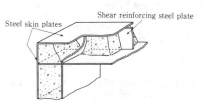

Steel skin plates

Shear reinforcing steel plate

Fig.8 Corner connection

Shear Connector

Shear connectors are to be located at appropriate intervals for full composite action. Equation(10) may be used to determine arrangement of shear connectors.

$$\gamma_i H_d \Big/ \sum_{i=1}^{N_{sc}} V_{scdi} \leq 1.0 \tag{10}$$

where　H_d : design shear force transferred between skin plate and core concrete at portion L

$H_d = t_f \sigma_f$

γ_i : structure importance factor

V_{scdi} : design shear capacity of individual shear connector

N_{sc} : total number of shear connectors at portion L

　L : portion between maximum flexural moment and zero flexural moment sections

t_f : thickness of skin plate at maximum flexural moment

σ_f : tensile stress in skin plate at maximum flexural moment section ($= f_{yd}(M_d/M_{ud})$)

M_d : design flexural moment at maximum flexural moment section

M_{ud} : design flexural capacity of maximum flexural moment section

Design shear capacity of shape steel may be calculated by Eq.(11).

$$V_{scd} = 5.59 h_{sc} W_{sc} f'^{1/2}_{cd} k_1 k_2 k_3 / \gamma_{b1} \tag{11}$$

but $\leq t_{sco} W_{sc} f_{scyd} / \sqrt{3} / \gamma_{b2}$

where　$k_1 = 2.2(t_{sc}/h_{sc})^{2/3}$ but ≤ 1.0

$k_2 = 0.4(t_f/t_{sc})^{1/2} + 0.43$ but ≤ 1.0

$k_3 = (s_{ch}/h_{sc}/10)^{1/2}$ but ≤ 1.0

f'_{cd} : design compressive concrete strength (in MPa)

h_{sc} : height of shear connector

W_{sc} : width of shear connector

t_{sco} : thickness of shear connector considering welding

f_{scyd} : design tensile yield strength of shear connector

t_{sc} : thickness of shear connector

s_{sc} : spacing of shear connector

γ_{b1} : member factor ($=1.3$)

γ_{b2} : member factor ($=1.15$)

γ_c : material factor for f'_{cd} ($=1.3$)

γ_s : material factor for f_{scyd} ($=1.05$)

Design shear capacity of shear reinforcing steel plate which is considered to be shear connector as well may be calculated by Eq.(12)

$$V_{scd} = t_{sco} W_{sc} f_{esd} / \gamma_{b2} \tag{12}$$

where $$f_{esd} = (f_{wyd}/\sqrt{3})(1 - \sigma_w/f_{wyd}) \tag{13}$$

Equation(12) indicates reduction in shear yield strength due to tensile stress acting as shear reinforcing steel plate.

Minimum Thickness of Steel Plates

In general minimum thickness is to be 8 mm.

Minimum Spacing of Steel Plates

Minimum spacing of steel plates should be determined so that concrete can be cast fully in spaces enclosed by steel plates.

Opening of Steel Plate

For construction, such as concreting, opening of steel plate is necessary. Size of opening should be minimum, and steel plate should be reinforced appropriately.

CONCLUDING REMARKS

JSCE Proposed Design Code of Steel-Concrete Sandwich Structure is the first comprehensive design code for composite structure, which is based on limit state design method. A trial design of submerged tunnel (JSCE Research Subcommittee) shows its competitiveness to reinforced concrete structure. English version of the proposed design code will be published in JSCE's Concrete Library International in December 1992.

ACKNOWLEDGEMENT

This paper has been written based on the report of the Research Subcommittee on Steel-Concrete Sandwich Structures of the Concrete Committee of the Japan Society of Civil Engineers (JSCE). The authors wish to express their thanks to the following members of the Subcommittee for their valuable contributions during the Subcommittee deliberations:

Research Subcommittee on Steel-Concrete Sandwich Structures

H. Okamura, Chairman   Y. Kakuta, Vice Chairman

T. Akimoto	N. Masui	I. Shimizu
R. Amano	S. Matsui	T. Shioya
M. Fujii	S. Matsumoto	K. Sonoda
T. Idemitsu	K. Minami	T. Tamura
S. Ikeda	T. Miura	T. Tanabe
Y. Imai	H. Mutsuyoshi	T. Ueda
H. Kawano	K. Nakajima	T. Uemura
O. Kiyomiya	H. Okamoto	H. Wakui
K. Kojima	H. Seki	H. Yokota
Y. Kumagai	T. Shima	O. Yoshikawa
A. Machida		

REFERENCE

JSCE Research Subcommittee on Steel-Concrete Sandwich Structures (1992). Proposed Design Code of Steel-Concrete Sandwich Structure. Concrete Library, Japan Society of Civil Engineers (JSCE) 73 (in Japanese).

Author Affiliations and Addresses

Affiliation et adresse des auteurs

K. Ando
ESI Asia
7-2-301, Oyama-chou
Shibuya-ku
Tokyo 151
Japan

T. Aoki
Institute of Engineering Mechanics
University of Tsukuba
1-1-1, Tennoudai, Tsukuba-shi
Ibaraki 305
Japan

C.A. Ballinger
Craig Ballinger & Associates
314 Ayito Rd. SE
Vienna, VA 22180-5983
USA

L.C. Bank
Department of Civil Engineering
The Catholic University of America
Washington, DC 20064
USA

D. Beaulieu
Département de génie civil
Université Laval
Ste-Foy, Québec G1K 7P4
Canada

G. Bélanger
C.E.M.P. Bélanger Ltée
C.P. 610
St-Germain-de-Grantham, Québec
Canada JOC 1K0

B. Benmokrane
Département de génie civil
Université de Sherbrooke
Sherbrooke, Québec J1K 2R1
Canada

L. Boire
Recherche en technologies
du réseau extérieur
Bell Canada
1818, Montée Ste-Julie
Varennes, Québec J3X 1T1
Canada

C.J. Burgoyne
Engineering Department
Cambridge University
Trumpington Street
Cambridge CB2 1PZ
UK

F. Buyle-Bodin
Département de génie civil
I.U.T.B.
Rue du Moulin-à-Tabac
62408 Béthune Cédex
France

J.-C. Carrière
Équipements de transport
Hydro-Québec
855, rue Ste-Catherine Est
Montréal, Québec H2L 4P5
Canada

O. Chaallal
Département de génie civil
Université de Sherbrooke
Sherbrooke, Québec J1K 2R1
Canada

M. Convain
Cousin Frères s.a.
B.P. 39
59117 Wervicq-Sud
France

B. Currie
Department of Civil Engineering
and Transport
University of Ulster at Jordanstown
Newtonabbey, Antrim BT37 0QB
Northern Ireland

S. Daniali
Department of Civil Engineering
Lamar University
P.O. Box 10024
Beaumont, TX 77710
USA

J. F. Davalos
College of Engineering
P.O. Box 6101
West Virginia University
Morgantown, WV 26506-6101
USA

M. Deblois
Département de génie civil
Université Laval
Ste-Foy, Québec G1K 7P4
Canada

M. Deuring
Swiss Federal Laboratories for
Materials Testing and Research
EMPA
Üeberlandstraße 129
CH-8600 Dübendorf
Switzerland

J.S. Ellis
Department of Civil Engineering
Royal Military College of Canada
Kingston, Ontario K7K 5L0
Canada

F. Ellyin
Department of Mechanical Engineering and
Advanced Engineered Materials Centre
University of Alberta
Edmonton, Alberta T6G 2G8
Canada

M.-A. Erki
Department of Civil Engineering
Royal Military College of Canada
Kingston, Ontario K7K 5L0
Canada

M. Faoro
SICOM GmbH
Grembergerstraße 151 a
D-5000 Köln 91
Germany

S.S. Faza
Constructed Facilities Center
West Virginia University
Morgantown, WV 26506-6101
USA

D.W. Fowler
Department of Civil Engineering
University of Texas
Austin, TX 78712
USA

T. Fujisaki
Shimizu Corporation
Seavans South
2-3, Shibaura 1-chome, Minato-ku
Tokyo 105-07
Japan

E. Fyfe
Fyfe Associates, Inc.
1341 Ocean Avenue
Del Mar, CA 92014
USA

H.V.S. GangaRao
Constructed Facilities Center
West Virginia University
Morgantown, WV 26506-6101
USA

A. Gerritse
Hollandsche Beton Groep nv
General Spoortlaan 489
2285 TA Rijswijk
The Netherlands

C.H. Goodspeed
Department of Civil Engineering
University of New Hampshire
Durham, NH 03824
USA

G. Goss
E.T. Techtonics
2117 Tryon Street
Philadelphia, PA 19146
USA

P. Hamelin
Laboratoire Mécanique et Matériaux
U.C.B. Lyon - I.U.T.A. Génie Civil
43, boul. du 11 novembre 1918
69622 Villeurbanne Cédex
France

Ch. Hankers
Institut für Baustoffe
Massivbau und Brandschutz
Beethovenstraße 52
D-3300 Braunschweig
Germany

M.W. Hargrave
Federal Highway Administration
Turner-Fairbank Highway Research Center
6300 Georgetown Pike
McLean, VA 22101-2296
USA

T.G. Harmon
Department of Civil Engineering
Campus Box 1130
Washington University
One Brookings Drive
St. Louis, MO 63130
USA

K. Hasuo
Technical Research Institute
Mitsui Construction Co. Ltd.
3-10-1, Iwamoto-cho, Chiyoda-ku
Tokyo 101
Japan

P. Head
Maunsell Structural Plastics Ltd.
Yeaman House
160 Croydon Road
Beckenham, Kent BR3 4DE
UK

S.V. Hoa
Department of Mechanical Engineering
Concordia University
1455 de Maisonneuve Blvd. West
Montréal, Québec H3G 1M8
Canada

H. Hodhod
Institute of Industrial Science
University of Tokyo
22-1 Roppongi, 7-chome, Minato-ku
Tokyo 106
Japan

J. Ida
Tokai Concrete Industrial Co. Ltd.
10, Shionagi-cho, Minato-ku
Nagoya
Japan

S.L. Iyer
Department of Civil Engineering
South Dakota School of Mines & Technology
Rapid City, SD 57701
USA

P. Jodin
Laboratoire de Fiabilité Mécanique
Faculté des Sciences
Université de Metz
57045 Metz
France

G.E. Johansen
E.T. Techtonics
2117 Tryon Street
Philadelphia, PA 19146
USA

S. Kaci
Institut de génie civil
Université de Tizi-Ouzou
Tizi-Ouzou 15000
Algérie

Y. Kakuta
Department of Civil Engineering
Hokkaido University
Sapporo 060
Japan

G.N. Karam
Department of Civil Engineering
Massachusetts Institute of Technology
Cambridge, MA 02139
USA

K. Katawaki
Public Works Research Institute
Ministry of Construction
Government of Japan
1, Asahi, Tsukuba-shi
Ibaraki-ken 305
Japan

Y. Kawamoto
Engineering Department
P.S. Corporation
Chiyoda-ku
Tokyo 101
Japan

M.A. Khalifa
Department of Civil Engineering
University of Nebraska-Lincoln
W348 Nebraska Hall
Lincoln, NE 68588-0531
USA

A. Khubchandani
Department of Civil Engineering
South Dakota School of Mines
and Technology
Rapid City, SD 57701
USA

D.H. Kim
Korea Composites
98 Gugi-Dong, Chongro-Gu
Seoul 110-011
Korea

Y. Kobayashi
Structure Mechanics Division
Ship Research Institute
Ministry of Transport
6-38-1, Shinkawa, Mitaka
Tokyo 181
Japan

M. Koga
Civil Engineering Technical Division
Obayashi Corporation
3-20, Kanda Nishikicho
Chiyoda-ku
Tokyo 101
Japan

M. König
Institut für Massivbau
Technical University Darmstadt
Alexanderstraße 5
D-6100 Darmstadt
Germany

D. Kujawski
Department of Mechanical Engineering and
Advanced Engineered Materials Centre
University of Alberta
Edmonton, Alberta T6G 2G8
Canada

S. Kumagai
Civil Engineering Department
Sumitomo Construction Co. Ltd.
13-4, Araki-cho Shinjyuku-ku
Tokyo 160
Japan

P. Labossière
Département de génie civil
Université de Sherbrooke
Sherbrooke, Québec J1K 2R1
Canada

K. Marran
E.T. Techtonics
2117 Tryon Street
Philadelphia, PA 19146
USA

R. Masmoudi
Département de génie civil
Université de Sherbrooke
Sherbrooke, Québec J1K 2R1
Canada

S. Matsubara
Technical Research Institute
Mitsui Construction Co. Ltd.
3-10-1, Iwamoto-cho, Chiyoda-ku
Tokyo 101
Japan

G. McClure
Department of Civil Engineering
and Applied Mechanics
McGill University
817 Sherbrooke Street West
Montréal, Québec H3A 2K6
Canada

K.S. McKay
Department of Civil Engineering
Royal Military College of Canada
Kingston, Ontario K7K 5L0
Canada

R.M. Measures
Institute for Aerospace Studies
University of Toronto
4925 Dufferin Street
Downsview, Ontario M3H 5T6
Canada

H. Meier
Swiss Federal Laboratories for
Materials Testing and Research
EMPA
Ueberlandstraße 129
CH-8600 Dübendorf
Switzerland

U. Meier
Swiss Federal Laboratories for
Materials Testing and Research
EMPA
Ueberlandstraße 129
CH-8600 Dübendorf
Switzerland

J. Mellen
E.T. Techtonics
2117 Tryon Street
Philadelphia, PA 19146
USA

J. Mizutani
Civil Engineering Department
Sumitomo Construction Co. Ltd.
13-4 Araki-cho Shinjyuku-ku
Tokyo 160
Japan

H.-J. Miesseler
SICOM GmbH
Grembergerstraße 151a
D-5000 Köln 91
Germany

S. Mochida
Building Engineering Department
Kajima Technical Research Institute
Kajima Corporation
19-1, Tobitakyu, 2-chome, Chofu-shi
Tokyo 182
Japan

H. Mori
Takenaka Civil and Construction Co. Ltd.
1-18-22, Nishiki, Naka-ku
Nagoya
Japan

A.A. Mufti
Department of Civil Engineering
Technical University of Nova Scotia
P.O. Box 1000
Halifax, Nova Scotia B3J 2X4
Canada

K. Mukae
Institute of Research and Development
Sumitomo Construction Co. Ltd.
13-4 Araki-cho, Shinjuku-ku
Tokyo 160
Japan

U. Munipalle
College of Engineering
P.O. Box 6101
West Virginia University
Morgantown, WV 26506-6101
USA

E. Munley
Federal Highway Administration
Turner-Fairbank Highway Research Center
Structures Division HNR-10
6300 Georgetown Pike
McLean, VA 22101
USA

T. Nakatsuji
Shimizu Corporation
Seavans South
2-3, Shibaura 1-chome, Minato-ku
Tokyo 105-07
Japan

694

A. Nanni
Department of Architectural Engineering
104 Engineering 'A' Building
The Pennsylvania State University
University Park, PA 16802
USA

I. Nishizaki
Public Works Research Institute
Ministry of Construction
Government of Japan
1, Asahi, Tsukuba-shi
Ibaraki-ken 305
Japan

M. Nofal
Department of Civil Engineering
Carleton University
Ottawa, Ontario K1S 5B6
Canada

K. Noritake
Civil Engineering Division
Sumitomo Construction Co. Ltd.
13-4 Araki-cho, Shinjuku-ku
Tokyo 160
Japan

S. Ohno
Research Laboratory
Takenaka Corporation
3-1-8, Mokuzai-dori, Mihara-cho
Minami-kawachi-gun
Osaka 587
Japan

H. Okamura
Department of Civil Engineering
University of Tokyo
7-3-1 Hongo, Bunkyo-ku
Tokyo 113
Japan

M. Okano
Technical Research Institute
Obayashi Corporation
Kiyose-city
Tokyo 204
Japan

D.A. Owens
Department of Civil Engineering
Royal Military College of Canada
Kingston, Ontario K7K 5L0
Canada

M.D. Pandey
Department of Civil Engineering
University of Waterloo
Waterloo, Ontario N2L 3G1
Canada

D.R. Paul
Department of Chemical Engineering
University of Texas
Austin, TX 78712
USA

A. Picard
Département de génie civil
Université Laval
Ste-Foy, Québec G1K 7P4
Canada

G. Pluvinage
Laboratoire de Fiabilité Mécanique
Faculté des Sciences
Université de Metz
57045 Metz
France

D.A. Pope
E.T. Techtonics
2117 Tryon Street
Philadelphia, PA 19146
USA

M.J.N. Priestley
Department of Applied Mechanics
and Engineering Sciences
University of California, San Diego
Mail Code 0411
9500 Gilman Drive
La Jolla, CA 92093-0411
USA

A.H. Rahman
Institute for Research in Construction
National Research Council Canada
Building M-20, Montreal Road
Ottawa, Ontario K1A 0R6
Canada

695

E.-H. Ranisch
Institut für Baustoffe
Massivbau und Brandschutz
Beethovenstraße 52
D-3300 Braunschweig
Germany

A.G. Razaqpur
Department of Civil Engineering
Carleton University
Ottawa, Ontario K1S 5B6
Canada

K.S. Rebeiz
Department of Civil Engineering
Lafayette College
Easton, PA 18042-1775
USA

P. Ritchie
E.T. Techtonics
2117 Tryon Street
Philadelphia, PA 19146
USA

S.H. Rizkalla
Department of Civil Engineering
University of Manitoba
Winnipeg, Manitoba R3T 2N2
Canada

F. Roll
E.T. Techtonics
2117 Tryon Street
Philadelphia, PA 19146
USA

C.N. Rosner
Department of Civil Engineering
University of Manitoba
Winnipeg, Manitoba R3T 2N2
Canada

F.S. Rostásy
Institut für Baustoffe
Massivbau und Brandschutz
Beethovenstraße 52
D-3300 Braunschweig
Germany

H. Sakai
Kurosaki Plant Engineering Department
Mitsubishi Kasei Corporation
Kitakyushu-city
Fukuoka Prefecture 806
Japan

H.A. Salim
College of Engineering
P.O. Box 6101
West Virginia University
Morgantown, WV 26506-6101
USA

I. Sasaki
Public Works Research Institute
Ministry of Construction
Government of Japan
1, Asahi, Tsukuba-shi
Ibaraki-ken 305
Japan

G. Schwegler
Swiss Federal Laboratories for Materials
Testing and Research
EMPA
Üeberlandstraße 129
CH-8600 Dübendorf
Switzerland

D.W. Scott
School of Civil Engineering
Georgia Institute of Technology
Atlanta, GA 30332
USA

F. Seible
Department of Applied Mechanics
and Engineering Sciences
University of California, San Diego
Mail Code 0411
9500 Gilman Drive
La Jolla, CA 92093-0411
USA

K. Sekijima
Shimizu Corporation
Seavans South
2-3, Shibaura 1-chome, Minato-ku
Tokyo 105-07
Japan

696

A.N. Sherbourne
Department of Civil Engineering
University of Waterloo
Waterloo, Ontario N2L 3G1
Canada

T.M. Sippel
Institut für Werkstoffe im Bauwesen
Universität Stuttgart
Pfaffenwaldring 4
7000 Stuttgart 80
Germany

R.C. Slater
Engineering Department
School of Engineering
Computing and Mathematical sciences
Lancaster University
Lancaster, Lancashire LA1 4YR
UK

K.T. Slattery
Department of Civil Engineering
Campus Box 1130
Washington University
One Brookings Drive
St. Louis, MO 63130
USA

D. Sleeth
E.T. Techtonics
2117 Tryon Street
Philadelphia, PA 19146
USA

P. Spanek
École d'architecture de Bordeaux
Domaine de Raba
33405 Talence Cédex
France

M.B. Stetson
Department of Civil Engineering
University of New Hampshire
Durham, NH 03824
USA

M. Sugita
Shimizu Corporation
Seavans South
2-3, Shibaura 1-chome, Minato-ku
Tokyo 105-07
Japan

A.L. Svenson
U.S. Department of Transportation
Federal Highway Administration
Turner-Fairbank Highway Research Center
6300 Georgetown Pike
McLean, VA 22101-2296
USA

C.A. Szücs
Departamento de Engenharia Civil
Universidade Federal de Santa Catarina
88049 Florianópolis, Santa Catarina
Brazil

L. Taerwe
Magnel Laboratory for Reinforced Concrete
University of Ghent
Grotesteenweg-Noord 6
B-9052 Ghent
Belgium

K. Tanaka
Research Laboratory
Takenaka Corporation
3-1-8, Mokuzai-dori, Mihara-cho
Minami-kawachi-gun
Osaka 587
Japan

T. Tanaka
Research Center Advanced Composite
Material Laboratory
Mitsubishi Kasei Corporation
Midori-ku
Yokohama
Japan

Y. Tanaka
Structure Mechanics Division
Ship Research Institute
Ministry of Transport
6-38-1, Shinkawa, Mitaka
Tokyo 181
Japan

697

D.A. Taylor
Institute for Research in Construction
National Research Council Canada
Building M-20, Montreal Road
Ottawa, Ontario K1A 0R6
Canada

T.C. Triantafillou
Department of Civil Engineering
Massachusetts Institute of Technology
Cambridge, MA 02139
USA

N. Turkkan
École de génie
Université de Moncton
Moncton, Nouveau-Brunswick E1A 3E9
Canada

G.J. Turvey
Engineering Department
School of Engineering
Computing and Mathematical Sciences
Lancaster University
Lancaster, Lancashire LA1 4YR
UK

T. Ueda
Department of Civil Engineering
Hokkaido University
Sapporo 060
Japan

T. Uomoto
Institute of Industrial Science
University of Tokyo
22-1 Roppongi, 7-chome, Minato-ku
Tokyo 106
Japan

L.D. Wegner
Department of Civil Engineering
Technical University of Nova Scotia
P.O. Box 1000
Halifax, Nova Scotia B3J 2X4
Canada

R. Wilson
E.T. Techtonics
2117 Tryon Street
Philadelphia, PA 19146
USA

R. Wolff
SICOM GmbH
Grembergerstraße 151a
D-5000 Köln 91
Germany

A.R. Woodside
Department of Civil Engineering
and Transport
University of Ulster
Newtonabbey, Antrim BT37 0QB
Northern Ireland

W.D.H. Woodward
Department of Civil Engineering
and Transport
University of Ulster
Newtonabbey, Antrim BT37 0QB
Northern Ireland

Z. Xi
Department of Civil Engineering
The Catholic University of America
Washington, DC 20064
USA

K. Yagi
Carbon Products Division
Mitsubishi Kasei Corporation
5-2, Marunouchi 2-chome
Chiyoda-ku
Tokyo
Japan

K. Yagi
Research Center Advanced Composite
Material Laboratory
Mitsubishi Kasei Corporation
Midori-ku
Yokohama
Japan

T. Yoda
Department of Civil Engineering
Waseda University
3-4-1, Okubo, Shinjuku-ku
Tokyo 160
Japan

S.J. Yoon
School of Civil Engineering
Georgia Institute of Technology
Atlanta, GA 30332
USA

M. Zink
Institut für Massivbau
Technical University Darmstadt
Alexanderstraße 5
D-6100 Darmstadt
Germany

A. Zureick
School of Civil Engineering
Georgia Institute of Technology
Atlanta, GA 30332
USA

AUTHOR INDEX
INDEX DES AUTEURS